IDEOLOGY IN U.S. FOREIGN RELATIONS

Ideology in U.S. Foreign Relations

NEW HISTORIES

EDITED BY

Christopher McKnight Nichols and David Milne

Columbia University Press
New York

Columbia University Press
Publishers Since 1893
New York   Chichester, West Sussex
cup.columbia.edu

Columbia University Press wishes to express its appreciation for assistance given by the Richard Lounsbery Foundation in the publication of this book.

Library of Congress Cataloging-in-Publication Data
Names: Nichols, Christopher McKnight, editor. | Milne, David, 1976– editor.
Title: Ideology in U.S. foreign relations : new histories / edited by
Christopher McKnight Nichols and David Milne.
Description: New York : Columbia University Press, [2021] |
Includes bibliographical references and index.
Identifiers: LCCN 2021053367 | ISBN 9780231201803 (hardback) |
ISBN 9780231201810 (trade paperback) |
ISBN 9780231554275 (ebook)
Subjects: LCSH: Ideology—United States—History. | Democracy. | United States—
Foreign relations—Philosophy. | United States—Politics and government—Philosophy.
Classification: LCC E183.7 .I34 2021 | DDC 327.73—dc23/eng/20211216
LC record available at https://lccn.loc.gov/2021053367

Columbia University Press books are printed on permanent and durable acid-free paper.
Printed in the United States of America

Cover design: Milenda Nan Ok Lee

To the memory of Carolyn Nichols, Rodney Nichols, and Matthew Dey

Contents

IDEOLOGY IN U.S. FOREIGN RELATIONS

Introduction

In the heated 2008 Democratic primary, Barack Obama's national security advisory team chose a pithy formulation to characterize his prospective approach to foreign policy: "pragmatism over ideology."[1] The tagline implied that Obama as president would respond to opportunities and crises with recourse to practical reasoning rather than theory or abstraction. Emphasizing the dangers of ideology in U.S. foreign policy on the campaign trail, Obama consistently reminded voters of one of his own principal strengths in foreign affairs—his opposition to the 2003 invasion of Iraq.

In contrast to Hillary Clinton and every serious Republican presidential candidate, Obama rejected President George W. Bush's ideological rationale for toppling Saddam Hussein. Bush claimed that a liberated Iraq would eventually foster a more democratic and peaceful Middle East. During the run-up to Bush's war, Obama denounced the "cynical attempt by Richard Perle and Paul Wolfowitz and other armchair weekend warriors in this administration to shove their own ideological agendas down our throats, irrespective of the costs in lives lost and in hardships borne."[2] From Obama's perspective, an ideologically driven foreign policy ignored practical obstacles, local circumstances, and history. A variant on grandiose Wilsonian ideology had led the United States to pursue an unrealizable abstraction— that military intervention could catalyze a wave of democratization in a region with no history of participatory democracy—and the consequences had been disastrous.

In 2014, after several years in office, Obama offered a blunter, earthier version of pragmatism over ideology: "Don't do stupid shit."[3] On the ground in Syria, for example, that meant not committing U.S. military power to a civil conflict when the party in power was backed by Russia and Iran. Obama's choice to break with the so-called Washington playbook—the militarized ideology of the U.S. foreign policy establishment—drew criticism from his national security team and, especially, from his former secretary of state, Hillary Clinton. In the long run–up to her second presidential bid, Clinton registered her disapproval of Obama's caution in the pages of *The Atlantic*: "Great nations need organizing principles, and 'don't do stupid stuff' is not an organizing principle for a great nation." It was a mistake to think that ideological struggle ended with the Soviet collapse, Clinton said, because "history never stops . . . nationalisms were going to assert themselves, and then other variations on ideologies were going to claim their space." In Clinton's assessment, Obama failed to counter the Assad regime's aggression, and that had empowered ISIS in Syria and Iraq and opened the space for Putin to fulfill "his vision of Russian greatness" by illegally annexing Crimea in 2014. It was not enough for Obama to avoid doing "something crazy" because the "world in which we are living right now" required a worldview strong enough to contain the hostile ideologies competing for dominance on the world stage.[4]

Reportedly, Obama became "ripshit angry" at Clinton's statement. After all, in the midst of a never-ending ideologically driven war, he asked, how was "don't do stupid shit" a misguided or myopic foreign policy? In the words of Obama's closest foreign policy advisor, Benjamin Rhodes, "Who's exactly in the stupid shit caucus? Who is pro–stupid shit?"[5] Of course, that depends on the definition of "stupid shit," which is where ideology comes in.

The historian Michael Hunt wrote that ideology is "an interrelated set of convictions or assumptions that reduces the complexities of a particular slice of reality to easily comprehensible terms and suggests appropriate ways of dealing with that reality." Furthermore, he argued, a truly critical understanding of the "web of ideology" that informed U.S. policy must consider "systematically the dimensions of that ideology, the roots that sustain it and may render it resistant to change, and the precise relationship it bears to policy." Hunt was responding sympathetically but critically to New Left historians, whose scholarship was indelibly shaped in the 1960s and 1970s by the calamity that was the Vietnam War and who had focused their interpretations of the history of U.S. foreign policy on material drivers and self-interest. Hunt insisted that an "open-minded inquiry into the roots of ideology should leave room for noneconomic impulses, in particular those stemming from racial or ethnic identity, strong nationalistic preoccupations, an evangelical faith, and pronounced regional concerns."[6] Inspired by the cultural anthropologist Clifford Geertz and political scientists such as Gabriel Almond and Sidney Verba, Hunt emphasized the utility of "political culture," in which "ideologies are integrated and coherent systems of symbols, values, and beliefs" are based on "socially established structures of meaning." According to Hunt, this approach foregrounds the complexity of ideological formation and guards against finding a "single, simple reason for the origins and persistence of a particular ideology."[7]

Hunt warned policy makers and their critics against dismissing or minimizing ideology or assuming they could somehow avoid it (as Obama claimed) by attending to the purported "real substance" of international affairs. Unless they made the effort to untangle the ideological drivers of U.S. foreign policy, Hunt cautioned, they would produce a "false diagnosis of the problems afflicting U.S. foreign policy, a misinterpretation of the roots of the problem and misdirected proposals for solving it." Instead of the "fresh insights on the problems of U.S. policy that we seek," they would repeat the mistaken policies of their predecessors.[8]

In other words, it was a profound miscalculation for Obama and his advisors to think they could transcend ideology and still resolve conflicts on the world stage. Obama's team looked at Russia in 2014, for example, and determined that it represented no real, material threat to U.S. core interests, even though Russia had invaded Crimea and publicly supported Bashar al-Assad. From Obama's perspective, by April 2016, Russia was "overextended," "bleeding," "significantly diminished" in world affairs, and on the verge of economic collapse under the weight of sanctions. "Real power means you can get what you want without having to exert violence," Obama said, whereas Putin's belligerence betrayed his weakness.[9] But Obama's realism—his tendency to overvalue economic factors and material conditions and to downplay ideology—made him underestimate Putin's wider ambitions in Ukraine and overestimate the coercive potential of economic sanctions. Obama rejected ideology, oblivious to the fact that he was being led by an ideology of economic determinism..

Long before Putin ordered the annexation of Crimea, his vast network had begun a strategy that would allow Russia to remain on the front foot. That strategy was sustained ideological warfare. In 2013, Putin's chief of the general staff, General Valery Gerasimov, observed that "nonmilitary means" have "exceeded the power of force of weapons in their effectiveness" in meeting Russia's political objectives. Conflicts in the twenty-first century were instead decided in the "information space," which opened "wide asymmetrical possibilities for reducing the fighting potential of the enemy."[10] While sowing chaos in Ukraine and Syria, Putin had contributed to the rise of far-right populist movements in Europe and the United States. As planned, this ideological warfare wreaked havoc on European domestic politics. It weakened their resolve to oppose Russian aggression in Ukraine, and it cultivated allies for the Kremlin among radical nationalist groups. It also informed the cyberoperations that had an impact on the 2016 U.S. presidential election.[11]

Obama may have configured his foreign policy as anti-ideological, but it wasn't. In fact, it was the underexamined ideologies informing his and his administration's own worldview that prevented them, at least in part, from anticipating the real, material, domestic, and geopolitical threat Russia posed to U.S. interests, and indeed to world peace.[12] 2014 was the beginning of a multiyear assault on Ukraine that culminated in the Russian invasion of February 2022. Ideologies set the terms of engagement; they shape politics; and they are not static. They order and explain the world and project the illusion of controllable outcomes. They define and explain success or failure, justify and set boundaries, and compel sacrifice, aggression, or inaction. And, sometimes, their very function hides the fact that they are ideologies.

Foreign policies emerge from and produce ideologies out of necessity. The Monroe Doctrine of 1823 is a good example. Issued by James Monroe, conceived in part by John Quincy Adams, and ostensibly designed to forestall European interventionism in the Western Hemisphere, the doctrine arose from and bequeathed enduring variants on imperialism, unilateralism, and hegemonism, developed during a critical period of anticolonial revolutions across south and central America. The dynamic of foreign policies emerging from as well as generating ideologies is further confirmed by the case of the Bretton Woods system of 1944, designed to help the world recover from the Second World War and to avoid the mistakes made following the First World War. The restructuring of the world order—what one scholar calls a "New Deal for the world"—and creation of institutions such as the United Nations and the International Monetary Fund (IMF) were clearly ideological projections of power, premised on a U.S. leadership role in the postwar world.[13] Ideologies are an inborn facet of foreign relations because, in Hunt's words, "to move in a world of infinite complexity, individuals and societies need to reduce that world to finite terms."[14] It is these "finite terms"—and the history of the larger implications of reducing the world to them—that this volume explores.

On Ideology

The term *ideology* has a long and contested history. It was introduced by the Idéologues of the French Revolution. They construed it as a science of thought aimed at constructing a system of ideas that reflected material reality.[15] Fifty years later, Karl Marx wrote that ideology instead articulated the relationship between culture and political economy, providing an essential mechanism by which societies managed and reproduced themselves. For Marx, a society's "legal, political, religious, aesthetic or philosophic" form ensured that members of the different classes viewed their positions in the social system (and the system itself) as natural.[16] Marx's varied positions on ideology almost always revolved around some kind of falsity and obfuscation, which in turn legitimizes capitalist forms of hegemony. This led him to identify and critique what he saw as the ideological superstructures that prop up capitalist society. In short, Marxist views of ideology focus on the way they serve as cover for exploitative economic systems.

In the twentieth century, the French Marxist philosopher Louis Althusser shifted this perspective slightly to make the case that ideology is better understood as worldmaking through reason and language, more of an imaginary set of relationships that do in fact correspond in many ways to real conditions of existence. He wrote that "human societies secrete ideology as the very element and atmosphere indispensable to their historical respiration and life." For Althusser, ideology performed the social function of masking the structures of power and naturalizing the hierarchies that supported them. In this sense, ideology defined the real for the subjects of a particular society—or, at least, their lived reality (in Althusser's terms, the subjects' "'lived' relation to the real"). Althusser emphasized the role of the state and social institutions as the "apparatus" that helps to reproduce ideology. One need not agree with all of Althusser's claims—the English historian E. P. Thompson skewered his theoretical pretensions and political naivete in *The Poverty of Theory*—to appreciate the impact his work has exerted on subsequent generations of scholars.[17]

This volume shows that U.S. foreign policy is ideological in each of these three senses. As the French Idéologues conceived it, ideology functioned as a self-conscious system of ideas constructed by experts. As Marx believed, it reinforces and naturalizes hierarchical structures of capital and operates through forms that privilege particular and historically situated interests, while at the same time presenting those interests as natural, universal, and moral. And, in Althusser's terms, it relies on "a system (with its own logic and rigor) of representations (images, myths, ideas or concepts, depending on the case) endowed with a historical existence and role within a given society."[18]

Because of his influence on our understanding of language and its role in shaping reality, Althusser's framing opens up a broad field of inquiry.[19] To name two examples from this book, Emily Conroy-Krutz and Daniel Immerwahr analyze representations of empire in popular culture, tying them into the larger framework of meaning with historical resonance and agency. In chapter 10, Conroy-Krutz turns to nineteenth-century missionary magazines with youth sections that manifested a Christian nationalist and evangelical destiny for American children in its pages. In chapter 21, Immerwahr mines George Lucas's cinematic universe to excavate the tension between tradition and modernization in his films. Immerwahr states that Star Wars and Indiana Jones evince an ideological reaction to the inherently hostile growth of the military-industrial complex during the Vietnam era and the ways that the United States marshaled that technological empire against "traditional" societies. In both examples, the vehicle for the ideology—the magazines and the movies—purposely reproduced identifiable and historically trenchant ideologies related to American empire while generating some unexpected outcomes.

The legacy of the French Idéologues is also discernible in this volume. In chapter 19, Daniel Bessner examines the ideological motives behind the objective "scientific" inquiry of certain think tanks. The founders of the RAND corporation set out to institutionalize a progressive vision of the military-intellectual complex in which experts "scientifically" deduced the guiding principles for U.S. foreign policy. From its origins, RAND expressly pursued the kind of ideological production imagined by the French Idéologues.

In chapter 15, Penny Von Eschen examines the U.S. neoliberal reaction to Soviet collapse, its attempt to secure international hegemony by marshaling the tools of capital to dominate the post–Cold War landscape, and the alternative ideologies that developed to contest that worldview. Conforming to ideology in the Marxist sense, U.S. foreign policy after the Cold

War sought to shore up a liberal-capitalist world order that privileged its own historical interests. By equating "freedom with the free market," Von Eschen argues, the authors of this policy fortified structural hierarchies of capital and accomplished the "ideological work of constructing unregulated markets and U.S. power as natural."

Although ideology as the "science of ideas"—studying ideas, their origins, and their development, in line with the notions of the French Idéologues—arose in the eighteenth century, the ways in which many of the scholars in this volume tend to examine ideology is more in keeping with the approaches and assumptions of the twentieth century and how historians tend to examine ideology. That is to say, the contributors do not always agree on definitions, or moments of false consciousness. But they do tend to characterize ideology as a system of ideas or a method of thinking—individual as well as collective—that assists in discerning interests, ascertaining principles, and justifying actions.[20]

A New Field, a New History

Ideology in U.S. Foreign Relations has an ambitious aim. We have brought together some of the foremost specialists in U.S. intellectual history and U.S. foreign relations to show how ideology shapes the United States in the world.[21] The essays in this volume explore the specific ideologies that produced discrete foreign policies and the concepts that these foreign policies in turn reinforced and reproduced. The contributors also examine the "intermestic"—the vital intersection of the international and the domestic—to identify the ideological functions of U.S. foreign policy at home and to trace these policies and their embedded ideas as they operate abroad. Together we map the vast ideological contours of U.S. foreign policy: the concepts, their impacts, and their repercussions.

The contributions to this book have been developed collaboratively with a central goal of establishing the state of a new field. A new area of diplomatic history has emerged in the past decade that explores the roles of ideas, ideologies, and intellectuals in U.S. foreign policy. Often referred to as the "intellectual history of U.S. foreign relations," this field has generated scholarship on people, groups, and ideas usually considered outside the bounds of traditional diplomatic history. With a focus on human rights, anti-imperialism, the culture of "wartime," missionary movements, indigeneity, science diplomacy, racism, white supremacy, Black internationalism, peace activism, and gender—to name a few key examples—this scholarship has already stimulated a fresh look at the historically explicit (if underexamined) intellectual architecture of U.S. foreign policy. It has excavated theories of nationalism, internationalism, liberal interventionism, isolationism, neutrality, realism, and grand strategy as they inform U.S. foreign relations. We bring these new contributions to the scholarly literature together in a single volume for the first time.

Looking beyond the usual suspects of highly placed policy makers, contributors illuminate the role of previously neglected figures and groups and consider ideologies that not only influence U.S. foreign policy but also challenge prevailing assumptions about the nation's global purpose. In a series of brief, incisive chapters, *Ideology in U.S. Foreign Relations* demonstrates how varied and disparate ideologies, from before the birth of the republic to today, have indelibly shaped the foreign and domestic affairs of the United States.

Exploring Ideology

At the outset, we asked our contributors a few questions to guide their exploration, a mode of common inquiry to connect the chapters. There were methodological questions: What is the most coherent way to tell this history? What approaches most accurately reveal the influence and impact of ideologies? What about the conception, transmission, and reception of ideas and ideologies?

Then there were questions of premise and definitions: What counts as an ideology and does it matter? Do we distinguish between the intentional and the incidental production of ideology? Does the source or site of ideological production matter? If so, how? The diversity of views across the contributors on how best to define ideology is revealing. The concept is unveiled in a fascinating variety of ways.

Then there were questions of context, both historical and political: Does a country's political system provide a distinctive cast to its foreign policy? What effect might an institutionally democratic-republican political system and the attendant ideas of representation and republicanism have on U.S. foreign policy or in similar systems? Did the reality of constant U.S. military engagement have a formative role on the ideologies shaping U.S. foreign policy?

Writing about ideologies forces us to turn abstract (and sometimes unreal) concepts into subjects. How do we ground our analysis in human actors and material agents while acknowledging the real and material agency of ideas? In this book, we define foreign policy and foreign relations very broadly, to include a wide range of actors, texts, and topics outside the narrower confines of "diplomatic" history. And it is worth asking whether that approach also illuminates what we still might be missing.

What are the moments when ideology forecloses options or debate? And overall, what are the pivotal moments for the crucial ideologies explored in this book? (Revolution, wars, and peace, to be sure—but what about other moments, turning points, acts, decisions, movements, and eras beyond the most obvious social and international relations ruptures?)

The book is divided into five sections that explore how ideology interacts with five broad categories: people, power, the international, democracy, and progress.

Ideologies and the People

Part 1, "Ideologies and the People," contains four chapters that delve into the interplay between people and the state: how "subjecthood" functioned as a lever to gain power and agency with a colonial state; ideological assimilation (in the guise of "civilization"), citizenship, and state sovereignty; the agency of the subject in the democratic imaginary; and the role played by women in shaping U.S. public culture.

In the first chapter, Matthew Kruer traces the historical tension between Indigenous and white colonial notions of subjecthood in the British empire. Treating subjecthood as "an ideology, an imaginative construction of the proper order of things that naturalizes relations of power and guides collective action," Kruer explores the "improvisational forms" Indigenous subjecthood took in an effort to safeguard Indigenous interests. In the seventeenth-century colonies, Indigenous groups leveraged the political designation of "subjecthood" to gain agency (legal rights as well as protections) with colonial British power, which incidentally created a mechanism for British authorities to intercede and exert imperial control over the colonies. As conditions changed in the eighteenth century, white colonial subjects, who enjoyed a different kind of subjecthood under British law, increasingly imagined their interests were in conflict with the interests of Indigenous subjects. When this ideological attitude shifted into a more "populist persuasion" in the 1760s, it turned to violence, resulting in the Paxton massacre of 1763. And most significantly, it inspired what Kruer argues came to be the "racially coded definitions of citizenship" that dominated the United States after independence.

In chapter 2, Benjamin Coates explores how U.S. presidents have deployed "civilization" as an ideological justification for particular actions. He contends that civilization "has functioned both as an ideology that reads difference as backwardness, and as a political language that justified domination on the grounds of universal values." Unlike ideologies such as "freedom" or "manifest destiny," which carry a distinctly American flavor, "civilization" is European in origin and universalist in implication, raising provocative questions about the nation's place in the world. Coates concludes bracingly that "while 'civilization' projects peace and inclusion, its invocation has in practice often accompanied exclusion and violence." In a world that is heating to a point of no return, portending civilizational collapse, Coates also wonders whether the time has come to expand our conception of civilization to encompass the nonhuman realm.

In chapter 3, Michaela Hoenicke-Moore examines a realm that is woefully understudied in the history of U.S. foreign relations: the views of ordinary people. Through revealing firsthand testimony, Hoenicke-Moore explores how ideologies and concepts such as universalism, national security, and a sense of mission were apprehended and acted upon at the grassroots level. Responding to the historian Robert Westbrook's appeal to look for the articulation of important ideas not only among intellectuals and elites but within the more broadly conceived civil society, Hoenicke-Moore demonstrates that ordinary Americans were better informed and more attentively involved in the major debates on U.S. foreign policy than is generally recognized. She observes that a bottom-up approach reveals a diversity of foreign policy perspectives "that defies conventional binaries of isolationism/internationalism, elites vs. masses, hawks vs. doves, Republicans/Democrats, or even, conservatives/liberals." Interestingly, one ideology that does recur frequently throughout her sample—although it is never defined as such by the letter writers—is realism. This revelation presents an irony that George Kennan and Walter Lippmann—those unabashed elitists and realist skeptics of participatory democracy—would have found surprising.

In the final chapter of part 1, Katharina Rietzler focuses on female actors and analyzes the role of women public intellectuals in debates on U.S. foreign policy and international affairs during the three decades after passage of the Nineteenth Amendment. In the aftermath of the expansion of the franchise, elite women mobilized to incorporate knowledge of international affairs into female citizenship. From the mid-1920s, women also emerged as public intellectuals commenting on international affairs, even though some institutions such as elite think tanks or universities excluded them. In the 1930s and 1940s, women were interviewed on the radio, gave talks, and taught at universities and colleges. Sometimes they referred to themselves as "lady authorities," secure in their knowledge that they had a receptive audience for their public speaking and writing on international affairs. From the late 1940s, however, this largely liberal internationalist women's public culture had to contend with an emerging counterpublic: conservative women who challenged the notion that liberal internationalists were "speaking for all women." Centering "gender" and "publicness," the chapter explores how women were constructed and constructed themselves across the political spectrum as responsible but international citizens in the era before international relations was professionalized as a discipline.

Ideologies of Power

Part 2, "Ideologies of Power," consists of five chapters that examine the dynamics of power within four interconnected themes: economics, race, empire, and unilateralism. These chapters explore connections among the radical free trade tradition, the antislavery movement, and anti-interventionism; trade imperialism (in the guise of "free trade") and hierarchies of power on the international stage; antislavery politics and the antebellum critique of imperialism; and the ideology of fear and insecurity as instrumental to U.S. intolerance for global threats. Permeating so many facets of U.S. power is an impulse toward freedom of action that takes ideological shape in the unilateralism that so often justifies and modulates its application.

In chapter 5, Marc-William Palen explores the divide between economic nationalists and economic cosmopolitans in U.S. history—something of a live issue today. He focuses specifically on the ideology of Cobdenism, which encapsulated the insights of Richard Cobden, the powerful British parliamentarian who led the overthrow of the protectionist Corn Laws in 1846 and helped to guide Britain's adherence to free trade principles in the century that followed. As Palen demonstrates, Cobden and Cobdenism were inspired by Adam Smith's *Wealth of Nations* and David Ricardo's theory of competitive advantage, and it advocated foreign policy restraint, the pursuit of peace, and a principled opposition to slavery. After "freeing the world from slavery," Palen writes, "freeing trade was but the next universalist step in the emancipation of humankind." Unsurprisingly, Cobden's American devotees included antebellum abolitionists in the industrializing Northeast. Following the decimation of the Jeffersonian proslavery southern position during the Civil War, it was American Cobdenites who opposed U.S. economic nationalism and foreign policy interventionism in the decades that followed. The movement's apogee arrived in the 1930s when Secretary of State Cordell Hull—nicknamed the "Tennessee Cobden"—sought to pursue Cobdenite goals regarding free trade.

In chapter 6, Nicholas Guyatt upends the notion that John Quincy Adams—President Monroe's secretary of state, author of the doctrine that bears his name, and the sixth president of the United States—was an antiimperialist. During a lecture to the Massachusetts Historical Society in 1846, Adams declared that Great Britain had the "righteous cause" in its tawdry war with China over the opium trade. In seeking to outlaw the trade of opium—British imports had addicted millions of Chinese to the drug—Adams suggested that China's leaders were committing an "enormous outrage on the rights of human nature," chief among which was the right to free trade. Guyatt uses Adams's speech as a springboard to discuss American ideas about world order in the mid-nineteenth century, particularly in reference to Britain's conception of international law, and the likely role of the United States in expanding and enforcing it.

In chapter 7, Matthew Karp examines U.S. antislavery politics and empire in the mid-nineteenth century, focusing on the 1850s Republican Party and how its leadership understood the relationship among slavery, imperialism, and what might today be termed "global development." Contrary to historians who identify antislavery positions as a fig leaf to justify the expansion of empire and exploitive capitalism, Karp contends that in the United States "opposition to bondage also produced a significant critique of imperialism—in its proslavery American and aristocratic European forms—and the rudiments of an alternative vision of global order, based crucially on political democracy and the protection of free labor." Karp explores these ideas as they were expressed by leading Republicans William Seward, Charles Sumner, and Carl Schurz alongside antislavery thinkers Frederick Douglass and Wendell Phillips. Karp makes a persuasive case that both the

Civil War and "the reconstruction of the former Confederacy should be understood as episodes in international relations." The popular ideology that someone like Seward espoused—combining a strong commitment to "free labor and democracy—both at home and abroad"—helped shape the violent manner of slavery's end in the United States.

In chapter 8, Andrew Preston examines "fear and insecurity" and centers on a paradox that has been evident since 1945: How is it that the United States, one of the most secure and powerful hegemonic nations in history, has been so beset by fear when considering its place in the world? Protected by two vast oceans to the east and west and with generally friendly (or at least, relatively weak) immediate neighbors to the north and the south, the United States has nonetheless been a surprisingly skittish nation. Preston observes that, ironically, this tendency to fear the worst was never more acute than when U.S. power was at its height, through the middle decades of the twentieth century. From this psychological frailty (writ large) stem large consequences for the world system. Whereas most states attempt to manage or mitigate threats through diplomacy and other nonmilitary means, Preston explores how the United States too often attempts to preemptively eliminate them, even when the threat is inchoate or even sometimes phantom.

The final chapter of part 2, chapter 9, explores a counterpoint to the sorts of fears Preston lays out: the pursuit of unilateralism. For Christopher McKnight Nichols, this unilateralism characterizes a constellation of ideas about how U.S. power should function. Fundamentally, this power should serve American interests single-mindedly, and the nation ought to be able to pursue those interests without constraints—whether that takes the form of a binding alliance, international law, or other external force. Nichols identifies and untangles the "long, deeply rooted history of unilateralism as an ideology and as an enduring strain in the constellation of foundational concepts that have informed and shaped U.S. foreign policy from the nation's earliest moments." Nichols concludes with a claim that can well be applied to other concepts and practices analyzed in part 2 and across this volume: "unilateralism does not have to amount to an ideology in order to function ideologically in U.S. history."

Ideologies of the International

Part 3, "Ideologies of the International," encompasses four chapters, each of which explores a distinct ideological system of representation built to justify the priorities of state and nonstate actors: white Christian missionary visions of the international targeted at young people; the ideology of the Global South as developed by Eugenia Charles, the former prime minister of Dominica, and in tension with the self-described "benevolent" forces of U.S. empire; the pragmatic internationalism of the African American academic and policy advisor and activist Flemmie Kittrell; and Catholic internationalists and the moral debate over U.S. war power.

In chapter 10, "'For Young People,'" Emily Conroy-Krutz introduces the voice of America's youth—not often heard in histories of the United States and the world. The foreign mission movement positioned itself as a source of expert information on the world for its American adherents and readers, and Conroy-Krutz explores the measures that missionaries took to ensure that the next generation would take up the mantle of education and world evangelization. In the *Missionary Herald*, for example, a monthly column headlined "For Young People" began to appear in the 1870s. Each month children learned about the world and the role they were supposed to play in it as American Christians. Conroy-Krutz explores how the ideology of Christian uplift was tailored, transmitted, and received: "Appealing to their readers as children, the letters understood that children grow into adults. The ideas that were planted as seeds now would grow to shape the ideology of the adults the children would become." But the seeds did not necessarily grow as expected. The missionary movement took racial hierarchy as a given yet held true to the notion that all souls were equal under God. Conroy-Krutz shows how missionary elders and their publications helped to generate new forms of intergenerational antiracist missionary internationalism.

In chapter 11, Imaobong Umoren explores the role that actors in the Global South played in shaping U.S. foreign policy. Umoren's focal point is Eugenia Charles, the prime minister of the Caribbean island of Dominica from 1980 to 1995. To the degree that Charles is known, it is principally for her role as leader of the Organization of Eastern Caribbean States in calling upon President Reagan to launch an invasion of Grenada to depose a Marxist leader in October 1983. Yet Umoren shows that Charles—alongside other conservative leaders such as Jamaica's Edward Seaga and Barbados's Tom Adams—worked to encourage the United States to act as a benevolent imperial power in the Eastern Caribbean at a time when its hemispheric attention was focused more on Central and Latin America. Umoren discusses Charles's career with close reference to three ideologies that recur throughout this volume: neoliberalism, neocolonialism, and unilateralism.

As she concludes, "exploring Charles is important because it foregrounds her as an agent, not a puppet of U.S. foreign policy."

In chapter 12, Brandy Thomas Wells investigates the fascinating life of the home economist and Howard University professor Flemmie Kittrell. Hewing closely to an ideology and worldview that might be described as "pragmatic internationalism," Kittrell argued that sound global politics required a practical approach that focused on the family, education, and women's social and economic life. She pursued and championed these beliefs from India to Africa and during the tenure of five U.S. presidents and six secretaries of state. While Kittrell deeply valued working with the U.S. State Department and would do so in numerous capacities throughout the Cold War, she contended that she had dual tasks. Wells demonstrates that Kittrell, as a Black American woman, worked as a bureaucratic infighter who served national interests while also seeking to undermine the global legitimacy of colonialism and white supremacy. She crossed boundaries—national, racial, and gender—to do battle with white supremacy, to combine domesticity with foreign affairs, and to develop a distinct brand of international thought. Wells illuminates the ways in which Kittrell's archival record reflects her worldview and the paradoxical tensions within. Hints, nuances, and silences analyzed throughout the chapter reveal that Kittrell's ideas about what it meant to be international were symbiotic rather than synonymous with the state.

In chapter 13, the final chapter in part 3, Raymond Haberski Jr. examines Catholic church teachings and the influential role played by just war theory: the notion that a series of criteria must be met before a war might be considered morally justifiable. In 1983 the National Council of Catholic Bishops published a pastoral letter, "The Challenge of Peace," that encouraged the increasingly bellicose and anticommunist Reagan administration to rethink a military posture built on the threat of thermonuclear war. This was an important moment in two significant ways. First, the Catholic Church had hitherto been a reliable Cold War ally against atheistic communism, but the "peace pastoral," as it became known, changed all that. Second, on issues of America's role in the world, the Catholic Church was divided between liberals who bemoaned the militarization of U.S. foreign policy and conservatives who believed the United States was engaged in noble global struggles against an insidious ideology. As Haberski lays out, the introduction of just war theory into debates about the purpose of U.S. global power ushered in a period in which discussions of its relevance and applicability—the moral debate about whether the United States was justified in going to war—increased in frequency (its apex came between Operation Desert Storm in 1991 and Operation Iraqi Freedom in 2003). However, the debates that ensued rarely took the United States down a more peaceful path.

Ideologies and Democracy

Part 4, "Ideologies and Democracy," addresses the tension between democracy as an ideology and the reality of the United States as a nation with a spotty, oscillating history in relation to democratic norms and practices in actions at home and abroad. Its four chapters all unpack the "intermestic," where concepts of democracy and its attendant ideologies move dialogically between domestic and foreign politics and policy. More specifically, they examine domestic ideologies of freedom marshaled in the framing and execution of U.S. foreign policy; multilateralist resistance to neoliberal capitalist imperialism; and the foreign policy ideologies that define and help to determine domestic immigration policy.

In chapter 14, Jeremi Suri investigates the notion of "freedom" as an ideology, which he describes as "a base alcohol for Americans that changes over time, mixing well with certain additives in some moments but not in others." In every era of American history, presidents have claimed that their foreign policies both promote freedom abroad and protect it at home. Suri examines three varieties of freedom that have been particularly influential at different periods: "freedom from," "freedom to," and "freedom over." The Monroe Doctrine is the classic example of freedom from—in this case, freedom from European meddling in the Western Hemisphere. Suri dates the period when freedom to was dominant to the late-nineteenth century, when the U.S. economy was developing at breakneck speed. Woodrow Wilson was the most influential advocate of bringing freedom to the rest of the world, according to Suri. The Second World War and the beginning of the Cold War marked a period when purposefully extending freedom over other nations—or as Jean-Jacques Rousseau might have phrased it, forcing them to be free—became the essential task of U.S. foreign policy. Suri writes that the "National Security Act of 1947 is one of the crucial moments in this new phase, when Americans self-consciously built a permanent military-industrial complex to guard freedom on a global scale." He concludes that the United States is currently transitioning out of this phase and into uncharted ideological territory.

In chapter 15, Penny Von Eschen explores how two ideologies—unilateralism and neoliberalism—deeply influenced the U.S. response to the end of the Cold War. In what Von Eschen calls a "road not taken," Mikhail Gorbachev and India's president, Rajiv Gandhi, issued what became known as the Delhi Declaration on November 27, 1986. They unveiled a vision for a "new world order" (a phrase later appropriated by—and often attributed to—President George H. W. Bush), which entailed strengthening the United Nations and pursuing multinational cooperation for a peaceable and ultimately nuclear-free world. Emergency environmental measures were proposed, and sustainability was championed. Three years later, in 1989, Václav Havel and Nelson Mandela echoed the declaration in calling for a rejection of unilateralism and the renascence of multilateralism, emphasizing the virtues of the genuinely mixed economy. But the United States, flush from victory in the Cold War, chose a different path born of triumphalism. Through the International Monetary Fund, the United States encouraged a disastrous course of "shock therapy" for the soon-to-be former Yugoslavia that had calamitous consequences for the stability of the Balkans. In addition, the "Defense Policy Guidance" document of 1992, sometimes known as the Wolfowitz Doctrine, outlined the principal goals of U.S. foreign policy as preventing the emergence of a peer competitor, whether friend or foe, and complete freedom of action in projecting and maintaining full-spectrum dominance. That corrosive ideological diptych, neoliberalism and unilateralism, foreclosed the realization of a more humane vision proposed by Gorbachev, Gandhi, Mandela, and Havel.

In chapter 16, Melani McAlister examines how a large bloc of American Jews positioned themselves as part of what she depicts as a "global pro-Biafra movement," which supported the majority-Christian and Igbo region in the wake of its attempt to break away from the rest of Nigeria. McAlister explores not only the ideology and politics of Holocaust memory as it played out in the wake of Biafra but also how American Jewish organizations (led by the American Jewish Committee) took up the Biafran cause in the aftermath of the Arab-Israeli war of 1967, which began just a week after the Nigeria-Biafra war. McAlister tackles problems with humanitarianism (as a politics of abjection and rescue) through the lens of the multiple, overlapping, and sometimes contradictory meanings the Biafra conflict had for American Jews and Americans more broadly. Connections between religious thought and action are revealed—groups like the AJC conceived Biafra as an ecumenical Judeo-Christian project—and anticolonialism is examined, including parallel views of the perils of U.S. involvement in Vietnam and the causes and consequences of the Arab-Israeli wars. Biafran relief was, according McAlister, a nonpolitical politics clothed in ecumenism that served a group still uncertain about its own whiteness and its rapidly evolving status as an ethnic-religious minority.

Chapter 17 by Daniel Tichenor concludes part 4 on democracy by looking at groups within and outside the American body politic and spotlighting "immigration as ideology." Immigration is often thought to sit squarely in the realm of domestic politics, but Tichenor shows that immigration policy is foreign policy, whether it is understood in terms of enhancing economic competitiveness, gaining or maintaining superiority in science and technology, or simply as a means to strengthen the nation's image in the world. Tichenor identifies four ideas about immigration that have profoundly influenced U.S. foreign relations. The first two, cosmopolitan visions of an open society and instrumental liberal notions of nation building, have combined to encourage an open immigration system. The second two, traditions of economic protectionism and nativist conceptions of security informed by notions of racial hierarchy, have combined to restrict and reject immigrants. Both sets of ideas are shaped by larger, familiar notions of isolationism and internationalism: meta-ideologies that lie at the heart of so many debates about the nature of U.S. foreign policy. Tichenor demonstrates that any discussion of ideology in foreign policy must count immigration among its most critical components.

Ideologies of Progress

Part 5, "Ideologies of Progress," branches out in three directions to register different configurations of ideas about progress across time. This concluding section explores the relationship among U.S. frameworks for progress, global policy, and its reception: emigration and the global image of American prosperity; white power, anti-Blackness, and western expansion; progressivism, scientism, and the military-intellectual complex; and dystopian visions of modernization in reaction to U.S. hegemony abroad.

In chapter 18, "Capital and Immigration in the Era of the Civil War," Jay Sexton concurs with Daniel Tichenor on the centrality of immigration policy to the history of U.S. foreign relations. Sexton examines the era of the Civil War, when the nation vacillated between shutting and opening its borders to migrants and capital. Sexton contends that the opening and ideological pull of the United States, as a nation of vast economic opportunity, was the major geopolitical event of the mid-to-late nineteenth century. That is, the very concept of the United States as a "land of opportunity" performed ideologically in foreign and domestic politics. More than any other single factor, Sexton asserts, it was mass immigration and the economic prospects that met those new arrivals that created the world's most powerful nation. The outward projections of power that followed 1865 were important, Sexton concedes, but it deflects "attention away from the headline story of the nineteenth century: the importation of power to North America from abroad." Lincoln's observation that the United States represented the "last, best hope of earth" resonated globally. The allure of post–Civil War America facilitated its rise to economic preeminence in the final quarter of the nineteenth century.

In chapter 19, Daniel Bessner addresses similar themes related to projections of power and progress in the mid-twentieth century as seen through the institutions and practitioners at an epochal Cold War moment of foreign policy ideology formation. Bessner focuses on the RAND corporation's role in generating ideas, informed by the positivist social sciences, that shaped U.S. foreign policy during the Cold War. Bessner states that RAND and its subsequent think tank progeny were undergirded by a distinct strand of American progressivism contending that rational administration by experts is the only sure way to guarantee the nation's security and prosperity in a world of ever-increasing complexity. Unlike the Council on Foreign Relations, whose membership was drawn from the WASPocracy of the American establishment and a broad cross-section of past and current leaders in politics, corporate and nonprofit worlds, academia, and beyond, RAND hired its scientists and intellectuals from a wider (religious if not racial) demographic that included Jews and Catholics in significant numbers. Driven by notions of postwar "meritocracy," and infused with the confidence and buoyed by the funding that coursed through the postwar social sciences, RAND ushered in the era of the Beltway foreign policy think tank—or "the blob," to deploy the pejorative term coined by the Obama advisor Ben Rhodes. Bessner demonstrates the power that two ideologies—Progressivism and scientism—exerted on RAND and consequently on U.S. foreign policy that continue to have dramatic influences today.

In chapter 20, Daniel Steinmetz-Jenkins and Michael Franczak examine the period between Cold War liberalism's ascent in the 1950s and its transformation into a doctrine of neoconservatism by the 1970s. The "end of ideology" is the key ideology, they argue, for understanding this transformation. First, it explains the political and economic conditions that gave rise to the end of ideology, as the notion appeared in the writings of Cold War intellectuals such as Daniel Bell, Seymour Martin Lipset, Edward Shils, Raymond Aron, Arthur Schlesinger Jr., and Reinhold Niebuhr. In turn, end-of-ideology defenders were divided as to whether it was more of a local or global condition. Steinmetz-Jenkins and Franczak then turn to the domestic and international factors of the late 1960s that left Cold War liberalism in a state of crisis. Some Cold War liberals developed a new faith: neoconservatism. Daniel Patrick Moynihan and others declared themselves "Truman Democrats" to emphasize their fidelity to moderate redistributive liberalism and anticommunism. In 1980, most Cold War liberals-cum-neoconservatives did the unthinkable—vote Republican. Many joined the Reagan administration and played key roles in U.S. foreign policy, particularly regarding human rights and the Soviet Union. Far from its "end" in the 1950s and 1960s, Cold War liberalism was rediscovered and repurposed by neoconservatives in the 1970s and 1980s for a new project: restoring American power overseas to its 1950s glory days.

In a surprising turn, chapter 21, Daniel Immerwahr's "The Galactic Vietnam: Technology, Modernization, and Empire in George Lucas's Star Wars," teases out some of the most significant ideological dimensions of George Lucas's hugely popular cinematic oeuvre. Immerwahr explores how Lucas's work speaks directly to the way the United States can be said to collectively view the nation's place and role in the world. Through his Star Wars and Indiana Jones trilogies, George Lucas became the most prominent and popular interpreter of the relationship between traditional and modern societies. Rejecting an ideology of modernization that had long been dominant, Lucas depicted universes in which past societies were fragile, in need of protection (or, in pathological cases, destruction), but not in need of "modernization" as led by supposedly benign empires. Even in his works of science fiction, Lucas displayed serious skepticism about technology and its benefits. The result was an extremely popular set of films consolidating a post-Vietnam worldview that doubted the prospects of modernization and that, time and again, articulated an unbridgeable gap between the traditional and the modern. Immerwahr demonstrates that popular culture is fertile ground in which to identify ideologies that explain the United States and the world it shapes.

In chapter 22, "Dual-Use Ideologies: How Science Came to Be Part of the United States' Cold War Arsenal," Audra Wolfe culminates our analysis by drawing attention to definitions of technology and technologies of ideas, namely ideologies, that allow human beings to manipulate or at least attempt to control and make sense of the world around them. She analyzes the ideology of scientific freedom as a dual-use technology of war that served both to empower marginalized voices and to preserve elite control. This essay reveals a hidden history: ideologies may not be inherently liberatory or oppressive but they still have consequences, often unanticipated or unaccounted for in their execution and deployment. "The problem," Wolfe concludes, is not with ideology but "with who is using it, and for what purpose."

Closing Thoughts

Before turning to the main text, we offer a few observations that frame the chapters that follow. The early American republic emerged in large part from the intellectual milieu of European diplomatic traditions, ideas about democracy located in antiquity and Enlightenment rationalism, and through a set of colonial experiences that privileged common sense, autonomy, and adaptability, fusing dynamic notions of individualism to varied conceptions of community. As the nation endured, moving from precarious revolutionary origins to more defined and eventually hegemonic power, stability provided fertile ground for ideological growth.

Despite being involved in a civil war and two world wars, the United States avoided some of the worst ravages of revolution, war, and hostile invasion that have assailed many other nation-states and peoples since the late eighteenth century. Two important outcomes from this stand out in terms of the formation of foreign policy ideologies. First, there has been a pronounced measure of ideological persistence, though far from static, over the breadth of U.S. history. Second, as Michael Hunt suggested, foreign policy ideologies in the United States have been marked at times by a peculiar "absence of self-consciousness about that ideology" (perhaps causally related to that relative stability of political culture and ideological persistence).[22] The often less-reflective process of ideological formation, even the outright rejection of ideology, in the United States is amply demonstrated by the opening story about Barack Obama. However, as we have emphasized, that apparent absence demonstrates the opposite: the profound influence of ideologies in U.S. foreign relations.

At work across the chapters is a central ideological struggle over competing visions of democracy and of American democracy's place in the long arc of civilization(s), variously defined and vigorously contested. Crucial to these competitions has been the relationship among capitalism, morality, democracy, and liberalism and thus the notion of U.S. "civilization" as a mission, a project, and an organizing worldview. In sweeping through this history, we must attend to ideas of labor and to class aspirations and assumptions, and, as this book shows, to a free/unfree divide that has characterized the United States since before the revolution.

The evolution of ideas about national security, including vociferous debates over what constitutes the national interest, is clearly identifiable in the historical record. At the intersection of national interest and national security can also be said to be another peculiar set of ideological commitments that center around what Hunt referred to as the "nagging preoccupation with perils of revolution."[23] Consider just one aspect of the U.S. foreign relations record from the early nineteenth century that encapsulates and illuminates the contradictions inherent in a nation struggling for security, seeking to advance interests, yet skeptical of revolution and beset by deep-seated racism. That is the decision not to recognize Haitian independence. The revolution lasted from 1791 to 1804, creating the second democracy in the hemisphere. Haitian revolutionaries led by Toussaint Louverture cast off the chains of slavery along with those binding the island colony to French rule. The first U.S. president, George Washington, opposed the Haitian Revolution, siding with the French. In contrast, his vice president and the nation's second president, John Adams, shifted gears to send aid, including funds as well as critical food and material. However, once in office, the third American president, Thomas Jefferson, overturned the Adams administration's policies. The United States refused to recognize Haiti during the early 1800s. Jefferson cut off essential assistance to Haiti, shifting in 1806 to implement a full trade embargo, largely out of a fear of revolution spreading to the slaveholding American South. These policies continued for almost seventy years. It was not until 1862 that the United States formally recognized the sovereign independent status of Haiti.[24]

As with the nonrecognition of Haiti, racist hierarchical thinking in many forms has been embedded in the ideologies that have shaped U.S. foreign policy. These forms of thinking are entangled with visions or structures of white supremacy, Western hegemony, and Christian nationalism; entangled with commerce, as in the Haitian example; and often imbued with contradictory claims and motivations around morality, democracy, and religious faith as drivers of foreign relations. In the history of U.S. foreign relations, ideologies of racism, antiracism, and racial hierarchies have often pivoted on contested notions of freedom and liberty, particularly in times of crises, wars, and economic downturns. Thus we find an enmeshed history in which ostensibly universal notions of equal rights and equal capacity derived from Enlightenment thought developed, coexisted, and competed alongside conceptions of improvement and perfectibility (teleologies of progress) against settler colonial projections of civilizational racio-religious power and ascendancy.

What some now refer to as "exceptionalism" has been a driving idea in U.S. relations with the world, although the motivations and key concepts as well as key terms related to such an orientation have changed over time. We see this in the providentialism of the "city on a hill" in the colonial era and the mission of "Manifest Destiny" in westward expansion during the nineteenth century as well as in the positioning of the United States as an "arsenal of democracy" or even as the "indispensable nation" from the Second World War through the Cold War to the present.[25] Mission, of course, and providentialism, in particular, have strong tones of Protestantism, suggesting as they do that the United States has a unique role in events and outcomes determined by God.[26] The sense of the United States as divinely ordained with a world-historical mission forms a palpable, potent subtext of many ideologies in U.S. foreign relations. We find these themes most evident in heated debates over the degree and type of U.S. continental and international "mission" at the turn of the twentieth century that fell under the rubric "Republic or Empire?" This included reinforcing a geographic sense that the United States was invulnerable (the twin "moats" of the Atlantic and Pacific), in making the case for unilateral action on the nation's "own" terms, on the ethics of slavery and colonization, and in debates over interventionism and extracontinental alliances and conflicts.

Coursing throughout this volume is the history of American settler colonialism and imperial practices, which intersect with notions of mission and racism, civilizational thinking and democracy, and national security and interests. At times "exceptionalism" and "empire" have been conceived of as alternatives, and at other moments they have been synonyms. What we find throughout U.S. history is a push and pull between types of anticolonialism rooted in the rejection of British and European systems of monarchy and aristocracy and new iterations of imperialism founded in colonial (and later republican) assumptions about free land, free security, freedom, and racial hierarchy.

These are but a few of the central themes and questions we have discerned in the ideologies that have served to guide U.S. foreign policy. But it is possible that the reader will detect entirely different patterns to the ones identified here. In a volume as varied and rich as this one, such an outcome would indeed be welcome.

Ultimately, this book is about the ideas at stake in the meaning of America and how they have been manifested in foreign policy. The chapters in this volume locate arguments over the ideological roots of patriotism, national identity, and visions of—and tensions between—nationalism and internationalism. The book illuminates the most significant ideologies and ideas that have driven U.S. foreign policy in the past, that propel U.S. foreign relations in the present, and that will shape it in the future.

Notes

1. In 2008 Barack Obama aimed to operate as a "principled" pragmatist, and his proposed efforts to deploy pragmatism over or against ideology generated a tremendous amount of reporting, praise, and criticism. On how this affected U.S. foreign policy, see David Milne, "Pragmatism or What? The Future of US Foreign Policy," *International Affairs* 88, no. 5 (September 2012): 935–51.
2. Barack Obama, "Senator Barack Obama's Speech Against Iraq War," NPR, October 2, 2002, https://www.npr.org/templates/story/story.php?storyId =99591469.
3. Barack Obama as quoted in Jeffrey Goldberg, "The Obama Doctrine," *Atlantic*, April 2016, https://www.theatlantic.com/magazine/archive/2016/04/the-obama -doctrine/471525/.
4. Hillary Clinton as quoted in Jeffrey Goldberg, "Hillary Clinton: 'Failure' to Help Syrian Rebels Led to the Rise of ISIS," *Atlantic*, August 10, 2014, https://www .theatlantic.com/international/archive/2014/08/hillary-clinton-failure-to -help-syrian-rebels-led-to-the-rise-of-isis/375832/. It is relevant to consider how many synonyms Clinton used for *ideology*—including "overarching framework," "worldview," and "organizing principle"—as a critique of Obama administration policy and in envisioning her own proposed approach as president. Reports after the Obama presidency, and contemporaneous coverage as

well, suggested that Joe Biden believed ideology usefully set the conditions for a pragmatic approach and thus he cautioned against a surge in Afghanistan and against larger interventions in Syria or Libya. In the early months of his presidency, Biden aimed to achieve those policy goals by withdrawing troops from Afghanistan in July and August 2021 despite the blowback and ensuing chaos.

5. Goldberg, "The Obama Doctrine."

6. Michael H. Hunt, *Ideology and U.S. Foreign Policy* (New Haven, CT: Yale University Press, 1987),12. The main contrast here would be to the prominent foreign relations historian and New Left critic William Appleman Williams, who emphasized economic self-interest as the principal driver of U.S. foreign policy—and often struggled to locate robust causal links in so doing. William Appleman Williams, *The Tragedy of American Diplomacy* (Cleveland, OH: World, 1959).

7. Hunt, *Ideology and U.S. Foreign Policy*, xi, 12. See Clifford Geertz, *The Interpretation of Cultures* (New York: Basic Books, 1973); Gabriel Almond and Sidney Verba, *The Civic Culture: Political Attitudes and Democracy in Five Nations* (Princeton, NJ: Princeton University Press, 1963).

8. Hunt, *Ideology and U.S. Foreign Policy*, 5.

9. Obama as quoted in Gerard Toal, *Near Abroad: Putin, the West, and the Contest Over Ukraine and the Caucasus* (New York: Oxford University Press, 2017), 296.

10. Molly K. McKew, "The Gerasimov Doctrine," *Politico*, September/October 2017.

11. On U.S. investigations into Russian interference in the U.S. presidential election in 2016, see Special Counsel Robert S. Mueller III, "Report on the Investigation Into Russian Interference in the 2016 Presidential Election," vol. 1, U.S. Department of Justice, March 2019, https://www.justice.gov/archives /sco/file/1373816/download.

12. This assessment is not to suggest that a Hillary Clinton presidency would have necessarily led to better outcomes simply because she took a more aggressive stance against Putin and Assad. In a 2014 interview, Clinton emphasized that political messaging should focus on America first. "First things first," she said. "If we don't restore the American dream for Americans, then you can forget about any kind of continuing leadership in the world. . . . You've got to take care of your home first." Hillary Clinton as quoted in Goldberg, "Hillary Clinton."

13. Elizabeth Borgwardt coined this term in a book of the same name. See Elizabeth Borgwardt, "Franklin Roosevelt, the New Deal, and Grand Strategy: Constructing the Postwar Order," in *Rethinking American Grand Strategy*, ed. Elizabeth Borgwardt, Christopher McKnight Nichols, and Andrew Preston (New York: Oxford University Press, 2021), 201–17. On the building of the new world order during WWII, see Stephen Wertheim, *Tomorrow the World: The Birth of US Global Supremacy* (Cambridge, MA: Harvard University Press, 2020).

14. Michael H. Hunt, "Ideology," *Journal of American History* 77, no. 1 (June 1990): 108.

15. The French Enlightenment thinker Antoine Destutt de Tracy first coined the term ideology, describing it as the "science of ideas." For an account of his life and thought, see Brian W. Head, *Politics and Philosophy in the Thought of Destutt de Tracy* (London: Taylor & Francis, 2019).

16. Karl Marx, preface to *A Contribution to the Critique of Political Economy*, as quoted in Raymond Williams, *Marxism and Literature* (Oxford: Oxford University Press, 1977), 67.

17. Louis Althusser, *For Marx*, trans. Ben Brewster (London: Verso, 2005), 232; E. P. Thompson, *The Poverty of Theory* (London: Merlin, 1978).

18. Althusser, *For Marx*, 231.

19. See Daniel T. Rodgers, *Atlantic Crossings: Social Politics in a Progressive Age, 1870–1945* (Cambridge, MA: Harvard University Press, 1998); Daniel T. Rodgers, *Age of Fracture* (Cambridge, MA: Harvard University Press, 2011); James T. Kloppenberg, *Uncertain Victory: Social Democracy and Progressivism in European and American Thought, 1870–1920* (New York: Oxford University Press, 1988); James T. Kloppenberg, *Toward Democracy: The Struggle for Self-Rule in European and American Thought* (New York: Oxford University Press, 2016); Jennifer Ratner-Rosenhagen, *American Nietzsche: A History of an Icon and His Ideas* (Chicago: University of Chicago Press, 2011); Jennifer Ratner-Rosenhagen, *The Ideas That Made America: A Brief History* (New York: Oxford University Press, 2019). For more on the burgeoning field of intellectual history, including approaches to ideology, see the new compilations Ray Haberski Jr. and Andrew Hartman, eds., *American Labyrinth: Intellectual History for Complicated Times* (Ithaca, NY: Cornell University Press, 2018); and Joel Isaac, James T. Kloppenberg, Michael O'Brien, and Jennifer Ratner-Rosenhagen, eds., *The Worlds of American Intellectual History* (New York: Oxford University Press, 2016).

20. The *Oxford English Dictionary*, 5th ed. (2002), s.v. "ideology," dates the etymology of the term to origins in the late eighteenth century with key developments regarding systems thinking in the early twentieth century. To help tease out some of the ways that intellectual historians approach the history of ideas, the definition and role of ideology, and intellectuals, see Dominick LaCapra, "Intellectual History and Its Ways," *American Historical Review* 97, no. 2 (April 1992): 425–39. Political theorists tend to examine ideologies and how intellectuals relate to the ideological traditions embedded in and developing out of political cultures, for example, see Craig Berry and Michael Kenny, "Ideology and the Intellectuals," in *The Oxford Handbook of Political Ideologies* (Oxford: Oxford University Press, 2013). See also *The Stanford Encyclopedia of Philosophy*, https://plato.stanford.edu.

21. Other books that investigate the connections between ideas/ideologies and U.S. foreign policy include Elizabeth Borgwardt, *A New Deal for the World* (Cambridge,

MA: Belknap Press of Harvard University Press, 2005); H. W. Brands, *What America Owes the World: The Struggle for the Soul of Foreign Policy* (Cambridge: Cambridge University Press, 1998); Mary L. Dudziak, *War Time: An Idea, Its History, Its Consequences* (Oxford: Oxford University Press, 2012); Norman A. Graebner, ed., *Ideas and Diplomacy: Readings in the Intellectual Tradition of American Foreign Policy* (New York: Oxford University Press, 1964); Michaela Hoenicke-Moore, "Ideology as a Factor in U.S. Foreign Relations," in *The Oxford Encyclopedia of American Military and Diplomatic History*, ed. Timothy Lynch, David Milne, and Christopher McKnight Nichols (New York: Oxford University Press, 2013), 498–504; Richard H. Immerman, *Empire for Liberty: A History of American Imperialism from Benjamin Franklin to Paul Wolfowitz* (Princeton, NJ: Princeton University Press, 2010); Bruce Kuklick, *Blind Oracles: Intellectuals and War from Kennan to Kissinger* (Princeton, NJ: Princeton University Press, 2006); David Milne, *Worldmaking: The Art and Science of American Diplomacy* (New York: Farrar, Straus and Giroux, 2015); Knud Krakau, "American Foreign Relations: A National Style?," *Diplomatic History* 8 (July 1984): 253–72; Melvyn P. Leffler, *A Preponderance of Power: National Security, the Truman Administration, and the Cold War* (Stanford, CA: Stanford University Press, 1992); Robert E. Osgood, *Ideals and Self-Interest in American's Foreign Relations: The Great Transformation of the Twentieth Century* (Chicago: University of Chicago Press, 1953); Anders Stephanson, *Manifest Destiny: American Expansion and the Empire of Right* (New York: Hill and Wang, 2995); and Ian Tyrrell, "American Exceptionalism in an Age of International History," *American Historical Review* 96, no. 4 (October 1991): 1031–72.

22. Hunt, *Ideology and U.S. Foreign Policy*, 13.

23. Hunt, *Ideology and U.S. Foreign Policy*, 124.

24. Brandon R. Byrd, *The Black Republic: African Americans and the Fate of Haiti* (Philadelphia: University of Pennsylvania Press, 2019); Tim Matthewson, "Jefferson and the Nonrecognition of Haiti," *Proceedings of the American Philosophical Society* 140, no. 1 (March 1996): 22–48.

25. Madeleine K. Albright, interview by Matt Lauer, *The Today Show*, February 19, 1998; John O'Sullivan, "Annexation," *United States Magazine and Democratic Review* 17 (1845): 5–6, 9–10; Michael Parker, *John Winthrop: Founding the City Upon a Hill* (New York: Routledge, 2014); Franklin D. Roosevelt, "Great Arsenal of Democracy," Fireside Chat December 29, 1940, in Samuel I. Rosenman, ed., *The Public Papers and Addresses of Franklin D. Roosevelt, 1940* (New York: Macmillan, 1941), 633–44.

26. Two contributors to this volume who have examined this subject in detail elsewhere are Nicholas Guyatt, *Providence and the Invention of the United States, 1607–1876* (Cambridge: Cambridge University Press, 2007); and Andrew Preston, *Sword of the Spirit, Shield of Faith: Religion in American War and Diplomacy* (New York: Knopf, 2012).

PART ONE

Ideologies and the People

CHAPTER 1

Indigenous Subjecthood and White Populism in British America

MATTHEW KRUER

In 1831, Supreme Court Chief Justice John Marshall ruled in *Cherokee Nation v. Georgia* that Indigenous peoples within the claimed boundaries of the United States were "domestic dependent nations." Indigenous peoples were paradoxically included in and excluded from the political community, both the objects of diplomacy as though foreign polities and the subjects of governance as colonized peoples.[1] The ruling built on *Johnson v. M'Intosh* (1823), which determined that Europeans acquired the right to Indigenous land by right of discovery, rendering Native peoples mere occupants in their own territory at the moment of contact. Marshall's so-called Doctrine of Discovery undermined Indigenous sovereignty, paved the way for removal, and consolidated the United States as an expansionist white republic. It was also a legal fiction based on intellectual sleight of hand. The right of discovery appeared in the papal bull *Inter caetera* (1493), which donated the Western Hemisphere to the Iberian crowns, but the Spanish jurist Francisco Vitoria invalidated it in 1539. No one invoked it again until John Marshall. His opinion cited no authority other than his own unfinished biography of George Washington, which upon publication was panned by critics not only for being long-winded and obtuse but also for lacking good primary sources. Marshall's academic skullduggery might be amusing if it were not the engine of enormous tragedy and ongoing injustice.[2]

In this chapter, I explore the evolution of Indigenous peoples' political membership in the British empire in North America from Jamestown to the U.S. Constitution—a history that Marshall erased.[3] I examine the relationship between independent Native nations, tributary nations that acknowledged themselves subjects of the British monarch, and colonists within a broad imperial framework, with attention to both commonalities across geographic regions and differences among distinct juridical spaces. I treat subjecthood as an ideology, an imaginative construction of the proper order of things that naturalizes relations of power and guides collective action. Rather than abstractions floating in mental space, such ideological constructions continually take shape through the grounded realities of political practice and social experience.[4] In this sense, ideology both informed and was transformed by British attempts to demarcate the boundary between the foreign and the domestic, distinguishing between members of the empire and those outside of it—distinctions central to the process of settler colonialism. Native Americans engaged in a similar process of negotiating the line between insiders and outsiders, kin and enemies, in ways that challenged British presumptions and altered the terms of the debate. This ideological dialogue determined the changing shape of bodies politic in early America.

The story of Indigenous subjecthood illuminates the influence of Indigenous struggles to define their political futures within the constraints of colonialism. It also invites a reconsideration of the shift in colonists' imagination of themselves from subjects of a monarch to citizens of a republic. The British empire was a composite entity that embraced multiple kingdoms of several languages, cultures, and ethnicities, with a growing cohort of overseas settlers whose status under the law was anything but clear. Like all polities in the early modern Atlantic, it was governed by legal pluralism—an agglomeration of juridical regimes that allowed for overlapping and never fully consistent definitions of political status. In the legal margins, struggles over power constituted law and empire, subjecthood and citizenship. Indigenous peoples struggled to protect their rights and pursue their interests within the ambit of imperial rule, and so did Scots and Irish; Indigenous peoples fought for recognition of their sovereignty at the same time that colonists fought for recognition that they were entitled to the "rights of Englishmen." The evolution of Indigenous subjecthood and British subjecthood profoundly shaped each other as different groups of subjects jostled to define themselves relative to their neighbors as well as to a distant imperial power. As those struggles became entwined with populist politics in the Age of Revolution, they fashioned the early definitions of racial citizenship in the United States.[5]

The ideology of English settler colonialism had a fantasy at its heart: that overseas empire would benefit not only themselves but also the Indigenous peoples it incorporated. William Strachey, the secretary of Virginia, wrote, "we shall by degrees chaunge their barbarous natures" by converting Natives to Protestant Christianity and "teach them obedience to the king's majestie." Early colonists therefore sought to transform independent Indigenous peoples into subjects of the king. Viewing the Powhatan paramount chiefdom as a "monarchicall governement," Virginia Company agents determined to turn the mamanatowick (paramount chief) Powhatan into a vassal by bestowing upon him a crown and red coat in the name of King James I. His acceptance, company spokesmen claimed, signaled "full acknowledgment of dutie and submission."[6] Similarly, in 1621 Plymouth colonists concluded an agreement with Ousamequin, the Wampanoag Massasoit (chief), claiming that it confirmed his submission. According to Nathaniel Morton, Ousamequin "acknowledged himself content to become the Subject of our Soveraign Lord the King . . . and gave unto them all the Lands adjacent, to them and their Heirs forever."[7] Because diplomatic agreements required consent under the law of nations, an ideological precursor to modern international law, English colonizers sought to legitimize their imperial claims by convincing Indigenous peoples to choose subjecthood willingly.[8]

One might expect fierce resistance to these colonizing gestures, but some Indigenous leaders cooperated with, or even welcomed, them. Coastal Algonquians interpreted "subjection" as tributary status, a familiar power relationship in which subordinate nations paid tribute to a more powerful group in exchange for protection and trade.[9] In 1620, the Wampanoags were tributaries of the Narragansetts, a relationship that Ousamequin sought to renegotiate through alliance with the English. He was pleased with the results: after colonists defended Wampanoags from the Narragansetts, Ousamequin proclaimed himself "King James his man" and Wampanoag territory "King James his country." Other sachems (chiefs) followed suit, viewing the benefits of submission to the English more desirable than paying tribute to the Narragansetts.[10] Powhatan, who received tribute rather than paying it, likewise viewed the English as an asset. He accepted the crown and robe, keeping them in the sacred space of the chiefly mortuary and wearing the crown on ceremonial occasions to receive tribute from subordinate werowances (chiefs). However, he insisted that subjection was not the same as submission. "I also am a King," he told company agents, "and this is my land." Indigenous leaders could embrace subjecthood because it augmented their power without diminishing their sovereignty.[11]

Incommensurate understandings of subjection bred conflict. Virginia colonists, insistent that Powhatans were subordinate, expanded aggressively after the introduction of tobacco. In 1622, Powhatan's successor, Opechancanough, defended his people's sovereignty through an orchestrated assault that killed one-quarter of Jamestown's population, followed by a siege that brought the colony to the brink of collapse.[12] In the years that followed, charters for new colonies, such as the 1632 Maryland charter, asserted that English immigrants were the land's true inhabitants. By royal decree, territory "not yet cultivated and planted" was merely "inhabited by certaine barbarous people." Indigenous people launching "incursions" into their own territory could be met with unlimited violence as "pyrates and robbers . . . by the Law of warre." This language echoed the writings of the Oxford jurist Alberico Gentili, who argued that brigands, rebels, and brutes were outside the *societas gentium* (community of states) and thus without sovereignty or the protection of law. Armed with such charters, English subjects could carry their sovereign status with them into the territories rendered uninhabited by ideology.[13]

Formal definitions of Indigenous subjecthood evolved out of a cauldron of violence with peacemaking in its aftermath. After two decades of war, Powhatans accepted defeat in a 1646 treaty that dissolved the paramount chiefdom and made each of its constituent nations subject to the crown. The treaty stipulated that Necotowance, Opechancanough's successor, pay annual tribute and "acknowledge to hold his kingdome from the King's Ma'tie of England." Although the treaty's punishing terms cannot be understood as anything other than conquest, it nevertheless established that Indigenous subjects were entitled to rights and protections. Virginia's 1662 legal code stated, "they shall have equall justice with our owne nation," and guaranteed Indigenous rights to own property, obligated county sheriffs to protect that property from squatters, and allowed freedom to enter English properties to gather traditional foods. Natives and settlers were legally distinct, yet both had a place in the legal regime of England's empire.[14] Such distinctions should not surprise us. As Mahmood Mamdani and Ann Laura Stoler have noted, defining different classes of subjects, each with its own rights and privileges, is one of the principal techniques of imperial rule.[15]

Canny Indigenous leaders could use their legal toehold to pull the levers of transatlantic power. In 1643, the Narragansett sachems Canonicus and Pessacus, having accepted subjection but chafing against the demands of Massachusetts Bay magistrates, enlisted the dissident Puritan Samuel Groton to carry a petition to the king. Canonicus and Pessacus underlined their sovereign status in Indigenous terms, asserting they were "the chief Sachems . . . of the country, time out of mind." They also declared submission in an idiom legible to the English, pledging obedience "*upon condition of His Majesties' royal protection*" against "some of His Majesty's pretended subjects," the overweening rulers of Boston.[16] Although England was embroiled in a civil war that ended with Charles I beheaded by radical puritans in Parliament, his son Charles II was only too happy to support Indigenous "Princes" as a means of bringing New England puritans to heel. In 1664, his agents communicated "Our Fatherly affection towards all Our Subjects," Native and settler alike. In subsequent disputes royal agents sided with New England sachems, forcing colonial officials to grudgingly respect their position as fellow subjects. When given the opportunity to craft a legal regime from whole cloth in newly conquered New York, agents of James, Duke of York, wrote the rights of Indigenous subjects into the legal code: "All injuryes done to the Indians of what nature whatsoever shall . . . have speedy redress . . . as if the Case had been betwixt Christian and Christian." Sachems such as Canonicus and Pessacus embraced their status as subjects of the king to defend Indigenous sovereignty and independence, and they found a sympathetic audience in a monarch who used Indigenous petitions to extend royal power.[17]

Despite some successes by Native leaders, colonization was an inherently violent process.[18] The rights and protections enshrined in treaties were often honored in the breach, and Indigenous subjects suffered under English rule. Nevertheless, Native peoples carved out a place within colonial regimes resilient enough that it could only be assaulted in legalistic terms, even in moments of crisis. In 1675, the Wampanoag sachem Metacom (King Philip) went to war against Plymouth, which had executed three Indigenous men charged with the murder of another Indigenous man in Indigenous territory—an egregious violation of the Wampanoags' sovereign right to adjudicate justice when neither colonists nor colonial space was involved. Colonists seeking to portray themselves in the right were forced to argue that Wampanoag attacks constituted unlawful rebellion by subjects of the crown. William Harris, cofounder of Rhode Island, described it as "high treason against the king," led by a man Plymouth governor Josiah Winslow called "Phillip the grande Rebell."[19]

Colonists who felt their own rights imperiled, however, progressed from accusing fellow subjects of treason to denying their subjecthood altogether. In 1676, Virginia colonist Nathaniel Bacon convinced himself that tributary Algonquians were conspiring with foreign nations at war with the colony and gathered an illegal militia "to ruine and extirpate all Indians in General." Governor Sir William Berkeley ordered these self-styled "Volunteers" to stand down, insisting that loyal Indigenous subjects were the best bulwark to colonial security. Bacon and the Volunteers refused and plunged Virginia into civil war because they believed their rights as Englishmen were at stake. From the Volunteers' perspective, Berkeley's insistence on treating Natives as subjects of the crown betrayed the sovereign's obligation to protect English subjects from harm. Bacon, no doubt recalling Gentili from his legal studies, declared that Indigenous peoples were "Robbers and Theeves and Invaders of his Majesties Right," and therefore were "wholly unqualifyed for the benefitt and Protection of the law." For Bacon's less erudite followers, political philosophy was less important than the experience of life and death on a frontier at war. For the "voluntiers who fight for their own Lives and Liberties" by pursuing a campaign of genocide, the rallying cry was "the just defence of ourselves, wives and children." A populist movement coalesced around an incendiary idea: the English empire had room for only one kind of subject.[20]

The Anglo-Indian wars of the 1670s devastated Native communities and might have closed the door on the possibility of Indigenous subjecthood. Instead, it was revived through Indigenous initiative and imperial intervention. Cockacoeske, the Pamunkey weroansqua (female chief), used her friendship with the Virginian Francis Moryson to gain a sympathetic ear in the Privy Council and orchestrate the landmark 1677 Treaty of Middle Plantation. The treaty stated that Indigenous people within Virginia were crown subjects with all the rights and obligations implied by that status. Cockacoeske and other Native leaders—one of whom took the name of the queen Catherine to honor the occasion—"have their immediate Dependency on, and owne all subjection to, the great King of England." The treaty acknowledged their rights to land and property "in as free and firme manner as others his Majesties Subjects have" and promised that the

Figure 1.1 Seal of the Dominion of New England, 1686.
Source: William Cullen Bryant and Sydney Howard Gay, *A Popular History of the United States*, vol. 3 (New York: Scribner, 1879), 9.

government would defend them from would-be Bacons. Signed by Herbert Jeffreys, handpicked by the king to replace Governor Berkeley and reshape the colonial order according to royal desires, the treaty established a legal framework for a multicultural empire.[21]

Support for Indigenous subjecthood was part of a broader agenda of imperial centralization during the reigns of Stuart monarchs Charles II and James II. Both saw intervention in Indigenous affairs as a tool for undermining colonial autonomy in the service of creating an integrated empire ruled by absolute monarchs. Defending Native rights, therefore, was less a beneficent vision of intercultural harmony than a cudgel to beat recalcitrant colonists into submission. The Stuarts' dream was emblazoned on the seal of the Dominion of New England (figure 1.1), a bold experiment in consolidation into a viceregal supercolony that depicted English and Indigenous subjects as equals, side by side on their knees before King James II.

Most opportunities to build on the foundations laid by the Treaty of Middle Plantation came crashing down with James II's abdication and the fall of the Dominion during the Glorious Revolution (1688–1689). Anti-Indigenous sentiment was a common thread in the revolutionary movements that swept through New England, New York, and Maryland; conspiracy theories that royal governments were secretly colluding with hostile Indigenous nations—thus betraying their duty to protect English subjects—fueled popular uprisings. Room for Native peoples to maneuver narrowed in an era that saw colonists forging a common identity as Britons in part through opposition to Indigenous enemies.[22]

Nonetheless, Indigenous peoples living within colonial jurisdictions still used their subject status to defend their communities. Many eighteenth-century Native leaders continued to treat sovereignty and subjection as complementary. The Chowanoke headman John Hoyter, for example, called himself a king and characterized Chowanoke land as his "Netev ples," suggesting a claim to sovereignty dating to before European contact. Yet in a 1705 petition, Hoyter stressed his history of solidarity with colonists, calling the governor his "Brother," part of the web of kin that constituted political community. Hoyter claimed the same rights that colonists enjoyed under the law, pointing out that he performed the same obligations, such as military service. Chowanokes, in other words, were both an ancient nation with sovereign rights and part of the British body politic. Hoyter and other representatives of Algonquian tributary nations apparently did not consider these two positions contradictory. Colonists, who were themselves part of a composite polity consisting of multiple kingdoms and colonies with a diverse array of peoples who had little in common except allegiance to the same monarch, apparently did not think so either.[23]

Indigenous articulations of sovereignty intersected with ongoing debates about the constitution of the British empire, challenging colonial claims to powers that superseded Native rights.[24] In 1703, the Mohegan sachem Oweneco complained to Queen Anne that Connecticut was illegally dispossessing his people. His petition was carried by Nicholas Hallem, a settler with his own axe to grind against Connecticut, who conveyed Oweneco's claim to "Hereditary Right to the Soyll and Royalltys of our Dominion and Territorys before the English came into the Country."[25] The attorney general and Board of Trade decided in his favor, agreeing that Mohegans were both a sovereign nation with original title to their territory and a subject people with legal rights and protections. Mohegan leaders used the ruling to defend against later land grabs, culminating in a 1743 commission that decided that not only was the Mohegan nation a political body distinct from Connecticut but also that the Mohegan nation's standing relative to the crown was equivalent to Connecticut's. According to the historian Craig Yirush, this decision adopted a definition of subjecthood frequently endorsed by Indigenous leaders: "a conditional subjection in which they ceded some of their original rights in return for being treated as coequal polities in the empire."[26]

Mohegans, like Narragansetts in 1643 and Pamunkeys in 1677, were heard because sympathetic Englishmen amplified their voices. Nations lacking such allies, however, could fall prey to rapacious locals and imperial indifference. The Meherrin nation was among the many signatories of the 1677 Treaty of Middle Plantation establishing them as subjects of the crown. In the early eighteenth century, however, the North Carolina government asserted that the Meherrins had signed a treaty making them tributaries of North Carolina, a spurious claim unsupported by any documentation. Because the crown's representative in the 1677 treaty negotiations had been the Virginia governor, the Meherrin leadership petitioned Virginia for protection. The Virginia Council protested that the Meherrins "are not to be Considered as a Nation of Savages . . . but as her Majestys Subjects who are as much under her protection as any of her Subjects of Virginia."[27] But Meherrin proximity to North Carolina settlers left them vulnerable to eviction at gunpoint, forcing them to accept tributary status to North Carolina and confinement to a reservation. Although their rights as subjects were technically ratified at the imperial level, those rights evaporated when the crown and its representatives abdicated their duty to enforce the protections due to subjects.[28]

British colonists could afford to trample over the complex legalities of Indigenous subjecthood in the case of nations such as the Meherrins, who were too small to pose a serious threat, but settlers were more constrained when dealing with populous nations that possessed the power to insist on their understanding of subjecthood. Native peoples of the Delaware and Susquehanna valleys had crafted treaties with William Penn establishing their incorporation into Pennsylvania. Their 1701 treaty stipulated that they "shall have the full and free privileges and Imunities of all the Said Laws as any other Inhabitants, they Duly Owning and Acknowledging the Authority of the Crown of England and Government of this Province."[29] When later generations of Pennsylvanians demonstrated contempt for Indigenous rights through fraudulent dealings, Delawares did not need to resort to the posture of supplicating subjects. Complaining of illegal squatters to agents of Governor Thomas Penn, Delaware sachems warned, "We never Sold him this land" and therefore "We Desire Thomas Penn Would take these People off . . . that we May not be at the trouble to drive them off."[30]

By the eighteenth century, Indigenous subjecthood in most of British North America had many local variations but a strong central theme: Native nations were both sovereign and subject, with rights rooted in their ancient integrity as peoples as well as rights and obligations as members of a transatlantic empire. This understanding of nested power structures was expressed by Native leaders, and it was neither objectionable nor exotic to administrators overseeing an increasingly expansive imperial state. The problem was not that imperial administrators rejected Indigenous ideas of subjecthood as a species of divided sovereignty but that settlers came to reject Indigenous peoples themselves. To a significant extent, as many historians have shown, the cause was the formation of racial hatred in the fires of war.[31] No less important, as imperial crisis rumbled toward revolution in the 1760s, colonial struggles for the rights of British subjects became predicated on the denial of those rights to Indigenous peoples.

By the mid-eighteenth century, the problems that Indigenous subjecthood posed to the British empire came from the combination of independent Native nations and nations within colonial jurisdiction. British defenses of territorial claims against an expanding French empire required establishing that nations of the continental interior were British subjects. However, making claims strong enough to ward off French officials without alienating Indigenous leaders was a tricky business. Attempts to walk that line produced such documents as New York Governor Thomas Dongan's 1687 letter to the governor of New France, in which he called the Haudenosaunee (Iroquois League) "the king of England's Subjects," but which the secretary emphatically annotated, "not Sent to the Indians."[32] Over time, Haudenosaunee sachems came to embrace the convenient diplomatic fiction of subjection: while the British claimed Indigenous spaces for its empire by asserting that the Haudenosaunee were subjects of the crown, the Haudenosaunee extended their influence over Indigenous neighbors with British support. British and Haudenosaunee both prospered in the first half of the eighteenth century thanks to this relationship, which came to be known as the Covenant Chain, but both sides knew that the Covenant Chain was an alliance rather than subjection. Sir William Johnson, superintendent of Indian affairs, told his superiors, "they have been represented as calling themselves subjects, altho, the very word would have startled them, had it ever been pronounced by any Interpreter."[33] Sachems may have had few qualms about performing subjection when it suited their interests, but they bristled when British officials took their own fantasies too seriously.

The British conquest of New France rendered this useful ambiguity untenable. On paper, the French surrender of North America in 1763 reduced all of the French-allied Indigenous nations to inhabitants of territory under the dominion of the British crown. The Proclamation of 1763 established a framework for imperial governance based on a cold clarity. East of the line, British subjects lived under a patchwork of colonial governments established by charter. West of the line, Indigenous nations were not subjects but wards of the crown. Their full inclusion into the body politic was contingent on gradual assimilation under the watchful eye of superintendents, who would govern through tribal leaders elected to serve as "Guardian for the Indians and protector of their Rights."[34] The goal of the system was to create conditions by which independent Indigenous nations could become like the eastern tributaries, who Johnson called "small domesticated Tribes," and its structure was not unlike the forms of indirect imperial governance that British officials were creating in South Asia around the same time.[35]

From an imperial point of view, it was a solid plan with humane motivations. From both settler and Indigenous perspectives, however, it was an intolerable assault on their rights. Native nations ranging from Odawas in the Great Lakes to Delawares in Pennsylvania defended their sovereignty in the face of an empire that claimed a dominion it could not enforce. "Englishman, although you have conquered the French," Anishinaabe (Ojibwe) chief Minweweh declared, "you have not yet conquered us!" He added, in language that colonists would soon hurl toward Parliament in defense of their own rights, "We are not your slaves." Indigenous warriors besieged nearly every western garrison, took several major forts, and tactically deployed terror to reduce illegal settlers to panicked refugees.[36]

Settlers closest to the frontier responded much as Virginians had nearly a century earlier: with ferocious violence against Indigenous peoples of any nation, refusing to distinguish between foreign belligerents and fellow subjects. In Pennsylvania, a group of vigilantes who called themselves Volunteers but came to be known as the Paxton Boys massacred the Conestogas, one of the signatories of the 1701 treaty. There is no question that racialized Indian-hating was central to the Paxton Boys' atrocities.[37] But they also articulated a vernacular understanding of subjecthood in the British empire. In a pamphlet defending their actions, the Paxton Boys rejected the model of divided sovereignty that allowed Indigenous nations such as the Conestoga to live in a composite empire:

> no Nation could be safe especially in a Time of War, if another State or Part of a State be allowed to live among them, free and independent, claiming and exercising within themselves all the Powers of Government. . . . No such Privilege has been granted to any Commonwealth in any civilized Nation in the World. But this had been allowed to Indians amongst us, and we justly complain of it as the Source of many of our Calamities.

When Governor John Penn declared the Paxton Boys outlaws and charged them with murder, they declared, "we insulted no lawful Authority, nor flew in the Face of Government, but acted as loyal Subjects of his Majesty when we cut off these his Enemies."[38] Their supporters insisted that anyone brought to trial must be prosecuted in their home counties, where juries packed with Indian-hating frontiersmen were guaranteed to acquit. To do otherwise would "take away from his Majesty's good Subjects, a Privilege so long esteemed sacred by *English Men*," an unacceptable affront even if it violated Indigenous rights to equal protection under the law.[39]

British officials, as well as elite colonists in the coastal cities, rejected these arguments. Benjamin Franklin inverted the tropes of civility when he called the Paxton Boys "Christian white savages" whose lawless actions threatened good government.[40] But metropolitan fear of frontier anarchy proved far more vigorous than horror at the frontiersmen's atrocities. As squatters, surveyors, and speculators streamed into the territory optimistically labeled "Land reserved for Indians" on imperial maps, military officers realized that they could only prevent chaotic warfare by policing the frontier. Natives considered the soldiers' presence to violate the 1763 Proclamation, and settlers interpreted it as evidence that standing armies paved the road toward tyranny. In 1765, Pennsylvania settlers known as the "Black Boys" ambushed a military convoy on a diplomatic mission to western nations. They announced that diplomacy was illegitimate unless endorsed by county magistrates, and they would oppose any British subject willing to tolerate peace with Indigenous peoples, even the imperial army. The Black Boys, asserted Commander-in-Chief Thomas Gage, demonstrated that "the Reins of Government are too lose to enforce an Obedience to the Laws," whereas Johnson considered them equal to the Sons of Liberty as "Enemies to the British Constitution."[41] Much like the urban rioters protesting the Stamp Act that same year, the Black Boys were staking a claim for the rights of colonists in terms that threatened to rupture the empire. In the west, however, colonists' conception of the rights of subjecthood excluded Indigenous peoples, and they enacted a populist policy of undeclared race war.[42]

The empire in the west unraveled in part through the strain of trying to enforce coexistence between two kinds of subjects. Rather than promoting restraint after the outbreak of revolution in 1775, British officials called upon Natives to quell white resistance. Indigenous leaders such as the cosmopolitan Mohawk Joseph Brandt, calculating that service to the crown would secure sovereignty for his nation, organized "volunteer" corps that coordinated with loyalist irregulars. Indigenous-British raids led western communities to fuse emerging notions of independence—notions that had much more to do with local self-sovereignty than solidarity with distant state capitals—with genocidal Indian hating.[43] The embattled states stoked that rage to drum up support for the common cause of independence. The British were not content to commit their own atrocities, thundered the Continental Congress in a broadside to the people, but have "excited the Indians against us; . . . whole Hosts of Savages, whose Rule of Warfare is promiscuous Carnage, who rejoice to murder the Infant smiling in its Mother's Arms, to inflict on their Prisoners the most excruciating Torments, and exhibit Scenes of Horror from which Nature recoils."[44] After U.S. victory in 1783, westerners made it clear that their loyalty to the new nation was predicated on its ability to protect them from Indigenous peoples, and the government had little interest in seeking the kind of delicate balancing act that had hastened the collapse of the British empire in North America.[45]

The concurrent processes of forging a nation of citizens and waging war against Indigenous peoples led the founders to endorse populist demands for Natives exclusion. By 1790, the only kinds of Indigenous rights that white Americans cared about were land rights, and then only insofar as it mattered to the sale of that land to white citizens. Squatters and speculators, state governments and federal governments, all struggled in a protean legal landscape to show that their claim to land title was legitimate based on past transactions with Native peoples.[46] Although it took more than a century to accomplish those transfers, the political exclusion of Indigenous peoples was immediate. The first session of Congress—the same session that ratified the Bill of Rights—reserved citizenship for "free white person[s]."[47] As colonists threw off their bonds of subjecthood and began forging new bonds of citizenship, one of their axioms was that Indigenous peoples were not, and could not be, a part of that civic brotherhood.

If there is such a thing as an originary moment to U.S. foreign policy, its defining feature was a commitment to settler colonialism encapsulated by that racialized definition of citizenship. The first foreign policy crisis faced by the United States was not in the Atlantic but in the Ohio Valley, and the "foreign" polities in question were not the empires of Britain or France or Spain but the "United Indian Nations" that destroyed two American armies and represented a viable alternative to U.S. expansion.[48] The crisis was provoked by settlers whose willingness to defy any authority that dared to recognize Indigenous rights threatened the coherence—and even the survival—of the American state. Secretary of War Henry Knox predicted that Anglo-Indian hostilities in Ohio, inspired in large part by Indian-hating settlers "possessing an equal aversion to all bearing the name of Indians," created a crisis that "will deeply injure, if not utterly destroy, the interests and government of the United States in the Western territory."[49] The force propelling the engine of settler colonialism was the belief that Native peoples ought to be removed to create opportunities for white citizens, a commitment to white supremacy that may have been the only solid bond linking western settlers to policy makers in the capital.[50] Rather than conciliate the Indigenous confederation, the Washington administration chose to treat foreign spaces of Indigenous nations as domestic ones. The alchemy of ideology transmuted invading settlers into endangered citizens entitled to the protection of the federal government and rendered Native peoples defending their sovereign homelands as rebels against the legitimate authority of the United States. This fiction of the foreign-as-domestic built on decades, or even centuries, of experience, woven into the nation's foreign policy DNA long before its inception, when it was still a little imperial zygote in an empire of many subjects.

Indigenous peoples were not the only people excluded from citizenship in the early republic. As revolutionary notions about who could bear the rights of the citizen solidified into juridical categories, white men stripped Black

Americans of political rights on a national consensus of white supremacy, and reduced women to incubating citizenship rather than practicing it.[51] Unlike Native peoples, however, neither women nor peoples of African descent constituted nations themselves. Their demands for recognition could only be articulated from within the edifice of the American state. Indigenous peoples, on the other hand, continued to claim rights that stemmed from their existence as sovereign nations long before Europeans first sighted the American coastline. "The land was given to us by the Great Spirit above as our common right, to raise our children upon, and to make support for our rising generations," women of the Cherokee Republic insisted in 1818; "we therefore claim the right of the soil."[52]

The legal determination that Indigenous peoples had no right of the soil, and that they were neither citizens nor aliens but wards of the state, was not preordained. Early modern political theorists ranging from Hugo Grotius to Emmerich de Vattel argued that sovereignty could be divided among multiple political bodies. Their arguments inspired revolutionaries such as James Madison to link sovereign states in a confederation through the federal Constitution.[53] Citizens of the early republic often referred to "these United States" with a plural pronoun, and until the Civil War it was a mainstream political position to insist that the states retained their sovereign powers and could leave the Union at will. There was nothing inherent to Indigenous sovereignty that made tribal nations incompatible with the federal structure of the United States. Perhaps this explains the repeated attempts of Native nations to join the United States as equals, from the Delaware chief Koguetagechton (White Eyes) joining the American rebellion against the crown in exchange for a Delaware state in the Ohio Valley, to the Cherokees' insistence on retaining sovereignty as a nation within a nation in the early republic, to the 1905 petition of tribal nations in Indian Territory for admission as the state of Sequoyah, and even to the modern Kanaka (Native Hawaiian) struggle to serve as an exemplar of alternative futures in an era of neoliberal capitalism and the climate crisis.[54]

Just as Indigenous leaders articulated visions of Indigenous membership in the United States in ways that respected their nations' sovereignty, so did their ancestors struggle to define their place in the British empire. To modern eyes, their definitions may seem paradoxical in claiming both subjection and independence, coming from speakers acting as much like foreign diplomats as community leaders. That paradox reflects Native understandings of subjecthood and its meanings that evolved as Indigenous political theory met the realities of European colonization. It also highlights the instability of the "subject" category among the British. Constitutional debates about the relationship between colony and empire and the legal standing of colonial creoles were ferocious in the seventeenth and eighteenth centuries, a running transatlantic argument that shaped the evolution of the empire.[55] Colonists in the haphazardly growing imperium also struggled to define the nature of their subjecthood, insisting that even subjects born at the farthest limit of the monarch's sovereignty were as entitled to the same rights as those in the shadow of the throne. The arguments of Natives defending their sovereignty were always entangled with colonial arguments about the "rights of Englishmen." The empire contained both kinds of subjects for decades. Until, that is, one of the liberties colonists claimed as Englishmen was the right to be free of Indigenous peoples.

Notes

1. In this chapter I avoid use of the terms *Indian*, which some Indigenous people consider pejorative or inaccurate, and *Native American*, which suggests a monolithic racial or ethnic subdivision of U.S. society rather than diverse members of many sovereign nations. When discussing the original peoples of North America as a whole, I generally use the term *Indigenous*, or occasionally *Native*, which are capitalized to reflect their constitution as nations (just as *German* and *European* are capitalized). Whenever possible I use the proper name for specific peoples as it is preferred by modern tribal nations. On these terminological issues, see Michael Yellow Bird, "What We Want to Be Called: Indigenous Peoples' Perspectives on Racial and Ethnic Identity Labels," *American Indian Quarterly* 23, no. 2 (Spring 1999): 1–21; Gregory Younging, *Elements of Indigenous Style: A Guide for Writing By and About Indigenous Peoples* (Edmonton, Canada: Brush, 2018).
2. Tim Alan Garrison, *The Legal Ideology of Removal: The Southern Judiciary and the Sovereignty of Native American Nations* (Athens: University of Georgia Press, 2002), 125–50; Lindsay G. Robertson, *Conquest by Law: How the Discovery of America Dispossessed Indigenous Peoples of Their Lands* (New York: Oxford University Press, 2005), esp. 96–103.
3. The Marshall rulings, perhaps because of the evident grasp of settler colonialism they reveal, have led most historians to gloss over the complexities of Indigenous peoples' political status, usually assuming that the law was a cynical tool for conquest or focusing on land as the sine qua non of Indigenous sovereignty and giving little attention to rights related to speech, religious

practice, individual property, and bodily integrity. See Francis Jennings, *The Invasion of America: Indians, Colonialism, and the Cant of Conquest* (Chapel Hill: University of North Carolina Press, 1975), esp. 105–27; Robert A. Williams Jr., *The American Indian in Western Legal Thought: The Discourses of Conquest* (New York: Oxford University Press, 1990). There are several fine-grained studies of Indigenous tributaries that have illuminated the varieties of Indigenous political experience but are understandably limited to particular times and places. Bradley J. Dixon, "'His one Netev ples': The Chowans and the Politics of Native Petitions in the Colonial South," *William and Mary Quarterly* 76, no. 1 (January 2019): 41–74; Katherine A. Hermes, "'Justice Will Be Done Us': Algonquian Demands for Reciprocity in the Courts of European Settlers," in *The Many Legalities of Early America*, ed. Christopher L. Tomlins and Bruce H. Mann (Chapel Hill: University of North Carolina Press, 2001), 123–49; Michelle LeMaster, "In the 'Scolding Houses': Indians and the Law in Eastern North Carolina, 1684–1760," *North Carolina Historical Review* 83, no. 2 (April 2006): 193–232; Jenny Hale Pulsipher, *Subjects Unto the Same King: Indians, English, and the Contest for Authority in Colonial New England* (Philadelphia: University of Pennsylvania Press, 2005); Dylan Ruediger, "'Neither Utterly to Reject Them, Nor Yet to Drawe Them to Come In': Tributary Subordination and Settler Colonialism in Virginia," *Early American Studies* 18, no. 1 (Winter 2020): 1–31; Craig Yirush, "'Chief Princes and Owners of All': Native American Appeals to the Crown in the Early-Modern British Atlantic," in *Native Claims: Indigenous Law Against Empire, 1500–1920*, ed. Saliha Belmessous (Oxford: Oxford University Press, 2011), 129–51.

4. My conception of ideology draws from Louis Althusser's Marxian approach to the production of ideology through practice; see Louis Althusser, "Ideology and Ideological State Apparatuses (Notes Towards an Investigation)," in *Mapping Ideology*, ed. Slavoj Žižek (New York: Verso, 1994), 100–40. Indigenous knowledge systems operated through ontologies and epistemologies distinct from those of colonizers, but they were no less complex and evolved in dialogue with European intellectual traditions. Although the concept of "ideology" does not adequately capture the nature of those thoughtways (particularly given Althusser's focus on the state), I use it here as a shorthand to indicate the work of Indigenous intellectuals in shaping political practice. See, for example, Lisa Brooks, *The Common Pot: The Recovery of Native Space in the Northeast* (Minneapolis: University of Minnesota Press, 2008); Gabriela Ramos and Yanna Yannakakis, eds., *Indigenous Intellectuals: Knowledge, Power, and Colonial Culture in Mexico and the Andes* (Durham, NC: Duke University Press, 2014); Alyssa Mt. Pleasant, Caroline Wigginton, and Kelly Wisecup, "Materials and Methods in Native American and Indigenous Studies: Completing the Turn," *William and Mary Quarterly* 75, no. 2 (April 2018): 207–36.

5. J. H. Elliott, "A Europe of Composite Monarchies," *Past & Present* 137 (November 1992): 48–71; Lauren A. Benton, *Law and Colonial Cultures: Legal Regimes in World History, 1400–1900* (Cambridge: Cambridge University Press, 2004).

6. William Strachey, *The Historie of Travaile Into Virginia Britannia: Expressing the Cosmographie and Comodities of the Country, Togither with the Manners and Customes of the People*, ed. Richard Henry Major (London: Hakluyt Society, 1849), 85; John Smith, *The Complete Works of Captain John Smith (1580–1631)*, ed. Philip L. Barbour, 3 vols. (Chapel Hill: University of North Carolina Press, 1986), 1:173–74; Council for Virginia, "True Declaration of the Estate of the Colonie in Virginia (1610)," in *Tracts and Other Papers Relating Principally to the Origin, Settlement, and Progress of the Colonies in North America: From the Discovery of the Country to the Year 1776*, ed. Peter Force, 4 vols. (Washington, DC: Peter Force, 1836–1846), 3:6; Edmund S. Morgan, *American Slavery, American Freedom: The Ordeal of Colonial Virginia* (1975; repr. New York: Norton, 2003), 3–24.

7. Dwight B. Heath, ed., *A Journal of the Pilgrims at Plymouth, or Mourt's Relation* (New York: Corinth, 1963), 56–57; Nathaniel Morton, *New Englands Memorial*, ed. Howard J. Hall (New York: Scholars' Facsimiles and Reprints, 1937), 24.

8. Jeffrey Glover, *Paper Sovereigns: Anglo-Native Treaties and the Law of Nations, 1604–1664* (Philadelphia: University of Pennsylvania Press, 2014), 7–15.

9. Kathleen J. Bragdon, *Native People of Southern New England, 1500–1650* (Norman: University of Oklahoma Press, 1996), 147–50; Margaret Holmes Williamson, *Powhatan Lords of Life and Death: Command and Consent in Seventeenth-Century Virginia* (Lincoln: University of Nebraska Press, 2003), 148–53.

10. Heath, *Mourt's Relation*, 66, 78; Morton, *New Englands Memorial*, 29; Neal Salisbury, *Manitou and Providence: Indians, Europeans, and the Making of New England, 1500–1643* (New York: Oxford University Press, 1982), 114–16.

11. Smith, *Complete Works*, 2:183; Glover, *Paper Sovereigns*, 65–70.

12. Karen Ordahl Kupperman, *The Jamestown Project* (Cambridge, MA: Harvard University Press, 2007), 278–328.

13. William Hand Browne et al., eds., *Archives of Maryland* (Baltimore: Maryland Historical Society, 1883–1972), 549:10, 21; Christopher Tomlins, *Freedom Bound: Law, Labor, and Civic Identity in Colonizing English America, 1580–1865* (Cambridge: Cambridge University Press, 2010), 120–21, 128–31, 175–77.

14. William Waller Hening, ed., *The Statutes at Large: Being a Collection of All the Laws of Virginia, from the First Session of the Legislature, in the Year 1619*, 13 vols. (Richmond: R. & W. & G. Bartow, 1809–1823), 1:323, 2:138–43, 194.

15. Mahmood Mamdani, *Define and Rule: Native as Political Identity* (Cambridge, MA: Harvard University Press, 2012); Ann Laura Stoler, "On Degrees of Imperial Sovereignty," *Public Culture* 18, no. 1 (December 2006): 125–46.

16. John Russell Bartlett, ed., *Records of the Colony of Rhode Island and Providence Plantations in New England*, 10 vols. (Providence: A. Crawford Greene and

Bro., 1856–1865), 1:134–35 (emphasis in original); Yirush, "'Chief Princes and Owners of All,'" 129–35.

17. Peter R. Christoph and Florence A. Christoph, eds., *Books of General Entries of the Colony of New York*, 2 vols. (Baltimore, MD: Genealogical, 1982), 1:5; Charles Z. Lincoln, William H. Johnson, and A. Judd Northrup, eds., *The Colonial Laws of New York From the Year 1664 to the Revolution*, 5 vols. (Albany: J. B. Lyon, 1894–1896), 1:40; Pulsipher, *Subjects Unto the Same King*, 37–69.

18. Patrick Wolfe, "Settler Colonialism and the Elimination of the Native," *Journal of Genocide Research* 8, no. 4 (December 2006): 387–409.

19. "William Harris to [Sir Joseph Williamson], 12 August 1676," The National Archives of the UK, Colonial Office, 1/37/47, f. 171r; "Governor Josiah Winslow to the King, 26 June 1677," The National Archives, Colonial Office, 1/40/116, f. 269r; Pulsipher, *Subjects Unto the Same King*, 101–34.

20. "Proclamations of Nathaniel Bacon," *Virginia Magazine of History and Biography* 1, no. 1 (July 1893): 57–58; "The humble Appeale of the Voluntiers to all well minded, and Charitable People," The National Archives, Colonial Office, 5/1371, 251; "Charles City County Grievances 1676," *Virginia Magazine of History and Biography* 3, no. 2 (October 1895): 137–38; Matthew Kruer, *Time of Anarchy: Indigenous Power and the Crisis of Colonialism in Early America* (Cambridge, MA: Harvard University Press, 2021), 50–144.

21. John Berry and Francis Moryson, "Names and Characters of and Presents to the Indians &c.," 267–68; Michael Leroy Oberg, ed., *Samuel Wiseman's Book of Record: The Official Account of Bacon's Rebellion in Virginia* (Lanham, MD: Lexington, 2005), 135; Martha W. McCartney, "Cockacoeske, Queen of Pamunkey: Diplomat and Suzeraine," in *Powhatan's Mantle: Indians in the Colonial Southeast* (1989), rev. ed. (Lincoln: University of Nebraska Press, 2006), 254–57.

22. James D. Rice, *Tales from a Revolution: Bacon's Rebellion and the Transformation of Early America* (New York: Oxford University Press, 2012), 170–201; Owen Stanwood, *The Empire Reformed: English America in the Age of the Glorious Revolution* (Philadelphia: University of Pennsylvania Press, 2011).

23. Dixon, "'His one Netev ples,'" 41–74.

24. Important works on settler constitutionalism include Jack P. Greene, *Peripheries and Center: Constitutional Development in the Extended Polities of the British Empire and the United States 1607–1788* (Athens: University of Georgia Press, 1986); Daniel J. Hulsebosch, *Constituting Empire: New York and the Transformation of Constitutionalism in the Atlantic World, 1664–1830* (Chapel Hill: University of North Carolina Press, 2005).

25. Oweneco, "Letter of Instruction from Oanhekoe, Sachem of the Mohegan Indians in New England, 14 July 1703," in *Early Native Literacies in New England*, ed. Kristina Bross and Hilary E. Wyss (Amherst: University of Massachusetts Press, 2008), 19.

26. Yirush, "'Chief Princes and Owners of All,'" 145.

27. Robert J. Cain, ed., *Records of the Executive Council, Colonial Records of North Carolina*, 2nd ser., vol. 7 (Raleigh: Department of Cultural Resources, Division of Archives and History, 1984), 419.

28. LeMaster, "In the 'Scolding Houses'," 214–16; Shannon Lee Dawdy, "The Meherrin's Secret History of the Dividing Line," *North Carolina Historical Review* 72, no. 4 (October 1995), 394–410.

29. Samuel Hazard, ed., *Minutes of the Provincial Council of Pennsylvania*, 10 vols. (Harrisburg: Theo. Fenn, 1838–1853), 2:16.

30. Alden T. Vaughan, ed., *Early American Indian Documents: Treaties and Laws, 1607–1789*, 20 vols. (Washington, DC: University Publications of America, 1979–), 2:24; Amy C. Schutt, *Peoples of the River Valleys: The Odyssey of the Delaware Indians* (Philadelphia: University of Pennsylvania Press, 2007), 62–93.

31. Daniel K. Richter, *Facing East from Indian Country: A Native History of Early America* (Cambridge, MA: Harvard University Press, 2001), 189–236. On "nested sovereignty," see Audra Simpson, *Mohawk Interruptus: Political Life Across the Borders of Settler States* (Durham, NC: Duke University Press, 2014).

32. Lawrence H. Leder, ed., *The Livingston Indian Records, 1666–1723* (Gettysburg: Pennsylvania Historical Association, 1956), 117–18.

33. "Sir William Johnson to the Lords of Trade, 25 September 1763," *Pennsylvania Archives*, ed. Samuel Hazard et al., 138 vols. (1852–1935), 2nd ser., 6:595; Francis Jennings, *The Ambiguous Iroquois Empire* (New York: Norton, 1984).

34. "Plan for the Future Management of Indian Affairs," *Documents Relative to the Colonial History of the State of New York*, ed. E. B. O'Callaghan, 15 vols. (Albany: Weed, Parsons & Co., 1853–1887), 7:638–39.

35. William Johnson, "Review of the Trade and Affairs of the Indians in the Northern District of America," *Documents Relative to the Colonial History of the State of New York*, 7:957; Daniel K. Richter, "Native Americans, the Plan of 1764, and a British Empire That Never Was," in *Cultures and Identities in Colonial British America*, ed. Robert Olwell and Alan Tully (Baltimore, MD: Johns Hopkins University Press, 2006), 269–92.

36. Alexander Henry, *Travels and Adventures in Canada and the Indian Territories, Between the Years 1760 and 1776*, ed. James Bain (Toronto: George N. Morang & Co., 1901), 44; Gregory Evans Dowd, *War Under Heaven: Pontiac, the Indian Nations, and the British Empire* (Baltimore, MD: Johns Hopkins University Press, 2002); Peter Silver, *Our Savage Neighbors: How Indian War Transformed Early America* (New York: Norton, 2008), 39–71.

37. Krista Camenzind, "Violence, Race, and the Paxton Boys," in *Friends and Enemies in Penn's Woods: Indians, Colonists, and the Racial Construction of Pennsylvania*, ed. William Pencak and Daniel K. Richter (University Park: Pennsylvania State University Press, 2004), 201–20; Silver, *Our Savage Neighbors*, 177–90; Patrick

Spero, *Frontier Country: The Politics of War in Early Pennsylvania* (Philadelphia: University of Pennsylvania Press, 2016), 165.

38. *The Apology of the Paxton Volunteers Addressed to the Candid and Impartial World* (1764), 9–10, 17, http://digitalpaxton.org/works/digital-paxton/apology-of-the -paxton-volunteers.

39. *A Declaration and Remonstrance of the Distressed and Bleeding Frontier Inhabitants of the Province of Pennsylvania* (1764), 12, http://digitalpaxton.org/works/digital -paxton/a-declaration-and-remonstrance (emphasis in original).

40. *A Narrative of the Late Massacres, in Lancaster County, of a Number of Indians, Friends of This Province* (1764), 27, http://digitalpaxton.org/works/digital-paxton/a -narrative-of-the-late-massacres.

41. "Thomas Gage to Henry Seymour Conway, 6 May 1766," in *The Correspondence of General Thomas Gage with the Secretaries of State, 1763–1775*, ed. Clarence Edwin Carter, 2 vols. (New Haven, CT: Yale University Press, 1931), 1:91; "Sir William Johnson to Lords of Trade, 22 November 1765," The National Archives, Colonial Office, 5/66, ff. 324–25.

42. Patrick Griffin, *American Leviathan: Empire, Nation, and Revolutionary Frontier* (New York: Hill and Wang, 2007), 72–94; Patrick Spero, *Frontier Rebels: The Fight for Independence in the American West, 1765–1776* (New York: Norton, 2018).

43. Griffin, *American Leviathan*, 152–70; Jeffrey Ostler, *Surviving Genocide: Native Nations and the United States from the American Revolution to Bleeding Kansas* (New Haven, CT: Yale University Press, 2019), 44–81.

44. Silver, *Our Savage Neighbors*, 252; Robert G. Parkinson, *The Common Cause: Creating Race and Nation in the American Revolution* (Chapel Hill: University of North Carolina Press, 2016).

45. Griffin, *American Leviathan*, 165–67; Jessica Choppin Roney, "1776, Viewed from the West," *Journal of the Early Republic* 37, no. 4 (Winter 2017): 655–700.

46. Williams, *American Indian in Western Legal Thought*, 287–324.

47. *United States Statutes at Large*, 126 vols. (Washington, DC: United States Government Printing Office, 1848–), 1:103.

48. "Speech of the United Indian Nations, at Their Confederate Council, 28 November 1786," *American State Papers: Indian Affairs* (Washington, DC: Library of Congress, 1832), 1:8; Gregory Ablavsky, "The Savage Constitution," *Duke Law Journal* 63, no. 5 (February 2014): 999–1089; Colin G. Calloway, *The Victory with No Name: The Native American Defeat of the First American Army* (New York: Oxford University Press, 2015); Gregory Evans Dowd, *A Spirited Resistance: The North American Indian Struggle for Unity, 1745–1815* (Baltimore, MD: Johns Hopkins University Press, 1992), 90–115.

49. "Report from H. Knox, Secretary of War . . . Relative to the Northwest Indians, 15 June 1789," *American State Papers: Indian Affairs*, 1:13.

50. David J. Silverman, "Racial Walls: Race and the Emergence of an American White Nationalism," in *Anglicizing America: Empire, Revolution, Republic*, ed. Ignacio Gallup-Diaz, Andrew Shankman, and David J. Silverman (Philadelphia: University of Pennsylvania Press, 2015), 181–204.

51. Martha S. Jones, *Birthright Citizens: A History of Race and Rights in Antebellum America* (Cambridge: Cambridge University Press, 2018); Rosemary Zagarri, *Revolutionary Backlash: Women and Politics in the Early American Republic* (Philadelphia: University of Pennsylvania Press, 2007).

52. "Petition, 30 June 1818," in *The Cherokee Removal: A Brief History with Documents*, 3rd ed., ed. Theda Perdue and Michael D. Green (Boston: Bedford/St. Martin's, 2016), 126.

53. Alison L. LaCroix, *The Ideological Origins of American Federalism* (Cambridge, MA: Harvard University Press, 2010).

54. Hermann Wellenreuther, "White Eyes and the Delawares' Vision of an Indian State," *Pennsylvania History* 68, no. 2 (Spring 2001): 139–61; Nicholas Guyatt, *Bind Us Apart: How Enlightened Americans Invented Racial Segregation* (New York: Basic Books, 2016), 225–46; Robert L. Tsai, "The Sequoyah Convention, 1905," in *America's Forgotten Constitutions: Defiant Visions of Power and Community* (Cambridge, MA: Harvard University Press, 2014), 152–84; Dean Itsuji Saranillio, *Unsustainable Empire: Alternative Histories of Hawai'i Statehood* (Durham, NC: Duke University Press, 2018), 171–196.

55. Lauren Benton, *A Search for Sovereignty: Law and Geography in European Empires, 1400–1900* (Cambridge: Cambridge University Press, 2010).

CHAPTER 2

American Presidents and the Ideology of Civilization

BENJAMIN A. COATES

mpires need ideologies, and the American empire is no exception. Its power spread under the guise of imperial catchphrases: liberty, manifest destiny, security, and the "liberal world order," to name but a few. Ideological concepts such as race and national greatness also proved generative.[1] In this chapter, I focus on another motivating ideology: civilization. Unlike "freedom," which Jeremi Suri points out Americans arrogated as a particularly national virtue (see chapter 14), "civilization" had transatlantic connotations. Even national variants—"our civilization" or "American civilization"—conjured visions of values that transcended domestic space. To invoke civilization was to justify American behavior by a universal standard that inevitably raised questions about the relation of the United States to the rest of the world. As American power changed, the vocabulary of civilization shifted with it even as the underlying hierarchical grammar remained the same.[2] As an ideology, civilization proved a capacious container for empire.[3]

Americans did not invent civilization. Its intellectual roots stretch back to ancient distinctions between a civilized inside and a wild, barbaric outside.[4] In medieval Europe, courtly "civility" meant self-control and sophistication.[5] The term *civilization* first appeared in the late eighteenth century, combining "civility" with the verb "to civilize," from the French *civiliser*, meaning to transfer a matter from criminal to civil jurisdiction and by extension to bring something from a state of violent nature into a rule-bound society.[6]

By the nineteenth century, civilization had become a common European concept for ordering the world. In short, it had become an ideology.

By ideology I mean a set of assumptions and assertions that shapes understanding of the world. I do not wade into the debate about the relationship between language and reality. Suffice it to say that an actual physical world does exist, but it becomes "real" to humans through our language and concepts. An ideology gathers a complex of related concepts within a single framework that purports to offer a "true" accounting of the world. Ideology exists as a mutually constitutive relationship between belief and rhetoric: ideological concepts shape how we interpret events, whereas ideological rhetoric describes those events and reinforces the conceptual framework. Multiple ideologies can exist simultaneously and struggle with one another. Consciously or unconsciously, by controlling rituals, information, and state practices, the powerful seek to make dominant an ideology that favors their interests. A hegemonic ideology then becomes "common sense."[7]

The ideology of civilization was simultaneously descriptive and normative. It assumed and asserted that the world could be differentiated into "civilized" and "uncivilized" peoples. The precise characteristics that defined the standard of civilization could be elusive, but they generally included certain forms of social organization. Civilized societies had settled agriculture, urban settlements, organized religion and the arts, and distinct gender expectations.[8] They possessed the rule of law, differentiated labor roles, and individual property rights; the growth of capitalism marched alongside the expansion of civilization.[9] The civilized settled disputes through juridical and rational means rather than through emotional or violent ones—or at least so they claimed—however, self-proclaimed civilized states often deployed violence on the grounds that the barbarians' lack of rationality required it. Behind the language of civilization lurked deeper assumptions about the importance of self-control over one's own bodily impulses, which enabled an abstract, intellectualized separation from the physicality of nature.[10] No wonder that cannibalism marked the antithesis of civilization.[11]

Unlike *race*, civilization was nonessentialist and inclusive in theory; that is, with proper tutelage the uncivilized might become civilized. In practice, essentialist assumptions and exclusionary practices often accompanied civilizing projects, and suspicions lurked that only white people—perhaps only white men—could truly embody civilization.[12] Barbarians defined as such threatened the civilized and required either uplift or extermination.[13] Crucially, the powerful maintained the right to decide who was civilized.

For Europeans, civilization functioned as a colonial ideology that justified domination from Ireland to India and beyond.[14] Still, the possibility of assimilation strengthened the ideology of civilization because it suggested that non-Western peoples might become full members of the international community if they adopted certain practices, a promise that attracted some colonized elites even as it flattered their colonizers.[15]

Studying the ideology of civilization is complicated by the fact that the word *civilization* could be used to mean different things. In the early twentieth century, a pluralist conception emerged that used civilization to mean society or culture.[16] Western scholars led by Oswald Spengler and Arnold Toynbee posited the existence of multiple civilizations rising and falling over time.[17] Colonial elites made claims for the distinctiveness or even superiority of non-Western civilizations, claims that found some adherents in the West.[18] This pluralistic vision in theory rejected hierarchical distinctions; Western Europe, India, and the pre-Colombian Americas each had its own civilization, none fundamentally superior to the next, all "philosophically equivalent."[19] Yet in practice an assumption of the superiority of Western civilization persisted. Thus, as Jean Starobinski put it, "the word could take on a pluralist, ethnological, relativistic meaning yet retain certain implications of the most general sort, implications that made 'civilization' a unitary imperative and determined the unique direction of 'march' of all humankind."[20] In short, civilization continued to function as an ideological standard against which societies could be measured and found wanting.

The ideology of civilization also could exist even in the absence of the term. In the wake of decolonization, colonizers no longer cited "civilizing missions," but new formulations of "development" and "modernization" relied on similar assumptions about difference and tutelage.[21] Debates over the laws of war recapitulated distinctions between "civilized" and "savage" combatants.[22]

In this chapter, I examine this evolving ideology of civilization as it manifested in American foreign relations through an analysis of presidential statements.[23] What presidents have written or said for public consumption is not necessarily coterminous with their inner thoughts, but presidential rhetoric is where ideology meets the politics of foreign relations. "Public words are calculated words," and the use of the term *civilization* reflected presidential expectations about the impact it would have on its audience.[24] It presumed (and enhanced) a shared ideological commitment. Presidential rhetoric is thus a valuable guide to how the term *civilization* functioned in political discourse.

What follows is a mostly chronological account of important shifts over time: from a messianic optimism inscribed in a variety of nineteenth-century civilizing missions to an anxious defensiveness in the face of successive twentieth-century threats. Along the way, presidents transformed the notion of civilization from a universal category to a more complex mixture of American and universal civilizations that justified American global power. Civilization projected American identity in world-historical time, revealing the mixture of anxiety and arrogance that characterized American empire.

In the early to mid-nineteenth century, presidents invoked civilization to assert America's membership in a transatlantic society of nations while simultaneously justifying expansion at the expense of racialized others.[25] By "imparting to them the blessings of civilization," George Washington claimed, Americans would bring benefits to the same Indigenous Americans whose lands they seized.[26] Thomas Jefferson agreed on the need to lead Indigenous peoples "to agriculture, to factures, and civilization";[27] and James Monroe found it "proper to persevere in our efforts to extend to them the advantages of civilization."[28] This rhetoric reflected government policy; in the Civilization Fund Act of 1819, for instance, Congress appropriated resources for missionary settlements on Indigenous peoples' lands that were designed to bring Indigenous people into the capitalist market.[29] Although a common narrative stretching from Paine's *Common Sense* to the Monroe Doctrine stressed fundamental differences between "old" Europe and the "new" world, invoking "civilization" here echoed European rhetorical strategies dating to the sixteenth century.[30] Mindful of this context, secretary of war Henry Knox fretted that exterminating the Indigenous people would invite "reproach" on "the American character" in world opinion.[31]

However, when the Cherokee claimed ownership of ancestral lands on the grounds of already being civilized—pointing to their adoption of written languages, Christianity, and slave-based agriculture—they found that in practice civilization was reserved primarily for white settlers. Andrew Jackson simply rejected Cherokee claims to civilization: "It seems now to be an established fact that they can not live in contact with a civilized community and prosper," he said in 1835.[32] Revealingly, Old Hickory promised that educational and missionary efforts would continue in the West so that Indigenous people might still "share in the blessings of civilization."[33]

Civilization also infused debates about military conduct and the law of war. During the War of 1812 Madison charged that England showed "a deliberate disregard of the principles of humanity and the rules of civilized warfare."[34] Although Europeans' barbarity inspired diplomatic protests, Americans responded to alleged savagery by non-Europeans with horrific violence. Describing Indigenous people of Sumatra as "piratical perpetrators belonging to tribes in such a state of society that the usual course of proceedings between civilized nations could not be pursued," Andrew Jackson dispatched U.S. marines to destroy their villages in retribution for an attack on an American merchant ship.[35] After Mexican troops executed Texan captives, President John Tyler accused Mexico of committing acts "equaled only in savage barbarity by the usages of the untutored Indian tribes," thus leaving "an indelible stain on the page of civilization."[36] James K. Polk cited Mexican barbarousness as justification for seizing Mexican territory and justified American atrocities as being in line with the actions of European states:"The Mexicans having thus shown themselves to be wholly incapable of appreciating our forbearance and liberality, it was deemed proper to change the manner of conducting the war, by making them feel its pressure according to the usages observed under similar circumstances by all other civilized nations."[37] Although it served national aims, Polk's appeal to the "civilized world" highlights continuing desires to convince imagined or real international audiences that America belonged within the society of nations.[38]

In the late nineteenth and early twentieth centuries, the ideology of civilization helped presidents make sense of America's place in an industrializing and imperialist world. Breathtaking technological and economic transformations brought nations ever closer, manifesting civilization and progress with every telegraph wire strung and railroad track laid. The upheavals of industrial capitalism reinforced discourses of the evolution—or devolution—of civilization. At home, socialists, immigration restrictionists, and eugenicists alike explained their projects as preserving or advancing civilization.[39] Abroad, colonizers cited a duty to civilize the inferior.[40] U.S. leaders found it natural to justify policy in civilizational terms.

Presidential statements portrayed the United States as both heir and successor to European civilization, both richer and more politically advanced. Unlike European aristocracies trapped in outdated wars of prestige, America promised to substitute law for violence, reserving force solely to promote civilization. Hence, in 1897, Grover Cleveland praised a treaty of general arbitration with Great Britain as advancing the "experiment of substituting civilized methods for brute force as the means of settling international questions" and marking "the beginning of a new epoch in civilization."[41] The following year William McKinley called for war against Spain "in the name of civilization."[42] After a quick victory, he demanded control over the Philippines, promising to "uplift and civilize and Christianize" their inhabitants.[43] The supposed duty of civilization remained a treasured trope of U.S. imperialists; as late as 1924, Calvin Coolidge denied Filipino petitions for independence on the grounds that the United States had not yet "discharged all of its obligations to civilization."[44]

Theodore Roosevelt was the ideology of civilization come to life, a man who read hundreds of books during his sanguinary hunting expeditions, combining manliness and masculinity into a life of intellectual achievement and strenuous physical exertion. According to his secretary of state, Elihu Root, Roosevelt interpreted diplomacy "against the background of those tendencies through which civilization develops."[45] "Uncivilized" peoples required a strong hand and imperial tutelage. U.S. occupation of the Philippines, Roosevelt claimed, would "help them to rise higher and higher in the scale of civilization and of capacity for self-government."[46] In his corollary to the Monroe Doctrine, Roosevelt called for the United States to play the role of an "international police" to prevent the "general loosening of the ties of civilized society."[47] His intervention in Panama was "justified by the interests of collective civilization."[48]

At the same time, Roosevelt called on civilized states to settle their disputes peacefully. "As civilization grows warfare becomes less and less the normal condition of foreign relations," he observed in 1902.[49] He supported the expansion of arbitration and international law, ultimately hoping for "something like an organization of the civilized nations."[50] Pacifists admired his call, in 1904, for a second Hague Peace Conference. Both Roosevelt and his secretary of state won the Nobel Peace Prize. Portraying their nation as an avatar of civilization helped Americans reconcile promotion of peace with imperial war.[51] Yet leaders in Africa, Asia, and Latin America found it difficult to translate their claims to be civilized into equal treatment under international law.[52]

Even criticism of American society could be framed in civilizational terms. William McKinley condemned lynching as unbecoming for a "great and civilized country,"[53] and Roosevelt complained that child labor formed "a blot on our civilization."[54] Some critics challenged the ideology directly, as when Mark Twain dismissed the imperial justifications of the "Blessings-of-Civilization Trust" as hypocritical nonsense or when a young W. E. B.

Du Bois noted in 1890 that if Jefferson Davis was a "Representative of Civilization" then "there is something fundamentally incomplete about that standard."[55] These dissents aside, the ideology of civilization remained hegemonic. Even Black nationalists such as Bishop Henry Turner praised emigration to Africa for its civilizing effects on the locals.[56]

Thus, in 1914, the shocking carnage of World War I represented a threat to civilization itself. From relative safety across the Atlantic, Americans marveled at the horrible ferocity of the war's industrialized violence: the millions of dead, the ruined cathedrals, universities, and libraries. Destruction at the heart of civilization's European birthplace inspired shock in some, a sad recognition in others. For Du Bois, the war's "brutality and inhumanity" merely revealed Europe's murderous tendencies. "The Great War is the lie unveiled," he pronounced.[57] Yet most Americans (ultimately including Du Bois) sought to save civilization rather than to bury it. How best to do this? Theodore Roosevelt wanted war with Germany, whose submarines resembled "the pirates of the Barbary Coast" in their flouting of civilized rules of warfare. But Roosevelt was no longer president, and Woodrow Wilson generally avoided public appeals to civilization.[58] Privately Wilson fretted about defending civilization from destruction but thought that this was best served by keeping the United States out of the war. As late as January 1917, he wrote to his confidante Edward House, "There will be no war. We are the only one of the great white nations that is free from war to-day, and it would be a crime against civilization for us to go in."[59] On January 31, Wilson said "he had been more and more impressed with the idea that 'white civilization' and its domination in the world rested largely on our ability to keep this country intact."[60] But after the United States entered the war, Wilson portrayed the struggle as "the forces of civilization" against "the forces of reaction."[61]

Wilsonianism is often portrayed as a crusading messianism, but Wilson's rhetoric emphasized defending civilization rather than expanding its reach. He invoked civilization most frequently after the war's end, when he stumped for U.S. entry into the League of Nations. With greater clarity than before, he identified the war in retrospect as one to protect civilization from Germany. Germany "tried to commit a crime against civilization," he told an audience in Montana.[62] In resisting, Belgium "did nothing less than underwrite civilization."[63] Now it was America's turn. Joining the League would promote peace through reasoned discussion. "It is the business of civilization to get together by discussion and not by fighting.

That is civilization," Wilson explained.[64] The United States faced a choice: "Either we are going to guarantee civilization or we are going to abandon it."[65] Alas for Wilson, the U.S. Senate rejected membership in the League of Nations.

After World War I, presidents spoke more frequently about defending civilization rather than promoting it. Here lie early precedents of the ideology of fear that Andrew Preston explores in chapter 8 in this volume. Presidents also began to preface civilization with new modifiers: American, Western, modern, etc. For the most part, this was not about promoting a pluralistic conception of multiple civilizations, all equal in their own way. Rather, it reflected struggles between universalistic and particularistic visions of America's role in the world. By the 1940s, the ideology of civilization would underwrite an argument that American security required global defense.

Wilson's Republican successors agreed that civilization needed defending. "We do not mean to shun a single responsibility of this republic to world civilization," promised Warren Harding.[66] Although Harding praised the League of Nations for its aim "to prevent war, preserve peace, and promote civilization," he resisted being "shackled by a written compact which surrenders our freedom of action and gives the military alliance the right to proclaim America's duty to the world."[67] Instead, the United States—which Harding and Calvin Coolidge portrayed as a "new civilization" that alone had survived the Great War intact—had a duty to maintain its own vitality.[68] This did not rule out advocating membership in the Permanent Court of International Justice: "The principle effort of civilization, after all," explained Coolidge, "is to bring the world under obedience to law."[69] But it did mean remaining out of the League of Nations.

The Great Depression, like World War I, once again threatened "the very safety of civilization," as Herbert Hoover put it in 1932. His solution, rhetorically at least, was to double down on traditional values, to find ways to "build up men and women in their own homes, on their own farms, where they may find their own security and express their own individuality."[70] Excessive government intervention in the economy would be "the negation of the ideals upon which our civilization has been based."[71] "Our civilization," in this formulation, suggested a particular constellation of property rights and capital; Harding had decried interference with strikebreakers as "crimes against civilization."[72] Franklin D. Roosevelt took the opposite approach, portraying the Depression as a threat to "modern civilization," which by virtue of being modern required new solutions. "Government in a modern civilization has certain inescapable obligations to its citizens," he explained.[73] The New Deal promised to "civilize our industrial civilization."[74] In FDR's eyes, the great transformations wrought by war and industrial capitalism required rethinking civilized values.

In response to the rise of Nazi Germany and imperial Japan, FDR reshaped the language of civilization to advocate for a new globalist foreign policy. The Nazis and the Japanese represented a threat to global civilization, he contended, because they "have attempted to drive history into reverse, to use all the mechanics of modern civilization to drive humanity back to conditions of prehistoric savagery."[75] They threatened a "bandit assault upon civilization" and were "endeavoring to enslave the entire world. . . . Never before has there been a greater challenge to life, liberty, and civilization."[76] Yet FDR also invoked civilization in national terms. The war posed a threat to "our American civilization" greater than any since "Jamestown and Plymouth Rock," he argued in 1940.[77] Once the United States entered the war, the conflict became a defense of "our type of civilization" or "our type of democratic civilization" or simply "the survival of our civilization." Yet he continued to claim generally that "the future of the world and civilization" hung in the balance.[78] In this context, to defend "democratic civilization" was to defend civilization as a whole. The slippage between the universal and national implicitly indentified civilization with democracy and the United States and laid rhetorical groundwork for asserting American global primacy.[79]

Despite the proliferating variants of civilization, the term continued to carry with it certain universal meanings connected to sociopolitical development. Decolonization discredited European colonialism and removed "civilizing missions" from the vocabulary of American leaders who sought allegiances with developing countries, but appeals to civilization in the abstract continued. Even as "Western civilization" blossomed from its WWI-era roots as an identity that justified transatlantic commitment, U.S. presidents often invoked civilization in an inclusive sense that made common cause not only with Europeans—incorporating Germany inside NATO and locating the birth of "Western civilization" on "the banks of the Tiber" (JFK) or in Greece (Eisenhower)—but also with allies in the wider world.[80] Harry Truman told the shah in 1949 that Iran was "the fountain of Western civilization," and Ronald Reagan called Egypt "a nation which cradled Western civilization in its arms" and said of Japan and Korea, "We're civilized nations believing in the same virtues of freedom and democracy."[81] U.S. modernization projects, with their ideologies and institutions steeped in assumptions about hierarchy, progress, and tutelage, traced the paths of earlier colonial projects of "benevolent" assimilation, but presidents rarely discussed these projects in terms of civilization per se.

The Cold War also mostly resisted being defined in civilizational terms. Although Truman warned of "the plans of the Kremlin to conquer the civilized world," for the most part the Soviet threat was not to civilization but to newer constructs such as "the free world" or "the West."[82] George Kennan avoided the term *civilization* entirely in both the Long Telegram and the "X" article, and NSC-68 used the term just once.[83] It was difficult to place the Soviet Union in the customary geographic and temporal space reserved for the uncivilized. Posing a Soviet "East" against an American-led "West" did some of this work, but Soviet communism could not be convincingly labeled "backward" or "traditional." It was instead a deviant modernity. Thus one finds Dwight Eisenhower imploring "all the world that calls itself civilized, *including the Soviets*," to address global poverty.[84] Jimmy Carter declared that "we Americans and Russians belong to the same civilization whose origins stretch back hundreds of years."[85] Even after the Soviets shot down a civilian airliner in 1983, Reagan admitted that "all of us had hoped that certain irreducible standards of civilized behavior, nonetheless, obtained."[86]

Nuclear weapons ruled out fighting a total war for civilization. Echoing concerns about the disastrous effects of the two world wars, presidents habitually warned of the "end of civilization as we know it."[87] "One miscalculated, impulsive, reckless move of a dingle finger," warned Lyndon Johnson, "could incinerate our civilization and wipe out the lives of 300 million men before you could say 'scat.'"[88] Carter predicted that any survivors of an "all-out nuclear war" would "live in despair amid the poisoned ruins of a civilization that had committed suicide."[89] Reagan professed hope for the "total elimination of nuclear weapons" because "they have no real place in a civilized world."[90] The Cold War was less about defending civilization from the uncivilized and more about preventing its destruction as a by-product of conflict.

Although the Soviet threat was not cast in civilizational terms, other developments were. Conservative presidents warned of challenges to a particular American civilization characterized by free enterprise, liberty, and piety. Here presidents drew on notions of the cyclical rise and fall of civilizations since antiquity. Richard Nixon returned often to what he called "the history of civilization," which was "strewn with the wreckage of nations that were rich" but collapsed because they "lost their drive, lost their desire, lost their dynamism, lost their vitality."[91] Among other threats, pornography "can corrupt a society and a civilization," the president argued.[92] More broadly, Reagan claimed that "if you look back to the collapse of great civilizations like the Greek and the Roman and all, you'll find that one of the characteristics of those civilizations was they began to desert and abandon their gods."[93] By invoking the term *civilization* as a grandiose substitution for "society" or "culture," conservatives hoped to demonstrate the timelessness of their values.

The rise of international terrorism led presidents to cast hijackings, kidnappings, and bombings in the 1970s as threats to civilization. Nixon claimed that "a civilized society cannot tolerate terrorism," and Carter frequently described the seizure of American hostages in Iran as shocking the "civilized world" or violating the "principle of civilized behavior and the rule of law."[94] Reagan's claim that the "civilized world" had no place for "assassinations, terrorist bombings, and other mindless violence" was a selective one, exempting for instance U.S.-backed Contra fighters in Nicaragua.[95] Nonetheless it is instructive that even as presidents feared a threat to the national American civilization at home they constructed a universal civilization abroad menaced by terrorists and assassins.

The end of the Cold War brought renewed talk of civilizing missions, albeit in conflicting formulations that mapped onto debates over American power. The collapse of the Soviet Union removed barriers to UN Security Council activism and humanitarian interventions. Observers wondered if human rights could serve as a new "standard of civilization."[96] Public intellectuals contended that the collapse of communism left liberal capitalism as the sole viable model for modern, successful societies. Terminologically the "developed world" replaced the "civilized nations," but the players remained mostly the same. A universalist, teleological sense of progress animated these visions, echoing ideological formations from one hundred years ago. For Francis Fukuyama, the emergence of a singular global civilization at the "End of History" seemed inevitable.[97] Renewed globalization promised a world in which everyone consumed fast food and pop music.

For others, the end of bipolar Cold War competition signaled descent into a chaotic clash of multiple cultural and political entities. In a widely read article and book, the Harvard political scientist Samuel Huntington predicted a "clash of civilizations."[98] He defined civilizations by religion most of all, but also by various cultural, linguistic, and political values that remained immune to modernization and globalization. "Somewhere in the Middle East," Huntington wrote, "a half-dozen young men could well be dressed in jeans, drinking Coke, listening to rap, and, between their bows to Mecca, putting together a bomb to blow up an American airliner."[99] In theory, Huntington echoed Toynbee: all civilizations were equal. In practice, he clearly favored the West but predicted that attempts to universalize Western civilization were bound to fail. Thus Huntington called for restraint abroad and a rejection of multiculturalism at home. "A multicivilizational United States will not be the United States," Huntington warned; "it will be the United Nations."[100] The nativist implications of this diagnosis would prove more enduring than its anti-interventionism.[101]

The 9/11 attacks and the War on Terror boosted Huntington's thesis, but George W. Bush's foreign policy ideology seemed more akin to Fukuyama with guns—a call to remake the Middle East in the image of the West. "When it comes to the common rights and needs of men and women, there is no clash of civilizations," Bush affirmed.[102] Echoing presidential rhetoric since the 1970s, Bush described the fight against terrorism as a war against those who threatened humanity: America fought "civilization's fight."[103] There was only "a single sustainable model for national success: freedom, democracy, and free enterprise," his administration's national security strategy averred.[104] Fukuyama posited this single model as the end point of natural historical development; the Bush administration would use war to accelerate its arrival. As one neoconservative writer had put it before 9/11, to advance civilization, the United States needed to move beyond its "civilized desire to minimize the body count."[105]

The failure of the Iraq war discredited this vision, and Bush's successors combined its rhetorical leftovers in quite different ways. Although still asserting the universality of liberal democratic principles and America's exceptional role in promoting them, Barack Obama acknowledging that "we're not always going to be right" and "other people may have good ideas."[106] Denying the existence of a "clash of civilizations," he praised "Persian civilization" as part of his attempted rapprochement with Iran.[107]

Donald Trump, on the other hand, combined nativist particularism with assertions of Western superiority. Echoing Huntington, candidate Trump said, "instead of trying to spread universal values that not everybody shares or wants, we should understand that strengthening and promoting Western civilization and its accomplishments will do more to inspire positive reforms around the world than military interventions."[108] Trump's insistence on referring to "radical Islamic terrorism" signaled a desire to draw ineradicable lines between the West and the rest.[109]

Over the last two hundred years, presidents have relied on the ideology of civilization to help mobilize U.S. power and justify its use. They have occasionally used "civilization" in a particularistic way, as a synonym for culture, to rally defense for an allegedly superior American way of life. Yet civilization's universalistic pretensions have never disappeared, making its associated ideology useful for portraying self-interest as humanitarian policy: perfect for a global empire that dare not speak its name. The ideology of civilization has rarely served humanity well, but a transformed version—one that expanded its claims beyond the human species—might have value. As scientists warn, an obsession with human squabbles that ignores the threat of climate change may mean "the collapse of our civilizations and the extinction of much of the natural world."[110] Civilization means little without human society present to appreciate it.

Notes

1. Michael H. Hunt, *Ideology and U.S. Foreign Policy* (New Haven, CT: Yale University Press, 1987).
2. Ntina Tzouvala, "Civilization," in *Concepts for International Law: Contributions to Disciplinary Thought*, ed. Jean d'Aspremont and Sahib Singh (Cheltenham, UK: Edward Elgar, 2019), 97.
3. Brett Bowden, *The Empire of Civilization: The Evolution of an Imperial Idea* (Chicago: University of Chicago Press, 2009).
4. Bruce Mazlish, *Civilization and Its Contents* (Stanford, CA: Stanford University Press, 2004), 2.
5. Joep Leerssen, *National Thought in Europe: A Cultural History* (Amsterdam: Amsterdam University Press, 2006), 26–27.
6. Jean Starobinski, "The Word *Civilization*," in *Blessings in Disguise; or, The Morality of Evil*, trans. Arthur Goldhammer (Cambridge, MA: Harvard University Press, 1993), 1–35.
7. For one exploration of how the dialectic between formal beliefs and state practice can internalize ideology as common sense, see Slavoj Žižek, "Introduction:

The Spectre of Ideology," in *Mapping Ideology*, ed. Slavoj Žižek (London:Verso, 1994), 12–15.

8. Emily Conroy-Krutz, *Christian Imperialism: Converting the World in the Early American Republic* (Ithaca, NY: Cornell University Press, 2015), 14–15.

9. Tzouvala, "Civilization," 99–103.

10. Andrew J. Rotter, "William Howard Taft's Drawers," in *The Familiar Made Strange: American Icons and Artifacts After the Transnational Turn*, ed. Brooke L. Blower and Mark Philip Bradley (Ithaca, NY: Cornell University Press, 2015), 46–58.

11. Nancy Shoemaker, *Pursuing Respect in the Cannibal Isles:Americans in Nineteenth-Century Fiji* (Ithaca, NY: Cornell University Press, 2019), 9.

12. Roxanne Lynn Doty, "The Logic of *Différance* in International Relations: U.S. Colonization of the Philippines," in *Post-Realism:The Rhetorical Turn in International Relations*, ed. Francis A. Beer and Robert Hariman (East Lansing: Michigan State University, 1996), 331–45.

13. Robert A. Williams Jr., *Savage Anxieties: The Invention of Western Civilization* (New York: Palgrave MacMillan, 2012).

14. Mazlish, *Civilization and Its Contents*, 22.

15. Ntina Tzouvala, *Capitalism as Civilisation:A History of International Law* (Cambridge: Cambridge University Press, 2020); Jennifer Pitts, *Boundaries of the International: Law and Empire* (Cambridge, MA: Harvard University Press, 2018); Gerrit W. Gong, *The Standard of "Civilization" in International Society* (Oxford: Clarendon Press, 1984).

16. Raymond Williams sees the popularity of the relativistic form arising in the late nineteenth century; however, it did not achieve broad usage until the early twentieth century. Raymond Williams, "Civilization," in *Keywords: A Vocabulary of Culture and Society*, rev. ed. (New York: Oxford University Press, 1983), 59–60.

17. William H. McNeill, *Arnold J. Toynbee: A Life* (New York: Oxford University Press, 1989); Arnold J. Toynbee, *A Study of History*, 2nd ed. (London: Oxford University Press, 1935).

18. Prasenjit Duara, "The Discourse of Civilization and Pan-Asianism," *Journal of World History* 12, no. 1 (2001): 99–130; Prasenjit Duara, "The Discourse of Civilization and Decolonization," *Journal of World History* 15, no. 1 (March 2004): 1–5; Michael Adas, "Contested Hegemony:The Great War and the Afro-Asian Assault on the Civilizing Mission Ideology," *Journal of World History* 15, no. 1 (2004): 31–63.

19. McNeill, *Arnold J. Toynbee*, 164.

20. Starobinski, "The Word *Civilization*," 6.

21. Sundhya Pahuja, *Decolonising International Law: Development, Economic Growth and the Politics of Universality* (Cambridge: Cambridge University Press, 2011);

Michael E. Latham, *Modernization as Ideology: American Social Science and "Nation Building" in the Kennedy Era* (Chapel Hill: University of North Carolina Press, 2000). In this volume, chapter 21 by Daniel Immerwahr highlights challenges to this ideology.

22. Frédéric Mégret, "From 'Savages' to 'Unlawful Combatants': A Postcolonial Look at International Humanitarian Law's 'Other,'" in *International Law and Its Others*, ed. Anne Orford (Cambridge, UK: Cambridge University Press, 2006), 265–317.

23. Most of these statements were found via the American Presidency Project (https://www.presidency.ucsb.edu), a database that collects presidential public documents, including from *Messages and Papers of the Presidents of the United States* and *The Public Papers of the Presidents*.

24. Roderick P. Hart, *Verbal Style and the Presidency: A Computer-Based Analysis* (Orlando, FL: Academic Press, 1984), 7.

25. On how the United States sought to become a "treaty worthy" state, see Eliga Gould, *Among the Powers of the Earth: The American Revolution and the Making of a New World Empire* (Cambridge, MA: Harvard University Press, 2012).

26. George Washington, "Third Annual Address to Congress," October 25, 1791, https://www.presidency.ucsb.edu/documents/third-annual-address-congress-0.

27. Thomas Jefferson, "Confidential Message to Congress Regarding the Lewis and Clark Expedition," January 18, 1803, https://www.presidency.ucsb.edu/documents/confidential-message-congress-regarding-the-lewis-and-clark-expedition.

28. James Monroe, "Inaugural Address," March 4, 1817, https://www.presidency.ucsb.edu/documents/inaugural-address-23.

29. Lori J. Daggar, "The Mission Complex: Economic Development, 'Civilization,' and Empire in the Early Republic," *Journal of the Early Republic* 36, no. 3 (2016): 467–91.

30. Matthew Restall, *Seven Myths of the Spanish Conquest* (New York: Oxford University Press, 2003), 131–45.

31. Henry Knox as quoted in Daggar, "The Mission Complex," 476.

32. Andrew Jackson, "Seventh Annual Message," December 8, 1835, https://www.presidency.ucsb.edu/documents/seventh-annual-message-2.

33. Andrew Jackson, "Farewell Address," March 4, 1837, https://www.presidency.ucsb.edu/documents/farewell-address-0.

34. James Madison, "Inaugural Address," March 4, 1813, https://www.presidency.ucsb.edu/documents/inaugural-address-22; James Madison, "Proclamation—Calling All Citizens to Unite in Defense of the District of Columbia," September 1, 1814, https://www.presidency.ucsb.edu/documents/proclamation-calling-all-citizens-unite-defense-the-district-columbia.

35. Andrew Jackson, "Third Annual Message," December 6, 1831, https://www.presidency.ucsb.edu/documents/third-annual-message-3.

36. John Tyler, "Special Message," December 18, 1844, https://www.presidency.ucsb.edu/documents/special-message-4272.

37. James K. Polk, "Third Annual Message," December 7, 1847, https://www.presidency.ucsb.edu/documents/third-annual-message-6.

38. Deborah A. Rosen, *Border Law: The First Seminole War and American Nationhood* (Cambridge, MA: Harvard University Press, 2015).

39. Daniel E. Bender, *American Abyss: Savagery and Civilization in the Age of Industry* (Ithaca, NY: Cornell University Press, 2009).

40. Alice Conklin, *A Mission to Civilize: The Republican Idea of Empire in France and West Africa, 1895–1930* (Stanford, CA: Stanford University Press, 1997).

41. Grover Cleveland, "Message Regarding Treaty with Britain," January 11, 1897, https://millercenter.org/the-presidency/presidential-speeches/january-11-1897-message-regarding-treaty-britain.

42. William McKinley, "Message to Congress Requesting a Declaration of War with Spain," April 11, 1898, https://www.presidency.ucsb.edu/documents/message-congress-requesting-declaration-war-with-spain.

43. General James Rusling, "Interview with President William McKinley," *Christian Advocate* 22 (January 1903): 17.

44. Calvin Coolidge, "Letter to the Hon. Manuel Roxas, Chairman, the Philippine Mission, on Relations with the Philippine Islands," February 21, 1924, https://www.presidency.ucsb.edu/documents/letter-the-hon-manuel-roxas-chairman-the-philippine-mission-relations-with-the-philippine.

45. Elihu Root, "Roosevelt's Conduct of Foreign Affairs," in *The Works of Theodore Roosevelt*, national ed. (New York: Scribner,1926), 16: xiii.

46. Theodore Roosevelt, "Fourth Annual Message," December 6, 1904, https://www.presidency.ucsb.edu/documents/fourth-annual-message-15.

47. Roosevelt, "Fourth Annual Message."

48. Theodore Roosevelt, "Special Message," January 4, 1904, https://www.presidency.ucsb.edu/documents/special-message-438.

49. Theodore Roosevelt, "Second Annual Message," December 2, 1902, https://www.presidency.ucsb.edu/documents/second-annual-message-16.

50. Theodore Roosevelt, "Fifth Annual Message," December 5, 1905, https://www.presidency.ucsb.edu/documents/fifth-annual-message-4.

51. Benjamin A. Coates, *Legalist Empire: International Law and American Foreign Relations in the Early Twentieth Century* (New York: Oxford University Press, 2016).

52. Liliana Obregón Tarazona, "The Civilized and the Uncivilized," in *The Oxford Handbook of the History of International Law*, ed. Bardo Fassbender and Anne Peters (Oxford: Oxford University Press, 2013), 917–41.

53. William McKinley, "Inaugural Address," March 4, 1897, https://www.presidency.ucsb.edu/documents/inaugural-address-43.

54. Theodore Roosevelt, "Sixth Annual Message," December 3, 1906, https://www.presidency.ucsb.edu/documents/sixth-annual-message-4.

55. Mark Twain, "To the Person Sitting in Darkness" (1901), in *Mark Twain's Weapons of Satire: Anti-Imperialist Writings on the Philippine-American War*, ed. Jim Zwick (Syracuse, NY: Syracuse University Press, 1992), 22–39; W. E. B. Du Bois, "Jefferson Davis as a Representative of Civilization," June 1890, W. E. B. Du Bois Papers (MS 312) Special Collections and University Archives, University of Massachusetts Amherst Libraries, http://credo.library.umass.edu/cgi-bin/pdf.cgi?id=scua:mums312-b196-i029.

56. Keisha N. Blain, *Set the World on Fire: Black Nationalist Women and the Global Struggle for Freedom* (Philadelphia: University of Pennsylvania Press, 2018), 50.

57. W. E. B. Du Bois, "Lusitania," *The Crisis* 10, no. 2 (June 1915): 81.

58. Woodrow Wilson's proclamation of neutrality made no reference to civilization. Aside from a passing reference to "civilized nations," neither did his "Peace Without Victory" speech of January 1917.

59. Woodrow Wilson as quoted in Trygve Throntveit, *Power Without Victory: Woodrow Wilson and the American Internationalist Experiment* (Chicago: University of Chicago Press, 2017), 208.

60. Woodrow Wilson as quoted in Adam Tooze, *The Deluge* (New York: Viking, 2014), 60.

61. Woodrow Wilson to George V, c. August 4, 1918, printed in *Official Bulletin* II, August 5, 1918.

62. Woodrow Wilson, "An Address in the Billings Auditorium," September 11, 1919, in *Papers of Woodrow Wilson* (Princeton, NJ: Princeton University Press, 1966–1994), 63:171.

63. Woodrow Wilson, "An Address in the Tacoma Armory," September 13, 1919, in *Papers of Woodrow Wilson* (Princeton, NJ: Princeton University Press, 1966–1994), 63:242.

64. Woodrow Wilson, "An Address to the Coliseum in Sioux Falls," September 8, 1919, in *Papers of Woodrow Wilson* (Princeton, NJ: Princeton University Press, 1966–1994), 63:114.

65. Woodrow Wilson, "An Address in the Tabernacle in Salt Lake City," September 23, 1919, in *Papers of Woodrow Wilson* (Princeton, NJ: Princeton University Press, 1966–1994), 63:454.

66. Warren Harding, "Speech Accepting the Republican Nomination," June 12, 1920, https://millercenter.org/the-presidency/presidential-speeches/june-12-1920-speech-accepting-republican-nomination.

67. Warren Harding, "Address to a Joint Session of Congress on Urgent National Problems," April 12, 1921, https://www.presidency.ucsb.edu/documents/address-joint-session-congress-urgent-national-problems; Warren Harding, "Speech

Accepting the Nomination for President," June 1920, https://www.wsj.com/articles/SB118971877847426817.

68. Calvin Coolidge, "Address at the Celebration of the 150th Anniversary of the Declaration of Independence," July 5, 1926, https://www.presidency.ucsb.edu/documents/address-the-celebration-the-150th-anniversary-the-declaration-independence-philadelphia.

69. Calvin Coolidge, "Address at Gettysburg Battlefield," May 30, 1928, https://www.presidency.ucsb.edu/documents/address-gettysburg-battlefield.

70. Herbert Hoover, "Address at the Coliseum in Des Moines, Iowa," October 4, 1932, https://www.presidency.ucsb.edu/documents/address-the-coliseum-des-moines-iowa.

71. Herbert Hoover, "Veto of the Muscle Shoals Resolution," March 3, 1931, https://www.presidency.ucsb.edu/documents/veto-the-muscle-shoals-resolution.

72. Warren Harding, "Address to Congress on Railroad and Coal Strikes," August 18, 1922, https://www.presidency.ucsb.edu/documents/address-congress-railroad-and-coal-strikes.

73. Franklin Roosevelt, "Acceptance Speech for the Renomination for the Presidency," June 27, 1936, https://www.presidency.ucsb.edu/documents/acceptance-speech-for-the-renomination-for-the-presidency-philadelphia-pa.

74. Franklin Roosevelt, "Fireside Chat," September 30, 1934, https://www.presidency.ucsb.edu/documents/fireside-chat-20.

75. Franklin Roosevelt, "Armistice Day Address," November 11, 1942, https://www.presidency.ucsb.edu/documents/armistice-day-address.

76. Franklin Roosevelt, "Statement on War and Peace," January 1, 1943, https://www.presidency.ucsb.edu/documents/statement-war-and-peace; Franklin Roosevelt, "Message to Congress Requesting War Declarations with Germany and Italy," December 11, 1941, https://www.presidency.ucsb.edu/documents/message-congress-requesting-war-declarations-with-germany-and-italy.

77. Franklin Roosevelt, "Fireside Chat," December 29, 1940, https://www.presidency.ucsb.edu/documents/fireside-chat-9.

78. Franklin Roosevelt, "Press Conference," August 7, 1942, https://www.presidency.ucsb.edu/documents/press-conference.

79. On Roosevelt and foreign policy globalism, see David Reynolds, *From Munich to Pearl Harbor: Roosevelt's America and the Origins of the Second World War* (Chicago: Ivan R. Dee, 2001).

80. John F. Kennedy, "Remarks on the Occasion of the Celebration of the Centennial of Italian Unification," March 16, 1961, https://www.presidency.ucsb.edu/documents/remarks-the-occasion-the-celebration-the-centennial-italian-unification. On Germany, see Patrick Thaddeus Jackson, *Civilizing the Enemy: German Reconstruction and the Invention of the West* (Ann Arbor: University of Michigan Press, 2006).

81. Harry Truman, "Toast of the President at a Dinner Given in His Honor by the Shah of Iran," November 18, 1949, https://www.presidency.ucsb .edu/documents/toast-the-president-dinner-given-his-honor-the-shah -iran; Ronald Reagan, "Remarks at the Welcoming Ceremony for President Anwar el-Sadat of Egypt," August 5, 1981, https://www.reaganlibrary .gov/research/speeches/80581a; Ronald Reagan, "Radio Address to the Nation on the President's Trip to Japan and the Republic of Korea," November 12, 1983, https://www.presidency.ucsb.edu/documents/radio-address-the-nation -the-presidents-trip-japan-and-the-republic-korea.

82. Harry Truman, "Address at the Jefferson-Jackson Day Dinner," April 14, 1951, https://www.presidency.ucsb.edu/documents/address-the-jefferson-jackson -day-dinner-1. On the relative absence of civilization as a justification for the Cold War, see John Fousek, *To Lead the Free World: American Nationalism & the Cultural Roots of the Cold War* (Chapel Hill: University of North Carolina Press, 2000), 2.

83. For LT, George Kennan to Secretary of State, February 22, 1946, https:// nsarchive2.gwu.edu/coldwar/documents/episode-1/kennan.htm For X article: X [George Kennan], "The Sources of Soviet Conduct," *Foreign Affairs* July 1947, https://www.foreignaffairs.com/articles/russian-federation/1947-07-01 /sources-soviet-conduct. For NSC-68: "National Security Council Report, NSC 68, 'United States Objectives and Programs for National Security'," April 14, 1950, History and Public Policy Program Digital Archive, U.S. National Archives, http://digitalarchive.wilsoncenter.org/document/116191

84. Dwight Eisenhower, "Radio and Television Broadcast with Prime Minister Macmillan in London," August 31, 1959, https://www.presidency.ucsb.edu /documents/radio-and-television-broadcast-with-prime-minister-macmillan -london. Emphasis added.

85. Jimmy Carter, "Charleston, South Carolina Remarks at the 31st Annual Meeting of the Southern Legislative Conference," July 21, 1977, https://www .presidency.ucsb.edu/documents/charleston-south-carolina-remarks-the-31st -annual-meeting-the-southern-legislative.

86. Ronald Reagan, "Remarks to Reporters on the Soviet Attack on a Korean Civilian Airliner," September 2, 1983, https://www.presidency.ucsb.edu /documents/remarks-reporters-the-soviet-attack-korean-civilian-airliner.

87. Fousek, *To Lead the Free World*, 105.

88. Lyndon Johnson, "Remarks at an Airport Rally in Detroit," October 30, 1964, https://www.presidency.ucsb.edu/documents/remarks-airport-rally-detroit.

89. Jimmy Carter, "Farewell Address," January 14, 1981, https://www.presidency .ucsb.edu/documents/farewell-address-the-nation-0.

90. Ronald Reagan, "Radio Address to the Nation on Nuclear Weapons," April 17, 1982, https://www.presidency.ucsb.edu/documents/radio-address-the

-nation-nuclear-weapons-0; Ronald Reagan, "Interview with Reporters on Domestic and Foreign Policy Issues," December 23, 1983, https://www.presidency.ucsb.edu/documents/interview-with-reporters-domestic-and-foreign-policy-issues.

91. Richard Nixon, "Remarks at the Veterans of Foreign Wars Annual Convention, in Dallas, Texas," August 19, 1971, https://www.presidency.ucsb.edu/documents/remarks-the-veterans-foreign-wars-annual-convention-dallas-texas.

92. Richard Nixon, "Statement About the Report of the Commission on Obscenity and Pornography," October 24, 1970, https://www.presidency.ucsb.edu/documents/statement-about-the-report-the-commission-obscenity-and-pornography.

93. Ronald Reagan, "Remarks and a Question-and-Answer Session with Local High School Honor Students," May 23, 1983, https://www.presidency.ucsb.edu/documents/remarks-and-question-and-answer-session-with-local-high-school-honor-students.

94. Richard Nixon, "Statement on Signing the Instrument of Ratification of the Convention for the Suppression of Unlawful Acts Against the Safety of Civil Aviation," November 1, 1972, https://www.presidency.ucsb.edu/documents/statement-signing-the-instrument-ratification-the-convention-for-the-suppression-unlawful; Jimmy Carter, "Visit of Prime Minister Thatcher of the United Kingdom White House Statement," December 18, 1979, https://www.presidency.ucsb.edu/documents/visit-prime-minister-thatcher-the-united-kingdom-white-house-statement.

95. Ronald Reagan, "Radio Address," November 9, 1985, https://www.presidency.ucsb.edu/documents/radio-address-the-nation-and-the-world-the-upcoming-soviet-united-states-summit-meeting.

96. Jack Donnelly, "Human Rights: A New Standard of Civilization?," *International Affairs* 74, no. 1 (1998): 1–23.

97. Francis Fukuyama, *The End of History and the Last Man* (New York: Avon, 1992).

98. Huntington's original article in *Foreign Affairs* was translated into twenty-six languages. James Dunkerley, "Chaotic Epic: Samuel Huntington's *The Clash of Civilizations and the Remaking of World Order* Revisited," in *American Foreign Policy: Studies in Intellectual History*, ed. Jean-Francois Drolet and James Dunkerley (Manchester: Manchester University Press, 2017), 137.

99. Samuel Huntington, *The Clash of Civilizations and the Remaking of World Order* (New York: Simon & Schuster, 1996), 58.

100. Huntington, *Clash of Civilizations*, 306.

101. Samuel Huntington, *Who Are We? The Challenges to America's National Identity* (New York: Simon & Schuster, 2004).

102. George W. Bush, "Commencement Address at the United States Military Academy in West Point," June 1, 2002, https://www.presidency.ucsb.edu

/documents/commencement-address-the-united-states-military-academy
-west-point-new-york-1.

103. George W. Bush, "Address Before a Joint Session of the Congress on the United States Response to the Terrorist Attacks of September 11," September 20, 2001, https://www.presidency.ucsb.edu/documents/address-before-joint -session-the-congress-the-united-states-response-the-terrorist-attacks.

104. National Security Strategy of the United States (2002), 1, https://georgewbush -whitehouse.archives.gov/nsc/nss/2002/.

105. Andrew Bacevich, *America's War for the Greater Middle East: A Military History* (New York: Random House, 2016), 209.

106. "News Conference by President Obama," April 4, 2009, https://obamawhitehouse .archives.gov/the-press-office/news-conference-president-obama-4042009.

107. Barack Obama, "Interview with Hisham Melhem of Al Arabiya," January 27, 2009, https://www.presidency.ucsb.edu/documents/interview-with-hisham -melhem-al-arabiya; Barack Obama, "Remarks at the White House Summit on Countering Violent Extremism," February 18, 2015, https://www .presidency.ucsb.edu/documents/remarks-the-white-house-summit-countering -violent-extremism.

108. Donald Trump, "Remarks on Foreign Policy," April 27, 2016, https://www .presidency.ucsb.edu/documents/remarks-foreign-policy.

109. Jon Greenberg, "Donald Trump and Islam: Then and Now," *Politifact*, https:// www.politifact.com/truth-o-meter/article/2017/may/21/donald-trump-and -islam-then-and now/.

110. "David Attenborough Warns of 'Collapse of Civilizations' At U.N. Climate Meeting," NPR, December 3, 2018, https://www.npr.org/2018/12/03 /672893695/david-attenborough-warns-of-collapse-of-civilizations-at-u-n -climate-meeting.

CHAPTER 3

Containing the Multitudes

Nationalism and U.S. Foreign Policy Ideas at the Grassroots Level

MICHAELA HOENICKE-MOORE

In his groundbreaking 1987 study, in typically jargon-free prose, Michael Hunt defined ideology as "an interrelated set of convictions or assumptions that reduces the complexities of a particular slice of reality to easily comprehensible terms and suggests appropriate ways of dealing with that reality."[1] This formulation freed the concept from its stigma of other people's false beliefs and rendered it centrally important to the study of American foreign relations. Hunt observed, "to move in a world of infinite complexity, individuals and societies need to reduce that world to finite terms," acknowledging that observer and observed, historians and historical actors, are both enmeshed in ideologies, neither one free from history or the rich soil in which convictions, assumptions, beliefs, and prejudices are rooted.[2]

Hunt described three areas as constitutive of U.S. foreign policy ideology. First, a *nationalism* that deemed territorial expansion and overseas intervention as essential for domestic economic well-being and also as beneficial to others. Expanding the Jeffersonian empire for liberty became the declared duty of a state-empire that saw itself, much like its European counterparts and Soviet Russia, as an agent of progress. Second, this vision of national greatness was supported by a belief in *racial hierarchies* that proved responsive to changing international realities and a successive cast of enemies but remained securely rooted in white, Christian, supremacy. Third, a sanctified notion of private property and an unwavering faith in capitalism expressed in ambivalence toward other peoples' *revolutions* and hardened by the twentieth century into a clear aversion to radical, transformative socioeconomic change and outright hostility toward those who supported such change.

The function of ideology is to naturalize, that is, make invisible, as well as justify and perpetuate socioeconomic racial power arrangements. The second and third pillars, white supremacy and unfettered capitalism, are constitutive of the first, nationalism. Both received a new lease on life during the American Cold War and beyond, when the political theorist Corey Robin stated that "market society . . . [became] not a complement to democratic rule but its replacement." Fusing the second and third pillars, Nikhil Pal Singh notes that American cold warriors recognized "that the animating logic was not strictly anti-communist but counterrevolutionary—indeed even racial."[3]

All three components—an expansionist, interventionist nationalism, racial anxieties and violence, and fear of revolution and market fetishism—not only highlighted the European roots of the American project in which empire trumped exceptionalism but also linked domestic arrangements with overseas errands. The racial, social, economic, and political orders at home shaped and manifested policies and practices abroad. Yet the impact of empire is multidirectional: blowback, unintended consequences, and forces beyond the state-empire's control affected people and institutions back home.[4]

Two aspects of this national-international dynamic have to be acknowledged before I pivot toward the domestic. On a civil society level, the varied *transnational* experiences of ordinary Americans through military deployment, missionary work, immigration, marriage, and living and working abroad challenge and even counteract nationalist ideologies. On the level of great power politics, observers from mid-century theologian Reinhold Niebuhr to Vietnam War historian Marilyn Young have highlighted that the United States leaves a heavier footprint on the world than vice versa but sometimes responds with acute frustration and resentment to an indomitable world.[5]

Hunt identified three constitutive elements, whereas others cut and slice the evidence in different ways. The foreign affairs specialist Walter Russell Mead identified *four* strains dominating American foreign policy ideology at different times—Jeffersonian, Hamiltonian, Jacksonian, and Wilsonian—with Wilsonian liberal interventionism switching party lines in 2001 and Jacksonianism, a right-wing populist nativist strain of "America First," coming back in vogue with the Tea Party movement and to power in 2016.[6] The British policy analyst Anatol Lieven condensed these trends into *two* camps. On one hand, the American creed offers an optimistic, messianic nationalism, along the lines of an exceptionalist-universalist axis, prompting the country to spread its good fortune around the world. This is accomplished by efforts to shape and control the global environment, ensuring American national security, often under the guise of fighting for other people's freedom and democracy. On the other hand, the antithesis, corresponding roughly to Mead's Jacksonianism, is a resentful backlash to the creed, an aggrieved chauvinism fed by racial, religious, and class anxieties Lieven locates in the "embittered heartland" of the American Midwest, previously disparaged for its isolationist tendencies, as well as the white South.[7] By 2008, the last year of the George W. Bush administration, scholars painted an exceedingly dark picture of U.S. foreign policy ideology: Walter Hixson was not the only one who distilled various strains down to *one* pathological DNA of violence, racism, and the will to dominate.[8]

Others focused on how foreign policy ideology has corrupted American democracy and freedom. Walter McDougall and Andrew Bacevich, for example, have argued that national security ethos and requirements have undermined, even destroyed, American core values.[9] These jeremiads stand in a long proud tradition of foreign policy critiques, but they tend to downplay the republic's origins as a European settler-colony and, correspondingly, the long history of violence against and suppression of freedom and rights of Native Americans and African Americans.[10]

By 2020, the ideological incoherence of American foreign relations had once more come into full view. U.S. global influence and reputation had reached a new all-time nadir, accelerated by a reactionary-nativist agenda, incompetence, and betrayal of democratic values at the highest level. Yet simultaneously, people across the world expressed their solidarity with African Americans and multiracial coalitions of mostly young people, outraged by police brutality and white supremacist violence.[11] Reminiscent of similar episodes during the Civil Rights movement and the protests against the wars in Vietnam and Iraq, the situation highlighted the global resonance of century-old U.S. political discourse, infused with ideals against which its actions are measured. It also exposed that the United States is not the author but, at best, an exemplar of these ideals that hold broad, even universal appeal: sanctity of life, freedom from want and fear, right to assemble and free speech, and pursuit of happiness. In the midst of a heightened sense of decline and uncertainty, the debate on the scope and purpose of U.S. international leadership and foreign policy confirmed Hunt's original appraisal of domestic concerns and conceits shaping and hampering U.S. foreign policy.[12]

From a different angle, Susan Brewer added depth to this literature by showing how U.S. war propaganda has integrated ideals and interests into a publicly compelling compound.[13] On the historiographical disputes over whether ideals or interests drive U.S. foreign policy, McDougall comments, "What a fortunate country to have such luxury; most countries are slaves to geopolitics."[14] Ideals such as to make the world safe for democracy, the four freedoms, or the American way of life sound persuasive enough on their own, but the need to fight for American interests overseas was often reinforced with linkages to national security, no matter how far-fetched. By 1965, Jack S. Swender, a twenty-two-year-old Marine fighting and soon to be killed in Vietnam, had internalized the message: "The way I see the situation, I would rather fight to stop communism in South Vietnam than in Kincaid, Humboldt, Blue Mound, or Kansas City." The theme has persisted into the twenty-first century with President George W. Bush arguing that by fighting the terrorists over there we would not have to fight them at home.[15] Official narratives in times of war pitted Allied civilization, modernity, and humanitarianism against backward barbarians who raped, tortured, and oppressed women, children, and minorities. Although Americans accepted that truth might be the first casualty of war, Brewer concludes that official manipulation, abuse of power, and outright lies have, if anything, become more heavy-handed over time. This and the fact that some wars were seen in retrospect as "mistakes," "tragedies," or "crimes," i.e., illegitimate, has had consequences for how citizens regarded their government and its global militarized internationalism.[16]

The cumulative effect of governmental unresponsiveness and the nation's inability to learn from the past has resulted in strong reactions by the public that have been captured in the literature under two different headings: backlash and disconnect. On one hand, loss of trust, cynicism, anger, and resentment have corroded the underpinnings of democratic faith and practice. On the other hand, citizens have continued to express their preferences for prioritizing "security of *domestic* well-being and international justice, not just security from attack," for diplomatic and political solutions over military ones, and if military, then multilateral—but apparently to no avail. Over the past decades, a growing number of public opinion studies have documented how domestic costs and consequences of U.S. military globalism have created a gap between confident elites and a skeptical public, between determined political leaders and wary military and diplomatic professionals.[17]

By the twenty-first century, the literature on U.S. foreign policy ideologies had so grown in depth and breadth that Hunt suggested *nationalism* might serve as a unifying concept.[18] But as contributions to this volume reveal, why force new insights and perspectives generated by a more consistent focus on ideas in the practice of U.S. foreign relations under one "umbrella ideology"? The extant literature on ideas and foreign policy culture has opened important fresh vistas, has invited a more sustained engagement with critical theory, and has directed our attention to new sources, methodologies, and themes. However, it has also encouraged essentializing interpretations and a reductionist impulse, searching for and finding recurring and persistent patterns, often promoted through elite culture, marginalizing and dismissing the many voices and movements that resisted, questioned, and rejected official rhetoric. Reading the national record for coherence and continuity has led to the pitfall of reviving a discarded approach of national character studies.

How does the picture change if we incorporate voices at the grassroots level as legitimate participants in foreign policy debates? Taking in a broader spectrum of voices and plumbing the sometimes dark, always rich depths from which they arise, we get a clearer sense of the *varieties* of American patriotism and the kind of "convictions or assumptions" in which Hunt says they are grounded. This broader conceptualization enables us to understand nationalism as an expression of national belonging and identity that underlies the legitimization as well as the *contestation* of U.S. foreign policy. Studying foreign policy debates from the bottom up brings underexposed and unsettling questions about the compatibility of American democracy and military globalism into clearer focus. It reveals wider and deeper controversies over the question of what purpose and whose interests does U.S. foreign policy serve.[19]

Ordinary citizens were part of U.S. foreign policy debates to a much larger extent than previously acknowledged. Oral histories, memoirs, and especially letters to elected officials, to editors, and to family members show how Americans at the grassroots level vigorously participated in domestic controversies, expressing their views on the need, expediency, or futility of fighting overseas, and adapting, resisting, and challenging official versions, all the while articulating their own conceptions of "what America is all about." The tradition of *great debates* conventionally depicted as an elite affair—Jane Addams and William James against Teddy Roosevelt and Woodrow Wilson—is, in fact, much more broadly based. It is also not easily confined to the many binaries and dualistic alternatives we have used to characterize foreign policy debates: pro- and antiexpansionist, interventionists and isolationists, hawks and doves, Democrats and Republicans, conservatives and liberals.[20] How Americans have expressed loyalty, hope, and sorrow for their country in response to world events and official policies cuts across these dichotomies and reveals a continuous practice of patriotic dissent and a deep reservoir of alternative forms of international engagement.

Moreover, the nationalist ideology that Hunt uncovered is grounded in white supremacy. A different conception of American exceptionalism comes into focus when Black nationalism and African American patriotism are no longer segregated into separate historiographies but are recognized as an integral, although continually marginalized, maligned, and violently suppressed, part of the histories of U.S. foreign policy ideas. Correspondingly, the study of U.S. internationalism, often a euphemism for military globalism, and the ideological motivations that feed it are more productively understood in critical dialogue with African American internationalism, cosmopolitanism, and transnational anticolonial activism, exposing the incoherence and hollowness of white supremacist universalist claims.[21]

What had been missing from Hunt's original analytical framework and has been fleshed out not least by several contributors to this volume is *religion*, a concept and practice central to the exploration of nationalism and foreign policy ideas. Indeed, dissent and objection at the grassroots level, beyond protest marches, sit-ins, and letter campaigns, were often prompted by one or both of these two malleable and dynamic components: patriotism and faith. Religious language and arguments have been used both to affirm and uphold white supremacy, capitalism, and empire and to challenge and undercut these practices.[22]

The government calling on its citizens to go to war—with the double implication of doing harm and being harmed—is the starkest demand any authority can make. It parallels and often draws support from the similarly absolutist claims that a religion or a church makes on its followers.

Seeking to be part of something bigger, better, and longer-lasting than our ephemeral selves is as integral to the human psyche as our selective filters and susceptibility to ideological narratives. The two obvious choices that fulfill this longing for transcendence are religion and nationalism, "man's other religion" (E. Shillito). Both share a strong affective dimension, an appeal to emotions, as well as an opportunity to perform emotions. Once we start reading for emotions, the sources reveal a more nuanced tapestry

of American varieties of patriotism and grassroots visions for this country'
international role. The alloyed nature of citizens' patriotism is articulated,
over and over, especially by soldiers and veterans, as historians who have
listened closely to them, have shown:

> At a very early age Bob Foley learned about alcoholism, divorce, vio-
> lence, unemployment, loss, and fear: the realities of life. He associ-
> ated these realities with family life. Somehow "the country" seemed
> unconnected to these realities. Bob believed the nation as a whole—as
> represented by the government and the military—possessed the very
> traits his family had lacked: wealth, power, predictability, and organi-
> zation. That very contrast contributed to Bob's assumption that the
> government could be trusted to have a good reason for sending its
> boys to war [in Vietnam].[23]

The study of nationalism—whether state-centered or civil society
focused—is not without its own often unacknowledged emotions, normative assumptions, and attempts at partisan appropriations. In the 1990s, the
philosopher Richard Rorty urged the American political Left not to abandon the topic and practice of patriotism to the Right.[24] Other philosophers,
such as George Kateb, have called patriotism "a mistake twice over."[25] Martha
Nussbaum charts a middle path by recognizing that patriotism is rooted in
a form of love, like other core emotions, necessary for ethical behavior.
Love of country, or one's people, enables solidarity, compassion, altruism. Yet
"the exclusionary values, coerced conscience, and uncritical homogeneity"
of patriotism spur fear, hatred, and violence.[26] In sum, both sides are correct:
it appears inescapable and the source of much of our trouble.

Most scholars agree with Hunt's conclusion that by the dawn of the
twentieth century the big debate over whether the United States was a
republic or an empire, whether it would perfect democracy at home or
go abroad in search of monsters to destroy, had been settled in favor of the
latter—the activist-interventionists had won. The anti-imperialists had lost
not only the battle but the war, although they served their fellow citizens
well "by emphasizing the steady drift from professed values."[27] On one
level that is true. Over the course of the twentieth century, increasingly and
with accelerated speed, the imperial presidency and the growing tentacles
of the national security state shifted the balance between state and civil
society—never an equal one when it comes to foreign policy—even more

dramatically toward the former.[28] But that makes the project of recording, interpreting, and reintegrating the voices of those who resisted and challenged—at all levels of civil society—an expansionist, interventionist, and militant U.S. foreign policy all the more important.[29]

Popular skepticism regarding *worldmaking*, in David Milne's apt phrase, is not always well captured in public opinion polls with their questions pertaining to the issue of the day, formulated to gauge support for official policies, appealing to citizens' loyalty. Yet in 1945 approval rates for U.S. participation in the proposed United Nations Organization were high among regular citizens, at 81 percent, and reached 99 percent among GIs. In other words, soldiers were nearly unanimous in support of their country's "active participation in an international organization to keep the peace"—so they wouldn't have to do so.[30] Radio listeners and newspaper readers registered the shift from FDR's antifascist war and alliance-based multilateralism of the Four Policemen to Truman's U.S.-centered anticommunist global crusade and leadership. Some welcomed it; others were wary. In either case, Americans picked up and commented in their letters on the different emotions both presidents evoked, from "the only thing to fear is fear itself" pronouncement by a president who reassured people by exuding supreme confidence (in himself and in the nation) to the Truman administration's many worries and anxieties.[31]

In the first half of the twentieth century, popular preferences with regard to foreign policy tended toward neutrality—staying internationally engaged but out of war. Leaders responded to this with fearmongering. Striking examples include FDR warning Iowans in 1938 that Nazi Germany might attack them, the Truman administration's often apocalyptic language, and the Alsop brothers' breathless attempt to strike panic in the hearts of *Saturday Evening Post* readers at the beginning of the Korean War. FDR had been famous for translating complex and abstract geopolitical considerations into homespun images of lending a garden hose to one's neighbor, whereas postwar leaders favored a language of imminent and mortal threats, of individual and collective responsibilities, the shirking of which betrayed weakness, immaturity, and naivete.[32]

By 1945 Americans were not yet afraid of communism, which they could neither define nor explain; nor did they see the Soviet Union as a threat to their security. Those fears had to be and were effectively manufactured by the separate efforts but combined effects of the Truman administration "scaring hell out of the American people" and the longer-standing anti–New Deal hostility and defamation campaigns on the Right. In the early 1950s, the future battle cry of "let's fight communism over there, so we don't have to fight them in Kansas City" had not yet been internalized. Instead, antiwar parents, often conservative and suspicious of FDR's successor, asked: If fighting communism was so important to their government, why did they not fight it at home, specifically in the State Department, rather than sending "our boys" halfway around the globe?[33]

Letters to President Truman from 1945 through the Korean War show that citizens often drew different lessons from World War II than did their political leadership. In contrast to the newly emerging national security ideology, popular thinking and preferences congealed around two poles: multilateral cooperative internationalism centered on the United Nations or a focus on national well-being and a strong preference for staying at home. During the debate over universal military training (UMT) from 1945 through 1948, many Americans rejected military preparedness as un-American, undemocratic, and un-Christian.[34]

Much of the dissent was expressed in a religious vernacular, distinct from the public version of American civil religion. At the beginning of the "police action" in Korea, forty-three-year-old devout conservative Mrs. Irma Rockwell of Springville, Iowa, asked her senator, Bourke Hickenlooper, ranking Republican on the Senate Foreign Relations Committee: "Why on earth does any person think that war can destroy Communism?" From the other end of the political spectrum, seventy-five-year-old Charles Chilberg of Portland, Oregon, also wrote to protest the war in Korea and admonished President Truman not to give in to anti-Leftist hysteria: "Here in our 'Christian America' any church that practices what it preaches is promptly branded with the same old 'RED' brush. Your enemies would prefer another WORLD WAR as a means of stopping your social program." From this evidence it is neither apparent that Reinhold Niebuhr had entirely succeeded "in making war safe for Protestants" nor that the public shifted to Cold War religious militantism as easily as did their leaders.[35] Opposition to UMT and criticism of the "police action" in Korea are just two examples of significant ideological gaps between the public and its government in a postwar era. Similar chasms opened after the U.S. Civil War, the war in Vietnam, and the end of the Cold War: citizens struggling to assert different lessons from recent conflicts than the ones propagated by the men at the helm of the nation.[36]

Taking African American commentaries and critiques into account, the picture changes once more. Most of the critical voices cited here came from white people at whom the patriotic ideology that Hunt dissected had been aimed in an effort to plaster over the contradiction of increasing militarization when the country was not under threat. Throughout this period, from the 1940s through the 1960s, Black activists, intellectuals, and soldiers pinpointed the hypocrisy and problematic assumptions about freedom, democracy, and national security with greater lucidity than their white counterparts. Specifically, African Americans articulated succinctly the hazards that a hysterical anticommunism (McCarthyism) posed to American democracy, racial justice, and a rational U.S. foreign policy.[37]

Just as the New Deal began to restore hope for millions of Americans, Mittie Gordon, a Chicagoan Black nationalist organizer, sought federal aid to support African American emigration to Liberia. In a petition to Franklin D. Roosevelt, signed by an estimated 400,000 Black citizens, she explained that "hungry, cold and miserable, the pursuit of life, liberty and happiness in America appears futile," evoking the rhetoric of the American Dream to make a case for escaping from the nightmare that the United States had become to Depression-era African Americans.[38] If working-class Black nationalist women organizers were looking abroad to escape poverty and racial violence in the United States, young Black men came to understand white nationalist fallacies in the context of being sent abroad to fight for a country that claimed to liberate and defend the rights of other peoples but was unwilling to do so for its own.[39]

Qualitative evidence shows that the connection between official discourse and grassroots foreign policy views is more dynamic than the political science model of elite or partisan cues suggests.[40] The literature on U.S. foreign policy ideology, moreover, complicates the hypocrisy charge: often there was no simple gap between bromidic or hyperbolic public justifications and actual motives articulated behind closed doors. Exceptionalist beliefs and historical analogies that fueled American hubris and imperial overstretch not only worked in public speeches but were decisive in deliberations at the highest level. As studies of foreign policy makers and intellectuals have shown, national security elites drank their own nationalist Kool-Aid and then were often slower to shed delusions of grandeur than the young people fighting in the jungles and deserts of foreign countries.[41]

An enabling factor here is the security-insecurity irony, or more accurately inversion. Expansive threat scenarios have regularly been evoked in official rhetoric to shore up domestic mobilization and have become a mainstay in U.S. foreign policy ideology. However, in a nation that has militarily outspent various combinations of enemies and allies over the past seventy years, most white Americans enjoyed a high degree of security, waning only in the original sense of socioeconomic security.[42] From the post–World War II debates about UMT and the Soviet threat, through Korea and Vietnam, some Americans expressed skepticism about how much security a heavily armed nation could obtain. Others doubted that wars and military interventions could effectively solve successive international challenges. Many more reproached their leaders for sacrificing the national welfare to ever-expanding national security exigencies.

Nativist discourses on the dangers emanating from politically, religiously, or racially defined others have formed a malleable but persistent leitmotif in the American foreign policy imaginary from the beginning, connecting the enemy within to an outside military threat. Whether Bolshevism or the Civil Rights movement, Catholicism or Islam, African Americans or Asians, groups and belief systems deviating from WASP or white supremacist culture have been pathologized, marked as carriers of disease and un-American ideas and practices. The very people associated with external threats were most liable to experience violence and insecurity at home. Beyond these demographics but partially overlapping with them, only American soldiers confronted existential threats. Insights and conclusions that citizens, as soldiers and civilians, drew from wars were often subverted when a generation later another group of Americans was called upon to shoulder the responsibilities of world leadership. The impact and legacies of wars on civil society are difficult to measure and have more often been studied as "public memory"—already carefully curated and sanitized.[43]

From the Munich crisis in 1938 through the Tet offensive in 1968, generations of citizens articulated insights for which realist foreign policy experts were subsequently celebrated: a tragic conception of human endeavors, the need for humility, the recognition and acceptance of other peoples' nationalism and pride (Morgenthau, Niebuhr), warnings of overextension (Lippmann), and militarization (Kennan). In contrast to the artists and scientists in Milne's magisterial *Worldmaking*, many Americans clearly stated their beliefs that their country could not or should not attempt to shape the course and outcome of human history.

The reasons for such realism among the populace, often combined with warnings against the arrogance of power, were manifold. Sometimes they were grounded in veterans' firsthand experiences with war as tragic and traumatic, engendering a sense of solidarity and empathy even across enemy lines. Often citizens shared religious notions with theologians such as Reinhold Niebuhr and King, according to which their country was not in charge of history; many more quoted Bible verses to their leaders reminding them of their savior's commandment not to wage war. African Americans, at all levels of society, offered some of the most trenchant anti-imperial critiques and punctured the pretension of white supremacist universalism, insisting that only if Americans confronted racism at home could they aspire to leadership. Over and over citizens questioned the need to fight other people's wars in faraway places and worried about contradictions between stated war aims and strategies. Young and old, liberals and conservatives doubted that military interventions could adequately address the most pressing problems. Across the political spectrum and in each generation, Americans showed themselves invested in the American dream and prioritized its realization at home over any ambition to export it.

There is, of course, no greater truth than vox populi. Amid the antiwar, pro-UN letters, and alongside Black Americans' lucid analyses of the newly emerging American Cold War empire, are the hate-filled screeching voices of white southerners, often women, in reaction to President Truman's partial desegregation order of the U.S. military, rejecting any notion of racial equality and democracy and, at times, even the humanity of their fellow citizens.[44]

As with earlier studies of foreign policy nationalism, the picture that emerges when we include the multitudes isn't always pretty, but it is more nuanced, complex, and ultimately instructive. By adding "the people" back in, we recover the diversity and range of views in the public sphere, the varieties of American patriotism where the views of expert critics and elite dissenters, from Robert Taft to Andrew Bacevich, were, in fact, duly noted and amplified. Tracking a wider spectrum of foreign policy views over time, enables us to understand how the content of these debates and specific arguments for and against military intervention changed. And by bringing out the incoherence and contradictions within the American nationalist discourse, we get a better sense of the dynamic interaction between state and society in defining nationalism, even if the latter's efforts appear doomed. To expect civil society to curb the national security state is too high a bar and primarily reflects our field's obsession with power and impact.[45]

In the end we may find citizens, foot soldiers, elites, and government officials caught in a similar dynamic. At the close of World War II, Dwight Macdonald grappled, valiantly if inconclusively, with the question of "the [moral] responsibility of peoples" for their country's policies, especially in times of war.[46] He offered relevant insights into the "cog in the machine" phenomenon that characterized, in his view, the modern soldier and citizen in democracies and dictatorships alike. He showed how the nation-state, especially as empire, implicates its citizens in its crimes.[47] The political scientist Herfried Münkler has called this "the logic of empire." The logic of imperial ideology manifests both in the more resigned version of midlevel military officers, "now that we are here . . . ," and in the cockier version of "We are an empire now . . . we create our own reality.[48] As Milne and Hollinger have shown, even those at the highest level or on the ground who suspect that their nation has strayed and are casting about for a course correction are as helpless as the sorcerer's apprentice in reining in the forces they have conjured.[49]

Notes

1. Michael H. Hunt, *Ideology and US Foreign Policy*, 2nd ed. (New Haven, CT: Yale University Press, 2009), xi.
2. Hunt, *Ideology and US Foreign Policy*, 221.
3. Corey Robin, "Eric Hobsbawm, the Communist Who Explained History," *New Yorker*, May 9, 2019, https://www.newyorker.com/books/under-review /eric-hobsbawm-the-communist-who-explained-history; Nikhil Pal Singh, "Banking on the Cold War," *Boston Review*, March 14, 2019, https://bostonreview .net/print-issues-war-security/nikhil-pal-singh-banking-cold-war.
4. Paul Kramer, "Power and Connection. Imperial Histories of the United States in the World," *American Historical Review* (December 2011): 1348–91; Paul Kramer, "The Geopolitics of Mobility: Immigration Policy and American Global Power in the Long Twentieth Century," *American Historical Review* (April 2018): 392–438.
5. Marilyn B. Young, "The Age of Global Power," *Rethinking American History in a Global Age* (Berkeley: University of California Press, 2002), 274–94; Reinhold Niebuhr, "Awkward Imperialists," *Atlantic* 145, no. 5 (May 1930): 670–75.
6. Walter Russell Mead, *Special Providence: American Foreign Policy and How It Changed the World* (New York: Routledge, 2002); Walter Russell Mead, "The Jacksonian Revolt: American Populism and the Liberal Order," *Foreign Affairs* 96, no. 2 (March/April 2017): 2–7.
7. Anatol Lieven, *America Right or Wrong: An Anatomy of American Nationalism* (Oxford: Oxford University Press, 2004).
8. Walter Hixson, *The Myth of American Diplomacy: National Identity and US Foreign Policy* (New Haven, CT: Yale University Press, 2008).

9. William O. Walker III, *National Security and Core Values in American History* (Cambridge: Cambridge University Press, 2009); Walter A. McDougall, *Tragedy of US Foreign Policy: How America's Civil Religion Betrayed the National Interest* (New Haven, CT: Yale University Press, 2019); Andrew J. Bacevich, *Washington Rules: America's Path to Permanent War* (New York: Metropolitan, 2010).

10. Robert Mickey, Steven Levitsky, and Lucan Ahmad Way, "Is America Still Safe for Democracy?," *Foreign Affairs* 96, no. 3 (May/June 2017): 20–29. On the function of Jeremiads in U.S. foreign policy discourse, see Vibeke Schou Tjalve, *Realist Strategies of Republican Peace: Niebuhr, Morgenthau, and the Politics of Dissent* (New York: Palgrave, 2008).

11. Brenda Gayle Plummer, "How Allies Abroad Help the Fight Against Racism at Home," *Foreign Affairs*, June 19, 2020, https://www.foreignaffairs.com/articles /united-states/2020-06-19/civil-rights-has-always-been-global-movement; David Pilling, "'Everybody Has Their Eyes on America': Black Lives Matter Goes Global," *Financial Times*, June 20, 2020, https://on.ft.com/2Ysmv67.

12. Among many others, see Daniel W. Drezner, "This Time Is Different: Why US Foreign Policy Will Never Recover," *Foreign Affairs* 98, no. 3 (May/June 2019): 10–17; Stephen Wertheim, "The Price of Primacy: Why America Shouldn't Dominate the World," *Foreign Affairs* 99, no. 2 (March/April 2020): 19–29; Peter Beinart, "The US Doesn't Have to Lead the World," *New York Times*, December 6, 2020.

13. Susan Brewer, *Why America Fights: Patriotism and War Propaganda from the Philippines to Iraq* (Oxford: Oxford University Press, 2011).

14. McDougall, *Tragedy of US Foreign Policy*, 31. Similarly, see John A. Thompson, *A Sense of Power: The Roots of America's Global Role* (Ithaca, NY: Cornell University Press, 2015).

15. Jack S. Swender, enlisted man in the First Marine Division, letter to uncle and aunt, September 20, 1965, as quoted in Michael H. Hunt, ed., *A Vietnam Reader. A Documentary History from American and Vietnamese Perspectives* (Chapel Hill: University of North Carolina Press, 2010), 126; George W. Bush as quoted in Nikhil Pal Singh, *Race and America's Long War* (Oakland: University of California Press, 2017), 101.

16. Brewer, *Why America Fights*, 277–83.

17. Quote, emphasis my own, from Benjamin Page, with Marshall Bouton, *The Foreign Policy Disconnect: What Americans Want from Our Leaders but Don't Get* (Chicago: University of Chicago Press, 2006), 227. See also Ole R. Holsti, *Public Opinion and American Foreign Policy* (Ann Arbor: University of Michigan Press, 1996); Stewart Patrick, *The Sovereignty War: Reconciling America with the World* (Washington, DC: Brookings Institution, 2018), 254–56.

18. Michael H. Hunt, "Nationalism as an Umbrella Ideology," in *Explaining the History of American Foreign Relations*, 3rd ed., ed. Frank Costigliola and Michael J. Hogan (New York: Cambridge University Press, 2016), 217–31.

19. Daniel Bessner and Stephen Wertheim, "Democratizing US Foreign Policy: Bringing Experts and the Public Back Together," *Foreign Affairs* (April 5, 2017), https://www.foreignaffairs.com/articles/united-states/2017-04-05/democratizing-us-foreign-policy; Lloyd Kramer, *Nationalism in Europe and America: Politics, Cultures, and Identities Since 1775* (Chapel Hill: University of North Carolina Press, 2011), 16–21.

20. Peter H. Gries, *The Politics of American Foreign Policy: How Ideology Divides Liberals and Conservatives over Foreign Affairs* (Stanford, CA: Stanford University Press, 2014).

21. Nikhil Pal Singh, *Black Is a Country: Race and the Unfinished Struggle for Democracy* (Cambridge, MA: Harvard University Press, 2004).

22. Andrew Preston, *Sword of the Spirit, Shield of Faith: Religion in American War and Diplomacy* (New York: Knopf, 2012); Melani McAlister, *The Kingdom of God Has No Borders: A Global History of American Evangelicals* (New York: Oxford University Press, 2018); Raymond Haberski, *God and War: American Civil Religion Since 1945* (New Brunswick, NJ: Rutgers University Press, 2012).

23. Christian G. Appy, *Working-Class War: American Combat Soldiers & Vietnam* (Chapel Hill: University of North Carolina Press, 1993), 72; Christian G. Appy, *American Reckoning: The Vietnam War and Our National Identity* (New York: Viking, 2015); and the oral history by Christian G. Appy, *Patriots: The Vietnam War Remembered from All Sides* (New York: Penguin, 2003). See also John Bodnar, "Moral Patriotism and Collective Memory in Whiting, Indiana, 1920–1992," in *Bonds of Affection: Americans Define Their Patriotism* (Princeton, NJ: Princeton University Press, 1996), 290–304; Gerald Lindermann, *The World Within War: America's Combat Experience in World War II* (New York: Free Press, 1997).

24. Richard Rorty, *Achieving Our Country: Leftist Thought in Twentieth Century America* (Boston: Harvard University Press, 1998). Compare with Jill Lepore, "A New Americanism: Why a Nation Needs a National Story," *Foreign Affairs* (March/April 2019): 10–19.

25. George Kateb, *Patriotism and Other Mistakes* (New Haven, CT: Yale University Press, 2006), 3.

26. Martha C. Nussbaum, *Political Emotions: Why Love Matters for Justice* (Cambridge, MA: Belknap, 2013), 208–39.

27. Hunt, *Ideology and US Foreign Policy*, 44.

28. How the state at war affects the behavior of citizens is brilliantly analyzed in Christopher Capozzola, *Uncle Sam Wants You! World War I and the Making of the Modern American Citizen* (Oxford: Oxford University Press, 2008), The kind of egalitarian envy and resentment his sources reveal is also discussed as "Envy's Empire" in Martha C. Nussbaum, *The Monarchy of Fear: A Philosopher Looks at Our Political Crisis* (New York: Simon & Schuster, 2019), 135f. Samuel Stouffer's World War II social science study registered the same egalitarian vigilantism.

Samuel Stouffer, *The American Soldier*, 2 vols. (Princeton, NJ: Princeton University Press, 1949).

29. Christopher McKnight Nichols and other antiwar and anti-interventionist positions were not concentrated on the Left. Chris Nichols, *Promise and Peril: America at the Dawn of a Global Age* (Cambridge, MA: Harvard University Press, 2011); Bill Kauffman, *Ain't My America: The Long, Noble History of Antiwar Conservatism and Middle American Anti-Imperialism* (Dallas: Metropolitan, 2008).

30. "Current Opinions #12, 10 May 1945," Office of War Information, Research Division, Philleo Nash Papers, box 5, Harry S Truman Library; compare to R. Alton Lee, "The Army 'Mutiny' of 1946," *Journal of American History* 53, no. 3 (December 1966): 555–71.

31. Michael Hogan, *The Cross of Iron: Harry S. Truman and the Origins of the National Security State 1945–1954* (New York: Cambridge University Press, 1998), 419–62.

32. Brooke L. Blower, "From Isolationism to Neutrality: A New Framework for Understanding American Political Culture, 1919–1941," *Diplomatic History* 38, no. 2 (2014): 345–76. For press conference with Associated Church Press, April 20, 1938, see Edgar B. Nixon, ed., *Franklin D. Roosevelt and Foreign Affairs* (Cambridge, MA: Belknap Press of Harvard University Press, 1969–1983), 9:443–45. For more hysterical, apocalyptic language, compare George F. Kennan, "Article X," *Foreign Affairs* (July 1947); Paul Nitze, "United States Objective and Programs for National Security," NSC-68, April 7, 1950; Joseph and Stewart Alsop, "The Lessons of Korea," *Saturday Evening Post*, September 2, 1950, 17–19, 96–98, 100; Elaine Tyler May, *Fortress America: How We Embraced Fear and Abandoned Democracy* (New York: Basic Books, 2017), 1–59.

33. Michaela Hoenicke Moore, "'It's Not Too Late, Heed Your People' Foreign Policy Views at the Grassroots Level from World War II to Korea," article in preparation for *Diplomatic History* Forum; Walter LaFeber, "American Policy-Makers, Public Opinion, and the Outbreak of the Cold War, 1945–1950," in *The Origins of the Cold War in Asia*, ed. Yonosake Negai and Akira Iriye (Tokyo: University of Tokyo Press, 1977), 43–65; John Fousek, *To Lead the Free World: American Nationalism and the Cultural Roots of the Cold War* (Chapel Hill: University of North Carolina Press, 2000).

34. Letters in PPF 200, boxes 280–285, OF 471, box 1453, OF 190, box 800, Harry S. Truman Papers, Harry S. Truman Library, Independence, MO.

35. Handwritten letter by Irma Rockwell to Senator Bourke Hickenlooper, August 1950, Bourke B. Hickenlooper Papers, Topical Files Foreign Policy, General, 1945–1950 (September/December), box 24, Herbert Hoover Presidential Library, West Branch, IA; Charles Kinsey Chilberg, June 27, 1950, capitalized in original; similarly, P. W. Caton of Chicago; E. T. Becker, OF 471 Korea, box 1461, Harry S. Truman Library, Independence, MO. Rev.

Dean L. Farringer, Fredricksburg, IA, September 1950, box 12, Topical Files "Communism," Herbert Hoover Presidential Library, West Branch, IA; David Hollinger, *After Cloven Tongues of Fire: Liberal Protestantism in Modern American History* (Princeton, NJ: Princeton University Press, 2013), 211; Michaela Hoenicke Moore, "'Are We Going to Fight Wars in All These Nations?' Citizen Responses to Korea and Vietnam," article in preparation for *Journal of American East-Asian Relations*.

36. For post–World War II, see Laura McEnaney, *Postwar: Waging Peace in Chicago* (Philadelphia: University of Pennsylvania Press, 2018); John Bodnar, *The Good War in American Memory* (Baltimore: Johns Hopkins University Press, 2010); compare with Jennifer E. Brooks, *Defining the Peace: World War II Veterans, Race, and the Remaking of the Southern Political Tradition* (Chapel Hill: University of North Carolina Press, 2004). For the post–Civil War era, see Cecilia Elizabeth O'Leary, *To Die For: The Paradox of American Patriotism* (Princeton, NJ: Princeton University Press, 1999). For post–Vietnam War, see Appy, *American Reckoning*. For the post–Cold War, see chapter 15 in this volume, "Roads Not Taken," by Penny Von Eschen.

37. Brenda Gayle Plummer, *Rising Wind: Black Americans and US Foreign Affairs, 1935–1960* (Chapel Hill: University of North Carolina Press, 1996); Penny M. Von Eschen, *Race Against Empire: Black Americans and Anticolonialism, 1937–1957* (Ithaca, NY: Cornell University Press, 1997); Carol Anderson, *Eyes Off the Prize: The United Nations and the African American Struggle for Human Rights, 1944–1955* (New York: Cambridge University Press, 2003); and Carol Anderson, *Bourgeois Radicals: The NAACP and the Struggle for Colonial Liberation, 1941–1960* (New York: Cambridge University Press, 2015).

38. Keisha N. Blain, *Set the World on Fire: Black Nationalist Women and the Global Struggle for Freedom* (Philadelphia: University of Pennsylvania Press, 2018), 71f; Keisha N. Blain, "Confraternity Among All Dark Races: Mitte Maude Lena Gordon and the Practice of Black (Inter)nationalism in Chicago, 1932–1942," in *To Turn the Whole World Over: Black Women and Internationalism*, ed. Keisha N. Bland and Tiffany M. Gill (Urbana: University of Illinois Press, 2019), 171–91.

39. Kimberley L. Phillips, *War! What Is It Good For? Black Freedom Struggles and the US Military from World War II to Iraq* (Chapel Hill: University of North Carolina Press, 2012), 112–87, zeroes in on the divide between "elite blacks who saw their participation in war as an opportunity to advance racial equality at home and working-class blacks who rejected Jim Crow in the military and the nation."

40. Adam Berinsky, *In Time of War: Understanding American Public Opinion from World War II to Iraq* (Chicago: Chicago University Press, 2009).

41. Yuen Foong Khong, *Analogies at War: Korea, Munich, Dien Bien Phu, and the Vietnam Decisions of 1965* (Princeton, NJ: Princeton University Press, 1992); David Milne, *Worldmaking: The Art and Science of American Diplomacy* (New

York: Farrar, Straus and Giroux, 2015); Bruce Kuklick, *Blind Oracles: Intellectuals and War from Kennan to Kissinger* (Princeton, NJ: Princeton University Press, 2006). Compare with Robert McNamara, *In Retrospect: The Tragedy and Lessons of Vietnam* (New York: Vintage, 1996); George Packer, *Our Man: Richard Holbrooke and the End of the American Century* (New York: Vintage, 2020).

42. Compare with Andrew Preston, "The Fearful Giant: National Insecurity and U.S. Foreign Policy," chapter 8 in this volume. See also David Campbell, *Writing Security: United States Foreign Policy and the Politics of Identity*, rev. ed. (Minneapolis: University of Minnesota Press, 1998).

43. Bodnar, *The Good War in American Memory*; Appy, *American Reckoning*; Patrick Hagopian, *The Vietnam War in American Memory: Veterans, Memorials, and the Politics of Healing* (Amherst: University of Massachusetts Press, 2009).

44. Letters in response to Truman's message to Congress on Civil Rights, Feb 2, 1948, PPF 200, box 356, Harry S. Truman Library, Independence, MO.

45. Although there are some striking exceptions to this view. See Katherine A. Scott, *Reining in the State: Civil Society and Congress in the Vietnam and Watergate Eras* (Lawrence: University of Kansas Press, 2013).

46. Dwight Macdonald, *The Responsibility of Peoples and Other Essays in Political Criticism* (1945; repr. London: Victor Gollancz, 1957), 9–45.

47. As one noncommissioned Vietnam War officer confronting his instructor at Fort Benning put it: "Sir, in all your examples, the nation seems to have less responsibility than individual soldiers. . . . Sir, what you're saying is you have the right to hang us, but we don't have the right to question the nation." Bernd Greiner, *War Without Fronts. The USA in Vietnam* (New Haven, CT: Yale University Press, 2009), 353f.

48. Herfried Münkler: *Empires: The Logic of World Domination from Ancient Rome to the United States* (Cambridge: Polity, 2007). Ron Suskind, "Faith, Certainty and the Presidency of George W. Bush," *New York Times Magazine*, October 17, 2004.

49. Milne, *Worldmaking*; David A. Hollinger, *Protestants Abroad: How Missionaries Tried to Change the World but Changed America* (Princeton, NJ: Princeton University Press, 2017), 288.

CHAPTER 4

"Mrs. Sovereign Citizen"

Women's International Thought and American Public Culture, 1920–1950

KATHARINA RIETZLER

In the mid-twentieth century, technological innovations and ideological polarization transformed American public culture. As aggressive ideologies and "isms" threatened the established international order in the volatile 1930s, Americans were exhorted to act as responsible citizens, willing to listen to "both sides" of any given issue. Public service broadcasting, mandated by new legislation, created innovative programs to involve ordinary Americans in political debate, including on international affairs. One of these was America's Town Meeting of the Air, a radio show that incorporated responses and questions from the public in the form of a live question and answer period. Its roster of speakers included prominent Americans and foreigners, such as the journalist Clarence Streit, the pacifist activist Dorothy Detzer, the Egyptian feminist Esther Fahmy Wissa and the Czech diplomat Jan Masaryk.[1] Although women were underrepresented as speakers, a professed egalitarianism permeated the show's design. Audience members who asked questions were always identified as either "woman" or "man" in the published transcripts, and name, occupation, and ethnicity were omitted.[2] George V. Denny, the inventor of Town Meeting of the Air, had joined forces with a discussion forum established by pro–woman suffrage activists, and he imagined his listeners as "Mr. and Mrs. Sovereign Citizen," an idealized heterosexual married couple.[3] And as listeners across the United States heard Dorothy Detzer denounce Clarence Streit's best-selling proposals for a federation of democracies as a recipe for the perpetuation of colonialism and war, they could not have doubted that women were an integral part of the American public debate on pressing foreign policy issues of the day.[4]

Although theorists of the public sphere have traditionally acknowledged women's exclusion as a constitutive constant of the discursive practices that shaped publicness in modern Western societies, women's active and organized participation in public debate on international affairs became part of a midcentury ideology of white female citizenship in the United States.[5] International affairs and foreign policy formed a discursive field that was entwined with women's citizenship claims in distinct and novel ways after the securing of suffrage for all white women and some women of color in 1920. The ideology of women's *international* citizenship opened pathways to intellectual production for women in traditionally feminized fields such as education but also in new professional locations such as the foreign policy think tank. Public understandings of the responsibility of citizens to understand and acknowledge the place of the United States in the world were gendered and rooted in participatory conceptions of citizenship that emphasized responsibilities instead of rights. Notions of women's responsibility to become "citizens of the world" went beyond the ideological confines of U.S. liberal internationalism. Right-wing women and their organizations also took seriously their responsibility to research and write on foreign nations and cultures and the U.S. relationship with them—whether this relationship was marked by mutual understanding or antagonism.[6]

After passage of the Nineteenth Amendment and drawing on older notions of women's public responsibilities, American discourses on women's citizenship emphasized their responsibilities as citizens of the world, including the notion that knowledge of the world would both benefit the United States and contribute to the regulation of global military conflict. This went beyond well-known women's activist organizations such as the feminist pacifist Women's International League for Peace and Freedom (WILPF), and incorporated scholarship, journalism, think tank work, teaching materials and curricula, and the writings and broadcasts of public intellectuals.[7] In this chapter, I highlight the role of a minority of women who became cultural producers—being able to interpret world politics was something open to only a small number of Americans in the mid-twentieth century— and who occupied a range of ideological positions, notably on the Right of U.S. politics, in an era in which women's issues became international issues, and vice versa.[8]

Women's International Citizenship

The ideology of women's international citizenship postulated that women, as female citizens, had a duty to care and know about world politics. What was at stake in ideologies of women as international—and sovereign—citizens were contested normative claims around citizenship, underpinned by Anglophone liberalism's ambivalent relationship with "the public."[9] Liberalism exalted rational debate and public discourse, but at the same time it tried to rein in the unruly aspects of mass politics, especially from the 1930s, when psychological theories and the rise of foreign dictatorships seeded doubts about the future of (liberal) democracy in America and abroad.[10] Indeed, the ideology of (white) women's international citizenship was most but not exclusively aligned with liberal and ameliorative conceptions of international relations—not least the idea that a transformation of individual consciousness could prevent interstate conflict.

The intellectual traditions of U.S. citizenship have always made specific demands on women, whether in the form of republican motherhood, the "female dominion" of social welfare in the progressive era, or the notion that wives and mothers had to safeguard the nation's security during the Cold War.[11] Compared to more narrow, rights-based approaches to citizenship, civic republicanism offered women opportunities by justifying their engagement as citizens in the world, but did not give them the same access to political decision-making and power as it did to men.[12] It is thus no surprise that within the American women's movement the tensions between republican participatory conceptions of citizenship and those focused on equal rights often led to deep disagreements, for instance, during the debate on female suffrage, and whether it would expand or circumscribe women's agency as citizens.[13] These tensions are also visible in the postsuffrage debates on women's international citizenship.

Rights-based citizenship has also been marked by exclusions on the basis of property, sex, and race. The First Red Scare, the racist backlash against civil rights activism, but also the betrayals by white suffragists in the wake of World War I mobilized African American women as citizens seeking recognition for their contributions. Some of them became prominent cultural and intellectual producers for a politicized Black counterpublic, defined by its being in "tension with a larger public." But, as Michael Warner has argued, counterpublics need not necessarily consist of oppressed subalterns.[14] Antiradical and socioeconomically privileged white women also came to regard themselves as a counterpublic in the era of women's international citizenship. They forged mechanisms of opinion and exchange that sought to undermine what they regarded as a fabricated consensus, couched their attacks on liberal women reformers and pacifists in terms of national security and offered a trenchant critique of the discursive culture of women's liberal internationalism.[15] Often characterized as antifeminist, right-wing women were an integral part of the American women's movement, with their own mass organizations, publications, and interpretations of the responsibilities of women's international citizenship.[16]

Even recent accounts of the role of foreign policy issues in shaping a hegemonic public in mid-twentieth-century America continue to foreground the role of male public intellectuals such as the journalist Henry Luce or the politician Wendell Willkie. Women are credited as mere diffusers of messages because they "rarely got to generate the big ideas."[17] Although it may be debatable whether a well-published and highly paid journalist such as Dorothy Thompson, one of the few American public intellectuals who understood the threat of Nazi Germany, was really bereft of "big ideas," such implicit assumptions of hierarchies among cultural producers point to a larger methodological issue when writing about publics, especially in the context of women's intellectual history. Historians may expect the process of constructing a "women's public" to be contested and striated by various ideological projects. The recovery of the work of female thinkers will not only reveal liberal, progressive, antiracist, or feminist voices. Women's political allegiances ranged across the political spectrum, certainly after the U.S. women's movement fragmented after 1920, when deep political divisions split even established organizations. Fierce ideological battles impeded the formation of a hegemonic consensus. Indeed, paying closer attention to liberal female publics as well as their right-wing counterparts may highlight international thinking that, although influential, is often neglected.[18]

Suffrage's Fractures

The fight for suffrage and its global ramifications linked international relations and women's citizenship. The ratification of the Nineteenth Amendment to the U.S. Constitution in 1920 represented the culmination of a decades-long struggle that had connected American activists to reformers across the globe. In the era of World War I, the international women's movement embedded the suffrage question in the question of whether the conflict's end would bring about a "people's peace," a slogan that feminists pressed into service throughout the postwar period.[19] Women made political arguments that couched their demands in the intellectual frameworks of a newly democratic age. WILPF member Emily Greene Balch argued that the new world order demanded the "rejection of such obsolete doctrines as the divine right of kings, but also the negation of racial subordination and exploitation, whether internally or in a colony, the end of sex domination—women are also people—and of class domination and exploitation."[20] Others interpreted Woodrow Wilson's promise for national self-determination in terms of the recognition of women's independent citizenship, a point developed by the international lawyer Sarah Wambaugh in her groundbreaking work on international plebiscites.[21] American suffrage activists were, by necessity, familiar with the world of diplomacy and statecraft, and they became acquainted with the new structures of international governance in the shape of the League of Nations. The league was uniquely open to appointing women in senior roles and turned "women's issues" into "international issues" through its international policy making and standard setting.[22] Thus began a long alliance between American (progressive) women's organizations and international organizations, an alliance that would come under fire by the middle of the twentieth century.

Once suffrage was achieved, the American women's movement fractured, and it did so along several axes.[23] Most women of color were denied the ballot. After 1920, women in American territories such as Puerto Rico remained disenfranchised, and the Jim Crow system ensured that most African American women remained second-class citizens, excluded not only from the vote but also from education, civic associations, and professions, all of which were pathways to international thinking.[24] Barred from Congress, women such as Amy Ashwood Garvey or Eslanda Robeson sought leadership roles in civil rights and Pan-Africanist organizations, often explicitly articulating their civic duties to "make the world safe for democracy" by fighting the global color line. They also shaped the print culture of mass membership organizations dedicated to racial liberation, writing prolifically in periodicals, newsletters, and other publications. The Pan-Africanist Amy Jacques Garvey, for instance, introduced a women's page, "Our Women and What They Think," to the magazine of the Universal Negro Improvement Association.[25] Others built parallel institutions and conducted research that shaped antiracist and anticolonialist international thought and pedagogy, for instance, Nannie Helen Burroughs who led a training school for African American and African women missionaries, or Anna Julia Cooper who gained a doctorate from the Sorbonne with a dissertation on French colonialism.[26] Black women excluded from the benefits of U.S. citizenship nonetheless articulated notions of civic internationalism based on engagement in an African American public world that saw itself in opposition to a white supremacist American public.

But suffrage also brought to the fore political differences among white women. The Bolshevik Revolution, which had enfranchised women in Russia in 1917, had already induced antiradical white women to distance themselves from the broader movement. As Julia Mickenberg has argued, "a significant proportion" of suffrage activists had been sympathetic to the Bolshevik project and its welfare provisions for women, at least in its pre-Stalinist days when a Soviet model of equal, rights-based citizenship seemed viable.[27] These sympathies contributed to a steady disintegration of the broader umbrella of maternalist middle-class reform that had been synonymous with women's public engagement in the progressive era. Although antiradical women's organizations such as the Daughters of the American Revolution (DAR) were still making common cause with their more progressive counterparts such as the League of Women Voters just after World War I, by the middle of the 1920s they had performed a remarkable volte-face. This could undermine entire organizations, for instance, the National Council of Women, which folded after the DAR withdrew its participation. DAR members also disrupted the 1924 WILPF congress, accusing the internationalist organization of disloyalty. (This contrasted markedly with the DAR's 1919 plans to introduce study groups on the League of Nations and world governance.) And an infamous publication, the so-called Spider Web Chart of 1924, indicted progressive women's organizations as subversive elements in the American body politic. Faced with what they regarded as a compromised movement that purported to speak for their sex, antiradical women founded new organizations such as the Women's Patriotic Conference on National Defense, which gained the support of over a million members through its constituent groups. By 1925, the movement that had supported white women's suffrage was no longer united by a single issue but had splintered in two.[28] And both camps had much to say about U.S. foreign policy and world politics.

One of the salient issues was pacifism. The interwar American peace movement featured a significant number of women as rank-and-file members and intellectual figureheads such as Jane Addams or Emily Balch.[29] Established organizations such as the League of Women Voters and the American Association of University Women (AAUW) supported the peace movement. These groups were close to the corridors of power, organized in the Women's Joint Congressional Committee. Antiradical women denounced pacifists as subversives who endangered the nation.[30] Another salient issue was propaganda and the notion that women were particularly prone to becoming dupes of foreign manipulation. In the context of the 1920s, when public intellectuals frequently debated the perils of propaganda in mass democracies and the importance of fact-based foreign policies, concerns over women as targets of propaganda formed an important part of a wider discourse that centered on the public's capacity to process and evaluate information relevant to making foreign policy.[31] Propaganda scares justified the surveillance that progressive women's organizations such as WILPF were subjected to and in which antiradical organizations such as the DAR engaged.[32] Yet both camps subscribed to a participatory understanding of women's citizenship. They shared a belief in women as rational and informed citizens—and that commonality was at least as significant as their substantive ideological differences. On the Left and on the Right, women broke with a liberal and patriarchal tradition that downplayed their participation as citizens in public debate. In the area of international thought, women's involvement often took the shape of various forms of pedagogy.

Women as Producers of International Thought

Recent research on women's international thinking in the Anglophone world has revealed multiple professional contexts as pathways for intellectual production. These included, among others, teaching, social work, librarianship, journalism, political activism, the academy, and think tank research.[33] Of course, whether women had access to these contexts was a question that was inextricably entwined with their status as citizens. Married women's employment bars, elite universities that only accepted male students, and bans on women in certain professions all functioned as barriers. These barriers were historically contingent; marriage bars, for instance, became more common during the Depression of the 1930s.[34]

Women's higher education became more open during this period, however; and university women were better organized, not least in the AAUW, founded in 1921.[35] New institutions specifically designed to provide resources to women academics who intended to conduct international relations research also opened their doors in the interwar years. The Harvard/Radcliffe Bureau for International Research is the most important of these. Its women graduates included the African American scholar Merze Tate and the German American scholar Louise Holborn, both of whom went on to successful academic careers.[36] More academic-adjacent, the AAUW published foreign policy–related briefings and pamphlets through its Committee on International Relations, which was run from 1927 by Esther Caukin Brunauer, a California native with a Stanford PhD on German and Austrian peace proposals in World War I.[37]

Brunauer represents a classic example of a woman thinker in the highly networked progressive female foreign policy public. At the AAUW, Brunauer published study courses, outlines, and bibliographies on international relations for individual AAUW and WILPF branches and delivered lectures to many of them. She was a graduate of the Geneva School of International Studies, a summer school run by two prominent liberal internationalists, Lucie and Alfred Zimmern, and she sought a research grant from the pacifist National Committee on the Cause and Cure of War for a research project on European politics. To right-wing women, these connections would have been disconcerting—and indeed, Brunauer would, in the 1950s, become a victim of McCarthyism. Brunauer was a serious intellectual with a considerable public impact. She wrote short books, articles, and a treatise on methods of adult education in international relations. She conducted surveys of AAUW branches "to reveal to our members the inadequacy of the international news services in their own localities, and to supply for the country at large a little more accurate information than we have at present about the state of American public opinion on foreign affairs."[38] In sum, Brunauer was both an expert on a topical aspect of interwar international relations (the problem of Germany in Europe) and a concerned woman citizen who used her academic training to improve the public's understanding of international affairs.

Such a civic orientation was not at all unusual among progressive women graduates who occupied key positions in American public debate on foreign policy. Also academic-adjacent, a new roster of specialist foreign policy think tanks became an important location for the production of women's international thought. The most important of these, the Council on Foreign Relations and the Foreign Policy Association, embraced very different attitudes when it came to including women in public debate on foreign policy, but both offered a variety of pathways for intellectual production. The Foreign Policy Association maintained strong relationships with organizations such as the League of Women Voters and businesswomen's associations. Its public events were open to, and sometimes dominated by, women. Many of its organizational networks relied on structures established during the fight for women's suffrage. The association also offered unique research opportunities to women with doctoral degrees, some of whom became influential foreign policy intellectuals, for instance, Vera Micheles Dean. The more masculinist Council on Foreign Relations excluded women as members but relied on the services of a specialist librarian, Ruth Savord. In the 1950s, a former council researcher, Ellen Hammer, reaped considerable commercial success with a book on Vietnam written for a broader audience.[39]

Another profession that considerably increased pathways for women's international thought was journalism. Even before the interwar period, Mary Baker Eddy's *Christian Science Monitor* set standards for reporting international affairs and boasted a circulation of more than 120,000 during World War I. Numbers of female reporters in the United States increased considerably after 1920, from just over seven thousand to more than double that by 1940. It was the foreign correspondent Anne O'Hare McCormick who became the first woman to serve on the *New York Times* editorial board, winning a Pulitzer Prize in 1937, and Dorothy Thompson's syndicated columns reached more than seven million readers.[40] Some foreign correspondents moved between the world of think tanks and the international press, for instance, Helen Kirkpatrick, who worked for both the Foreign Policy Association and the *New York Herald Tribune* in the 1930s. Armed with an international relations degree, Kirkpatrick then set up a weekly foreign affairs magazine, the *Whitehall Letter*. These are just a few examples of women foreign correspondents who shaped public perceptions of international politics.[41]

Among them Thompson remains the best known. In the 1930s and 1940s, she published not only in newspapers (her column "On the Record" ran for twenty-two years) but also in the house journal of the Council on Foreign Relations, *Foreign Affairs*. Here she dissected the inner workings of the Nazi regime but also analyzed other pressing international matters, such as the growing refugee crisis.[42] Although Thompson's assessment of Nazi Germany was prescient (here she was in the good company of another female foreign correspondent, Sigrid Schultz), her stances taken after World War II sometimes went against the mainstream, for instance, when she opposed the creation of Israel. From 1937, Thompson wrote a monthly column for the *Ladies Home Journal*, but this did not mean she abandoned international politics as her subject. On the contrary, she brought fairly technical diplomatic matters to the attention of her female readership, commenting, for instance, on U.S. diplomatic appointments.[43] The mix of "serious" and "soft" publications Thompson wrote for did not diminish her stature as a public intellectual.[44]

Thompson was not above putting her female audience in its place in her political writings, however. In a book chapter titled "The World—and Women," she argued that "the object of women's emancipation" was "not to make them more like men, but more powerfully womanly, and therefore of greater use to men and themselves and society." Thompson linked a service-focused notion of women's citizenship to the regulation of international conflict, putting the responsibility for "a world based, not on mechanical but on human principles . . . a renascence of liberalism and humanism" on women whom she asked to work for and demand such a world.[45] Thompson's explicitly hierarchical evaluation of women's usefulness in terms of the needs of men and society at large (the shrinking of which due to low birth rates she also blamed on women) made demands on women without granting them full and equal political subjectivity.

Thompson was one of several women public authorities on international affairs—others that could be mentioned here are Pearl S. Buck, Freda Kirchwey, and, of course, first lady Eleanor Roosevelt—and it was professions that drew on the labor of large numbers of women as shapers of citizenship that offered most opportunities for producing and disseminating ideals of international citizenship. Teaching was arguably the most important profession in this regard, with women making up more than 85 percent of teachers by the end of World War I. At the same time, professional teaching associations sought to enhance women teachers' status in terms of pay and training. By the 1930s, post–high school qualifications were the norm for teachers.[46] Some women international thinkers who went on to gain PhDs in the academy trained as teachers, for instance, Merze Tate, the historian Bessie Louise Pierce, and the educational reformer Fannie Fern Andrews. Those who remained in the profession produced curriculum materials that sought to shape children's understanding of citizenship, both American and international citizenship.

Some of this teaching focused on race, ethnicity, and Americanization as a consequence of an increasingly interconnected world in the form of international migration. Teachers were crucial agents when it came to defining what an educated American ought to think about race, and they increasingly highlighted contributions made by minority groups to American civilization. Rachel DuBois (no relation to W. E. B. Du Bois) pioneered the intercultural education movement, developing her Woodbury plan in the mid-1920s before studying at Columbia's Teachers College. The ultimate aim was to sensitize children to human diversity on a global scale, to both fortify them against militaristic propaganda and offer an alternative perspective on international relations to one that focused on great power rivalries. The intercultural education movement suffered from a big blind spot— institutional racism against African Americans. Although DuBois was a racial progressive, she included little acknowledgment of the unique impact of slavery on African Americans.[47] Other initiatives to educate schoolchildren for world citizenship shared this blind spot, for instance, the experiment in the public schools of Los Angeles under school superintendent Susan Miller Dorsey. Dorsey was a standard bearer for "world friendship," and her teachers wrote a book on including the international in the curriculum and ran essay contests. Following the example of Los Angeles, World Friendship Clubs were rolled out across California's high schools. These clubs valorized pan-Americanism but had comparatively little to say about racial minorities in the state, even if Dorsey spoke out against a 1931 attempt to segregate children of Mexican heritage in California schools.[48]

Education for world citizenship left less of an imprint than its practitioners desired. Bessie Louise Pierce, a historian who studied four hundred school textbooks in the 1920s, found that they contained stereotypical descriptions of other nations, reinforced patriotic loyalty and portrayed the United States as "generous in spirit in her relations with weaker peoples and as a benefactor of mankind." Positive portrayals of ethnic minorities and foreign nations remained few and far between.[49] This was partly owed to right-wing influence.

Right-Wing Critiques of International Citizenship

Right-wing women tried to assert dominance and entrench white supremacy in public schools in the American South, where they joined forces with antiradical women's organizations in the interwar years. Educators such as Mildred Lewis Rutherford, a former Historian General of the United Daughters of the Confederacy (UDC), an organization that cooperated with similar groups such as the DAR and the American Legion, introduced citizenship education that entrenched patriotism and Jim Crow segregation. Schoolchildren were presented with a narrative that undermined Reconstruction and lauded American imperialism as a project for uplifting people of color around the world. The contributions of African Americans to the nation's development were systematically erased. Women's organizations tried to wrestle control from academic experts and professional educators and argued that celebratory narratives in school textbooks were essential for crafting patriotic citizens. As Elizabeth Gillespie McRae has argued, antiradical groups proved to be far more successful than progressive ones when it came to capturing the American textbook market. They ran textbook censorship campaigns and influenced legislatures, and they worked together with northern activists such as Margaret Robinson of the Women's Patriotic Conference on National Defense. They also copied some of the methods of their progressive counterparts, with the UDC sponsoring essay contests for white schoolchildren on topics such as the contribution of Confederate organizations to the First World War.[50]

Education was a key battleground in which alliances between rightwing women were forged and their political demands articulated. This process only intensified in the 1940s and 1950s when liberal and progressive women's groups became more organized and even more willing to work with the institutions of the American state to further its foreign policy aims. A conference organized by the Committee on the Cause and Cure of War and sponsored by Eleanor Roosevelt produced a "roster of qualified women" who were put forward for employment in foreign policy making roles, thus ensuring their adequate representation as citizens.[51] Rightwing women's groups railed against the perceived progressive bias when it came to such appointments and also targeted education, for instance, on the United Nations, in their grassroots mobilizing. An influential 1948 pamphlet produced by two Californian activists, Lucille Cardin Crain and Anne Burrows Hamilton, argued that the "principal women's organizations consistently and uncritically support the government's foreign policy," often using adult education to indoctrinate their members. Crain and Hamilton alleged that the Women's Joint Congressional Committee colluded with the U.S. government to "sell women the idea of universal military training," and that women's organizations cooperated with public education specialists such as George V. Denny of America's Town Meeting of the Air to bolster the work of advocacy groups promoting the liberalization of world trade. In Crain and Hamilton's view, liberal and progressive women's organizations did not represent the "authentic" voice of American women. To oppose such misrepresentations, Crain and Hamilton exhorted right-wing women to be wary of propaganda, to oppose big government and, above all, to "think for yourself."[52]

Some right-wing women who came to prominence during the advent of second-wave feminism began their public careers as specialists on international affairs, before transitioning to grassroots political advocacy that opposed rights-based conceptions of women's domestic citizenship in favor of republican motherhood. Phyllis Schlafly, the undisputed leader of the campaign against the Equal Rights Amendment (ERA) in the 1970s, made her reputation as a DAR operative who organized educational activities for Republican clubs and high schools. Foreign policy was her field of expertise. In the 1950s, when Schlafly joined, the DAR was both anticommunist and anti-internationalist, seeking to implement its own ideals of American citizenship that emphasized vigilance against foreign threats and limited government. In her writings and speeches of these years, Schlafly denounced what she called the "John Dewey school of education" that distorted the lessons of American history and left students unable to resist communist brainwashing. Together with her husband, she authored an influential 1957 report on underhanded communist tactics and what she regarded as the weak response of the liberal Warren Court. Schlafly also regularly commented on national security issues on radio, and forged links to opponents of communism outside the United States. When she supported Barry Goldwater's 1964 presidential campaign, she argued that neither Democrats nor liberal Republicans could keep Americans safe from communism. This, Schlafly argued, concerned women and mothers in particular, and she explicitly encouraged them to get involved in politics. As David Farber has noted, here Schlafly "walked a thin line between a protofeminist engagement with the public world on egalitarian terms and a traditionalist understanding of women's roles." It was only in 1972 that Schlafly shifted her attention from anticommunism and national security to the fight against the ERA, a political campaign that successfully implemented principles of participatory democracy among scores of so-called housewife activists.[53]

Conclusion

From the 1920s, engaging with international affairs became a feature of women's citizenship across the political spectrum. Women produced and consumed international knowledge in different locations, such as teaching, academe, or journalism. Women's political activism was another important location, but it is important to recognize that this activism was not necessarily synonymous with liberal internationalism but included right-wing, antiradical, and anticommunist aims. Whether related to scholarly debates on international law or the integration of immigrants into the American body politic via the intercultural education movement, international issues inflected key questions of women's citizenship. Before the civil rights legislation of the 1960s, this ideal of citizenship mostly excluded African American women. Black women also formulated political demands in terms of increased participation, and their intellectual labor shaped Black nationalist and Pan-African public cultures and rallied antiracist counterpublics.

After ratification of the Nineteenth Amendment in 1920, women's citizenship remained politically contested. Although often regarded as emblematic of women's international thought and political activism, liberal internationalist and pacifist women were always opposed by a well-organized and resourceful female counterpublic that questioned the identification of women's political commitments with causes such as disarmament or peace. The international thought of right-wing women's organizations such as the DAR remains incompletely understood, but it is striking to what extent it revolved around key questions of citizenship, such as race, nation, and assimilation, and their links to U.S. national security. Prominent right-wing women intellectuals such as Phyllis Schlafly began their public life as foreign policy experts. It was not only Schlafly's organizational experience as an anticommunist activist but also her analysis of what she regarded as the communist threat to U.S. family life that informed her efforts to mobilize American women against the ERA.

Future research should take women public intellectuals seriously but also be attentive to the political substratum from which they emerged. In particular, this means that future research ought to take right-wing women more seriously, their publications, organizations, and their thought. Recent syntheses of the conservative intellectual tradition have mostly neglected women.[54] Moreover, there remains a tendency within the history of international thought to idealize women intellectuals as progressives and to assume that right-wing thought was inward-looking and anticosmopolitan, and thus was not relevant.[55] But the increasingly sophisticated analysis of the internationalism of the Right should refocus attention on the complexity and ideological versatility of American women's international thought.[56]

Notes

1. "Would a Union of Democracies Save World Peace?," *America's Town Meeting of the Air* 4, no. 18 (March 13, 1939); "What Price Must We Pay For Peace?," *America's Town Meeting of the Air* 2, no. 3 (November 19, 1936); "How Can Europe Avoid War?," *America's Town Meeting of the Air* 4, no. 13 (February 6, 1939).

2. On the history of Town Meeting of the Air, see David Goodman, "Programming in the Public Interest: America's Town Meeting of the Air," in *NBC: America's Network*, ed. Michele Hilmes (Berkeley: University of California Press, 2007), 44–60; Barbara D. Savage, *Broadcasting Freedom: Radio, War, and the Politics of Race, 1938–1948* (Chapel Hill: University of North Carolina Press, 1999), 206–22.

3. George V. Denny, "America's Town Meeting and the Library," *Bulletin of the American Library Association* 32, no. 11 (October 1938): 753–59, at 757.

4. "Would a Union of Democracies Save World Peace?," 8–11.

5. On gender and theories of the public sphere, see Jürgen Habermas, "Further Reflections on the Public Sphere," in *Habermas and the Public Sphere*, ed. Craig Calhoun (Cambridge, MA: MIT Press, 1992), 421–61; Nancy Fraser, "Rethinking the Public Sphere: A Contribution to the Critique of Actually Existing Democracies," in *Habermas and the Public Sphere*, ed. Craig Calhoun (Cambridge, MA: MIT Press, 1992), 109–42; Joan B. Landes, "The Public and the Private Sphere: A Feminist Reconsideration," in *Feminists Read Habermas*, ed. Johanna Meehan (New York: Routledge, 1995), 91–116.

6. Conceptual slippage between categories such as "right-wing," "conservative," and "reactionary" is frequent. In this chapter, I use "right-wing" as an umbrella term for ideological commitments that include conservatism, antiradicalism, nationalism, and white supremacism, with the understanding that right-wing coalitions may shift over time. For an instructive debate on this matter, see Corey Robin and Mark Lilla, "'The Reactionary Mind': An Exchange," *New York Review of Books*, February 23, 2012.

7. The literature on WILPF is vast. For accounts that emphasize intellectual production, see Linda K. Schott, *Reconstructing Women's Thoughts: The Women's*

International League for Peace and Freedom Before World War II (Stanford, CA: Stanford University Press 1997); Catia C. Confortini, *Intelligent Compassion: Feminist Critical Methodology in the Women's International League for Peace and Freedom* (New York: Oxford University Press, 2012). For an overview of the multiple locations and genres of Anglophone women's international thinking, see Patricia Owens, Katharina Rietzler, Kimberly Hutchings, and Sarah Dunstan, eds., *Women's International Thought: Towards a New Canon* (Cambridge: Cambridge University Press, 2022.

8. Benjamin Alpers, *Dictators, Democracy, and American Public Culture: Envisioning the Totalitarian Enemy, 1920s-1950s* (Chapel Hill: University of North Carolina Press, 2003), 2–3. Alpers defines "cultural producers" as those inhabiting a social space that provides hegemonic access and outlets and argues that only a "comparatively small group of men and women has been in a position to interpret events abroad to American mass audiences."

9. On liberalism, the public, and international thought, see Duncan Bell, *Reordering the World: Essays on Liberalism and Empire* (Princeton, NJ: Princeton University Press, 2016), chap. 4.

10. Alpers, *Dictators, Democracy, and American Public Culture*; Edward A. Purcell Jr., *The Crisis of Democratic Theory: Scientific Naturalism and the Problem of Value* (Lexington: University Press of Kentucky, 1973).

11. Linda K. Kerber, *No Constitutional Right to Be Ladies: Women and the Obligations of Citizenship* (New York: Hill and Wang, 1999); Robin Muncy, *Creating a Female Dominion in American Reform, 1890–1935* (New York: Oxford University Press, 1991); Andrea Friedman, *Citizenship in Cold War America: The National Security State and the Possibilities of Dissent* (Amherst: University of Massachusetts Press, 2014).

12. Ruth Lister, "Citizenship: Towards a Feminist Synthesis," *Feminist Review* 57, no. 1 (Autumn 1997): 28–48.

13. Manuela Thurner, "'Better Citizens Without the Ballot': American Antisuffrage Women and Their Rationale During the Progressive Era," *Journal of Women's History* 5, no. 1 (Spring 1993): 33–60.

14. Michael Warner, *Publics and Counterpublics* (New York: Zone Books, 2005), 56, 57. See also Catherine Squires, "Rethinking the Black Public Sphere: An Alternative Vocabulary for Multiple Public Spheres," *Communication Theory* 12, no. 4 (November 2002): 446–68.

15. On right-wing women's activism, see Mary Brennan, *Wives, Mothers, and the Red Menace: Conservative Women and the Crusade Against Communism* (Boulder: University Press of Colorado, 2008); Catherine E. Rymph, *Republican Women: Feminism and Conservatism from Suffrage Through the Rise of the New Right* (Chapel Hill: University of North Carolina Press, 2005); Ronnee Schreibner, *Righting Feminism: Conservative Women and American Politics* (New York: Oxford University Press, 2008).

16. Some historians reject the term *right-wing feminist* as an oxymoron, identifying feminism as inherently left-liberal or progressive, which is why I use "women's movement." However, it is worth noting that the perception of ideological gatekeeping by liberal women's groups has been a motivating factor for right-wing women's political mobilizing since the 1920s. Kim E. Nielsen, "Doing the 'Right' Right," *Journal of Women's History* 16, no. 3 (Fall 2004): 170.

17. Andrew Buchanan, "Domesticating Hegemony: Creating a Globalist Public, 1941–43," *Diplomatic History* 45, no. 2 (January 2021): 319

18. On the comparative absence of intellectual histories of reactionary international thought, see Joseph MacKay and Christopher David LaRoche, "Why Is There No Reactionary International Theory?," *International Studies Quarterly* 62, no. 2 (June 2018): 234–44. For other attempts to bring "the public" back into the study of ideas and ideology in U.S. foreign policy, see chapter 3 in this volume by Michaela Hoenicke-Moore.

19. Mona L. Siegel, *Peace on Our Terms: The Global Battle for Women's Rights After the First World War* (New York: Columbia University Press, 2020), 25.

20. Emily Greene Balch as quoted in Catia Confortini, "Race, Gender, Empire, and War in the International Thought of Emily Greene Balch," in *Women's International Thought: A New History*, ed. Patricia Owens and Katharina Rietzler (Cambridge: Cambridge University Press, 2021), 256.

21. Sarah Wambaugh, *A Monograph on Plebiscites* (Washington, DC: Carnegie Endowment for International Peace, 1920); Karen Knop, *Diversity and Self-Determination in International Law* (Cambridge: Cambridge University Press, 2002), 284.

22. Glenda Sluga, "Women, Feminisms and Twentieth-Century Internationalisms," in *Internationalisms: A Twentieth-Century History*, ed. Glenda Sluga and Patricia Clavin (Cambridge: Cambridge University Press, 2017), 61–84.

23. Kirsten Delegard, *Battling Miss Bolsheviki: The Origins of Female Conservatism in the United States* (Philadelphia: University of Pennsylvania Press, 2012), 4–5.

24. Linda K. Kerber, "The Meanings of Citizenship," *Journal of American History* 84, no. 3 (December 1997): 833–54.

25. Keisha N. Blain, *Set the World on Fire: Black Nationalist Women and the Global Struggle for Freedom* (Philadelphia: University of Pennsylvania Press, 2018), 32–36, at 35; Barbara Ransby, *Eslanda: The Large and Unconventional Life of Mrs. Paul Robeson* (New Haven, CT: Yale University Press, 2013); see also Michelle Rief, "Thinking Locally, Acting Globally: The International Agenda of African American Clubwomen, 1880–1940," *Journal of African American History* 89, no. 3 (Summer 2004): 203–22; Lisa G. Materson, "African American Women's Global Journeys and the Construction of Class-Ethnic Racial Identity," *Women's Studies International Forum* 32, no. 1 (January–February 2009): 35–42.

26. Angela Hornsby-Gutting, "'Woman's Work': Race, Foreign Missions, and Respectability in the National Training School for Women and Girls," *Journal of Women's History* 31 no. 1 (2019): 37–61; Vivian M. May, "Anna Julia Cooper on Slavery's Afterlife: Can International Thought 'Hear' Her 'Muffled' Voice and Ideas?," in *Women's International Thought: A New History*, ed. Patricia Owens and Katharina Rietzler (Cambridge: Cambridge University Press, 2021), 29–51.

27. Julia Mickenberg, "Suffragettes and Soviets: American Feminists and the Specter of Revolutionary Russia," *Journal of American History* 100, no. 4 (2014): 1049.

28. Delegard, *Battling Miss Bolsheviki*, 3–11, 48, 79–89; on DAR study groups, see Florence Guertin Tuttle, *Women and World Federation* (New York: McBride, 1919), 174. For a history of the DAR in the context of American nationalism see Simon Wendt, *The Daughters of the American Revolution and Patriotic Memory in the Twentieth Century* (Gainesville: University Press of Florida, 2020).

29. Cecelia Lynch, *Beyond Appeasement: Interpreting Interwar Peace Movements in World Politics* (Ithaca, NY: Cornell University Press, 1999), 32–33, 132.

30. Delegard, *Battling Miss Bolsheviki*, 17.

31. On propaganda concerns and foreign policy, see Sarah E. Graham, *Culture and Propaganda: The Progressive Origins of American Public Diplomacy, 1936–1953* (Farnham, UK: Ashgate, 2015), chap. 1; J. Michael Sproule, *Propaganda and Democracy: The American Experience of Media and Mass Persuasion* (Cambridge: Cambridge University Press, 1997).

32. Delegard, *Battling Miss Bolsheviki*, 40, 49, 146.

33. Valeska Huber, Tamson Pietsch, and Katharina Rietzler, "Women's International Thought and the New Professions," *Modern Intellectual History* 18, no. 1 (March 2021): 121–45; Patricia Owens and Katharina Rietzler, eds., *Women's International Thought: A New History* (Cambridge: Cambridge University Press, 2021).

34. Claudia Dale Goldin, *Understanding the Gender Gap: Economic History of American Women*, new ed. (New York: Oxford University Press, 1992), 174, 178.

35. Susan Levine, *Degrees of Equality: The American Association of University Women and the Challenge of Twentieth-Century Feminism* (Philadelphia, PA: Temple University Press, 1995); Christine von Oertzen, *Science, Gender and Internationalism* (London: Palgrave, 2014).

36. Mary Ann Dzuback, "Gender, 'Professional Knowledge, and Institutional Power: Women Social Scientists and the Research University'," in *The 'Woman Question' and Higher Education: Perspectives on Gender and Knowledge Production in America*, ed. Ann Mari May (Cheltenham, UK: Edward Elgar, 2008), 59–62. On Merze Tate's critical stance toward U.S. foreign policy in the 1950s, see chapter 12 in this volume by Brandy Thomas Wells.

37. Jonathan M. Schoenwald, "Brunauer, Esther," American National Biography Online (Oxford University Press, 2018), https://doi.org/10.1093/anb

/9780198606697.article.0700039; Esther Caukin Brunauer, "The Peace Proposals of December, 1916–January, 1917," *Journal of Modern History* 4, no. 4 (December 1932), 544–571.

38. Esther Caukin [before marriage] to Mary Woolley, 2 March 1931, *American Association of University Women Archives, 1881–1976* (microfilm), reel 1, 1:17; Esther Caukin Brunauer, *Has America Forgotten? Myths and Facts About World Wars I and II* (Washington, D.C.: American Council on Public Affairs, 1940); Esther Caukin Brunauer, "Power Politics and Democracy," *Annals of the American Academy of Political and Social Science* 216 (July 1941), 109–116.

39. Katharina Rietzler, "U.S. Foreign Policy Think Tanks and Women's Intellectual Labor, 1920–1950," *Diplomatic History* 46, no. 3 (June 2022).

40. Jan Whitt, *Women in American Journalism: A New History* (Urbana: University of Illinois Press, 2008), 5, 16–19. On African American journalists see Rodger Streitmatter, ed., *Raising Her Voice: African-American Women Journalists Who Changed History* (Lexington, KY: University Press of Kentucky, 1994). On journalism and other public-oriented writing as a medium for international thought, see Edward Keene, "Where Should We Look for Modern International Thought?," *Contemporary Political Theory*, 13, no. 4 (November 2014): 397–402.

41. Nancy Caldwell Sorel, *The Women Who Wrote the War* (New York: Arcade, 1999), 13–14, 52.

42. Dorothy Thompson, "National Socialism: Theory and Practice," *Foreign Affairs* 13, no. 4 (July 1935): 557–73; Dorothy Thompson, "Refugees: A World Problem," *Foreign Affairs* 16, no. 3 (April 1938): 375–87; Dorothy Thompson, "The Problem Child of Europe," *Foreign Affairs* 18, no. 3 (April 1940): 389–412. On Thompson's role in the U.S. debate on Nazism, see Michaela Hoenicke-Moore, *Know Your Enemy* (Cambridge: Cambridge University Press, 2010), 52–58.

43. Dorothy Thompson, "Who Represents America?," *Ladies Home Journal*, August 1937, 8, 54.

44. Peter Kurth, *American Cassandra: The Life of Dorothy Thompson* (Boston: Little Brown, 1990), 218–219, 239, 331–335, 385–387.

45. Dorothy Thompson, *Political Guide: A Study of American Liberalism and Its Relationship to Modern Totalitarian States* (New York: Stackpole, 1938), 96–97; on birth rates, see 114.

46. Ellen L. Berg, "'To Become GOOD MEMBERS OF CIVIL SOCIETY and PATRIOTIC AMERICANS': Mass Education in the United States, 1870–1930," in *Mass Education and the Limits of State Building, c. 1870–1930*, ed. Laurence Brockliss and Nicola Sheldon (London: Palgrave Macmillan, 2012), 177–201; Wayne Urban, *Gender, Race, and the National Education Association: Professionalism and Its Limitations* (New York: Routledge, 2000), chaps. 1–2.

47. Zoe Burkholder, *Color in the Classroom: How American Schools Taught Race, 1900–1954* (New York: Oxford University Press, 2011); Diana Selig, *Americans All: The Cultural Gifts Movement* (Cambridge, MA: Harvard University Press, 2008).

48. John Eugene Harley, *Agencies Educating for a New World* (Stanford, CA: Stanford University Press, 1931), 81–82; Evaline Dowling, ed., *World Friendship* (Los Angeles, CA: Committee on World Friendship, Los Angeles City School District, 1931); "New Jim Crow Bill Denounced," *Los Angeles Times*, April 4, 1931; Suzanne Borghei, "Internationalism at the Grassroots: Los Angeles and Its City Schools, 1916–1953" (PhD diss., University of Southern California, 1995).

49. Bessie Louise Pierce, *Civic Attitudes in American School Textbooks* (Chicago: University of Chicago Press, 1930), 255; Murray R. Nelson, "Bessie Louise Pierce and Her Contributions to the Social Studies," in *Bending the Future to Their Will: Civic Women, Social Education, and Democracy*, ed. Margaret Smith Crocco and O. L. David Jr. (Lanham, MD: Rowman & Littlefield, 1999), 149–68.

50. Elizabeth Gillespie McRae, *Mothers of Massive Resistance: White Women and the Politics of White Supremacy* (New York: Oxford University Press, 2018), 41–51; see also Robert J. Cook, *Civil War Memories: Contesting the Past in the United States Since 1865* (Baltimore, MD: Johns Hopkins University Press, 2017), 210.

51. Helen Laville, *Cold War Women: The International Activities of American Women's Organizations* (Manchester: Manchester University Press, 2002), 32.

52. Michelle Nickerson, *Mothers of Conservatism: Women and the Postwar Right* (Princeton, NJ: Princeton University Press, 2012), chap. 3; Lucille Cardin Crain and Anne Burrows Hamilton, "Packaged Thinking for Women," *American Affairs*, Supplement to Autumn 1948 issue, 23, 10, 17, 29.

53. Donald T. Critchlow, *Phyllis Schlafly and Grassroots Conservatism: A Woman's Crusade* (Princeton, NJ: Princeton University Press, 2005), 71–79, at 77; Wendt, *Daughters of the American Revolution and Patriotic Memory*, 183, 188; David Farber, *The Rise and Fall of Modern American Conservatism: A Short History* (Princeton, NJ: Princeton University Press, 2018), chap. 4, at 128. For critiques of progressive education see Nickerson, *Mothers of Conservatism*, 74–80.

54. See, e.g., Edmund Fawcett, *Conservatism: The Fight for a Tradition* (Princeton, NJ: Princeton University Press, 2020), 447–466, which lists two women, Ayn Rand and Phyllis Schlafly, among seventy-six "thinkers."

55. Laville, *Cold War Women*, 8.

56. Madeleine Herren, "Fascist Internationalism," in *Internationalisms: A Twentieth-Century History*, ed. Glenda Sluga and Patricia Clavin (Cambridge: Cambridge University Press, 2017), 191–212; David Motadel, "The Global Authoritarian Moment and the Revolt Against Empire," *American Historical Review* 124, no. 3 (June 2019): 843–77; Martin Durham and Margaret Power, eds., *New Perspectives on the Transnational Right* (New York: Palgrave Macmillan, 2010).

PART TWO
Ideologies of Power

CHAPTER 5

Competing Free Trade Traditions in U.S. Foreign Policy from the American Revolution to the "American Century"

MARC-WILLIAM PALEN

ree trade's monolithic portrayal within the historiography of U.S. foreign policy has hidden the nation's multiple, often competing, free trade ideological traditions.[1] This has resulted in a mixture of confusion and indifference regarding the stark ideological differences between and within political parties regarding U.S. foreign trade policy. It also minimizes economic nationalism's central political and ideological role amid the heyday of the U.S. imperial project—the late nineteenth and early twentieth centuries. In this chapter, I challenge these common misconceptions by putting into context a long-overlooked Anglo-American free trade tradition, then famously known as the "Manchester School" or "Manchester liberalism" or "Cobdenism."[2] I argue that Cobdenism played a fundamental role in shaping U.S. foreign policy from the mid-nineteenth century to the present.

The dominant historiographical relationship between free trade ideology and U.S. foreign policy owes a particular intellectual debt to Charles Beard's *The Idea of the National Interest* (1934) and *The Open Door at Home* (1934); W. A. Williams's *Tragedy of American Diplomacy* (1959); and Michael Hunt's *Ideology and U.S. Foreign Policy* (1987). All put forward an ideological interpretation for U.S. imperialism and contributed to conceptualizing "open-door imperialism." Beard, the most influential of progressive era scholars, kicked things off in 1934 with an economic ideological interpretation of U.S. foreign policy that emphasized the long-term contestation between Hamiltonian "industrial statecraft" and Jeffersonian "agrarian statecraft" in shaping the Open Door

Empire from the turn of the twentieth century.[3] Williams (and his former students, the so-called Wisconsin School) reframed the Open Door as a bipartisan free trade imperial search for new markets to export surplus capital. In so doing, Williams and the Wisconsin School have achieved what Frank Ninkovich describes as "the most impressive results in their employment of ideology as a historical variable."[4] And whereas Williams made the Open Door the centerpiece of *Tragedy*, for Hunt it provided a more indirect inspiration stemming from his previous studies of U.S.-China relations and the enduring influence of *Tragedy*'s free trade imperial argument.[5] Hunt instead took Williams to task for his "excessively narrow conception of ideology," which overlooked other ideological forces that were "neither rooted in nor sustained by economic forces or calculations": namely, paternalism, racism, and nationalism.[6]

New histories of economic ideologies and U.S. foreign policy are helping to bridge the divide between Beard, Williams, and Hunt. This stems from a broader attempt to reconnect "international thought with modern politics."[7] First, recent scholarship has gone a long way in showing that Hunt's presumed noneconomic ideologies were in many ways inseparable from America's capitalist imperial raison d'être.[8] Second, the presumed bipartisan free trade character of the Wisconsin School's Open Door Empire has come under scrutiny from scholars who have highlighted the partisan, nationalist, and protectionist frame of U.S. imperialism at its late-nineteenth- and early-twentieth-century zenith. The U.S. empire during this period was an expansive Closed Door Empire.[9] Opening markets through free trade became pronounced only from the 1930s and 1940s onward.[10]

The predominantly economic nationalist political and ideological makeup of the American empire project becomes even more pronounced through the recovery of the Anglo-American free trade tradition of Cobdenism, which arose in Britain as well as within Boston and New York City in the 1830s and 1840s. Named after Richard Cobden (1804–1865), Victorian England's radical "apostle of free trade," this northeastern-based free trade ideology was born from within the era's entwined transatlantic antislavery movement and was the dominant economic ideology underpinning the country's burgeoning peace and anti-imperialist movements. Cobdenism was the ideological belief that worldwide adoption of free trade would make the world's markets so interdependent that wars would become obsolete; hunger would be eradicated through the expansion of the global supply of cheap food; and democracy would flourish once the inefficient, militant, and atavistic protectionist interests were removed from their monopolistic positions of political influence. In other words, for American Cobdenites, freeing trade was the next peaceful step toward the emancipation of mankind following the eradication of American slavery.[11] This same free trade ideology of the antislavery Northeast played a more sizable role in shaping U.S. foreign policy in the century and a half that followed the U.S. Civil War than did its more widely studied Jeffersonian competitor.

The history of U.S. foreign policy is therefore better understood as having had a handful of oft-competing free trade ideologies that challenged the protectionist ideas and policies of the "American System." The tangible results of Jeffersonianism were, of course, on full display within the Democratic Party's antebellum proslavery, Anglophobic, agrarian, and expansionist politics, culminating in military interventionism in Mexico (1846–1848). But the competing free trade tradition of Cobdenism, underpinning the late-nineteenth- and early-twentieth-century U.S. anti-imperialist and peace movements, was far more prevalent from the 1860s until the present day. American Cobdenism's grassroots influence eventually sprouted more radical branches amid a seventy-year period dominated by Republican economic nationalist presidencies and foreign policies (1861–1933). These same American free trade idealists of the American Cobdenite tradition—anti-imperialists, pacifists, socialists, feminists—thereafter felt some degree of vindication following Woodrow Wilson's pacifistic enunciation of his internationalist Fourteen Points in 1918, followed by the more concrete trade liberalization reforms of Democratic secretary of state Cordell Hull, the "Tennessee Cobden" and "Father of the United Nations," in the 1930s and 1940s. Subsequent post-1945 neo-Cobdenite activism has more recently placed itself in opposition to "neoliberal" globalization. This century-and-a-half ideological evolution of Cobdenite activism admittedly shares some theoretical links with the neoliberal free trade tradition that began making its mark on U.S. foreign policy making from the 1970s. However, the right-wing neoliberal tradition's willingness to support military interventionism and antidemocratic governments on behalf of freeing foreign markets demonstrates a much stronger resemblance to the Jeffersonian tradition in practice.[12]

Jeffersonianism v. Cobdenism, c. 1846–1898

Jeffersonianism has become the all-too-common all-encompassing catchword used to describe a single U.S. free trade ideological tradition stretching back to the nation's founding. Jeffersonianism's southern, agrarian, military interventionist, Anglophobic, antidemocratic, proslavery characteristics might work well when describing the Democratic free trade ideology of the antebellum period, but much less so after 1865. Because of a limited understanding of the post-1865 U.S. free trade movement, the three pro–free trade Democratic presidencies between the U.S. Civil War and the Second World War—Grover Cleveland, Woodrow Wilson, and Franklin Roosevelt—have inaccurately been branded as Jeffersonian. Rather, the free trade ideology most prominently at work within these administrations—and indeed throughout much of the century that followed the Civil War—was a different free trade tradition: Cobdenism. American Cobdenism first arrived on U.S. shores in the 1830s and 1840s, whereupon it began transforming Anglo-American relations, U.S. party politics, and the U.S. anti-imperialist and peace movements.

The unilateral British embrace of free trade in 1846 followed nearly a decade of activism by Richard Cobden, his man-at-arms John Bright, and their middle-class pressure group, the Anti–Corn Law League (ACLL, 1838–46). Britain's turn to free trade represented a radical break from the mercantilist status quo among the European empires. Up to this point, the European powers had taken to violently divvying up much of the world, with the imperial metropoles dictating the terms of trade within their separate colonial spheres of influence. In other words, until 1846, imperial trade policies were mercantilist, wherein one's colonies provided raw materials to the metropole, which in turn produced finished goods to be sold back to its own protected colonial market. The mercantilist makeup of this period of "imperial globalization" discouraged the flow of trade between rival imperial markets, with one consequence being the competitive scramble for colonies both as outlets for surplus capital and as new sources of manpower (both free and unfree) and raw materials. The decision of the mid-nineteenth-century world's most powerful manufacturing nation to scrap its protectionist policies just over a decade after it had abolished slavery across its empire represented a decisive challenge to the mercantilist system.

Keep in mind, too, that free trade had a different meaning in the nineteenth and early twentieth centuries. Free trade in the mid-nineteenth century was interchangeable with a "tariff for revenue only" rather than a near complete absence of tariffs, as free trade is more commonly thought of today. Britain, as well as every other industrializing nation at that time, obtained most of its revenues from tariff duties. Separating what some contemporaries called a free trade tariff from a protective tariff, then, was the latter's explicit use of tariffs to discriminate against foreign imports in order to shelter "infant" domestic agricultural or manufacturing interests. Free traders instead sought nondiscriminatory tariffs, which were to be made as low as possible through decreasing government and military expenditures, with the savings passed on to the consumer.

But the cosmopolitanism of Cobdenism promised far more than cheap food and goods: nothing less than a world without war. Cobdenites argued that wars and other unnecessary military expenditures perpetuated an unholy monopolistic alliance between protectionist industrial interests and the militant and atavistic aristocracy: a symbiotic relationship that only caused empires to raise their tariff walls ever higher, leading to trade wars, the imperial search for new markets, and heightened geopolitical conflict. The economic interdependence of international markets wrought from free trade, Cobdenites believed, would thus eliminate the main causes of imperialism and war. Some British policy makers saw no contradiction between free trade and imperial expansion, but for Cobdenites the two were antithetical.[13]

The mid-century political, economic, and ideological waves created from Britain's newfound free trade advocacy rippled across the Atlantic in both the U.S. South and North. Although Cobden and his ACLL allies abhorred the U.S. system of slavery, Britain's turn to free trade at first gave succor to embattled proslavery Jeffersonian expansionists in the U.S. South. For Jeffersonians such as South Carolina's John C. Calhoun, the end of British protectionism portended a new era for the exportation of southern slave-grown products to the import-hungry British isles, a prospect that was given a further boost when Britain repealed the import tariff on West Indian slave-grown sugar and as British demand grew for U.S. slave-grown cotton. These transatlantic developments also strengthened Jeffersonian pro-slavery imperial designs on the Caribbean.[14]

But the British successes of Cobden's ACLL and the liberal ideas the movement extolled also guided some of the most radical abolitionists in New York and Massachusetts. For American Cobdenite abolitionists such as Ralph Waldo Emerson, William Cullen Bryant, Reverend Joshua Leavitt, Edward Atkinson, and William Lloyd Garrison, the abolition of the Corn Laws was seen as the next step in the universal emancipation of mankind and the dawn of a more peaceful and prosperous interdependent world order if coupled with the abolition of American slavery. In the early 1840s,

Leavitt, the founder of the antislavery Liberty Party, went so far as to establish anti–corn law leagues in the U.S. north and west as both a show of solidarity with the movement's British counterparts and to make a forceful case to British radical reformers that ethically produced U.S. free-grown wheat could soon supplant slave-grown cotton as Britain's main U.S. import. The lowering of U.S. rates that same year through the Walker Tariff, in turn, gave hope to Richard Cobden and the ACLL that a new transatlantic moral economy of free trade internationalism had arrived.[15]

Such hopes, however, proved short-lived. The founding of the antislavery Republican Party in the 1850s muddied the political and ideological waters surrounding transatlantic free trade and antislavery until after the Civil War. Northeastern Cobdenites were naturally drawn to the new party of anti-slavery and free labor, and they believed that they could work from within to replicate the successes of the British ACLL and so add "free trade" to the Republican slogan "free soil, free labor, and free men." But they were wrong. Greatly outnumbered from the outset by the new party's Whig protectionist members such as Abraham Lincoln and Henry Carey, the Republican Party instead embraced the American System of economic nationalism. The American System was in no small part an attempt to separate and protect the developing U.S. economy from the British-dominated international economic order; implementation of the American System proved to be an effective countermovement to British free trade hegemony in the United States.[16] Anglophobic conspiracy theories were commonplace, driven by fears that U.S. industries would be snuffed out in their infancy if American tariff walls were lowered and cheaper British goods came pouring into the United States. In early 1861, the Republicans were able to push through Congress the Morrill Tariff, the first of many infant industrial tariff policies (in contrast to a tariff for revenue only). The Morrill Tariff's passage was made possible thanks mostly to the secession of various southern states, whose pro–free trade Jeffersonian senators could otherwise have blocked the tariff's congressional passage.

The close timing of southern secession and the Morrill Tariff's passage proved unfortunate for Anglo-American relations at the outset of the Civil War, requiring the concerted efforts of Cobdenites on both sides of the Atlantic to undo the political damage. Southern Jeffersonian propagandists sought to play on British free trade sympathies and thus sour Union-British relations and gain British recognition of the Confederacy. When President Abraham Lincoln, a Whig protectionist supporter of the new tariff, did not immediately make the Civil War explicitly about ending southern slavery, Confederate agents and diplomats sold the conflict to the British—heady with their newfound free trade ideas—as one being fought between greedy protectionist industrialists of the North versus agrarian free traders of the South, who just wanted to sell their cotton and tobacco to European markets as peacefully and cheaply as possible. Only after about a year of grassroots Cobdenite antislavery diplomacy and Lincoln's September 1862 Emancipation Proclamation was the "fake news" surrounding the Civil War tariff myth finally busted in Britain.[17]

From this economic ideological perspective, Union victory meant the end of southern slavery, which also signaled the beginning of the end of Republican antislavery activism. This ideological shift in focus within the party heralded a new era of Republican-dominated economic nationalist foreign policy making (Closed Door imperialism), to the dismay of the party's hapless Cobdenite minority.

Following Cobden's 1865 death, his close friends and disciples founded the Cobden Club in London, with international honorary members dedicated to its creed "free trade, peace, goodwill among nations" scattered across the globe, but with the greatest bunching within the American Northeast. The first batch of U.S. luminaries to join the Cobden Club included, among others, Republican abolitionists Garrison, Atkinson, Leavitt, Emerson, Charles Sumner, and Charles Francis Adams Sr.

Disillusioned with the GOP's increasingly expansionist anti-British adherence to the American System in the years immediately following the Civil War, and bolstered with the notable addition to their free trade ranks by the likes of Reverend Henry Ward Beecher, Charles Francis Adams Jr., and David Ames Wells (U.S. secretary of the Cobden Club), American Cobdenites decided to run their own pro–free trade Liberal Republican presidential candidate in 1872. Their political naivety and ineptness, however, proved their undoing; outmaneuvered by protectionist elements led by *New York Tribune* editor Horace Greeley, the Liberal Republican ticket ended up endorsing Greeley for president rather than the Cobdenites' preferred choice, Charles Francis Adams Sr. Amid the turmoil, the GOP's economic nationalist incumbent and war hero, Ulysses Grant, won reelection in a landslide.[18]

Still smarting from the sting of 1872, when Cobdenites were faced with the even more detestable GOP presidential nomination of James G. Blaine in 1884—by far the most progressive and imperial-minded protectionist of the Gilded Age—they decided instead to back the Democratic nominee,

Grover Cleveland, because the New York governor and civil service reformer seemed receptive to the Cobdenite message of free trade, prosperity, ameliorative Anglo-American relations, and international peace. Cleveland won thanks in part to the support of the Cobdenites in close-fought northeastern swing states; their party treachery also earned the Cobdenite turncoats the moniker "Mugwumps." Cleveland quickly went about filling key cabinet positions with some of the era's leading Cobdenites, including his secretaries of state, war, agriculture, treasury, and interior, as well as his administration's economic advisors. His two nonconsecutive administrations (1885–1889; 1893–1897) accordingly took a much less hostile posture toward the British; sought North American commercial union; opposed various Republican imperial designs in North America, Africa, Latin America, and the Asia-Pacific; and initiated numerous unsuccessful attempts to lower U.S. tariff walls.[19]

For their part, the Gilded Age Republican protectionist majority instead preferred coercive market expansion into Latin America and the Asia-Pacific alongside twisting the British lion's tail. Owing to the strong ties between U.S. and British free trade movements, Republican politicians and the GOP press were prone to insinuating that Cleveland and his Cobdenites were secret agents of the British, who, through their free trade activities, were seeking to return the U.S. market to its former position as a British colony.[20] The GOP coupled their particular brand of Anglophobic conspiratorial politics with an ever-more strident economic nationalist platform of protective tariffs and subsidies to support U.S. infant industries and to inflate the wages of the nation's industrial laborers.[21] The presidential victory of William McKinley—the GOP's "Napoleon of Protection"—in 1897 meant that the leading protectionist ideologues of the American System also would oversee the acquisition and maintenance of America's overseas colonial empire, with the country's Cobdenite anti-imperialists and peace activists on the outside looking in.[22]

Competing Cobdenisms: Orthodox Cobdenism, Henry Georgism, and Free Trade Socialism, c. 1898–1945

Following the outbreak of the war with Spain in 1898, a new generation of even more radical Cobdenites brought about a closer politico-ideological alignment between free trade and other liberal prodemocracy causes, such as women's suffrage and the early Civil Rights movement. This same radical confluence also intersected with the country's turn-of-the-century anti-imperialist and peace movements. America's leading Cobdenites spearheaded the grassroots anti-imperial opposition to the Republican Party's Closed Door Empire through the Anti-Imperialist League (AIL, 1898–1920), the Carnegie Endowment for International Peace (1910–present), the World Peace Foundation (1909–present, now the Fletcher School at Tufts University), the New York-based American Free Trade League (AFTL, c. 1865–early 1930s), the Boston-based International Free Trade League (IFTL, c. 1919–1930), American socialist internationalist groups, and what Christopher Nichols refers to as the "pacifist internationalism" of the women's peace movement, particularly the Woman's Peace Party (WPP, founded in 1915), the Women's Peace Society (WPS, c. 1919–1933), the Women's International League for Peace and Freedom (WILPF, 1919–present), and the U.S. branch of the Young Women's Christian Association (YWCA, 1858–present).[23] And from within these organizations can be gleaned competing Cobdenite traditions. The older cohort of orthodox Cobdenites, many now in their sixties and seventies, was rejuvenated by a new generation of even more radical Cobdenites within the growing Georgist, socialist, and women's movements.

Georgism was a more radical free trade variant of Cobdenism that arose in the United States following publication of the San Francisco journalist Henry George's internationally popular *Progress and Poverty* (1879) and *Protection or Free Trade* (1886), both of which built on the economic ideas of Richard Cobden and Herbert Spencer. George himself had converted from protectionism to Cobdenism in the 1860s, at which point he put his faith "in the international law of God as Cobden called free trade." George thereafter became an American member of London's Cobden Club in 1881, and he took an active role in various American Cobden Clubs, including the AFTL and the New York Free Trade Club. George and his disciples were even more radical than orthodox Cobdenites because Georgists believed a direct tax on the estimated value of land—what became known as the Single Tax—would break up monopolies while at the same time providing enough of a revenue stream to fully fund state and federal governments. Hence Georgism was far more extreme in calling for a new system of direct taxation of land alongside the complete elimination of tariffs (in contrast to the orthodox Cobdenite advocacy of tariffs for revenue only), thereby promising to bring about an even more interdependent and peaceful world order. Georgists also included numerous officers of the AIL, and dominated the Boston-based interwar peace organization, the IFTL, as well as dozens of Henry George leagues spread across the United States in the late nineteenth and early twentieth centuries. The country's main Georgist news organ, the *Public*, was founded in 1898 in Chicago largely to protest the war with Spain. But more broadly the paper was dedicated to the principles of peace, equality, and democracy along Georgist free trade principles. Some notable Georgist acolytes included AIL officers William Lloyd Garrison (a son of the radical abolitionist of the same name); satirist Mark Twain; and Louis F. Post, founding editor of the *Public* and subsequently Woodrow Wilson's assistant secretary of labor.[24]

From within turn-of-the-century socialist internationalist circles grew a further radical U.S. Cobdenite branch. The socialist internationalist free trade tradition had come a long way since Karl Marx and Friedrich Engels had given it their qualified support from their home base in 1840s "Free Trade England." By the turn of the century, more and more socialist internationalists began associating free trade far less with a progressive development of the capitalist system to bring closer the proletarian revolution and far more with world peace: the Marx-Manchester free trade tradition.[25] This came about thanks in no small part to American socialist radicals and the continued salience of the Manchester School within radical peace and anti-imperial circles. American socialist internationalists first began contributing to the issue during the Great Debate of 1888, when Pennsylvania's Marxist feminist Florence Kelly, with the aid of her friend Friedrich Engels, undertook the first English translation of Marx's 1848 "Speech on the Question of Free Trade" to encourage socialists to throw their support behind Cleveland's reelection bid.[26]

Owing to the evolving Marx-Manchester tradition, by the time of the First World War, free trade was a key plank within American socialist internationalist platforms. Boston Marxist radical, feminist, women's peace activist, and IFTL officer Crystal Eastman, for example, began pushing free trade and the League of Nations as prerequisites for postwar peace in the pages of her Communist magazine the *Liberator*. The Socialist Party of America's 1918 congressional program, in turn, demanded "no economic nationalism, no war after the war." That same year, prominent socialist academic Scott Nearing presided over the National Conference of Labor, Socialist, and Radical Movements in Harlem, which laid out its peace program calling for free migration, disarmament, self-determination, freedom of the seas, and that "free trade should prevail." And thanks to the continued leadership of Nearing and six-time Socialist Party presidential nominee Norman Thomas, the party thereafter lashed out at the GOP's "monstrous" 1930 Smoot-Hawley Tariff for having "declared economic war against the rest of the world" and for having aggravated "the instability of world economy and world trade." The Socialist Party's free trade and peace activism spilled over into the post-1945 years as well.[27]

The rise of the international women's peace movement between the War of 1898 and the First World War further bolstered the American Cobdenite fight, as the aforementioned roles of feminist radicals such as Florence Kelley and Crystal Eastman already suggest. Only a handful of women numbered among AIL officers, but those that did were avowed free traders. This included more orthodox Cobdenites such as Chicago social reformer Jane Addams and New York City's Fanny Garrison Villard, as well as Georgist's Carrie Chapman Catt. These same feminist Cobdenites spearheaded the woman's suffrage movement as well as numerous women's peace organizations during and after the First World War, particularly the WPP, WPS, WILPF, and YWCA. For all these women's peace organizations, free trade was an explicit prerequisite for avoiding another world war, eradicating global hunger, and thus making the world more conducive to political equality and women's empowerment. As Fanny Garrison Villard, daughter of William Lloyd Garrison, put it in 1921 as the head of the WPS: "Our members are devoted to the principle of Free-Trade and assert the right of every human to buy in the cheapest market and to sell in the dearest, and regard the constant infringement of this right as a chief cause of friction between nations. Richard Cobden . . . saw clearly the intimate connection between Free-Trade and Peace."[28] These women's peace organizations accordingly supported Woodrow Wilson's Fourteen Points in 1918, as well as the trade reforms of FDR's secretary of state Cordell Hull, in the 1930s and 1940s.[29]

Anglophile Democratic president Woodrow Wilson considered himself "of the brand of the Manchester School." His favorite authors from student days were Richard Cobden and John Bright, and Grover Cleveland and William Gladstone were his most revered statesmen. Understanding Wilson's Cobdenite ideological leanings and American Cobdenism's longer history helps inform his support for the low Underwood-Simmons Tariff (1913) and the free trade elements of the Fourteen Points, the latter of which received strong backing from orthodox Cobdenites, Georgists, socialist internationalists, and the American leaders of the women's peace movement alike.[30]

Many of the leaders of these same Cobdenite groups even believed they were partly responsible for Wilson's internationalist declaration owing to their persistent lobbying efforts throughout the war.

After yet another decade of Republican Closed Door imperialism, American Cobdenites of all stripes waxed even more enthusiastic over the free trade and peace politics of Democratic secretary of state Cordell Hull (1933–1944). Hull provided the ideological impetus behind what would become a U.S.-led post-1945 trade liberalization program. This multilateral trading system that arose in the 1930s and 1940s——Hull's "tariff revolution," as Alfred Eckes calls it—was explicitly established to foster a more integrated, prosperous, and peaceful world. And it owed much to America's Cobdenite traditions.[31]

Hull first encountered the Cobdenite free trade movement amid the Gilded Age battle over U.S. trade policy. He got his start in U.S. Democratic politics as a seventeen-year-old stump speaker to reelect Cobdenite president Grover Cleveland amid the "Great Debate" of 1888. The international connection between tariffs and war crystalized more fully for Hull as a congressman (D-TN) during the First World War. By the war's outbreak, he had come to the realization "that you could not separate the idea of commerce from the idea of war and peace." War was "largely caused by economic rivalry conducted unfairly." At this time, he recollected,

> I embraced the philosophy that I carried throughout my twelve years as Secretary of State. . . . unhampered trade dovetailed with peace; high tariffs, trade barriers, and unfair economic competition with war. . . . I reasoned that, if we could get a freer flow of trade—freer in the sense of fewer discriminations and obstructions—so that one country would not be deadly jealous of another and the living standards of all countries might rise, thereby eliminating the economic dissatisfaction that breeds war, we might have a reasonable chance for lasting peace.[32]

As FDR's state secretary and with the strong support of the Cobdenite-dominated U.S. peace movement, the "Tennessee Cobden" thereafter began redirecting America's long-standing protectionist course on its freer-trade path from 1934 onward, culminating in the multilateral General Agreement on Tariffs and Trade (GATT) in 1947, which led to a dramatic lowering of U.S. and foreign tariff rates.[33]

Neoliberalism v. Neo-Cobdenism, c. 1945–Present

The GATT would eventually morph into the World Trade Organization in 1995, which today is commonly (m)aligned with a particular strand of neoliberalism associated closely with U.S. foreign policy elites: the so-called Washington Consensus. As a result, American free trade ideas and policies in the latter decades of the century are more often labeled as part of the neoliberal free trade tradition. This era of "neoliberal globalization" also sparked additional grassroots neo-Cobdenite opposition.

Neoliberal ideas first arose in Europe during the interwar years in an effort to reconcile nineteenth-century liberal economic principles with a zealous belief in protecting private property rights and a belief that only strong state and supranational governance could maintain free markets worldwide.[34] One of neoliberalism's founding founders, Ludwig von Mises, reflecting on the subject in 1927, was quite explicit in connecting his ideas with Manchester liberalism.[35]

Although the American neoliberal belief that free trade brings prosperity and peace shares a common theoretical heritage with the radical mid-nineteenth-century Cobdenite tradition, in practice American neoliberalism has demonstrated a stronger affinity with the antebellum antidemocratic Jeffersonian free trade tradition. Whereas throughout its history the American Cobdenite tradition remained committed to strengthening democracy and political equality through free trade and a noninterventionist foreign policy, American neoliberals instead supported antidemocratic regimes, and even military interventionism to prop them up, on behalf of freeing markets and protecting the property rights of U.S. multinational corporations. U.S. backing of the Chilean dictatorship of Augusto Pinochet from 1973, and the neoliberal reformation of the Chilean economy under the direction of the "Chicago Boys" (Chilean economists who trained at the University of Chicago under neoliberal intellectual Milton Friedman), provides an apt early illustration of this antidemocratic and militaristic tendency.[36]

The growing antidemocratic and prointerventionist influence of neoliberalism within U.S. foreign policy making from the early 1970s helped invigorate the grassroots international cooperative and Fair Trade counter-movements, whose neo-Cobdenite ethical roots also stretch back to mid-nineteenth-century Britain.[37] Through international cooperatives and the fair trade movement, U.S. neo-Cobdenites worked toward creating an alternative multilateral trade liberalization regime more in line with the vision of

GATT's pacifistic progenitors such as Hull, coupled with elements enshrined within the proposed new international economic order of the 1960s and 1970s: a trade regime that encouraged free trade in the Global North in order to strengthen economic development in the Global South, all of which would also help foster peace, equality, and social justice.[38] Neo-Cobdenite support for supranational regulation of multilateral trade through the United Nations, the International Labour Organization, the proposed International Trade Organization, and the GATT; allowances for temporary protectionist measures for developing nations, often accompanied by solidarity boycotts in the Global North; and a willingness to pay more for ethically produced Fair Trade goods illustrates the evolution of American Cobdenism from its more moderate mid-nineteenth-century beginnings. These neo-Cobdenite efforts have since come to represent, as Gavin Fridell puts it, "an innovative challenge to neoliberal globalization."[39] Neo-Cobdenism has thus made key progressive contributions to the broader post-1945 "fair globalization" movement.[40]

Competition between free trade ideologies over U.S. foreign policy has continued in recent decades, with American neo-Cobdenite grassroots activists once again largely on the outside looking in as American neoliberals have taken the reins of power in Washington. But this ideological state of affairs is once again in flux. Neoliberalism, widely held to be the dominant economic ideology at work within U.S. foreign policy circles since at least the 1980s "Reagan Revolution," has recently fallen on hard times with the election of an avowedly economic nationalist GOP president, Donald Trump (2017–2021), who in this respect reflected a return to late-nineteenth- and early-twentieth-century Republican foreign policy making akin to that which earlier generations of American Cobdenites had worked so long and hard to thwart. Amid a worldwide pandemic that has strained global supply chains to near breaking point, the economic nationalist plan of Joe Biden, Trump's successful 2020 Democratic presidential challenger, "to Ensure the Future is 'Made in All of America' by All of America's Workers" suggests that the neoliberal Washington Consensus is being replaced by a protectionist ideological consensus among Washington policy makers.[41]

Conclusion

The history of U.S. foreign policy's competing free trade ideologies challenges long-standing "consensus" interpretations of U.S. foreign economic expansion, from the rise of the ill-named Open Door Empire in the late nineteenth century to the post–Cold War neoliberal Washington Consensus. American Cobdenism's competition with the American System of protectionism as well as its free trade ideological rivals—Jeffersonianism and neoliberalism—often intersected with ideas of race, gender, and (inter)nationalism. Cobdenism thus helped shape U.S. foreign policy in five key ways: (1) laying the economic ideological foundations of the Gilded Age noninterventionist foreign policy of the two Cleveland administrations; (2) driving the U.S. anti-imperial and peace movements that developed between the War of 1898 and the First World War; (3) providing ideological inspiration to Woodrow Wilson's Fourteen Points; (4) creating the more liberal post-1945 multilateral trading regime; and (5) underpinning subsequent grassroots alt-globalization opposition to neoliberalism.

The implications of the nation's competing free trade traditions are proving to be even more salient today because, remarkably, neoliberal globalization has come under assault from within. A global economic nationalist resurgence—heralded by Republican Donald Trump's and Democrat Joe Biden's "America First" foreign trade policies alongside Britain's political economic break from the European Union and a worldwide pandemic—now seems to be transforming more than seventy years of regional and global market integration into a more illiberal economic order punctuated by perpetual trade wars and geopolitical conflict that increasingly resembles that of the late nineteenth and early twentieth centuries. American and international critics of today's protectionist retreat from free trade are once again warning that the world is facing a catastrophe for global consumers and producers alike, as well as an existential threat to regional and world peace.[42] It remains to be seen whether the country's neoliberals and neo-Cobdenites will find common cause in opposing this new era of economic nationalism.

Notes

1. Ideology is a doctrine or belief that provides the basis for an ideal political, economic, social, or cultural system.
2. On Cobdenism and British politics, see especially Anthony Howe, *Free Trade and Liberal England, 1846–1946* (Oxford: Oxford University Press, 1997); Frank

Trentmann, *Free Trade Nation: Commerce, Consumption, and Civil Society in Modern Britain* (Oxford: Oxford University Press, 2008).

3. On Beard's intellectual influence on the Open Door Empire, see David Milne, *Worldmaking: The Art and Science of American Diplomacy* (New York: Farrar, Straus and Giroux, 2015), chap. 3; Emily S. Rosenberg, "Economic Interest and United States Foreign Policy," in *American Foreign Relations Reconsidered, 1890–1993*, ed. Gordon Martel (London: Routledge, 1994): 37–51; H. W. Brands, *What America Owes the World: The Struggle for the Soul of Foreign Policy* (Cambridge: Cambridge University Press, 1998), chap. 5; Marc-William Palen, "The Open Door Empire," in *A Companion to U.S. Foreign Policy*, ed. Christopher Dietrich, 2 vols. (Hoboken, NJ: Wiley-Blackwell, 2020): 1:271–87; Richard Drake, *Charles Austin Beard: The Return of the Master Historian of American Imperialism* (Ithaca, NY: Cornell University Press, 2018).

4. Frank Ninkovich, "Ideology, the Open Door, and Foreign Policy," *Diplomatic History* 6, no. 2 (April 1982): 185, 207.

5. William Appleman Williams, *The Tragedy of American Diplomacy* (1959; repr. New York: Norton, 1972), 97, 55–56; Michael Hunt, *Ideology and U.S. Foreign Policy* (New Haven, CT: Yale University Press, 1987), xiii, 9, 133.

6. Hunt, *Ideology and U.S. Foreign Policy*, 11.

7. Glenda Sluga and Patricia Clavin, eds., "Rethinking the History of Internationalism," in *Internationalisms: A Twentieth-Century History* (Cambridge: Cambridge University Press, 2016), 5.

8. See, for example, the work of Sven Beckert, Edward Baptist, Brian Schoen, and Walter Johnson.

9. On the Closed Door Empire, see Mary Speck, "Closed-Door Imperialism: The Politics of Cuban-U.S. Trade, 1902–1933," *Hispanic American Historical Review* 85, no. 3 (2005): 449–83; April Merleaux, *Sugar and Civilization: American Empire and the Cultural Politics of Sweetness* (Chapel Hill: University of North Carolina Press, 2015); Marc-William Palen, "The Imperialism of Economic Nationalism, 1890–1913," *Diplomatic History* 39, no. 1 (January 2015): 157–85; Marc-William Palen, *The "Conspiracy" of Free Trade: The Anglo-American Struggle over Empire and Economic Globalization, 1846–1896* (Cambridge: Cambridge University Press, 2016); Benjamin O. Fordham, "Protectionist Empire: Trade, Tariffs, and United States Foreign Policy, 1890–1914," *Studies in American Political Development* 31 (October 2017): 170–92; Marc-William Palen, "Empire by Imitation? US Economic Imperialism Within a British World System," in *The Oxford Handbook of the Ends of Empire*, ed. by Martin Thomas and Andrew S. Thompson (Oxford: Oxford University Press, 2018): 195–211.

10. Michael Patrick Cullinane and Alex Goodall, *The Open Door Era: United States Foreign Policy in the Twentieth Century* (Edinburgh: Edinburgh University Press, 2017); Palen, "The Open Door Empire."

11. Marc-William Palen, "Free-Trade Ideology and Transatlantic Abolitionism: A Historiography," *Journal of the History of Economic Thought* 37, no. 2 (June 2015): 291–304.

12. Nancy Mclean has even conspiratorially argued for a direct antidemocratic line of thought between South Carolina's antebellum proslavery politician John C. Calhoun and neoliberal intellectuals. See Nancy Mclean, *Democracy in Chains: The Deep History of the Radical Right's Stealth Plan for America* (New York: Penguin, 2017).

13. See John Gallagher and Ronald Robinson, "The Imperialism of Free Trade," *Economic History Review* 6, no. 1 (1953): 1–15; Oliver MacDonagh, "The Anti-Imperialism of Free Trade," *Economic History Review* 14, no. 3 (April 1962): 489–501.

14. Matt Karp, *This Vast Southern Empire: Slaveholders at the Helm of American Foreign Policy* (Cambridge, MA: Harvard University Press, 2016), chap. 6.

15. Palen, *The "Conspiracy" of Free Trade*, chap. 1.

16. Marc-William Palen, "Economic Nationalism in an Imperial Age, c. 1846–1946," in *The Cambridge History of Nationhood and Nationalism*, ed. Aviel Roshwald, Matthew D'Auria, and Cathie Carmichael (Cambridge: Cambridge University Press, 2022).

17. Marc-William Palen, "The Civil War's Forgotten Transatlantic Tariff Debate and the Confederacy's Free Trade Diplomacy," *Journal of the Civil War Era* 3, no. 1 (March 2013): 35–61.

18. Palen, *The "Conspiracy" of Free Trade*, chap. 4.

19. Palen, *The "Conspiracy" of Free Trade*, chaps. 5 and 9.

20. On American Anglophobia, see Stephen Tuffnell, "'Uncle Sam Is to Be Sacrificed': Anglophobia in Late Nineteenth-Century Politics and Culture," *American Nineteenth Century History* 12, no. 1 (March 2011): 77–99; Jay Sexton, "Anglophobia in Nineteenth-Century Elections, Politics, and Diplomacy," in *America at the Ballot Box: Elections and Political History*. ed. Gareth Davies and Julian E. Zelizer (Philadelphia: University of Pennsylvania Press, 2015): 98–117.

21. Marc-William Palen, "Foreign Relations in the Gilded Age: A British Free-Trade Conspiracy?" *Diplomatic History* 37, no. 2 (April 2013): 217–47.

22. See Benjamin Allen Coates, *Legalist Empire: International Law and American Foreign Relations in the Early Twentieth Century* (Oxford: Oxford University Press, 2016); Merleaux, *Sugar and Civilization*; A. G. Hopkins, *American Empire: A Global History* (Princeton, NJ: Princeton University Press, 2018); Daniel Immerwahr, *How to Hide an Empire: A History of the Greater United States* (New York: Farrar, Straus and Giroux, 2019).

23. Marc-William Palen, "Transimperial Roots of American Anti-Imperialism: The Transatlantic Radicalism of Free Trade, 1846–1920," in *Crossing Empires: Taking U.S. History Into Transimperial Terrain*, ed. Jay Sexton and Kristin

Hoganson (Durham, NC: Duke University Press, 2020), 59–82; Marc-William Palen, "British Free Trade and the Feminist Vision for Peace, c. 1846–1946," in *Imagining Britain's Economic Future, c. 1800–1975: Trade, Consumerism, and Global Markets*, ed. David Thackeray, Andrew Thompson, and Richard Toye (London: Palgrave Macmillan, 2018), 115–31. On the AIL's transatlanticism, see Michael Patrick Cullinane, "Transatlantic Dimensions of the American Anti-Imperialist Movement, 1899–1909," *Journal of Transatlantic Studies* 8, no. 4 (2010): 301–14; Michael Patrick Cullinane, *Liberty and American Anti-Imperialism, 1898–1909* (London: Palgrave Macmillan, 2012), chap. 4.

24. Palen, "Transimperial Roots of American Anti-Imperialism."

25. Marc-William Palen, "Marx and Manchester: The Evolution of the Socialist Internationalist Free-Trade Tradition, c. 1846–1946," *International History Review* 43, no. 2 (February 2020): 381–98.

26. Karl Marx, "Free Trade: A Speech Delivered Before the Democratic Club, Brussels, Belgium, January 9, 1848," trans. by Florence Kelley (1888).

27. Palen, "Marx and Manchester."

28. *Report of the Third International Congress of Women, Vienna, July 10–17, 1921* (Geneva, 1921), 149.

29. Palen, "British Free Trade and the International Feminist Vision for Peace."

30. Clifford F. Thies and Gary M. Pecquet, "The Shaping of the Political-Economic Thought of a Future President: Professor Ely and Woodrow Wilson at 'The Hopkins,'" *Independent Review* 15, no. 2 (Fall 2010): 257–77; Palen, *The "Conspiracy" of Free Trade*, 275; Palen, "Marx and Manchester."

31. Alfred E. Eckes, *Opening America's Market: U.S. Foreign Trade Policy Since 1776* (Chapel Hill: University of North Carolina Press, 1995). See also F. W. Hirst, "Cobden and Cordell Hull," *Contemporary Review* 155 (1939): 10–17; Anthony Howe, "Free Trade and the International Order," in *Anglo-American Attitudes: From Revolution to Partnership*, ed. Fred M. Leventhal and Roland Quinault (London: Routledge, 2000); Anthony Howe, "From Pax Britannica to Pax Americana: Free Trade, Empire and Globalisation, 1846–1946," *Bulletin of Asia-Pacific Studies* 13 (2003): 137–59; Howe, *Free Trade and Liberal England*, 274, 299, 304.

32. Cordell Hull, *The Memoirs of Cordell Hull* (New York: Hodder & Stoughton, 1948), 81, 84.

33. Palen, "British Free Trade and the International Feminist Vision for Peace," 123–25. On the politico-ideological conflict surrounding the GATT regime, see especially Thomas W. Zeiler, *Free Trade, Free World: The Advent of GATT* (Chapel Hill: University of North Carolina Press, 1999); Douglas A. Irwin, *Clashing over Commerce: A History of US Trade Policy* (Chicago: University of Chicago Press, 2017), 483–508; and Francine McKenzie, *GATT and Global Order in the Postwar Era* (Cambridge: Cambridge University Press, 2020).

34. Quinn Slobodian, *Globalists: The End of Empire and the Birth of Neoliberalism* (Cambridge, MA: Harvard University Press, 2018).

35. Ludwig von Mises, *The Free and Prosperous Commonwealth: An Exposition of the Ideas of Classical Liberalism* (Princeton, NJ: Van Nostrand, 1962). See also, Edwin van de Haar, *Classical Liberalism and International Relations Theory: Hume, Smith, Mises, and Hayek* (London: Palgrave Macmillan, 2009), 95–97. George H. W. Bush and Bill Clinton have even been given the moniker "Cobdenite" owing to their pacifistic free trade rhetoric and trade liberalization reforms. See Eckes, *Opening America's Market*, 280; Alfred E. Eckes, "Cobden's Pyrrhic Victory," *Chronicles*, October 1995, 14–16.

36. Slobodian, *Globalists*; Simon Reid-Henry, *Empire of Democracy: The Remaking of the West Since the Cold War, 1971–2017* (New York: Simon & Schuster, 2019); Tobias Rupprecht, "Global Varieties of Neoliberalism: Ideas on Free Markets and Strong States in Late Twentieth-Century Chile and Russia," *Global Perspectives* 1, no. 1 (July 2020), https://doi.org/10.1525/gp.2020.13278.

37. On the mid-nineteenth-century Cobdenite entanglements with cooperativism, see Palen, "Marx and Manchester," 10–11. On Fair Trade, see Bronwen Everill, *Not Made by Slaves: Ethical Capitalism in the Age of Abolition* (Cambridge, MA: Harvard University Press, 2020); Frank Trentmann, "Before 'Fair Trade': Empire, Free Trade, and the Moral Economies of Food in the Modern World," *Environment and Planning D: Society and Space* 25, no. 6 (2007): 1079–1102; Matthew Anderson, *A History of Fair Trade in Contemporary Britain: From Civil Society Campaigns to Corporate Compliance* (London: Palgrave Macmillan, 2015).

38. Florence E. Parker, "The International Cooperative Congress, September 1948," *Monthly Labor Review* 67 (December 1948): 600–602; Jagdish Bhagwati and Robert E. Hudec, eds., *Fair Trade and Harmonization: Prerequisites for Free Trade?* Vol. 2, *Legal Analysis* (Cambridge, MA: MIT Press, 1997); Johanna Bockman, "Socialist Globalization Against Capitalist Neocolonialism: The Economic Ideas Behind the New International Economic Order," *Humanity* 6 (Spring 2015): 109–12.

39. Gavin Fridell, "The Fair Trade Network in Historical Perspective," *Canadian Journal of Development Studies* 25, no. 3 (January 2004): 412.

40. Paul Adler, *No Globalization Without Representation: U.S. Activists and World Inequality* (2021).

41. "The Biden Plan to Ensure the Future Is 'Made in All of America' by All of America's Workers," https://joebiden.com/made-in-america/. On pandemics and U.S. protectionist politics, see Marc-William Palen, "Pandemic Protectionism: Revisiting the 1918 'Spanish' Flu in the Era of COVID-19," *Diplomatic History* 45, no. 3 (June 2021): 571–79.

42. See, among many others, Mark Thompson, "Brexit's Existential Threat to Europe," *CNN Business*, June 24, 2016; Ingram Pinn, "Peace and Prosperity:

It Is Worth Saving the Liberal Order," *Financial Times*, February 8, 2017; Clodagh Kilcoyne and Padraic Halpin, "Fearing for Post-Brexit Prosperity and Peace, Farmers Demand Invisible Irish Border," *Reuters*, December 1, 2017; Josh Wingrove, "Economists Invoke Great Depression in Warning to Trump on Trade," *Bloomberg*, May 2, 2018; Martin Kettle, "Trump's Trade War Threatens Global Peace," *Guardian*, June 1, 2018; "Countries Team Up to Save the Liberal Order from Donald Trump," *Economist*, August 4, 2018; Catherine Porter, "For Canada and U.S., 'That Relationship Is Gone' After Bitter NAFTA Talks," *New York Times*, October 3, 2018.

CHAPTER 6

The Righteous Cause

John Quincy Adams and the Limits of American Exceptionalism

NICHOLAS GUYATT

On a rainy night in November 1841, John Quincy Adams took to the stage at Masonic Hall in Boston to tell his audience what they didn't want to hear. The former president had been invited by the Massachusetts Historical Society to address the leading international crisis of the moment: the escalating conflict between Britain and China. According to one local newspaper, opium had been "raised by oppression, purchased with injustice, taken to China contrary to law, and sold there with extortion, to carry death to millions, all for avarice." Masonic Hall was packed "to overflowing" with Bostonians who expected Adams to say something similar. Instead, he blamed China for refusing to accept free trade with Western powers, and he insisted that a war to force the Chinese to open their markets would benefit the entire civilized world. "Which has the righteous cause?," Adams asked the audience in conclusion. "You have perhaps been surprised to hear me answer Britain: Britain has the righteous cause."[1]

The Opium Wars of the 1840s and 1850s have occupied an outsized position in Chinese historical consciousness. They've supplied China with a view of itself as abruptly and unfairly conquered by a Western vision of global order, and in our own historical moment they've served as a rallying cry for Chinese who believe that that order is unraveling. China's state-controlled newspapers responded to the Trump administration's pugilistic language on trade with a simple question: "Is it now 1840?" China's leaders, meanwhile, have presented their massive Belt and Road initiative—a developmental scheme luring partners from Malaysia to Djibouti to Italy—as definitive proof that the ghost of the Opium Wars has been laid to rest.[2]

In contrast, John Quincy Adams's fervent defense of British imperialism merits barely a footnote in the history of the United States in the world, or even in studies of John Quincy Adams. In 1841, the former president was in the middle of his vaunted second career as a congressman and staunch opponent of slavery. He had just helped to win the *Amistad* case before the Supreme Court and was leading the fight in the House of Representatives against the gag rule and the annexation of Texas. Adams's hostility to proslavery expansionism—along with his increasingly critical assessment of U.S. Indian policy—has allowed historians to present him as a late convert to the cause of anti-imperialism. For William Earl Weeks, Adams's later years "can in large part be understood as a repudiation of the achievements of his first career as a national leader." This essay takes a different view. I argue that Adams's striking position on the Opium War was grounded in ideas about race, law, and "civilization" that were deeply imperial, and I suggest that his defense of the British empire in East Asia was bound up with his thinking about the American empire at home. Adams's engagement with China clearly illustrates the role of ideology in shaping American understandings of unfamiliar places. It also shows us how this archetypal elder statesman struggled to adapt venerable assumptions to new circumstances.[3]

The First Opium War (1839–1842) had many causes. Chief among them was the determination of Lord Palmerston, the British prime minister, to employ what became known as "gunboat diplomacy" to open Chinese markets to British merchants. Since Lord Macartney's flamboyantly unsuccessful embassy to the Qing emperor in 1793, China had tantalized and infuriated Britons in equal measure. Its products—porcelain, silk, and tea—were coveted by British consumers. But China's rulers were determined to keep economic relations with the West under tight control. Qing governments established Canton in southern China as the entrepôt for all Western trade and further confined westerners to a series of "factories" outside the walls of the city. (The Qing also insisted that Western merchants could trade only with the Hong, a group of Chinese merchants who facilitated still tighter control over foreign commerce.) From the 1780s, U.S. merchants had formed part of the Western community outside Canton, and the interests (and frustrations) of British and American traders were closely aligned.

Christian missionaries from both countries in turn saw commerce (and merchants) as integral to the broader project of "opening" China to the full benefits of Western influence.[4]

Britain's opium peddling reflected a double weakness: British merchants were embarrassed not only by Qing trade restrictions but by the fact that ordinary Chinese seemed uninterested in anything they had to sell. The China trade required a hemorrhaging of silver on the British side until the East India Company realized the potential of opium (grown in India) to create an expanding customer base. Qing officials were initially complicit in the opium craze that was engineered by British commerce. But when Qing emperor Daoguang demanded in the mid-1830s that opium's influence be curbed, and (more important) when he found an official who would enact prohibition without succumbing to corruption, the conditions for the Opium War were in place. In 1839, British merchants and officials in Canton were left aghast when the Chinese seized and destroyed their (illegal) stocks of opium. Fortified by Palmerston's commitment to a war for "free trade," British forces moved onto the offensive. Across nearly three years, a series of mismatched battles killed hundreds of British sailors and perhaps twenty thousand Chinese. The 1842 Treaty of Nanjing brought China squarely into the orbit of the British empire, "opening" the nation's commerce to British domination and closing a half-century or more in which Western ambition was restrained by Chinese sovereignty and law.[5]

Why would John Quincy Adams laud the actions of the British? Adams was, after all, a prominent defender of "benevolent" causes in the House of Representatives and an intermittently vocal opponent of empire. For much of the early republic, American critiques of imperial formations were muted. Particular empires could be guilty of overreach or oppression, but relatively few American public figures identified empire itself as an illegitimate political form. Although Adams was hardly a zealot in the anti-imperial cause—he was notoriously reluctant to support the Greek revolt against the Ottoman empire during his years in the White House (1825–1829)—the revolutions in Latin America had strengthened his view that the maintenance of "colonial establishments" was impolitic and probably unjust. It was Adams who pushed James Monroe to issue his famous doctrine in 1823, with its prohibition on further European settlement in the Western Hemisphere. In his conversations with British ministers over the future of Latin America in the early 1820s, Adams was blunt about the course of empire in the Atlantic world. "The whole system of modern colonization was an abuse of government," he told the British minister to Washington in 1822, "and it was time that it should come to an end."[6]

Adams applied the same logic to the United States, rejecting the notion that the republic should extend its borders via colonies or protectorates. The equal footing doctrine—the principle that U.S. expansion would produce new states with the same rights and privileges as existing states—was included in the Northwest Ordinance, rejected by the Constitutional Convention of 1787, then established as precedent during the 1790s. It remained murkily understood by American politicians and commentators, and as late as the 1850s one could find enthusiasts in Congress and the media for the idea of seizing Cuba and retaining the island as a protectorate. Adams, however, was one of the most consistent and vocal defenders of equal footing.

Consider his outspoken opposition to Liberia, the Black colony founded by the American Colonization Society in 1821. Adams doubted that Black colonization would solve the problem of slavery at home, and he fretted that Liberia would eventually entail "the engrafting of a Colonial Establishment upon the Constitution of the United States." Many of Adams's contemporaries—such as the writer and historian Jared Sparks—were excited to explore what Sparks termed in 1824 "the constitutional question, whether the United States have power to establish such a colony." Sparks was willing to be creative about terminology: "Let us denominate our colony a Territory, if we will, and then it will not differ from other Territories, except in being separated from the confederated States by an ocean, instead of a river, or lake." Adams had no patience for casuistry on this question. Although he didn't doubt the benevolence of Liberia's white sponsors, he feared that a formal embrace of colonialism—"an accession of power to the National Government transcending all its other powers"—constituted an even greater threat to the republic than slavery.[7]

The same anxieties informed Adams's response to proslavery expansionism in the 1830s and 1840s. "The annexation of Texas to this Union is the first step to the conquest of all Mexico, of the West India Islands, of a maritime, colonizing, slave-tainted monarchy, and of extinguished freedom," he wrote in his diary in 1844. A few days later, he posited the annexation of Texas as "the turning point of a revolution which transforms the North American Confederation into a conquering and warlike nation." As Ian Tyrrell and Jay Sexton have argued, what we would now call antiimperialism in the early American republic was usually expressed as a form of antimonarchism. When Adams contemplated the nightmare of proslavery imperialism, he warned of "a military government, a large army, a costly navy, distant colonies, and associate islands in every sea." The Constitution would be "a menstruous rag, and the Union . . . a military monarchy." The concept of "a president for four years will be a laughing stock," he warned; Americans would owe allegiance instead to "a Captain-General for life, [with] a Marshal's truncheon for a scepter."[8]

The idea that Adams retreated from his youthful expansionism in his later years—that he became, to borrow again from William Earl Weeks, an enlightened northern sectionalist to set against the depraved sectionalists of the South—has an obvious appeal. But Adams never stopped being an expansionist. When James Monroe had asked in 1819 if the United States should conceal its territorial ambitions from Europe, Adams breezily answered that Americans should simply get on with the business of conquering the continent without worrying about the old world. Europeans were bound to "alarm the world at the gigantic grasp of our ambition," he told his colleagues. "Nothing that we could say or do would remove this impression until the world shall be familiarized with the idea of considering our proper dominion to be the continent of North America." In the same vein, even as the Polk administration readied for war with Mexico, Adams insisted that Oregon should be wrested from Great Britain—and aligned himself with the ultras on this question who forged the memorable slogan "Fifty Four Forty or Fight!"[9]

Adams harbored two fears about Texas annexation and the cascade of proslavery conquests he expected it to trigger: that these acquisitions would bring people of color in large numbers into the American republic, and that the blood and treasure required to seize and govern this territory would destroy republican government. In this respect, Adams recognized a basic distinction between the work of deleting Indigenous sovereignty within North America—of which more later—and the challenge of extending American power over the newly independent societies of Latin America and the complicated polities of the Caribbean. Adams was an anti-imperialist in the sense that he did not want the United States to sacrifice republican government for the lure of distant colonies. But he had little fear that this would take place in the process of establishing the United States as a continental power; hence his relaxed assurance to James Monroe in 1819 that it would soon be "a settled geographical element that the United States and North America are identical." His committed, even brutal advocacy of settler colonialism coexisted with revulsion at the prospect of an "American

Mediterranean" in which the entire Gulf of Mexico region came under the sway of American slaveholders. Adams's real fear was that the highly stratified forms of government required by an empire of slavery would ultimately subjugate white Americans as surely as people of color.[10]

When the Opium War broke out in 1839, it divided the American community of merchants and missionaries in Canton. Some viewed the British action as an opportunity to sweep away China's restrictions on trade, benefiting the United States as much as Britain. Others were cautious about the goals and especially the methods of the British, not least because the United States lacked the capacity to launch its own version of gunboat diplomacy. One American merchant, Charles W. King, prepared a memorandum on the iniquities of the British effort that ended up in John Quincy Adams's personal papers. King implored Washington to send a "competent representative" to China who could demonstrate that the United States "has no sympathies on the side of the Contraband trade, no part in opium indemnities, no interest, in short, but in a legal, honorable, and mutually beneficial commerce." Even if the British won the war, or the Qing sued for peace, King thought it "greatly for the interest of the American people that they be ably represented in China." King even supplied a would-be emissary with lines to "whisper in the imperial ear": "Take our concessions, make a voluntary treaty with us, instead of an extorted one with the English." If the State Department and Congress could seize the opportunity, the United States might emerge with the greater prize of commercial primacy in China.[11]

Americans who wrote about China in the 1830s found it "civilized" but also deeply strange. "Its inhabitants are almost as different from other nations," wrote one magazine, "as if they belonged to another planet." American travelers and newspapers gently mocked the Chinese for their perceived insularity and their "arrogance." Lord Macartney's mission in 1793, and subsequent American attempts to open diplomatic relations, had been derailed by the "kowtow," the expectation that foreign visitors would prostrate themselves before the emperor. American commentators on China roundly disapproved, but virtually no one considered this a casus belli for Britain. "By what color of right can England assume to dictate to China the terms on which that nation shall regulate its intercourse with the civilized or uncivilized world," asked one New York newspaper in 1841. "The conduct of England in China, has been the counterpart of that of Mehemet Ali in Syria."[12]

John Quincy Adams engaged with Chinese affairs on multiple fronts during the Opium War. He discussed the future of American involvement in China with congressional colleagues, and he read British accounts of the Macartney mission of 1792–93 to learn more about Chinese self-regard. In December 1840, not long after the House of Representatives received a request for assistance from American merchants in Canton, Adams rose in Congress to protest China's "boasted superiority above every nation on earth." Historians have usually framed his 1841 lecture as an isolated and eccentric exercise. In fact, Adams was a key figure in the network of merchants, missionaries, and politicians who were pressing Washington officials to adopt a similar China policy to the one being championed by Britain.[13]

Adams became a particular object of interest for the Presbyterian missionary and surgeon Peter Parker, who had been sent by the American Board of Commissioners for Foreign Missions to Canton in 1834. Parker had impressed the Chinese by founding a hospital and acquiring an unusually good grasp of their language. As the dispute with Britain moved toward war in 1839, Parker wrote to Lin Zexu, the emperor's commissioner in Canton, to urge him to accept the "opening" of China and the good wishes of the United States. In the summer of that year, Parker told his sister that "the storm probably must and will come, but He who rides thereon and controls the tempest has a regard for His world, and out of evil is wont to bring good." The particular good Parker foresaw was "the putting of foreign intercourse with China upon a more honorable and safe footing." When he and the other Americans in Canton were forced out in 1840, Parker returned to the United States and approached John Quincy Adams with a big idea— Adams should be the first U.S. minister to China. Emperor Daoguang would, after all, feel a "strong sympathy and regard for one approaching his own advanced age, and of similar rank." Being compared to the ruler of the celestial empire was hardly disagreeable to the one-term president, but Adams advised Parker that the war with Britain needed to play out a little further before the United States made a diplomatic overture. The two men agreed that the United States would benefit from the geopolitical realignment that a British victory seemed certain to produce.[14]

Most of Adams's interventions on China took place behind closed doors. However, it's not quite true to suggest, as Adams did in his diary, that his Masonic Hall address in November 1841 was "so adverse to the prevailing prejudices of the time and place that I expect to bring down a storm upon my head." In fact, his lecture developed arguments he had already deployed in Congress and tested on other powerful Americans who shared his disdain for China's "boasted superiority." In the weeks after his address, Adams bragged that "the excitement of public opinion and feeling by the delivery of this lecture far exceeds any expectation that I had formed." When lecturing to the public, Adams often imagined himself in the prophetic mode, speaking truth to power and expecting praise only from posterity. On China, though, his views were already becoming mainstream.[15]

The lecture did three things. First, it maintained that the Opium War wasn't really about opium. "This is a mere incident to the dispute," Adams insisted, "but no more the cause of the war, than the throwing overboard of the tea in Boston Harbor was the cause of the North American Revolution." Second, it urged Americans to recognize that the war was "of deep interest to the human race, and of pre-eminent interest to the people of the North American Union." Finally, and most important, it argued that "the cause of the war is the pretension on the part of the Chinese, that in all their intercourse with other Nations, political or commercial, their superiority must be implicitly acknowledged, and manifested in humiliating forms." By refusing to open its markets to free trade, China had violated a basic principle of the international order. This was, in short, a war not for the advantage of the British empire but for "the natural equality of mankind."[16]

Was China equal to the "spirited, enlightened and valourous Nations of Christendom?" In an anonymous 1839 article, the *Princeton Review* had admitted that China "preceded Europe in what are justly considered three of the most important inventions or discoveries of modern times: the art of printing, the composition of gunpowder, and the magnetic compass." American travelers noted the politeness of the Chinese and the richness of their culture, even as they acknowledged "excessive arrogance" (the *Review*, again) and fretted about Confucianism or the place of women in Chinese society. Unlike in South Asia or Africa, where the British, French, and Portuguese had coopted or coerced local rulers into facilitating the extension of Western law and commerce, China remained sovereign and separate from an emerging European order. China's status mattered because European and American statesmen of the mid-nineteenth century increasingly felt the need to align their actions with international law. Although the key texts in this tradition licensed projections of Western power into "uncivilized" spaces, they were maddeningly restrictive in governing relations between "civilized" nations.[17]

It's not a surprise, then, that Adams spent a large portion of his 1841 speech developing a highly partial understanding of China's legal status. Having argued that international law was actually a misnomer because the nations of the Earth were not subject to the enforcement mechanisms of any higher power (at least, not a terrestrial one), he worked to undo the inconvenient conclusions of the most famous authority of the age, the Swiss jurist Emer de Vattel. In his celebrated *Law of Nations* (1758), Vattel had declared that it was every nation's right "to carry on commerce with another, or to let it alone." Nations had a right to "renounce and prohibit" any form of trade, and Vattel invoked the Chinese to prove both the fact and the justice of this position. As Jennifer Pitts has argued, Vattel pitched his legal theory into a fascinatingly ambiguous zone: he assumed non-European societies could be "members of the society of states bound by the law of nations," and yet "his legal system was unselfconsciously European in origin."[18]

Adams's strategy for undoing Vattel was extraordinary. First, he insisted that the universalism of the *Law of Nations* was mistaken. In reality, there was no single law governing all societies but a series of distinct legal systems tied to religion:

There is also a Law of Nations between *Christian* communities, which prevails between the Europeans and their descendants throughout the globe. This is the Law recognised by the Constitution and Laws of the United States, as obligatory upon them in their intercourse with the European States and Colonies. But we have a separate and different Law of Nations for the regulation of our intercourse with the Indian tribes of our own Continent; another Law of Nations between us, and the woolly headed natives of Africa; another with the Barbary Powers and the Sultans of the Ottoman Empire; a Law of Nations with the Inhabitants of the Isles of the Sea wherever human industry and enterprise have explored the Geography of the Globe; and lastly a Law of Nations with the flowery land, the celestial Empire, the Mantchoo Tartar Dynasty of Despotism, where the Patriarchal system of Sir Robert Filmer flourishes in all its glory.

According to Adams, Vattel had been wrong to offer nations the right to reject the trade of other nations; moreover, the "hereditary, patriarchal despotism" of the Chinese government made the emperor a terrible judge of the national interest of his people. (Here Adams tried to skirt a central precept of modern international law, that states had no right to intervene in the internal affairs of other states.) At the heart of Adams's argument was the claim that a universal law of nations depended on a common religion. Since the Chinese had refused Christianity, they had no access to the protections and indemnities defined by Vattel. "The moral obligation of commercial intercourse between nations is founded entirely, exclusively, upon the Christian precept to love your neighbor as yourself," Adams claimed. The "selfish" principles that animated Chinese religion could only result in "the assumption of a pretension to superiority over other nations." Here Adams's dissent from Vattel assumed a strangely circular logic: China had to be excluded from the realm of civilized nations to have any chance of eventually taking its place among them.[19]

As Benjamin Coates demonstrates in chapter 2 in this volume, American leaders frequently assumed the right to define or deny civilized status to non-American peoples. China—a society that seemed both civilized and alien—presented a particular challenge in this regard, one that John Quincy Adams surmounted by insisting that the Chinese had haughtily rejected the true universalisms of Christianity and the Enlightenment. The arrogance of the Qing, with their "pretensions" of cultural exceptionalism, had been "too long connived at and truckled to by the mightiest Christian nations of the civilized world." It was a cause for celebration that Palmerston had finally found the courage to act: "I cannot forbear the hope that Britain, after taking the lead in the abolition of the African Slave Trade and of slavery, and of the still more degrading tribute to the barbary African Mahometans, will extend her liberating arm to the farthest bounds of Asia." Britain, as many scholars have pointed out, had spent the first decades of the nineteenth century building a new imperial-legal order around its opposition to the slave trade. Although its actions often drew criticism from Vattel's successors—including the American legal theorist Henry Wheaton—Britain's projections of Christian power and principle offered John Quincy Adams a simple solution for East Asia. Instead of a world in which China "utterly denies the equality of other nations with itself" and "holds itself to be the centre of the terraqueous globe," a British victory would ensure that "future commerce shall be carried on upon terms of equality and reciprocity."[20]

In fact, the projection of British power in China produced the first of a series of "unequal treaties"—the Treaty of Nanjing (1842)—that effectively erased Vattel's principle that the Chinese could regulate their own commerce. Britain received $21 million in compensation for the destroyed opium and for the loss of other property and lives; five Chinese ports were opened to British trade; the Hong merchants lost their monopoly, allowing British merchants to trade with anyone; and Hong Kong was ceded to Britain. A pair of annexes to the treaty (signed the following year) gave British subjects the right to live and work in Chinese ports under the jurisdiction of British rather than Chinese officials. John Quincy Adams had insisted not only that the war had nothing to do with opium but that the "natural equality" that would follow a British victory would allow the Chinese to confirm their prohibition of the drug. In fact, opium appeared only once in the treaty text, in the context of the indemnities owed by China to the merchants whose stocks had been destroyed. British officials tactfully avoided overt support for the continuation of the trade, but the same pattern of illegal commerce brought Britain and China into another conflict barely a decade later.[21]

In his study of the First Opium War, the historian Stephen Platt insists that Adams's 1841 lecture represented "absolute heresy in the eyes of the American public at the time." In fact, American audiences had long viewed Britain with creative ambivalence: a reflexive critique of British aggression coexisted with an acknowledgment of shared religious and cultural values between the American republic and its former colonial parent. Adams invited his compatriots to look beyond the moral messiness of opium and shelling to a deeper understanding of Anglo-American world order. Adams also worked to promote his distinctive formulation of the "natural equality of mankind" in Washington. In 1842 he met again with Peter Parker to discuss sending an "intelligent and discreet and spirited" American minister to China. Following Parker's earlier hint, Adams imagined that he himself would be perfect for this role. To his irritation, it went instead to Caleb Cushing, a former congressman from Massachusetts. Ironically, in a speech in Congress in 1840, Cushing had lamented Britain's "violation of the laws of nations and of humanity" in the Opium War. "God forbid," he told the House of Representatives, "that I should entertain the idea of co-operating with the British Government in the purpose . . . of upholding the base cupidity and violence, and high handed infraction of all law, human and divine, which have characterized the operations of the British." But Cushing, like other Americans, was already coming around to Adams's imaginative understanding of "the equality of nations." With the missionary-diplomat Peter Parker as his secretary and translator, Cushing traveled to Canton in 1843 (after a pep talk from Adams) with a remarkable determination to open China to

American commerce and religion. In the Treaty of Wanghia, signed in 1844, Cushing and Parker extracted even more concessions from the Chinese than the British had done at Nanjing.[22]

When Cushing returned in triumph to the United States, Adams reminded him that he had previously held "a position adverse to mine" on China and asked why he'd changed his mind. Obligingly, Cushing told Adams that "on reading my lecture he had procured the papers laid before the British Parliament, upon which my opinion had been formed, and that he fully concurred with it." Adams then rehearsed his theory that "there were differences of international law between nations, modified by their system of religion." Had Cushing been able to determine "what was the fundamental principle of morals" among the Chinese? Adams wasn't entirely happy with Cushing's answer that "it was the relation of authority and obedience between parent and child." When Cushing followed this claim with the more outlandish assertion that "the words of Jesus upon the cross . . . were to the very letter in the Cryopaedia of Xenophon," Adams began to doubt whether Cushing could help him with the search for an underlying grammar of human morality. Absent this deeper system, China would remain in subsequent decades where Adams had placed it in 1841: exiled from the promises of Vattel, properly subject to a "Christian law of nations," and relegated to a subordinate place in the emerging Euro-American world order.[23]

China, according to Adams, contained "the extremes of civilization and of the savage state blended together in one condition of human existence." As Duncan Bell has reminded us, British thinkers in the mid-nineteenth century were similarly perplexed by the question of whether "liminal" peoples such as the Japanese, Chinese, and Ottomans could realize their "potential for full inclusion" in a new world order. For Adams, though, the problem of China and the "natural equality of the human race" also pointed backward to his flawed vision of U.S. continentalism. In the first part of his career, leading up to his assumption of the presidency in 1825, Adams imagined a United States that might abolish slavery, assimilate Native Americans by bringing them to "civilization," and live in harmony with the newly independent republics of Latin America. There would be no need for "colonial establishments" in a Western Hemisphere dedicated to liberty, republicanism, and racial and religious uplift.[24]

When this vision was challenged—as, for example, by Tecumseh and his pan-Indian confederacy before the War of 1812, or the Seminole Indians after 1815—Adams followed an old trick of Thomas Jefferson's: he insisted that Britain or Spain had manufactured Indigenous resistance. Hence his zeal in denying Indian sovereignty at the peace negotiations with Britain in Ghent in 1814, or his extraordinary defensiveness in 1830 when asked to explain why he had supported Andrew Jackson's operations in Spanish Florida during the First Seminole War: "Were it to go over again, I would do the same, should the retribution reserved for me, instead of that which I endure, be crucifixion." The source of Adams's righteousness in both cases was his belief that the United States was defending its territory from European encroachment. When Native Americans were left alone, he maintained, they would resume the process of civilizing and become full members of the American family.[25]

After 1820 it became more difficult to blame Europe for the failures of American Indian policy. But during his single term in the White House, Adams did little to protect Native Americans from cascading white encroachment. At a cabinet meeting in 1825, his secretary of state, Henry Clay, insisted that it was "impossible to civilize the Indians." (Adams noted in his diary that there was "too much foundation" for this view.) Adams's secretary of war, James Barbour, reaffirmed the Monroe administration's chimerical plan to "colonize" Native Americans west of the Mississippi. The cabinet had "nothing more effective to propose," so Adams signed off on this but doubted it would work. The crisis over Andrew Jackson's removal bill in 1830 allowed Adams once again to shift responsibility to another party: now it was the southern states, rather than Europe, that were destroying the dream of Indigenous assimilation. But when proposals reached Congress in 1834 to create a formal territory west of the Mississippi that might incubate the first exclusively Indigenous state in the American republic, Adams—now returned to the House of Representatives—bitterly opposed it. Was Congress "ready to declare that these people were to be admitted, in their collective capacity, as a state of the Union?" If lawmakers passed the bill, "they would be bound to admit not only one, but two or three, or half a dozen such states." The bill's proponents—especially in the missionary community—were amazed at Adams's opposition. His contribution to the debate was to speak elegiacally of the lost potential of Indian "civilization" while directing the House to dismiss the prospect of Indigenous statehood in the West.[26]

As for the nations of Latin America, Adams had hoped that they would form part of an "American System" of hemispheric commerce and liberty.

But Adams's vision was opposed by proslavery southerners unnerved by the abolitionist sentiment of many Latin American regimes, and by northern Democrats who rejected "entangling alliances" and new forms of hemispheric government. Falling back on the idea that the nations of the Americas would at least defend their independence from Europe, Adams watched the events of the 1830s with considerable unease. Adams was an inveterate opponent of Texas annexation, but he nursed increasing anxiety about the "helpless weakness" of Mexico and the limited capacity of Mexicans to play their role in a system of civilized states. In 1845, he confided to his diary that the public was being distracted from the clear injustice of Texas annexation by "the anarchy and civil war into which, precisely at this moment, Mexico had fallen." The defenders of republicanism in the United States needed Mexico to be strong, Adams noted wistfully, and yet "she cannot maintain her own identity; she is falling to pieces, and if Texas were restored to her she could not hold it." Adams's understanding of the continental United States as a republican space required both Indigenous peoples and Mexicans to consolidate their claims to civilized status. By the 1840s, Adams doubted the capacity of either group to hold back the forces of an expanding and increasingly chauvinistic United States.[27]

One of the most strident critics of Adams's China lecture was the Harvard professor William Adam, who had been born in Britain and had worked as a missionary and colonial official in India before relocating to the United States. In a long essay for the *Christian Examiner*, Adam noted that the former president had been "unable to rise superior to the prejudices of European and American civilization." It was incredibly tempting to universalize from one's own culture and experience; Americans were bound to think as "men glorying in the civilization of the nineteenth century, as it has been developed and matured in Europe and America." But they should also make "a strong effort of the reason and imagination combined" to conceive how the world might appear to a Chinese person "living under his peculiar form of civilization, and deriving all his prepossessions and idiosyncrasies, all his habits of feeling, thought, and action from its influence." With a mischievous nod to the golden rule, Adam insisted that "it is only thus that we may hope to do to others as we would that they should do to us."[28]

John Quincy Adams was moving in the other direction. Having lived long enough to see the universalisms of his youth embarrassed by the persistence of racial and cultural difference, Adams faced an awkward choice between the moral relativism (and geopolitical restraint) outlined by William Adam and an acknowledgment that racial, religious, and cultural hierarchies would lead inexorably toward imperialism. Adams never stopped believing that the United States should eschew "colonial establishments," but in his final years he was tugged toward the belief that racial and cultural differences were immutable. Managing their influence would require force as well as persuasion, an insight that inspired Adams to glimpse the "natural equality of mankind" only on the other side of British aggression in China.

Notes

1. John Quincy Adams, "Lyceum Lecture," *Cambridge Magnolia*, December 30, 1841, 39. Charles Francis Adams, ed., *Memoirs of John Quincy Adams*, 12 vols. (Philadelphia: J. B. Lippincott, 1874–1877), 11:30–31. The fullest version of Adams's lecture appears in "J. Q. Adams on the Opium War," *Proceedings of the Massachusetts Historical Society* 43 (February 1810): 295–325.

2. Julia Lovell, *The Opium War: Drugs, Dreams and the Making of China* (London: Picador, 2011); Alan Rappeport, "19th-Century 'Humiliation' Haunts China–U.S. Trade Talks," *New York Times*, March 27, 2019.

3. William Earl Weeks, *John Quincy Adams and American Global Empire* (Lexington: University Press of Kentucky, 1992), 5.

4. Stephen R. Platt, *Imperial Twilight: The Opium War and the End of China's Last Golden Age* (New York: Knopf, 2018), 15–44; Dael Norwood, "Trading in Liberty: The Politics of the American China Trade, c. 1784–1862" (PhD diss., Princeton University, 2012); Christa Dierksheide, "Creating a 'Treaty-Unworthy' State: Anglo-Americans in China in the Age of Jefferson," in *Ireland and America: Empire, Revolution, and Sovereignty*, ed. Patrick Griffin and Francis D. Cogliano (Charlottesville: University of Virginia Press, 2021), 285–300.

5. Lovell, *Opium War*, 17–240. Platt, *Imperial Twilight*, 285–400.

6. Adams, *Memoirs of John Quincy Adams*, 6:104; Jay Sexton, *The Monroe Doctrine: Empire and Nation in Nineteenth-Century America* (New York: Hill and Wang, 2011).

7. Adams, *Memoirs of John Quincy Adams*, 4:292–93. Jared Sparks, "Sixth Annual Report of the American Society for Colonizing the Free People of Color," *North American Review* 18 (January 1824): 40–92, 89–90; Brandon Mills, "Situating African Colonization Within the History of U.S. Expansion," in *New Directions in the Study of African American Recolonization*, ed. Beverly C. Tomek and Matthew J. Hetrick (Gainesville: University Press of Florida, 2017), 166–83.

8. Adams, *Memoirs of John Quincy Adams*, 12:49, 57, 171; Jay Sexton and Ian Tyrrell, eds., introduction to *Empire's Twin: U.S. Anti-Imperialism from the Founding Era to the Age of Terrorism* (Ithaca, NY: Cornell University Press, 2015), 1–18, 10.

9. Weeks, *John Quincy Adams and the Global Empire*, 176–99; Charles N. Edel, *Nation Builder: John Quincy Adams and the Grand Strategy of the Republic* (Cambridge, MA: Harvard University Press, 2014), 249–89; Adams, *Memoirs of John Quincy Adams*, 4:438. On Oregon, see Adams's remarks to George Bancroft, December 6, 1812, in Adams, *Memoirs of John Quincy Adams*, 12:218–19.

10. Adams, *Memoirs of John Quincy Adams*, 4:439. On proslavery expansionism, see Matthew Pratt Guterl, *American Mediterranean: Southern Slaveholders in the Age of Emancipation* (Cambridge, MA: Harvard University Press, 2008); and Matthew J. Karp, *This Vast Southern Empire: Slaveholders at the Helm of American Foreign Policy* (Cambridge, MA: Harvard University Press, 2016).

11. Charles W. King, "Memoranda in the Position of the Government of the United States, with Respect to Negotiations with China," c. 1840, in Adams Family Papers, reel 516; Dierksheide, "Creating a 'Treaty-Unworthy' State."

12. "The Chinese," *Princeton Review* 11, no. 2 (1839): 147–80, at 148; Edwin Crosswell, "China and England," *Northern Light*, May 1841, 29. On the "kowtow," see James L. Hevia, "'The Ultimate Gesture of Deference and Debasement': Kowtowing in China," *Past & Present* 203, suppl. 4 (2009): 212–34.

13. "J. Q. Adams on the Opium War," 296. Adams, *Memoirs of John Quincy Adams*, 10:367, 373–74, 375, 424; John Quincy Adams, December 16, 1840, Congressional Globe, 26th Cong., 2nd Sess., 28–29.

14. George B. Stevens, ed., *The Life, Letters, and Journal of the Rev. and Hon. Peter Parker, M.D.* (Boston: Congregational Sunday School and Publishing Society, 1896), 170–72; Adams, *Memoirs of John Quincy Adams*, 10:444–45; Michael C. Lazich, "American Missionaries and the Opium Trade in Nineteenth-Century China," *Journal of World History* 17, no. 2 (2006): 197–223; Louis Fu, "Healing Bodies or Saving Souls? Reverend Dr Peter Parker (1804–1888) as Medical Missionary," *Journal of Medical Biography* 24, no. 2 (2016): 266–75.

15. Adams, *Memoirs of John Quincy Adams*, 11:30, 31.

16. "J. Q. Adams on the Opium War," 314, 303, 310.

17. "J. Q. Adams on the Opium War," 311; "The Chinese," 168, 151. On the relationship between empire and international law, see Antony Anghie, *Imperialism, Sovereignty and the Making of International Law* (Cambridge: Cambridge University Press, 2004); Lisa Ford and Lauren Benton, *Rage for Order: The British Empire and the Origins of International Law, 1800–1850* (Cambridge, MA: Harvard University Press, 2016); and Jennifer Pitts, *Boundaries of the International: Law and Empire* (Cambridge, MA: Harvard University Press, 2018). See also Teema Ruskola, "Canton Is Not Boston: The Invention of American Imperial Sovereignty," *American Quarterly* 57, no. 2 (2005): 859–84.

18. "J. Q. Adams on the Opium War," 304; Emer de Vattel, *The Principles of the Law of Nations* (London: G. G. and J. Robinson, 1797), 39–40; Pitts, *Boundaries of the International*, 72.

19. "J. Q. Adams on the Opium War," 307, 309, 308, 310; Pitts, *Boundaries of the International*, 135–36.

20. "J. Q. Adams on the Opium War," 313–14. On slave trade abolition and international law, see Lauren Benton, "Abolition and Imperial Law, 1790–1820," *Journal of Imperial and Commonwealth History* 39, no. 3 (2011): 355–74; Jenny S. Martinez, *The Slave Trade and the Origins of International Human Rights Law* (New York: Oxford University Press, 2014); and Padraic X. Scanlan, *Freedom's Debtors: British Antislavery in Sierra Leone in the Age of Revolution* (New Haven, CT: Yale University Press, 2017).

21. Lovell, *Opium War*, 241–66; Platt, *Imperial Twilight*, 401–27; Dong Wang, *China's Unequal Treaties: Narrating National History* (Lanham, MD: Lexington, 2005), 9–16.

22. Platt, *Imperial Twilight*, 415–16; Adams, *Memoirs of John Quincy Adams*, 11:166–67, 289–90, 296–97, 300, 337, 388; Caleb Cushing, March 16, 1840, Congressional Globe, 26th Cong., 1st Sess., 275; Stevens, *Life, Letters, and Journals of Peter Parker*, 249–57.

23. Adams, *Memoirs of John Quincy Adams*, 12:227. On U.S. ambivalence toward Britain, see Samuel W. Haynes, *Unfinished Revolution: The Early American Republic in a British World* (Charlottesville: University of Virginia Press, 2010). On the development of U.S. extraterritoriality, see Eileen P. Scully, *Bargaining with the State from Afar: American Citizenship in Treaty Port China, 1844–1942* (New York: Columbia University Press, 2001); and Teemu Ruskola, *Legal Orientalism: China, the United States, and Modern Law* (Cambridge, MA: Harvard University Press, 2013).

24. Adams, *Memoirs of John Quincy Adams*, 10:374. Duncan Bell, with Casper Sylvest, "International Society in Victorian Political Thought," in *Reordering the World: Essays on Liberalism and Empire*, by Duncan Bell (Princeton, NJ: Princeton University Press, 2016), 237–64; 259.

25. Lynn Hudson Parsons, "'A Perpetual Harrow upon My Feelings': John Quincy Adams and the American Indian," *New England Quarterly* 46, no. 3 (1973): 339–79, 341, 348; Nicholas Guyatt, *Bind Us Apart: How Enlightened Americans Invented Racial Segregation* (New York: Basic Books, 2016), 107–8.

26. Adams, *Memoirs of John Quincy Adams*, 7:90, 113; John Quincy Adams, June 25, 1834, Register of Debates, 23rd Cong., 1st Sess., 4768–69. For Adams's efforts to southernize the "Indian problem," see Adams, *Memoirs of John Quincy Adams*, 10:491–92.

27. Adams, *Memoirs of John Quincy Adams*, 11:353, 12:171.

28. William Adam, "Great Britain and China," *Christian Examiner*, July 1842, 281–319, 282–83. On William Adam, see Christopher Clark, "The Communitarian Moment," in *A Place Called Paradise: Culture and Community in Northampton, Massachusetts, 1654–2004*, ed. Kerry W. Buckley (Amherst: University of Massachusetts Press, 2004), 301–42, 309–12; and Andrea Major, *Slavery, Abolitionism and Empire in India, 1772–1843* (Liverpool: University of Liverpool Press, 2012), 321–23.

CHAPTER 7

Antislavery and Empire

The Early Republican Party Confronts the World

MATTHEW KARP

The central ideological struggle in mid-nineteenth-century America was the struggle over the future of slavery. This titanic conflict, which broke apart antebellum social and religious institutions and consumed American politics for nearly two decades, culminated in a revolutionary war of emancipation that left a major impact on American foreign relations as well. Historians of U.S. foreign policy have recently returned to questions of slavery, abolition, and disunion—bringing rich life to the "Great American Desert," as Kinley Brauer once called the study of American foreign relations during the antebellum decades—but the relationship between slavery and ideology remains relatively unexplored. In Michael Hunt's classic account of the ideological contours of U.S. foreign policy, "racial hierarchy" assumes a central position, but the fierce conflict over slavery, like the Civil War itself, scarcely receives a mention.[1]

Of course, slavery's impact on U.S. foreign relations was profound. During the antebellum decades, proslavery ideology played a vital role in the annexation of Texas, the Mexican-American War, and U.S. foreign policy across the Western Hemisphere.[2] Yet this only represented one half of the larger ongoing ideological struggle over slavery. *Antislavery* ideology also shaped this history. To be sure, proslavery figures dominated the executive branch and controlled the levers of American state power before 1861.[3] Nevertheless, the campaign against slavery in the United States—first as a social movement, and later as a part of American politics—developed a distinctive ideological vision that ultimately left a major impact on U.S. foreign policy. Indeed, for antislavery figures from William Seward to Frederick Douglass, the struggle against bondage was an ideological anchor of sorts—a way of understanding political, social, and economic relations at home and around the world. Beyond national borders, antislavery intellectuals and activists found themselves relating their opposition to human bondage to geopolitical questions about war and peace, international law, and free trade and commercial relations.[4]

Historians since Eric Williams have sought to understand the intimate but often complex relationship between antislavery ideology, the rise of industrial capitalism, and Euro-American imperial expansion in the nineteenth century.[5] This work has often centered on the British experience, and with good reason, given Britain's central role in the history of abolition, capitalism, and imperialism alike. But a glimpse at the international politics of antislavery in the United States, where circumstances were very different from those in Britain, presents an alternative view of the problem. It may also help illuminate some particularities of the American experience. One key difference, as we have seen, was that nineteenth-century American antislavery struggles developed in almost total opposition to the dominant forces inside the national government.

A second particularity is that after 1854, when antislavery emerged as a force capable of shaping government policy, it did so in the context of mass partisan politics. This marks a significant difference from parallel struggles in monarchical Britain and Brazil or revolutionary Haiti, France, and Spanish America, where antislavery forces either lobbied an essentially aristocratic government or came into power through armed insurrection.[6] The contrast with the British experience, which has formed the backbone for most analysis of antislavery ideology in global terms, is particularly acute. British abolitionism certainly involved a mass movement of petitioners, tract-writers, and meeting attendees, but it took place in a political system in which no more than 20 percent of the adult male population had the right to vote (and many fewer actually did vote).[7] In the United States, the antislavery movement won power in a limited but nevertheless popular electoral democracy, and mass parties debated the question of bondage in heated election campaigns marked by high and increasing voter turnout. When Abraham Lincoln was elected president in 1860, he received 1.8 million votes, more than any previous American presidential candidate.[8]

I suggest that the oppositional and mass democratic character of American antislavery politics helped produce an antislavery worldview considerably different from the ideology developed by genteel parliamentarians and imperial officials in early and mid-nineteenth-century Britain. This essay highlights two major aspects of that antislavery vision as they were elaborated by activists and politicians in and around the Republican Party in the 1850s. First, a commitment to what Eric Foner influentially called "free labor ideology" did not just help Republicans frame the domestic conflict between the free North and slave South but formed the basis of an international view of political economy. As opposed to aristocratic Europe or the rapacious slaveholders of the South, Republicans celebrated "intelligent labor"—not heredity, status, or capital—as the engine that drove global economic progress.[9] Second, Republicans understood this egalitarian free labor economy, in global as well as domestic terms, to be inextricable from the rights and freedoms guaranteed by political democracy. Again, in contrast to monarchical Europe and the slave South, antislavery leaders argued that only popular government—anchored by "the changeless natural equality of human rights"—could advance the cause of civilization all across the world.[10]

The ideological compound that formed in the 1850s, fusing free labor and democratic politics, had major consequences for both the United States and the broader Atlantic world. On one hand, this distinctively American antislavery ideology shared some features of the bourgeois liberal capitalism that was beginning to emerge on both sides of the Atlantic, a worldview that ultimately proved compatible with the late-nineteenth-century world of empires. On the other hand, that same ideology provided a popular ideological foundation for perhaps the most revolutionary transformations of that same nineteenth-century Atlantic world—the violent mass emancipations and enfranchisements of the American Civil War era.

Free Labor and Soulless Capital

Early Republican ideas about the world, and the role of the United States within it, were organized around opposition to what antislavery activists had long called "the Slave Power" in Washington. This attack on the concentrated strength of slavery had a global dimension too. Slaveholding politicians boasted about the productivity of enslaved labor in Cuba, Brazil, and the United States, whereas antislavery leaders argued that bondage was in retreat all across the globe. Not only had Western European nations freed their bondspeople, declared Charles Sumner, but in India, "slavery has been condemned"; in Constantinople, "the Ottoman Sultan has fastened upon it the stigma of disapprobation"; the rulers of Morocco and Tunis "have been changed into abolitionists"; and even "despotic Russia," with its millions of serfs, had issued a "positive prohibition" against the expansion of bondage into Bessarabia or Poland.[11]

Like many abolitionists before him, Sumner presented the international decline of slavery as a moral awakening. But other Republicans also linked this principled rejection of bondage to a broader rejection of a global economy based on bound labor and cheap staples. This formulation took aim at a transatlantic ruling class of landlords, aristocrats, and "slaveholding capitalists," from Ukraine to Texas, who all lived "upon the forced labor of others." And it placed the Republican Party, as the German American politician Carl Schurz put it, on the side of the global "laboring classes." To escape the fate of Europe's oppressed, toiling masses, Republicans called on northern farmers and workers to wrest their national government from the slaveholding oligarchs who had seized it—and who threatened to shape the entire American economy in their image. "They enslave the blacks," declared Cleveland's leading Republican newspaper, "not because they are *black*, but because they are laborers—and they contend that the highest civilization demands that the laboring class should be subjected and owned by the '*higher* class.'" Republicans framed their own economic vision as the diametric opposite of this aristocratic nightmare. An economy centered on small producers, argued Abraham Lincoln, "will be alike independent of crowned-kings, money-kings, and land-kings."[12]

In the same 1859 speech, Lincoln memorably framed the conflict between the slave South and the free North as a battle over the true relationship between "capital" and "labor." While southern advocates of the "mud-sill theory" believed that "labor is only available in connection with capital," Lincoln declared, northerners understood that "labor is prior to, and independent of, capital. . . . Hence they hold that labor is the superior—greatly the superior—of capital." Later socialist propaganda notwithstanding, Lincoln's words did not signify a rejection of the competitive marketplace, never mind the individual right to property.[13] But neither should we ignore the frequency with which Lincoln and other Republicans denounced "class" rule, demoted "capital," and celebrated "labor." Sometimes dismissed as no more than an awkward euphemism for slavery—or a bland glorification of northern society in its current form—this language of capital and labor expressed a distinct political-economic worldview. Whereas American slaveholders and their allies touted trade for its own sake—boasting over export statistics and cheering the dissemination of goods—Republicans generally stressed the importance of labor in the productive process. "It is not traffic, but labor alone, that converts the resources of the country into wealth," argued New York senator William Henry Seward. If this free labor vision of the 1850s was in some respects a provincial one, celebrating a particular form of small-scale agriculture and industry in the northern United States, it had larger implications too.[14]

Its chief expositor in global terms was not Lincoln but Seward, who, as Foner recognized, "brought the Republican ideology to a kind of culmination." Like Lincoln, Seward built his career as a reform-minded Whig and a champion of activist government economic policy: tariff-funded internal improvements, subsidized public postage, and public investment in education. For the New York senator, the true measure of progress was not simply the "great accumulation of wealth"—whether in the hands of a Louisiana sugar planter or a Manhattan merchant—but balanced, "diversified," economic development. Slavery, serfdom, and other forms of dominated labor might produce enormous fortunes for the ruling elite, but they inhibited actual growth. Despite his vast wealth and power, Tsar Nicholas of Russia needed "a Massachusetts engineer" to design his railroads, "a Baltimore mechanic" to build his locomotive engines, and "a carriage-maker of Troy" (New York) to construct his train cars. It was not coercion or commerce but skilled labor that made the global economy hum. Indeed, whether in Russia, Latin America, or the U.S. South, an emphasis on raw material exports was a deadly mistake: "This false economy crowds the culture of a few staples with excessive industry; thus rendering labor dependent at home, while it brings the whole nation tributary to the monopolizing manufacturer abroad."[15]

Seward embraced a range of Whiggish development policies, but after becoming a Republican in 1855 he too attacked slavery with a highly un-Whiggish rhetoric that seized on international divisions of class, capital, and labor. According to Seward, the American sectional struggle was best understood in world-historical terms: "In every state," he declared in 1856, "all the property classes sympathize with each other, through the force of common instincts of fear, cupidity, and ambition, and are easily marshaled under the lead of one which becomes dominant and represents the whole."

Such was the case with "the patricians in old Rome, the noblesse and the clergy in France," the "landholders in Ireland," "the landed aristocracy in England," and, of course, the slaveholders in the American South. The Republican Party's battle against this last "property class" was thus part of a global struggle against the unchecked power of economic elites. By 1860 Seward could speak of the entire American sectional crisis as the product of a "worldwide" conflict between "capital states," such as the proslavery South, and "labor states," such as the antislavery North: "in the one case, capital invested in slaves becomes a great political force; while in the other, labor, thus elevated and enfranchised, becomes the dominating political power." Seward lamented the apparent triumph of the former over the latter in the American politics of the 1850s: "Did ever the government of a great empire, founded on the rights of human labor, slide away so fast and so far, and moor itself so tenaciously on the basis of capital, and that capital invested in laboring men?"[16]

Seward's sincere view of the relationship between capital and slavery is far from clear. As he once told Jefferson and Varina Davis (jokingly, perhaps), he did not always believe his own aggressive antislavery speeches but knew that such rhetoric was "potent to affect the rank and file of the North."[17] In any case, the force of this class-conscious attack on slavery did not depend on personal conviction but on its effectiveness in mass partisan politics, as Seward's political opponents understood. The Republicans, charged the leading northern Democrat Stephen Douglas, were attempting to turn the slavery debate into "a question between capital and labor, and take the side of the numbers against the few."[18] In the election of 1860, Republicans hammered away at this theme, consistently identifying the abusive power of slaveholders with the abusive power of "capital." Speakers and newspapers lambasted Herschel V. Johnson of Georgia, Douglas's running mate, for suggesting that "Capital should own Labor"; Republican banners responded, defiantly, that "CAPITAL SHALL NOT OWN US."[19] With Democrats in power, warned one editor, the "class that controls and directs the capital of the country" might well seek to extend the domination of slavery, or something like slavery, over the "mechanics and laborers" of the North. "Democracy places men above property," ran one formula; "the democratic party believes in making property of men."[20]

If antebellum "free labor" ideology could serve, in some contexts, as a kind of bourgeois alibi for wage labor, it could also function as a populist rhetoric that summoned an international cast of workers against the dangerous domination of slave capital.[21] "Put the brand of degradation upon the brow of one working-man," Henry Wilson told an audience in East Boston, "and the toiling millions of the globe share in that degradation." The same militancy infused the Republican advocacy for western homesteads, another issue with potent appeal for "the rank and file of the North." "The struggle between capital and labor is an unequal one at best," declared Pennsylvania's Galusha Grow, whose speech in favor of "Free Homes for Free Men" became a key Republican campaign document in 1860. For Grow, federal homesteads were necessary to fight "the power of soulless capital," whether southern or northern: "It will weaken the system of chattel slavery, by making war upon its kindred system of wages slavery, giving homes and employment to its victims, and equalizing the condition of the people." In this sense, a free-soil homestead act was not a mere safety valve, designed to alleviate class conflict, but an actual weapon of class conflict, resisted by speculators and slaveholders alike, and demanded by a party that sought to use "the broad shield of government" to guarantee an economic "right to land" and a more equal "distribution" of wealth.[22]

"Emancipation Is a Democratic Revolution"

This belligerent language of class, capital, and labor not only separated Republicans from Whigs but also distinguished the political-economic worldview of American antislavery from the most influential antislavery leaders in nineteenth-century Britain.[23] A related difference—and a defining feature of Republican antislavery politics in national and international terms—was the celebration of "democracy." In the free states of the American North, Seward declared, "labor, being emancipated, seizes upon the Democratic machinery of the Government, and works out the results of political and social equality with a great rapidity of success. Thus labor rules in the free States. In the slave States, labor being enslaved, the operation of a pure Democratic principle is hindered, and the consequence is, that capital is more successful in retaining its ancient sway." Democracy, the natural political form of free labor, was innately incompatible with the rule of slavery, aristocracy, and capital.[24]

Since Edmund Morgan at least, U.S. historians have been less interested in any elemental conflict between American slavery and American democracy than in their ironic and tragic inextricability.[25] And across the eighteenth and early nineteenth centuries, slavery's elected representatives in government gave slaveholders in the United States more political power than their counterparts almost anywhere else in the Atlantic world. In a very concrete sense, American democratic institutions thus fortified the power of bondage. Visiting Ireland and England in 1845, Frederick Douglass was hardly the only abolitionist to note the contrast between "American republican slavery" and British "monarchical liberty."[26]

In the 1850s, however, Republican leaders articulated a rather different view of the relationship between American bondage and America freedom. The dominance of the Slave Power, for Seward, did not reveal any intractable "paradox" between slavery and democracy: it showed, rather, that large portions of the country were simply not democratic at all. "If there is any part of the United States where the land or the labor is monopolized by capital," he argued, referring to the South, "there is a place in which the democratic element has not yet had its introduction." Southern politicians, said Carl Schurz, "speak of democracy, but the despotic spirit of slavery and mastership combined pervades their whole political life like a liquid poison." Schurz compared the enslaved South to the kingdom of Naples; both were governments organized around "a social institution which is in antagonism with the principles of democratic government." At times, Seward could be even more explicit about the relationship between slavery and democracy. "Emancipation," he declared in 1850, "is a democratic revolution."[27]

This critique of slavery as oligarchic tyranny both drew on and outstripped an older seventeenth- and eighteenth-century rhetoric of republicanism.[28] By the 1850s, American antislavery leaders did not merely counterpose liberty and power, virtue and corruption, or the court and the commonwealth: they spoke the language of nineteenth-century political economy, in which "labor" vied with "capital" and popular government meant nothing less than "democracy" itself. American freedom, Seward avowed, can only be preserved "by maintaining the democratic system of government. There is no other name given under heaven by which, in this generation, nations can be saved from desolation and ruin, than democracy. This, to many conservative ears, would seem a strange proposition; and yet it is so simple." Nor was this vision confined simply to the United States. The European revolutions of 1848 had been suppressed, but Republicans cheered the partial and erratic moves toward popular government in Britain and France, while noting that Germany and Italy still demanded "the principle of universal suffrage." Seward, a warm advocate of the Hungarian revolutionary Lajos Kossuth, confidently predicted that all Europe would soon become "democratic," while imagining the birth of "future republics on the islands and continents on the Pacific Ocean, and on the heretofore neglected coasts of Africa." The "supreme law" of world history, he avowed, "is necessarily based on the equality of nations, of races, and of men."[29]

To be sure, most Republicans were not true racial egalitarians, either inside or outside the borders of the United States. Some opposed even basic civil rights for African Americans; others toyed with the idea of the federal government encouraging emancipated slaves to resettle in Africa or Latin America. Even Seward, never a real advocate of such colonization schemes, asserted that Black and Native Americans, due to "their peculiar condition," constituted "inferior masses," incapable of easy assimilation within the United States. In foreign affairs, amid an 1856 Anglo-American dispute over Central America, Seward cited "the universal custom of European and American States," which asserted that "savage tribes . . . have no actual or high sovereignty." Yet the terms of this Republican racial hierarchy—governed by geographic circumstance and contingent social condition—departed from the fixed ladder of color and blood conjured by proslavery leaders. "Philosophy," Seward informed the Senate, "meekly expresses her distrust of the asserted natural superiority of the white race." Euro-Americans may have been justified in asserting their economic and political power over the rest of the world, but that justification lay in their superior institutions, not their superior genealogy.[30]

For the Indigenous peoples of the Great Plains or Central America, this was often an imperial distinction without a difference. But it mattered a great deal to Black leaders in the United States, many of whom also spoke in the language of global free labor and democratic progress. Frederick Douglass, for all his sarcasms about "monarchical liberty," consistently defended the principle of true popular sovereignty. The "assertion of the wickedness of the masses," he declared, belonged to the "kings and despots" of Europe; his preference was for a "righteous democratic government" of "the whole people."[31] Although Douglass frequently criticized the limits of the Republican platform, he and other Black abolitionists saw the party's rise as evidence that American democracy did not make slavery powerful, but vulnerable. As long as "the ballot-box is open to the people of the sixteen free States," he argued in 1857, "while the slaveholders are but four hundred thousand in number, and we are fourteen millions . . . we are really the strong and they are the weak." Lincoln's election in 1860, Douglass later declared, proved "the masses at the North (the power behind the throne) had determined to take and keep this Government out of the hands of the slave-holding oligarchy, and to administer it hereafter to the advantage of free labor against slave labor." For Douglass, no less than for Seward, the triumph of American antislavery politics was the triumph of both free labor and popular democracy.[32]

How did this American antislavery ideology actually shape U.S. foreign policy? In the 1850s, with slaveholders and their allies in power in Washington, D.C., Republicans practiced the politics of opposition, working with varying effectiveness to block southern-led plans for military and diplomatic expansion in the Caribbean. In Congress, the press, and on the campaign trail, their specialty was the blistering rebuke of proslavery imperialism. "In the eyes of all civilized peoples," said Ohio's James Ashley in 1856, "we are, to-day, regarded as a nation of liars and hypocrites . . . with the avowed purpose of reducing to slavery all the weak and defenseless who can labor, whether Africans, South Sea Islanders, Chinese Coolies, Indians, or white men."[33]

Yet after Lincoln entered the White House, the prospects for a tangible foreign policy of antislavery became real. And in the mind and the person of William Seward, secretary of state from 1861 to 1869, the antebellum Republican celebration of global free labor and democracy eventually left a deep imprint in Washington and across the world. For many historians, the course of late-nineteenth- and even twentieth-century U.S. foreign policy—its emphasis on economic rather than territorial expansion, its embrace of "democratic imperialism"—flowed, more or less directly, from the free labor ideology of the antebellum Republicans, Seward most of all. From this perspective, the ideological struggle against American slavery evolved alongside a sharpened sense of national power, an ever-expanding search for global markets, a hardening view of racial difference, and a new-found belief in imperial destiny.[34]

But treatments of late-nineteenth-century foreign relations often fail to reckon fully with by far the most consequential U.S. foreign policy initiative of the 1860s: the revolutionary war of emancipation waged against the Confederate States of America. By fleeing the Union, Frederick Douglass observed in 1861, slaveholders "invited armed abolition to march to the deliverance of the slave." The Civil War quickly ripened into a relentless war on the Confederate master class; it ended with federal troops, including two hundred thousand former slaves, enforcing the uncompensated expropriation of $3 billion in antebellum American property. This too was a kind of "democratic imperialism," but of a rather different character than anything in the British imperial experience. From the perspective of Richmond or Atlanta, Lincoln hardly made good on his 1860 pledge to make "no war against capital": in fact, he presided over perhaps the single largest seizure of private capital in world history to date. As slaveholders had understood all along, the populist rhetoric of Republicans on the campaign trail—in which the power of government could be turned against the depredations of a vicious "property class"—offered a far more realistic preview of free labor ideology in action.[35]

If wartime emancipation itself, as Seward had promised, was a "democratic revolution," then the era of Reconstruction offered an even more vivid demonstration of the Republican commitment to popular government. In the years after 1865, as part of their effort to reorganize the conquered Confederacy, Republicans collaborated with freed people in an unprecedented struggle to expand democracy. The American antislavery commitment to popular self-determination—Douglass's vision of a "righteous democratic government" of "the whole people"—framed this project from the start. Although Reconstruction ultimately fell far short of this aim, its attempt to reengineer southern society, incorporate ex-slaves into national politics, and rewrite the federal Constitution amounted to a democratic revolution with few parallels in the global history of emancipation: "the finest effort to achieve democracy for the working millions," concluded W. E. B. Du Bois, "which this world had ever seen."[36]

These epochal transformations are seldom included in the scholarly literature on ideology and U.S. foreign policy, except perhaps as domestic disturbances that produced a midcentury American "paralysis."[37] But there is a case to be made that both the war and the reconstruction of the former Confederacy should be understood as episodes in international relations. And although Seward himself did not lead the drive for emancipation or Radical Reconstruction, it may be that the popular ideology he enunciated before the war, with its aggressive commitment to free labor and democracy—both at home and abroad—played a significant role in the distinctive violence and radicalism of slavery's end in the United States. Indeed, the particular conditions under which American antislavery developed in the 1850s—as a mass partisan politics, enlisting "the rank and file of the North" in a struggle against an aristocratic Slave Power—can help explain the particular course of American emancipation in the 1860s. If the Civil

War was ultimately a "people's contest," as Lincoln described it, it became that way in part because antislavery, in the United States, had become a people's movement.

Notes

1. Kinley Brauer, "The Great American Desert Revisited: Recent Literature and Prospects for the Study of American Foreign Relations," *Diplomatic History* 13, no. 3 (Summer 1989): 395–417; Michael Hunt, *Ideology and U.S. Foreign Policy* (New Haven, CT: Yale University Press, 1987).
2. Among many works, see Gerald Horne, *The Deepest South: The United States, Brazil, and the African Slave Trade* (New York: New York University Press, 2007); Matthew Pratt Guterl, *American Mediterranean: Southern Slaveholders in the Age of Emancipation* (Cambridge, MA: Harvard University Press, 2008); Robert E. Bonner, *Mastering America: Southern Slaveholders and the Crisis of American Nationhood* (New York: Cambridge University Press, 2009); Matthew Karp, *This Vast Southern Empire: Slaveholders at the Helm of American Foreign Policy* (Cambridge, MA: Harvard University Press, 2016).
3. Don E. Fehrenbacher, *The Slaveholding Republic: An Account of the United States Government's Relations to Slavery* (New York: Oxford University Press, 2001).
4. On American abolitionists and international politics, see Manisha Sinha, *The Slave's Cause: A History of Abolition* (New Haven, CT: Yale University Press, 2016), 97–129, 339–80; Edward Crapol, "The Foreign Policy of Antislavery, 1833–1846," in *Redefining the Past: Essays in Diplomatic History in Honor of William Appleman Williams*, ed. Lloyd C. Gardner (Corvallis: Oregon State University Press, 1986), 85–103; Marc-William Palen, "Free Trade Ideology and Transatlantic Abolitionism: A Historiography," *Journal of the History of Economic Thought* 37, no. 2 (June 2015): 291–304.
5. On antislavery, capitalism, and empire generally, see Eric Williams, *Capitalism and Slavery* (Chapel Hill: University of North Carolina Press, 1944); David Brion Davis, *The Problem of Slavery in the Age of Revolution, 1770–1823* (Ithaca, NY: Cornell University Press, 1975); Howard Temperley, "Capitalism, Slavery, and Ideology," *Past & Present* 75, no. 1 (May 1977): 94–118; Catherine Hall, *Civilising Subjects: Metropole and Colony in the English Imagination, 1830–1867* (Cambridge: Polity Press, 2002); Christopher L. Brown, *Moral Capital: Foundations of British Abolitionism* (Chapel Hill: University of North Carolina Press, 2006), esp. 314–30; Richard Huzzey, *Freedom Burning: Anti-Slavery and Empire in Victorian Britain* (Ithaca, NY: Cornell University Press, 2012), 132–202; Howard Temperley, *White Dreams, Black Africa: The Antislavery Expedition to the River*

Niger, 1841–1842 (New Haven, CT: Yale University Press, 1991); Lisa Ford, "Anti-Slavery and the Reconstitution of Empire," *Australian Historical Studies* 45, no. 1 (February 2014): 71–86.

6. David Brion Davis, *Inhuman Bondage: The Rise and Fall of Slavery in the New World* (New York: Oxford University Press, 2006), 141–296; Seymour Drescher, *Abolition: A History of Slavery and Antislavery* (New York: Cambridge University Press, 2009), 146–372; Robin Blackburn, *The American Crucible: Slavery, Emancipation and Human Rights* (London: Verso, 2011), 171–390.

7. Frank O'Gornan, "The Electorate Before and After 1832," *Parliamentary History* 12, no. 2 (1993): 171–83. On British abolitionism as mass social movement, see Seymour Drescher, "History's Engines: British Mobilization in the Age of Revolution," *William & Mary Quarterly* 66, no. 4 (October 2009): 737–56.

8. The election of 1860 saw the highest turnout in any U.S. election to date, bringing more than 81 percent of eligible voters to the polls: John P. McIver, "Voter Turnout in Presidential Elections, By State: 1824–2000," *Historical Statistics of the United States, Millennial Edition*, ed. Susan B. Carter and Scott Sigmund Gartner (Cambridge: Cambridge University Press 2006), series Eb62–113.

9. Carl Schurz, "The Doom of Slavery," August 1, 1860, in *Speeches, Correspondence, and Political Papers of Carl Schurz*, vol. 1, ed. Frederic Bancroft (New York: Putnam, 1913), 150; Eric Foner, *Free Soil, Free Labor, and Free Men: The Ideology of the Republican Party Before the Civil War* (1970; repr. New York: Oxford University Press, 1995), esp. 11–72, 301–17.

10. Edward Wade, August 2, 1856, Congressional Globe Appendix, 34th Cong., 1st Sess., 1076–77. On the transformation of free labor democracy in the age of industrial capitalism, see Sven Beckert, *The Monied Metropolis: New York City and the Consolidation of the American Bourgeoisie, 1850–1896* (Cambridge: Cambridge University Press, 2001), 111–236.

11. Charles Sumner, *The Landmark of Freedom: Speech of the Hon. Charles Sumner . . .* (Washington, DC: Buell & Blanchard, 1854), 4.

12. Schurz, "The Doom of Slavery," 137, 149–50; *Cleveland Morning Leader*, August 21, 1856; Abraham Lincoln, "Speech in Milwaukee, September 30, 1859," in *The Collected Works of Abraham Lincoln*, vol. 3, ed. Roy P. Basler (New Brunswick, NJ: Rutgers University Press, 1953), 481.

13. Lincoln, "Speech in Milwaukee," 478–79; Gabor S. Borritt, *Lincoln and the Economics of the American Dream* (Urbana: University of Illinois Press, 1978).

14. William Henry Seward, "The True Basis of American Independence," October 20, 1853, in *The Works of William H. Seward*, vol. 4, ed. George E. Baker (Boston: Houghton Mifflin, 1884) 153–54.

15. Seward, "The True Basis of American Independence," 149–57; Foner, *Free Soil, Free Labor, and Free Men*, 316. On 1850s tariff politics and free labor ideology

in international terms, see Marc-William Palen, *The "Conspiracy" of Free Trade: The Anglo-American Struggle over Empire and Economic Globalization* (Cambridge: Cambridge University Press, 2016), chap. 1; Jay Sexton, *A Nation Forged by Crisis: A New American History* (New York: Basic Books, 2018), 69–79. On Seward, see Glyndon G. Van Deusen, *William Henry Seward* (New York: Oxford University Press, 1967); Walter G. Sharrow, "William Henry Seward and the Basis for American Empire, 1850–1860," *Pacific Historical Review* 36, no. 3 (August 1967): 325–42.

16. Seward, "The Slaveholding Class Dominant in the Republic," October 2, 1856, *Works of Seward*, vol. 4, 254–55, 272; Seward, "The State of the Country," February 29, 1860, *Works of Seward*, vol. 4, 619–43. Political historians have universally depicted this last speech as a tactical embrace of conservative rhetoric, aimed at reassuring moderates of Seward's fitness for the presidential nomination in 1860: see, e.g., David M. Potter, *The Impending Crisis: America Before the Civil War, 1848–1861* (New York: Harper, 1976), 419–20. But for Seward to discuss slavery and freedom in terms of capital and labor was neither especially new nor intrinsically "conservative": see Karl Marx, *Capital*, vol. 1, trans. Ben Fowkes (1867: repr. London: Penguin, 1990), 344–45.

17. Varina Davis, *Jefferson Davis, Ex-President of the Confederate States of America: A Memoir by His Wife*, vol. 1 (New York: Belford, 1890), 579–82; Van Deusen, *William Henry Seward*, 259–61.

18. Stephen Douglas, February 29, 1860, Congressional Globe, 36th Cong., 1st Sess., 915.

19. Madison *Wisconsin State Journal*, August 27, 1860; *Freeport* (Ill.) *Wide Awake*, November 17, 1860, Brown Digital Repository, Brown University Library, https://repository.library.brown.edu/studio/item/bdr:80549/.

20. *Cleveland Morning Leader*, August 8, 1860; *New York Evening Post*, in *Buffalo Weekly Express*, Oct 23, 1860.

21. For the traditional view of free labor as an ideological expression of "laissez-faire" economics and bourgeois capitalism, see William Appleman Williams, *The Contours of American Empire* (1961; repr. London: Verso, 2011), 284–300; Temperley, "Capitalism, Slavery, and Ideology"; John Ashworth, "Free Labor, Wage Labor, and the Slave Power: Republicanism and the Republican Party in the 1850s," in *The Market Revolution in America: Social, Political, and Religious Expressions, 1800–1880*, ed. Melvyn Stokes and Stephen Conway (Charlottesville: University of Virginia Press, 1996), 128–46. For vigorous counterpoints, see James Huston, *The British Gentry, the Southern Planter, and the Northern Family Farmer: Agriculture and Sectional Antagonism in North America* (Baton Rouge: Louisiana State University Press, 2015), xi–xvi, 183–242; Adam Tuchinsky, *Horace Greeley's* New-York Tribune: *Civil War-Era Socialism and the Crisis of Free Labor* (Ithaca, NY: Cornell University Press, 2009).

22. Henry Wilson as quoted in Elias Nason and Thomas Russell, *The Life and Public Services of Henry Wilson* (Boston: B. B. Russell, 1876), 277; Galusha Grow, "Free Homes for Free Men . . ." (Washington, DC: Republican Executive Congressional Committee, 1860); Tuchinsky, *Horace Greeley's New-York Tribune*, 126–64.

23. On British abolitionists and various forms of aristocratic, capitalist, and imperial labor coercion, see Eric Williams, *Capitalism and Slavery* (1944; repr. Chapel Hill: University of North Carolina Press, 1994) 178–96; Blackburn, *American Crucible*, 334–336; Davis, *Problem of Revolution*, 443–96; Huzzey, *Freedom Burning*, 132–76.

24. William Henry Seward, July 2, 1856, Congressional Globe Appendix, 34th Cong., 1st Sess., 791; Seward, "The Irrepressible Conflict," October 25, 1856, in *Works of Seward*, vol. 4, 291.

25. Edmund S. Morgan, "Slavery and Freedom: The American Paradox," *Journal of American History* 59, no. 1 (June 1972): 5–29. For important recent scholarship in this vein, on the deep interrelationship between democratic expansion and racial oppression in the early United States, see Aziz Rana, *The Two Faces of American Freedom* (Cambridge, MA: Harvard University Press, 2010); Nicholas Guyatt, *Bind Us Apart: How Enlightened Americans Invented Racial Segregation* (New York: Basic Books, 2016); Robert G. Parkinson, *The Common Cause: Creating Race and Nation in the American Revolution* (Chapel Hill: University of North Carolina Press, 2017).

26. Frederick Douglass, speech in Ireland, October 23, 1845, in *The Frederick Douglass Papers: Series One—Speeches, Debates, and Interviews*, vol. 1, ed. John Blassingame et al. (New Haven, CT: Yale University Press, 1979), 59.

27. Seward, "Democracy the Chief Element in Government," September 12, 1860, *Works of Seward*, vol. 4, 322; Carl Schurz, "True Americanism," April 18, 1859, in *Speeches, Correspondence, and Political Papers of Carl Schurz*, vol. 1, ed. Frederic Bancroft (New York: Putnam, 1913), 59–60; Schurz, "Doom of Slavery," 126; Seward, *Speech of William H. Seward on the Admission of California* (Washington: Buell and Blanchard, 1850), 42. On Republican antislavery and European democratic revolutions, see Andre Fleche, *The Revolution of 1861: The American Civil War in the Age of Nationalist Conflict* (Chapel Hill: University of North Carolina Press, 2012), 11–37.

28. On the Republican debt to "republicanism," see especially Michael F. Holt, *The Political Crisis of the 1850s* (New York: Wiley, 1978).

29. Seward, "Democracy the Chief Element," 320–21; Seward, "The Pilgrims and Liberty," December 21, 1855, in *Works of Seward*, vol. 4, 198–99; Seward, "Destiny of America," 127–29; Van Deusen, *William Henry Seward*, 139–40, 200–213.

30. Seward, *Speech . . . on the Admission of California*, 8, 43; William H. Seward, speech in Senate, January 31, 1856, Congressional Globe Appendix, 34th

Cong., 1st Sess., 75–80; on early Republican racial attitudes, see Foner, *Free Soil, Free Labor, and Free Men*, 261–300.

31. Douglass, "Is Civil Government Right?" On Douglass's commitment to popular democracy, see Nicholas Buccola, *The Political Thought of Frederick Douglass: In Pursuit of American Liberty* (New York: NYU Press, 2012), 65–75; on the importance of democracy in radical American abolitionist thought, see W. Caleb McDaniel, *The Problem of Democracy in the Age of Slavery: Garrisonian Abolitionists and Transatlantic Reform* (Baton Rouge: Louisiana State University Press, 2013).

32. Douglass, "The Dred Scott Decision," May 11, 1857, in *Life and Writings of Frederick Douglass*, vol. 2, ed. Philip S. Foner (New York: International, 1950), 415; Douglass, "The Inaugural Address," *Douglass' Monthly*, April 1861; John Mercer Langston, "The World's Anti-Slavery Movement: Its Heroes and Triumphs," August 3, 1858, in *Freedom and Citizenship: Selected Lectures and Addresses of John Mercer Langston* (Washington, DC: Rufus H. Darby, 1883), 41–67. For a more developed version of this argument, see Matthew Karp, "The Mass Politics of Antislavery," *Catalyst* vol. 3, no. 2 (Summer 2019): 131–78.

33. James Ashley, "Speech in Ohio," September 1856, in *Souvenir of the Afro-American League of Tennessee to Hon. James M. Ashley of Ohio*, ed. Benjamin W. Arnett (Philadelphia: Publishing House of the A.M.E. Church, 1894), 613.

34. On Seward and "democratic imperialism," see Sharrow, "William Henry Seward and the Basis for American Empire," 325; Anders Stephenson, *Manifest Destiny: American Expansionism and the Empire of Right* (New York: Hill and Wang, 1996), 58–63; Richard Immerman, *Empire for Liberty: A History of American Imperialism from Benjamin Franklin to Paul Wolfowitz* (Princeton, NJ: Princeton University Press, 2010), 99–126; Robert Kagan, *Dangerous Nation: America's Foreign Policy from Its Earliest Days to the Dawn of the Twentieth Century* (New York: Vintage, 2006), 301–56; Jay Sexton, "William H. Seward in the World," *Journal of the Civil War Era* 4, no. 3 (September 2014): 398–430.

35. Douglass, "Nemesis," *Douglass' Monthly*, May 1861. On the Republican war of emancipation and its cost, see James Oakes, *Freedom National: The Destruction of Slavery in the United States* (New York: Norton, 2012); Thomas Piketty, *Capital in the Twenty-First Century* (Cambridge, MA: Harvard University Press, 2014), 158–63. The generous compensation packages received by British slaveholders form a stark contrast to this history: see Nicholas Draper, *The Price of Emancipation: Slave-Ownership, Compensation and British Society at the End of Slavery* (Cambridge: Cambridge University Press, 2010).

36. W. E. B. Du Bois, *Black Reconstruction in America, 1860–1880* (1935: repr. New York: Free Press, 1998), 727; Peter Kolchin, "Comparative Perspectives on Emancipation in the U.S. South: Reconstruction, Radicalism, and Russia," *Journal of the Civil War Era* 2, no. 2 (June 2012): 203–32.

37. See, for example, Hunt, *Ideology and U.S. Foreign Policy*, 36. But for valuable commentary on the Civil War and global politics, see Sexton, *A Nation Forged by Crisis*, 99–140; David T. Gleeson and Simon Lewis, eds., *The Civil War as Global Conflict* (Columbia: University of South Carolina Press, 2014); Sven Beckert, *Empire of Cotton; A Global History* (New York: Knopf, 2014), 242–311; Don H. Doyle, *The Cause of All Nations: An International History of the American Civil War* (New York: Basic Books, 2015).

CHAPTER 8

The Fearful Giant

National Insecurity and U.S Foreign Policy

ANDREW PRESTON

Tensions on the Korean peninsula are perennially on edge. Ever since the outbreak of the Korean War in 1950, the North and South have been locked in an existential struggle over who will determine the fate of the Korean people. North Korea has been especially provocative, most notably in January 1968 when its special forces stormed the Blue House, South Korea's presidential palace, and attempted to assassinate President Park Chung-hee; two days later, it seized the USS *Pueblo*, a U.S. Navy intelligence vessel, and held its eighty-three crew members captive for several months. A year after that, a North Korean fighter jet shot down a U.S. reconnaissance plane, killing all thirty-one personnel aboard. Since then, North Korea has bombed a Korean Air Lines passenger jet (killing 115 civilians), sunk a South Korean warship, and covertly developed a nuclear weapons program.[1]

Despite all these incidents, however, North Korea and the United States were probably never closer to going to war than they were in the spring and summer of 2017.[2] The reason for the sudden escalation in tensions was simple: after several years of nuclear weapons testing, in 2017 North Korea made unexpectedly rapid progress in developing an intercontinental ballistic missile that was capable of both carrying a nuclear warhead and reaching the United States. Roger Cohen, a *New York Times* columnist not normally known for his bellicosity, argued that North Korea was "working furiously" to develop technology "that would enable it to fire a nuclear-tipped intercontinental ballistic missile at Los Angeles. To put that in perspective, a 33 year-old tyrant who specializes in macabre family executions would hold a gun to America's head. Santa Monica would never feel quite the same." Despite the extreme unlikelihood of such a calamity actually occurring, Cohen declared this "unacceptable." Christopher Hill, a former ambassador to South Korea, concurred: "We can't live with that country pointing nukes at us."[3] Calls for preventive military action against North Korea, including regime change in Pyongyang, that had been circulating among foreign policy analysts since at least 2013 intensified during the crisis of 2017.[4]

Leaders of both countries stoked tensions further. U.S. President Donald Trump and North Korean Supreme Leader Kim Jong-un traded insults and threats while their militaries readied for battle. In April, Trump predicted that a "major, major conflict" with North Korea was possible and later declared that the U.S. military was "locked and loaded."[5] In August, he warned that "North Korea best not make any more threats to the United States. They will be met with fire and fury like the world has never seen."[6] Those close to the president chimed in. Senator Lindsey Graham told NBC's *Today* program that the United States could not tolerate North Korea possessing a weapon that could "hit America." Graham partly justified preventive military action because it would mean war would occur in Korea, not the United States. "If there's going to be a war to stop [Kim Jong-un], it will be over there," he explained. "If thousands die, they're going to die over there. They're not going to die here." When pressed over whether a military strike would be effective, Graham responded that it would be: "There is a military option to destroy North Korea's program and North Korea itself."[7] National Security Advisor H. R. McMaster claimed the United States had the right to launch a "war that would prevent North Korea from threatening the United States with a nuclear weapon."[8] John Bolton, who would soon replace McMaster, said that the "way to end North Korea's nuclear weapons program is to end North Korea."[9] U.S. ambassador Nikki Haley called a special session of the United Nations Security Council and leveled the remarkably undiplomatic charge that North Korea was "begging for war."[10] War-gaming for a preventive strike, which had been "accelerated" in the spring, proceeded apace throughout August and into September.[11] Polling showed that a solid majority of Americans supported the Trump administration's tough stance even if it would lead to armed conflict.[12]

South Koreans would presumably have the most to fear. They had been living next door to an unpredictable, volatile North Korea for decades, and they would of course bear the brunt of a second Korean war. It was widely predicted that Seoul, which was close to the border and well within range of thousands of pieces of North Korean heavy artillery, would be devastated soon after the outbreak of hostilities. As Stratfor reported, even if North Korea held much of its artillery fire in reserve, and even if much of its artillery was not all that advanced, it could still inflict catastrophic damage on South Korea's capital.[13] And, of course, North Korea was already able to use nuclear weapons against its southern neighbor.[14] South Koreans certainly realized their peril. As one woman in Seoul told an American reporter, "her elderly mother had begun stockpiling bottled water in a corner of their apartment. 'I don't have the heart to tell her: This is not the war you remember anymore. If the worst happens, we're just gone. Wiped out. We're not going to be worrying about staying hydrated.'"[15]

Yet South Koreans viewed the crisis rather differently from Americans. In the spring of 2017, the reaction in Seoul was much more measured and far less fearful than the reaction in Washington; according to one poll, 58 percent of South Koreans did not believe North Korea would ever initiate an attack.[16] Indeed, South Koreans' fears seemed to be more aggravated by the rhetoric of their ally, the United States, than by their adversary, North Korea, and they urged leaders in Washington, notably President Trump, not to inflame an already sensitive situation.[17] Choe Sang-Hun, a South Korean reporter for the New York Times, noted that as Americans girded themselves for war South Koreans reacted with "a shrug . . . a prevailing calm, even a nonchalance." His experience of living in Seoul as an American journalist was surreal: "I feel as if I am living in two different realities," a Korean one that was calm and an American one that had slipped into full-blown panic mode.[18]

What explains this paradox? Americans, who lived far from the danger and had the ability to respond overwhelmingly to any North Korean attack, seemed more fearful of the situation than South Koreans, who had already faced an existential threat from North Korea for decades. In the highly unlikely event North Korea decided to use its entire arsenal to launch a nuclear strike against California, the United States would be able to respond immediately, with a small fraction of its arsenal, in a manner that would lay waste to North Korea and definitively end the Kim regime. Santa Monica might never be the same, but North Korea would cease to exist. So why would a country as powerful as the United States—more powerful, in both absolute and relative terms, than virtually any other state in world history—be so concerned about a country as impoverished as North Korea?

The answer, I suggest, is an inordinate prevalence of fear that sits at the heart of the American worldview and provides the basis for thinking about U.S. foreign policy. This is not to say that such fears are inherently either beneficial or harmful, warranted or unfounded—they may be irrational overreactions to minimal threats or prudent assessments of real dangers. Perhaps Trump and his national security officials were thoroughly justified in their view that North Korea presented a clear and present danger; perhaps not. In this chapter, I examine fear as a source of American insecurity, but I do not seek to judge U.S. foreign policy one way or another. I call attention to the fear factor that scholars have alternatively ignored, taken for granted as natural, or fetishized as artificial and manufactured. Americans seem to have intense fears about the wider world, and those fears are an integral part of U.S. foreign policy. In this chapter, I seek to understand why.

Fear, Culture, and Ideology

It is uncertain whether fear should be classed as an ideology because fear itself is an instinct, and not necessarily programmatic, conceptual, or visionary. As theorists from Thomas Hobbes to Judith Shklar have pointed out, fear is distinct in being so elemental, even primal, while also being the wellspring of sophisticated political thought. This facet of culture and emotion has suffused American political culture, and it has evolved in ways that exaggerate risk and foster insecurity. As William Reddy, a historian of the emotions, points out, "fear brings excitement, rapid thinking, a readiness for action."[19] This is highly ironic because fear provides the basic motivation for policies designed to enhance security even as those very policies end up further stimulating feelings of insecurity. If security regimes are shaped by ideological priorities and objectives, the fear that underpins them is driven more by various cultural assumptions about the world. Recognizing and comprehending those fears, and appreciating the history of emotions that runs through U.S. foreign relations but has only recently been excavated, will in turn help us come to a better understanding of U.S. foreign policy.[20]

Ideas help provide the foundations for U.S. foreign policy, but so too do emotions, even (especially) those emotions that seem grounded in fact. Fear falls into this category. This simple point is worth considering in more detail because much of the literature on the United States and the world from the last three decades takes Michael Hunt's *Ideology and U.S. Foreign Policy* as a conceptual starting point. Yet what if Hunt's book is actually more an analysis of culture than of ideology? Even if both terms—"culture" and "ideology"—are notoriously difficult to define, Hunt's examination of exceptionalism, race, and revolution would seem to owe more to the anthropology of culture than to the sociology of ideas. Perhaps tellingly, from the outset of his book, Hunt alternates between referring to "cultural values" and "policy ideas."[21] This is probably because he based much of his own approach on the cultural/ideological theories of Clifford Geertz, who famously perceived of "ideology as a cultural system," which in turn led him to elide the distinction between cultural behavior and social action, emotions and ideas.[22] Hunt's capaciousness is, to be sure, almost certainly the more fruitful approach. But it's worth considering in more depth here because it has been ignored by most historians who examine fear. Instead, much of the recent literature on fear in American politics, culture, and society—perhaps working under the influence of long-standing suspicions about McCarthyism, a period David Caute memorably called "the great fear"[23]—portrays fear in starkly ideological terms by positing it as a political construct used by elites for the purposes of legitimating their political dominance, economic advantage, and social control.[24]

I offer a somewhat different perspective. I take as a given the sincerity of fears as expressed by policy makers at key moments in the Cold War and use them to theorize more generally about the sources of American conduct.

Fear Itself

Fear, and a resultant sense of insecurity, have long been a presence in American political culture; it is one of the most powerful forces binding Americans together as an "emotional community."[25] Fears of domestic subversives have run high throughout U.S. history, often about gender, race, and religion that mixed in highly combustible ways: white fears of rebellious slaves, supposedly savage Indians, and allegedly criminal African Americans after 1865; Protestant fears of conspiratorial Catholics and Jews; middle-class fears of moral degradation from alcoholism, drug abuse, and sexual depravity. It's clear that these centuries-old domestic fears have not gone away. In foreign policy, by contrast, the predominance of fear is relatively recent, a product of the era since World War II. Americans almost never spoke of "security" as an objective of foreign or military policy before the late 1930s, a curious fact that in turn reveals an inverse truth: Americans rarely felt a sense of insecurity in the world.[26]

This is because, until 1941, the United States benefited from a freak of geopolitical good fortune that scholars call "free security."[27] This term is contentious because it is often mistakenly assumed to mean that Americans enjoyed *total* or *perfect* security before World War II, when of course they did not.[28] There were threats to U.S. security, and particular groups of Americans at particular moments feared for their safety: western states and territories on the nation's expansionist edge feared Indian raids, for example, and southern planters feared abolitionist Britain's Royal Navy.[29] Free security simply means that, for a long period of history, Americans could assume they would not be invaded or occupied. I would delineate the era of free security as between 1815 and 1941, although other end points are plausible (an earlier origin date is not plausible given that the period between independence and the War of 1812 was a time of constant threat). Beginning sometime after the War of 1812, Americans could take the basic integrity of their national sovereignty for granted. In modern world history, this was not just an unusual situation but a unique one. It was not just a product of fortunate geography either: U.S. neighbors Canada and Mexico could not make similar claims to free security, not least because they were frequently threatened and invaded by the United States itself.

Americans at the time appreciated their advantage, and in their relations with foreign nations they more often spoke optimistically of their power rather than pessimistically of their fears. "Shall we expect some transatlantic military giant, to step the Ocean, and crush us at a blow?" Abraham Lincoln rhetorically asked in 1838. "Never!—All the armies of Europe, Asia and Africa combined, with all the treasure of the earth (our own excepted) in their military chest; with a Buonaparte for a commander, could not by force, take a drink from the Ohio, or make a track on the Blue Ridge, in a trial of a thousand years."[30] Sixty years later, secretary of state Richard Olney was no less brash during a standoff with Great Britain, the only power with a navy that could do significant damage to the United States. "To-day," Olney declared, "the United States is practically sovereign on this continent, and its fiat is law upon the subjects to which it confines its interposition." U.S. hegemony in the region was not due to the "pure friendship or good will" felt by its neighbors, nor to its "high character as a civilized state. It is because," he explained, "its infinite resources combined with its isolated position render it master of the situation and practically invulnerable as against any or all other powers."[31]

Scholars have in part attributed a range of phenomena, for example, America's colossal industrial revolution, to free security.[32] Michael Hunt himself argued that it enabled the ideological consistency he detected in U.S. foreign policy to initially emerge and subsequently flourish.[33] But what free security also did was lead Americans to assume they would always be that secure. However, by the middle of the twentieth century, it was clear that as U.S. power grew free security vanished. And thus was created a paradox that continues, as recently seen on the Korean peninsula, to shape U.S. foreign policy: with great power comes great fear.

This is another way in which fear does not conform to Hunt's ideological typology: unlike republicanism, race, and revolution, fear has not been a consistent presence in U.S. foreign policy. The heady mix of great power and chronic fear was a product of the Great Depression, when economic collapse at home and abroad triggered a global political crisis and the rise of fascism, Nazism, and authoritarianism in Europe and Asia.[34] At home, President Franklin D. Roosevelt constructed the New Deal to overcome economic insecurity: his response was exemplified by Social Security, a program designed to take care of citizens in their time of need, such as in old age or unemployment. In foreign affairs, after 1937 FDR began positioning the United States as the democratic bulwark of last resort, an "arsenal of democracy" embodied in what I call the "national security revolution."[35]

The main obstacle to this revolution was the fact that, in the late 1930s, most Americans had no interest in joining FDR on a global crusade. Despite the growing power of Nazi Germany, fascist Italy, and imperial Japan, Americans resisted the call to become more involved in the world crisis mostly because they did not feel threatened by these revisionist and expansionist powers, however objectionable they might be. As the historian John A. Thompson has shown, Roosevelt and other like-minded interventionists responded by grossly exaggerating the scale of U.S. vulnerability—that is, by raising new fears that the United States could no longer assume it had free security, that Americans were now vulnerable to physical attack and ideological subversion, and that they had to either go on the offensive and resist these new threats or eventually succumb to them entirely.[36] As Roosevelt put it in June 1940, in a speech at the University of Virginia that signaled the reversal of a century of American self-perception, the United States could no longer stand as "a lone island in a world dominated by the philosophy of force."[37]

With Great Power Comes Great Fear

After Pearl Harbor, the United States fought to prevent a world dominated by force from succeeding. When World War II ended, that goal seemed to have been achieved. The United States was not only the world's dominant military power and its leading economic power by some distance (as the only country to prosper from the war), it was also the only major belligerent to have suffered virtually no physical damage to its home nation/metropole. Only Britain had also avoided invasion and occupation, but the British suffered tremendous damage from heavy bombing (consider that more Britons died on their home soil from German bombing than U.S. military personnel died fighting in Korea or Vietnam). The United States had a monopoly of nuclear weapons and had demonstrated their awesome destructive power against Japan. If any nation could feel secure, it was the United States after World War II.

Yet as numerous historians have shown, Americans felt a great sense of fear in the decade following the end of the world war. Despite their overwhelming advantages (military, economic, geographic), insecurity pervaded U.S. perceptions of the wider world. It was in fact Americans' very security that made them feel insecure because it was a rare thing in a world devastated by the most destructive war in history. Preserving that security became the overriding objective. The United States, as we have seen, had possessed this level of security for well over a century, but after 1941 security no longer seemed to be free: preserving it would require tremendous effort, funds, and vigilance. Circumstances were ideal for creating a highly insecure foreign policy that expressed much less willingness to tolerate the kinds of perennial threats other states had to contend with on a constant basis.

Accentuating this heightened threat perception was the fact that U.S. policy makers now considered their parameters for self-defense on a much grander scale. As Melvyn Leffler has shown, policy makers in the Truman administration believed they needed to secure American safety and prosperity against global threats. Doing so required them to use America's "preponderance of power" to establish a system, initially in Europe and then in Asia, conducive to U.S. interests. It is crucial to remember Leffler's point that the imposition of American preponderance was largely motivated not by confidence or optimism but by fear and alarmism.[38]

Moreover, on such a vast terrain, the chances for threats to emerge were virtually limitless. Strength, indeed supreme strength, ironically made

Americans feel more vulnerable because maintaining supremacy became an end in itself. In this culture of fear, ideology became conflated with physical safety, so that protecting the "American way of life"—not coincidentally, a recent phrase from the New Deal era[39]—against all enemies in an interconnected world became the ultimate if never-quite attainable goal of U.S. foreign policy. By this point, Americans' tolerance for acceptable risk was close to zero, its military capabilities were powerful and easy to project globally, and its economic resources were vast. It was this combination that led to the panic over the Chinese Revolution in 1949, even though President Truman and Secretary of State Dean Acheson themselves were not that concerned. In 1950, it similarly led to the surprising intervention in a region, the Korean peninsula, that until then was peripheral to U.S. interests and that Acheson himself had seemed to exclude from America's sphere of influence in his infamous National Press Club speech that January.

With its tendencies toward zero-sum thinking, the Cold War deeply embedded the circular logic of security-through-supremacy in the American worldview. But instead of real security, or even a sense of security, the "national security revolution" triggered an endless series of nightmares about potential enemies who may have appeared to be small and distant but could theoretically inflict grievous harm on the United States. This worldview gave rise to the conceptual Cold War, driven by metaphor and analogy precisely because the threats themselves were logical but, in reality, unlikely. Only under the influence of something like the domino theory could Americans see the Vietnamese communists—who lived more than eight thousand miles away, represented only one half of one of the world's poorest countries, and lacked the ability to project power beyond Indochina—as any kind of a threat to the United States.[40]

In Cuba, the American fear factor, and the intolerance for even small risks, led to the most dangerous crisis of the Cold War. The story of the 1962 missile crisis is familiar,[41] but what is important to remember is that Kennedy and his advisors found the mere presence of the missiles in Cuba to be unacceptable even though, as JFK argued to one of his more hawkish advisors who was calling for a strike against the Soviet missile sites followed by an invasion of Cuba, "it doesn't make any difference if you get blown up by an ICBM flying from the Soviet Union or one that was ninety miles away. Geography doesn't mean that much." After some further debate, Kennedy pressed his point again: "What difference does it make? They've got enough to blow us up now anyway."[42] Nonetheless, some even advised

Kennedy to launch an invasion on the basis that it was a justifiable act of self-defense[43]—despite the fact that the United States was not attacked and was not being threatened with attack.

This marked a sharp break with how most other states perceived threat during the Cold War for the simple reason that most other states did live beside hostile nuclear weapons. Perhaps because he was Kennedy's ambassador to the United Nations, and therefore spent much of his time surrounded by foreign perspectives, Adlai Stevenson argued that a U.S. invasion of Cuba would be condemned internationally if the justification was to remove the missiles. "While the explanation of our action may be clear to us it won't be clear to many others," Stevenson wrote in a private letter to JFK. "Unless the issue is very clear there may be sharp differences with our Western Allies who have lived so long under the same threat of Soviet attack from bases in the satellite countries by the same IRBMs [intermediate-range ballistic missiles]."[44] Stevenson's point wasn't based on idle speculation or grand theorizing: the Soviets themselves had been surrounded by American nuclear missiles based in Europe, and before that they had been vulnerable to U.S. air power. Even America's closest allies had to strain to see things from Washington's alarmist perspective. At the height of the crisis, for instance, British prime minister Harold Macmillan pointedly told Kennedy that "many of us in Europe have lived so long in close proximity to the enemy's nuclear weapons of the most devastating kind that we have got accustomed to it."[45] It's no surprise that the crisis ended when Kennedy agreed to remove U.S. Jupiter missiles in Turkey in exchange for the removal of the Soviet missiles in Cuba. In the end, though, the Cuban missile crisis was resolved due to the power of fear—this time, Kennedy's and Khrushchev's shared fears of nuclear war.

Strong fears, elevated threat perception, and a low tolerance for risk all combine to powerful effect in the conduct of modern U.S. foreign policy—so powerful, perhaps, that the fear factor may now be embedded at the very heart of America's identity. As one astute observer of U.S. foreign relations has argued, "America needs enemies and would be lost in its identity without them."[46] But this is probably overstating things. This chapter has instead argued that structural and ideological factors combine to make American threat perception unusually high and American threat tolerance exceedingly low. It's not impossible to see this baseline fear receding if international circumstances change over time, but the change would have to be dramatic and fundamental.

For the foreseeable future, at least, whenever the United States feels a global shock, Americans are likely to elevate their threat perception out of proportion to the severity of the threat—especially when the shock is traumatic and the resultant fear real and understandable. Recent history is a guide. The 9/11 attacks spurred the George W. Bush administration into a disastrous invasion of Iraq, and even though the war itself was planned with incompetence and justified by a dubious rationale and little evidence, that doesn't negate the very intense and sincerely held fears Bush and his advisors felt for the safety of the United States.[47] That those fears were overblown, exacerbated by power and hubris, only supports the overall point that the American propensity for an exaggerated sense of insecurity is systemic and enduring.

This returns us to the Korean peninsula, where the potential for conflict remains as high as it ever has been. In words that provided a front-page headline in the *New York Times*, Robert S. Litwak, a nuclear weapons expert and North Korea watcher at the Woodrow Wilson International Center for Scholars, likened the ongoing standoff to "the Cuban missile crisis in slow motion."[48] This analogy is apt for more reasons than Litwak intended; there is certainly the presence of dangerous weapons and aggressive rhetoric on both sides, but there is also an alarmism coursing through the United States that is not found in South Korea. South Koreans have instead normalized the fear because it is in response to a threat that is real and immediate.[49] Americans have yet to normalize their fear, however, because it is mostly in response to a threat that is abstract and distant. Or perhaps the inverse is true: Americans *have* normalized their fear, in the sense that heightened threat perception is the default condition. Extreme worst-case scenarios are assumed to be the most likely outcome—"we don't want the smoking gun to be a mushroom cloud," as Condoleezza Rice infamously put it during the run-up to the invasion of Iraq.[50] Either way, it's clear that our current era is hardly uniquely fearful. When it comes to foreign affairs, every era since World War II has been "defined by fear."[51]

Notes

1. For a superb history of bilateral Korean tensions, see Sheila Miyoshi Jager, *Brothers at War: The Unending Conflict in Korea* (New York: Norton, 2013).
2. On how this unfolded, see Van Jackson, *On the Brink: Trump, Kim, and the Threat of Nuclear War* (New York: Cambridge University Press, 2019).

3. Roger Cohen, "Making Kim Jong-un Sweat," *New York Times*, August 25, 2017, https://www.nytimes.com/2017/08/25/opinion/trump-kim-jong-un-north-korea.html.

4. For a preventive military strike, see Jeremi Suri, "Bomb North Korea, Before It's Too Late," *New York Times*, April 12, 2013, https://www.nytimes.com/2013/04/13/opinion/bomb-north-korea-before-its-too-late.html; and Edward Luttwak, "It's Time to Bomb North Korea," *Foreign Policy*, January 8, 2018, https://foreignpolicy.com/2018/01/08/its-time-to-bomb-north-korea/. For regime change, see Bret Stephens, "On North Korea, Trump's on the Right Track," *New York Times*, July 7, 2017, https://www.nytimes.com/2017/07/07/opinion/on-north-korea-trumps-on-the-right-track.html.

5. Gerry Mullany, "Trump Warns That 'Major, Major Conflict' with North Korea Is Possible," *New York Times*, April 27, 2017, https://www.nytimes.com/2017/04/27/world/asia/trump-north-korea-kim-jong-un.html; Peter Baker, "Trump Says Military Is 'Locked and Loaded' and North Korea Will 'Regret' Threats," *New York Times*, August 11, 2017, https://www.nytimes.com/2017/08/11/world/asia/trump-north-korea-locked-and-loaded.html.

6. Donald J. Trump, "Remarks Prior to a Briefing on the Opioid Crisis and an Exchange With Reporters in Bedminster, New Jersey," American Presidency Project, August 8, 2017, https://www.presidency.ucsb.edu/node/330849.

7. "Sen. Lindsey Graham: Trump Says War with North Korea an Option," NBC News, August 1, 2017, https://www.nbcnews.com/news/north-korea/sen-lindsey-graham-trump-says-war-north-korea-option-n788396.

8. Jason Le Miere, "U.S. Prepared to Launch 'Preventive War' Against North Korea, Says H. R. McMaster," *Newsweek*, August 5, 2017, https://www.newsweek.com/us-north-korea-war-mcmaster-646942.

9. Max Fisher, "The North Korea Paradox: Why There Are No Good Options on Nuclear Arms," *New York Times*, April 17, 2017, https://www.nytimes.com/2017/04/17/world/asia/north-korea-nuclear-weapons-missiles-sanctions.html.

10. David Smith, "North Korea 'Begging for War' Says US, Calling for Strongest Possible Sanctions," *Guardian*, September 4, 2017, https://www.theguardian.com/world/2017/sep/04/north-korea-nikki-haley-sanctions-nuclear-test-begging-for-war.

11. William M. Arkin, Cynthia McFadden, Kevin Monahan, and Robert Windrem, "Trump's Options for North Korea Include Placing Nukes in South Korea," NBC News, April 7, 2017, https://www.nbcnews.com/news/us-news/trump-s-options-north-korea-include-placing-nukes-south-korea-n743571; David Sanger, "Talk of 'Preventive War' Rises in White House over North Korea," *New York Times*, August 20, 2017, https://www.nytimes.com/2017/08/20/world/asia/north-korea-war-trump.html.

12. Lydia Saad, "More Back U.S. Military Action vs. North Korea Than in 2003," Gallup, September 15, 2017, https://news.gallup.com/poll/219134/back-military -action-north-korea-2003.aspx.

13. "How North Korea Would Retaliate," Stratfor, January 5, 2017, https://worldview .stratfor.com/article/how-north-korea-would-retaliate.

14. Rob Crilly, "North Korea 'Could Kill Almost Four Million People in Seoul and Tokyo with Retaliatory Nuclear Attack,'" *Daily Telegraph*, October 6, 2017, https://www.telegraph.co.uk/news/2017/10/06/north-korea-could-kill -almost-four-million-people-seoul-tokyo/.

15. Maya West, "Brit-Pop for a Nuclear Standoff," *New York Times*, August 26, 2017, https://www.nytimes.com/2017/08/26/opinion/sunday/brit-pop-for -a-nuclear-standoff.html.

16. "Most South Koreans Doubt the North Will Start a War: Poll," *Reuters*, September 8, 2017, https://www.reuters.com/article/us-northkorea-missiles -southkorea-poll/most-south-koreans-doubt-the-north-will-start-a-war-poll -idUSKCN1BJ0HF.

17. Choe Sang-Hun, "South Korea's Leader Bluntly Warns U.S. Against Striking North," *New York Times*, August 15, 2017, https://www.nytimes.com /2017/08/15/world/asia/south-korea-moon-jae-in-trump.html; Choe Sang-Hun, "Allies for 67 Years, U.S. and South Korea Split over North Korea," *New York Times*, September 4, 2017, https://www.nytimes.com/2017/09/04/world /asia/north-korea-nuclear-south-us-alliance.html.

18. Choe Sang-Hun, "North Korea Threatens; South Shrugs," *New York Times*, August 17, 2017, A2. See also Motoko Rich, "Worry About War? 'I Am Too Busy,' South Koreans Say," *New York Times*, April 27, 2017, https://www .nytimes.com/2017/04/27/world/asia/north-korea-south-tensions.html.

19. William M. Reddy, *The Navigation of Feeling: A Framework for the History of Emotions* (Cambridge: Cambridge University Press, 2001), 3.

20. Much of that excavation work has been done by Frank Costigliola, whose publications on the subject are too numerous to list here. But for a clear and concise overview, see Frank Costigliola, "Reading for Emotion," in *Explaining the History of American Foreign Relations*, 3rd ed., ed. Frank Costigliola and Michael J. Hogan (New York: Cambridge University Press, 2016), 356–74. International relations theorists have also recently begun paying attention to a range of emotions. See, for example, Todd H. Hall, *Emotional Diplomacy: Official Emotion on the International Stage* (Ithaca, NY: Cornell University Press, 2015); and Steven Ward, *Status and the Challenge of Rising Powers* (New York: Cambridge University Press, 2017).

21. Michael H. Hunt, *Ideology and U.S. Foreign Policy* (New Haven, CT: Yale University Press, 1987), xii, xiii.

22. Hunt, *Ideology and U.S. Foreign Policy*, 11–17; Clifford Geertz, *The Interpretation of Cultures* (New York: Basic Books, 1973), esp. 14, 17, 89, 193–233.

23. David Caute, *The Great Fear: The Anti-Communist Purge Under Truman and Eisenhower* (New York: Simon & Schuster, 1978).

24. See, for example, Corey Robin, *Fear: The History of a Political Idea* (New York: Oxford University Press, 2004), esp. 16, 28, 33, 119, 140, 162, 181–91; and Elaine Tyler May, *Fortress America: How We Embraced Fear and Abandoned Democracy* (New York: Basic Books, 2018). On McCarthyism specifically—which, not coincidentally, features heavily in the otherwise chronologically broad accounts by Robin and May—see Robert Griffith, "The Political Context of McCarthyism," *Review of Politics* 33, no. 1 (January 1971): 24–35; James T. Patterson, *Grand Expectations: The United States, 1945–1974* (New York: Oxford University Press, 1996), 201–3; and Ellen Schrecker, *Many Are the Crimes: McCarthyism in America* (Boston: Little, Brown, 1998).

25. That is, the community shares certain emotions, not that the community is emotional; and that each community conditions its own emotional responses and determines which emotions should be embraced and which should be avoided. Barbara H. Rosenwein, *Generations of Feeling: A History of Emotions, 600–1700* (Cambridge: Cambridge University Press, 2015), 3–10.

26. Andrew Preston, "Monsters Everywhere: A Genealogy of National Security," *Diplomatic History* 38, no. 3 (June 2014): 490.

27. In the context of U.S. foreign relations, see Campbell Craig and Fredrik Logevall, *America's Cold War: The Politics of Insecurity* (Cambridge, MA: Harvard University Press, 2009); and Preston, "Monsters Everywhere." In the context of nineteenth-century U.S. military history, see Allan R. Millett and Peter Maslowski, *For the Common Defense: A Military History of the United States of America* (New York: Free Press, 1994), 248–83.

28. For an example of this criticism, see Fareed Zakaria, "The Myth of America's 'Free Security,'" *World Policy Journal* 14, no. 2 (Summer 1997): 35–43. At times, however, U.S. foreign policy planners did attempt to achieve total security. See James Chace and Caleb Carr, *America Invulnerable: The Quest for Absolute Security from 1812 to Star Wars* (New York: Summit, 1988).

29. Matthew Karp, *This Vast Southern Empire: Slaveholders at the Helm of American Foreign Policy* (Cambridge, MA: Harvard University Press, 2016).

30. Abraham Lincoln, "The Perpetuation of Our Political Institutions: Address Before the Young Men's Lyceum of Springfield, Illinois," January 27, 1838.

31. Richard Olney to Thomas Francis Bayard, July 20, 1895, *Foreign Relations of the United States, 1895*, Part I (Washington, DC: Government Printing Office, 1896), 558.

32. See Paul Kennedy, *The Rise and Fall of the Great Powers: Economic Change and Military Conflict from 1500 to 2000* (New York: Random House, 1987), 242–43; Michael Mann, *The Sources of Social Power*, vol. 2. *The Rise of Classes and Nation-States, 1760–1914* (Cambridge: Cambridge University Press, 1993),

377, 490–91; Charles S. Maier, *Among Empires: American Ascendancy and Its Predecessors* (Cambridge, MA: Harvard University Press, 2006), 195.

33. Hunt, *Ideology and U.S. Foreign Policy*, 13.

34. A point made most powerfully by Ira Katznelson, *Fear Itself: The New Deal and the Origins of Our Time* (New York: Liveright, 2013).

35. Franklin D. Roosevelt, "Fireside Chat, December 29, 1940," American Presidency Project, https://www.presidency.ucsb.edu/node/209416; Andrew Preston, *American Foreign Relations: A Very Short Introduction* (New York: Oxford University Press, 2019), 72.

36. John A. Thompson, "The Exaggeration of American Vulnerability: The Anatomy of a Tradition," *Diplomatic History* 16, no. 1 (January 1992): 23–43. See also John A. Thompson, *A Sense of Power: The Roots of America's Global Role* (Ithaca, NY: Cornell University Press, 2015), 151–92.

37. Franklin D. Roosevelt, "Address at the University of Virginia," June 10, 1940, *Public Papers and Addresses of Franklin D. Roosevelt, 1940* (New York: Macmillan, 1941), 261.

38. Melvyn P. Leffler, *A Preponderance of Power: National Security, the Truman Administration, and the Cold War* (Stanford, CA: Stanford University Press, 1992).

39. See Wendy L. Wall, *Inventing the "American Way": The Politics of Consensus from the New Deal to the Civil Rights* (New York: Oxford University Press, 2008).

40. The literature is enormous, but a good conceptual overview history is Frank Ninkovich, *Modernity and Power: A History of the Domino Theory in the Twentieth Century* (Chicago: University of Chicago Press, 1994).

41. The best one-volume account remains, despite its age, Aleksandr Fursenko and Timothy J. Naftali, *"One Hell of a Gamble": Khrushchev, Castro, and Kennedy, 1958–1964* (New York: Norton, 1997).

42. Off the Record Meeting on Cuba, October 16, 1962, Document 21, *Foreign Relations of the United States, 1961–1963*, vol. 11, https://history.state.gov/historicaldocuments/frus1961-63v11/d21.

43. See, for example, Senator Richard Russell's comments in "Minutes of Meeting, October 22, 1962," in *The Kennedy Tapes: Inside the White House During the Cuban Missile Crisis*, ed. Ernest R. May and Philip D. Zelikow (Cambridge, MA: Harvard University Press, 1997), 270–71.

44. Letter From the Representative to the United Nations (Stevenson) to President Kennedy, October 17, 1962, Document 25, *Foreign Relations of the United States, 1961–1963*, vol. 11, https://history.state.gov/historicaldocuments/frus1961-63v11/d25.

45. Harold Macmillan as quoted in Nigel Ashton, *Kennedy, Macmillan and the Cold War: The Irony of Interdependence* (Basingstoke, UK: Palgrave Macmillan, 2002), 75. However, as Ashton rightly explains in further detail, Macmillan's views during the missile crisis shifted and were often inconsistent.

46. David C. Hendrickson, *Republic in Peril: American Empire and the Liberal Tradition* (New York: Oxford University Press, 2018), 59.

47. A point convincingly made by Melvyn P. Leffler in two essays: Melvyn P. Leffler, "The Foreign Policies of the George W. Bush Administration: Memoirs, History, Legacy," *Diplomatic History* 37, no. 2 (April 2013): 190–216; and Melvyn P. Leffler, "The Decider: Why Bush Chose War in Iraq," *Foreign Affairs* 99, no. 6 (November/December 2020): 144–52.

48. "U.S. Faces 'Cuban Missile Crisis in Slow Motion,'" *New York Times*, April 17, 2017. For another version of this analogy, see also Graham Allison, "Thinking the Unthinkable with North Korea," *New York Times*, May 30, 2017, https://www.nytimes.com/2017/05/30/opinion/north-korea-nuclear-crisis-donald-trump.html.

49. Haeryun Kang, "In South Korea We're Scared but We've Normalised the Fear," *Guardian*, August 9, 2017, https://www.theguardian.com/commentisfree/2017/aug/09/south-korea-normalised-fear-north-korea-missile-kim-jong-un.

50. Wolf Blitzer, "Search for the 'Smoking Gun,'" CNN, January 10, 2003, https://edition.cnn.com/2003/US/01/10/wbr.smoking.gun/.

51. David Brooks, "An Era Defined by Fear," *New York Times*, April 29, 2019, https://www.nytimes.com/2019/04/29/opinion/politics-fear.html.

CHAPTER 9

Unilateralism as Ideology

CHRISTOPHER McKNIGHT NICHOLS

Former national security advisor John Bolton's book, *The Room Where It Happened*, chronicled the inner workings of arguably the most unilateralist foreign policy presidency in U.S. history. Donald Trump's singular, transactional focus, argued Bolton, lay at the intersection of domestic policy and foreign policy. "I am hard-pressed to identify any significant Trump decision during my tenure that wasn't driven by reelection calculations," Bolton wrote.[1] Although the 2020 reelection focus might have been anathema to Bolton, the core impulse for the United States to act on its own in the world was not. "If John Bolton had his way he would, in his own words, remake the UN Security Council with 'one permanent member: the United States'," wrote the *Financial Times* Editorial Board in September 2018. "Trump's foreign policy, to the extent that he has one, tends toward isolationism, while Bolton's is expansive but heavily unilateral," declared journalist Dexter Filkins in 2019, accusing Bolton of "spurning allies when necessary."[2] Headlines such as "Trump Administration Extends Its Assault on Multilateralism" and "Attack on the ICC Marks an Escalation of Washington's Unilateralism" are characteristic of scores of comparable articles written over the last five years. Like so many others, accounts of the Trump administration dovetail with the *Financial Times* piece in their focus on what editors, journalists, and many foreign policy experts understand as an abrupt change in U.S. foreign policy thought and practice.[3]

This reporting sits alongside insider accounts and scholarly analysis that all tend to seize on certain Trump administration actions that seem to smack of "America First" priorities: pulling out of the Iran Nuclear Accord and the Paris Agreement, formal withdrawal and termination of the intermediate-range nuclear forces treaty, and the threat to withdraw from NATO. But many of these reports diverge on the origins of this phenomenon. Some provocatively trace unilateralism to the Obama administration. Others claim its genesis was in the George W. Bush years and the War on Terror. Yet others imply that a turn toward unilateralism began after the end of the Cold War, under George H. W. Bush and Clinton, and sped up in the wake of the Gulf War, which modeled a feeling (militaristic) for post–Cold War multilateralism.[4] What these evaluations all have in common is that they almost monolithically deride the "unilateral" mode of diplomatic, economic, and military conduct and accuse it of being selfish and short-sighted—entirely insufficient to meet the challenges of what appears so obviously to be a multilateral world.[5]

In sharp contrast, the Biden administration's foreign policy has centered largely on what Secretary of State Anthony Blinken argued in 2020 would be "stepping back from unilateralism."[6] Journalists and analysts around the world during Biden's first few months in office examined what they believed amounted to a major turn "back" toward multilateralism. In keeping with perceived precedents, those guiding policy in the Biden administration pledged to develop specific ideas and policies that would guide "putting four years of Donald Trump's erratic unilateralism behind them."[7] Headlines asked, "How Will Biden Manage Unilateral Tariff Legacy?" and "Will Biden's Iraq Policy Signal the End of US Unilateralism?"[8] Some, such as the foreign policy scholar Stewart Patrick, suggested that Trump's presidency "repudiated seven decades of US internationalism" and that Biden "has reasserted American global leadership and rededicated the United States to *multilateral cooperation*, including at the *United Nations* and other major international bodies."[9] Still, a smaller set of commentators, largely on the political right, saw continuity. They suggested that in his early actions, such as canceling the Keystone Pipeline project, "Biden signal[ed] unilateralism" and that "leading the world" might be more important than "consulting with allies" for his administration. Some wondered, "Is Biden committed to unity or unilateral action?"[10] Abroad, similar questions about unity and unilateralism were building, centering on the Biden administration's rapid withdrawal from Afghanistan, itself precipitated by the diplomatic efforts by Donald Trump and secretary of state Mike Pompeo to pull U.S. forces out of Afghanistan, both administrations apparent lack of communication or coordination with allies in the region, and the resulting chaos of U.S. retrenchment through the summer and fall of 2021. One observer referred to those actions as amounting to a kind of "America First-lite." "This is the sort of thing you would have expected under Trump but not under Biden—the unilateralism," remarked Ian Bremmer, president of the Eurasia group.[11]

There can be no doubt that the Biden Administration's efforts in late 2021 into 2022 to work with allies across Europe and around the world to avert a Russian war in Ukraine and then to backstop Ukraine after the shocking unprovoked Russian invasion amount to evidence of a renewed commitment to multilateralism. The United States' recent support of free peoples and nations, particularly working with NATO, are reminiscent of the early Cold War. Still, given the contradictory and countervailing actions and statements of the past two administrations there are undeniable undercurrents of unilateralism at work as well. So, are there other, better, perhaps richer ways to understand the historical development and contemporary power of the ideas and impulses at stake in unilateralist arguments and actions?

Unilateralism, the Long View

The questions raised by journalists covering the Biden administration today are representative of longer-standing conceptual issues and underlying confusion of what exactly constitutes unilateralism. And how should we best understand unilateralism: as a concept or an ideology?

The analysis framing debates about both unilateralism and its perceived diametric opposite, multilateralism, is plagued by one of the most significant misconceptions about the ideologies guiding U.S. foreign relations and misses at least two central facts.

First, it mistakes unilateralism for a recent phenomenon when it is, in many ways, the oldest, most formative ideological instrument in the U.S. foreign relations tool kit. After all, George Washington, James Madison, Thomas Jefferson, and John Adams all argued vociferously, in surprisingly similar ways, for national autonomy. They held it as a "maxim" that the United States should not be "entangled" with other nations. In the words of John Quincy Adams, American "happiness consists in independence, disconnected from all European interests and European politics." Even Alexander Hamilton, who was instrumental in securing the first Anglo-American treaty in U.S. history, sought to spurn the "fatal heresy of a close alliance."[12]

Second, and closely related, this analysis tends to misunderstand the ideological and material roots of contemporary unilateralism. Most significant, such assessments manifest a presentist fixation (perhaps even a presentist fallacy) that overlooks the long intellectual and institutional tradition on which unilateralism rests. Even if its origins and duration are neither appreciated nor meaningfully conceptualized by recent presidential administrations, unilateralism remains trenchant as an ideology of U.S. foreign policy, in large part because of its pedigree and purchase. That is, unilateralism has historically shaped persuasive evaluations of the country's core commitments, values, material conditions, and directions.

Do recent events herald an outpouring of U.S. unilateralism? Should we fear them? Embrace them? Why is this such a contentious topic, generating tremendous fear or praise of a United States "going it alone"? Is unilateralism ultimately a coherent political philosophy, an idea, a guiding concept, or something else altogether?

I probe these questions in this chapter and seek provisional answers in locating, tracking, and tracing what we might call an intellectual genealogy of unilateralism as a core ideology in the United States and its relations to the world.

Unilateralism, Defined

As an adjective, *unilateral* is best understood as a tactic. As a noun, *unilateralism* clearly connotes much more. It is not unthinking or an impulse, although a visceral unilateral response to external challenges has certainly been elemental to some U.S. foreign policies.

The crux of unilateralism is the aim to prioritize U.S. "interests" in conducting foreign policy by leveraging singular action that is not constrained by allies, enemies, or neutrals. The historian Melvyn Leffler argues that there is relative continuity in how unilateralism has clarified America's "core values" even in eras or for administrations often thought of as being multilateral. Leffler reminds us, for example, "When they perceived threats, especially in the Third World, U.S. officials did not refrain from acting unilaterally."[13] In balancing threats and interests, the historical record suggests that preferred, often hotly contested, "vital interests"—nurturing domestic industry or gaining access to markets or fossil fuels or stopping communist revolutions—were most significant in determining behaviors, chosen instruments, and approaches, starting with whether or not, or how much, to pursue a unilateral policy. In the abstract, such evaluations of policy options refuse to subordinate whatever the unilateralist position judges to be the core values, aims, or actions to the demands of other groups (be they peoples, nation-states, organizations, or leagues) or to the constraints imposed by binding agreements and alliances. In the particular, the precise "interests" must be specified, matching means to ends. Of course, vital interests have varied over time and were often hotly debated. In the historical record, however, what stands out in defining unilateralism is the intense inward emphasis on vital interests, which is the very essence of unilateralism and unilateralist worldviews.

As a policy approach, unilateralism has been more nuanced than a superficial reading of the history tends to imply. Unilateralism's advocates—those viewing policy challenges through the lens of unilateralism—have often aimed at adopting a cautiously realist strategy to build an ideal equilibrium between autonomy from other nation-states while increasing control of (or influence over) their actions and outcomes. Such a foreign policy was generally developed without alliances—or at least without giving much credence to the views of allies—and with an eye to limiting the dimensions by which other actors beyond the United States can or might determine the nation's course in the world. Unilateralism has provided touch points for policy makers to consider, debate, and navigate which foreign issues, alliances, and agreements would increase the country's relative power and thus its capacity to act unilaterally on the international scene. Its primary concern revolves around maintaining U.S. autonomy, sovereignty, and leverage, with a strong historical tendency to privilege economic leverage to military or diplomatic leverage, enabling private enterprise to flourish while avoiding entangling alliances, bureaucratic buildup, or increases in institutional oversight or authority. To the extent that unilateralist approaches have been open to international agreements, the past clarifies that it has been only if they enable the United States to maintain (near or complete) control and flexibility in its foreign policy. As an "ism," however, "unilateralism" in U.S. foreign policy thought has meant taking the side of a theory or philosophy, and it implies components that are more expansive than the sometimes simple caricature of one-sidedness or mono-directionality indicate.

My main goals for this brief chapter are to clearly define unilateralism as an ideology in U.S. foreign policy, establish a baseline historical trajectory from the 1770s to the present, and examine some of the ideas at stake today refracted through the clarifying prism of the past. A long, deeply rooted history of unilateralism as an ideology *and* as an enduring strain in the constellation of foundational concepts has informed and shaped U.S. foreign policy from the nation's earliest moments. Nor does it have to amount to "an ideology" in order to function ideologically.

On Unilateralism

Remarkably little has been written about unilateralism. Political scientists and public commentators have done the bulk of exploring unilateralism, largely as a modern, postwar phenomenon. Few historians have focused attention on the subject, and you would be hard-pressed to find more than a few paragraphs on unilateralism in any recent historical works on U.S. foreign relations. Perhaps at most one chapter would address this issue in works from 1990s to the present, with virtually no mention at all prior to that time.

What work has been done by political scientists and international relations theorists has tended to focus on the late Cold War and post–Cold War years, particularly in making cases to public audiences decrying the Bush administration's unilateralism in the wake of 9/11. Much of this analysis bears titles such as "The Case Against Unilateralism" or "US Unilateralism and Its Dangers" or "Unilateralism: Anatomy of a Foreign Policy Disaster."[14] G. John Ikenberry has written rather prolifically about how U.S. unilateralism is somehow new and deeply problematic. He has also made the fairly persuasive case that the United States has—especially in the unprecedented bipolar and then unipolar moments of the mid-twentieth century and post–Cold War era—as a hegemonic state, exercised unilateral leadership to fashion and benefit from a favored form of international order in the wake of wars.[15] Rejections of the doctrine of preemption from 2002 and 2003 aside, prescriptions about hegemonic powers using unilateral action to direct multilateral activities in their interests makes the present moment of denial and rejection of international institutions, agreements, structures, and so on all the harder to fathom.

For most of its history, the United States did not have the freedom of action it enjoys today. Nor could the United States ever fully subscribe to "isolation." That is a connotation we must cast off. Still, it was weakness, not strength, that guided American policy makers, activists, intellectuals, and citizens in organizing their ideas about the proper U.S. role in the world through more than the first half of its history. Unilateralism, therefore, offered advantageous guidance. Neutrality, noninterventionism, rejecting entangling alliances, and aiming at self-sufficiency were all crucial to existing long enough to advance across the continent and eventually be strong enough to at least not appear weak relative to European nations in commercial and military arenas. The arguments from geography operate along similar lines. The United States enjoyed a unique strategic advantage in its access to the Atlantic and Pacific oceans. Despite empires and threats abounding across the hemisphere, these vulnerabilities were nowhere near those of the European states. During the "interwar years," Charles Beard made the argument, for example, that to keep the United States out of a future catastrophic war the nation must embrace unilateralism and near-complete autonomy in diplomacy *outside* the hemisphere but act with more of a consensus-building and security-oriented leadership approach *within* the hemisphere.[16]

Walter McDougall, one of the few historians to give sustained attention to the concept of unilateralism, suggests that the Beardian notion might be seen as the apotheosis of a longer trend. If one maps the patterns of nineteenth-century history in terms of unilateralism, he argues, the lessons for policy makers seem certain and obvious: "The first twenty years [of the American Republic] proved the utility of Unilateralism over and over again," and despite temptations and coercion, the Monroe Doctrine's unilateralist bent held, and no U.S. administration "even considered another foreign entanglement, much less an alliance, for the rest of the century."[17] What fundamental concepts did American policy makers and citizens alike carry in their heads? Although this search can be difficult in many cases, and establishing the causal effects of ideas on actions and outcomes is notoriously problematic, unilateralism as ideology may be one of the clearer cases in U.S. foreign policy thought, debate, and action.

The crux of this historical project to trace unilateralism as an ideology is to define and chronicle its development and application. The task is not to argue whether it made a difference but rather to explain what sort of difference it made in shaping policy, intention, and actions at key moments. As George Herring has suggested, the unilateral impulse was made possible by geographical distance from major foreign threats. In his sweeping history of U.S. foreign relations since the founding, Herring states that a "unilateralist approach seemed natural and essential to a people who saw themselves as morally superior and understandably fear entanglement in Europe's wars and contamination from its cancerous politics."[18] Now let's turn to that history.

Unilateralist from the Cradle

The specific grievances of the American colonists that grew out of the politico-diplomatic and intellectual maneuvers of asserting independence and national sovereignty bore a nationalist agenda. This agenda supported one-sided action (in the positive frame) or minimized longer-term commitments and vulnerabilities (in the negative), and rejected or negated foreign ties and entreaties. Unilateralism goes back to the revolutionary era; it is one of and perhaps *the* most basic ideological traditions in American foreign policy.

Consider, for example, the Model Treaty of 1776, a template treaty drafted largely by John Adams for prospective diplomacy aimed at regulating commercial and wartime ties with France and Spain. This treaty was the new nation's first attempt to make a diplomatic statement about the core principles that would guide U.S. foreign relations; it was written simultaneously with the Declaration of Independence. This template for future agreements for the new nation and world powers emphasized the ideals of free and reciprocal trade and rejected formal binding of political or military alliances. Although the United States did rapidly ally with France and Spain soon thereafter to help wage and win the Revolutionary War, the Model Treaty is a useful point of departure because it illuminates some foundational ideas of democratic foreign policy. As Michael Hunt and others have shown, the early seeming consensus of the place of the United States in international affairs fragmented fairly rapidly; however, it did not totally dissipate, and a set of core values emerged and deepened across the eighteenth century. These core values ran right along the lines of the Model Treaty's aims, centered on autonomy and flexibility (especially in commerce), to collectively wield strong influence over policy.[19]

As the historian Jennifer Ratner-Rosenhagen has recently suggested, the intellectual innovations of the founding era were many, and separation from Europe was a crucial element intrinsic to these notions, as evidenced by Thomas Paine's *Common Sense*.[20] The "world-historical grandeur" of the fight of independence and potent democratic ideas imbricated therein, however, was rooted less in transcendence, I would argue, and more in exceptionalist-provincialism: independence, a novus ordo seclorum. "Enlightened" republicanism, yes, but for "us" Americans. We can see early forms of unilateralism in many of the first national sentiments and diplomatic practices.

During the presidencies of Washington, Jefferson, and Monroe, three formative policy pillars emerged. In turn, they framed what options lay beyond the formal exercise of power. Each position coupled what we might now term "cautious realism" with the imperatives of unilateral action or inaction, guided by an imperative for the fledgling United States to stay out of power politics, foreign wars, and binding international treaties. From the 1770s onward, American thinkers and policy makers and citizens forged a tradition of autonomy-based isolation in an effort to protect the world's first democracy from what they perceived as a world of corrupt monarchies. Potential enemies were within and without—enslaved people, Indigenous peoples, European empires—and the United States negotiated a tenuous position.[21] Some theorists argue that power is essential for unilateralism and that such a policy orientation is likely to be more of a preferred course of action for more powerful nations. However, the U.S. case seems to suggest that significant power in terms of other nation-states need not be a prerequisite for a unilateralist ideological basis to foreign relations.[22]

George Washington's 1796 Farewell Address laid one key foundation in making the case for unilateralism: "to steer clear of permanent alliances with any portion of the foreign world." Even before that speech, however, Washington established the nation's neutrality as a formal policy tradition with the Proclamation of Neutrality (1793) and the Neutrality Act (1794). These were as much about keeping a free hand for unilateral action as subscribing to a reductive notion of mere neutrality. They also contravened the alliance with France that had helped win the Revolutionary War. Officially, they asserted the guiding position that America would pursue "a conduct friendly and impartial towards the Belligerent powers," distancing the United States from allies and enemies alike. In his Farewell Address (partly written by Alexander Hamilton and James Madison and read in Congress almost every year until quite recently), Washington set an explicitly isolationist tone—but more than that the central imperative was to preserve the United States' freedom of action: unilateralism. This was not a simple set of ideas, and the goals were not what is sometimes caricatured as seeking a walled-and-bounded nation but rather emphasized the limits of U.S. power in light of its commercial, cultural, and intellectual interests in the world.[23]

This became what some have referred to as Washington's "Great Rule" or an "instant tradition." But it took Thomas Jefferson confirming those ideals in his 1801 inaugural address, and James Monroe later reasserting and amplifying them for the hemisphere in his 1823 State of the Union, for this unilateralist orientation to become firmly established in U.S. foreign relations ideology. Because the French did not formally invoke the terms of the 1778 treaty in the 1790s or thereafter, the new U.S. stance was not challenged at the outset. Indeed, the battle between Jeffersonians and Hamiltonians, heated though it was, about competing U.S. allegiances to England or France resulted in nothing official. By 1800, when the United States abrogated the Franco-American Alliance, the master diplomatic strategist Charles Maurice de Talleyrand and Napoleon Bonaparte surveyed the scene and came to expect nothing from the United States even if Jefferson came to power. "Mr. Jefferson will make it his duty to unite around himself the true Americans," wrote Talleyrand in 1800, "and to resume in all its force the system of perfect equilibrium between France and England, which alone suits the United States."[24] In this, Talleyrand presciently summed up the American unilateralist-neutralist ethos. This set of ideas and sensibilities seemed more and more wise in a world of threats, wars, and uncertainty. It came together and distilled what we might call *unilateral neutrality*, which policy makers and citizens invoked as an essential tradition in virtually every major conflict until the attack on Pearl Harbor brought the United States into World War II.

But that moves us too far, too fast, because the rapid crystallization of a unilateralist ideology began under Jefferson, not just in affirming "peace, commerce, and honest friendship with all nations, entangling alliances with none." Although his inaugural address stressed the practicality of avoiding alliances or conflicts in the Old World, he propelled what was often conceived as a great mission of continental purpose with the purchase of the Louisiana Territory in 1803, doubling the nation's territory. The purchase limited the amount of North American land European powers could claim, but it also pushed an "empire for liberty" upon the Indigenous peoples and others who occupied large swaths of the newly acquired land.[25] Jefferson's unilateralist efforts rejected the prospect of a Napoleonic empire in the Mississippi Valley, represented a first new step for unilateral foreign policy made by the president and not Congress, and remained consistent with the idea of a sort of isolation from the corruptions of European power politics (alliances as well as conflicts) as a best means to protect national sovereignty.[26]

In 1812, with the Napoleonic Wars broiling, violations of maritime rights overlapped with assertions of neutrality, and the United States under Madison went to war with Britain. One logical reason for this is found in a version of realpolitik: the enemy of my enemy, who also previously was an ally, should again be a friend and ally. Still, unilateralism was affirmed. Even though France and the United States were both at war with Britain, Madison and his cabinet debated the proper course of action and pursued no formal alliance.

In fact, the United States did not even "associate" with France to coordinate the war effort as Woodrow Wilson did upon entering World War I (in 1917 the United States joined in "association" to fight but not in "alliance").

Just over ten years later, President James Monroe articulated a slightly revised, similarly circumspect view of American power in what came to be known as the Monroe Doctrine. Largely the grand strategic vision of secretary of state John Quincy Adams, the Monroe Doctrine offered an ambitious expression of American hemispheric power that evolved as the guiding view for later foreign policy advocates of both intervention and isolation. "With the movements in this hemisphere we are of necessity more immediately connected," Monroe declared. Therefore, "we should consider any attempt on their part to extend their system to any portion of this hemisphere as dangerous to our peace and safety."[27] For many of its later proponents, the doctrine authorized unilateral involvement across the Americas, while reinforcing the proscription against foreign entanglements beyond the Western Hemisphere, and, especially, Washington's warning to avoid the corruptions of Old World political intrigues. But also in the doctrine is the rejection of a joint Anglo-American pronouncement as suggested by the British. Adams and Monroe rejected that entreaty. Yes, the United States engaged in Pacific trade and naval expansion in the late 1830s and early 1840s, pursuing trade with China in the 1840s and Japan in the 1850s; from 1846 through 1848 the United States fought the Mexican War and secured another enormous territorial land grab, again unilaterally. For the remainder of the century, no administration or serious national politician really contemplated another foreign entanglement. Unilateralism was established, and it was ascendant. What we observe, as the historian Walter McDougall aptly summed up, is that "a look at nineteenth-century American history is a nation convinced of the wisdom of Unilateralism."[28]

The hemispheric dimensions of unilateralism after the age of revolutions across the Americas is crucial to understanding its transformation and geographical directionality. A constituent part of the broader isolationist framework in which it was often embedded reveals that U.S. unilateralism was premised on an Old World–New World divide. As such there were significant limits to U.S. engagement with Europe that were rarely breached in war and treaty-making until the end of the nineteenth century and really not fundamentally overturned until the mid-twentieth century. But there were far fewer such limits—especially after the Monroe Doctrine—in the Western Hemisphere, and the increasing regional dominance of the United States, with its unique capacity to formal and informal imperial forms, hard and soft power, led the Argentine jurist Manuel Ugarte to call the United States a "New Rome" by the 1920s.

The relationship between unilateralism and executive power is worth keeping in mind as we march across the centuries. Unilateralism as an operating ideology and a policy option (or set of options) was established early on and has been in ascent alongside the rise of the imperial president and executive power. With the rise of U.S. commercial and military power, this pattern tracks to the McKinley and Roosevelt years at the dawn of the twentieth century and the global age, but it becomes pronounced as undeclared wars and interventions proliferated after the Korean War. It reached an ideal form, its apotheosis, in the wake of the Cold War during the George W. Bush administration. So, too, it is important to consider the historical trajectory of tensions between unilateralism and internationalism. By the 1910s, we can see a clear opposition between unilateralism and transnationalism, as evident in cultural critic Randolph Bourne's pacifist isolationist argument in 1916 against the "reverberatory effect of the war" and his argument for a "Trans-national America," in which connections and overlapping citizenships undermined parochial, bellicose notions of nationalism.[29]

Multilateralism, Unilateralism, and Isolationism

Multilateralism is, of course, the antithesis of unilateralism. This is clear. The *Oxford English Dictionary* and other etymological sources suggest that the former gave rise to the latter as phenomena in the real world collided with ideology. The term *unilateralism* was coined in the mid-1920s amid the swirling impulses of global integration and organization in the wake of World War I as an antonym to multilateralism. Usage of the term regarding foreign policy did not begin appreciably until the 1960s, and it was not until the 1980s and especially the early Cold War years of the 1990s that the term was employed regularly, with use rising dramatically from the 1990s through the 2000s.[30] But in the longer historical trajectory, what is more interesting to observe and explore is how far back unilateralism goes in U.S. foreign relations. Unilateralism functioned as an ideology and discursive framework on which to hang seemingly obvious imperatives for the nation-state: securing borders, avoiding foreign wars, keeping a free hand in trade, and being wary of special interests. In this way, unilateralism has served as a bulwark against facile internationalism and transnationalism and generated debates about what Leffler calls "core values" and how to preserve them against foreign encroachment, and reinforced related notions of nationalism, exceptionalism, and mission.

This all revolved around a primordial kind of American "autonomism"—a way of viewing potential opportunities and threats that prioritizes national autonomy and sovereignty. It is the freedom to act or not act in virtually any arena at the expense of making friends or enemies, rejecting or embracing profitable trade relationships, and adhering to or distancing from even the most advantageous security alliances. Multilateralism, in contrast, involves the cooperation of three or more nations or groups in an area of international relations. It has much higher costs in diplomatic connections and overall compromise but likely lower absolute costs because it distributes burdens across nations and groups. It is premised on binding, or at least temporary coalitions for collective action, be they in trade, immigration, or war. As such, multilateralism has been rightly depicted as "a highly demanding institutional form." Several scholars grappling with the attractiveness presented by unilateral approaches argue that it is "unsurprising that great powers would find such generalized principles of conduct constraining."[31]

On the Relationship Between Unilateralism and Isolationism

With respect to the practice of foreign policy, isolationism as it developed in the United States can best be understood as a constellation of ideas. In my own multipart definition of isolationism, one of the core elements of any isolationist position is a firm adherence to unilateral action. This is, as isolationist politicians tended to put it, "the doctrine of the free hand."[32] Americans who opposed restrictions on national sovereignty—that is, any limits imposed by entering into global agreements, permanent alliances, and interventions in foreign conflicts—have advocated for political isolationism.

Two main isolationist strains of thought emerged during the late nineteenth century. One would permit nonbinding international dialogues; the other would favor acting alone. In either case, such views of global diplomacy were essentially unilateral. To preserve national autonomy, proponents of isolation have often proposed a unilateralist "going it alone" option. Consider "Irreconcilable" Idaho Republican senator William Borah, who from the 1910s through the 1930s rejected entering the League of Nations and even most binding economic, diplomatic, and military pacts. Or consider

"Mr. Republican" Ohio senator Robert Taft, who from the 1930s through 1953 opposed NATO, the Korean War (off and on), and wanted to limit U.S. commitments to Western Europe, including objections to the Marshall Plan as well as the stationing of U.S. troops in Europe.[33] The degree, type, and aggressiveness of unilateralism have often been fiercely debated, but the unilateral impulse has undergirded much of modern isolationist thought and practice since the 1890s. Even when we leap forward to the twenty-first century, we find, for example, George W. Bush, who argued against signing the Kyoto Protocol in part because of economic costs for domestic growth and a preference not to be constrained by multinational pledges or oversight.

Historically, seeking the freedom to act alone could and frequently did lead to an embrace of unilateral military action. Thus the Bush Doctrine of preemptive war as applied in Iraq in 2003 can be seen as archetypal. But there are other somewhat comparable examples, including John F. Kennedy's unilateral quarantine of Cuba during the Cuban missile crisis in 1962 or the McKinley administration's move for war with Spain after the sinking of the USS *Maine* in 1898. In these sorts of wartime unilateralist moves, rather than coalition-building we find the interrelated elements of unilateralism and nonentanglement, which both emphasize national autonomy and have been two of the most prominent and widely shared isolationist points of empha-sis.[34] Going back to Washington's and Jefferson's fears of being pulled into European wars, nonentanglement as a goal need not be seen—and U.S. politicians have rarely done so—as a preventative to war or cooperative action or binding collective security agreements. Indeed, unilateralism may be the dominant ideology in U.S. foreign policy for militant "hawks" across eras. A glance at these moments and this history suggests that what may be most fascinating about how conceptions of unilateral action intersected with events in U.S. history may be the ways in which it served to underscore suspicions about international organizations and agreements, xenophobia, and indifference and often hostility to other peoples and cultures.

Unilateralist logics are so powerful that even after almost three-quarters of a century of large-scale U.S. global commitments and an even longer set of increasing worldwide interconnections, it has resurfaced with a vengeance in the wake of 9/11 and remains strong in the third decade of the twenty-first century. Another fascinating connection to draw out further is that taking a unilateral action—for example, raising tariffs in the late nineteenth century, in the 1920s, or in the 2020s—has a tendency to generate reciprocal actions and to undermine soft power alternatives. Thus it would appear that unilateralism has an unsteady relationship to soft power in that unilateral actions and policy proposals generally have been coercive by design rather than premised on notions of shaping preferences or behaviors through values and culture. The defensive posture of the United States, however, can sometimes be seen as an exemplar rather than a crusader. That was the case when former president Herbert Hoover called in 1950 for the United States to be like a "Gibraltar" defensively but not intervene in Korea or work through the United Nations to do so and instead serve as a beacon for democracy. This fits the pattern from a century before, when President Millard Fillmore met with Hungarian revolutionary Louis Kossuth at the end of 1851 and early 1852. Fillmore and many from a receptive Congress explained the nation's formative foreign policies regarding nonentanglement and neutrality, enmeshed as they were in a unilateralist prescription of moral sentiment supporting democratic values abroad while not sending direct aid or intervening.

Conclusions About the Vital Intersection of Ideals, Self-Interest, and Power

What we are left with in this intellectual tradition is a vital intersection, a meeting and perhaps a battle between what we might rightly depict as power, ideals, and self-interest. A significant element of national self-interest, of course, is self-sufficiency, which has manifested in efforts to carry out formal and informal relations with the world without regard to other nations or actions outside of unilateral control. In a classification of isolationist strains of thought that have helped to guide U.S. foreign relations, I place unilateralism, nonentanglement, neutrality, and the urge for self-sufficiency as the most influential.

The historian Robert Osgood noted that "when self-sufficiency is motivated by passive egoism, by an urge to withdraw and a longing to be left alone, it is commonly known as isolation. To be sure, isolationism may also spring, in part, from idealistic motives, but historically its determining aspect has always been a conception of national self-interest." But Osgood also cautioned that a more aggressive cast to self-sufficiency in the unilateralist mode is evident in the historical record of "national self-assertion and not simply out of a passive yearning for withdrawal."[35] On the spectrum of seeking greater or lesser self-sufficiency, acting with allies and assessing threats and opportunities, U.S. military and commercial power has been essential, but so have been debates and evaluations of that power's balance relative to other nations and blocs, along with questions ranging from issues of national precarity and survival to the responsibility to protect fellow human beings from suffering.

The core principles at work in unilateralism have provided positive and negative rhetorical ammunition for political supporters. On the positive side of the ledger we find active, proactive, and enlarging policy arguments, such as to intervene abroad (e.g., in the Mexican American War, the Spanish American War), as articulated by "large policy" advocates at the dawn of the twentieth-century, including Massachusetts senator Henry Cabot Lodge and Theodore Roosevelt; the vision of active unilateralism helped to elaborate the case for intervention and expansion, as well as to pursue aggressive bilateral trade agreements or push for tariffs and trade protections unilaterally. Indeed, William McKinley's 1896 campaign slogan "Patriotism, protection, prosperity" maps on to what we might depict as a central unilateralist set of connections between foreign and domestic policy. On the negative side of the ledger we find more reactive claims, arguments for ignoring, denying, rejecting, closing down, along the lines of Osgood's insights. These negative positions have undergirded rejection of or withdrawal from a variety of multilateral treaties, agreements, and organizations (e.g., U.S. entry into the League of Nations in 1919–20, fight or limit of U.S. membership in the World Court and International Criminal Court in varied eras, opposition of the North Atlantic Treaty Organization in the early Cold War and recent past, pulling out of the Trans Pacific Partnership and Paris Climate Accord). In this sense, the positive and the negative are about orientation, not normative judgments. If we examine the intersection of the positive and negative valences of unilateralism, we find arguments for economic policies of raising protectionist barriers and rationales often for restricting immigration. In the 1920s, for example, both valences of unilateralism were in ascendency under presidents Warren Harding, Calvin Coolidge, and Herbert Hoover. Republicans rejected the League of Nations and pushed for the United States to be involved in the world without being committed, to adapt a phrase from the historian George Herring.[36] The United States dodged membership in the World Court as well. Business-first priorities made politicians skeptical of canceling World War I war debts. A similar logic of insularity combined with a priority for self-sufficiency undergirded two of the most protectionist pieces of tariff legislation in U.S. history: the 1922 Fordney-McCumber Tariff and the 1930 Smoot-Hawley Tariff. Each raised barriers on tens of thousands of import goods. Such thinking is exemplified by the most sweeping immigration restriction acts in U.S. history from the same era: the 1921 Emergency Quota Act and the draconian Johnson-Reed Immigration Act of 1924, which reduced immigration into the nation to a trickle, setting national immigration quotas on ratios from 1890, discriminating against immigrants from southern and eastern Europe and virtually all Asian peoples (in effect until the 1960s). Here we see some of the most important antecedents of the sorts of unilateral protectionist, restrictionist, probusiness polices advocated by Trump and his allies. A glance at a range of flashpoint moments makes the historical case for the enduring power and remarkable adaptability of unilateralism as an ideology.

One reason to tackle unilateralism as ideology in the early twenty-first century is that it seems to have come roaring back, yet so many commentators and citizens seem amnesiac about just how powerful, enduring, and appealing it has been in the historical record. The recent "turn" toward unilateralism in rhetoric and action, and perhaps a new or renewed turn against it, makes it all the more incumbent on historians to examine patterns of thought and practice, to determine an intellectual genealogy, and to diagnose successes, failures, appeals, and transformations over time. In other words, we must historicize the "unilateral shift" of Trump and his administration. And when we do, we see that unilateral arguments and actions abound, from "America First" nationalist unilateralism from 2017 to the present, including in some of the Biden administration's actions, and that similar invocations and policies go all the way back to the Model Treaty of the Founders. They took first form in bedrock ideas and approaches to American foreign policy, firmly moored to George Washington's injunctions to "not quit our own to stand upon foreign ground . . . [and not] interweaving our destiny with that of any part of Europe" and Adams's rationale that "we should calculate all our measures and foreign negotiations in such a manner, as to avoid a too great dependence upon any one power of Europe."[37] Indeed, from the eighteenth century to the present, unilateralist motivators were present in the international arena, enmeshed in a system that has rested on foundational principles of sovereignty and the boundaries of the nation-state that acknowledge few limits on their independence since the Peace of Westphalia in 1648. This is hardly a uniquely American diplomatic ideology, although there is a strong case to be made that unilateralist ideology has taken on a unique form as it developed in the U.S. context. Despite the ascent of multilateralism over the U.S.'s history and current interdependent and multilateral world, multilateral institutions tend to be less flexible and slower to act. Therefore, unilateral persuasion, leadership, or threats have tended in recent history to generate action—for better and for worse.

One goal of this chapter has been to start a conversation about how unilateralism, as a limited but persuasive set of principles, can stand—and has stood—on its own in large part as ideology and in part as tactic (or behavior).[38] Unilateralism, as we have seen, operated as ideology as an influence on foreign policy thought, debate, or policy.

In the cases examined briefly in this chapter, we must acknowledge the narrowness of unilateralism as ideology, at least in how it has functioned in the history of U.S. foreign relations, and the often repugnant outcomes it has justified. Nationalism, civilizational hierarchy, exceptionalism, and empire are centrally at stake in the development and application—as well as the appeal—of unilateralism. Within this, a process of "othering" is critical to the one-sidedness of unilateral action, such as against or for specific ethnic, racial, and religious groups.

In this way, too, the history of unilateralism as foreign policy ideology, wrapped up as it is in ideals and values related to democracy—anticolonialism, exceptionality, and equality— simultaneously has been implicated in some of the worst excesses of American uniqueness and projections of national greatness: racial hierarchy, hegemonic practices, and settler colonialism. The Janus-faced nature of unilateralism suggests its function might be best understood in terms of what French minister and diplomatic thinker Charles-Maurice de Talleyrand called the "equilibrium" state. Unilateralism has been and continues to be the default setting or "orthodoxy test" by which all other policy options and ideological approaches can be measured in the formation of U.S. foreign policy.[39]

Notes

1. John Bolton, *The Room Where It Happened: A White House Memoir* (New York: Simon & Schuster, 2020), 485. This emphasis on unilateralism is borne out in the recent spate of books on the Trump administration such as those by journalists Michael Bender, Carol Leaning and Phil Rucker, and Michael Wolff, and insiders such as Bolton, Cliff Sims, Sean Spicer, and Alexander Vindman.
2. Dexter Filkins, "John Bolton on the Warpath," *New Yorker*, May 6, 2019, https://www.newyorker.com/magazine/2019/05/06/john-bolton-on-the-warpath.

3. Board of Editors, "Trump Administration Extends Its Assault on Multilateralism—Attack on the ICC Marks an Escalation of Washington's Unilateralism," *Financial Times*, September 14, 2018.

4. Christopher S. Kelley, " Rhetoric and Reality? Unilateralism and the Obama Administration," *Social Science Quarterly* 93, no. 5 (Special Issue, December 2012): 1146–60. The Bush Doctrine of preemption, inscribed in the National Security Strategy of 2002, is almost always depicted by scholars as well as diplomats as fundamentally unilateralist. For example, see Strobe Talbot, "Unilateralism: Anatomy of a Foreign Policy Disaster," *YaleGlobal Online*, February 21, 2007, https://www.brookings.edu/opinions/unilateralism-anatomy-of-a-foreign-policy-disaster/. There is a large body of scholarship on the "unilateralist turn" after 9/11, or perhaps as evident in the 1990s and post–Cold War; see David Skidmore, "Understanding the Unilateralist Turn in U.S. Foreign Policy," *Foreign Policy Analysis* 1, no. 2 (July 2005): 207–28; Maria Kiani, "US Unilateralism Versus Post-Cold War Multilateralism," *Strategic Studies* 23, no. 3 (Autumn 2003): 103–24; John G. Ruggie, "Doctrinal Unilateralism and Its Limits: America and Global Governance in the New Century," Corporate Social Responsibility Initiative Working Paper No. 16, John F. Kennedy School of Government, Harvard University, 2006, https://www.hks.harvard.edu/sites/default/files/centers/mrcbg/programs/cri/files/workingpaper_16_ruggie.pdf.

5. Across journalism and scholarship, a few representative pieces over time include critiques of "unilateral" Obama administration policies, most notably regarding drones, and scholarly accounts such as Christopher S. Kelley, "Rhetoric and Reality? Unilateralism and the Obama Administration," *Social Science Quarterly* 93, no. 5 (Special Issue, December 2012): 1146–60. In the George W. Bush years this criticism is vast, for example, see Thomas Ricks, *Fiasco: The American Military Adventure in Iraq* (New York: Penguin, 2006). Andrew Bacevich and Samantha Power had criticism similar to that of Talbott, "Unilateralism: Anatomy of a Foreign Policy Disaster." But there was also praise for unilateralism, such as Charles Krauthammer's coinage of the "Bush Doctrine" as a useful application and extension of "unilateralism" in policy, treaty-making, and treaty-breaking. See Charles Krauthammer, "The Bush Doctrine: ABM, Kyoto, and the New American Unilateralism," *Weekly Standard*, June 4, 2001; and Charles Krauthammer, "Charlie Gibson's Gaffe," *Washington Post*, September 13, 2008. There has been a good amount of debate about how best to characterize the Clinton administration's foreign policy on the shift from multilateralism to unilateralism; those writing during the Clinton years and before 9/11 were more firm about the underlying unilateralism (contrasts to George W. Bush made it seem less clear): see Bernd W. Kubbig, Matthias Dembinski, and Alexander Kell, "The Primacy of Unilateralism:

The American Superpower and the International Organizations in the Clinton Era" *Amerikastudien/American Studies* 46, no. 4 (2001): 629–46. Similar analysis of Clinton building in part on a legacy bequeathed by George H. W. Bush appears in the *American Prospect* and a range other publications and as tracked by scholars, such as in "The US: The Unilateralist Temptation," *Strategic Survey* 95, no. 1 (1994): 53–63, doi 10.1080/04597239408460968.

6. Anthony Blinken, "Stepping Back from Unilateralism," Arms Control Today, January/February 2021, https://www.armscontrol.org/act/2021-01/features /stepping-back-unilateralism.

7. Barbara Plett Usher, "Up Close with Biden and Trump's Top Diplomats," BBC News, May 7, 2021, https://www.bbc.com/news/world-us-canada-57022920.

8. Lu Feng, "How Will Biden Manage Unilateral Tariff Legacy?," *Global Times*, March 21, 2021, https://www.globaltimes.cn/page/202103/1218960.shtml; Ibrahim Al Marashi, "Will Biden's Iraq Policy Signal the End of US Unilateralism?," TRT World, February 22, 2021, https://www.trtworld.com/opinion /will-biden-s-iraq-policy-signal-the-end-of-us-unilateralism-44396.

9. Stewart Patrick, "The Biden Administration and the Future of Multilateralism," *Council on Foreign Relations* (blog), April 21, 2021, https://www.cfr.org /blog/biden-administration-and-future-multilateralism (emphasis added).

10. Post Editorial Board, "Biden Signals Unilateralism and Other Commentary," *New York Post*, January 26, 2021, https://nypost.com/2021/01/26/biden -signals-unilateralism-and-other-commentary/; Kay C. James, "Is Biden Committed to Unity or Unilateral Action?," Heritage Foundation, January 29, 2021, https://www.heritage.org/political-process/commentary/biden-commited -unity-or-unilateral-action.

11. In the withdrawal from Afghanistan, many observers suggest that they have seen the emergence of a Biden Doctrine, "a cautious worldview that prizes alliances but also narrows the aperture of American influence." Matt Viser, Anne Gearan, and Reis Thebault, "'America First Lite': Afghanistan Withdrawal Brings a Biden Doctrine Into Focus," *Washington Post*, August 21, 2021, https:// www.washingtonpost.com/politics/biden-doctrine-afghanistan/2021/08/21 /df07e02a-0106-11ec-85f2-b871803f65e4_story.html. Ian Bremmer as quoted in Ashley Parker, Tyler Pager, and Annie Linskey, "72 Hours at Camp David: Inside Biden's Lagging Response to the Fall of Afghanistan," *Washington Post*, August 17, 2021, https://www.washingtonpost.com/politics/biden-afghanistan -camp-david/2021/08/16.

12. Christopher McKnight Nichols, "U.S. in the World: The Significance of an Isolationist Tradition," in *American Labyrinth: Intellectual History for Complicated Times*, ed. Raymond Haberski Jr. and Andrew Hartman (Ithaca, NY: Cornell University Press, 2018), 296–340. Here I draw upon some insightful older work and draw quotes from Samuel Flagg Bemis, "Washington's Farewell

Address," *American Historical Review* (1934); John Quincy Adams, *Writings of John Adams*, ed. Worthington C. Ford (1913–1917; repr. Ithaca, NY: Cornell University Library, 2009).

13. Melvyn P. Leffler, "9/11 and American Foreign Policy," *Diplomatic History* 29, no. 3 (June 2005): 398.

14. Stephen G. Brooks and William C. Wohlforth, "International Relations Theory and the Case Against Unilateralism," *Perspectives on Politics* 3, no. 3 (September 2005): 509–24; Charles William Maynes, "US Unilateralism and Its Dangers," *Review of International Studies* 25, no. 3 (July 1999): 515–18; Jagdish Bhagwati and Patrick Hugh, *Aggressive Unilateralism: America's 301 Trade Policy and the World Trading System* (Ann Arbor: University of Michigan Press, 1990); Joseph Nye Jr., "America Can't Go It Alone: Unilateralism vs. Multilateralism," *New York Times* and *International Herald Tribune*, June 13, 2002; Talbot, "Unilateralism: Anatomy of a Foreign Policy Disaster." For a characteristic view in the 2017–2021 period, see Peter Gibbon and Jakob Vestergaard, "US Trade Policy Under Trump: Assessing the Unilateralist Turn," *Danish Institute for International Studies* 8 (2017): 24.

15. G. John Ikenberry, *After Victory: Institutions, Strategic Restraint, and the Rebuilding of Order After Major Wars* (Princeton, NJ: Princeton University Press, 2000); G. John Ikenberry, "Is American Multilateralism in Decline?," *Perspectives on Politics* 1, no. 3 (2003): 533–50; G. John Ikenberry, *Liberal Order and Imperial Ambition* (Cambridge: Polity, 2006); and G. John Ikenberry, *Liberal Leviathan: The Origins, Crisis, and Transformation of the American World Order* (Princeton, NJ: Princeton University Press, 2012).

16. This argument is detailed at length in Christopher McKnight Nichols, "Beyond Hemispherism: Charles Beard's Vision of World Order," in *Progressivism and U.S. Foreign Policy Between the World Wars*, ed. Cornelia Navarri and Molly Cochran (London: Palgrave, 2017), 241–68.

17. Walter McDougall, *Promised Land Crusader State: The American Encounter with the World Since 1776* (New York: Mariner, 1997), 43, 49.

18. George Herring, *From Colony to Superpower: U.S. Foreign Relations Since 1776* (New York: Oxford University Press, 2008), 6.

19. On coming to terms with ideology, see Michael Hunt, *Ideology and U.S. Foreign Policy* (New Haven, CT: Yale University Press, 1987), 17–18.

20. Jennifer Ratner-Rosenhagen, *The Ideas That Made America: A Brief History* (New York: Oxford University Press, 2019), 48–49.

21. Michael Kammen, *Empire and Interest: The American Colonies and the Politics of Mercantilism* (Philadelphia: Lippincott, 1970).

22. For example, William Wallace, "U.S. Unilateralism: A European Perspective," in *Multilateralism and U.S. Foreign Policy: Ambivalent Engagement*, ed. Stewart Patrick and Shepard Forman (Boulder, CO: Lynne Rienner, 2002), 141–64;

R. Wedgwood, "Unilateral Action in a Multilateral World," in *Multilateralism and U.S. Foreign Policy: Ambivalent Engagement*, ed. Stewart Patrick and Shepard Forman (Boulder, CO: Lynne Rienner, 2002), 167–89.

23. George Washington, *Farewell Address* (1796; repr. New York: Bedford, 2002), 29–30.

24. Charles Maurice de Talleyrand as quoted in Albert Hall Bowman, *Struggle for Neutrality: Franco-American Diplomacy During the Federalist Era* (Knoxville: University of Tennessee Press, 1974), 415.

25. It is incumbent on us to recognize the alliances forged with Indigenous peoples, and then, of course, the Revolutionary French alliance, which was discarded when it was no longer self-serving; there is some superb scholarship being done on American-Native relations as U.S. foreign relations and understood as part of the intellectual/ideological makeup of American foreign policy, for example, the work of Brian DeLay, Sasha Harmon, Andrew Lipman, and Daniel Richter.

26. On Jefferson's limited foreign policy perspective but expansive "continental" understanding of expansion and America's "republican empire," see Peter Onuf, *Jefferson's Empire: The Language of American Nationhood* (Charlottesville: University of Virginia Press, 2000). See also Thomas Jefferson, *Writings: Autobiography / Notes on the State of Virginia / Public and Private Papers / Addresses / Letters* (New York: Library of America, 1984). On Franklin, "Benjamin Franklin to Lord Kames, January 3, 1760," in Leonard W. Labaree, ed., *The Papers of Benjamin Franklin*, vol. 9 (New Haven, CT: Yale University Press, 1966), 9:7. On British debates about expansion and America's so-called empire, see Felix Gilbert, *To the Farewell Address: Ideas of Early American Foreign Policy* (Princeton, NJ: Princeton University Press, 1961), 33–35. Gerald Stourzh, *Benjamin Franklin and American Foreign Policy*, 2nd ed. (Chicago: University of Chicago Press, 1969), 120.

27. James Monroe, "*Monroe Doctrine*," Annual Address to Congress on December 2, 1823. For the Monroe Doctrine's ideological development in later narratives of American empire, see Gretchen Murphy, *Hemispheric Imaginings: The Monroe Doctrine and Narratives of U.S. Empire* (Durham, NC: Duke University Press, 2005).

28. Walter McDougall, *Promised Land, Crusader State: The American Encounter with the World Since 1776* (Boston: Houghton Mifflin, 1997), 51.

29. Randolph Bourne, "Trans-National America," (*Atlantic Monthly*, vol. 118 [July, 1916]: 86–97), in *War and the Intellectuals: Essays by Randolph S. Bourne, 1915–1919*, ed. Carl Resek (New York: Harper and Row, 1964), 107–23.

30. This trajectory has been established by reviewing the relevant literature and through basic Google Books N-Gram Viewer and a range of word and phrase searches performed by the author.

31. John Gerard Ruggie, ed., *Multilateralism Matters: The Theory and Praxis of an Institutional Form* (New York: Columbia University Press, 1993), 12; David M.

Malone and Yuen Foong Khong, eds., *Unilateralism and U.S. Foreign Policy: International Perspectives* (Boulder, CO: Lynne Riener, 2003), 3.

32. Nichols, article in progress on the "doctrine of the free hand" in the early Cold War, with special focus on the foreign policies of Robert A. Taft.

33. This is evident in my current book project on conservative foreign policy thought in the early Cold War with a focus on the pivotal 1952 election (Oxford: Oxford University Press, forthcoming).

34. Christopher McKnight Nichols, "Strains of Isolationism, "in *Promise and Peril: America at the Dawn of a Global Age* (Cambridge, MA: Harvard University Press, 2011), 347–52. I argue for protectionism and political isolationism as the two types, with eight main strains or points of emphasis: unilateralism, nonentanglement, and neutrality are the three most vital (also included are self-sufficiency, hemispherism or continentalism, temporary/ad hoc alliances, exceptionalism, and minimizing war). Christopher McKnight Nichols, "The Enduring Power of Isolationism: An Historical Perspective," *Orbis* 57, no. 3 (Summer 2013): 390–407; Christopher McKnight Nichols, "Isolationism, Internationalism, and the USA's 'America First' Policy in Historical Perspective," *Journal of International Affairs* 3, no. 2 (March 2019): 1–22. There appear to be connections in the U.S. historical record between unilateralism and populism.

35. Robert Osgood, *Ideals and Self-Interest in America's Foreign Relations* (Chicago: University of Chicago Press, 1953), 5–6.

36. George Herring termed the overriding U.S. foreign policy orientation in the 1920s and into the 1930s as one of "involvement without commitment." George Herring, *From Colony to Superpower: U.S. Foreign Relations Since 1776* (New York: Oxford University Press, 2008), 436.

37. The Adams quote comes from *The Papers of John Adams*, Vol. 14. "To the President of Congress" (Paris Feby. 5th, 1783), Massachusetts Historical Society, Adams Papers Digital Edition, p. 241, 1783, https://www.masshist.org /publications/adams-papers/index.php/view/ADMS-06-14-02-pb-0238.

38. To be clear, my point is not to say that unilateralism is the same as isolationism, nor is it to make the case that unilateralism is the right way to understand what is sometimes construed "mistakenly" as isolationism, as Walter McDougall and George Herring suggest at various times in their work. Instead, I am making the case that unilateralism can and does stand on its own in the historical record as an ideology, albeit one linked closely as part of a broader set of isolationist core ideological points of emphasis, in keeping with my argument and historical findings in Nichols, *Promise and Peril: America at the Dawn of a Global Age*.

39. George Tucker, *The History of the University States from Their Colonization to the End of the Twenty-Sixth Congress, in 1841*, 4 vols. (Philadelphia, 1856), as cited by Jerald A. Combs, *American Diplomatic History: Two Centuries of Changing Interpretations* (Berkeley: University of California Press, 1983), 15.

PART THREE

Ideologies of the International

CHAPTER 10

"For Young People"

Protestant Missions, Geography, and American Youth at the End of the Nineteenth Century

EMILY CONROY-KRUTZ

In 1880, the *Morning Star* made its seventh trip between Micronesia and Hawaii, carrying supplies and teachers to this mission field in the Pacific. This had been an exciting trip. As the ship traveled her familiar path, she noticed the "crowds of children that gather along the coral strands, waving their feathery palm boughs, singing just the sweetest welcomes ever sung," and the ship was happy. The children were delighted to welcome their new teachers, recent Christian converts from Ponape, and the ship, too, was delighted to carry them. But she soon felt "twinges of fear" as she pulled into a new and unfamiliar lagoon. Making her way carefully through the reefs and flats, the ship recalled the "bloody deeds" that had occurred there in the past. It seemed suspicious to her that "no natives came off to meet" her. Through the bushes, she could see some people "dodging in and out," "darting" into darkness and hiding. It was "an hour or two of solemn suspense" as the ship worried that she "had got [her] friends into a tight place." As she told this story to the young American Christians who had long been her sponsors, she emphasized the twin emotions of the joy of coming together and the fear of the unknown. Missionaries, converts, and natives alike were all the "friends" of the ship—except for when those natives did not seem happy to meet her and the cargo she carried. Luckily in this instance, she made it out safely and soon heard shouts of "joyous welcome" to herself and the teachers she carried. Young American readers could sigh with relief that their ship lasted another day to return to Ponape again. Usually, when the *Morning Star* wrote to her young American correspondents, she ended her letter with a call to action. If it seems odd that a ship was writing to American youth, the reasons could be found in those closing appeals.[1]

The *Morning Star* was a missionary ship, and a special one at that. Funded largely through donations from American children and youth, she was the special contribution of American Protestant young people to the foreign mission movement (figure 10.1). This was the third such ship; *Morning Star I* had been built a generation earlier by American children in the mid-1850s. Perhaps it was the children of those first donors who had begun contributing to this third ship in 1870, sending in pennies for "a plank, or a nail, or a spar, or a rope" in service of the mission cause. In return, they were taught about the places that the *Morning Star* went. The people of Micronesia, these readers learned, were "wild and dark, both in mind and body." Before the missionaries came, they "were all liars and thieves, and were cruel to old people and to women. They believed in spirits, and set up stones in honor of them, to which they brought offerings." But twenty-six years of missionary work had been transformative: now there were thirty-four churches with 1,500 members. Illustrations showed converts in western-style clothing, bibles in hand.[2]

The *Morning Star*'s letters encouraged children to send in their contributions to its work and to the mission cause in general. Appealing to its readers as children, the letters understood that children grow into adults. The ideas that were planted as seeds now would grow to shape the ideology of the adults the children would become. They asked the children to think about whether they, too, would serve as missionaries one day, carried to their new stations by the *Morning Star* herself. The ship promised that if they did they could be assured of "a hearty welcome and a glorious work." The *Morning Star*, in turn, loved these "younger friends" and wrote several letters to them in the 1870s and 1880s. These were published in "For Young People," a monthly column in the *Missionary Herald*, the American Board of Commissioners for Foreign Missions (ABCFM) periodical, alongside brief missionary biographies, geographic reports on mission lands, and updates on the project of global missions intended for young readers and illustrated by maps and photographs of mission buildings, landscapes, and people from mission stations all around the world.[3]

All missionary writing was supposed to be at once didactic and inspiring, informing readers about the world and calling them to take action in it.[4]

WELCOME OF THE MORNING STAR.

Figure 10.1 "Welcome of the Morning Star" accompanied a "For Young People" column on Micronesia.
Source: *Missionary Herald* (May 1882), 205.

Missionary literature aimed at young readers provides us with a distilled version of these larger messages. It both exemplifies a missionary ideology and works to reproduce that ideology over a new generation, providing young readers with a lens through which to see the world and their place within it. Two elements of that ideology are important for our understanding of the relationship of this story to a broader history of ideology and foreign relations. First is the active evangelistic impulse that insisted upon American Christians' right and duty to intervene in the world. Second, and far more complicated, is the tension inherent in the mission movement's simultaneous focus on racial hierarchy and belief in the ultimate equality of all souls. It was a contradictory message that animated missionaries and their supporters throughout the nineteenth and well into the twentieth centuries. When packaged for young readers, it resulted in a literature that claimed to be a central authority for explaining the world and its people. By the end of the century, it included both racist outlooks and the beginnings of the tools to challenge them.

The ultimate success of the foreign mission project demanded its continuation across the generations, so it was especially important to the movement's leaders that American children grew up invested in missions—both spiritually and financially.[5] In the final decades of the nineteenth century, juvenile missionary writing worked to raise up children dedicated to the conversion of the world and secure in their position as American Christians. To inspire a new generation of missionary supporters, the first step was to educate them. "For Young People," like so much missionary writing, did so by taking readers into the global mission field from the comfort of their armchairs.[6] As they did so, we can see the ways in which nineteenth-century missionaries navigated a transitional era from a nineteenth-century emphasis on the "heathenism" of the non-Christian world to the beginnings of a twentieth-century kind of appreciation for foreign cultures and peoples. As they sought to raise a new generation to embrace missionary ideology, these writers worked to resolve tensions between their assumption of the cultural and religious superiority of the United States and new understandings of the value and legitimacy of the foreign cultures they hoped to transform.

By the time the "For Young People" column launched in 1879, the ABCFM had been disseminating "missionary intelligence" to audiences young and old for nearly seven decades. From its beginnings in 1810, missionary leaders had understood that a key part of their work would be to educate the American public about the world. If Americans did not know about foreign places and people, how could they care about the salvation of foreign souls? Accordingly, missionaries became prolific authors who claimed expertise on the places where they lived and worked. In their writings for adults and youth, missionaries provided information about the geography, history, culture, and politics of the places where they lived and worked. They claimed to fully understand who these people were, just as they claimed to know what it was that they really needed: transformation. For much of the century, missionaries were unique among Americans abroad for their long residences in particular foreign spaces and their resultant familiarity with foreign languages, cultures, and people. On this basis, they claimed to be sources who could be trusted to tell Americans the truth about the world.

Missionary literature was shaped by, and in turn helped to reinforce, an evangelistic outlook that we can identify as missionary ideology. This ideology helped its adherents to make sense of the world around them, to borrow Michel Hunt's explanation of ideological constructs, serving "as an indispensable guide to an infinitely complex and otherwise bewildering present, and as a basis for moral action intended to shape a better future."[7] This missionary ideology was predicated, first and foremost, on the supremacy of Protestant Christianity and the identity of the United States as a Christian nation. These basic tenets influenced the responses to all sorts of questions and challenges that missionaries and their American supporters would confront over the course of the century. Perhaps most significant, missionary ideology assumed that the United States would and should be a "sending" nation—intervening in the world to further the work of the gospel.

By the 1870s, young readers of missionary literature were being raised by parents who had themselves had access to the missionary vision of the world for their whole lives. When directed at children, the ideology within missionary literature became all the more evident. The stakes were, quite simply, higher: here was the opportunity to train the next generation of missionaries and donors, without whom the movement would fail. Accordingly, in the vast sea of missionary literature, a healthy quantity was always aimed directly at young readers.[8] By the early twentieth century, religious educators turned to emerging social science research on children's development to consider what missionary writers had long known about young readers: children wanted narrative and characters. Preferably, they should have heroes and vibrant tales of adventure. Missionary literature provided precisely this. With gripping tales of missionaries in exotic climes, authors sought to shape young people's ideological framework on a range of issues: the centrality of their faith to their life and actions, the meaning and significance of human difference, and the role that their country should take in the world. Exposure to these stories from a young age could, writers hoped, set the direction for a person's whole life.[9]

Mid-nineteenth-century missionary children's literature tended to take the form of tracts written for Sabbath-School students. An 1843 tract by missionary J. Scudder, *Letters to Sabbath-School Children on the Condition of the Heathen*, is exemplary of the genre. His reason for writing, he explains to the reader, was "to tell you something of the people among whom I have been dwelling."[10] The tone throughout emphasized his perception of the depravity of India. Individual letters discussed thugs, human sacrifice, self-torture, and *sati*, each emphasizing violence and wickedness. In particular, Scudder dwelt on the ways that Hinduism was bad for women and children. It made for disturbing reading, especially with Scudder's direct appeals to his readers that reminded them that they, too, might have been born into such a place.

The book's overarching goal was to prime young readers to feel grateful that they had been born in a Christian land, and thus to call them to action and their duties as missionaries or missionary supporters. Three of the ten letters explicitly addressed the question of what American children could do, and the answer was clear: donate money, pray, and perhaps even become a missionary yourself when you grow up. Scudder included messages from American children who had saved money by abstaining from tea, sugar, coffee, and other small luxuries, or who had formed sewing and knitting societies to raise money. As Scudder encouraged children to give, he reminded them that people were literally burning to death for want of the gospel. He saved his most gruesome story of sati for this section, telling his readers of a fourteen-year-old widow who had tried to escape the flames of her husband's funeral pyre, only to have her family members trick her into thinking they would help but then forcing her back to her death. Only then did readers learn of Indian children who were able to attend mission schools and become Christians themselves.[11]

Scudder positioned himself as an authority on India. As he told his readers in the opening, this was where he lived. His position as a missionary at Madras was on the book's title page. First-person reporting loaned him the veneer of intimate knowledge and expertise that so many missionary writers of this era claimed. This model would be followed by many of the writers in "For Young People." The column did not always include a byline, but when it did, it was from missionaries in the field whose locations were included alongside their names. Missionaries used such geographic markers as signals of their authentic knowledge. They knew the people they were writing about personally. They walked these streets and spoke the language. Over years of residence, they came to know what mattered in the places they wrote about, and they trusted that their readers would grant them authority as a result.

"For Young People" debuted in the *Missionary Herald* in 1879 and remained a monthly staple into the early twentieth century. After lengthy reports, letters from the mission field, updates on finances and world politics, three to five pages were reserved for children. These were short pieces in simple language, directly addressed to a young reader who may or may not have perused the "adult" section of the magazine. If the front of the *Herald* featured a letter from a particular mission station, "For Young People" might tell children more about that place. In a text-heavy periodical, these were the pages where readers could find images: drawings, photographs, and maps. The *Herald* had no images until "For Young People" debuted; once the column began, it remained the home of most of the illustrations in the magazine.

In contrast to the images that illustrated earlier tracts, these were much more specific and detailed. Earlier juvenile missionary literature included stock illustrations of Bibles, children praying and going to church, or children surrounded by animals in an image of the blessed kingdom. Images that related directly to the text existed but were rarer. Of ten illustrations in Scudder's tract, for example, only four related directly to the text itself. All of these depicted negative portrayals of India and its culture.[12] In contrast, "For Young People" included multiple illustrations that related directly to the text. Making good use of technological innovations as the years progressed, these illustrations showed missionaries, students, mission buildings, street scenes from around the world, and landscapes (figure 10.2). They were much less negative in tone and seemed intended to make the foreign feel more immediate and real to American youth. Maps were similarly included to help ground readers in the geographic specifics of the places they were learning about. In this, they were not dissimilar to secular juvenile travel and adventure writing. Mission stories were designed to be similarly exciting, entertaining, and educational.

Over the years, the articles took on a wide range of themes. Many introduced young readers to places of missionary interest. These were quite similar in tone and content to what readers might have seen in their geography schoolbooks. Indeed, readers of other juvenile missionary periodicals reported that children who studied such missionary sources were "the best students" in their geography and history.[13] The geographic coverage of the columns was quite wide-ranging, with articles discussing most of the ABCFM's mission stations in Africa, Turkey, India, China, Japan, and Micronesia, in addition to a few pieces on Spain, Prague, Hawai'i, Fiji, Madagascar, and North America. These articles featured a combination of general description of population size, landscape, and environment with a good amount of ethnographic detail and cultural commentary. For example, an

ZULUS AT HOME.

Figure 10.2 This depiction of Zulu life was typical of the ways that "For Young People" illustrated its articles over the course of its existence. Realism was the goal. Engravings like this were often modeled from photographs.
Source: Missionary Herald (November 1881), 467.

1881 article, "India and Its Wild Tribes," opened with a discussion of the size and location of India, its population size relative to the recent U.S. census, and a brief history of British rule. With illustrations of hook-swinging, a Parsee man, a landscape, and a Hindu woman, the text then proceeded to describe the different ethnic groups within the country. The changes since missionary work had begun were, the article beamed, "wonderful." Despite the illustration, the writers informed young readers that "hook-swinging is unknown now," and sati had been abandoned. To labor as a missionary in such a field was "a blessed privilege," readers learned.[14] This format was typical of the geographical entries, from its provision of facts to its judgment about cultural values.

Figure 10.3 This map of Central and Southern Africa noted the location of mission stations throughout the region as an illustration of "For Young People: Across Africa." *Source: Missionary Herald* (June 1879), 274.

Two years earlier, "Across Africa" had provided readers with a new map of Africa, based on the explorations of Henry Morton Stanley (figure 10.3). This, too, used the language and tone of scientific information to provide judgment on the peoples whom the ABCFM hoped to evangelize. In comparison to old "quite worthless" maps, young American readers could now look over a map that was "in the main correct" and could help them to understand the location and perhaps the lives of the people of Africa. The article described the people of Uganda as "deceitful, thievish, and quite regardless of human life." Yet the land itself was "marvelous . . . rich and fertile" and would soon "open to trade." These young readers were to understand that the promise of future trade was an important sign of the potential for transformation here; economic hopes were paired with evangelistic hopes. This was a place of promise, and the author concluded the article by assuring young readers that though the people "are rude and cruel . . . they can be reached by the gospel of Jesus Christ." For readers too young to read Stanley's book themselves, "For Young People" provided them with a helpful summary, tailored to missionary interests, accompanied by seven illustrations from the book itself.[15]

Once young readers had been introduced to a general understanding of a place, they could meet some of the people who lived and worked there. Articles introduced readers to missionaries and converts alike. Harriet Newell, whose memoir had been continuously printed since its original 1814 edition, appeared in the "For Young People" column in 1884.[16] Less prominent missionaries were profiled when their stories were particularly inspiring for young American readers. For example, Rev. Richardson, a missionary in Madagascar, was the subject of an article several months after his letters had been published in the main section of the *Herald*. Richardson was only seven years old when he had been called to missionary work. Looking at an illustration of Christians being martyred in Madagascar in the *Juvenile Missionary Magazine*, a mid-century publication of the London Missionary Society, had so moved him that he knew he wanted to travel there some day. Seventeen years later, he did in fact go to Madagascar. "That story made me a missionary," he wrote. Considering that this article was titled "A Picture That Made a Missionary," the writers at the *Missionary Herald* clearly saw it as an inspiring story about the power of the sort of print venture that they were undertaking to power the mission movement. They hoped that their young readers would be similarly inspired to embrace the mission cause from a young age.

In addition to introducing young readers to Richardson, they described the place where he worked. In Madagascar, the government had been "determined to crush out the new religion" and threatened Christian converts with death. Although the new queen had converted and ended this practice, the column ended the article with a poignant tale of martyrdom. To drive home the point of the power of young believers, readers were introduced to a little girl who was killed for her faith. The executioners had planned to spare her because she was just a child, but she had insisted, "No, sir, I am no

A JAPANESE FAMILY.

Figure 10.4 An article celebrating the "First Protestant Baptisms in Japan" included this illustration of a Japanese family.
Source: *Missionary Herald* (January 1887), 44.

fool; but I love the Lord Jesus Christ. Throw me over." Her killers complied. The readers of "For Young People" may have been comforted to read that she "may have accomplished more by her early death than she could have done by a long life."[17] But what had her death accomplished? Perhaps nothing if these young American readers did not respond to her story with action. Like Richardson in his youth, these readers were to respond to the sacrifice of martyred converts with their own embrace of missionary ideology.

Converts and students in mission schools made for particularly exciting topics in these columns. If the articles on missionaries were designed to inspire and model how young Americans ought to live in the world, articles on converts could play a similar role. Here, American youth could read of children facing incredible difficulties who had embraced Christianity regardless of barriers (figure 10.4). These foreign Christians were celebrated for their piety and held up as models of faith for American readers. If foreign children could do so, the implication went, how much more might these young Americans be expected to act as good and true Christians. Articles such as "Ruth of Micronesia," "Chieh-Ni: Maiden, Wife, and Mother," "Tei Ming, the Boy Without Any Feet," and "Blind Wong" were written to inspire pity and sympathetic giving in American readers. Yet they were also marked by racist depictions of the people whom they celebrated. Tei Ming was repeatedly described as an animal, and the missionaries doubted whether he could even feel, never mind convert to, Christianity. Ruth's childhood, too, was compared to that of wild animals before she met the missionaries. Chieh-Ni's husband was praised as gentle and beautiful, but with the important caveat "Chinaman though he was."[18]

Simultaneously celebrating and denigrating converts signaled one of the central tensions of missionary ideology. Missionaries were driven to seek conversion because they believed that Christianity was the true faith. Conversion was necessarily built on the idea that one could change; after converting, the new Christian was a brother or sister in Christ of the American missionary. But missionaries had a difficult time delineating Christianity from other aspects of their culture that they understood to be superior, and their racism had profound effects on the ways that they understood what kinds of changes were possible through conversion. After decades of foreign experience and general shifts in American appreciation of foreign cultures, the 1870s saw missionaries less insistent on changing the cultures they met while still holding on to an assurance of American superiority. In children's literature, these dynamics could produce a dual message.

The complex missionary relationship to world cultures in the last decades of the nineteenth century is well demonstrated in a "For Young People" article by Rev. J. H. DeForest, stationed in Osaka. He had come to Japan in 1875 and filled his days as a teacher and a preacher, but he also became something of a collector of idols. As he told his young readers, one of his seminary classmates at Yale had told him to "remember I want the first bushel of idols you persuade the heathen to give up." Six years later, he began collecting them, first announcing his interest at a gathering of students at the end of the school year, then discussing it with converts he met as he preached around town (figure 10.5). In the *Herald*, he shared illustrations and textual descriptions of the "jolly idols" and stories of their donors as well. One after another, he wrote, converts were getting rid of their idols to make space for Christian worship. The man who gave DeForest

A LOAD OF IDOLS FOR THE MISSIONARY.

Figure 10.5 "A Load of Idols for the Missionary" accompanied the article on DeForest's efforts to collect "rejected idols" that had been cast off by Chinese converts for an eager American audience.

Source: *Missionary Herald* (September 1881), 374.

his *Bishamon* had replaced it with a new lantern that read "The True Way Taught Here," ready to light the way for those who were coming to study Christianity. Another had turned over his home to become a permanent church building.[19]

One doctor had, upon his baptism, planned to throw away, sell, or burn his collection of idols until the missionary offered to take them from him. Now that he had a fine collection, DeForest planned to send them to Yale for the edification of students at his alma mater. He was not the only missionary engaged in collecting work, nor was he the only one to present such materials to a juvenile audience. Rather, he was part of a late-nineteenth-century missionary cohort that was in the midst of a transition from the scorn of "heathen" culture of earlier in the century to what historian Gale Kenny has called "Christian cosmopolitanism."[20] Japan had only opened to Americans in the 1850s, and American interest was high. As with many other parts of the "eastern world," the consumption of Japanese goods and art was an important part of American engagement. For missionaries and their supporters, however, a long-standing commitment to cultural change could result in some uncomfortable dissonance as they tried to make sense of how to at once condemn and celebrate (even collect) the objects of a culture that they were determined to change.

In this late-nineteenth-century moment, missionaries were demanding that converts cast off idols, only to collect them and send them back to the United States to satisfy curious Americans with evidence of what Japanese culture was like. As DeForest explained to his young readers, he regularly discussed idols in his preaching. "Man is naturally covetous," he would preach, "and the Japanese are no exception. The wide worship of *Bishamon*, *Yebisu*, *Daikoku*, and the rest of your gods of luck, shows, beyond any need of argument, that the hearts of the Japanese are covetous, and that they need the gospel of giving as an antidote." That Americans coveted these objects as well, if for other purposes, went unexplored.[21] DeForest hoped that his idols would be displayed in the Peabody Museum, where "they may speak so perpetually of the lust and lies, the folly and moral degradation" of those who had not yet been evangelized. These particular objects, of course, had belonged to those who *had* received the Christian message. Transformed but still represented by the objects of their formerly held beliefs, these Japanese Christians and their representation in the pages of "For Young People" speak to the difficult ways that American missionaries understood conversion and the possibilities or even benefits of cultural change in this transitional moment.

The strangeness of the foreign world was something that some of these missionaries emphasized to young readers. Dr. Emily Smith, a medical missionary bound for China in 1902, for example, emphasized the difficulty of describing "this strange people" as she tried to record her first impressions of her new mission station. She found Shanghai to be too influenced by foreign life. She wanted to find the "real China" that she had read about at home—a place marked by "narrow dirty streets, the sights and sounds and smells." This she found in Foochow, where she described a palanquin ride surrounded by "a wildly shouting, jabbering, gesticulating mob of the strangest looking people I had ever seen, who gazed at me as though I were still stranger than themselves." Smith soon found that she, like all the other China missionaries, "love[d]" the Chinese, although it took "a great deal of patience to put up with all of their peculiarities and apparent stupidities, besides certain dishonesties for which a stronger adjective than 'apparent' must be used." She praised the "rare souls" she met who led lives of "purity and righteousness" and counted herself privileged to live among them.[22]

How might a young reader respond to such a piece? Smith's overwhelming message concerned the importance of the work and the excitement of discovering a new place. The tone was enthusiastic, and she closed with a call for assistance to the station, even as she pointed out that other mission fields surely needed help as well. Like other writers for the column, her story was meant to attract attention and interest in the world, and to plant the seeds for readers to imagine their own entry into the mission field as missionaries or as donors. Such work could have been done without dwelling on difference, but Smith was not alone in this emphasis. China, like so much of the world that missionaries sought to evangelize, was *strange* in "For Young People." Even as writers sought to find the lines of connection and similarity that a Christian understanding of the unity of the kingdom of God required, the strangeness of the foreign world was one of its attractions. Smith's writing is typical for its awkwardness in describing this strangeness and whether or not it implied some sort of hierarchy. After all, she acknowledged that even as she found the Chinese strange, they found *her* to be even stranger.

One of the major shifts in late-nineteenth-century missionary children's literature was the introduction of a more relativistic approach to the descriptions of overseas cultures. Earlier in the century, it would not have been unusual for writers to ask readers to put themselves in the shoes of the "heathen." This framing was often used as a fear tactic, however, and to make a very clear statement of the duty to become involved in mission work. If you had been born in India, your mother might have thrown you into the Ganges, young readers were told. But they had been born in America, thanks to some combination of luck and grace. This demanded a proper response. "God expects of you some return for his goodness to you," Scudder told his readers. As they were lucky enough to be born in America and raised with knowledge of true Christianity, they had a duty to repent of their sins and give their hearts to Christ. Failure to do so would lead to a worse punishment than the "heathen" they were reading about, for these American children should have known better.[23]

Such a harsh tone was significantly lessened by the end of the century, when missionaries writing for a young audience approached the same themes with a different message (figure 10.6). By 1895, one juvenile

A CHILD BEFORE GANESHA.

Figure 10.6 This illustration, depicting a mother and child in front of Ganesha, accompanied a column on "Idolatry in India." It is in marked contrast to the violent images of Hindu mothers and children in earlier juvenile missionary literature, such as Scudder's tract. *Source: Missionary Herald* (December 1879), 516.

missionary periodical, the *Heathen Children's Friend*, even changed its name out of the understanding that the word "heathen" had become "a term of reproach" in the mission fields.[24] Within the "For Young People" column, an article that profiled Stanley's tour of Africa included quotations from Kassanga, Chief of Ruanda, musing about the apparent wickedness of white men: "How can the white men be good when they come for no trade, whose feet one never sees, who always go covered from head to foot with clothes. Do not tell me they are good and friendly. There is something very mysterious about them; perhaps wicked." In the column, these questions were taken seriously, as the author reminded the readers that Africans surely had "as much right to question whether we are men as we have to question whether they are."[25] For all that authors of these pieces clearly believed in the superiority of American Christian culture, they were increasingly ready to discuss the ways in which white Americans had failed to live up to their potential and had failed to act as examples in various ways.

Similarly, an article on Chinese superstition could easily compare rituals of birth and death in that country to those of "some foolish people in America" who likewise associated good or bad luck with certain places and dates. The Chinese, the column was sure to explain, took things further than their fellow superstitious Americans, but the comparison was pointed.[26] When describing the ways in which some Muslims "reverence but do not obey" the Koran, they were similarly quick to compare this practice to Christians who "reverence the Bible as a holy book, but do not follow its commands." Here, perhaps most directly, the writer's comparisons between American Protestantism and other religions were designed to prick at the conscience of young American readers. The comparison, then, could both create connections and also shame Americans for the likeness.[27]

This dynamic is the key to the ideological work that the column set out to do. American children, the articles implied, should be ashamed precisely because they should be better than these others. Their role in the world, the articles collectively argued, was to intervene and to bring the good news of both the gospel and the modern world. Adult writers in this transitional era held to this ideological framework even as their writings revealed aspects of a pluralistic appreciation of foreign cultures and people.

The politics of these columns lives between the lines. Explicit discussion of major political events is absent, despite their obvious presence elsewhere in missionary writing. Although adult missionary literature was full of hand-wringing, planning, theorizing, and self-justifications in the years between the Spanish-American War and the Boxer Uprising, "For Young People" continued in its tradition of didactic and inspirational writing for American Christian youth. The Philippines are largely absent here. Certainly there is no discussion of this new colony as a missionary opportunity, even as adults in the mission movement emphasized this idea.[28] It is in looking at the type of education these authors tried to provide their child readers, and at the ways they sought to energize them to go into the world, that we can see the politics of "For Young People."

In the early years of the new century, the column expanded into a Young People's Department. With the new department, young people could find a new slate of articles designed to support the young leaders of missionary organizations in the United States. The emphasis of these new features was missionary methodology, reading suggestions, spiritual development advice, and announcement of activities in other denominational groups.[29] The didactic and inspirational writing for children and youth continued to be found in other venues but was absent in the *Missionary Herald* in the same form. Throughout the nineteenth century and well into the twentieth, young American Christians could find an introduction to the people, cultures, and landscapes of the world through missionary introductions.

Notes

1. "For Young People: Report of the Morning Star," *Missionary Herald* (May 1880): 197–99; "For Young People: The Morning Star's Report to Her Stockholders," *Missionary Herald* (May 1879): 197–99; "For Young People: The Last Words of Morning Star No. III," *Missionary Herald* (March 1885): 129–32. Emphasis in original.
2. "For Young People: Micronesia," *Missionary Herald* (January 1879): 37–40.
3. "For Young People: The Morning Star's Report to Her Stockholders"; "For Young People: The Last Words of Morning Star No. III."
4. On missionary periodicals more generally, see David Golding, "Superstitions of the Heathen: Foreign Missions and the Fashioning of American Exceptionalism, 1800–1861" (PhD diss., Claremont Graduate University, 2016); Terry Barringer, "What Mrs. Jellyby Might Have Read: Missionary Periodicals: A Neglected Source," *Victorian Periodicals Review* 37, no. 4 (Winter 2004): 46–74.
5. On the moral and political work of nineteenth-century children's religious literature, see Gale L. Kenny, "Mastering Childhood: Paternalism, Slavery, and the Southern Domestic in Caroline Howard Gailman's Antebellum Children's Literature," *Southern Quarterly* 44, no. 1 (Fall 2006): 65–87; Karen Keely, "'Let the Children Have Their Part': 'The Young Christian Soldier' and the Domestic Missionary Army," *Anglican and Episcopal History* 79, no. 3 (September 2010): 200–237.
6. On armchair tourism in this era, see Kristin Hoganson, *Consumer's Imperium: The Global Production of American Domesticity, 1865–1920* (Chapel Hill: University of North Carolina Press, 2007), chap. 4.
7. Michael Hunt, *Ideology and U.S. Foreign Policy*, rev. ed. (New Haven, CT: Yale University Press, 2009), 12.

8. The ABCFM was a Congregationalist organization whose members and supporters would, by the early twentieth century, be active in the ecumenical movement. Rennie Schoepflin's survey of nearly a dozen American children's missionary magazines across ecumenical and evangelical denominations from 1880 to 1980 found remarkable similarities in the ways that they portrayed mission work to young readers. Rennie B. Schoepflin, "Making Doctors and Nurses for Jesus: Medical Missionary Stories and American Children," *Church History* 74, no. 3 (September 2005): 557–90. See also Karen Li Miller, "The White Child's Burden: Managing the Self and Money in Nineteenth-Century Children's Missionary Periodicals," *American Periodicals* 22, no. 2 (2012):1390157.

9. Sophia Lyons Fahs, "Missionary Biography in the Sunday School," *Biblical World* 27, no. 5 (May 1906): 362–70.

10. J. Scudder, *Letters to Sabbath-School Children on the Condition of the Heathen* (Philadelphia: American Sunday-School Union, 1843), Letter 1.

11. Scudder, *Letters to Sabbath-School Children on the Condition of the Heathen*, Letters 9–10.

12. The book included illustrations of Juggernaut, an Indian mother throwing her baby into the Ganges, a devotee throwing himself under the wheel of a Juggernaut cart, and a person performing a hook vow. These India-specific illustrations accompanied illustrations of a Bible with rays of light, a small white child surrounded by animals, a small white child praying, a man in a top hat, white children going to church, and a missionary preaching in an unspecified location. Scudder, *Letters to Sabbath-School Children on the Condition of the Heathen*, 5, 9, 13, 17, 19, 25, 26, 29, 39, 45.

13. Quotation from *Heathen Children's Friend*, as quoted in Miller, "The White Child's Burden," 148. Compare missionary writings with, for example, Samuel Griswold Goodrich, *Peter Parley's Geography for Beginners; with Eighteen Maps and One Hundred and Fifty Engravings* (New York: Huntington and Savage, 1847); Roswell C. Smith, *Smith's New Geography, Containing Map Questions Interspersed with Such Facts as an Observing Tourist Would Notice, Which Are Followed by a Concise Text and Explanatory Notes. Based on a Combination of the Analytical, Synthetical and Comparative Systems; Designed to Be Simple and Concise, but Not Dry; Philosophical, yet Practical for the Use of Common Schools in the United States and Canada* (Philadelphia: Lippincott, 1861).

14. "For Young People: India and Its Wild Tribes," *Missionary Herald* (February 1881): 81–84.

15. "For Young People: Across Africa," *Missionary Herald* (July 1879): 273–80.

16. "For Young People: Harriet Newell," *Missionary Herald* (December 1884): 531–34; Mary Kupiec Cayton, "Canonizing Harriet Newell: Women, the Evangelical Press, and the Foreign Mission Movement in New England, 1800–1840," in *Competing Kingdoms: Women, Mission, Nation, and the American*

Protestant Empire, 1812–1960, ed. Barbara Reeves-Ellington, Kathryn Kish Sklar, and Connie A. Shemo (Durham, NC: Duke University Press, 2010), 69–93.

17. "For Young People: A Picture That Made a Missionary," *Missionary Herald* (September 1880): 365–66.

18. Mrs. Sarah J. Price, "For Young People: Ruth of Micronesia," *Missionary Herald* (January 1899): 41–44; Rev. Charles A. Nelson, "For Young People: Blind Wong," *Missionary Herald* (March 1901): 133–36; Mrs. Arthur H. Smith, "For Young People: Tei Ming, the Boy Without Any Feet," *Missionary Herald* (December 1899): 553–56; Mrs. Sarah B. Goodrich, "For Young People: Chieh-Ni; Maiden, Wife, Mother," *Missionary Herald* (April 1899): 168–72.

19. J. H. DeForest, "For Young People: Rejected Idols," *Missionary Herald* (September 1881): 371–74.

20. Gale Kenny, "The World Day of Prayer: Ecumenical Churchwomen and Christian Cosmopolitanism," *Religion and American Culture* 27, no. 2 (Summer 2017): 129–58.

21. DeForest, "For Young People: Rejected Idols."

22. Miss Emily D. Smith, M.D., "For Young People: Some First Impressions of China," *Missionary Herald* (May 1902): 221–24.

23. Scudder, *Letters to Sabbath-School Children on the Condition of the Heathen*, 32.

24. Miller, "The White Child's Burden,"143.

25. "For Young People: Across Africa," *Missionary Herald* (July 1879): 273–80.

26. "For Young People: China," *Missionary Herald* (March 1879): 113–20.

27. "For Young People: The Followers of the False Prophet," *Missionary Herald* (November 1879): 481–84.

28. The only mention of the Philippines in the column is in "Spanish Friar and Evangelist in the Philippines," an article by Esther Alonso, the daughter of a deceased Philippine missionary of the London Bible Society. Miss Esther Alonso, "For Young People: Spanish Friar and Evangelist in the Philippines," *Missionary Herald* (March 1899): 129–32.

29. "Young People and Missions," *Missionary Herald* (May 1903): 216.

CHAPTER 11

Eugenia Charles, the United States, and Military Intervention in Grenada

IMAOBONG UMOREN

On the morning of October 25, 1983, Eugenia Charles appeared alongside President Ronald Reagan at the White House press briefing room. The sixty-four-year-old prime minister may have been relatively unknown to American audiences, but three years earlier she made international headlines when she became the first female prime minister in the Anglophone Caribbean, following her victory in the 1980 election in Dominica. In her role as head of the Organisation of Eastern Caribbean States (OECS), a seven-nation coalition, Charles and Reagan informed audiences that nineteen hundred U.S. marines and army rangers alongside three hundred Caribbean troops had staged an invasion of Grenada following the assassination of its prime minister, Maurice Bishop. After hearing news of the violence, the OECS reached out for assistance to other islands in the region, namely Jamaica and Barbados, and later to the United States. The events in Grenada served as the principal reason for Charles's presence at the White House, but it also marked a significant step in her strategic attempt to persuade a seemingly reluctant United States to set its sights more broadly on the former British Caribbean and, in particular, on the eastern islands, many of which were among the poorest in the region.

When Charles took office, Dominica was on the brink of collapse. Known as the nature island, Dominica was not typical of islands in the Caribbean due to its agrarian economy and its rugged mountainous terrain. With a small population of around 73,795 in 1981, the island suffered from a substantial public debt and a severe lack of necessary infrastructure.[1] Due to the absence of white sandy beaches, Dominica could not develop mass Western tourism. The island depended on bananas, which accounted for 60 percent of export earnings in 1978.[2] But Hurricane David destroyed the industry in 1979, causing a 42 percent drop in exports. Weeks after Charles took office in 1980 Hurricane Allen caused further structural damage.

According to Charles, the only way Dominica could survive was with the help of Western powers. As a conservative, Charles did not resent Britain's colonial influence nor was she opposed to U.S. investment in the region. Following decolonization in 1978, Britain disengaged with Dominica and other former Caribbean colonies, forcing many new states and their leaders, like Charles, to focus on gaining aid elsewhere. Although she did not give up trying to receive British support, Charles looked beyond Great Britain to the United States, France, Germany, and Taiwan for aid. These actions shaped what scholars have labeled Charles's "donor-driven" economic strategy.[3] Throughout her time as prime minister, Charles approached Western countries and the International Monetary Fund (IMF) for aid and loans but did not present a long-term vision for economic development. Charles's lack of a coherent policy was twinned with her laissez-faire economic attitude and allegiance to free market ideology. Charles believed in the state's importance in providing citizens with education, health care, and infrastructure but "firmly believed the private sector should be the engine of economic growth."[4] However, she failed to grasp that the private sector in Dominica had a limited ability to stimulate the economy. Nonetheless, with these ideas leading Charles's economic and foreign policy, she looked heavily to the United States for support.

Charles repeatedly expressed the need for the United States to engage more closely with the Caribbean. She lamented that "the United States presence in our region is not enough" and encouraged leaders to remember that "we are not your backyard, we are the front door, and you should help us to keep it clear."[5] In 1981, the United States did precisely that when the FBI provided Dominica with essential intelligence and security assistance that helped prevent the so-called Bayou of Pigs, a coup plotted by white supremacists and former Dominican prime minister Patrick John that sought to transform the island into a "drug, gambling and offshore banking empire."[6] Charles was not the only conservative Caribbean politician calling for the United States to play more of a role in the region, so too did Jamaica's Edward Seaga, Tom Adams from Barbados, and John Compton of

St. Lucia. Together these influential leaders openly denounced communism and socialism and embraced neoliberal economics, in part, to court the United States.

Taking Charles as a case study, I foreground her role in increasing U.S. power and influence in the eastern Caribbean broadly and in Dominica specifically. I focus primarily on the impact of neoliberalism and anticommunism. In the 1970s, as the opposition leader in the Dominica Freedom Party (DFP), Charles used the language of anticommunism to smear her opponents in the left-leaning Dominica Labour Party (DLP) and stressed the importance of neoliberalism as a viable option in aiding Dominica's development. As prime minister in the 1980s, Charles continued to preach anticommunism and neoliberalism, which she hoped would help develop closer ties to the Reagan administration. In some respects, her advocacy did have results, which were evident in the Caribbean Basin Initiative (CBI) and in the aftermath of the U.S. invasion of Grenada when U.S. aid to Dominica increased. Although Charles clung close to following the U.S.-led neoliberal and anticommunist agenda in the Caribbean, it resulted in few meaningful political gains.

In the short term, neoliberalism and anticommunism united Charles with U.S. security interests, but in the long term it hindered relations between the two states, exposing Dominica's vulnerability and undermining Caribbean unity. The two ideologies also came to have negative consequences for Charles's leadership as she increasingly came to be viewed as merely a puppet for the United States. Focusing on the effects of neoliberalism and anticommunism for Charles and Dominica illuminates the seminal role they played in shaping U.S.-Dominica relations and provides a more nuanced understanding of the difficulties Charles faced as the leader of a small state. They also offer further context for explaining the changing tide of U.S. interests in the eastern Caribbean in the 1980s.

Early in his presidency, Reagan recognized the Caribbean's significance as a space where the United States could continue its Cold War assault and containment of Cuba. His administration promoted a policy that recognized the Caribbean as America's third border.[7] First introduced in the Bahamas in 1981, the CBI served as the central piece of Reagan's foreign policy in the Caribbean. The CBI aimed to "stimulate foreign and domestic investment, to diversify local economies, and to augment export earnings by eliminating U.S. customs duties on most items manufactured or assembled" throughout the Commonwealth Caribbean and Latin and Central America.[8] Reagan contrasted the CBI "designed to help the nations there help themselves through trade and private investment" with what he called the "Soviet and Cuban Caribbean Basin Initiative" that sought "to brutally impose Communist rule and deny individual freedom."[9] The CBI enabled the United States to maintain economic and political hegemony in the region while also convincing Caribbean economies to be receptive to U.S. ideas of enterprise and freedom.

Although Charles and other Caribbean Community (CARICOM) leaders welcomed the CBI, they also voiced criticism. Established in 1973, CARICOM promoted regional cooperation and economic integration among the British empire's former Caribbean colonies. It served as a seminal organization within the Caribbean and formed connections to other regional institutions such as the OECS and the Organization of American States (OAS). One of the central critiques CARICOM leaders made of the CBI was its treatment of Grenada. They attacked "the economic aggression being waged by the United States against the left-wing government of Grenada," which was prohibited from joining the CBI.[10] Grenada's exclusion undermined regional unity because the island was a member of both CARICOM and the OECS. CARICOM leaders insisted that the United States respect the sovereignty of all states in the region, including Cuba and Nicaragua, which were also excluded from the CBI.[11]

Reagan's refusal to include Grenada within the CBI served as part of a broader strategy to destabilize the island. After Bishop and others in the socialist New Jewel Movement (NJM) overthrew former prime minister Eric Gairy in the revolution of 1979, they installed the People's Revolutionary Government (PRG). Initially, the United States recognized Bishop's government, but when Reagan entered the White House, he asked him to stop his anti-U.S. rhetoric, break ties with Cuba, hold general elections, and show a commitment to nonalignment. When Bishop refused, tensions between Grenada and the United States escalated.[12] Despite calls from CARICOM, the CBI remained unavailable to Grenada, leading to divisions among member states.

Leaders of small states also criticized the CBI for its alleged favoritism toward larger states, such as Jamaica. After Seaga's election in 1980, commentators considered Jamaica "the most committed 'client-state'" of the United States in the Caribbean.[13] Upon taking office, Seaga cut links with Cuba that former prime minister Michael Manley had maintained and opened up the island to increased U.S. investment, especially of the tourist industry. The preference given to Jamaica exacerbated long-standing tensions within CARICOM between large and small nations. Feelings of marginalism among small states in CARICOM encouraged the formation of the OECS. Created to bring together the small islands of Antigua and Barbuda, Dominica, Grenada, Montserrat, St. Kitts and Nevis, St. Lucia, and St. Vincent and the Grenadines, the OECS worked to combat their isolation from the larger CARICOM states and address common problems in the neighboring islands such as development, jobs, and migration. Those from smaller islands in the OECS stated that the CBI was too focused on trade and investment sought by larger islands and did not pay enough attention to providing aid for infrastructural improvements on smaller islands.[14] In the wake of hurricanes David and Allen, Dominica was in desperate need of funds to build roads and improve electrical and water systems. In 1982, amid ongoing talks about the CBI, Charles, Adams, and others in the eastern Caribbean approached Reagan directly for aid to develop these necessities, but Dominica did not receive support. Although Charles and Seaga were close allies, she recognized that he would not challenge the United States on the CBI's scope. But Charles publicly and privately argued that Jamaica's preferential treatment was detrimental to the eastern Caribbean.[15] Charles also called on U.S. policy makers to ensure that the CBI did not show favoritism toward Latin America at the expense of the Caribbean, reminding them that the Caribbean "shouldn't be confused with Central America because we have different hopes and aspirations."[16] From the outset and once the CBI had passed the U.S. Congress, most of the funds targeted Latin and Central America.

Ultimately, the CBI's neoliberal focus had little positive impact in Dominica,[17] and the island's small economy was not able to take advantage of the CBI's initiatives.[18] Dominican senator Charles Savarin gave voice to the CBI's limitations in 1984, stating that "there is an opportunity for us in the C.B.I. to attract investment to create industry. . . . But we would first have to create products we could sell. It would take a long gestation period before we would be able to take advantage of the trade program. So its impact in the short run on our economy will be minimal."[19] Although the CBI did not provide Charles with the expanded influence of the United States in Dominica that she sought, the October 1983 U.S. invasion of Grenada gave her a renewed opportunity.

Charles took a pragmatic approach to the PRG and Bishop. She did not endorse the 1979 revolution or make favorable statements about the PRG, but she recognized the necessity of peaceful coexistence, stating that "we didn't think that we would agree with the things he was doing but we felt that we had to work together if these islands were going to get anywhere."[20] Charles put aside Bishop's animosity toward right-leaning leaders in the Caribbean and worked with him to form the OECS. When Charles heard of Bishop's murder, she released statements condemning the violence and military take over. On Friday, October 21, OECS leaders convened in Barbados and compiled a list of sanctions against Grenada. Adams first raised the prospect of military intervention and arranged for Charles to meet Milan Bish, the U.S. ambassador to the Eastern Caribbean, to talk about U.S. military assistance.[21] The next day the leaders ventured to Trinidad to attend an emergency CARICOM meeting to discuss military intervention. By Sunday, October 23, Charles had returned to Barbados with a note asking for U.S. assistance under the defense and security article eight of the OECS treaty. Following talks with Reagan, the U.S. military invasion of Grenada began.

During the press conference on October 25, Reagan justified the attack as part of an attempt to save the lives of eleven hundred Americans and prevent the spread of communism, describing the island as a "Soviet-Cuban colony being readied as a major military bastion to export terror and undermine democracy."[22] Charles echoed much of Reagan's argument and stressed how Grenada jeopardized the security of the eastern Caribbean. According to Charles, those in the OECS were "greatly concerned that the extensive military build-up in Grenada over the last few years had created a situation of disproportionate military strength between Grenada and other OECS countries. This military might in the hands of the present group has posed a serious threat to the security of the OECS countries and other neighboring states."[23] Charles's words spoke to her real concerns regarding Dominican security, which had increased following the Bayou of Pigs, the Dominican Defense Force's subsequent attempt to release John from prison, the rise of the Dreads, a small but significant group of Black Power influenced Rastafarians some of whom were involved in violence, and the island's lack of a standing army. In her remarks, Charles evoked a sense of mutual responsibility that guided the action of the OECS, arguing that member states in the region considered themselves "kith and kin," which justified their action.[24] But debates raged about the legality of the invasion and the use of article eight in the OECS treaty. Charles and supporters of the intervention argued that article eight gave them the authority to ask for help from the United States. Those who opposed the invasion pointed out that article eight relied on a unanimous decision by member states, and in this case, Grenada had not formally requested assistance. But Charles stated that the OECS had received a secret request for intervention from Grenadian Governor-General Sir Paul Scoon when it met in Barbados on October 21. In the days following Bishop's assassination, a copy of the letter was discussed, and its contents were later revealed. Ultimately, U.S. and Caribbean intervention led to the deaths of eighteen U.S. soldiers, twenty-four Cubans, and forty-five Grenadians.[25]

Although joint action to restore democracy in Grenada was quick and polls indicated that most Americans supported Reagan's actions, U.S. intervention sparked a contentious debate across the Americas. In the United States, questions arose concerning the 1973 War Powers Resolution, which some argued had been violated due to the Reagan administration not fully consulting the U.S. Congress before sending troops to the island.[26] Democrats voiced opposition to the invasion that some saw as violating Grenada's sovereignty. Members of the Congressional Black Caucus (CBC), especially those with links to the Caribbean, reacted negatively to the invasion because a week earlier Reagan administration officials had informed them that they had no plans for military action. Also, following the decision to intervene, briefings were not extended to Black legislators. In previous years, the CBC had expressed vocal support for Bishop and lobbied Reagan to recognize the legitimacy of the Grenadian government. In an address to the CBC in Washington, D.C., Charles repeated that U.S. and Caribbean action in Grenada was a "rescue mission," and some members who attended walked out in protest. Democratic representative Gus Savage from Illinois called Charles a puppet for U.S. military aggression and stated that he did not want to "listen to a pack of lies."[27] Savage also described Charles as representing "Aunt Jemimism in geopolitics."[28]

Savage's comment reflected how race factored into criticism of Charles's relationship with the United States. Charles's attempt to develop close bonds with Reagan led to accusations that she overlooked the long historical and racist legacy of U.S. influence in the Caribbean and ignored the racist views that Reagan and others in his administration exhibited toward African Americans in particular. However, Charles refuted allegations that she was simply Reagan's pawn, maintaining that she was not speaking on behalf of him, and stating that she did not know that some African Americans opposed him.[29] Charles's response indicates a degree of ambivalence and naivete evident in her understanding of race in U.S. domestic and international relations. It is likely that she was aware of Reagan's opposition to critical civil rights issues and his repeated use of racist stereotypes toward African Americans, but she was willing to overlook this to gain his support. In contrast to Savage, some CBC members with ties to Caribbean leaders who supported the invasion muted their criticism of the administration.[30]

Opposition to the invasion came from the Caribbean too.[31] George Chambers, prime minister of Trinidad and Tobago, disagreed with the invasion based on article eight. Meanwhile, Guyanese president Forbes Burnham disputed "the claim that there was a massive arms build-up in Grenada, concentration of Cubans in that country or that a military airport was being built."[32] Burnham put pressure on the OECS and the United States through the United Nations Security Council by proposing a resolution that the UN condemn "'armed intervention in Grenada' as a violation of international law."[33] At a UN General Assembly, the invasion was deemed illegal by a vote of 108 to 9.[34]

Latin American countries also spoke out against the invasion. At the OAS meeting in late October 1983, fifteen out of the twenty-eight members condemned U.S. action.[35] Angered at this response, Charles refused to debate the invasion with the OAS. In an interview with her biographer, Janet Higbie, Charles admitted that she was not "really concerned about whether they like it or not. It's done. And all I owe them is a statement, an explanation. I don't need to sit down and listen to other talk from people who know nothing about the situation. I haven't got time."[36] Charles and the OECS received additional criticism from African members of the Commonwealth, especially Zambian president Kenneth Kaunda and Zimbabwean prime minister Robert Mugabe, who feared that the invasion could set a dangerous precedent for conflict on the continent. This criticism caught many Caribbean leaders by surprise, with Adams describing it as "unprecedented."[37] The Commonwealth response frustrated Charles, who admitted that it had left her having less "respect for the Commonwealth than I had before."[38] To reassure their African allies, Charles and other Caribbean leaders repeatedly stressed that the invasion was a rescue mission.[39] Opposition to the invasion by the UN, OAS, and the Commonwealth had a lasting legacy for Charles, leading her to have a certain distrust of international organizations.

The U.S. invasion fractured opinion in the Americas and the Commonwealth, and it also briefly soured relations with Britain. Before approaching the United States, the OECS reached out to British prime minister

Margaret Thatcher for military assistance, but she believed military intervention was unnecessary. Thatcher also tried to persuade Reagan not to intervene but was rebuffed by the U.S. secretary of state George Shultz, who stated that "the Caribbean is in our neighborhood."[40] Britain's refusal to intervene symbolically signaled a fundamental shift in postcolonial relations. At a speech in December 1983 at the Royal Commonwealth Society in London, Adams stated that "in hemispheric terms, 1983 is bound to be seen as the watershed year in which the influence of the United States, willy-nilly, came observably to replace that of Great Britain in the old British colonies."[41] Charles, too, shared this sentiment but throughout the 1980s remained Thatcher's friend and ally.

Although Charles's actions created divisions, it did provide her with benefits. Decisions taken by Charles and the OECS legitimized U.S. action and strengthened its military credibility, leading to Reagan describing the invasion as "one of the highest of the high points of my eight years."[42] The two leaders developed a good friendship, and Reagan later called Charles a "truly great lady."[43] Bob Woodward's claim that the CIA provided $100,000 for Charles as a payoff for her role in Grenada, which she disputed, speaks to her closeness with the Reagan administration.[44] Charles's actions reaped rewards in Dominica; it increased her popularity, and on her return to the island after visiting Washington, D.C., fifteen thousand Dominicans lined the streets to show their appreciation for her.[45] On November 9, 1983, politicians in the Dominican House of Assembly passed a motion to endorse the actions of the OECS. Savarin criticized the UN, OAS, and CARICOM for their impotence and stated that it was "encouraging, heart warming and something that we as a people in this corner of the world should be proud that an organization established by the people of the Eastern Caribbean, merely two years ago, could find the moral courage to respond to a very real situation existing in one of the Member States and to be able to take action swiftly."[46] Although members of the DLP questioned the legality of the invasion, Charles received widespread praise. Her actions brought more international attention to Dominica following her appearance on the U.S. television show *Sixty Minutes*.[47]

Charles sought to capitalize on this moment. In 1984, she and other leaders in the region approached Reagan to show his support for their role in Grenada by increasing aid to the eastern Caribbean. At a conference held at the University of South Carolina, Reagan and U.S. trade and regional officials met with Caribbean leaders "in what one Caribbean diplomat called 'clearly a symbol of commitment' to fulfill promises of economic and security assistance." The *Washington Post* remarked that "many of the governments represented at the meeting have supported administration security concerns in the region, but all have been gently critical of what they view as the slow pace of U.S economic assistance." Many at the conference hoped to ask the administration for more funds and call for a change in the direction of the CBI. After the Kissinger Commission recommended an $8 billion economic aid and military package for Central America alone, those in the Caribbean, echoing Charles's previous warning, wanted the CBI to focus more on their region.[48]

On this occasion, the Reagan administration was receptive to calls for aid. Dominica received $9.6 million to construct roads, schools, and public buildings and to upgrade airport facilities.[49] Also, in September 1984, the U.S. Agency for International Development (USAID) provided US$7,651,424 to finance the Roseau Pond Casse-Hatton Garden Project.[50] Charles also asked Reagan for funds to boost regional security. She led the way in calling for the creation of a joint military force consisting of Jamaica, Barbados, Dominica, St. Vincent, St. Lucia, Antigua, and St. Kitts-Nevis that was aided by financial and training support from the United States.[51] Charles hoped that "the U.S. training and equipment their police forces already are receiving in Grenada and their home islands can provide a nucleus for the inter-island force."[52] British, Australian, and Canadian leaders supported the creation of the security force, and U.S. military aid to the eastern Caribbean increased from $1.2 million in 1982 to $7.2 million in 1984 and $8.5 million in 1985.[53] By shoring up security on the island, Charles hoped that this would attract U.S. investors, and in 1984 she passed the State Security Act and the Treason Act. The latter, designed to increase faith in investors that Dominica was a safe island, imposed the death penalty on Dominicans who tried to overthrow the government.[54]

Charles also increased her anticommunist rhetoric during the 1985 Dominican election, both as a way to undermine her opposition and to advance U.S. support. Although the communist threat in Dominica remained minimal, in a June 1985 rally Charles argued that "the Labour Party at the present moment is a Labour Communist Party no matter how long they deny it, and in a true manner of Communism, they tell lies." Going further, she stated that "we do not want Communism in Dominica, because under Communism we will lose our freedom, we would lose our choice as to what we want to do with our lives."[55] Charles relayed her fears of a communist threat to the U.S. State Department and accused DLP politicians of receiving funds from North Korea and Libya.[56] To what extent Charles genuinely believed there was a viable communist presence in Dominica is questionable. Michael Douglas, the DLP's leader, disputed Charles's accusations, describing himself as a social democrat and favored continuing Dominica's close ties to the United States, but he accused Charles of being "too slavish" to the United States.[57]

Despite millions in U.S. aid and Charles's renewed emphasis on anticommunism, it was not enough to address the island's economic challenges, nor did it help increase American investment. Indeed, the preferential treatment the United States gave to Grenada after the invasion further increased Caribbean tensions. The United States provided Grenada with $18.5 million in aid, and in 1984, $57 million.[58] Seaga spoke for others in the Caribbean when he stated that "there is no way these investments can be put into Grenada and not into the rest of the OECS . . . otherwise, all islands will look to having a revolution and being rescued."[59] Charles, too, queried the high costs and believed that the United States would have to increase its aid to other islands.[60] However, with security no longer a significant concern, U.S. aid to countries in the OECS declined from $214 million in 1984 to $127 million in 1987.[61]

Using Charles as a case study provides a useful set of reflections on neoliberalism and anticommunism. Charles hung close to the two ideologies in both a genuine belief in their relevance and importance for U.S.-Dominican relations and Dominica's domestic policies. In the short term, the ideologies brought Dominica and the United States closer, especially regarding their shared security concerns. The relationship between Reagan and Charles proved mutually beneficial. It allowed Charles to attract U.S. interest in Dominica and enabled Reagan to fight Cold War battles in the eastern Caribbean. But one of the consequences was that U.S. influence in the Caribbean undermined regional unity. By the mid-1980s, the significance of security threats waned as the limited impact of U.S.-led neoliberal economic policies came to light. Once the Cold War threat in the Caribbean subsided, U.S. attention quickly turned away from the Caribbean, increasing difficulties for Charles's donor-driven strategy. By 1986, Charles had come to recognize the limits of her foreign policy, saying in the annual independence day address, "During the first three years of our administration we spent a lot of time and resources in putting forward a program for attracting foreign investment. . . . This has not been very successful. Until we are able to overcome the physical constraints that make it difficult for visitors to come to and remain in Dominica we cannot depend too heavily on foreign investment." Rather than relying on external support, Charles stressed the importance of Dominicans needing to "rely on our own resourcefulness, on our own entrepreneurship to create employment for ourselves and for the many young persons who leave school every year. We must see ourselves as the owners and exploiters of the resources that are around us. We must find opportunities in everything that can be developed and sold."[62]

Although Charles recognized the limits of neoliberalism and the declining power of anticommunist rhetoric in the late 1980s and 1990s, she did not entirely abandon the United States. When Reagan left the White House, she continued to look to the new administration for help. But as Patsy Lewis has so aptly said, by the 1990s, Dominica and other small Caribbean states became "a far cry from their heyday in the 1980s when they were successful in getting an international power to act on their behalf. The irony is that in the international climate in whose creation they were complicit they have been relegated to mere anachronisms."[63] Concentrating on the impact of neoliberalism and anticommunism allows for a richer understanding of the complex ideas guiding Charles's relations with the United States, underscoring how the struggles she faced as a leader of a small, poor state could not be entirely undone by courting U.S. power.

Notes

1. Eudine Barriteau, "The Economic Philosophy of Eugenia Charles and Dominica's Development, 1980–1995," in *Enjoying Power: Eugenia Charles and Political Leadership in the Commonwealth Caribbean*, ed. Eudine Barriteau and Alan Cobley (Kingston: University of West Indies Press, 2006), 189, 201.
2. Irving W André and Gabriel J Christian, *In Search of Eden: Essay's on Dominican History* (Brampton, Ontario: Pond Casse Press, 2002), 263.
3. Barriteau, "Economic Philosophy," 206–7.
4. Barriteau, "Economic Philosophy," 198.
5. Seth Mydans, "Caribbean Nations Felt Grenada Threatened Stability," *New York Times*, October 26, 1983.
6. Jo Thomas, "Dominica Unsettled in Wake of Thwarted Invasion," *New York Times*, June 7, 1981.

7. Eudine Barriteau, "Enjoying Power, Challenging Gender," in *Enjoying Power: Eugenia Charles and Political Leadership in the Commonwealth Caribbean*, ed. Eudine Barriteau and Alan Cobley (Kingston: University of West Indies Press, 2006), 16.

8. Michael Campbell, "The Impact of the Caribbean Basin Initiative Program on the Economic Growth and Development in the English Speaking Caribbean Region," *Journal of Economic and Economic Education Research* 15 no. 3 (2014): 39.

9. "Public Papers of the President: Ronald Reagan, August 15, 1983," as quoted in Cynthia Weber, "Shoring Up a Sea of Signs: How the Caribbean Basin Initiative Framed the US Invasion of Grenada," *Environment and Planning D: Society and Space* 12 (1994): 556.

10. Anthony Payne, "Whither CARICOM? The Performance and Prospects of Caribbean Integration in the 1980s," *International Journal* 40 (Spring 1985): 213.

11. Payne, "Whither CARICOM?," 214–15.

12. Gary Williams, "The Tail That Wagged the Dog: The Organisation of Eastern Caribbean States' Role in the 1983 Intervention in Grenada," *European Review of Latin American and Caribbean Studies* 61 (December 1996): 96–97.

13. Anthony Payne, *Politics in Jamaica*, rev. ed. (New York: St Martin's Press, 1994), 84.

14. Payne, "Whither CARICOM?," 214.

15. Payne, "Whither CARICOM?," 214–15.

16. Lou Cannon, "Working Hard at Vacation in the Caribbean: Reagan Relaxing in Caribbean Amid Scoffs at Marxist Threat," *Washington Post*, April 10, 1982.

17. Campbell, "The Impact of the Caribbean Basin Initiative Program," 40–41.

18. Sheila Rule, "Dominica on the Map Now, Hopes for Better Days," *New York Times*, May 28, 1984.

19. Rule, "Dominica on the Map Now."

20. Alan Cobley, "'We Are Kith and Kin': Eugenia Charles, Caribbean Integration and the Grenada Invasion," in *Enjoying Power: Eugenia Charles and Political Leadership in the Commonwealth Caribbean*, ed. Eudine Barriteau and Alan Cobley (Kingston: University of West Indies Press, 2006), 123 (Interview with Alan Cobley and Eugenia Charles, July 9, 2002, Roseau, Dominica.)

21. Cobley, "'We Are Kith and Kin,'" 124–25.

22. Transcript of address by President (Reagan) on Lebanon and Grenada, *New York Times*, October 28, 1983.

23. "Statement by Prime Minister Charles, Chairman of OECS," box 104, no date, 1–2 M Eugenia Charles Collection, Special Collection, University of West Indies, Cave Hill, Barbados.

24. Cobley, "'We Are Kith and Kin,'" 126; Francois Dominique, ed., *Grenada: Intervention? Invasion? Rescue Mission?*, TS Pamphlet (1984), 30–31. Copy held in the Main Library, University of West Indies, Cave Hill, Barbados.

25. Michael Rubner, "The Reagan Administration, the 1973 War Powers Resolution, and the Invasion of Grenada," *Political Science Quarterly* 100 no. 4 (Winter 1985): 628.

26. Rubner, "The Reagan Administration," 630.

27. Howard Kurtz, "Black Legislators Seek Withdrawal of American Forces from Grenada," *Washington Post*, October 29, 1983.

28. Alfreda L. Madison, "From Capitol Hill; Invasion Wrong for Russia, but Right for U.S.?," *Washington Informer* 20, no. 4 (November 1983): 17.

29. Madison, "From Capitol Hill," 17.

30. Kurtz, "Black Legislators."

31. For more on the effects of the Grenada invasion on CARICOM, see Payne, "Whither CARICOM?"

32. "Caribbean Heat and Dust on Grenada," *Times of India*, November 26, 1983.

33. Michael J. Berlin, "Dominica Says Governor General Urged Intervention Last Friday," *Washington Post*, October 27, 1983.

34. Cobley, "'We Are Kith and Kin,'" 126.

35. Howard Kurtz, "At OAS, Grenadan Denounces U.S.; 15 Members Join Condemnation," *Washington Post*, October 27, 1983.

36. Eugenia Charles as quoted in Janet Higbie, *Eugenia: The Caribbean's Iron Lady* (London: Macmillan, 1993), 238–39.

37. William Claiborne, "Commonwealth Rift on Grenada Widens," *Washington Post*, November 25, 1983.

38. Edward Cody, "Caribbean Aid," *Washington Post*, December 17, 1983.

39. Claiborne, "Commonwealth Rift."

40. Patrick E. Tyler and David Hoffman, "U.S. Invades Grenada, Fights Cubans," *Washington Post*, October 26, 1983.

41. Cody, "Caribbean Aid."

42. Ronald Reagan, *An American Life* (1990: repr. New York: Simon & Shuster, 2011), 458.

43. Higbie, *Eugenia*, 237; Reagan, *An American Life*, photo section.

44. Bob Woodward, *VEIL: The Secret Wars of the CIA, 1981–1987* (New York: Simon & Schuster, 1987), 279.

45. André and Christian, *In Search of Eden*, 262.

46. "Notice to Endorse the Action Taken by the Organisation of Eastern Caribbean States in Relation to Grenada-Charles Savarin," *Hansard*, November 9, 1983, 7, Dominica Documentation Centre, Dominica Archives.

47. André and Christian, *In Search of Eden*, 265.

48. Dana Priest, "13 Caribbean Leaders Seeking Aid from U.S.," *Washington Post*, July 19, 1984.

49. Williams, "The Tail That Wagged the Dog," fn90, 112.

50. André and Christian, *In Search of Eden*, 265; *The New Chronicle*, September 21, 1984.
51. Cody, "Caribbean Aid."
52. Cody, "Caribbean Aid."
53. Patsy Lewis, "Revisiting the Grenada Invasion: The OECS' Role and Its Impact on Regional and International Politics," *Social and Economic Studies* 48, no. 3 (1999): 106.
54. André and Christian, *In Search of Eden*, 268.
55. As quoted in Higbie, *Eugenia*, 246; Radio Debate, June 2 Speeches from State Department Cable, June 7, 1985.
56. Higbie, *Eugenia* 244. Joseph B. Treaster, "Pro U.S. Dominica Premier Wins a Second 5-Year Term," *New York Times*, July 2, 1985.
57. Treaster, "Pro U.S. Dominica Premier Wins."
58. Williams, "The Tail That Wagged the Dog," 107.
59. Cody, "Caribbean Aid."
60. Cody, "Caribbean Aid."
61. Anthony P. Gonzales, "Recent Trends in International Economic Relations of the CARICOM States," *Journal of Interamerican Studies and World Affairs* 31, no. 3 (1989): 69.
62. Eugenia Charles as quoted in Higbie, *Eugenia*, 254.
63. Lewis, "Revisiting the Grenada Invasion," 117.

CHAPTER 12

I Think of Myself as an International Citizen

Flemmie P. Kittrell's Internationalist Ideology

BRANDY THOMAS WELLS

I
n March 1946, the Howard University professor and home economist
Flemmie P. Kittrell shared a story with members of the National Council of Negro Women (NCNW) about family, health, and community.
Using the metaphor of "two rooms and a kitchen," she described the pre-
dicament of a Washington, D.C. family whose lives were severely affected
by the housing shortage that followed the second great migration that coin-
cided with World War II. Kittrell did not reveal how she knew the family, instead keeping readers' attention on how a scarcity of resources could
adversely affect families at the micro level and make a city volatile. When
the Johnson family came to terms with the fact that they could not afford to
move, she revealed how they learned to make efficient use of their existing
space. Kittrell hoped to convince readers that issues that could have beset
this family and broader society could be solved through practical solutions
and an emphasis on the home.[1]

Kittrell took this belief with her when she joined American foreign
policy circles in the 1940s. Although the nation's domestic "containment"
policy of the Cold War period held that women needed to return to the
home to protect the American way of life, its foreign component allowed
women with expertise on home, family, education, and the like to propel
themselves into global affairs.[2] In addition to exporting "technical" skills,
Kittrell looked forward to doing her part to contribute to peace, security, and progress, compelled by the belief that "the homes of today build

tomorrow's world."[3] From the 1940s through the 1970s, she embarked on a dizzying array of travel that took her to Asia, Europe, and Africa for the U.S. State Department, the United Nations, and many women's, religious, and philanthropic organizations. Most of Kittrell's appearances in the American press either announced her recent departure or her return from abroad or advertised her lectures on international topics during her lifetime.

Despite her remarkable travel schedule, service on three continents, and teaching and publishing on internationalism, Kittrell's name does not appear in works on U.S. foreign policy, international relations, or cultural diplomacy, nor does it appear in publications that increasingly interrogate the roles and the ideologies of thinkers in international politics. But it is clear that Kittrell had ideas that she tried to work into U.S. foreign policy.[4] As an academic, she published in journals for her specific discipline and those read by foreign policy experts and Black studies scholars. As a grant recipient and consultant, Kittrell authored reports that included policy suggestions that frequently stressed practical methods. As a public scholar and an activist, she used the podium and the press to increase public awareness and knowledge of foreign lands. When she feared that U.S. foreign policy was out of touch with oppressed people's lived realities, she protested as a private citizen. Allison Beth Horrocks, one of the few historians to consider Kittrell's work as an educator and an internationalist, succinctly labeled her as the "goodwill ambassador with a cookbook."[5] This apt description captures the State Department's positioning of Kittrell as a cultural ambassador with specialties in family, education, and the social and economic life of women. It also captures her personal commitment to advance a practical, but transformative internationalism that combated the ills of white supremacy broadly and improved the lives of the world's people of color immediately.

Kittrell has a lot to teach scholars of U.S. foreign relations and intellectual history about how we think, engage, and write about thinker-practitioners and their efforts, successes, and failures to shape policy and practice. Fortunately, many have begun the work to uncover a broader genealogy of international thinkers and doers, several of them women and women of color.[6] Even with this exciting trend, Kittrell's pragmatic approach to internationalism might never appear. In some circles, Kittrell might continue to go unseen because she was not a top-level federal administrator, politician, or foreign service officer—who were usually white and male. In others, she may never appear because she did not participate in anticolonial or anticapitalist transnational movements, which some argue are the truest forms of internationalism.[7]

Indeed, Kittrell and her ideological renderings were somewhere in the middle. She was, as the historian Carol Anderson explains, a "bureaucratic infighter—an activist, practitioner, thinker, who mastered the arcane rules and power relationships at the State Department, the United Nations, and the White House to undermine the global legitimacy of colonialism and white supremacy."[8] Kittrell's arguments about peace and security positioned her well within these circles, but she was not a blank slate that unthinkingly absorbed and regurgitated the state's ideas. That her internationalism was symbiotic rather than synonymous with the state emerges when we develop a broader view on how to discover ideology in the international and when we pay attention to nuance and silence.

Becoming an International Girl

Kittrell grew up in the small, Black rural town of Henderson, North Carolina. Although the eighth of nine children born to a farming family, she often described herself as her parents' favorite. As such, she claimed that she was frequently spared burdensome tasks around the farm. Although this may have been true, Kittrell was expected to make money just like her siblings. As young as eleven years old, she worked summer jobs, first as a nursemaid and later as a cook. But each fall Kittrell gleefully returned to her studies even when she admitted that some of her local teachers knew little more than the pupils. She counted herself as one of the lucky ones when she considered her family's circumstances relative to those of the larger Henderson community. Indeed, her older siblings grew up and made their living just as their parents had—in domestic work and menial jobs—but the younger three attended college. In 1919, Kittrell followed her older sister to Hampton Institute (now Hampton University), a small Black college in Virginia.[9]

Laboring alongside her sister to pay tuition that first year, Kittrell earned her high school diploma followed by her bachelor's degree. She had been loath to take up home economics as her field of study, believing that "the home was just so ordinary," but she was convinced by the pioneering career of Ellen H. Swallow Richards, whose work in sanitary engineering made her one of the nation's earliest female professional chemists. Seeing this,

Kittrell became convinced that the home was "really the center of all . . . learning" and that the study of home economics was "concerned with the whole of life," which meant that it was primed to develop "full understanding among people."[10] After her 1928 graduation, Kittrell became the director of home economics and dean of women at Bennett College, the newly transitioned women's college in Greensboro, North Carolina.[11]

Although her work on campus kept her busy, Kittrell's desire for education and her commitment to racial uplift led her to take up graduate studies at Cornell University. She deepened her knowledge of foods and nutrition, child studies, and rural education by taking classes at Columbia University. At both universities, Kittrell worked with faculty who conducted global work with the League of Nations and contended that the home was a critical international nexus where community and global politics met. As she matriculated with peers from other nations, including India and South Africa, and listened to speakers from around the world, Kittrell learned the value of international exchange.[12]

In 1936, Kittrell earned her PhD. Along with it came the distinction of becoming the first Black woman to earn a graduate degree in home economics.[13]

In 1944, Kittrell became the head of the Department of Economics at Howard University, a position she held for nearly thirty years. Situated in the nation's capital and one of the leading historically Black colleges that possessed a growing reputation in its global outreach, Kittrell became an "international girl."[14]

On Easy Terms with People at Home and Abroad

Given Kittrell's academic accolades, her path from a poor Black southern woman to a university professor, and her zeal to serve, it is little wonder that the U.S. State Department tapped her for a mission.[15] In December 1946, she traveled to Liberia to conduct a six-month study of "nutrition and family life problems of the Liberian people." President Franklin D. Roosevelt made clear the nation's interest in improving Liberia's health conditions because it would not only strengthen diplomatic relations but also serve military interests as American troops remained stationed there after World War II. Kittrell became the first person to explore the possibilities of international cooperation through home economics, but her work was part of a previously existing "all-Negro mission" American technical assistance program during World War II.[16]

Initially Kittrell was scheduled to begin her evaluation in November. She did not depart until December 22, when the academic semester ended. Thus, although Kittrell may have been ecstatic for the appointment and her first trip outside of the United States, she took up this work on terms that worked for her. She also expanded her visit to research medical facilities in the Gold Coast, arguing that the information was crucial for understanding Liberia's health needs. She also emerged as a lecturer in Liberia and five neighboring countries. The State Department warned Kittrell not to become "too familiar with the bush people, who would quickly lose respect for her and get out of control," but she responded that she "felt at home in the world" and "could easily be on terms with people at home and abroad."[17] In the years that followed, Kittrell often related a story to make this point. She told how a community chief verbally reprimanded her for wearing pants and told her that he did not trust nor like her. In response to being called a "bad woman," Kittrell claimed that she won him over by declaring, "I am a missionary ma!"[18] The State Department came to rely on Kittrell's flexible rhetoric in the years ahead.[19]

At the end of her stay, Kittrell produced a twenty-one-page report based on more than four thousand Liberians' diets. She detailed vitamin deficiencies and explained methods to combat them within the home and at the national level. Extending beyond her contract, she reported a good working relationship between Firestone Rubber Company and state leaders, thus commenting on a human rights disaster that captured global attention in the 1930s when news of the forced labor of Indigenous Africans went global.[20] While pointing out that a remarkable number of Firestone laborers still suffered from tuberculosis and other respiratory issues, Kittrell was careful not to offer additional comments that might frustrate state leaders in Liberia or the United States or jeopardize her future with the department. As a matter of strategy and out of a genuine belief that the local is also global, she implored the United States to pay attention to the "hidden" and "hollow" hunger occurring within its borders.

Two months later Kittrell received a commendation from the Liberian government when it opened its embassy in Washington, D.C. She was in the midst of a national lecture tour in which she praised the "friendly aid of the United States" as well as "the progressive admission of President Tubman." She declared that the "country was headed for a new day." In many ways,

Kittrell's statements that upheld and celebrated American involvement in Liberia were a bit ahead of a burgeoning trend in the 1950s when some liberal African American activists adopted what historian Penny von Eschen calls a "depoliticized vocabulary of modernization," a perspective or critique that ignored the political implications of U.S. investment in the affairs of foreign nations.[21]

Over the next few years, Kittrell's ideas about internationalism grew. She increasingly proclaimed that international relations should be centered on teacher exchange programs and that these teachers should be women. Her essentialist ideas about women as natural peacemakers and nurturers grew through her involvement with women's organizations such as the Women's International League for Peace and Freedom (WILPF). Born at the Hague in 1915 and in the tracks of women's suffrage, the organization espoused a leftist and feminist approach to war and imperialism. Kittrell's colleagues were so impressed by her Liberian work that they made her chair of WILPF's Committee of African Affairs.[22]

To Build Goodwill and Prevent War

In 1949, Kittrell's contacts at Cornell presented her with second opportunity to take up foreign work—this time in Asia. Hansa Mehta, delegate to the United National Human Rights Commission and vice-chancellor of the Maharaja Sayajirao University of Baroda, provided funding for her to build a home economics department. Going beyond American foreign relations experts, Kittrell contacted the Fulbright program to argue that it needed to send a home economist to India in its first year of independence. A year earlier, she posited that "in the face of transition, the family and the home must remain the cornerstone from which learning flows to enable society to handle change in a progressive way."[23] Many global or civil conflicts were rooted in other issues, but Kittrell wanted to defeat hunger and the fear to ensure peace. Fulbright leaders, too, believed in true globalism and international understanding, but they also held that its international programs needed to serve U.S. interests, which, they argued, served the world's interests.[24] As a visiting scholar of color, they expected Kittrell to aid the United States in staving off criticism about its problem with racism. She had no scruples with this mission even though she maintained a dual agenda to aid people of color both at home and abroad.

Historical records reveal that Kittrell was motivated to take leave to alleviate an ongoing funding problem at Howard. She would use her time away from the university to reduce expenses, which might help the university construct a new building for her department.[25] In August 1950, she became one of the earliest Black women in the Fulbright program and the first Black woman to go to Asia. She served Baroda University as an interim dean, educator, and strategic organizer.[26]

Kittrell was not the only Black home economist taking up global work, or even the only Howard faculty member to work globally. In November 1950, Merze Tate traveled to India. She was one of the earliest female professors in the university's history. Unlike Kittrell, Tate had lived abroad before, having first traveled to Switzerland in 1931, where she earned a diploma in international studies. In 1935, she earned a bachelor of letters degree in European diplomatic studies from Oxford University. In 1941, she became the first Black woman to earn a Harvard PhD in international relations. At Howard she taught in the international relations department alongside Alain Locke, Ralph Bunche, and E. Franklin Frazier. By the time she arrived in India, Tate had published two books on disarmament and the growing military-industrial complex.[27]

Soon after her arrival to the Rabindranath Tagore's World University in West Bengal, Tate expressed confusion about the financial terms of her award. A month later she charged that she and Kittrell received second-rate accommodations because they were Black. Tate also used several of her lectures at the university and in the community to discuss American race relations. The State Department labeled Tate a "public relations liability" and declared Kittrell an asset because she publicly avoided such topics.[28] After completion of her nine-month assignment, Tate's Fulbright was not renewed. She spent several months traveling through Western Europe and the Middle East before returning to the United States by way of Southeast Asia. Valuing the relationship she had built, Kittrell not only kept quiet about these matters but worked to draw closer to those in power. One part of this included publishing pieces on her experiences in the *American Reporter*, the United States Information Service organ.[29]

Consider This a Good Project

In August 1953, Kittrell again responded to a call for help from Baroda University. She was so eager to lend her services that she moved ahead of her clearance from the State Department. By the following March, she received clearance through the Point Four Program, a U.S. technical assistance program targeting newly independent countries. In considering the work of more than two thousand American specialists in the program, President Dwight D. Eisenhower declared it to be "the United States' most effective countermeasure to Soviet propaganda and the best method by which to create the political and social stability essential to lasting peace."[30]

The State Department put Kittrell to work in many ways all at once. She served as institution builder, consultant, and liaison. In January 1955, she became a group leader to twenty-two Indian women who traveled to Japan and Hawaii to study home economics.[31] Kittrell should have been able to rely on the State Department for her work, but she believed that Black women had a role to play in India and in November 1954 she reached out to fellow members of Delta Sigma Theta Sorority to alert them of Baroda's "great need for books."[32] By working with Black women's groups like this one, Kittrell found a receptive and supportive public. In fact, a few years earlier, she received an honor scroll for her dietetic work from the NCNW, one of the nation's prominent Black women's organizations. In 1960, she received another for her international activities.[33] In conferring such designations on ambassadors, heads of state, and nonstate actors, Black women made clear the activities they considered worthwhile and progressive in improving human relations at home and abroad. Even when this population did not always possess the means to travel or call upon the relationships Kittrell had, their actions revealed that they possessed a genuine interest in global affairs and had sustained a diasporic consciousness.[34]

Part of Their Progress

Rich correspondence reveals that Kittrell spent many of her years in India thinking about Africa. She often shared with close friends and colleagues that she considered terminating her service to take up African studies. Kittrell looked forward to spending time in Africa because she found it thrilling to "see the people going forward so dramatically" in newly independent countries such as Ghana, Morocco, and Guinea. And she was committed to "do[ing] something to be a part of their progress."[35]

In September 1958, Kittrell got her chance to go to Africa for a brief cultural tour through recommendations by "highly respected officers in the

[State] Department and the United States Information Agency." Undeniably, Kittrell's aim to support African countries to develop as democracies fell in line with the U.S. narrative and aims. Nevertheless, it also importantly fit her goal of fulfilling her moral obligation to the world. The venture took Kittrell to five African countries, including Ghana—a recently independent nation presided over by Kwame Nkrumah, a well-known Pan-Africanist.

Unlike what had occurred in her lectures in Liberia in 1947, Kittrell fielded several questions about U.S. race relations.[36] American diplomats steadily observed how Kittrell and other African American visitors, especially journalists, answered questions on this topic. Just shy of Kittrell's arrival, Marguerite Cartwright, a professor at Hunter College in New York and an NCNW life member, had been giving talks in Ghana at the invitation of the Ghanaian government; she had attended the Afro-Asian Conference in Bandung, Indonesia, the previous year. Although the State Department expressed initial concern, it soon decided that her "rambling" talks were not a foreign risk because she often attributed American racial inequality to local whites' actions.[37]

U.S. foreign relations experts and many Ghanaians appreciated Kittrell's attempt to present an "honest and balanced" picture of American race relations, but Kittrell also drew sharp criticism. One recorded incident involved Evelyn Amartefio of the Ghana Women's Association, who had just returned from the United States after an international exchange tour. Amartefio questioned Kittrell about the September 1957 Little Rock crisis and the Alabama State Court case involving Jimmy Wilson, a fifty-five-year-old African American male, who was initially sentenced to the electric chair for stealing $1.95.[38]

Slowly but deliberately, Kittrell admitted that there would likely be other racial incidents like these, but she also emphasizing that these injustices did not undo the progress that Black Americans had achieved since emancipation. Kittrell stressed, "At least we have a constitution as a way of working things out."[39] At the end of her talks, including those in Central Africa the following year, Kittrell usually made sure to say that she was "a specialist in family matters, not in political and living matters."[40] Kittrell talked politics, and she knew it. But in marketing and presenting her tours under a disciplinary guise, Kittrell escaped the harsh criticism that fell on Edith Spurlock Sampson, who was vilified in the Black press for her State Department tours in 1951 and 1952.[41] For its part, the NCNW lauded all of these women with awards, courted them for membership, and placed them before their bodies.[42]

What a World Citizen Would Do

In 1959 and 1961, Kittrell again traveled to Africa, first to West Central Africa and then to Guinea. Although little information appears in the State Department records on the latter trip, her private correspondence from Conakry shows that she extended her trip to take up academic research,[43] traveling from the Congo to Mozambique and Rhodesia and then on to South Africa. Here she used the home and the community study to draw more significant conclusions about the nation's future. She viewed her work as different from high-level folks because she did not rely on "stereotypes and cliché that oppressors have handed down for hundreds of years." In her service and research, Kittrell claimed that she let go of an America-first attitude. In reflecting on her work years later, she stated, "I'd like to think of myself as an international citizen," which meant doing "what one who is really a world citizen would do."[44]

As a self-professed citizen of the world, Kittrell set out to do everything. While working for the U.S. Information Service, the International Development Agency created her programs and widened her public. From 1962 through 1964, she hosted a Home Economics Workshop on African Life on the Howard Campus. The six-week program enrolled African women who were already students in American schools and was cosponsored by Howard University, the African American Institute of New York City, and the State Department.[45] Nearly every time Kittrell returned from abroad, she took up a heavy lecture schedule to share the trials and triumphs she had witnessed in India and Africa. These lectures increased her status and buoyed her income. She also found funding for international students to study in the United States and worked on publications using the information she gathered.

Kittrell continued to participate in international conferences called by the United Nations, professional bodies, and religious organizations. In 1959, she attended a UN Conference on Discrimination in Geneva and then made her way to the WILPF conference in Stockholm. Next, Kittrell traveled to Moscow with the Horizons Unlimited Tour of Russia where she viewed the exhibit of the infamous 1959 "kitchen debate" in which Richard Nixon and Nikita Khrushchev debated an American vs. Soviet future.[46] Kittrell kept busy in the 1960s, and one of her most interesting activities occurred in December 1967. Protesting conditions in South Africa and the ambivalent stance of the UN concerning them, she became one of five Americans to stage a fly-in as part of an Ad Hoc Committee for the Development of Independent South West Africa. Here Kittrell showed that she was willing to move ahead of American foreign policy. Only in 1986 did the United States impose sanctions.[47]

Not Afraid to Speak Against Evil

In 1977, Kittrell related details of some of her international adventures as part of the Black Women's Oral History Interviews Project. This 1976–1981 initiative of the Radcliffe Schlesinger Library collected the oral memoirs of seventy-two Black women who made substantial contributions to their communities and larger society through their civic activism or professional activities. Tate conducted the interview with Kittrell, which showed that the women crossed paths often, not just on Howard's campus but also abroad. It also made clear, if there was any doubt, that they conceived of internationalism differently. Kittrell still found value in the bulk of her work within the state and introducing her audiences to diverse cultures and places through journal length articles, whereas Tate took on larger book projects and theoretical arguments about the nexus between capitalism, empire, and race.[48]

Although Tate might have appeared to be a more obvious internationalist to some, given her education and writings, Kittrell wanted to make clear (likely to Tate especially) that from her field of home economics she, too, deserved this designation. She shared pictures and discussed campus events in Howard's home economics program that represented "scholarship as well as internationalism."[49] Kittrell also shared details of her trips that did not end up in the written records. One such trip was her 1961 journey to South Africa. She made clear that the U.S. embassy knew that her trip was motivated by her "desire to find out what was happening in the country."[50] Kittrell told how she called on contacts at the American consulate in Rhodesia and how the U.S. ambassador personally met her plane and welcomed her into his home. Kittrell then traveled throughout the country and witnessed the conditions of Black South Africans under apartheid.

One of her most memorable events was her meeting with Black male mine workers. In response to their call for a speech, she responded simply, but forcefully, "To my fellow citizens of the world, I'm glad to be here and so happy to have this chance to see how you live and work, and I will tell my people about this when I return, and the Americans will be glad to know about how you're getting along." Emphatically she stated, "Now that was a political speech." Tate and she both laughed heartily, but Tate soon retorted that Kittrell's speech was more "innocuous" than political. Kittrell insisted that it was political and then offered a second story she hoped would make her internationalist leanings clear. Having told her Afrikaner escorts that she did not enjoy her time in the Union, she expressed joy in not "whitewashing" her remarks. She also reported that the "American embassy was very pleased in the way I behaved, and what I said." Tate did not follow up.[51]

Kittrell's paradoxical explanation does much to reveal her internationalism as a bureaucratic infighter. She believed she could accomplish more by working with the state rather than being surveilled and attacked by it. She realized that this approach required her to be more subtle than sensational and more quiet than quarrelsome. This worldview and practice are reflected in the documentation she left behind. Kittrell's written record primarily focuses on her official activities, especially those with the State Department. Although her participation in the 1967 fly-in appears a few times—and likely would have impressed Tate if she shared it—Kittrell minimized this event when telling her life story. In addition, only once in her records is there a mention of the discrimination she experienced upon her return from a State Department trip in 1961. News of her being refused service in Laurel, Maryland, was carried on the front page of newspapers. Kittrell did not offer a personal reflection but chose to include letters of protest that people wrote on her behalf.[52]

Kittrell's true feelings about her internationalism are often just hints. Only once in her career, when she was in India, did she keep a diary, and even then she was careful not to dwell on the deep isolation she felt in her work or to record deeper thoughts about Tate's actions with Fulbright. However, in speaking with Tate, Kittrell hinted that she "was very fortunate not to have gotten into more trouble" in her international trips.[53] Considering this statement, alongside an interview at Howard that happened three years later (and six months before her death) in which she more boldly claimed that she "was not afraid to speak against evil as I see it," reveals that a great deal of Kittrell's internationalism is not in the records.[54] It also elucidates her commitment to curating her legacy: she hoped to demonstrate the transformative potential of home economics even when she ventured beyond these bounds.

As Kittrell sought all at once to be true to herself, remain in the good graces of the State Department, and advance progress and peace, she made several puzzling decisions and perhaps even some obvious errors. To grant space to these means to recognize that this international thinker-practitioner, like many others, was not always intellectually pure or right and that she was thinking her way through as she worked. One thing is clear, however. Given Kittrell's long engagement with U.S. foreign policy, which stretched across five presidents and six secretaries of state, she was committed to fighting for peace, equality, and freedom from within.

Kittrell's work toward these ends was recognized in the renaming of the Home Economics building upon her 1972 retirement from Howard. The American Home Economics Association (now the American Association of Family and Consumer Sciences) named a scholarship in her honor. Near the end of her life, Kittrell was invited to return to Cornell on a fellowship, and she spent two years there wrangling with her ideas.[55] She planned to produce a monograph about the lessons she had garnered in her world travels but did not do so before her death. Instead, Kittrell's ideas about internationalism live on in scattered publications, her lectures before various groups, the institutions she built, and the silences she left.

Notes

1. Flemmie P. Kittrell, "Two Rooms and a Kitchen: What One Family Did About Their Housing Problem," *AfraAmerican Woman's Journal* (March 1946): 14–15, box 1, folder 20, series 13, Council of Negro Women Papers, National Park Service–Mary McLeod Bethune Council House, Washington, D.C. Hereafter cited as NCNW Papers.

2. On American consumerism more generally, see Lizabeth Cohen, *A Consumers' Republic: The Politics of Mass Consumption in Postwar America* (New York: Vintage, 2003).

3. Flemmie P. Kittrell, "Today's Home Builds Tomorrow's World," box 104–2, folder 27, Flemmie P. Kittrell Papers, Howard University, Moorland-Spingarn Research Center. Hereafter cited as MSRC Papers.

4. See, for instance James Kessler et al., *Distinguished African American Scientists of the 20th Century* (Phoenix: Oryx Press, 1996); and Wini Warren, *Black Women Scientists in the United States* (Bloomington: Indiana University Press, 1999), 153–74.

5. Allison Beth Horrocks, "Good Will Ambassador with a Cookbook: Flemmie Kittrell and the International Politics of Home Economics" (PhD diss., University of Connecticut, 2016).

6. The scholarship on activism is extensive, and that on intellectualism is growing. For a recent work, see Patricia Owens and Katharina Rietzler, eds., *Women's International Thought: A New History* (Cambridge: Cambridge University Press, 2021); and Samuel Moyn and Andrew Sartori, eds., *Global Intellectual History* (New York: Columbia University Press, 2015).

7. Glenda Sluga and Patricia Clavin, *Internationalisms: A Twentieth-Century History* (Cambridge: Cambridge University Press, 2017), 3–14.

8. Carol Anderson, "The Histories of African Americans' Anticolonialism in the Cold War," in *The Cold War in the Third World*, ed. Robert McMahon (Oxford: Oxford University Press, 2013), 178–91.

9. Horrocks, "Good Will Ambassador with a Cookbook," 51–52.

10. "Flemmie P. Kittrell Interview by Merze Tate," August 29, 1977, *Black Women Oral History Project Interviews, 1974–1976*, transcript, 29, https://iiif.lib.harvard.edu/manifests/view/drs:45173968$1i.

11. "Kittrell Interview," 1–2.

12. Horrocks, "Good Will Ambassador with a Cookbook," 93–102.

13. "Kittrell Interview," 14.

14. "Kittrell Interview," 28.

15. "Loy W. Henderson to Dean Acheson, June 25, 1945," box 7138, General Records of the Department of State, record group 59, National Archives at College Park, Maryland.

16. "Dr. Flemmie P. Kittrell," *Telefact* (February 1947): 5, box 2, folder 4, series 13, NCNW Papers.

17. Esther Ottley, "Flemmie Pansy Kittrell, (1904–1980)," *Profiles* (Howard University, Graduate School of Arts and Sciences, December 1980), 13–14, box 104–1, folder 10, MSRC Papers.

18. Ottley, "Flemmie Pansy Kittrell, 10–11.

19. "Kittrell Interview," 30.

20. Flemmie P. Kittrell, "Preliminary Food and Nutrition Survey, December 1946–June 1947," box 104–13, folder 11, 2, MSRC Papers.

21. "Liberian Praised by Hampton Lecturer," *New Journal and Guide* (Norfolk, VA), July 26, 1947; and Brenda Gayle Plummer, *Rising Wind: Black Americans and U.S. Foreign Affairs, 1935–1960* (Charlotte: University of North Carolina Press, 2000), 164.

22. Lucian M. Ashworth, "Women of the Twenty Years' Crisis: The Women's International League for Peace and Freedom and the Problems of Collective Security," in *Women's International Thought: A New History*, ed. Patricia Owens and Katharina Rietzler (Cambridge: Cambridge University Press, 2021), 137; and Joyce Blackwell, *No Peace Without Freedom: Race and the Women's International League for Peace and Freedom, 1915–1975* (Carbondale: Southern Illinois University Press, 2004), 54–55.

23. Flemmie P. Kittrell, "The Health Status and Health Education of Negroes in the United States," *Journal of Negro Education* 18, no. 3 (Summer 1949): 422–28.

24. Sam Lebovic, "From War Junk to Educational Exchange: The World War II Origins of the Fulbright Program and the Foundations of American Cultural Globalism, 1945–1950," *Diplomatic History* (April 2013): 280–312.

25. "Kittrell Interview," 9–10; "Gilford W. Remington to Kittrell, January 18, 1950," box 104–11, folder 4, MSRC Papers.

26. Flemmie P. Kittrell, "Fourth and Final Report, September 3, 1951," box 104–8, folder 6, MSRC Papers.

27. Barbara Savage, "Beyond Illusions: Imperialism, Race, and Technology in Merze Tate's International Thought," *Women's International Thought: A New History*, ed. Patricia Owens and Katharina Rietzler (Cambridge: Cambridge University Press, 2021), 266–81.

28. "New Delhi to Secretary of State, November 7, 1950 [Confidential]," box 2534, General Records of the Department of State, record group 59, National Archives at College Park, Maryland; and "New Delhi to Secretary of State, December 14, 1950 [Confidential]," General Records of the Department of State, record group 59, National Archives at College Park, Maryland.

29. Flemmie P. Kitrrell, "1951 Asian Diary," box 104–1, folder 17, MSRC Papers.

30. Melvyn P. Leffler, *A Preponderance of Power: National Security, the Truman Administration, and the Cold War* (Stanford, CA: Stanford University Press, 1992), 291; and Stephen Macekura, "The Point Four Program and U.S. International Development Policy," *Political Science Quarterly* 128, no. 1 (May 2013): 127–60.

31. "General Report, Chief Home Economist, Govt. of India, Training Program in Allahad, Hawaii, Japan, Baroda, November 19, 1954–May 27, 1955," box 104–14, folder 15, MSRC Papers.

32. "Kittrell to Dorothy Height, November 16, 1954," box 3, folder 27, series 6, NCNW Papers.

33. "Untitled document, June 13, 1948," box 16, folder 270, series 2, NCNW Papers.

34. On Black women's many forms of internationalism, see Keisha Blain and Tiffany Gill, eds., *To Turn the Whole World Over: Black Women and Internationalism* (Urbana: University of Illinois Press, 2019).

35. "Dr. Flemmie Kittrell: U.S. Nutritionist with a Keen Interest in Africa, I.P.S./ Africa, June 23," box 104–1, folder 9, MSRC Papers.

36. Kenneth W. Heger, "Race Relations in the United States and American Cultural and Informational Programs in Ghana, 1957–1966, Part 2," *Prologue* (Winter 1999), http://www.archives.gov/publications/prologue/1999/winter/us-and-ghana-1957-1966-2.html.

37. "U.S. Journalist Visits Accra, April 21, 1958," Ghana Embassy, U.S. Department of State, box 2597, General Records of the Department of State, record group 84, National Archives at College Park, Maryland.

38. "Ghana Embassy to Department of State, October 9, 1958," Ghana Embassy, U.S. Department of State, box 2597, General Records of the Department of State, record group 84, National Archives at College Park, Maryland. On civil rights and foreign affairs, see Mary L. Dudziak, *Cold War Civil Rights: Race and the Image of American Democracy* (Princeton, NJ: Princeton University Press, 2011).

39. Ottley, "Flemmie Pansy Kittrell," 9–10.

40. Ottley, "Flemmie Pansy Kittrell," 13.

41. On Edith Spurlock Sampson, see Helen Laville and Scott Lucas, "The American Way: Edith Sampson, the NAACP, and African American Identity in the Cold War," *Diplomatic History* 20, no. 4 (Fall 1996): 565–90.

42. "Marguerite Cartwright to Francis M. Hammond," box 181, Marguerite Cartwright Papers, Amistad Research Center at Tulane University, New Orleans, Louisiana. At the time of my 2013 study in the Marguerite Cartwright collection, it was still largely unprocessed.

43. "Kittrell to Omar L. Hartzler, June 27, 1961," box 104–15, folder 1, MSRC Papers.

44. Kittrell, "Y.W.C.A. Frontiers in Uganda, East Africa," n.d. 104–14, folder 7, MSRC Papers; and "Kittrell Interview," 16.

45. Ottley, "Flemmie Pansy Kittrell," 13.

46. Women's International League for Peace and Freedom, *14th International Congress of Women's International League for Peace and Freedom*, Stockholm, Sweden, 1959; and "Howard University Press Release, June 24, 1959," box 104–1, folder 9, MSRC Papers.

47. Kittrell published six articles in the 1960s, including Flemmie Kittrell, "Foreign Needs I've Seen Around the World," *Methodist Women*, June 1963.

48. Savage, "Beyond Illusions," 276.

49. "Kittrell Interview," 30.

50. "Kittrell Interview," 38.

51. "Kittrell Interview," 40.

52. "Francis C. Murphy and Elizabeth Murphy to Gertrude Poe, June 11, 1961," box 104–8, folder 2, MSRC Papers.

53. "Kittrell Interview," 44.

54. Ottley, "Flemmie Pansy Kittrell," 12.

55. Ottley, "Flemmie Pansy Kittrell," 13; and "Kittrell Interview," 29.

CHAPTER 13

Just War as Ideology

A Militant Ecumenism of Catholics and Evangelicals

RAYMOND HABERSKI JR.

Vietnam threw the American experience with war into an existential crisis. The legacy of the Vietnam War, once dubbed the "Vietnam Syndrome," warns against launching large-scale ground warfare that almost by definition will descend into an immoral (or at best amoral) abyss without a clearly defined exit strategy and with diminishing popular support. Every president since Richard Nixon has heeded this warning, but all have attempted to find ways to moralize U.S. military power. Colin S. Gray, an accomplished and hawkish defense scholar, captured the heart of that campaign in an essay defending Ronald Reagan's Strategic Defense Initiative (SDI; or "Star Wars"): "The ability of a democracy to sustain an adequate military posture year after year (for decades and even longer) is not unrelated to the popularly perceived compatibility of moral values with defense policy."[1] But how? An idea that has provided moral ballast to U.S. military action since the mid-1970s is *just war theory*. The complex, abstract nature of just war has helped presidents avoid the most obvious pitfalls of the Vietnam Syndrome, but it has also underwritten, in the twenty-first century, what the reporter Scott Shane calls "unnecessary killing," the legal scholar Samuel Moyn criticizes as "humane war," and the war correspondent Dexter Filkins labels the "forever war."

Just War

Just war theory has long offered a moral language for describing how people can kill and die for a country. Three basic categories comprise the theory: (1) *jus ad bellum* (having a just cause to fight), (2) *jus in bello* (conducting a just war), and (3) *jus post bellum* (creating a just peace; a more recent addition). Just war sounds moral, but in the U.S. context it has operated as more of a blanket endorsement for, rather than a measured use of, military violence. Although just war has Catholic connotations, Americans of all faiths and political persuasions have used it since the seventeenth century.[2] Just war might be theological, but in the American experience it has most certainly also been ideological; indeed, because just war theory offers a moral guide for right action in the world, it also provides those who use it with the power to claim they are simply right. In the abstract, the effectiveness of just war should be measured by the way it operates independent of nations and their ideological commitments. In the American experience, just war has been effective as a defense for state violence and as a tool for silencing those who dissent against it—just war operates far more effectively as an ideology for going to war than as a theology to challenge it.

War organizes American life. The military historian Michael Sherry describes the relationship between war and American national identity bluntly: "War created the United States. Although many Americans professed genuine hostility toward it, war was central to their history, the instrument by which they forged and expanded their nation and often defined themselves."[3] In *God and War*, I argue that at least since the end of World War II a civil religion emerged around American experience with war that enabled Americans and their religious leaders to endorse the moral nature of their nation. Although Vietnam complicated that endorsement, neoconservative intellectuals in the late 1970s and 1980s came to see just war theory as a way not only to remoralize U.S. foreign policy but to shut down challenges to American moral authority from the left.

Ironically, among the most significant contributors to the popularity of just war after Vietnam was the political theorist and liberal-left intellectual Michael Walzer. "Almost against its will," Walzer writes, "the left fell into morality. All of us in the antiwar camp suddenly began talking the language of just war—though we did not know that that was what we were doing."[4]

Of course, Vietnam forced a broader discussion about the moral nature of the nation, and Walzer explains that "what happened then was that people on the left, many others too, looked for a common moral language. And what was most available was the language of just war."[5]

Adding further irony to just war's renewed popularity, the Catholic Church in the United States attempted to push a theological interpretation of just war that ultimately inspired an ideological cooptation of the term. The touchstone for the church's discussion of just war was the 1983 Pastoral Letter on War and Peace, titled "The Challenge of Peace: God's Promise and Our Response," issued by the National Conference of Catholic Bishops. This lengthy statement on war and peace addressed anxiety about Cold War militarism but also made just war more prominent than it otherwise might have been. By endorsing just war to critique the Reagan administration's bellicose foreign policy, the bishops invited a larger debate about the relationship between just war and American moral authority. And in the American context, ideology trumped theology.

The Challenge of Peace

The U.S. bishops released their peace pastoral in May 1983, and their 103-page letter laid out opposition to nuclear deterrence. "In simple terms," the bishops explained, "we are saying that good ends (defending one's country, protecting freedom, etc.) cannot justify immoral means (the use of weapons which indiscriminately threaten whole societies)." Rather than trust policies of nuclear deterrence, the bishops warned, "we fear that our world and nation are headed in the wrong direction. More weapons with greater destructive potential are produced every day. More and more nations are seeking to become nuclear powers." And with a direct jab at what many people viewed as the dangerous brinkmanship of the Reagan administration, the bishops concluded, "In our quest for more and more security we fear we are actually becoming less and less secure."[6]

The pastoral letter had gone through three substantial revisions before the conference officially issued it. The process that produced the final product included a good deal of debate between the more pacifist wing of the Catholic Church and those bishops who adhered to an interpretation of just war theory that, traditionally, counseled deferring to state authority in matters of war and peace. A committee of bishops and their advisors worked on the letter for more than a year, during which the group held hearings, issued drafts, and invited officials from the Reagan administration to contribute testimony. In the end, the conference knew the letter would "prove highly controversial, not least because [it] would almost certainly voice major criticisms of U.S. defense policy in the past and probably even more of the hawkish . . . Reagan administration." The American Catholic bishops, who overwhelmingly voted in favor of the 1983 letter, wanted to strike a prophetic stand toward their nation.[6]

In this way, the letter was very much a reflection of the struggle over American moral authority that emerged in the wake of Vietnam. The Catholic Church in the United States had a pacifist faction within it, but that faction had exerted little influence over the church hierarchy. In the 1970s, the wars in Central America, the Supreme Court's decision in *Roe v. Wade*, and the abject and existential terror many people felt living with a nuclear standoff emboldened Catholic leaders to go beyond decrying the immorality of the Vietnam War and to influence the agenda of the nation. Father J. Bryan Hehir, the Catholic priest who served as the key architect of "The Challenge of Peace," approached the issue of nuclear weapons from within a broad understanding of what Joseph Cardinal Bernardin had termed "the consistent ethic of life." That position embraced ending the threat of nuclear war, opposing abortion and the death penalty, and fighting against the kind of oppression and poverty that pervaded the developing world. Hehir attempted to find a point of collaboration between the pacifists, who had carried the day during the Vietnam War, and the just war advocates, who argued that nuclear deterrence was not an end in itself but a means to prevent Soviet expansion at the price of democratic freedom.

Hehir was sensitive to the criticism by conservative Catholics and observers outside the church that the letter presaged a move toward outright pacifism or the adoption of a position in direct conflict with that of the U.S. government. This was the era during which liberation theology inspired many Catholics to imagine the church as a vanguard institution standing with the poor of Central America to resist and perhaps even topple oppressive regimes.[7] The religious and secular Left in the United States lumped the Reagan administration in with regimes tagged as global oppressors. According to the historian Andrew Preston, "as during the Vietnam era, protest by otherwise respectable churches and clergy gave the movement a moral and political credibility it might otherwise have lacked."[8] So a letter from

American Catholic bishops that came out boldly against American defense policy demanded a response.

The response came from a group of conservative Catholic intellectuals, including Michael Novak (who wrote for *National Review*), George Weigel (who attacked Hehir for what they viewed as the priest's internationalist relativism), and their Lutheran ally Richard John Neuhaus. Standing by deterrence, Novak asserted in an essay titled "Moral Clarity in the Nuclear Age" that "to abandon deterrence is to neglect the duty to defend the innocent, to preserve the Constitution and the Republic, and to keep safe the very idea of political liberty." The sanctity of the American promise had to be protected, even at the price of endangering the material existence of the entire population.[9] Weigel also attacked Hehir, but did something else that vastly expanded how just war theory could be used. Weigel reclaimed the term by forging an alliance with other conservative religious leaders, especially evangelical Protestants, and by opposing liberal and leftist critiques of U.S. military power and the moral authority to use it.

Ecumenical Militarism

The immediate context for Weigel's outreach to evangelicals was Reagan's notorious "Evil Empire Speech" on March 8, 1983. The president gave an address to the annual convention of the National Association of Evangelicals (NAE) in Orlando, Florida, declaring Soviet leaders were the "focus of evil in the modern world." Reagan used this high-profile engagement to make two appeals: one was to evangelical Christians whom he wanted to secure for the 1984 election; a second was to those Americans who wanted reassurance that the Cold War continued to be a morally righteous cause. These two appeals were connected because, like many presidents before him, Reagan needed to make a convincing argument that U.S. foreign policy was inherently moral and that his administration's approach—although bellicose and militaristic—was part of that tradition.[10]

In November 1983, a few months after Reagan's speech, George Weigel contacted Billy Melvin, executive director of the NAE, a leader with tremendous political power. The NAE had considerable influence over forty-five thousand churches and nearly fifty million evangelical Christian Americans. Weigel had reached out to Melvin at the urging of Robert (Bob) Dugan, the NAE's director of the Office for Public Affairs, or the chief lobbyist for the NAE. Dugan had grown very concerned that the NAE had begun to drift politically leftward on U.S. foreign policy, just like, apparently, the mainline National Council of Churches and the Catholic Church in the United States. Dugan had been the one to encourage the president to address the 1983 NAE convention in Orlando with the hope that Reagan's speech would challenge NAE leadership to establish a more definitively conservative position on U.S. military policy. "Our concern, quite candidly," Dugan wrote in a letter to a former military official, "is that evangelicals not wind up, in a few years, with the same problems as the mainline Christian denominations—an elite, radical fringe dominating a sullen but coopted majority."[11] Weigel felt very similarly about his Catholic Church.

In his letter to Melvin, Weigel explained that as a scholar-in-residence at the World Without War Council (WWWC) of Greater Seattle he had developed a specific kind of moral justification for American military policy. "We combine a commitment to peace with a commitment to democratic values," Weigel asserted. "We marry a goal—not the end of conflict, but alternatives to war in resolving conflict—that is drawn from the best in the human story to a pessimistic assessment of what now blocks the way to peace." Sounding much like Dugan, Weigel concluded, "We are profoundly disturbed by currents of thought dominant in the National Council of Churches (and increasingly in the Roman Catholic Church) on issues of America and the world; we believe we can work with the NAE to both interdict such problems in the evangelical community, as well as positively modelling the kind of church engagement with war/peace issues that makes moral and political sense."[12] This project became the NAE's Peace, Freedom, and Security Studies (PFSS) program in 1984, and a bit later it influenced Dean C. Curry's "Philadelphia Statement" (1985) and, ultimately, the NAE's "Guidelines for Peace, Freedom, and Security" (1986). As the historian Axel Schäfer writes: "In short, PFSS connected 'peace' and 'freedom' in ways that anticipated the neoconservative agenda of the late 1990s."[13]

Weigel's emergence as a leading neoconservative has been well covered.[14] He and his friend Richard John Neuhaus, a Lutheran minister who converted to Catholicism in 1990 and founded the influential journal *First Things*, were among a core group of religious intellectuals who argued for religious endorsement of American power. For his part, Weigel sought to remoralize American foreign policy by deploying a novel interpretation of just war theory. Working with the NAE, Weigel intended to use just war not merely to make a case *for* American power but *against* an increasingly robust antinuclear movement and the Catholic bishops who supported it. But genuine and unresolvable theological differences remained between Catholicism and evangelical Christianity, so ultimately the goal of this alliance could not be theological but ideological. In other words, even though just war had clear theological roots within the Catholic Church, Weigel saw its utility in equally clear ideological terms.

George Weigel

Throughout the late 1970s and into the mid-1980s, George Weigel operated as a consultant for groups who wanted to craft ethical arguments for American Cold War strategies, as the founding director of the conservative James Madison Foundation and as a scholar-in-residence at the WWWC of greater Seattle, and later as a fellow at the Wilson Center in Washington, D.C. His most important position has been his role at the Ethics and Public Policy Center, where he served as president and then as senior distinguished fellow and William D. Simon Chair in Catholic Studies.

Damon Linker remarked that Weigel's major intellectual contribution to American life has been getting just war into policy statements of successive Bush administrations. This is true, but Weigel's influence has had broader cultural implications. He and Neuhaus both argued in the late 1970s that in the wake of Vietnam the United States needed a way to reinscribe a moral defense of the nation and its history. For example, in a 1976 essay published in the Carnegie Council's magazine *Worldview*, Neuhaus argued that an ideological counterrevolution needed to rise to combat waves of anti-Americanism across secular and religious communities. "In the last quarter of the twentieth century we do not need Christian Marxists," Neuhaus declared, "we need a Christian Marx. That is to say, for this century and the next, we need a definition of reality, an ideology, based on Judeo-Christian religion that is as creative, comprehensive, and compelling as was Marx's definition of reality for the century past."[15] Neuhaus made it his life's work to "clothe" what he saw as a "naked public square" in religious language that would validate the American experiment as he conceived it.

Likewise, Weigel found a role in Neuhaus's project by urging just war as way to the remoralization of American power. "We have formed a national political community," Weigel explained in 1982. "The problem we face is not to weaken it (as some in the public effort for peace would teach); the problem is to add to this existing community another layer of responsibility and obligation, and to make that real in international affairs through legal and political alternatives to war."[16] Weigel felt the imperative to act because his own church had severely questioned whether its values aligned with contemporary American defense policies. Trained in Catholic theology at St. Mary's Seminary and the University in Baltimore, he taught theology for a short period at the graduate school of St. Thomas Seminary. Weigel boldly spoke with authority on the question of Catholic thought on war and peace. In his capacity at the WWWC, he sought to use his position to engage both sides of the defense debate: the policy makers in the military and Reagan administration as well as their critics in and outside the Catholic Church.

To that end, Weigel promoted projects in the early 1980s that he imagined would help the U.S. avoid "totalitarianism or apocalypse."[17] One approach was an American foreign policy "course" called "The American Initiatives Project" that, according to Weigel, would "develop a portfolio of 10–15 policy proposals, non-military initiatives that the U.S. could take to advance the disarmament/law/human rights/development agenda, that would have the coercive capacity to compel Soviet reciprocation." The intention was to counter "peace-types" who, Weigel contended, were "allied to a politics and a moral arrogance that are obstacles, not aids, to a disarmed world under law, and American leadership toward that goal."[18] A second initiative was to debate the American Catholic bishops directly over U.S. military strategy, especially nuclear deterrence. In a small book titled *The Peace Bishops and the Arms Race*, Weigel collected a series of his previously published articles, statements from Catholic officials (mostly bishops), responses to his arguments from readers of his syndicated column, and a reply to his critics. Ostensibly, he meant the book to answer a question posed in the subtitle: "Can religious leadership help in preventing war?" More practically, Weigel hoped to sway American Catholic leaders, who at the moment of the book's publication were framing their peace pastoral, toward a more hawkish interpretation of just war theory.

If one theme unified both projects, it was Weigel's plea for the role Catholic thought might play in underwriting the "American Proposition," a term made famous by the Catholic theologian John Courtney Murray. "There has been no new 'consensus' in the American political community on even the goals, much less the tactics, of U.S. foreign policy," he concluded. And debates about American defense policy "testi[fied] to our continued inability to re-set the ground on which a common sense of purpose and direction in the world can be built."[19] He believed, as he laid out in *Peace Bishops*, that the Catholic Church had the capacity to help that nation rebuild its moral authority. "Our desperate need, as a Church and as a country, is for a third voice: a voice that faces our responsibilities; that does not weaken this political community; that gathers it for the job of changing our adversaries; and that in doing so points a way out of the twin dead-ends of accommodation and Armageddon."[20]

Despite connections to a few Catholic bishops, Weigel did not receive an invitation to speak formally to the United States Conference of Catholic Bishops. Weigel admitted to Cardinal James Francis Stafford that "I'm still not sure why they're not in touch with me, although I continue to suspect that Bryan [Hehir] has ruled me out of court."[21] This chilly reception prompted Weigel to offer his perspective in other ways. In 1987 he published *Tranquillitas Ordinis* (the tranquility of order), which was largely a collection of previously written (if not published) work on just war theory and a full-throated rebuttal of the bishops' position on nuclear deterrence and, especially, Hehir's criticism of U.S. foreign policy.

Throughout 1984 and midway through 1985, Weigel worked with the NAE and his handpicked representative at the NAE, Brian O'Connell, to launch a campaign to study how American evangelicals thought about issues of war and peace and then develop a "resource center" out of which would emerge "guidelines for evangelical organizational and institutional involvement in the war/peace field." The guidelines were meant to be proscriptive, indicating how evangelicals could make an "appropriate contribution to the defense of democratic values, to American and world security, and to progress toward the non-violent resolution of international conflict."[22] Dugan hoped this work might "avoid some of the pitfalls of ecumenical Protestantism and of the Roman Catholic Bishops." In a letter to O'Connell, Richard John Neuhaus was more blunt: "This is preventive action at its best and you [are] to be congratulated for your prescience."[23]

In 1985, Dean C. Curry, a member of the original advisory board of the PFSS program, drafted what he intended to be a concise statement that would consolidate the work Weigel and O'Connell had done up to that point. Curry called it "The Philadelphia Statement" and wanted the signatures of PFSS program advisors. Like Neuhaus, Curry saw NAE offering an ideological intervention: "We are looking not for a 'middle of the road' statement, but a wiser one that would synthesize the partial truths found at each end of the present war/peace debate—a statement capable of defining new ground ahead of the present polarization."[24] Weigel sent Curry a list of themes to emphasize in his final draft—almost all made an appearance. Among the most important suggestions from Weigel was his list of "principle defects in the religious community's present engagement with war/peace issues," which included "the survivalism problem; the mis-use and abuse of Scripture for pre-determined political ends; mirror-imaging of the US and the USSR; an excessive focus on weapons (especially American weapons) to the detriment of thought about alternative ways to settle conflict; a tendency to Third Worldisms when this agenda is addressed."[25] In a final draft of the statement, Weigel was especially pleased to see Curry defend just war theory, underlining the passage that read, "God has provided the means for humanity, collectively, to live free from war. This peace is not perfect, it is not predicated on the abolition of all human conflict; but, it is a realistic peace, a peace which recognizes the effects of sin and evil. It is a peace of public order and governed community." In his massive, four-hundred-page book on just war theory and Catholic thought, *Tranquillitas Ordinis*, Weigel made public order the central theme.[26]

Neuhaus took stock of the occasion for Bob Dugan, telling him that the campaign represented by the PFSS program was "something of potentially momentous importance." He contended that "if handled properly" it had the capacity to "significantly" change the "'church and society' map, with broad ecumenical ramifications." Indeed, by late 1985, the PFSS had become a vehicle for a larger shift in Christian ecumenism. "It has the potential," Neuhaus wrote, "of both broadening and deepening the conversation dramatically. It could provide a new option for Roman Catholics, Lutherans, and more reflective fundamentalists who are increasingly uncomfortable with the mainline liberal agenda—and, indeed, could draw considerable support from the liberal constituency that has wearied of tattered and ill-considered radicalisms."[27] Writing for the evangelical publication *Eternity: The Magazine of Christian Truth*, Weigel argued that as "neither cheerleaders nor cynics" American Catholics and American evangelicals embraced a "common love for the American proposition [that] places them in a distinctive position to be the agents of a reconsecration of the American experiment, a rebirth of freedom for all. The new ecumenism, then, will have as a primary task the generating of fresh thought about the right relationship of religiously-based values and public policy in America."[28]

This ecumenical endorsement did not impress the Christian left. Responses to the NAE's efforts illustrated the pivotal role Weigel played in shaping the ideological nature of the report and guidelines. Jim Rice, director of Sojourners Peace Ministry and a close colleague of Jim Wallis, pointed directly to Weigel as a serious problem. "Many of the report's basic assumptions were quite problematic for a sincere evangelical Christian concerned with Christian peacemaking in response to our nuclear world," Rice began. Beside calling out Weigel specifically in the first paragraph of his letter to Brian O'Connell, Rice also critiqued the report's clear pro-America orientation. "Our role as people of faith is not to provide sanction for whatever the state should choose to do," Rice wrote, "but rather to preach and live faithfully, speaking truth to power and wealth while working for justice for the poor."[29] In reply, O'Connell defended the NAE's PFSS program, claiming that Rice and his supporters have led to "politicization of the church's moral witness." Arguing that the NAE sought the middle ground between nuclear war and totalitarianism, O'Connell told Rice that the program intended to defend both "peace and freedom."[30] In a second letter, Rice again suggested to O'Connell that the problem was Weigel, suggesting he speak to those familiar with Weigel's work in Seattle and others in the Catholic peace movement who also saw Weigel as divisive in their community.[31]

O'Connell didn't necessarily need to look to Seattle for a critique of Weigel's work because he could witness a sharp rebuke from one of its central players. At a seminar called by the Carnegie Council on Ethics and International Affairs, the NAE released its set of guidelines based on the PFSS program. Fr. J. Bryan Hehir was on hand to provide comments on the document and clearly had Weigel in mind with his critique. He observed that NAE's guidelines were "stronger in its theory of ends than on its ethics of means" and that the drafters were "clearer about what you don't like than about how you will carry out the task." Not mincing words about the document's ideological bent, Hehir said "it combines political innocence with a view that is worthy of Dean Acheson." Other religious intellectuals, including Methodist Alan Geyer and Catholic Peter Steinfels, had sharp criticism for the anti-anti-American tone of the document. Geyer hit it for its "ecumenical estrangement, ideological taint, dubious facticity, and questionable prescriptions."[32] In an article for *Sojourners Magazine*, Jim Rice laid out his case for criticizing the guidelines as a product of Weigel's project. Rice argued that the NAE's leadership had become "troubled by the growing peacemaking activity among grassroots evangelicals." By turning to the WWWC, and to Weigel specifically, the NAE produced what Rice believed was an "opening salvo of the conservative attack against the growing evangelical peace movement. The effect of such sophistry is to confuse its readers rather than call them to action."[33] Rice hammered that ideology rather than theology mattered to Weigel and the NAE. He was far from alone on this front.

Just War for What?

The Christian theologian Stanley Hauerwas, a close friend of Richard John Neuhaus, expressed a great unease with this ideological alliance. Hauerwas was also a conservative—on theology, not on ideology. He profoundly disagreed with Neuhaus on the affirmational relationship neoconservatives supported between the Christian church and the United States. In an essay published in 1985 by the *Christian Century*, a leading evangelical intellectual outlet, Hauerwas and his coauthor and Duke colleague William Willimon decried the ideological implications at the heart of the remoralization of American power. Hauerwas and Willimon declared, "We are not at all interested, as Richard John Neuhaus is, in contending that the church is a useful component in keeping constitutional democracy afloat. It may be, but that is neither the church's nor the Christian's first task." The coauthors, like their neoconservative colleagues, had grappled with the role Christianity played in American life in the wake of costly wars and under the shadow of existential challenges from nuclear weapons. However, Hauerwas and Willimon came to a very different conclusion about their obligations to the United States. "We are children of Vietnam," they explained. "That experience taught us that one doesn't challenge Caesar's imperialism with open minded, soft liberalism, but through being so well formed that one is able to say No!"[34] Akin to the role the Catholic bishops played in their peace pastoral, Hauerwas and Willimon imagined a role for the Christian church as a check on, rather than an endorsement of, American moral authority.

In response, Neuhaus wondered if the "dismissive" tone of the essay didn't miss a major point. "I do believe," he wrote in an unpublished reply, "that the church has a great stake in and responsibility for the democratic idea (which is not to be equated with the embodiment of that idea in any social order, including the United States). Exploring, sustaining, and advancing that democratic idea is certainly not the 'first task' of the church, nor is it the task of all Christians. It is among the tasks to which I believe I am called." Neuhaus, Novak, and Weigel saw no way around contending with, and thereby endorsing, the American Proposition. "Hauerwas and Willimon are right," Neuhaus shot back, "the church of today and every day desperately needs to hear the word of repentance and return. Hauerwas and Willimon are wrong," he scolded them, "return does not mean turning away from the worldly tasks which, while fallibly perceived, are nonetheless urgently pursued. Even, please God, the task of advancing the democratic idea in a world that is overwhelmingly hostile to it."[35]

Not surprisingly, the intellectual trajectory of the two friends continued to diverge, but the issue that divided them most acutely was the use of just war in an era of "forever wars." Successive presidents from George H. W. Bush to Barrack Obama have invoked just war to defend a succession of U.S. military actions—from wars in Iraq and Afghanistan to bombing campaigns in the Balkans and drone strikes in the Middle East and Central Asia. The wars of Bush I and Bush II, however, revealed the ideological nature of the doctrine's growing popularity, and Hauerwas showed why.

In 1991, President George H. W. Bush began the rapid troop deployment in the Gulf ahead of what became Desert Storm. Bush invoked just war as a way to substantiate a moral case for an invasion of Iraq and used language that would become notorious in the war his son would launch in 2003. In an exchange with the bishop of the Episcopal Church, Edmond Browning, the elder Bush barked: "What is the morality of not doing anything?" America had to do something, Bush demanded, for it was the "only nation strong enough to stand up to evil."[36] And because World War II had defined Bush's view of just causes, he framed the battle against Saddam Hussein as part of the tradition of the United States fighting just and moral wars. A sizable number of religious leaders in the United States, including a handful of Catholic bishops, openly criticized the president's use of just war, which led Weigel and Neuhaus to pounce yet again. Weigel contended that "the leaders of the oldline Protestantism and American Catholicism cannot bring themselves to say that here is a situation in which the use of proportionate and discriminate armed force is morally justifiable."[37] Neuhaus added that the National Council of Churches' "condemnation of allied action in the Gulf was entirely predictable. The council and the bureaucracies of its chief member churches were thoroughly 'radicalized,' as it used to be said, in the Vietnam era."[38] Hauerwas considered himself a radical, but not mainline.

To Hauerwas, Neuhaus had given in to the anti-anti-Americanism of Weigel and by doing so compromised the power of remaining independent of an ideological construction of just war. "Consider . . . the difference between your application of the [just war] theory and its use to inform penitential practice by Christians for the examination of conscience," Hauerwas wrote. "The latter use requires the presumption that when Christians kill their souls are in jeopardy. In contrast, your use of the theory does not presume that salvation is at stake or that the church exists as part of that salvation. All you assume is the nation-state in a system of nation-states."[39]

This argument between old friends only deepened and ultimately split them apart in the second Bush presidency. In a bracing editorial titled "A Time of War," in his flagship conservative journal *First Things*, Neuhaus reflected on witnessing the collapse of the Twin Towers and the war that had to follow: "Those who in principle oppose the use of military force have no legitimate part in the discussion about how military force should be used. They only make themselves and their cause appear frivolous by claiming that military force is immoral and futile, and, at the same time, wanting to have a political say in how such force is to be employed. The morally serious choice is between pacifism and just war. Here, too, sides must be taken."[40] In response, Hauerwas left *First Things*: "I love many of the things *First Things* represents, but the politics of *First Things* is not really my politics," he explained. "Obviously, you take quite a different view about America and the democratic experiment than I do. Obviously our ecclesiologies don't exactly match."[41] Hauerwas's reflection confirmed what a conservative dependency on just war had created: it didn't foster debate about the moral criteria for war, it ended it. The use of just war had become more effective in silencing criticism of American wars than in preventing them. In the end, however, one might wonder with Stanley Hauerwas, "Which is the better option: to be a functional pacifist or a functionary for the state?"

Notes

1. Colin S. Gray, "Strategic Defense, Deterrence, and the Prospects for Peace," *Ethics* 95, no. 3 (April 1985): 661.
2. Raymond Haberski Jr., *God and War: Civil Religion in Postwar America* (New Brunswick: Rutgers University Press, 2010), 1–10; Stanley Hauerwas, *War and*

the American Difference: Theological Reflections on Violence and National Identity (Grand Rapids, MI: Baker Academic, 2011), 33.

3. Michael S. Sherry, *In the Shadow of War: The United States Since the 1930s* (New Haven, CT: Yale University Press, 1995), 1.

4. Michael Walzer, "The Triumph of Just War Theory (and the Dangers of Success)," *Social Research* 69, no. 4 (Winter 2002): 928.

5. Walzer, "The Triumph of Just War Theory," 929.

6. National Conference of Catholic Bishops, "The Challenge of Peace: God's Promise and Our Response," United States Catholic Conference, May 3, 1983, vii.

7. William J. Gould, "Father J. Bryan Hehir: Priest, Policy Analyst, and Theologian of Dialogue," in *Religious Leaders and Faith-Based Politics*, ed. Jo Renee Formicola and Hubert Morken (Lanham, MD: Rowman and Littlefield, 2001), 205, 210.

8. Gould, "Father J. Bryan Hehir," 207; William Au, *The Cross, the Flag, and the Bomb* (Westport, CT: Praeger, 1985), 237–39.

9. Andrew Preston, *Sword of the Spirit, Shield of Faith: Religion in American War and Diplomacy* (New York: Knopf, 2012), 591.

10. Michael Novak, "Moral Clarity in the Nuclear Age," *National Review* (April 1, 1983): 380, 383.

11. See also Preston, *Sword of the Spirit*, 584.

12. Robert Dugan as quoted in Axel R. Schäfer, *Piety and Public Funding: Evangelicals and the State in Modern America* (Philadelphia: University of Pennsylvania Press, 2012), 166, 167.

13. "George Weigel to Dr. Billy A. Melvin, November 8, 1983" [letter], box 8, folder 1, George Weigel Papers, Hoover Institution Library & Archives, Stanford University, Stanford, California. Hereafter cited as George Weigel Papers.

14. Schäfer, *Piety and Public Funding*, 171.

15. Damon Linker, *The Theocons: Secular America Under Siege* (New York: Anchor, 2007).

16. Richard John Neuhaus, "The Democratic Prospect," *Worldview*, July–August 1976, 20.

17. George Weigel, *The Peace Bishops and the Arms Race* (Chicago: World Without War, 1982), 46.

18. "George Weigel to Rev. P. Francis Murphy, September 11, 1981" [letter], box 8, folder 1, George Weigel Papers.

19. "Weigel to Murphy, October 13, 1980" [letter], box 8, folder 1, George Weigel Papers.

20. World Without War Council, *The American Initiatives Project: A New Course for American Foreign Policy* (Chicago: World Without War, 1981), 1.

21. Weigel, *The Peace Bishops and the Arms Race*, 50.

22. "Weigel to J. Francis Stafford, March 1, 1982" [letter], box 8, folder 1, George Weigel Papers.

23. "Peace, Freedom and Security Studies: An NAE Program on America's Role in World Affairs," n.d., box 6, folder 1, George Weigel Papers.

24. "Neuhaus to O'Connell, September 25, 1984" [letter], box 6, folder 1, George Weigel Papers.

25. "Dean C. Curry to Selected PFSS Program Advisers, April 3, 1985" [letter], box 6, folder 3, George Weigel Papers.

26. "Weigel to Curry, April 18, 1985" [memo], box 6, folder 3, George Weigel Papers.

27. George Weigel, *Tranquillitas Ordinis: The Present Failure and Future Promise of American Catholic Thought on War and Peace* (New York: Oxford University Press, 1987).

28. "Neuhaus to Dugan, October 11, 1985" [letter], box 6, folder 3, George Weigel Papers.

29. Weigel, "Catholics and Evangelicals: A New Ecumenism?," *Eternity: The Magazine of Christian Truth*, May 23, 1985; corrected draft in box 10, folder 1, George Weigel Papers.

30. "Jim Rice to Brian O'Connell, January 20, 1985" [letter], box 6, folder 1, George Weigel Papers.

31. "O'Connell to Rice, January 25, 1985" [letter], box 6, folder 1, George Weigel Papers.

32. "Rice to O'Connell, January 28, 1985" [letter], box 6, folder 1, George Weigel Papers.

33. Darrell Turner, "Critics Tear Into Evangelicals' Document on War and Peace," *Religious New Service*, December 12, 1986, box 6, folder 9, George Weigel Papers.

34. Jim Rice, "The Pretense of Peacemaking," *Sojourners Magazine*, April 6, 1987, box 6, folder 9, George Weigel Papers.

35. Stanley Hauerwas and William Willimon, "Embarrassed by God's Presence," *Christian Century*, January 30, 1985, 99.

36. Richard John Neuhaus, "Reader's Response: Encountered by God's Purpose," Richard John Neuhaus Papers, correspondence, box 32, Stanley Hauerwas, American Catholic Research Center and University Archives, Catholic University of America, Washington, D.C.

37.

38. Kenneth Walsh, "Bush's 'Just War' Doctrine," *U.S. News and World Report*, February 4, 1991, 52.

39. George Weigel, "The Churches and War in the Gulf," *First Things*, (March 1991), https://www.firstthings.com/article/1991/03/the-churches-war-in-the-gulf.

40. Richard John Neuhaus, "Just War and This War," *Wall Street Journal*, January 29, 1991.

41. Neuhaus, "Just War and This War."
42. Neuhaus, "Just War and This War."
43. "Richard John Neuhaus to Stanley Hauerwas, October 11, 2001, unset letter, Stanley Hauerwas (1999–2008), Richard John Neuhaus Papers, box 33, folder 9, American Catholic Research Center and University Archives, Catholic University of America, Washington, D.C.

PART FOUR
Ideologies and Democracy

CHAPTER 14

Freedom as Ideology

JEREMI SURI

To coerce a man is to deprive him of freedom—freedom from what?
—ISAIAH BERLIN, "TWO CONCEPTS OF LIBERTY"

In every era, U.S. leaders have claimed that their foreign policies promote freedom abroad as they also protect it at home. Eric Foner has written that "freedom" is *the* keyword of American history, and that holds equally true for American interactions with the wider world. Americans have always justified their possession and deployment of power and argued about it with reference to claims about freedom. There can be no legitimate power in American society without a connection—no matter how tenuous—to being "free."[1]

The centrality of freedom to the American language of politics and society makes it a highly contested concept—argued about and redefined by every generation in new ways. Foner reminds us: "The meaning of freedom has been constructed not only in congressional debates and political treatises but on plantations and picket lines, in parlors and bedrooms."[2] We might add on foreign battlefields and in diplomatic negotiations, international exchange programs, and postcolonial spaces to this capacious list.

Different figures and contexts have stretched the concept in various directions, often producing very "unfree" outcomes, but that only reaffirms how important American assumptions and imaginations of freedom have remained. Frequently, American obsessions with particular conceptions of freedom have blinded citizens and leaders to the repressive consequences of their actions. At other moments, American assumptions about freedom have justified inaction, even in the face of genocide and ethnic cleansing.

The pursuit of freedom does not necessarily elicit results that match intentions, and American intentions have often been deeply self-serving. The historian Edmund Morgan famously observed that from its early days the American pursuit of freedom made others unfree, particularly slaves, Indigenous peoples, and those who thwarted American ambitions.[3]

The United States, like other nations, has always pursued its own interests. In widely varying circumstances, those interests have reflected how particular leaders defined freedom, its subjects, and its pursuit. Although this observation does not make the United States necessarily exceptional (or humble), it distinguishes American policy making from other states that are not driven by similar conceptual obsessions. Countries whose survival is more consistency imperiled—Poland, Israel, and the Koreas, for example—emphasize their national sustenance above all. Island regimes with largely homogenous populations—Japan is the prime example—tend to prioritize racial and cultural purity. And societies with self-conscious histories of civilizational glory that long precede nationhood—China, India, and Persia are three of many—rarely make policy around a concept so modern in its formulation. Every society cares about freedom in one form or another, but American policy makers have obsessed about it in ways that are distinctive, enduring, and often quite problematic.

Obsession does not prevent dissembling; it might even encourage it. Donald Trump's presidency, filled with flagrant dishonesty, raises questions about whether American leaders really care about freedom—or is it just a convenient rationalization? The word *freedom* is used and abused frequently, but it is not the honesty or dishonesty of its invocation that matters. The fact that freedom is a necessary point of reference for all policy—that all uses of U.S. power must be justified in its terms—makes the concept central to American ideologies. U.S. leaders legitimize their power by claiming to enhance freedom. Uses of power that make the most persuasive claims about freedom endure, whereas uses of power with weak claims about freedom quickly lose popular support. Ideas of freedom encourage larger promises from leaders when they explain their actions. Realpolitik is never sufficient for the American polity.[4]

In this essay, I analyze some of the continuities and phase shifts in the invocation of freedom for foreign policy purposes. I examine how policy makers have used the concept, what they have meant, how meanings have changed over time, and how changed meanings have helped shape U.S. actions abroad. Ideas are tied to context, and in the case of U.S. foreign policy, the conceptions of freedom animating expressions of power have evolved in recognizable ways to address different historical moments in the nation's history and in the history of the wider world. The main point here is not to deconstruct the fine grains of policy making in any particular period but to understand and analyze how changing ideological climates have defined what freedom meant to U.S. policy makers and how those meanings in turn influenced policy. Many other motivations contribute to policy making, and many other factors determine outcomes on the ground. The concepts of freedom that have mattered for U.S. foreign policy have anchored a wider complex of influences.

Freedom is an unstable ideology because it is not prima facia. One group's freedom is another group's imprisonment. Both Morgan and Foner make this point: the freedom of many eighteenth-century white Americans required the enslavement of millions of Black bodies. Assumptions about whose freedom counts, and how it is defined, reflect wider debates about race, justice, and belonging. These are arguments about more than interest. They are questions of value: Who and what counts? Analyzing freedom as a shifting ideology behind foreign policy enables us to see how much the international projection of U.S. power has built upon and contributed to these fundamental questions. When the United States deploys its power, it also deploys changing ideas about what it means to be free. The foreign responses to American ideas push them in new directions back home.

If foreign policy is a complex cocktail of ingredients, ideas of freedom constitute a base alcohol for Americans that changes over time, mixing well with certain additives in some moments, but not in others. The final color and taste of the U.S. foreign policy cocktail is, in fact, often hard to predict. The leaders empowered as bartenders are constantly mixing the inherited ingredients in new ways.

Isaiah Berlin, a frequent consumer of cocktails himself, famously elucidated two political concepts of liberty: *negative* (freedom from) and *positive* (freedom for). In his famous essay on the subject, he argued that negative freedom was more individualistic and limiting, positive freedom more communal and expansive. He observed that the former tended to restrict government power, whereas the latter required government action on behalf of worthy goals. Free societies needed both conceptions, according to Berlin, and excess in pursuit of either could cause deprivation and tyranny. As in all things, Berlin sought balance and moderation. As a Russian émigré writing in the shadow of Soviet tyranny, he was especially wary of positivistic conceptions of freedom that justified state violence to change human behavior. The correct balance of negative and positive liberty—what some have called Berlin's "liberal" sensibility—was crucial in his eyes for preserving a just society. He perceived policy makers in Western Europe and the United States as struggling to find this correct balance after World War II.[5]

For the longer history of U.S. foreign policy and the intellectual roots behind it, Berlin's framework is a good start, but too narrow. The American language of freedom has a wider range beyond the negative and positive polarities articulated by Berlin. A growing, diverse country has more ways to think about freedom. Changes in capabilities, threats, and other circumstances make the pursuit of a liberal balance, as Berlin defined it, more multidimensional.

A layered historical understanding of freedom (less a balance of polarities and more an unstable mix) works better for analyzing the main currents in U.S. foreign policy. We can periodize U.S. foreign policy around three evolving conceptual frames that expand on Berlin's observations. Instead of negative and positive liberty, we can identify *restrictive* (freedom from), *expansive* (freedom for), and *hegemonic* (freedom over) conceptions that were present in all periods of U.S. history but alternated in their weight over policy making. The changing mix of these three concepts, in different periods, reflects the ongoing debate about what freedom meant to Americans, and the evolving circumstances of the country. The growing power of the American state, and rising expectations for the state in foreign policy, pushed thinking about freedom away from the early restrictive anchors to ever-more expansive and then hegemonic assumptions.

We can map this process in three historical phases. In each phase, an evolving discussion of freedom contributed to new foreign policies. Attention to freedom as an evolving ideology explains key shifts in U.S. power.

Restrictive Freedom

The first serious statement of American foreign policy doctrine was President George Washington's Farewell Address on February 22, 1796. Felix Gilbert has shown how this document—written in parts by Alexander Hamilton, James Madison, and the president himself—drew on a rich reading of Renaissance and Enlightenment thinking about freedom. The address was a self-conscious testament, designed to frame how citizens understood democratic freedoms and how leaders had to behave. Ceding power and articulating a vision for his successors, Washington liberated the nation from traditions of personalist and hereditary power. He replaced them with reasoned expectations about restrictions on how long and to what effect power could be used.[6]

Washington wanted the nascent United States to be a free society, which meant a society free from tyranny, war, and other impediments on community life. Early American republicanism emphasized community strongly, believing that the United States was a pluralistic collection of localities pursuing their distinctive traditions. People were free because they could work and pray in their communities. The Union represented the loose but vital connections the federal government provided to enhance communities in their chosen forms.[7]

For Washington, freedom grew from a trinity of basic order at home, trade with the wider world, and resistance to foreign coercion:

> If we remain one people under an efficient government, the period is not far off when we may defy material injury from external annoyance; when we may take such an attitude as will cause the neutrality we may at any time resolve upon to be scrupulously respected; when belligerent nations, under the impossibility of making acquisitions upon us, will not lightly hazard the giving us provocation; when we may choose peace or war, as our interest, guided by justice, shall counsel.[8]

Washington's Farewell Address called for a free society to pursue a foreign policy of caution, commerce, and disinterest ("neutrality") toward the political conflicts of other societies. The president emphasized protecting freedom at home, and he warned against trying to spread it abroad. The United States needed freedom from interference by others. Power served freedom by ensuring independence for communities within the new nation.

These ideas echoed Machiavellian concerns, according to J. G. A. Pocock, of a limited state for a dynamic society. For Washington, the sources that restricted freedom were excess, uniformity, and domination—all of which he warned against in the making of foreign policy. He did not want the United States to become a traditional diplomatic actor with aristocratic ambassadors playing the game of alliances for imperial acquisition.[9]

The first president defined a free society as one that self-consciously restricted its own uses of power to prevent the military excesses that would tempt policy makers in the short run but limit independence over time. Freedom meant security not just from foreign threats but also from foreign entanglements. To be free was to be cautious, separate, and humble. Washington associated freedom with commercial growth but with limited government power, a small military, and citizen diplomats.[10]

Washington's vision of freedom and foreign policy guided the United States for the nation's first century because it was so widely shared. His ideas matched the experiences and aspirations of literate elites in various communities. Washington's ideas also matched the conditions of a large landed nation, rich with resources, far from foreign threats, and lacking in established military and diplomatic institutions. His words made sense to Americans, and they used that sensibility to think about foreign policy.

One of the clearest manifestations of Washington's influence was the Monroe Doctrine, articulated by President James Monroe on December 2, 1823. As former Spanish and Portuguese colonies throughout South America successfully threw off foreign rule in the early nineteenth century, the United States faced a series of policy choices: actively defend the independence of these new states, negotiate with the European powers (particularly Britain and Spain) who sought to maintain influence in the region, or remain neutral.

Although widespread American sentiment favored the Latin American revolutionaries, the first option of offering active defense was impractical. The United States possessed limited naval capabilities, and conflict with a European power could spill back onto the North American continent. Americans remained traumatized by their military failures in the War of 1812 with Great Britain, and the burning of the Executive Mansion in particular. Even the most ardent American defenders of the South American revolutions wanted to remain free from war with the European powers—at almost all costs.

The British pushed for a negotiated alternative that would expand London's influence in the region and benefit from American support. The British offer made sense for traditional practitioners of diplomacy because it promised to give the larger powers, including the United States, more influence over the region as it also limited conflict. The American secretary of state John Quincy Adams seriously considered this option, but he ultimately rejected it. Adams recognized that Americans wanted the Western Hemisphere to remain free from expanded British power, even at the cost of American influence over the newly independent South American states. The United States had to avoid going forward alone "in search of monsters to destroy," but it also had to stop foreign imperialists from doing the same.[11]

Neutrality was not an option simply because the stakes were so large. If the South American revolutions were crushed by the Holy Alliance of conservative European monarchies, including Spain, the future of the American experiment would be imperiled by powerful hostile forces near North America. If the British inserted themselves on the South American continent, the United States would be stuck in a subordinate position to British trade and other influences throughout the Western Hemisphere. American freedom would suffer in both scenarios.

The language of the Monroe Doctrine, largely written by Adams, brought the wisdom of George Washington's Farewell Address to the problem. The United States remained free of alliances. It encouraged increased trade and other forms of commerce across the newly independent states and old imperial regimes. What the United States promised was that it would use its economic influences, short of war, to help newly independent states survive and resist the return of imperial powers defeated in their former colonies. The United States would neither join revolutionary struggles nor ally with their oppressors; it would support independence, once achieved, and it would act cautiously.

Above all, Monroe and Adams wanted freedom from colonial wars. They were convinced that South American societies were moving away from colonialism, and they supported that cause. They accepted incremental change that would limit war and remove repression over time. Adams, in particular, believed that a common hemispheric project of seeking freedom from European controls would establish American leadership, if wars and alliances could be avoided. This was a policy that reflected the first president's emphasis on commerce, independence, and restraint for limited objectives.[12]

The Monroe Doctrine became the classic assertion of American freedom from new European colonialism:

With the existing colonies or dependencies of any European power we have not interfered and shall not interfere. But with the Governments who have declared their independence and maintain it, and whose independence we have, on great consideration and on just principles, acknowledged, we could not view any interposition for the purpose of oppressing them, or controlling in any other manner their destiny, by any European power in any other light than as the manifestation of an unfriendly disposition toward the United States.[13]

American freedom meant a new American role in the Western Hemisphere as supporter of independence when possible and as a self-proclaimed leader of free peoples. The United States did not have the capabilities or the ambition to control the entire region, but it committed itself to freeing the hemisphere from potential challengers. American anticolonialism, therefore, was not concerned primarily with the content of other former colonized peoples' freedoms but was obsessed with removing threats to American freedoms.

Washington's Farewell Address, the Monroe Doctrine, and other major acts of foreign policy in the first U.S. century reflected restrained efforts to free American communities from foreign intruders. Restrictive American conceptions of freedom aimed at excluding those who defined freedom in monarchical, imperial, or other terms. When South American revolutionaries adopted their own radical alternatives to American capitalist and republican freedoms, they also elicited American opposition. The pursuit of freedom against threatening alternatives, as defined by American leaders, made the United States a restrained but still sometime aggressive unilateralist, as South American critics of the Monroe Doctrine would contend in later decades. The same was true at home, especially for slaves, Indigenous peoples, and other excluded groups.[14]

Expansive Freedom

The end of American slavery after a horrific Civil War expanded the vision of American freedom enormously, although stubborn limits surrounding economics, race, gender, and other categories remained strong—and were, in some ways, redoubled. The party of Abraham Lincoln (the Republican Party) defined American freedom as more than freedom from foreign interference.[15]

The Republican position was that freedom meant access to opportunity, defined largely through new land, capital, and other resources. The quintessential Lincoln policies, pursued with more consistency than slave abolition, included expedited westward settlement (the Homestead Act), increased higher education access (the Morrill Land Grant Act), and the spread of industry through massive federal railroad subsidies. "Free men," according to Republicans, required fertile "soil" and paid "labor," especially for white male citizens.[16]

Increased access to resources encouraged an expansive foreign policy. Americans had moved across the continent in prior decades with the assumption of continued freedom from "old world" entanglements. After the Civil War those assumptions began to change, beginning with secretary of state William Henry Seward's acquisition of Alaska and the Midway Islands in 1867. These acquisitions were unpopular among many citizens who still adhered to a more limited vision of foreign policy, and they were nearly rejected by Congress. Nonetheless, they were the first steps in a cohesive Republican policy of connecting expanded American freedoms at home with control over foreign areas. Democrats remained more attached to a restrictive vision of domestic and international freedoms, but they were the less powerful national party—largely because of the Civil War—for the next half century.[17]

Theodore Roosevelt and Woodrow Wilson inherited this legacy, and they made their political careers as exponents of expansive definitions of American freedom, and the presidency, although for different purposes. Roosevelt advocated the freedom to acquire resources for the United States to become a leading industrial power—a world capitalist leader. "The history of America," Roosevelt explained in 1910, "is now the central feature of the history of the world; for the world has set its face hopefully toward our democracy." In the worldwide competition among nations, Roosevelt argued, Americans needed a strong government and a forceful executive to bring citizens together, breakup corrupt "trusts," and push into foreign markets. "The American people," he asserted,

are right in demanding that New Nationalism, without which we cannot hope to deal with new problems. The New Nationalism puts the national need before sectional or personal advantage. It is impatient of the utter confusion that results from local legislatures attempting to treat national issues as local issues. It is still more impatient of the impotence which springs from over division of governmental powers, the impotence which makes it possible for local selfishness or for legal cunning, hired by wealthy special interests, to bring national activities to a deadlock. This New Nationalism regards the executive power as the steward of the public welfare.[18]

The "impotence" that Roosevelt criticized was the restrained vision of freedom that Washington, Adams, and others had defended in their formulation of American foreign policy goals before the Civil War. Now, in a rapidly industrializing nation, Roosevelt turned the nationalism of the Union cause into a "New Nationalism" of aggressive expansion that asserted American freedom to access resources far from the North American continent.[19]

What became known as the Roosevelt Corollary revised the Monroe Doctrine in these terms. In his Fourth Annual Message to Congress, on December 6, 1904, Roosevelt proclaimed:

> Chronic wrongdoing, or an impotence which results in a general loosening of the ties of civilized society, may in America, as elsewhere, ultimately require intervention by some civilized nation, and in the Western Hemisphere the adherence of the United States to the Monroe Doctrine may force the United States, however reluctantly, in flagrant cases of such wrongdoing or impotence, to the exercise of an international police power.[20]

To protect freedom within the United States, Roosevelt argued that the president had to act as a policeman, particularly in the Caribbean and other areas close to North America. The dangers of "chronic wrongdoing," including violent instability and financial mismanagement, threatened an industrializing United States, in Roosevelt's view. His predecessors' restraint was part of the dangerous "impotence" he condemned in his statement.[21]

Roosevelt's rival, Woodrow Wilson, condemned the New Yorker's emphasis on centralized power and militarism, but he shared Roosevelt's expansive conceptualization of American freedom. Wilson, in fact, intervened more frequently in Latin American societies to combat perceived threats to the United States. When Wilson reluctantly brought the country into World War I, he contended that the "world must be made safe for democracy." Echoing Roosevelt, he explained: "We desire no conquest, no dominion. We seek no indemnities for ourselves, no material compensation for the sacrifices we shall freely make. We are but one of the champions of the rights of mankind."[22]

Both Roosevelt and Wilson conceived of the United States as more than a continental power with limited interests. Now a world power with a growing industrial economy, they had ambitious domestic and foreign agendas for the promotion of freedom. They saw an unavoidable connection. They believed they had to bring American freedom to the wider family of nations to protect its progress at home. Wilson's Fourteen Points, written in the dual shadow of World War I and the Russian Revolution, sought to avert what Frank Ninkovich has identified as the president's nightmare of a world suffocating freedom. Wilson did not want the United States to dominate the globe, but he sought to ensure that it could spread key ideas and institutions.[23]

The trajectory of American political economy in the half century after the Civil War widened the range of ambitions attached to the American discourse of freedom. To be free meant to own land, earn a wage, get an education, and attain respect abroad. These attributes were still restricted to the most privileged, and denied to many, but they powerfully influenced how journalists, academics, and politicians talked about the United States. If Lincoln's America was dominated by debates about freedom and slavery, Roosevelt and Wilson's America was pervaded with debates about freedom and national power. A growing industrial country needed freedom to expand across the oceans and into foreign lands. Those assumptions guided unprecedented U.S. decisions to acquire foreign territory, enter a world war, and then try to redesign the international system.[24]

Hegemonic Freedom

An expanding America was not hegemonic before World War II. For all its growth, the United States remained detached from many international developments, particularly the rise of fascism. American economic and cultural influences spread widely, but the military capabilities of the United States were small, and American diplomats had a limited presence outside the Western Hemisphere.

World War II brought a sea change. Shaken by the worldwide devastation of the Great Depression, the militant rise of fascism, and the genocidal violence across the globe, American leaders believed they had no alternative but to make people free and prevent a return to the recent past. "Never again" referred to the nightmarish experience of the last decade and the inherited assumptions of American restraint and separation. The United States now had to lead, not just expand; it had to plant its vision of freedom abroad and eradicate the proven threats from fascism and communism. George Washington's warnings against foreign entanglements seemed terribly outdated, and opposition to American dominance in war-devastated areas appeared naïve, even treasonous.[25]

Woodrow Wilson had proclaimed that "the world must be made safe for democracy" to justify temporary participation—as an "associate power" (not a permanent ally)—in a war far from American borders. Franklin Roosevelt stretched Wilson's ideas much further to define American freedom after depression and world war as international hegemony. Roosevelt started to make this case on January 6, 1941, when he spoke to Congress about the overwhelming need to respond to a "foreign peril." Calling for measures to defeat the roots of fascism, Roosevelt looked "to a world founded upon four essential human freedoms." The United States would take the lead in promoting its conception of free speech, freedom of religion, "freedom from want," and "freedom from fear," without obvious geographic limits. "That is no vision of a distant millennium," Roosevelt explained. "It is a definite basis for a kind of world attainable in our own time and generation. . . . Freedom means the supremacy of human rights everywhere. Our support goes to those who struggle to gain those rights or keep them."[26]

The Atlantic Charter, imposed by Roosevelt on British prime minister Winston Churchill in August 1941 (before the United States had entered the military conflict), stamped this conceptualization of freedom on the allied effort. In return for Lend-Lease and other aid from the United States, Roosevelt forced the British empire, and later the Soviet Union, to embrace an American vision of freedom. The Atlantic Charter included:

- "the right of all peoples to choose the form of government under which they will live" with "sovereign rights and self-government restored to those who have been forcibly deprived of them;"
- "enjoyment by all States, great or small, victor or vanquished, of access, on equal terms, to the trade and to the raw materials of the world which are needed for their economic prosperity;"
- "collaboration between all nations in the economic field with the object of securing, for all, improved labor standards, economic advancement and social security;" and
- "a peace which will afford to all nations the means of dwelling in safety within their own boundaries, and which will afford assurance that all the men in all lands may live out their lives in freedom from fear and want."[27]

Roosevelt wrote these words to define American war aims, the conditions for American support, and the expectations for the postwar world. The United States would now join alliances unprecedented in its history. And the White House would lead the "free world," enforcing its conception of freedom as a guarantee for peace and prosperity.[28]

George Kennan's influential "Long Telegram" from Moscow in February 1946 sought to discipline this new American ambition, focusing on the containment of Soviet advances. As the first State Department director of policy planning, Kennan contributed to what was still a breathtaking and hegemonic agenda. Through the Marshall Plan and the Reverse Course in Japan, Washington funded the reconstruction of postwar Europe and East Asia, largely on American terms. Through the creation of the Central Intelligence Agency, the United States influenced foreign elections, particularly in Italy, encouraging the rise of pro-American "Christian Democracy" across Western Europe. And through the Truman Doctrine, Washington gave aid to anticommunist groups in Greece and Turkey, as well as to communist dissident leaders in Yugoslavia—a country of particular fascination for Kennan.[29]

Although he opposed the militarization of American foreign policy—including the development of thermonuclear weapons and the creation of the North Atlantic Treaty Organization (NATO)—Kennan's presumption that the United States had to dominate the "core" areas of military-industrial power encouraged the continual spread of anticommunist efforts. American leaders and citizens came to see the emergence of communism anywhere as a threat to their freedoms. The United States acted to impose its capitalist freedoms, often by supporting undemocratic regimes with force, to prevent the worse perceived danger of communist expansion. Freedom over foreign societies—from South Korea to Vietnam and Chile, among others—meant defeating communist sympathizers at all costs. Kennan later condemned these excesses, but they shared many of the same assumptions about freedom and American power that he articulated at the beginning of what became the Cold War.[30]

The National Security Act of 1947, supported by Kennan, institutionalized the hegemonic aspirations of American freedom. Breaking with inherited assumptions against a large standing military, Americans essentially rewrote the Constitution to create a permanent military-industrial complex, designed to promote American freedoms on a global scale. This mission included the spread of markets, the containment of communism, and the armed support for trusted leaders and parties abroad. The militarization and globalization of U.S. foreign policy grew from a boundless American-centered definition of freedom, more expansive than ever before.[31]

Despite recurring criticisms of American foreign policy for overreach and harm to democracy, assumptions of global hegemony became embedded in the basic definition of freedom for many Americans. When the

Soviet Union disintegrated and the Cold War ended, American policy makers could not imagine a "free world" that did not include American dominance—everywhere. Few leaders invested in a careful examination of U.S. national interests; the presumption was that the United States had to lead everywhere if the world was to remain peaceful, prosperous, and free.

This was the "end of history" with permanent hegemony for American freedom, according to one popular author. The remaining challenge was to defend free civilization in its "clash" with unfree civilizations, another famous author wrote. Continued American hegemony looked like the necessary, and inevitable, antidote.[32]

Epilogue: Freedom Exaggerated, Overturned, and Renewed

The September 11, 2001, terrorist attacks on the United States redoubled American commitments to hegemonic freedom and an "end of history." President George W. Bush contended that the terrorists targeted America because they hated freedom. The only solution was for the United States to make unfree lands free—"ending tyranny in our world." In his second inaugural address, President Bush preached "confidence because freedom is the permanent hope of mankind, the hunger in dark places, the longing of the soul." Bush announced: "We are ready for the greatest achievements in the history of freedom."[33]

This was the false prophecy at the root of the Global War on Terror. Drawing on a long tradition of difficult American nation-building efforts, with mixed results, the Bush administration promised messianic possibilities for the spread of freedom with overwhelming American military force. They would reap the whirlwind. Defeating the Taliban in Afghanistan and then overthrowing Saddam Hussein in Iraq were going to be the first, easy steps—a "cakewalk," one official bragged. Then would come coerced change in Iran and North Korea—the other pieces of what President Bush called the "axis of evil." The president believed American ideas of freedom were now so hegemonic that they could create their own power, turning the slow work of nation-building into hypertransformation through shock and awe.[34]

American failures in Iraq, combined with the global financial crisis of 2007–08, unmasked the shallowness of the Bush administration's conceptualization. The president and his "neoconservative" advisors had grossly exaggerated the power and appeal of hegemonic claims about American freedom, and their actions motivated mass resentments at home and abroad. The decline in goodwill toward the U.S. government was precipitous, and resistance to American claims about freedom multiplied globally. Leaders in Russia and China, in particular, took advantage of the circumstances to diminish the image advantage the United States had long maintained as a "free society." American freedom now looked militaristic, destructive, and self-defeating. Even some Americans agreed.[35]

The future of U.S. foreign policy will depend on a redefinition of American freedom, as in past eras. The United States will not be able to reconstruct its discredited hegemonic claims; it will need an ideological alternative. Americans will have to author a more persuasive narrative for what freedom means and how it should be pursued. The history of past adjustments is valuable because it shows why this is necessary and how it is possible.

That was Isaiah Berlin's point when he wrote about positive and negative freedoms. They are not static, and they are not self-contained. American uses of power gain legitimacy from conceptions of freedom that speak to a historical context—its aspirations and its capabilities. Those are the stakes in contemporary debates about what constitutes freedom at home and abroad. The course of these debates over ideas will drive the evolution of U.S. power.

Notes

1. Eric Foner, *The Story of American Freedom* (New York: Norton, 1998).
2. Foner, *Story of American Freedom*, xv.
3. See Edmund Morgan, *American Slavery, American Freedom: The Ordeal of Colonial Virginia* (New York: Norton, 1975).
4. This observation is the point of departure for this classic work: Michael H. Hunt, *Ideology and U.S. Foreign Policy* (New Haven, CT: Yale University Press, 1987).
5. Berlin, "Two Concepts of Liberty." See also Michael Ignatieff, *Isaiah Berlin: A Life* (New York: Metropolitan, 1998).
6. Felix Gilbert, *To the Farewell Address* (Princeton, NJ: Princeton University Press, 1961).
7. Gilbert, *To the Farewell Address*. See also Gordon S. Wood, *The Idea of America: Reflections on the Birth of the United States* (New York: Penguin, 2011), esp. 231–50.
8. "George Washington's Farewell Address," February 22, 1796, http://avalon.law .yale.edu/18th_century/washing.asp.

9. See J. G. A. Pocock, *The Machiavellian Moment: Florentine Political Thought and the Atlantic Republican Tradition* (Princeton, NJ: Princeton University Press, 1975); Don Higginbotham, *George Washington and the American Military Tradition* (Athens: University of Georgia Press, 1985); Jeremi Suri, *The Impossible Presidency: The Rise and Fall of America's Highest Office* (New York: Basic Books, 2017), chap. 2.

10. See Suri, *The Impossible Presidency*, chap. 2.

11. See Charles N. Edel, *Nation-Builder: John Quincy Adams and the Grand Strategy of the Republic* (Cambridge, MA: Harvard University Press, 2014), 107–84. See also the classic account in Samuel Flagg Bemis, *John Quincy Adams and the Union* (New York: Alfred Knopf, 1956).

12. The best recent account of the Monroe Doctrine is Jay Sexton, *The Monroe Doctrine: Empire and Nation in Nineteenth-Century America* (New York: Hill and Wang, 2011).

13. President James Monroe's Annual Message to Congress, December 2, 1823, http://avalon.law.yale.edu/19th_century/monroe.asp.

14. On this point, see, among many others, Lars Schoultz, *Beneath the United States: A History of U.S. Policy Toward Latin America* (Cambridge, MA: Harvard University Press, 1998), esp. 59–124.

15. See Matthew Karp, *The Vast Southern Empire: Slaveholders at the Helm of American Foreign Policy* (Cambridge, MA: Harvard University Press, 2016).

16. See, among many others, James M. McPherson, *Abraham Lincoln and the Second American Revolution* (New York: Oxford University Press, 1991); Eric Foner, *Free Soil, Free Labor, Free Men: The Ideology of the Republican Party Before the Civil War* (New York: Oxford University Press, 1970).

17. See Daniel Immerwahr, *How to Hide an Empire: A History of the Greater United States* (New York: Farrar, Straus, and Giroux, 2019), esp. 46–153.

18. Theodore Roosevelt, "New Nationalism," August 31, 1910, https://teachingamericanhistory.org/library/document/new-nationalism-speech/.

19. On this point, see Howard K. Beale, *Theodore Roosevelt and the Rise of America to World Power* (Baltimore, MD: Johns Hopkins University Press, 1956).

20. Theodore Roosevelt, "Fourth Annual Message to Congress," December 6, 1904, https://teachingamericanhistory.org/library/document/roosevelt-corollary-to-monroe-doctrine/.

21. On the influence of Alfred Thayer Mahan's advocacy for a strong navy to promote American freedom, see David Milne, *Worldmaking: The Art and Science of American Diplomacy* (New York: Farrar, Straus, and Giroux, 2015), 21–68.

22. Woodrow Wilson, "War Message to Congress," April 22, 1917, https://wwi.lib.byu.edu/index.php/Wilson%27s_War_Message_to_Congress.

23. Frank Ninkovich, *Modernity and Power: A History of the Domino Theory in the Twentieth Century* (Chicago: University of Chicago Press, 1994), esp. 37–68; Milne, *Worldmaking*, 105–22.

24. See Walter LaFeber, *The New Empire: An Interpretation of American Expansion, 1860–1898* (Ithaca, NY: Cornell University Press, 1963); Frank Ninkovich, *The Wilsonian Century: U.S. Foreign Policy Since 1900* (Chicago: University of Chicago Press, 1999), esp. 170–77. On the critics of U.S. expansion and expansive definitions of American freedom, see Christopher McKnight Nichols, *Promise and Peril: America at the Dawn of a Global Age* (Cambridge, MA: Harvard University Press, 2011), esp. 273–320.

25. See Melvyn P. Leffler, *A Preponderance of Power: National Security, the Truman Administration, and the Cold War* (Stanford, CA: Stanford University Press, 1992); Odd Arne Westad, *The Cold War: A World History* (New York: Basic Books, 2017), esp. 71–158.

26. Franklin Roosevelt, "Annual Message to Congress," January 6, 1941, http://docs.fdrlibrary.marist.edu/od4frees.html; Harvey J. Kaye, *The Fight for the Four Freedoms* (New York: Simon & Schuster, 2014); Jeremi Suri, "FDR Delivers the Four Freedoms," *Voices and Visions*, http://vandvreader.org/fdr-delivers -the-four-freedoms-january-6-1941/.

27. "Atlantic Charter," August 14, 1941, http://avalon.law.yale.edu/wwii/atlantic .asp. See also Elizabeth Borgwardt, *A New Deal for the World: America's Vision for Human Rights* (Cambridge, MA: Harvard University Press, 2005); Kiran Klaus Patel, *The New Deal: A Global History* (Princeton, NJ: Princeton University Press, 2016), esp. 261–300.

28. See Suri, *The Impossible Presidency*, chap. 6. This analysis draws on a classic account: Thomas Paterson, *On Every Front: The Making and Unmaking of the Cold War*, rev. ed. (New York: Norton, 1992).

29. See John Lewis Gaddis, *George F. Kennan: An American Life* (New York: Penguin, 2011), esp. 201–403; John Lewis Gaddis, *Strategies of Containment: A Critical Appraisal of American National Security Policy During the Cold War*, rev. ed. (New York: Oxford University Press, 2005), esp. 24–86; Wilson D. Miscamble, *George F. Kennan and the Making of American Foreign Policy, 1947–1950* (Princeton, NJ: Princeton University Press, 1992); Milne, *Worldmaking*, 217–67.

30. See, among many others, Odd Arne Westad, *The Global Cold War: Third World Interventions and the Making of Our Times* (New York: Cambridge University Press, 2005), esp. 110–57; Frank Costigliola, "'Unceasing Pressure for Penetration': Gender, Pathology, and Emotion in George Kennan's Formation of the Cold War," *Journal of American History* 83 (March 1997): 1309–39.

31. See, among many others, Grant Madsen, *Sovereign Soldiers: How the U.S. Military Transformed the Global Economy After World War II* (Philadelphia: University of Pennsylvania Press, 2018); Michael J. Hogan, *A Cross of Iron: Harry S. Truman and the Origins of the National Security State, 1945–54* (New York: Cambridge University Press, 1998); Douglas T. Stuart, *Creating the National Security State: A History of the Law That Transformed America* (Princeton, NJ: Princeton University Press, 2008).

32. See Francis Fukuyama, "The End of History?," *National Interest* 16 (Summer 1989): 3–18; Samuel P. Huntington, "The Clash of Civilizations?," *Foreign Affairs* 72, no. 3 (Summer 1993): 22–49.

33. George W. Bush, "Second Inaugural Address," January 20, 2005, https://www.presidency.ucsb.edu/documents/inaugural-address-13.

34. On the long and difficult history of American nation-building and the Bush administration's misuse of that history, see Jeremi Suri, *Liberty's Surest Guardian: American Nation-Building from the Founders to Obama* (New York: Free Press, 2011).

35. See James Mann, *Rise of the Vulcans: The History of Bush's War Cabinet* (New York: Penguin, 2004); Thomas Ricks, *Fiasco: The American Military Adventure in Iraq* (New York: Penguin, 2006); Dexter Filkins, *The Forever War* (New York: Random House, 2008); Milne, *Worldmaking*, 387–456; Jeremi Suri, "How 9/11 Triggered Democracy's Decline," *Washington Post*, September 11, 2017, https://www.washingtonpost.com/news/made-by-history/wp/2017/09/11/how-911-triggered-democracys-decline/?utm_term=.07038c5bbef3.

CHAPTER 15

Roads Not Taken

The Delhi Declaration, Nelson Mandela, Václav Havel, and the Lost Futures of 1989

PENNY VON ESCHEN

In 1993, the Czechoslovakian poet-turned-president Václav Havel warned that "if the West does not find the key to us . . . or to those somewhere far away who have extricated themselves from communist domination, it will ultimately lose the key to itself. If, for instance, it looks on passively at 'Eastern' or Balkan nationalism, it will give the green light to its own potentially destructive nationalisms, which it was able to deal with so magnanimously in the era of the communist threat."[1] Havel's fear that the West was losing its way stemmed from his immediate bewilderment over the failure of the United States to intervene in the growing atrocities in Bosnia, but this also captures the remarkably rapid shift from the buoyant hopes for democracy, disarmament, and environmental redress that accompanied the revolutions of 1989 to grave concerns about new conflicts.[2]

Taking to heart Havel's warning, and viewing the end of the Cold War as an interregnum in global affairs fraught with uncertainty, I focus on the historically specific projects of post–Cold War capitalist neoliberalism and U.S. unipolarity as intersecting ideological projects. The shift from the age of three worlds to a global order defined by U.S. unipolarity—that is, where the United States had outsized power to set the terms on which others acted—required a massive reshuffling, a rearticulation of the discursive practices by which the United States understood and projected its own particular interests as universal.

In addition to the ideological/political work attempting to naturalize neoliberalism, consolidating a new hegemonic bloc with the United States at the helm of unipolar order, necessitated a rearticulation of American exceptionalism in the face of robust calls for a multipolar and demilitarized world. U.S. unipolar hegemony was a highly self-conscious political project. Clearly articulated in what came to be known as the Wolfowitz Doctrine, leaked to the press in February 1992 and stating that no counterhegemonic challenge to U.S. political and economic dominance can be allowed to emerge in the former Soviet sphere, U.S. officials acted to promote a unipolar world undergirded by U.S.-led militarism. Moreover, U.S. policy makers consistently favored nationalist over multinational formations. From backing Boris Yeltsin's Russian nationalist breakaway from the Soviet Union, to relying on "clash of civilization" justifications for military spending and intervention and constructing new enemies at home, U.S. officials in Congress and the national defense establishment wittingly and unwittingly fueled the short and long-term development of xenophobic right-wing ethnic nationalisms within and beyond U.S. borders.

After a Cold War era structured around competition between blocs over which form of society could best deliver the good life to the masses, establishing a new hegemonic bloc based on restructuring and privatizing social goods in terms of market efficiency and profit was an enormous ideological undertaking. Understanding U.S. unipolarity as a self-conscious hegemonic foreign policy strategy as well as an ideological formation characterized by a will to totality undergirded by the assertion of timeless truths, I contend that the processes through which the politics of U.S. Cold War triumphalism prevailed over visions of multilateral cooperation are best understood in relation to the visions that it displaced.

In the wake of 1989 revolutions in Eastern Europe and the weakening of the South African apartheid government, Václav Havel and Nelson Mandela presented robust challenges to U.S. unilateralism as well as capacious visions of a just global society in their respective 1990 visits to the United States. The responses of the George H. W. Bush administration and Congress to these challenges resulted in a systematic undermining of multinational institutions. In this essay, I outline the visions displaced by U.S. unipolarity and then focus on hegemonic struggle and the displacement of those visions through the 1990–91 U.S. intervention in Iraq and responses to the end of apartheid in South Africa. But before turning to this history, I outline my understanding of the concept of ideology and the related concept of hegemony, not to attempt to fix a definition of these widely debated terms but to identify some of the understandings of ideology that I find particularly instructive for analyzing U.S. foreign policy.

Ideology

The concept of ideology has roots in early Marxist notions of false consciousness as well as sociological notions of totality or worldview. Both have been widely critiqued and debated. In the most basic sense, early Marxist theorists posited ideology as false consciousness, arguing that the working class misrecognized its true interests and correct subject position, often accepting instead the interests of elites as aligning with their own. Following the work of Ernesto Laclau and others working in a post-Marxist tradition, I reject the idea that any true or correct subject position exists a priori. Rather, subject positions and meaning are constructed and historically contingent.[3]

However, I also agree with Laclau that one cannot dispense with the notion of false consciousness entirely. Rather, to understand the notion of ideology and how ideological projects operate, we need an *inverted* sense of false consciousness. Ideologies assert timeless truths and fixed meanings, when, in fact, power, meaning, and social organization are always constructed, contingent, and inherently unstable. "The ideological would consist of those discursive forms through which a society tries to institute itself as such on the basis of closure, of the fixation of meaning, of the non-recognition of the infinite play of differences. The ideological would be the will to 'totality' of any totalizing discourse."[4]

In this sense, the work of historians is deeply connected to the notion of ideology critique. As historians we are fundamentally in the business of showing how power relations, ideas, people, and the organization of societies are historically contingent, changing, and contested. And we are particularly invested in critiquing any claims to the contrary—that is, the ideological.

I understand ideology then, as the ongoing work of naturalizing and normalizing power relations that are constructed and contingent. To my mind, this implies the primacy of politics in both its formal and informal senses, the imperative not to separate political history from cultural, economic, and social history, and the importance of locating and analyzing the sets of discursive practices in which meaning and power are produced and contested.[5]

Another common invocation of the concepts of ideology and hegemony among scholars involves positing ideology/hegemony as marking the limits of what can be uttered or even thought. A related view posits ideology as equivalent to worldview. To be sure, it would be impossible for any person or groups of people, however large or small, to operate without a worldview and assumptions that are necessarily bounded and limited. But a definition of ideology as worldview or ideas strikes me as inadequate if it does not also emphasize the critical element of the will to totality in ideology, *and* the acceptance, imposition, or struggles against totalizing discourses witnessed in ideological projects. Indeed, simply emphasizing the limiting boundaries of ideology leaves one unable to account for change and contestation.

Moreover, although the lenses through which one sees and acts in the world necessarily contain elements of ideology, not all worldviews are committed to notions of totality based on timeless truths. And worldviews that allow for ambiguity and posit humility regarding the limits of what can be known, and the extent to which we can understand our own assumptions, are not prone to totalizing ideological claims.

Here, I would contrast the drive to totalization that characterized neoliberals and the post–Cold War U.S. hegemonic projects with the democratic projects they replaced. The democratic projects of the 1980s and early 1990s, from Mikhail Gorbachev's calls for glasnost, to Eastern European dissidents, and the antiapartheid movement, contained self-conscious critiques of totalizing ideologies in both state-communist and capitalist-imperialist forms.

Writing about the possibilities in democratic projects at the moment of the crumbling of Cold War blocs, Chantelle Mouffe and Ernesto Laclau observed:

> We are living . . . one of the most exhilarating moments of the twentieth century: a moment in which new generations, without the prejudices of the past, without theories presenting themselves as "absolute truths" of history, are constructing new emancipatory discourses, more human, diversified and democratic. The eschatological and epistemological ambitions are more modest, but the liberating aspirations are wider and deeper.[6]

Like Mouffe and Laclau, the critics Judith Butler and Slavoj Žižek have emphasized the instability of the subject and incompleteness of ideological projects. All have been criticized for failing to provide any ethical foundation for democratic projects.[7] But I contend that a foundational democratic ethics, as well as a means of extending critiques of totalizing "false consciousness" in neoliberal ideology can be developed through following feminist emphases on reproduction and embodiment.[8] Although no a priori subject position or meaning exists prior to its discursive constitution in historically specific human societies, we must begin with the fact that humans are embodied, and must reproduce themselves with adequate water, food, and shelter on a daily basis. Moreover, humans are born completely dependent on others. The social organization whereby helpless infants/young are kept alive for an extraordinarily long period—long enough for a critical mass to reproduce the species—is historically contingent. But our extended period of dependence makes us fundamentally interdependent, fundamentally social beings. Our embodied existence is also porous, constituted by, and in continual interaction with our environment, including other living plant and animal species as well as with seemingly inanimate and inert matter. This fundamental relationality is denied in the neoliberal project and its assertion of homo economicus, positing a timeless human nature as inherently entrepreneurial, narrowly self-interested, and profit maximizing. Infamously captured in Margaret Thatcher's declaration that "there is no such thing as society, only individuals and families," in denying complex webs of interdependence, in denying the very fact of society, neoliberalism marks an especially pernicious ideological project, presenting an especially false and totalizing claim. Taking the individual as sprung from the head of Zeus, neoliberalism denies the elite's dependence on the labor of others and the violence that has entailed—violence committed on bodies and the earth—and further dispenses with human and interspecies interdependence altogether.

Ideologies then—those discursive acts of taking to be fixed, true, and permanent that which is in fact constructed and contingent—are not all created equal; some entail greater misrecognitions of necessarily embodied and social existence and more violent impositions of totalizing projects.

In the ideological work of constructing unregulated markets and U.S. power as natural, neoliberalism and its twin, "globalization," posited global economic integration as a natural development driven by supposedly inexorable market forces, masking the ways that global economic integration occurred and the violence that accompanied it. Accelerating in the 1970s, then assuming new forms after the collapse of the Soviet bloc, globalization was the outcome of the deliberate decisions and deregulatory policies of U.S. and Western politicians, bankers, and financiers. And from structural adjustment policies to the Reagan administration's weaponizing of global financial instruments to target socialist economies, their highly profitable actions dramatically increased economic inequality within their societies and globally.

Hegemony

The notion of hegemony is usefully understood not as a simple, forceful domination by the elite, nor a simple imposition of power, but as a process of making new political identities that "involves linking particular interests with wider, more universal social aims. The process through which this occurs is called hegemonic struggle."[9]

The U.S. unipolar project shared deep ideological continuities with the Cold War era, from assumptions of American exceptionalism to a conflation of capitalism and democracy. But the collapse of the communist bloc also demanded a remapping of the globe to specify new alliances and new articulations, threats, and antagonisms—the new enemy. Both elements, the rearticulation of particular U.S. interests to universal claims and the mapping of new antagonisms are evident in U.S. responses to reformers and U.S. arguments for military intervention in Iraq. Both reveal the work that went into rearticulating earlier forms of U.S. exceptionalism into new assertions of unipolarity.

Prior U.S. interventions had been done in the name of anticommunism. From Panama to Iraq, interventions were now carried out in the name of democracy.[10] But the "other of democracy" changed in keys ways. New antagonists were "rogue states," those that followed—in the words of George H. W. Bush as he made his case for intervention in Iraq—the "rule of the jungle" rather than the "laws of civilization." It was not so much that one could not think or act outside of the market and the U.S.-led world, but to do so marked the actor as anti- or premodern, a notion elaborated in ideas of the "clash of civilizations" and the notions of outlaw and rogue states. The violence imposed by neoliberal policies, whether in suffering and starvation caused by structural adjustment policies or wars ensuing from the destabilization caused by these policies, was masked by assumptions of a clash of civilizations. From those outlined by the political scientist Samuel Huntington to the popular claims of Robert Kaplan and Tom Clancy, the clash of civilizations invoked claims about ancient hatreds to distort the ways violence was an outgrowth of intertwined colonial and Cold War policies, afterlives of Cold War violence.

Examining projects to consolidate U.S. unipolar power reveals shape shifting and mutually constitutive ideological projects as neoliberalism and globalization triangulated with the reworking of "us versus them" binaries. As framings of enemy threats shifted from communist to those posited as antimodern and anti-Western, new articulations joining imperial discourses to a moment of new geopolitical possibilities justified military spending and interventions abroad and constructed new enemies at home. Powerful U.S. policy makers all worked in tandem to assert the righteousness and inevitability of a neoliberal U.S.-led unipolar and remilitarized world order.

Rival Visions: Glasnost vs. Victors' History

Western triumphalism displaced a much broader range of stories about the Cold War and what its ending might entail. The revolutions that brought down Eastern bloc regimes began as movements to reform and humanize socialism, certainly not as procapitalist movements, and the range of possible futures imagined in the mid-1980s far exceeded that voiced by triumphalist victors' histories.[11] In the United States and Europe, activists and the general public called for a "peace dividend," expressing hope that an end to escalating arms and military spending of the Cold War era would result in increased spending on education, health care, and the environment. Mikhail Gorbachev's call for glasnost, for a genuine political openness, appealed for national and international public self-examination among Soviet leadership and citizens about the assumptions and missteps of the Cold War past.

Bush's vision of a new world order maintained by U.S. power rested on the claim that all alternatives to liberal democracy rooted in free market capitalism, including socialism, had been discredited. But alternate ideas about the optimal organization of society were not simply swept away in a celebratory tide of neoliberal ascendency. Gorbachev sought new European institutions from the Atlantic to the Ukraine; and former Warsaw Pact dissidents, as heads of state, sought a demilitarized Central and Eastern Europe to serve as a bridge between the former East and West. Reformers such as Gorbachev and Havel joined with French President Francoise Mitterrand to promote strong multilateral institutions in a demilitarized Europe.

Václav Havel's distress over the inability of the West to "get" the East underscores the fundamental tension between the vision of Eastern bloc reformers of a multilateral and disarmed world and U.S. Cold War triumphalism—the insistence that the United States had won the Cold War and was now the sole superpower in a unipolar world. Bush self-consciously appropriated and diminished Gorbachev's vision of a "new world order" after Gorbachev revived the term—invoked by Woodrow Wilson after World War I—to lay out a vision of a demilitarized post–Cold War world. Elaborated in a joint statement with Rajiv Gandhi in "The Delhi Declaration," issued on November 27, 1986, calling for strengthening the United Nations and multinational cooperation to secure a nuclear weapon free and nonviolent world, Gorbachev and Gandhi emphasized emergency environmental measures and pointed to sustainable approaches to redress the military and environmental consequences of the Cold War race for weapons and consumption.[12] The declaration was widely praised by those in the West for its departure from rigid Soviet ideology and its eclectic inclusion of ideas from the nonaligned world and global South.

The importance of the Delhi Declaration's emphasis on addressing environmental damage should not be underestimated. As the Eastern bloc unraveled, many on both sides of the former divide confronted the environmental damage and sheer waste in towering landfills, incinerated garbage, discarded consumer goods, and nuclear waste. The sense that the race for superiority in weapons and appliances was unsustainable called for a radical rethinking of the good life, including a growing scientific consensus on climate change.

Gorbachev's acclaimed speech before the United Nations on December 7, 1988, emphasized environmental concerns in the context of announcing Soviet military cuts and a comprehensive plan for disarmament. Gorbachev elaborated his hopes for international cooperation toward alleviating "economic, environmental and humanistic problems in their broadest sense. I would like to believe that our hopes will be matched by our joint effort to put an end to an era of wars, confrontation and regional conflicts, to aggressions against nature, to the terror of hunger and poverty as well as to political terrorism."[13]

Time magazine characterized Gorbachev's UN speech as "compelling and audacious." Quoting Gorbachev's call for a "transition from the economy of armaments to an economy of disarmament," suffused with the romantic dream of "swords into plough-shares," for *Time* reporter Walter Isaacson, Gorbachev's vision had the potential to bring about a historic shift of the magnitude of George Marshall and Harry Truman.[14]

As late as 1989, there were reasons to hope that Bush might endorse international climate protection agreements. Ronald Reagan had fought environmental protections; in one of the first acts of his presidency, he removed thirty-two solar panels Jimmy Carter had installed on the White House roof, calling them a "joke." But in Bush's 1988 campaign, during the hottest summer ever recorded, Bush declared himself an environmentalist, doing a five-state environmental campaign tour that began on Lake Erie and ended in Boston. Challenging complacency in the face of climate change, Bush argued: "those who think we are powerless to do anything about the greenhouse effect are forgetting about the White House effect."[15] Once in office, Bush and a bipartisan group in Congress moved to immediately cut emissions in the United States.

Ultimately, however, not only did the Bush administration double down on protecting the fossil fuel economy but it did so by challenging scientific evidence on the relation between fossil fuels and climate change. On November 6, 1989, three days before the breaching of the Berlin Wall, an international group of scientists and diplomats met in Noordwijk in the western Netherlands with the intent to pass a comprehensive treaty to address climate change through strict emissions restrictions, the culmination of a decade of scientific and diplomatic cooperation. Quite unexpectedly, at the last minute, influenced by Bush political advisor John Sununu, the United States withdrew from the treaty, and with the acquiescence of Britain, Japan, and the Soviet Union, the United States "forced the conference to abandon the commitment to freeze emissions."[16]

The Noordwijk convention marked a major reversal in the perestroika era resolve of the major superpowers to clean up their Cold War mess. Although the Soviet Union and Eastern European countries were slow to acknowledge the environmental damage wrought by their arms and development race, by 1989 a "public awakening about environmental problems" was taking hold in the Soviet Union and Eastern Europe "comparable to that triggered by Earth Day in the United States in 1970."[17] In addition, Sununu's dismissal of the international scientific consensus as "technical poppycock" signaled a new attack on science that would soon manifest in climate change denial. Sununu's particular position undoubtedly reflected oil and gas executives' will to protect their enormous profits, but the fateful choice to side with extractive energy industries over the scientific community had unintended and far-reaching consequences. If conspiracy theories had long existed at the fringes of American culture, in the 1990s, as politicians and CEOs impugned the integrity of environmental scientists, widespread skepticism and paranoia about the status of truth itself entered the American mainstream.[18]

Redressing the environmental damage wrought by extractive Cold War economies was fundamentally tied to demilitarization. The breadth of the vision that placed demilitarized multilateral cooperation at the heart of an emerging "new world order" is illustrated in Václav Havel's February 1990 visit to the United States. After multiple arrests, including a stint in prison from 1979 to 1983, Havel had again been arrested by Czech police on October 27, 1989.[19] Two months later, on December 29, the Czech Parliament unanimously elected him president. Within weeks, he was in the United States to enlist support for the new government's reforms. Havel immediately set off alarm bells by voicing his hope that NATO and the Warsaw Pact would soon be abolished; this was ironic in retrospect because he later become an advocate of the expansion of NATO.[20] Havel sought to assure the skittish Americans, explaining that Europe, perhaps under a "new pan-European structure," would be able to "decide for itself how many of whose soldiers it needs so that its own security . . . may radiate peace into the whole world."[21]

The poet-philosopher befuddled the U.S. Congress with his insistence that "consciousness precedes being."[22] According to the *Guardian* reporter, one hungry congressperson heard the phrase as "nacho-cheese burrito." Other less famished and perhaps more geopolitically minded members of Congress thought Havel had said "Confucius precedes Beijing, thinking this supported the Taiwan lobby."[23]

Pushed by the White House to clarify or retract his speech's alarming implications that in a post–Cold War world NATO was irrelevant, Havel sought to assure Congress and the White House. But he also insisted on his vision of a new Europe free of the constraints imposed by a bipolar world.[24] Asserting his country's independence from the Soviet Union, Havel stated that "Czechoslovakia is returning to Europe" and, he explained, is no longer "someone's meaningless satellite." Havel desired "the quickest possible departure of Soviet troops from Czechoslovakia," insisting that "our freedom, independence and our new-born democracy have been purchased at great cost, and we will not surrender them."[25]

However, asserting autonomy from the Soviet Union did not mean replacing one relationship of dependency with another. Most fundamentally, Havel told Congress "these revolutionary changes will enable us to escape from the rather antiquated straitjacket of this bipolar view of the world, and to enter at last into an era of multipolarity."[26]

If much of the Congress had been perplexed by "consciousness precedes being," it may have been politically convenient to ignore, or mishear,

Havel's pleas to move beyond a bipolar world and, in particular, to support Gorbachev's reforms. "My reply" to the problem of how to create this multipolar world, Havel explained, "is as paradoxical as the whole of my life has been. You can help us most of all if you help the Soviet Union on its irreversible but immensely complicated road to democracy."[27] A staunch opponent of communism who supported market reforms, Havel wanted the United States to back Gorbachev's reforms, not turn the economy over to capitalist shock therapy, and certainly not to expand NATO. The Bush administration tacitly rejected Havel's (and Poland's Walesa's) appeal to the United States to support Gorbachev, whose reforms had facilitated the success of their own agendas. In backing Gorbachev's opponent, Boris Yeltsin, Bush dismissed Havel's belief that Soviet stability was critical to the success of Europe. Bush, and later Clinton, confused Yeltsin's promarket policies with "democracy," as Yelstin's autocratic government presided over the rise of a corrupt oligarchy in a frenzy of radical privatization. And Havel, despite his promarket orientation, later rued taking the advice of pro-free-market "experts," mourning the displacement of his Czech Velvet revolution by the right-wing politics of Václav Klaus; regrets compounded by his sense of the human toll of an ascendant untrammeled capitalism.

Many opted to mishear Havel in 1990, but the words of Nelson Mandela, aimed directly at the policies of the United States and its allies, rang out as an affront. When Mandela died in 2013, George H. W. Bush described Mandela's June 1990 visit to the White House as the "genuine highlight" of his presidency.[28] One need not doubt Bush's later heartful admiration for Mandela to recall that the sudden release of the world-renowned leader of the antiapartheid movement by the white minority South African regime and a strong U.S. ally throughout the Cold War presented vexing issues for Bush.

Only two years earlier, in 1988, Reagan placed Mandela and the ANC on the U.S. list of international terrorist organizations, where the antiapartheid leader remained until 2008. Just one year before Mandela's visit, a Defense Department publication with a foreword by then president-elect George H. W. Bush termed the ANC one of the "world's most notorious terrorist groups," citing Mandela as the "organization's leader."[29] Mandela's release was accompanied by reports (later confirmed) that a CIA tip had led to Mandela's 1962 arrest, and embarrassed government officials refused to comment.[30]

As international and U.S. press coverage reported on the CIA's role in Mandela's arrest and imprisonment, Bush went on the offensive, outlining his policy differences with Mandela and demanding that Mandela shift his objectives. Bush called on Mandela to renounce his defense of armed struggle in the fight against apartheid. Second, he demanded a full embrace of "democracy" defined as unencumbered free markets and privatization and asked Mandela to renounce his calls for selective nationalization and a mixed economy.

Visiting the White House, Mandela took exception to Bush's demands that the ANC renounce armed struggle. Mandela argued that no reasonable person could fail to understand the need for armed resistance given the thorough denial of political or civil rights within a violent and repressive police state. In a truly democratic, inclusive government, violence would be unnecessary and unjustified.

South Africans traveling with Mandela later recalled that Mandela was received "like a heroic military figure or one of the first astronauts, just back from space."[31] At stops in New York City, Boston, Miami, Atlanta, the Bay area, Detroit, Los Angles, and Washington, D.C, all were met by a roistering gaggle of thousands of broadcast and print journalists eager to capture every moment. If the trip, in the eyes of South Africans, was something of an "organizational disaster," it was simultaneously an "overwhelming public affairs triumph," turning Mandela into "a secular saint and political rock star, all rolled into one."[32]

But for Mandela, this was emphatically not a victory tour. The goal of the American trip and the European stops that followed was to lobby for the continuation of U.S. sanctions on South Africa.[33] In Detroit visiting a Ford Motor plant in Dearborn, Mandela donned a union cap and jacket he had received from the president of the UAW and expressed gratitude and solidarity with the workers. At an evening rally at Tiger Stadium, Mandela quoted Marvin Gaye's lyrics to condemn political violence in South Africa: "Brother, brother, there's far too many of you dying, Mother, mother, there's far too many of you crying." In Detroit as well as in New York addresses to the UN General Assembly and at Yankee Stadium, the message of Gaye's iconic antiwar anthem was clear: "Join us in the international actions we are taking. The only way we can walk together on this difficult road is for you to assure that sanctions are applied."[34] At rally after rally, the cheers rang out, "Keep the Pressure On."[35]

Ironically, as the Bush administration disavowed its earlier alliance with Saddam Hussein, media pundits in lockstep with the administration challenged Mandela about the aid the ANC had received from those now deemed "outlaw nations" by the United States. During a nationally televised

New York town hall interview on ABC's *Nightline*, Ted Koppel aggressively questioned Mandela's willingness to meet with Fidel Castro, Yassir Arafat, and Muammar Gaddafi. Mandela's retort left Koppel speechless: "They support our struggle to the hilt. Any man who changes his principles according to with whom he is dealing; that is not a man who can lead a nation."[36]

Mandela's defense of his Third World allies remained an affront to Bush— no doubt aware that his verbal battles with Mandela were over the power to name such nations as Cuba and Libya as "outlaw" as opposed to legitimate sovereign states. Mandela embraced allies who were outlaw nations in the eyes of the Bush administration and the key targets of his regional defense strategy. Mandela's friendship with Fidel Castro (whom he would visit in Cuba in 1991) was particularly irksome to Bush. In addition to Cuba's fundamental role in defeating U.S. interests in southern Africa, longtime Bush family investments in Cuba further ensured that Castro held a special place of enmity for George H. W. Bush. Walker and Prescott Bush had run several Havana companies during the 1920s and 1930s involved with the sugar and rum distilling industries, along with a major railroad that served these enterprises.[37]

In a conversation with Bush in March of 1991, Mandela directly confronted his differences with Bush over the U.S. war in the Gulf, explaining why the ANC had publicly backed the UN General Assembly resolution of December 6, 1990, that asked the Security Council to pursue a negotiated settlement toward Iraq withdrawing from Kuwait by convening an International Peace Conference on the Middle East. Mandela explained that the ANC position was "similar to the UN" in supporting the "withdrawal of Iraq from Kuwait" but also supporting the "convening of an international conference for a comprehensive settlement of the problems on the Middle East including the restoration of rights of the Palestinians and the withdrawal of Israel from the occupied territories." Bush responded that "we opposed Palestinian linkage from the beginning. It plays into the hands of the brutal dictator Saddam Hussein."[38]

As the historian Jeffrey A. Engel has shown, the first U.S.-Iraq war was the moment when Bush defined his notion of a new world order, a unipolar world defined first and foremost, as Brent Scowcroft put it, as "an ongoing process of improvement, as more and more of the world's peoples choose to follow America's lead."[39] Bush believed deeply in American exceptionalism—that American values were universal, superior, and would eventually be accepted around the world— and that only the United States could safely shepherd the world to a more peaceful and prosperous future.

But he also won backing for military intervention rather than a negotiated settlement through tough carrot and stick diplomacy. When George H. W. Bush and Mikhail Gorbachev jointly condemned the Iraqi invasion of Kuwait, some observers noted that the Cold War was now officially over. But as Engel also astutely notes, Iraq was also the last act of the Cold War for Bush. He made it clear to Gorbachev and to the world, as he had privately told congressional leaders, "there are no longer two super-powers in the world. There's only one."[40] But it was not just Gorbachev who was a casualty of the Gulf War as he was forced to accept U.S. leadership in a military action that was anathema to his demilitarization agendas in glasnost and perestroika. Another casualty was the vision, shared by Gorbachev, Havel, and Mandela, of a new world order based on multilateral cooperation and demilitarization.

In April of 1991, just weeks after the end of "Operation Desert Storm" and in the midst of escalating violence in South Africa, the twelve-member European Union ignored appeals from the ANC and lifted its remaining economic sanctions on South Africa.[41] In July of 1991, against opposition in Congress and the wishes of Mandela and the ANC, Bush followed suit, lifting U.S. sanctions on apartheid South Africa. Mandela chastised Bush, telling him that "your actions are premature." For Mandela, even on the terms set by the United States the conditions had not been met: "There are still political prisoners in prison. It is not correct for the U.S. to have its own definition." And with the abolition of apartheid incomplete, "violence is raging in the country and impeding free political activity."[42]

Mandela, along with other ANC leaders, was gravely disappointed with the international community for removing sanctions and outraged by the political violence in South Africa. The ANC had suspended armed resistance in August 1990 in favor of negotiations, but immediately began to worry about the existence of a "third force" fomenting violence with an intent to undermine negotiations. Mandela had appealed to Bush for assistance in halting the escalating violence in South Africa.

Indeed, subsequent inquiries by scholars and the South African Truth and Reconciliation Commission have demonstrated that the most significant violence occurring between 1990 and the 1994 elections resulted from security and ex-security force operations, often acting in collaboration with right-wing elements and members of the Inkatha Freedom Party. The "third force" violence continued to escalate right up until the elections, nearly plunging the country into a full a scale civil war.[43]

Bush had assured Mandela that he would talk with Buthelezi of the Inkatha Freedom Party about his role in the violence. Instead, referring to the ANC's support of negotiated withdrawal from Kuwait linked to a broader Middle East peace process, Bush told Buthelelzi that "we both have reservations about the ANC. I was concerned by the position they took during the war. I was disappointed by it." When Bush asked for Buthelezi's sense of future ANC leadership, Buthelezi played to what he clearly understood as Bush's antipathy toward communists, claiming "half of the Executive Committee of the ANC were card-carrying members of the SACP."[44] Bush appeared willing to ignore violence targeting ANC leadership in hopes that the elimination of communists would marginalize any remnant of the left in a new government.

As De Klerk continued to turn a blind eye to the complicity of his forces, in June 1992 Mandela announced that the ANC was suspending negotiations after the June 17 Biopatong Massacre, where over forty township dwellers died after an attack by Inkatha members assisted by government security members. The international furor that ensued led to some measures to curb government forces, but security and ex-security forces continued to be implicated in the murders that continued to mar negotiations.[45]

Violence continued to target ANC leadership. In October 1992, a prominent Natal ANC leader was shot and killed after contacting the *Natal Witness*, a Pietermaritzburg newspaper with evidence that RENAMO was behind the violence on Natal. In April of 1993, a Polish right-wing, anticommunist immigrant, Janusz Walús, assassinated Chris Hani, antiapartheid activist and head of the South African Communist Party, who had played a major role in suspending the armed struggle in favor of negotiations.

Many South African economists regret what they retrospectively view as their nation having succumbed to fear about how South Africa was being perceived by others, and thus accepting the terms of the "Washington consensus." Adam Habib argued that the ANC viewed the threat of an exodus of investors as more immediate than the challenges of the poor and excluded.[46]

The ANCs controversial acceptance of economic arrangements favorable to banking and investment—leading to bitter accusations of selling out— must be seen in the context of persistent state-sanctioned violence driven by those determined to undermine a negotiated peaceful end to apartheid and the international community's premature lifting of sanctions. More South Africans died between Mandela's 1990 release from prison and the first free elections in 1994 than in all the previous years of apartheid.

Bush later recalled with pride his relationship with Mandela. There is no reason to doubt that over time Bush came to see Mandela, as he wrote in 2013, as "one of the great moral leaders during that transformative and hopeful time of global change," or that he had genuinely come to see his twenty-seven years in custody as "wrongful imprisonment."[47] But such pride depended on selective memory, such as ignoring Mandela's grave disappointments with U.S. and European politicians and the Western business community as the ANC struggled to build a democracy on the flimsy foundations of white supremacist oligarchy and terror. A willed amnesia with regard to state violence on the part of apartheid South Africa to undermine ANC strategy and tactics had been critical to U.S. Cold War policy, and it remained critical to Bush's post-Soviet hegemonic ambitions.

The world rejoiced at the election and inauguration of Mandela in 1994. On a global level, Mandela won the moral battle over the story of the ANC and apartheid. But Bush and his free-market allies won the hegemonic war of position in two crucial ways. First, by publicly deflecting his differences with Mandela, Bush was able to claim Mandela as part of the story of a forward march of universal freedom based on the values of the West, thus severing for many the history of Mandela and the ANC from a broader story of the struggle for economic as well as political justice. Second, in his one-term presidency, Bush and his allies assured that future struggles for democracy, including South Africa's transition to democracy, would unfold on a neoliberal free market terrain.

Just as the projects and dreams of many developing countries had been hijacked by Cold War dynamics over which most had no say, the global imposition of neoliberalism commandeered and distorted the end of white supremacist regimes in southern Africa, erasing the history of apartheid South Africa and southern African white supremacist governments as part of the Western Cold War alliance. Radical privatization was enabled by claims about the Cold War that discredited even the most successful mixed economies. As reforms took place on a geoeconomic terrain controlled by IMF policies—shock therapy—of regulation and structural adjustment, the first democratically elected ANC government had remarkably ambitious redistributive policies. But fears of being seen as inhospitable for investment led to decisions that placed severe limitations on its ability to deliver the promise of economic justice along with political freedom. The equation of freedom with the free market undergirded devastating policies of neoliberalism, assuring that from Russia and the Eastern bloc to the end of apartheid in South Africa reforms that had been grounded in aspirations for economic justice as well as fundamental political change played out on a geopolitical terrain of radical privatization and a rapid escalation of inequality.

As dreams of a humane mixed market economy began to fade, so too did visions of a demilitarized world. In Václav Havel's 1993 admonition that the West "would ultimately lose the key to itself" if it underestimated the threat of Balkan nationalism, Havel offered insight into the workings of an earlier hegemonic project—mindful of how anticommunism had held American politics together—as he registered his profound dismay with the Western response to the breakup of Yugoslavia. As the country imploded, Bush's lofty rhetoric of humanitarian actions in Iraq and Somalia contrasted with his indifference to the political violence engulfing Yugoslavia, stating that "we don't want to put a dog in this fight."[48] Indeed, Bush had persuaded Havel to support intervention in Iraq by emphasizing Iraqi human rights violations against Kurds. Robert Kaplan's 1993 *Balkan Ghosts* depicted the entire region as seething with unsolvable ancient ethnic hatreds, which later "spooked" Clinton from putting troops in Bosnia. The administration would not act decisively until, as the historian Susan Woodward has argued, the Europeans tricked them into intervention through NATO obligations to defend the security of Europe.[49]

Many in the international community pleaded with the Bush administration for intervention to stop the Bosnian genocide. Bush had justified intervention in the Gulf and then Somalia on humanitarian grounds. Why Iraq and Somalia but not Bosnia? Bush told Turkey's President Turgot Ozal and Havel that his hands were tied in Bosnia because he was under pressure at home, and that Americans were looking inward and want a peace dividend. He further claimed that he did not want "to saddle Clinton with major new commitments. Somalia was so appalling."[50]

But the debacle in Somalia was not a failure of humanitarian aid per se. It was the consequence of the Bush administration's attempt to restore the ousted government of their ally, President Siad Barre, after his overthrown by Mohammed Farrah Aidid, in a context where neoliberal structural adjustment policies had destroyed food self-sufficiency. As Rania Khalek has argued, "the neoliberal dismantling of Somalia's agro-pastoralist economy" left Somalia "extremely vulnerable to famine when faced with a drought in 1992, causing the mass starvation of 300,000 people." U.S. attempts to restore Barre, who had received extensive support from the United States— at the time of his overthrow "nearly two-thirds of Somalia was allocated to the American oil giants Conoco, Amoco, Chevron, and Phillips"—fed sectarian violence.[51] Industry sources reported that the companies holding concessions are hoping that "the Bush Administration's decision to send U.S. troops to safeguard aid shipments to Somalia will also help protect their multimillion-dollar investments there." Indeed, critics charged that Bush, a former Texas oilman, sent in the troops to secure oil reserves. The Houston-based Conoco Oil company had been involved in extensive oil exploration in north-central Somalia since 1981. After U.S. intervention, Conoco aided in the U.S. relief efforts, profiting as the U.S. government subsidized the company's facilities.[52]

If Bush's cases for humanitarian intervention in Iraq and Somalia aligned all too neatly with oil interests, his unwillingness to act in Bosnia also speaks to the unipolar slant of his "new world order," his resistance to U.S. action in accord with the interests of a multipolar world or with Europe as an equal partner. Havel and Gorbachev had hoped for a strengthened UN and multilateral cooperation, but at the moment of the Bosnian crisis, the UN was weakened because the United States had not paid its bills. From 1985, with the Reagan administration and Republicans resentful at the perceived strength of a nonaligned bloc, the U.S. Senate withheld funds to the United Nations. Bush and Clinton squandered the chance to redress the neglect before Republicans took control of the House in 1994, making its hostility to United Nations peacekeeping actions a central tenet of its foreign policy.[53]

As noted above, in 1994, observing U.S. policy makers favoring national-ist over multi-nationalist formations, Havel worried that the United States would "give the green light to its own potentially destructive nationalisms." Indeed, the xenophobic nationalism on display at the January 6, 2021 insur-rection at the U.S. Capitol, with insurrectionists contending that the United States is under siege from nonwhites and non-Christians, offered a chilling display of what Laclau argues, constitutes the ideological: "those discursive forms through which a society tries to institute itself as such on the basis of closure, of the fixation of meaning."[54] The will to totality driving the ideological marriage of neoliberalism and neoconservatism has emboldened an anti-democratic minority in the United States. Intent on crippling the mechanisms of democracy, far-right falsifications of history promote new ideologies conflating local governments with totalitarianism and equating a duly elected government with authoritarian communism.

As the Covid-19 pandemic rapidly spread to six continents, it was clear that people throughout the globe were imperiled by long-standing contempt by Republican officials for multilateralism. This is compounded by the long record of Republicans of discrediting science, with George H. W. Bush's rejection of the 1989 Noordwijk climate treaty echoed in George W. Bush's withdrawal from the Geneva Climate Accords, and most recently in Trump's withdrawal of the United States from the Paris Climate Agreement, and then from the World Health Organization at the height of the pandemic. The nation's calamitous response to Covid-19 saw renewed demagogic attacks on science, global cooperation, and the common good, fostering mob anger against public health officials and medical professionals. As for vaccine distribution, the most robust attempts at international cooperation to date remain at the mercy of national priorities and the proprietary rights of corporations. In a global vaccine apartheid, putting profit before technology sharing has endangered the lives of millions worldwide by severely restricting the production and availability of vaccines.

As the neoliberal conflation of democracy and capitalism renounced social spending and ceded primacy to market solutions to social problems, such policies have robbed all but the world's most wealthy of a dignified future. The pandemic has underscored that the future of humanity depends on addressing social needs and recognizing our interdependence, amongst ourselves, and with all living species. If one can imagine any security in a postpandemic future, it will not be found in earlier models of American-style unipolar leadership, but in roads not taken of genuine multinational cooperation, demilitarization, and environmental justice.

Notes

1. Václav Havel, "The Co-responsibility of the West," written for *Foreign Affairs*, December 22, 1993, in Václav Havel, *The Art of the Impossible: Politics as Morality in Practice* (New York: Knopf, 1997), 141.
2. A fuller treatment of parts of this essay can be found in the first two chapters of Penny M. Von Eschen, *Paradoxes of Nostalgia: Cold War Triumphalism and Global Disorder Since 1989* (Durham, NC: Duke University Press, 2022).
3. Ernesto Laclau, *New Reflections on the Revolution of Our Time* (New York: Verso, 1990), 92; and Ernesto Laclau and Chantelle Mouffe, *Hegemony and Socialist Strategy: Towards a Radical Democratic Politics* (New York: Verso, 1985).
4. Laclau, *New Reflections*, 92.
5. Eric Foner, *Politics and Ideology in the Age of the Civil War* (Oxford: Oxford University Press, 1981).

6. Laclau and Mouffe, *Hegemony and Socialist Strategy*, 98.

7. For an introduction to the extensive debates between these critics a well as their debates with others, see Judith Butler, Ernesto Laclau, and Slavoj Žižek, *Contingency, Hegemony, Universality: Contemporary Dialogues on the Left* (New York: Verso, 2011).

8. The literature is vast. See Kathleen Canning, "The Body as Method: Reflections on the Place of the Body in Gender History," *Gender & History* 11, no. 3 (1999): 499–513.

9. Lynn Worshom and Gary A, Olson, "Hegemony and the Future of Democracy: Ernesto Laclau's Political Philosophy," *JAC* 19, no. 1 (1999), 4.

10. Amy Goodman, "'How the Iraq War Began in Panama': 1989 Invasion Set the Path for Future Interventions," with Humberto Brown, Greg Grandin, and Lawrence Wilkerson, *Democracy Now*, December 23, 2014, http://www .democracynow.org/2014/12/23/how_the_iraq_war_began_in_Panama.

11. Charity Scribner, *Requiem for Communism* (Cambridge, MA: MIT Press, 2003); Mary Serotte, *1989: The Struggle to Create a Post Cold War Europe* (Princeton, NJ: Princeton University Press, 2011); Kristen Ghodsee, *Red Hangover: Legacies of Twentieth-Century Communism* (Durham, NC: Duke University Press, 2017).

12. Vladimir Radyuhin, "Delhi Declaration Still Relevant, Says Mikhail Gorbachev," https://www.thehindu.com/todays-paper/tp-international/delhi-declaration -still-relevant-says-mikhail-gorbachev/article3157743.Also see Shri Nath Sahai, *The Dehli Declaration: Cardinal of Indo-Soviet Relations* (Columbia, MO: South Asia Books, 1990).

13. "The Gorbachev Visit; Excerpts from Speech to U.N. on Major Soviet Military Cuts," *New York Times*, December 8, 1988, https://www.nytimes.com /1988/12/08/world/the-gorbachev-visit-excerpts-from-speech-to-un-on -major-soviet-military-cuts.html.

14. Walter Isaacson, "The Gorbachev Challenge," *Time Magazine*, December 19, 1988, 16.

15. Nathaniel Rich, "Losing Earth: The Decade We Almost Stopped Climate Change," *New York Times*, August 1, 2018, https://www.nytimes.com/interactive /2018/08/01/magazine/climate-change-losing-earth.htm.

16. Nathaniel Rich, "Losing Earth."

17. Anthony Cortese, "Regulatory Focus: Glasnost, Perestroika, and the Environment," *Environmental Science & Technology* 23, no. 10 (October 1989): 1212–13, doi: 10.1021/es00068a601.

18. Rob Nixon, *Slow Violence and the Environmentalism of the Poor* (Cambridge, MA: Harvard University Press, 2011), 39–40.

19. Ravid Remnick, "Exit Havel: The King Leaves the Castle," *New Yorker*, February 17, 2003, https://www.newyorker.com/magazine/2003/02/17/exit -havel.

20. Martin Walker, "Havel's Congress Play a Box Office Hit," *Guardian*, February 22, 1990.

21. Al Kamen, "Havel Asks U.S. to Aid Soviet Democratization: In Hill Speech, Czech Calls for Creating 'Family of Man,'" *Washington Post*, February 22, 1990.

22. Walker, "Havel's Congress Play a Box Office Hit."

23. "Let's Hear It for Hegel!," *Washington Post*, February 23, 1990, https://www.washingtonpost.com/archive/opinions/1990/02/23/lets-hear-it-for-hegel/ed97d6fe-00a0-47f3-90cf-1fd9f940ee24/.

24. Kamen, "Havel Asks U.S. to Aid Soviet Democratization." For Edgar Beigel's reported hearing of "nacho before beans," see Jonah Ben-Joseph, "What Did Congress Hear? About Nacho Chips?," *Washington Post*, March 3, 1990.

25. Kamen, "Havel Asks U.S. to Aid Soviet Democratization."

26. Kamen, "Havel Asks U.S. to Aid Soviet Democratization."

27. "Upheaval in East: Excerpts from Czech Chief's Address to Congress," *New York Times*, February 22, 1990.

28. George H. W. Bush, "Honoring Nelson Mandela," Huffington Post, December 5, 2013, https://www.huffingtonpost.com/george-h-w-bush/honoring-nelson-mandela_1_b_4377877.html.

29. Robert Windram, "US Government Considered Nelson Mandela Terrorist Until 2008," NBC News, December 7, 2013, http://www.nbcnews.com/news/other/us-government-considered-nelson-mandela-terrorist-until-2008-f2D11708787.

30. Joseph Albright and Marcia Kunstel, "Ex-Official: CIA Helped Jail Mandela," *Chicago Tribune*, June 29, 2013.

31. J. Brooks Spector, "When Mandela First Met America," *Daily Maverick* (South Africa), December 9, 2013.

32. Spector, "When Mandela First Met America."

33. John Kifner, "The Mandela Visit: Mandela Gets an Emotional New York City Welcome," *New York Times*, June 21, 1990, http://www.nytimes.com/1990/06/21/nyregion/the-mandela-visit-mandela-gets-an-emotional-new-york-city-welcome.

34. Spector, "When Mandela First Met America."

35. Kifner, "The Mandela Visit."

36. Francis Njubi Nesbitt, "When American Met Mandela," *Nightline: Foreign Policy in Focus*, June 28, 2013, http://fpif.org/when_america_met_mandela/. For a discussion of the role of Yassir Arafat and the PLO in the disparate and "broad complex of liberationist forces scattered throughout the international system of the Cold War world," see Paul Thomas Chamberlin, *The Global Offensive: The United States, the Palestine Liberation Organization, and the Making of the Post-Cold War Order* (Oxford: Oxford University Press, 2012).

37. Kevin Phillips, *American Dynasty: Aristocracy, Fortune, and the Politics of Deceit in the House of Bush* (New York: Penguin, 2004), 202.

38. Memorandum of telephone conversation between George H. W. Bush and Nelson Mandela of South Africa, March 6, 1991, Oval Office, George H. W. Bush Presidential Library and Museum, https://bush41library.tamu.edu/files/memcons-telcons/1991-03-06--Mandela.pdf. On debates at the United Nations over negotiated withdrawal, see John Quigley, "The United States and the United Nations in the Persian Gulf War: New Order or Disorder," *Cornell International Law Journal* 25, no. 1 (1992): article 1.

39. Jeffrey A. Engel, *When the World Seemed New: George H. W. Bush and the End of the Cold War* (Boston: Houghton Mifflin Harcourt, 2017), 480.

40. Engel, *When the World Seemed New*, 412; Chase Untermeyer, *Zenith: In the White House with George W. Bush* (College Station: Texas A&M University Press, 2016), 149.

41. Alan Riding, "European Nations to Lift Sanctions on South Africa," *New York Times*, April 16, 1991, http://www.nytimes.com/1991/04/16/world/european-nations-to-lift-sanctions-on-south-africa.html.

42. "Telephone conversation, Bush with Nelson Mandela," July 10, 1991, Papers of George H. W. Bush, Presidential Library, Dallas, Texas.

43. Stephen Ellis, "The Historical Significance of South Africa's Third Force," *Journal of South African Studies* 24, no. 2 (June 1998): 261–99.

44. National Security Council memorandum of conversation 4461, Subject: Meeting with Gatsha Mangosuthu Buthelezi, Chief Minister of KwaZulu, South Africa, June 20, 1991, Old Family Dining Room, George H. W. Bush Presidential Library and Museum, https://bush41library.tamu.edu/files/memcons-telcons/1991-06-20--Buthelezi.pdf.

45. Matthew Graham, "Foreign Policy in Transition: The ANC's Search for a Foreign Policy Direction During South Africa's Transition 1990–1994, *Commonwealth Journal of International Affairs* 101, no. 5 (October 2012): 1–19.

46. Adam Hirsh, "Fatal Embrace: How Relations Between Business and Government Help to Explain South Africa's Low-Growth Equilibrium," *South African Journal of International Affairs* 27, no. 4 (2020): 473–92; Adam Habib, *South Africa's Suspended Revolution: Hopes and Prospects* (Athens: Ohio University Press, 2013).

47. George H. W. Bush, "Honoring Nelson Mandela," *Huffington Post* (blog), updated December 6, 2017, https://www.huffingtonpost.com/george-h-w-bush/honoring-nelson-mandela_1_b_4377877.html.

48. "Diary Entry July 2, 1991," in George H. W. Bush, *All the Best, George Bush: My Life in Letters and Other Writings* (New York: Scribner, 2013), 527.

49. Susan L. Woodward, *Balkan Tragedy: Chaos and Dissolution after the Cold War* (Washington, DC: Brookings Institution, 1995), 199.

50. Memorandum of telephone conversation between George H. W. Bush and President Turgut Ozal of Turkey, December 5, 1992, White House, George H. W. Bush Presidential Library and Museum, https://bush41library.tamu.edu/files/memcons-telcons/1992-12-05--Ozal.pdf.

51. Rania Khalek, "Food Emergency: How the World Bank and IMF Have Made African Famine Inevitable," Alternet.org, September 8, 2011, https://www.sott.net/article/235355-Food-Emergency-How-the-World-Bank-and-IMF-Have-Made-African-Famine-Inevitable.

52. Mark Fineman, "Column One; The Oil Factor in Somalia: Four American Petroleum Giants Had Agreements with the African Nation Before Its Civil War Began. They Could Reap Big Rewards If Peace Is Restored," *Los Angeles Times*, January 18, 1993, https://web.archive.org/web/20120224071029/http://bailey83221.livejournal.com/70509.html.

53. Richard Bernstein, "Why Does the United States Refuse to Pay Its U.N. Bill?," *New York Times*, August 7, 1988.

54. Laclau, *New Reflections*, 92.

CHAPTER 16

Not Just Churches

American Jews, Joint Church Aid, and the Nigeria-Biafra War

MELANI McALISTER

R abbi Marc Tanenbaum claimed to be hopeful, but his argument was pointed. In an essay written for *Religion News Service* in August 1968, he discussed the way that American Jews were responding to the suffering of civilians in the Biafra war. Tanenbaum was at the time the head of Interreligious Affairs at the American Jewish Committee (AJC), and he had been involved for some years in interreligious dialogue with American Christians. He pointed out that Jews had been moved by the news of suffering in Nigeria-Biafra and that they had chosen to contribute money especially *as* Jews, yet they donated that money through Catholic Charities and the (Protestant) Church World Service.

They did this, Tanenbaum said, as an expression of Jewish universalism. Jews were responding to pictures of suffering Biafrans that had been prominent in U.S. news media over the previous year as journalists covered the battles that pitted the Nigerian military against an underresourced and embattled army of separatists from the eastern Nigerian region of Biafra. Those struggles left many civilians in the Biafran region injured or dead from violence and, increasingly, from starvation brought about by the war. But Tanenbaum also made clear that the response to Biafra had a particular meaning in Jewish consciousness and historical memory. The images of starvation and suffering required action of Jews in particular, he said, so they would not be complicit in the ways that others had been in the past: Jews would not reproduce "the silence of governments, universities, and church institutions, among others, who, by and large, were spectators to the Nazis' 'final solution of the Jewish problem' in Europe. . . . 'Thou shalt not stand idly by the blood of thy brother' has become virtually the eleventh commandment in contemporary Judaism."

In addition, Tanenbaum commented, Jews remembered how American Christian organizations had responded during the Arab-Israeli war just one year earlier. Tanenbaum felt that many mainline Protestant and Catholic organizations had been unenthusiastic about Israel's victory and takeover of East Jerusalem, the West Bank, Gaza, and the Golan Heights:

> The straddling on the part of many church institutions and Christian leaders of the moral and humanitarian issues that were at stake in May and June 1967 when Arab governments were explicitly and publicly threatening to annihilate the two and a half million Jews of Israel has resulted in a radar-like sensitivity in the collective Jewish psyche to any threat of genocide or mass destruction against any group.[1]

For Tanenbaum, Jewish humanitarian action on the part of the largely Christian population in Biafra should teach a lesson to American Christians about interreligious cooperation in a transnational frame. It also was supposed to teach them a lesson about Israel.

In this essay, I examine U.S. Jewish responses to the Nigeria-Biafra war of 1967–1970, focusing on Rabbi Tanenbaum and the AJC but with the aim of highlighting some of the complex ways that the crisis in Nigeria affected different groups of Americans. The goal is *not* to make an argument about the ideological problems with humanitarianism as a politics of abjection and rescue—that important work has been done well by a number of scholars.[2] Instead, I explore the meanings of the Nigeria-Biafra conflict as ideologically significant along several different vectors. I show how, for the leading American Jewish activists on the issue, Biafra was imagined and presented (internally and externally) as a "nonpolitical" issue, a simple moral statement about Jewish humanitarianism. But in reality this humanitarianism functioned within a set of debates and performances, working in three distinct registers that interacted both ideologically and affectively.

First, it situated American Jews in relationship to American Christians as mainstream and liberal religious actors. It attempted to continue the work of interreligious dialogue that was part and parcel of the performance of new forms of "Judeo-Christian" civil religion, including the work of Jewish incorporation into U.S. whiteness. Second, it played a role in renarrating the very recent history of the 1967 Arab-Israeli war. Whereas some American activists on behalf of Biafra saw the war as a potential way for the United States to make amends for its failed policies in Vietnam by supporting those who fought for genuine freedom in Biafra, Tanenbaum and the AJC saw Biafra as a commentary on U.S. attitudes toward Israel. The activism worked to position Israel as being *like* Biafra—an underdog victim fighting for safety in a national home. And third, Jewish activism on Biafra complicated the already complicated relationship between American Jews and African Americans, particularly Black nationalists, at a time of rising decolonial sentiment in the United States that included increased support for Palestinians.

The critique I'm offering is specific to the Jewish community in some ways, but the cultural work—and political investments—of a "nonpolitical" humanitarian view of Biafra was common to a range of actors, at the time and since, who have narrated and renarrated the Biafra war as a morality tale. The meanings (and ideological freight) of Biafra in that context are varied. For some, it is a straightforward matter of a cry for justice that the world ignored. ("The world was silent when we died" is the title of the book-within-the-book in Chimamanda Ngozi Adichie's marvelous novel of the war.[3]) For others, Biafra was the opposite: a parable of the damage done by (Western) humanitarianism's binary logic, which framed a complex war as a seemingly simple case of suffering. On that model, Western humanitarians did not fail to respond; instead, they acted after falling victim to Biafran propaganda and perhaps did more harm than good in the process. For yet others, the war becomes a postcolonial cautionary tale—with Nigeria as Patient Zero in the epidemic of nationalist crises and division after the end of empire. My argument here is that, whatever else the Biafra war was, it was also an affectively charged figure in U.S. debates about race, power, and the nation's role in the world.

Background: Biafra-Nigeria War

From 1967 to 1970, the Nigerian civil war riveted the world's attention as a secessionist movement in the eastern province struggled to create an independent state. Nigeria had become independent from Britain in 1960, and already it was an admired model—large, populous, militarily strong, and with great potential wealth. But the regional and ethnic tensions were close to the surface as well. Commentators noted, at the time and since, that Nigeria, like many decolonizing states, had been molded into a state out of a collection of British colonial holdings. "Nigeria is not a nation, it is a mere geographical expression," commented the anticolonial leader Obafemi Awolowo.[4] Regional tensions and debates over how to rule a large and diverse democracy had been present since the beginning. It was no surprise, really, when ethnic divides and conflicts over power erupted into civil war.[5] Militarily, the war between Nigeria and Biafra was hardly a match. Within six months the tide had already turned against Biafra. Nigeria's victory seemed all but certain.

But when Nigeria began to blockade Biafra, European and U.S. activists responded with horror. By the spring of 1968, images of dead civilians and starving children were everywhere in the news, and the cause seemed straightforward: a draconian Nigerian government was intentionally starving a rebellious region into submission. In response, a transnational coterie of advocates, together with an activist global media, embraced Biafra's struggle as a humanitarian crisis and, ultimately, as a political project. Biafra became an international cause that helped forge a new form of popular humanitarianism—one that exhibited both the promise and the dangers of humanitarian sentiment writ large.[6]

Although the war began in 1967, it really did not reach U.S. consciousness until a series of newspaper and television reports appeared in the summer of 1968. The subsequent movement to "Keep Biafra Alive" was built on transnational networks that had been politically activated by the Vietnam War, civil rights, and opposition to apartheid. Globally, the movement included many hundreds of national and local groups in the United States, the United Kingdom, Ireland, and France, as well as transnational organizations such as Oxfam and the World Council of Churches. Religious activism was particularly notable. Most of the Igbo and other ethnic groups in the Biafra region were Catholics, many converted by Irish missionaries. (There were substantial numbers of Christians in other parts of Nigeria as well. The thriving Nigerian Baptist Convention, for example, based largely in western Nigeria, was associated with the U.S. Southern Baptist Convention.[7]) In both Europe and the United States, Catholic and Protestant institutions were notably responsive to the crisis in Biafra. In 1968, one of the five copresidents of the World Council of Churches (WCC) was Francis Akanu Ibiam, a former governor of Biafra, which put the war immediately on the organization's agenda. However, the WCC was deeply divided, in part because it included churches from the rest of Nigeria, as well as across Africa, where there was a great deal of concern about any conflict that threatened to divide a newly independent country. Like other groups, then, the WCC initially declared itself to be apolitical, interested only in humanitarian relief.[8]

As the war progressed, however, that apolitical stance soon became untenable. Nigeria blockaded Biafra from receiving aid except through its supervision. The International Red Cross complied, but others did not. Joint Church Aid, for example, was formed by an independent coalition of churches that were frustrated with the WCC's stance. Built out of an earlier group of Northern European Protestant Churches, the transnational coalition came to include the Catholic Caritas International. Later, national coalitions emerged under the Joint Church Aid umbrella; Joint Church Aid–USA, for example, was the umbrella group that the AJC joined. Joint Church Aid made the notable decision to hire mercenary pilots who began to deliver aid under cover of night in violation of Nigeria's blockade.[9]

In the United States alone, more than two hundred organizations took up the Biafran cause, some asking merely for more aid, others pushing for a U.S.-sponsored relief plan, and others, implicitly or explicitly, supporting Biafra's independence. The American Committee to Keep Biafra Alive, started jointly by a former Peace Corps volunteer and a British student at Cornell, became the most active and vocal, but political actions on behalf of Biafra included scores of groups doing actions from fund-raisers and media campaigns to candlelight vigils and sophisticated lobbying on Capitol Hill. The movement to "Let Biafra Live" was just that—a movement, uncoordinated, disunified, and improvisational, that spread across the country and crisscrossed a range of ideological positions. It was also very short-lived. The war ended with Biafra's defeat in January 1970; major activities in the United States lasted less than two years.[10]

There had been relatively little scholarship on the global response to the Nigeria-Biafra war prior to the last decade, but that is changing rapidly.[11] Not only do we have increasingly sophisticated work on the role of Biafra as part of the "founding myth" of Médecins Sans Frontières (Doctors Without Borders), but a number of scholars also offer transnational accounts that attend to state politics, nonstate actors, and the role of media.[12] The historian Lasse Heerten has written a marvelous transnational history of the global response to the Biafra war that examines, among other things, how Biafra's story was narrated in relationship to an evolving memory of the Holocaust in the late 1960s. Heerten argues, quite convincingly, that Biafra was understood by American Jews and others as being "another Holocaust" and thus something to which both Jews and non-Jews *must* respond. Heerten also points out that Biafra and Holocaust memory were being constituted together in the late 1960s. Michael Rothberg's notion of "multidirectional memory" helps us understand how the meaning of the Holocaust, which was being evoked and reworked in the late 1960s, was shaped in part, retroactively, by the Biafra crisis. That is, seeing the images of the emaciated children reminded people of the images they had seen of the liberation of the concentration camps, and the interweaving of these images helped to construct them both as being two instances of the same thing: genocide.[13]

But Heerten's story of Holocaust memory only partially shows the many resonances that Biafra had in the American Jewish community. To explore the additional ideological registers that the debate over Biafra held for American Jews, I draw on Bourdieu's notion of "position-taking"—an act in which agents operate in a cultural/political field in which they know the stakes and have a feel for the game.[14] Calling something an act of position-taking is not to say that it was not heartfelt; it only posits that people take their own positions in some awareness of what positions others are taking, and how their moves might situate them vis-à-vis those others—and also how, in inhabiting a particular position, they might change the field itself. In his most famous articulation of this argument, *The Field of Cultural Production*, Bourdieu is writing about the "field" of French literature in the 1890s, and he argues that the meaning of any specific literary work changes as other position-takers (novelists, intellectuals, consumers) enter the field. "The meaning of a work (artistic, literary, philosophical, etc.) changes automatically with each change in the field within which it is situated for the spectator or reader."[15] In the context of Biafra, this means that any individual's or group's ideology was not simply about what they believed or valued but was also inevitably relational—established and made meaningful in relationship to the total field of manifestations and actions. Humanitarianism can be viewed as an "apolitical" and "universal" ideology, but it also resides within a multivalent field of domestic and international civil society, which is not a world of rational actors so much as a mobile space of action in which material conditions, various forms of capital, political values, and affective objects embed and inform each other.

Position-Taking I: American Jews in
Interreligious Dialogue

The American Jewish Committee is one of the oldest Jewish civil society organizations in the United States. Founded in 1906, the group focused on civil rights activism, human rights promotion, and the push for a more inclusive American polity. Before the founding of Israel, AJC was officially "non-Zionist"—supportive of Jewish settlement in Palestine but not focused on Jewish sovereignty, which they saw as potentially dangerous to the cause of full integration of American Jews. After 1948, AJC shifted to a more pro-Israel policy—as long as Israel did not try to convince American Jews that their real home was elsewhere. The AJC pursued a human rights agenda, focused both on removing prejudice toward minorities of all types (a human relations model) and on a more legalistic model of supporting human rights against state infringement.[16] As Lawrence Grossman summarized it, "in the constellation of major American Jewish organizations [in the 1950s and early 1960s], AJC was distinguished for its scholarly tone, its programmatic moderation, and the priority it gave to the successful integration of Jews into the American mainstream."[17]

Rabbi Tanenbaum had been head of the Interreligious Program at AJC since 1960. Born in 1925 in Baltimore to Orthodox Jewish immigrants from Russia, he attended the Jewish Theological Seminary in New York, where he was a student and aide to famed Rabbi Abraham Joshua Heschel. Ordained in 1950, Tanenbaum developed an immediate and passionate interest in Christian-Jewish relations. When, in the early 1960s, it became clear that the planners of the Second Vatican Council were open to making new statements on Catholic-Jewish relations, Tanenbaum and the AJC began working with Catholic representatives, issuing a series of papers and reports that led into Vatican II. Tanenbaum himself became an official observer and an active behind-the-scenes organizer at the meeting. The final document, the *Nostra Aetate*, issued in October 1965, was a turning point in Jewish-Catholic relations.[18]

Tanenbaum's work on Vatican II was one aspect of the much larger push toward improving interfaith relations, both in the United States and internationally, during the 1950s and 1960s. AJC had been a mainstay of that work, but it also included the Anti-Defamation League (1913), and the National Conference of Christians and Jews (1928), which notably ran a series of Brotherhood summer camps for young people.[19] The goals of these programs was less theological education than a practical challenge to the casual antisemitism of many American Christians, including education about Jewish beliefs, limiting or ending attempts to convert Jews to Christianity, and, in the process, highlighting the value of "liberal" religion in a presumedly secular society.[20] The Cold War played a role as well. As sociologist Will Herberg pointed out in *Protestant, Catholic, Jew* (1955), Judaism was becoming one of three public religions in the United States, a signifier of a liberal-mindedness about faith that would mark the distinctiveness of the United States in the conflict with communism.[21] When Tanenbaum joined the AJC in 1960, he saw himself as an ambassador not only for the inclusion of American Jews in the mainstream of American religious and cultural life but also for the importance of religion in the public square.

Indeed, his first draft of the *Religion News Service* article that laid out Jewish investments in the Nigeria-Biafra war was originally titled "Biafra: A Test Case of Inter-Religious Relevance." Just a few weeks previously, Tanenbaum had called for the establishment of a specifically Jewish organization for raising money for Biafra—what became the twenty-one-member American Jewish Emergency Effort for Biafran Relief. (It would later change the name to include Nigeria as well as Biafra.) That organization raised $185,000 in its first year (about $1.3 million in 2019 dollars).[22] Tanenbaum soon argued that the Jewish organization should become part of the larger Joint Church Aid–USA, even though this meant having Jewish fund-raising subsumed under an organization called Joint *Church* Aid. That fact remained a concern for the AJC during the entire course of the war, but Tanenbaum was convinced that Jews needed to make their mark on the terrain on interreligious liberalism.[23] "The response of the religious communities in the United States and overseas to the plight of the victims of the Nigerian-Biafran struggle," he opined, "has been moving and marvelous: it is a landmark in the quest of the relevance of religion to life."[24]

Tanenbaum and others at the AJC insisted that their involvement in work on behalf of Biafra was inherently apolitical, motivated purely by humanitarian sentiment in the face of suffering. Catholic Relief Services made the same argument, as did the mainline Protestant Church World Service in the United States. However, almost every organization (except the International Red Cross) that was sending aid into Biafra after June 1967 was doing so against a blockade by Nigeria, supporting air flights that went under the cover of night to avoid being targeted by the Federal Military

Government. Joint Church Aid was originally founded in Europe, and it was broadly seen as being in support of Biafra's demand for independence, not just interested in responding to immediate need. For American Jews, Biafra carried a different kind of double-load: there was no question that part of the point of the aid for Tannenbaum and others at the AJC was not only to respond to the "never again" lesson of the Holocaust but also to demonstrate ways that American Jews were part of the kaleidoscope of religious humanitarianism in the United States. "Not the smallest of the rewards of this campaign," the AJC later commented, "was the spirit of cooperation and mutual understanding that developed between Christians and Jews."[25] In the field of interreligious Americanism, taking a position on Biafra also placed the position-taker as part of a liberal consensus about duty in the context of distant suffering.[26]

Position-Taking II: The 1967 Arab-Israeli War

Although Tanenbaum was committed to interreligious work, he made it clear that all was not rosy in terms of Christian-Jewish relations in the late 1960s, especially after the crucible of the 1967 Arab-Israeli war. For much of its existence, the AJC has been a non-Zionist organization; in the complex field of American (and global) Judaism in the early twentieth century, the AJC focused on civil rights for American Jews and showed little interest in, or support for, a sovereign Jewish state in the Middle East (although the organization did support Jewish settlement in Palestine). Working to end antisemitism in the United States, expand civil rights for Black Americans, and support church-state separation, the AJC guarded its position as a moderate, elite, mainstream voice for American Jews.

After Israel's founding in 1948, the organization generally supported the Israeli state but was not afraid to engage in quiet criticism and negotiation, especially regarding Israel's treatment of its Palestinian minority. For the AJC, this seemed consonant with its mission because it defined itself largely as a human rights organization and felt the need to speak about rights of minorities globally, including in Israel. The leadership also tended to feel that Israel's treatment of its Arab minority was bad for American Jews—it gave ammunition to anti-Jewish sentiment. When the AJC did open an office in Tel Aviv in 1960, it defined its mission there as one of promoting greater democracy and liberalism in Israel, helping in "develop[ing] greater understanding in Israel of the pluralistic nature of American society . . . increas[ing] the knowledge of American and Western traditions of civic responsibility and civil liberties in order to foster development of democratic institutions."[27] The paternalism of the sentiment was in line with AJC's reputation as an organization of liberal elites dedicated to civil rights.

Over time, the AJC moved to support Israel more fully and publicly when it recognized that the organization's rather hands-off view of Israel was out of step with many American Jews. Israel was not yet at the forefront of American Jewish identity, but most Jews outside the AJC's largely elite cohort felt real sympathy with Zionism. There was, according to Lawrence Grossman, "a broad AJC strategy in the early 1960s to reposition the organization closer to the American Jewish mainstream by place greater emphasis on Israel."[28] This closer-in position, however, was always paired with AJC's insistence that the Israeli government should not claim to speak for Jews outside of Israel.[29]

By May 1967, when tensions began to rise dramatically between Israel and Nasser's Egypt, the leadership of the AJC was prepared to move quickly—although not without some anxiety—in calling on the U.S. government to intervene on Israel's behalf. (Several leaders were acutely aware that the opposition of several major Jewish organizations to U.S. military involvement in Vietnam made calls for U.S. involvement in a Middle East war potentially fraught.[30]) Israel struck first against Egypt and Syria, and Jordan soon joined as well. In the very early days of the conflict, news was scarce, and the assumption among many Jews was that Israel might well be destroyed. In Arthur Hertzberg's oft-repeated formulation, "As soon as the Arab armies began to mass on the border of Israel, the mood of the American Jewish community underwent an abrupt, radical, and possibly permanent change . . . far more intense and widespread than anyone could have foreseen."[31] In fact, Israel won the war quickly and handily, but this did not erase the memory of those first few days in the American Jewish community. As Amy Kaplan has compellingly argued, the fact of Israel's remarkably rapid and complete victory left a complex legacy in U.S. popular culture more broadly, in which Israel was seen as both vulnerable and yet indomitable—an invincible victim.[32] Certainly for leaders such as Tanenbaum, the war was a turning point—he and the AJC as a whole became strongly and adamantly supportive of Israel, weaving the state into the fundamental narrative of what it meant to be Jewish.

In this context, Tanenbaum also found himself increasingly at odds with the ecumenical Protestants who were a key component of the interreligious work he did at AJC. American Protestants of all stripes had shown great interest in the founding of Israel twenty years earlier. Although some, such as the editors at Christian Century, had tended to be quite critical of Zionism, there was also a strong strain of pro-Israel sentiment among liberal Protestants—both at the leadership level and among people in the pews, who not only read about God's chosen people in the Bible but who likely also watched Hollywood's sepia-hued depictions of both ancient Hebrews and modern Israelis.[33]

The 1967 war, however, saw quite mixed reactions from major Protestant organizations. In particular, the National Council of Churches initially offered a brief neutral statement that simply expressed "compassion and concern for all the people of the Middle East" and called for the UN to play a role. A few weeks after the war's end, the NCC had criticized Israel's unilateral annexation of the Jordanian portion of Jerusalem.[34] Many individual denominations had strong connections in the region and had ties to Arab communities. The Lutherans, for example, raised money to assist Syrian and Jordanian war victims—areas where they had missionaries—and issued a statement saying simply that Israel would "make a mistake if it annexed conquered territory without negotiation."[35] Such statements angered a number of U.S. Jewish leaders, who saw their interreligious allies as having stood quietly aside while the threat of another Holocaust loomed. Rabbi Balfour Brickner, director of the Reform Judaism's Commission on Interfaith Activities, angrily told a conference of rabbis in late June that official Christendom has failed the "acid test of American inter-religious relations."[36] A few months later, Rabbi Brickner wrote in Christianity and Crisis magazine that over the previous months "Jewish leaders accused the Christian Establishment not only of a failure of moral nerve by their silence but also of failing the cause of world peace."[37] At AJC, too, there was a great deal of frustration; staffers prepared several memos that outlined what many saw as an ignoble Christian silence during the war.[38]

However much Tanenbaum was angered by such lack of support for Israel, he also insisted—correctly—that most Christians, including liberal ecumenical Protestants, had strongly supported Israel. Writing in Conservative Judaism in 1969, Tanenbaum pointed out that a number of individual Protestant and Catholic leaders had signed statements of support. One of the most widely circulated, signed by Reinhold Niebuhr; Martin Luther King Jr.; John Bennett, president of Union Theological Seminary; and a dozen others, called "Americans of all persuasions and groupings and the

[Johnson] Administration to support the independence, integrity, and freedom of Israel."[39] (Indeed, some liberal Protestants complained that their fellow believers were "hypocritical" in their enthusiasm for Israel after the 1967 war: "Arabs can be judged as bloodthirsty for their rhetoric no matter how little they actually do, while Israel could do no wrong no matter how far its conquests exceeded its provocation," complained one professor of theology at Yale.[40])

Tanenbaum wanted his fellow Jews to realize how much support Israel had—and he didn't want them to toss away what he saw as the great progress in creating a respectful space for Jews in U.S. civil society at a time when 92 percent of Americans still identified as Christian. In addition, Tanenbaum had come to believe that Israel was also dependent on the goodwill of the U.S. government and, thus, on American Christians. These are the "facts of our existence," he said, and we need to "relate to them seriously—which means to recognize the fundamental importance of strengthening cooperation and authentic solidarity with Christians and their institutions. It is they who constitute primary structures in our environment."[41]

Tanenbaum's complex views about the events of June 1967 very much shaped his response to the Biafra war in early 1968. (The Biafra war had begun in May 1967, at almost exactly the same time as the Arab-Israeli war, but it did not receive attention or coverage in the U.S. and European press until early 1968.) Tanenbaum did not think American Jews had the option to simply "give up" on liberal American Christians or interreligious dialogue, and Tanenbaum found in Biafra a way of reshaping the conversation about Israel. He used his close working relationship with the other members of Joint Church Aid-USA to articulate a position that linked not only the Holocaust and Biafra (which was being done more broadly) but that tied both of those to American Christian responses to the 1967 war. Tanenbaum did this in a series of steps.

Tanenbaum often spoke to audiences about what he saw as the fundamental moral imperative for Jewish generosity and activism in the case of Biafra. For example, he wrote: "The principle was . . . that this was the first time that the entire Jewish community volunteered to join with Catholics and Protestants on an international humanitarian endeavor, to serve people who were not Jewish and would not likely ever become Jews."[42] Here Tanenbaum was making a sly point: unlike Christians who might be acting in Biafra on behalf of fellow Christians, or who might act in other places and times in hope of missionary opportunity, Jews were acting out a Jewish universalism and understanding of humanity, on behalf of people who were "not Jewish and would not likely ever become Jews." But Tanenbaum also frequently presented Jewish action in Biafra as being specifically Jewish—not as a missionary opportunity, because Jews did not much engage in missionizing, but as nonetheless emerging from Jewish particularity and Jewish history.

Speaking at a joint conference of Southern Baptist and Jewish scholars in 1969, Tanenbaum first asked why Jews had been active on both Biafra and civil rights. He explained that this came from "an authentic Jewish expression of human conscience." It was a particularly Jewish universal. But the response to Biafra also had other sources. First, he said, the marches and quick action on behalf of distant Africans were, on the deepest levels, an act of delayed atonement for the marches Jews did *not* make in the 1930s and 1940s in Washington, Paris, Berlin, and Warsaw.[43] Second, Tanenbaum posited the familiar narrative about the 1967 war: "When, therefore, Jews heard the rhetoric and themes of genocide and 'final solution' in the May and June 1967 proclamations from Cairo, Amman, Damascus, and Baghdad, the sleeper reaction to the Nazi holocaust was instantly awakened."[44] And it was this Holocaust consciousness, reenlivened by the 1967 war, that, in Tannenbaum's view, led to the Jewish determination to fight for the oppressed in general and in Biafra specifically: "This transformed consciousness of the Jewish people and the bonds of solidarity between the diaspora and Israel amounted to a refusal to give Hitler and the Nazi murderers a final victory over both Jews and civilized humanity."[45]

Tanenbaum is working here to position Israel's military victory in 1967 as having the same kind of moral sanction that the Biafra crisis carried in 1968 and 1969. At that point, the Jewish Holocaust was just beginning to have the contemporary meanings that made one's response to it a measure of human moral sentiment.[46] Arguments about Israel facing a new Holocaust certainly were made in the 1967 war, but for many non-Jews they didn't have the profound familiarity and moral status they do for most Americans today. However, for at least some audiences in 1968, Biafra did.

It was not just American Jews who constructed a link between Judaism and the struggle in Biafra. A number of Biafra activists did exactly the same thing, especially in making appeals to the American Jewish community. For example, activists appealed to officials at the AJC in the language of a historical connection between the Igbo people of Eastern Nigeria and the Jewish experience in Europe and the Middle East. In the summer of 1968, for example, a writer for the *New York Amsterdam News*, Simon Anekwe, wrote a long and heartfelt letter jointly addressed to Yitzhak Rabin, then chief of staff of the Israeli Defense Forces, and AJC president Morris B. Abram. In it, Anekwe argued that Israelis in particular had every reason to support the largely Christian population of Biafra over the government of Nigeria. After all, he said, in the early days of Nigerian independence (just a few years previously), Golda Meir had been received far more warmly by President Azikiwe ("a Christian Easterner") than by Prime Minister Balewa ("a Muslim Northerner"). "I keep wondering why Israel and the Jews, a state and a people who have experienced the kind of suffering that Biafrans are now enduring, seemed so insensitive to the needs of Biafrans." How was it, he asked, that neither American Jews nor Israelis had sent aid? "I am puzzled to think that not a bottle of aspirin or a phial of penicillin; not a rubber ball or a dime, has gone from a state and a people possessed of such military and financial strength that they could stand up to the whole Islamic Middle East: not an ounce of aid to Biafra from those whom they thought of as friends."[47] (The American Jewish Emergency Effort for Biafran Relief was founded just a couple of weeks after Anekwe wrote his letter.)

This framing of Israelis and American Jews as sharing a common Muslim enemy with the Igbo was presented consistently, with more or less subtlety, in a range of venues. (Eighteen months later, Donatus U. Anyanwu, president of the Biafran Relief Services Foundation, would send a letter to the new AJC president, Phillip Hoffman, arguing, in a similar vein, that the Nigeria-Biafra war "brings to mind the struggle between the Jews and the Arabs in the 1947 War of Independence in which it was clearly understood that the only way the Jewish people could achieve their independence and live as free men was to establish their own nation with their own self-government. In this respect, the Igbos in Biafra are very similar to the Jews in Israel, and thus are often referred to as 'the Jews of Africa'."[48]) In this sense, Biafrans both in the United States and in Biafra itself made an argument based on a parallelism but acknowledged some differences. They agreed that Jews around the world should appreciate what it was like to be suffering and have the world not respond; the Holocaust analogy was at hand. Just as important, however, Biafrans argued that they had the same kind of right of self-determination that Jews had twenty years previously, in 1947. Why not split the territory with Nigeria in much the way the UN had split the territory that had been Palestine? And finally, there was the supposed Muslim threat: surely the Jews of Israel could understand why the Christians of eastern Nigeria felt fearful? (Interestingly, this framing of the conflict as a religious war had very little traction in the United States in 1967, which the leaders of the Republic of Biafra soon realized. Its propaganda changed course after 1968 to focus almost entirely on starvation as the key issue.[49])

Position-Taking III: Black-Jewish Alliance

Finally, American Jewish contributions to Biafran relief were a complicating factor for Black-Jewish relations. Black political activists in the United States were more ambivalent about the Nigeria-Biafra war than many other Americans. Nigeria, which had just received its independence in 1960, was one of the great postcolonial success stories in Africa, and many African Americans were concerned about any move to break up the country. As Brenda Plummer has argued, "the war marked in some respects the end of innocence for the champions of liberation because it could not be understood either literally or figuratively in black and white terms."[50] Now those trials were front and center.

Many Black leaders, from moderate civil rights groups such as the American Negro Leadership Council on Africa (ANLCA) to Black nationalist organizations, tended to support Nigeria or wanted to stay neutral in the conflict. Martin Luther King Jr. had attended the inauguration of Nigeria's Nnamdi Azikiwe as the first Governor-General after independence. He, like many other African American leaders, saw Nigeria as a model of African freedom – and a bulwark in the struggle against apartheid. So it was not perhaps surprising that the four cochairmen of ANLCA—Martin Luther King Jr., Roy Wilkins, J. Phillip Randolph, and Whitney Young—had volunteered themselves as mediators of the Nigeroia-Biafra conflict and were scheduled to go to Nigeria in April 1968. Just a week before their planned trip, King was assassinated.[51]

This broadly shared sense among African Americans of hoping to see the conflict resolved without breaking up Nigeria did not mean that African Americans were not interested in humanitarian support for Biafra. Many were, and groups such as the AME-Zion church raised funds for Biafran relief. Similarly, in September 1968, a group of African American leaders, including Kenneth Clark and Jackie Robinson, sent a telegram to President Johnson and UN General Secretary U Thant to express their concern for the "tragic condition" of children in Biafra.[52] There were also one or two strongly pro-Biafran organizations active among African Americans, most notably the Brooklyn-based Joint Afro Committee on Biafra, an "eclectic mix of civil rights activists, black nationalist militants, and other African Americans with experience in Africa."[53] Members of that group admired Biafra in the same terms that Biafra's leaders used to present themselves: as a democratic, anticolonial force, a model for self-empowerment standing up against the old imperial powers that were allied with Nigeria. In their initial position paper, the group argued that African Americans should support Biafra not only because its people were facing a "genocidal war" but because of the values they represented. Drawing obliquely on the Black Power rhetoric of the time and its links to various anticolonial struggles, the Joint Afro Committee's position paper posited Biafrans as people who were "not the 'Yes, Suh' type"; they were fighting their old colonial masters, the Russians and the United States, and they were not going to give in to being bullied by world powers.[54]

But a purely pro-Biafran position was uncommon in U.S. Black communities, and in fact, a number of African Americans were suspicious of any policy that seemed to support the breakup of Nigeria. In October 1968, when the Senate Committee on Africa held hearings on the Nigerian civil war, civil rights activist James Meredith testified that most of the other testimony in the hearings—almost all from white pro-Biafran activists— was "simply racism in disguise, in the disguise of humanitarianism."[55] The African American press, too, was generally dubious about Biafra's claims. The Baltimore *Afro-American*, for example, ran a number of articles hostile to those in the United States who advocated for recognition of Biafra, particularly the American Committee to Keep Biafra Alive. (One article attacking Simon Anekwe, who wrote the 1968 letter to Yitzhak Rabin and Morris B. Abram, commented angrily on what the author described as "the duplicity of Biafra and its supporters."[56])

For some supporters of Biafra, both Jewish and non-Jewish, such African American debates were baffling—and at times infuriating. They came in the wake of tensions that had emerged between Blacks and Jews over Israel in 1967, and were sometimes explicitly seen as related. For example, in an April 1969 memo from Sidney Liskofsky to Marc Tanenbaum, the AJC staffer sent a brief clipping from the *New York Times* about a pro-Nigerian protest by a group of Black high school students.

What earthly reason could there be for Negro High School students suddenly and spontaneously to decide to demonstrate in opposition to—of all things!—aid to starving children in Biafra? For Americans,

Negro or White, to make an intellectual judgment on the merits in favor of the Nigerian side, is perhaps even understandable, for the issues are complex. But is there any explanation for a demonstration of this nature other than that they were indoctrinated or incited to do so by certain militant groups who follow the communist . . . or "Third-World" line? . . . Undoubtedly, the manipulators are the same that influence these children along other lines, like supporting the Arab against the Israeli cause, and what-have-you.[57]

Here, Liskofsky is expressing yet another layer of the multiple connections that AJC staff and others saw between the politics of the Nigeria-Biafra war and the Arab-Israeli conflict. Writing fifteen years after the 1955 Asian-African conference at Bandung, the AJC activists were fully aware of the intertwined power of Third Worldism, Black internationalism, and domestic antiracism. Liskofsky imagines that these students were being indoctrinated—that they were being positioned on a field in which nationalisms of certain types were allied—the (pan-Africanist) nationalism of the Nigerians, the Arabs against Israel, and Black nationalists in the United States. The fact that there was indeed exactly such an alignment between Palestinian Arabs and Black Power advocates globally meant that the AJC's position was not incorrect.[58] And the fact that Israel (along with South Africa) was loosely supporting Biafra in the conflict lent a certain weight to the notion that the young Black students in the US might have some kind of transnational support for a pro-Nigeria position—if one ignored (as Liskofsky and Tannenbaum were both inclined to do) the long history of Black anticolonialism that made Nigeria matter so much to African Americans.[59] In other words, despite the expressions of befuddlement, the AJC activists had a feel for the game, and they realized that the ideological stance of being "against aid to starving children" was its own kind of position-taking in a much larger field of political conversation.

Conclusion

When I began this research, I assumed that any connections between the relationship between U.S. Christian and Jewish support for Biafra and the politics of the 1967 Arab-Israeli war would be oblique, hard to parse, requiring layers of analysis to reveal the political complexities and assumptions of the supposedly apolitical humanitarian activism in Biafra. As the AJC evidence makes clear, however, the matter of supporting starving Biafrans was, despite protestations, never apolitical – not in the cultural and political field of the late 1960s. Instead, it was freighted with multiple forms of ideological investment. The AJC's position was part of a larger conversation—about the Holocaust, the 1967 war, race in America, and African decolonization. In this case, the AJC's work on Biafra was imagined as a longed-for reproach to the world for failing to stop the Holocaust, but it also became a weapon in the struggle to craft a narrative about Israel that could, and would, be used against the cause of Palestinians. In the early 1970s, Tanenbaum began to cultivate more relationships with U.S. evangelicals. (This was not new; he had been friendly with Billy Graham since the early 1960s.) Those relationships made domestic sense—American's civil religion, whatever it was or might be, was no longer dictated by ecumenical Protestants. And those contacts were smart politics, too, because, as many scholars have shown, U.S. evangelicals would soon become the strongest and most powerful segment of pro-Israel activism in the United States.[60]

In January 1970, the Biafran leadership surrendered. Joint Church Aid continued to provide some support for the population over the next few months, but soon enough the committees were dismantled. There had already been a range of debates and doubts among various activists in the United States and Europe; current scholarship on the movement to "keep Biafra alive" gives a sense of just how fragile it ultimately was. Perhaps the most striking aspect, in retrospect, was how quickly the Nigeria–Biafra war was forgotten in the United States—along with the passions it inspired and the ways it positioned activists and movements in relationship to each other. The Nigeria–Biafra war and the Arab–Israeli war of 1967 started within a week of each other, and the first one was far more deadly. But historical memory is its own field, and the position of Biafra has been shaped by forces far larger than that small corner of Africa's most populous nation.

Notes

I would like to thank the editors of the collection for organizing the initial conference and for their advice at various points of the project. Thanks also to Samantha Silver for research assistance, and to Mark Bradley, Jamie Cohen-Cole, Arie Dubnov, and Penny Von Eschen for comments, as well as the members of the GWU Humanities Center.

1. Marc Tanenbaum, "Biafra: Test Case of Interreligious Relevance," August 9, 1968, manuscript for "Biafran Tragedy Accelerates: Christian Jewish Cooperation," *Religious News Service*, August 14, 1968. Interreligious Affairs, box 85, folder 3, American Jewish Committee Archives, New York.

2. Didier Fassin, *Humanitarian Reason: A Moral History of the Present* (Berkeley: University of California Press, 2011); Ilana Feldman and Miriam Ticktin, eds., *In the Name of Humanity: The Government of Threat and Care* (Durham, NC: Duke University Press, 2010); Michael Barnett, *Empire of Humanity: A History of Humanitarianism* (Ithaca, NY: Cornell University Press, 2011); Erica Bornstein and Peter Redfield, eds., *Forces of Compassion: Humanitarianism between Ethics and Politics* (Santa Fe, NM: School for Advanced Research Press, 2011).

3. Chimamanda Ngozi Adichie, *Half of a Yellow Sun* (New York: Anchor, 2007).

4. Obafemi Awolowo and Margery Perham, *Path to Nigerian Freedom* (1947; repr. London: Faber and Faber, 1967), 47. Awolowo was not an outside observer but a leading Yoruban activist and Nigerian nationalist.

5. Of the large volume of literature on Nigeria's colonial history, see particularly Toyin Falola, *Colonialism and Violence in Nigeria* (Bloomington: Indiana University Press, 2009); Max Siollun, *What Britain Did to Nigeria: A Short History of Conquest and Rule* (New York: Hurst, 2021); Chima J. Korieh, *Nigeria and World War II: Colonialism, Empire, and Global Conflict* (Cambridge: Cambridge University Press, 2020).

6. On Biafra as the "totem and taboo" of modern humanitarianism, see Alex de Waal, *Famine Crimes: Politics & the Disaster Relief Industry in Africa* (Bloomington: Indiana University Press, 1997).

7. I. Adedoyin, *A Short History of the Nigerian Baptist: 1850–1978* (Ibadan, Nigeria: Nigerian Baptist Bookstore, 1998); Travis Collins, *The Baptist Mission of Nigeria, 1850–1993: A History of the Southern Baptist Convention Missionary Work in Nigeria* (Ibadan: Y-Books/Associated Book-Makers Nigeria, 1993); Alan Scot Willis, *All According to God's Plan: Southern Baptist Missions and Race, 1945–1970* (Lexington: University Press of Kentucky, 2004).

8. Laurie S. Wiseberg, "Christian Churches and the Nigerian Civil War," *Journal of African Studies* 2, no. 3 (1975): 297–331; Ernest W Lefever, *Amsterdam to Nairobi: The World Council of Churches and the Third World* (Washington, DC: Georgetown University, 1979); John Briggs, *A History of the Ecumenical Movement*, Vol. 3. *1968–2000*, 3rd ed. (Geneva: World Council of Churches, 2004); Julius Gathogo, "Francis Akanu Ibiam (1906–1995): A Leader Who Had a Mission Beyond Ecclesia," *Studia Historiae Ecclesiasticae* 41, no. 1 (2015): 222–38; Mercy Oduyoye, "Biafra Faith-Based Humanitarian Intervention: Basis in the World Council of Churches," *CIHA Blog* (blog), May 24, 2016, http://www.cihablog.com/biafra-faith-based-humanitarian-intervention-basis-world-council-churches/; Hans von Rütte, "The Problem of How to Enact Diakonia:

The World Council of Churches and the Nigerian Civil War, 1967–1970," *CIHA Blog* (blog), May 19, 2016, http://www.cihablog.com/problem-enact -diakonia-world-council-churches-nigerian-civil-war-1967-1970/.

9. Thierry Hentsch, *Face au Blocus: Histoire de l'intervention du Comité International de la Croix-Rouge dans le Conflit du Nigéria, 1967–1970* (Genève: Droz, 1973); Denis Maillard, "1968–2008: Le Biafra ou le sens de l'humanitaire," *Humanitaire: Enjeux, Pratiques, Débats* 18 (Spring 2008), http://humanitaire .revues.org/182; Arua Oko Omaka, "Humanitarian Action: The Joint Church Aid and Health Care Intervention in the Nigeria-Biafra War, 1967–1970," *Canadian Journal of History* 49, no. 3 (December 2014): 423; Tony Byrne, *Airlift to Biafra: Breaching the Blockade* (Dublin: Columba Press, 1997); Stanley Meisler, "Food Pilots Risk Lives to Keep Biafrans Alive: Perilous Nightly Airlift of Joint Church Aid Now Almost Only Source of Relief," *Los Angeles Times*, October 7, 1969.

10. On the American Committee to Keep Biafra Alive, see Brian McNeil, "'And Starvation Is the Grim Reaper': The American Committee to Keep Biafra Alive and the Genocide Question During the Nigerian Civil War, 1968–70," *Journal of Genocide Research* 16, no. 2–3 (July 2014): 317–36.

11. Important earlier scholarship includes John J. Stremlau, *The International Politics of the Nigerian Civil War, 1967–1970* (Princeton, NJ: Princeton University Press, 1977); Laurie S. Wiseberg, "The International Politics of Relief: A Case Study of the Relief Operations Mounted During the Nigerian Civil War (1967–1970)" (PhD diss., University of California, Los Angeles, 1973); Suzanne Cronjé, *The World and Nigeria: The Diplomatic History of the Biafran War, 1967–1970* (London: Sidgwick and Jackson, 1972).

12. On Médecins Sans Frontières, see Peter Redfield, *Life in Crisis: The Ethical Journey of Doctors Without Borders* (Berkeley: University of California Press, 2013); Samuel Moyn and Jan Eckel, eds., *The Breakthrough: Human Rights in the 1970s* (Philadelphia: University of Pennsylvania Press, 2013); Marie-Luce Desgrandchamps, "Revenir Sur Le Mythe Fondateur de Médecins Sans Frontières: Les Relations Entre Les Médecins Français et Le CICR Pendant La Guerre Du Biafra (1967–1970)," *Relations Internationales* 146 (June 2011): 95–108. New scholarship on the war includes A. Dirk Moses and Lasse Heerten, eds., *Postcolonial Conflict and the Question of Genocide: The Nigeria-Biafra War, 1967–1970* (New York: Routledge, 2017); Brenda Gayle Plummer, *In Search of Power: African Americans in the Era of Decolonization, 1956–1974* (Cambridge: Cambridge University Press, 2013); Kevin O'Sullivan, *Ireland, Africa, and the End of Empire: Small State Identity in the Cold War 1955–75* (Manchester: Manchester University Press, 2014); Karen E. Smith, *Genocide and the Europeans* (Cambridge: Cambridge University Press, 2010); Michael Gould, *The Biafran War: The Struggle for Modern Nigeria* (New York: Tauris, 2013); Douglas Anthony, "'Resourceful and Progressive Blackmen':

Modernity and Race in Biafra, 1967–70," *Journal of African History* 51, no. 1 (2010): 41–61; McNeil, "'And Starvation Is the Grim Reaper.'"

13. Lasse Heerten, *The Biafran War and Postcolonial Humanitarianism: Spectacles of Suffering* (Cambridge: Cambridge University Press, 2017), 175; Michael Rothberg, *Multidirectional Memory: Remembering the Holocaust in the Age of Decolonization* (Stanford, CA: Stanford University Press, 2009).

14. Pierre Bourdieu, *The Field of Cultural Production: Essays on Art and Literature* (New York: Columbia University Press, 1993); Pierre Bourdieu, *The Logic of Practice* (Stanford, CA: Stanford University Press, 1990).

15. Bourdieu, *The Field of Cultural Production*, 30.

16. On the AJC's history and the relationship of Zionist to non-Zionist organizations, see Michael N. Barnett, *The Star and the Stripes: A History of the Foreign Policies of American Jews* (Princeton, NJ: Princeton University Press, 2016); Doug Rossinow, "'The Edge of the Abyss': The Origins of the Israel Lobby, 1949–1954," *Modern American History* 1, no. 1 (March 2018): 23–43; Menahem Kaufman, *An Ambiguous Partnership: Non-Zionists and Zionists in America, 1939–1948* (Detroit, MI: Wayne State University Press, 1991). On AJC and protecting minority rights, see Geoffrey P. Levin, "Liberal Whispers and Propaganda Fears: The American Jewish Committee and Israel's Palestinian Minority, 1948–1966," *Israel Studies Review* 33, no. 1 (Spring 2018): 81–101.

17. Lawrence Grossberg, "Transformation Through Crisis: The American Jewish Committee and the Six-Day War," *American Jewish History* 86, no. 1 (1998): 32.

18. Gerald S. Strober, *Confronting Hate: The Untold Story of the Rabbi Who Stood Up for Human Rights, Racial Justice, and Religious Reconciliation* (New York: Skyhorse, 2019); Magdalena Dziaczkowska, "American Judaism and the Second Vatican Council: The Response of the American Jewish Committee to Nostra Aetate," *U.S. Catholic Historian* 38, no. 3 (2020): 25–47.

19. Phyllis Palmer, *Living as Equals: How Three White Communities Struggled to Make Interracial Connections During the Civil Rights Era* (Nashville, TN: Vanderbilt University Press, 2008), chap. 1.

20. Yaakov Ariel, "Interfaith Dialogue and the Golden Age of Christian-Jewish Relations," *Studies in Christian-Jewish Relations* 6 (2011): 1–18.

21. Jonathan Magonet, "The Growth of Interfaith Dialogue," *European Judaism* 48, no. 2 (2015): 38–45; Yaakov Ariel, "Jewish-Christian Dialogue," in *The Wiley-Blackwell Companion to Inter-Religious Dialogue* (New York: Wiley, 2013), 205–23; Palmer, *Living as Equals*.

22. Member groups included the American Jewish Committee, American Jewish Congress, American Joint Distribution Committee, B'nai B'rith, Jewish Labor Committee, National Community Relations Advisory Council, National Council of Young Israel, the Union of American Hebrew Congregations, and the World Jewish Congress. "A Year Later: Summary of the American Jewish

Emergency Effort for Biafran Relief," July 1969, Interreligious Affairs, box 85, folder 4x, American Jewish Committee Archives, New York.

23. "Draft Memo from Rabbi James Rudin to Bert Gold," February 4, 1969, Interreligious Affairs, box 86, folder 3, American Jewish Committee Archives, New York. In the first year, the Emergency Committee initially made allocations to CRS (Catholic) and CWS (Protestant). In February 1969, it joined the coalition of CRS, CWS, and AJC, which became the channel for donations from the Emergency Committee.

24. Marc Tanenbaum, "Biafra: Test Case of Interreligious Relevance," Rabbi Tanenbaum Collection, doc 2, box 5, ms-603, American Jewish Committee Archives, New York.

25. AJC Press Release, October 12, 1969, box 86, folder 4x, American Jewish Committee Archives, New York.

26. Luc Boltanski, *Distant Suffering: Morality, Media and Politics*, trans. Graham D. Burchell (Cambridge: Cambridge University Press, 1999).

27. Levin, "Liberal Whispers and Propaganda Fears." See also Levin's forthcoming book on American Jewish organizations and Israel, *Seeing Another People: American Jews, Palestinian Rights, and the Early U.S.-Israel Relationship*.

28. Lawrence Grossman, "Transformation Through Crisis: The American Jewish Committee and the Six-Day War," *American Jewish History* 86, no. 1 (1998): 39.

29. As Doug Rossinow has made clear, this idea that Israeli leaders would not interfere in American Jewish affairs was not the policy of many of the major Jewish organizations and certainly was not a reality in practice. Rossinow, "'The Edge of the Abyss.'"

30. Grossman, "Transformation Through Crisis."

31. Arthur Hertzberg, "Israel and American Jewry," *Commentary* (August 1967): 69, https://www.commentary.org/articles/arthur-hertzberg/israel-and-american-jewry/.

32. Amy Kaplan, *Our American Israel: The Story of an Entangled Alliance* (Cambridge, MA: Harvard University Press, 2018).

33. Melani McAlister, *Epic Encounters: Culture, Media, and U.S. Interests in the Middle East Since 1945*, 2nd ed. (Berkeley: University of California Press, 2005); Michelle Mart, *Eye on Israel: How America Came to View Israel as an Ally* (Albany: State University of New York Press, 2007); Caitlin Carenen, *The Fervent Embrace: Liberal Protestants, Evangelicals, and Israel* (New York: New York University Press, 2012); Hillary Kaell, *Walking Where Jesus Walked: American Christians and Holy Land Pilgrimage* (New York: New York University Press, 2014).

34. NCC Resolution, July 1967, quoted in S. Shepard Jones, "The Status of Jerusalem: Some National and International Aspects," *Law and Contemporary Problems* 33, no. 1 (1968): 169–182.

35. Carenen, *The Fervent Embrace*, 137. As Carenen notes, the religious historian Martin Marty pushed back against the criticism of mainline Protestants as being unfair, particularly on the question of their silence during the very short period of the war itself. Martin E. Marty, "Christians and Jews: An Inconclusive Quest for Accord," *Christian Century* (February 12, 1969): 206–207.

36. John Dart, "Christians' Silence in Mideast Crisis Deplored by Rabbi: Rabbis' Meeting," *Los Angeles Times*, June 23, 1967.

37. Balfour Brickner, "No Ease in Zion for Us," *Christianity and Crisis* 27, no. 15 (September 1967): 200–204. See also Carenen, *The Fervent Embrace*, chap. 5.

38. Grossman, "Transformation Through Crisis." 49. For example, Lucy Dawidowicz, "American Public Opinion," in *The American Jewish Yearbook, 1968*, ed. American Jewish Committee (New York: Springer, 1969), 198–229.

39. Marc H. Tanenbaum, "Israel's Hour of Need and the Jewish-Christian Dialogue," *Conservative Judaism* 22 (Winter 1969): 112.

40. Carenen, *The Fervent Embrace*, 140.

41. Tanenbaum, "Israel's Hour of Need and the Jewish-Christian Dialogue," 118.

42. Tanenbaum, "Biafra: Test Case of Interreligious Relevance," 6.

43. Marc Tanenbaum, "The Meaning of Israel: A Jewish Voice," paper delivered at Southern Baptist-Jewish Scholar Conference," August 18–20, 1969, at Southern Baptist Theological Seminary, Louisville, Kentucky, ms 603, box 2, folder 14, 5, American Jewish Committee Archives, New York.

44. Tanenbaum, "The Meaning of Israel: A Jewish Voice," 6.

45. Tanenbaum, "The Meaning of Israel: A Jewish Voice."

46. Peter Novick, *The Holocaust and Collective Memory* (London: Bloomsbury, 2001); Edward Linenthal, *Preserving Memory: The Struggle to Create America's Holocaust Museum* (New York: Columbia University Press, 2001); Kaplan, *Our American Israel*.

47. "Simon Obi Anekwe letter to Y. Rabin & M. Abram," June 26, 1968, box 86, folder 3, American Jewish Committee Archives, New York.

48. "Donatus U. Anyanwu letter to Phillip Hoffman," November 7, 1969, box 86, folder 4x, American Jewish Committee Archives, New York.

49. McNeil, "'And Starvation Is the Grim Reaper.'"

50. Plummer, *In Search of Power*, 194. Or, as Meriwether put it, African Americans had "tended to focus on the travails of liberation struggles as opposed to the trials of newly independent Africa." James H. Meriwether, *Proudly We Can Be Africans: Black Americans and Africa, 1935–1961* (Chapel Hill: University of North Carolina Press, 2002), 240.

51. The most comprehensive analysis of African American responses is James Farquharson, "'Black America Cares': The Response of African Americans to the Nigerian Civil War, 1967–1970," dissertation at Australian Catholic University, 2019, which discusses both King's presence in Lagos in 1960 (65) and the history of the ANCLA (101–137). See also Farquharson, "'Black America

Cares': The Response of African-Americans to Civil War and 'Genocide' in Nigeria, 1967–70," in *Postcolonial Conflict and the Question of Genocide: The Nigeria-Biafra War, 1967–1970*, ed. A. Dirk Moses and Lasse Heerten (New York: Routledge, 2018), 301–25. In addition: "4 Top Rights Leaders Consider Africa Trip," *Chicago Daily Defender*, December 23, 1967; Wiseberg, "International Politics of Relief," 230. African American leaders' interest in mediating continued even after King's death: "Black Americans Urge Peace in Nigeria," *The Crisis*, July 1969, 246-247.

52. Farquharson, "'Black America Cares,'" 311. A contemporary argument for more attention to Igbo suffering is also in Charles L. Sanders, "The War Between Blacks Nobody Cares About: Oil Money, Tribal Customs Spur Terrible Civil War in Nigeria," *Jet*, July 27, 1967.

53. Farquharson, "'Black America Cares,'" 321.

54. "Position Paper of Joint Afro Committee on Biafra," n.d., box 3, folder 10, ACKBA Collection, Hoover Institution. See Sean L. Malloy, *Out of Oakland: Black Panther Party Internationalism During the Cold War* (Ithaca, NY; Cornell University Press, 2017); Keisha Blain, *Set the World on Fire: Black Nationalist Women and the Global Struggle for Freedom* (Philadelphia: University of Pennsylvania Press, 2018).

55. "Nigerian-Biafran Relief Situation," hearings before the United States Senate, Committee on Foreign Relations, Subcommittee on African Affairs, 19th Cong., 2nd Sess., October 4, 1968, 55–58.

56. Moses Newson, "Biafran Fails to Explain Relief Duplicity, Avoidable Costs," *Afro-American*, December 13, 1969.

57. Memo Sidney Liskofsky to Marc Tanenbaum, April 24, 1969, box 86, folder 3x, American Jewish Committee Archives, New York. Within a couple of years, Liskofsky would become the founding director of the Jacob Blaustein Institute for the Advancement of Human Rights to help institutionalize universal human rights standards and monitoring. "Paid Notice: Deaths: Liskofsky, Sidney," *New York Times*, June 12, 2005.

58. There is a rich scholarship on the Bandung conference, much of which challenges the mythical place it holds in some histories of the Third World. Recent work includes Amitav Acharya and See Seng Tan, eds., *Bandung Revisited: The Legacy of the 1955 Asian-African Conference for International Order* (Singapore: National University of Singapore Press, 2008); Frank Gerits, "Bandung as the Call for a Better Development Project: US, British, French and Gold Coast Perceptions of the Afro-Asian Conference (1955)," *Cold War History* 16, no. 3 (July 2, 2016): 255–72; Christopher J. Lee, ed., *Making a World after Empire: The Bandung Moment and Its Political Afterlives*, (Athens: Ohio University Press, 2010); Su Lin Lewis and Carolien Stolte, "Other Bandungs: Afro-Asian Internationalisms in the Early Cold War," *Journal of World History* 30, no. 1 (2019):

1–19; Gerard McCann, "Where Was the Afro in Afro-Asian Solidarity? Africa's 'Bandung Moment' in 1950s Asia," *Journal of World History* 30, no. 1 (2019): 89–123; Quỳnh N. Phạm and Robbie Shilliam, eds., *Meanings of Bandung: Postcolonial Orders and Decolonial Visions* (New York: Rowman & Littlefield International, 2016); Vijay Prashad, *The Darker Nations: A People's History of the Third World* (New York: New Press, 2008); Carolien Stolte, "'The People's Bandung': Local Anti-Imperialists on an Afro-Asian Stage," *Journal of World History* 30, no. 1 (2019): 125–56.; Robert Vitalis, "The Midnight Ride of Kwame Nkrumah and Other Fables of Bandung (Ban-Doong)," *Humanity* 4, no. 2 (2013): 261–88.

On the links between Palestinians and other revolutionary or radical movements, see Alex Lubin, *Geographies of Liberation: The Making of an Afro-Arab Political Imaginary* (Chapel Hill: University of North Carolina Press, 2014); Paul Chamberlin, *The Global Offensive: The United States, the Palestine Liberation Organization, and the Making of the Post-Cold War Order* (New York: Oxford University Press, 2012).

59. Zach Levey, "Israel, Nigeria and the Biafra Civil War, 1967–1970," in *Postcolonial Conflict and the Question of Genocide: The Nigeria-Biafra War, 1967–1970*, ed. A. Dirk Moses and Lasse Heerten (New York: Routledge, 2017), 177–97.

60. Melani McAlister, *The Kingdom of God Has No Borders* (New York: Oxford University Press, 2018); Yaakov Ariel, *An Unusual Relationship: Evangelical Christians and Jews* (New York: NYU Press, 2013); Stephen Spector, *Evangelicals and Israel: The Story of American Christian Zionism* (New York: Oxford University Press, 2008); Daniel G. Hummel, *Covenant Brothers: Evangelicals, Jews, and U.S.-Israeli Relations* (Philadelphia: University of Pennsylvania Press, 2019); Samuel Goldman, *God's Country: Christian Zionism in America* (Philadelphia: University of Pennsylvania Press, 2018).

CHAPTER 17

Contentious Designs

Ideology and U.S. Immigration Policy

DANIEL TICHENOR

A s underscored by recent refugee and asylum crises, targeted immigration bans, pandemic-related travel restrictions, and border security controversies, the centrality of international migration to foreign policy has been unmistakable during the past decade. In truth, this is far from novel. Immigration has long been a touchstone for debates over economic, security, and humanitarian concerns that are significant to international relations. From Cold War administrations melding immigration and refugee policy with geopolitical imperatives to congressional majorities focused on strengthening economic competitiveness or science and technology, immigration control lies at the intersection of domestic and international politics.[1] Immigration policy is formative not only of what a nation is and will become but also of what image and ideals it projects in the world. Across U.S. history, struggles over immigration have been influenced by rival notions of isolationism and internationalism, mingling easily with durable nativist and cosmopolitan traditions. The deep ideological tensions fueled by immigration in the United States over time has produced recurring conflict, key legal and policy contradictions, and notable distance between avowed democratic beliefs and illiberal practices.[2]

Amid partisan hyperpolarization of U.S. politics in general and of immigration policy in particular, one might logically assume that Americans largely fall into two warring ideological camps on this issue. On one side of this rendering are immigration restrictionists, including former president

Donald Trump, Senator Tom Cotton, and other Republicans whose ferocious attacks on undocumented Latin American immigrants and Muslim refugees energize their conservative base. On the other are immigration defenders, led by Dreamers and elected Democrats who resisted draconian initiatives such as the Muslim ban, efforts to "build the wall," and family separation. Indeed, one can trace this bifurcation over decades. Well before Trump's political ascendance, the Obama administration's Deferred Action for Childhood Arrivals (DACA) yielded similar polarization, eliciting celebration in progressive political circles and outrage among Tea Party activists. Six years earlier, in 2006, U.S. Senate movement on comprehensive immigration reform unleashed a furious backlash from conservative media and base voters at roughly the same time as immigrants and liberal supporters launched unprecedented nationwide protests against a tough House enforcement bill.[3] The problem with this interpretation, of course, is that the ideological underpinnings of U.S. immigration policy are anything but neat and clean.

In truth, the great partisan divide associated with immigration in American politics—both past and present—belies the contemporary and historical fact that Republicans and conservatives have supported robust immigration and that Democrats and liberals have advanced immigration restrictions. Immigrant rights activists grew so outraged by the vigor with which the Obama administration detained and deported record numbers of undocumented immigrants in its first term that they launched nationwide protests and rebuked the president as "Deporter-in-Chief."[4] Trump's GOP predecessor in the Oval Office, George W. Bush, embraced new immigration as he urged reforms that "match willing workers with willing employers."[5] In similar fashion, the core ideas that animate U.S. immigration politics often defy simple binaries such as restriction versus openness or xenophobia versus xenophilia. Consider, for example, the diverse ways in which prominent U.S. political leaders and policy activists have framed the cause of immigration restriction. Some argue that sharp distinctions should be drawn between welcoming legal immigrants who play by the rules and cracking down on unauthorized immigrants who disregard our laws. Others object to the legal immigration preference system, calling for limits on specific categories such as family-based visas or refugee relief. Classically, U.S. nativists have been hostile to "new" immigrants of particular national origins and pressed for policies that advance notions of ethnic, racial, and religious hierarchy. Many restrictionists have sought to keep out immigrants deemed too politically radical or threatening to national security. Some have targeted homosexual migrants and those with AIDS for exclusion. Still others have advocated decreased immigration to protect the economic well-being of American workers and vulnerable groups. This list does not include restrictionist rationales connected to environmental protection, public health, social welfare dependency, and other claims. In other words, immigration restriction has assumed varied forms and meant different things to political actors across the U.S. political spectrum over time.[6] Defenses of immigration reflect similar variegation championed by disparate opinion leaders. To better understand the U.S. immigration debate, it is useful to reach beyond reductionist binaries and identify the richer patterns of American thought on this contentious issue.

We might gain greater traction on core ideas at the heart of U.S. immigration discourse and policy by mapping ideological convictions along two dimensions. Consider, for example, one dimension that concentrates on immigration numbers and divides those who support expansive immigration opportunities and robust numbers from those who favor substantial new restrictions on alien admissions. Then consider a second dimension that focuses on the rights of noncitizens residing in the United States and distinguishes those who endorse the provision of a broad set of civil, political, and social rights to newcomers from those who advocate strict limitations on the rights accorded to noncitizens. These two dimensions of immigrant admissions and rights help us illuminate four durable ideological traditions on immigration in American political thought. We can discern *classic restrictionists* who ardently favor stringent limits on both immigrant numbers and rights, as well as *liberal cosmopolitans* who just as strongly believe in expansive immigration and the "democratic dignity" (to borrow Herman Melville's memorable phrase) of all new Americans. We also can identify *social justice restrictionists* who intriguingly call for less immigration while supporting broad membership rights for new arrivals, and *market expansionists* who inversely embrace large-scale immigration to meet the nation's labor needs while favoring significant limits on the rights of noncitizens. As we shall see, these perspectives reflect four rather durable ideological traditions that have found expression in national debates and political struggles over immigration.

This chapter is divided into two key parts. The first illuminates the interrelated set of ideas and beliefs that comprise each of the four U.S. ideological traditions on immigration. The second investigates these moving ideological parts in action. A number of influential works—from Michael

Hunt's *Ideology and U.S. Foreign Policy*, which helped inspire this conference, to Rogers Smith's *Civic Ideals*[7]—poignantly explore what powerful ideas mean for U.S. law and policy. Yet fewer studies address other key questions: What are the specific processes by which potent ideas become public policy, and how exactly do some key ideas influence policy choices and outcomes while others do not? Ideas are not translated into law on their own accord. In addition to analyzing the rival ideas and epic ideological clashes that immigration elicits in American politics, in this chapter I also discuss key reform periods in the early twentieth century and the Cold War era that capture ideological tensions, political struggle, and uneven policy reform.

U.S. Ideological Conceptions of Immigrant Admissions and Rights

For generations, Americans have woven immigration narratives and iconography into their collective cultural identity; indeed, the idea that the United States is "a nation of immigrants" has been popular at least since then senator John F. Kennedy penned a book of that title sixty years ago. Yet the resonance of Donald Trump's populist assaults on immigrant "others" also captures the tenacious power of nativist and xenophobic ideas in American political life. *Classic restrictionists* favor sweeping limits on both immigrant admissions and rights, often on ethnic, racial, and religious grounds. Benjamin Franklin's infamous 1750s attack on German immigrants for not adopting local customs, lacking intelligence, and being "swarthy" in complexion set the tone.[8] During the Federal Constitutional Convention, delegates such as Pierce Butler, Governeur Morris, and Elbridge Gerry warned that immigrants had divided loyalties and thus should not fully participate in the political process. Yet their concerns were tepid compared to the exclusionary views expressed by anti-Federalists such as Agrippa in the ratification process. Agrippa insisted that states have authority to sharply restrict immigration and naturalization "to keep their blood pure," adding that "keeping separate from the foreign mixtures" was crucial for guarding "religion and good morals."[9]

Since the nation's founding, significant shifts in the ethnic, racial, and religious composition of immigration have been viewed by classic restrictionists as perilous to the nation's well-being. Ohio missionary Josiah Strong warned, in his popular book *Our Country*, that new immigration was like "a peaceful invasion by an army more than four times as vast as the estimated number of Goths and Vandals that . . . overwhelmed Rome." Consistent with key elements of *classic restrictionism*, Strong associated new European immigrants with criminality, racial inferiority, religious zealotry, cultural degeneracy, poverty, and political corruption.[10] In the same period, the California Anti-Chinese Convention proclaimed that "the strong nations of the earth are now, as they always have been, the most thoroughly homogenous nations, that is to say, the most nearly of one race, language, and manners." Decades later, from the other side of the continent, Harvard president A. Lawrence Lowell invoked nearly identical language in response to new southern and eastern European immigration, underscoring "the need for homogeneity in a democracy." This need, he insisted, stands "as a basis for popular government . . . that justifies democracies in resisting the influx in great numbers of a widely different race."[11] In addition to narratives of immigration fueling "race suicide," classic restrictionists also highlight the economic dangers that "new" immigrants pose as job-takers and welfare-dependents. Immigration's challenges to law and order is another key tenet. Twentieth-century classic restrictionists, for example, warned that Italian and Jewish newcomers were prone to "personal violence," "criminality," and "radicalism in politics." From this perspective, illegal immigration looms as nothing short of an unprecedented breakdown of American sovereignty, and proposals for amnesty or legalization appear to be unethical rewards to those who break the rules. Knitting these themes together, Donald Trump's depiction of Mexicans, Muslims, "illegals," and migrant "caravans" as dire threats to public order—like Patrick Buchanan, Tom Tancredo, Samuel Huntington, and Steve King before him—is deeply rooted in a vision of ethnic nationalism in which nonwhite immigrants imperil the culture, security, and economic well-being of native-born white Americans.[12]

Liberal cosmopolitans endorse expansive immigrant admissions and the full inclusion of newcomers in the national political community. Their ideals found prominent expression in the early American republic. In 1776, for instance, Thomas Paine celebrated what he saw as the "triumph" of liberal brotherhood among Americans of diverse European origins. The strength of the new nation, he noted, stemmed from the equal liberty and political rights of English, Dutch, German, Swedish, and other groups in the United States. "In this extensive quarter of the globe, we forget the narrow limits of three hundred and sixty miles [the extent of England] and carry our friendship on a larger scale," Paine reveled. "We surmount the force of local prejudices as we enlarge our acquaintance with the world." In prototypical *liberal cosmopolitan* terms, Paine believed that the United States—precisely because of the history of its people and their devotion to self-government— has a special obligation to extend "asylum for the persecuted lovers of civil and religious liberty" from across the globe.[13] This revolutionary faith in a distinctively American asylum ideal was widely held among many of the founding leaders. "America is open to receive not only the Opulent and respectable Stranger," George Washington pledged in 1783, "but the oppressed and persecuted of all Nations and Religions."[14]

Liberal cosmopolitans believe that large-scale immigration is socially and economically beneficial to the United States and that the nation's assimilative capacities are vast. From Ralph Waldo Emerson and Jane Addams to Luis Gutierrez and Jose Antonio Vargas, these cosmopolitans have defended cultural pluralism and heterogeneous immigration. Contrary to classic restrictionist claims about homogeneity, they believe U.S. democracy is nurtured by diversity and an "open society," to borrow the phrase coined by Kennedy aid Abba Schwartz. These political actors and thinkers have ardently opposed efforts to make immigrant groups into marginalized and disenfranchised subclasses in American society. The abolitionist Senator Charles Sumner argued in 1855 that committed egalitarians should loathe both slavery and nativism. Denouncing those who "attaint men for religion and also for birth," he expressed faith that American nationhood was defined by "Civil Freedom" and the democratic inclusion of outsiders and their offspring. "Ourselves children of the Pilgrims of a former generation, let us not turn from the Pilgrims of the present," he proclaimed. "The history of our country, in the humblest as well as the most exalted spheres, testifies to the merit of foreigners."[15] A century later, the progressive labor leader Hyman Bookbinder directly challenged nativist visions of ethnic nationalism. "The true image of America is the kaleidoscope," he told Congress. "It is a mosaic of human beings that is always changing but encased in a basic framework of freedom, of brotherhood, of tolerance."[16]

Market expansionists embrace expansive immigrant admissions to meet labor demands and to promote national prosperity. In his "Report on Manufactures," Alexander Hamilton noted that it was in the country's fundamental interest "to open every possible avenue to emigration from abroad." Consistent with his ambition to build a commercial empire, he saw immigrants as "an important resource, not only for extending the population, and with it the useful and productive labor of the country, but likewise for the prosecution of manufactures."[17] Nearly a century later, steel magnate Andrew Carnegie lauded robust immigration as "a golden stream which flows into the country each year."[18] The integration and democratic inclusion of newcomers was not Hamilton's nor Carnegie's priority. Whereas liberal cosmopolitans have been deeply committed to extending broad membership rights to aliens living and working in the United States, market expansionists generally have not. As celebrants of entrepreneurial and self-sufficient newcomers, and as champions of employers benefiting from the flow of labor across borders, these probusiness actors have resisted immigrants organizing for worker rights or deemed "likely to become a public charge." Indeed, market-oriented defenders of expansive immigration numbers also have supported measures denying welfare and other public benefits for noncitizens. The telling political slogan of market expansionists in 1996, led by Republican lawmakers such as Senator Spencer Abraham and House Majority Leader Dick Armey, was "Immigration yes, welfare no!"[19]

For immigration defenders devoted to unregulated labor markets and business growth, the chief policy problem is that existing federal policies fail to address "the reality," as former president Bush put it, "that there are many people on the other side of our border who will do anything to come to America to work." In short, the U.S. economy has grown dependent on this supply of cheap, unskilled labor.[20] To market expansionists, the solution lies in regularizing employers' access to this vital foreign labor; if the back door is to be closed, then this labor supply must be secured through temporary worker programs and an expansion of employment-based legal immigration.

Social justice restrictionists favor reductions in immigration on the grounds that porous borders and an unfettered supply of foreign labor creates economic competition for the country's least advantaged citizens, undermines efforts to organize and protect American workers, and strains the welfare state. At the same time, they have tended to share with liberal cosmopolitans a strong belief that immigrants already living and working in the country should not be subjugated but rather should enjoy many of the same rights and freedoms of native-born citizens. The political thought of Frederick Douglass captures these convictions well. In the midst of Reconstruction, Douglass called for limits to be imposed on European immigration in frustration over the enormous economic challenges faced by African Americans. "Every hour sees the black man elbowed out of employment by some newly arrived immigrant whose hunger and whose color are thought to give him a better title and place," he lamented. However, Douglass had no tolerance for discrimination and violence against immigrants already living on American soil. He was especially disquieted by the fierce repression of Chinese and other Asian migrants on the West Coast. As the Chinese faced mob violence and repressive policies in the West and Congress mobilized for total exclusion, Douglass became a passionate advocate of Chinese rights. "There are such things in the world as human rights," he told audiences in language closely aligned to liberal cosmopolitans. "They rest upon no conventional foundation, but are external, universal, and indestructible." These rights, he asserted, should apply to the "Chinese and the Japanese, and for all other varieties of men. . . . I know of no rights of race superior to the rights of humanity."[21]

At the heart of Douglass's ideas about immigration and alien rights was lifelong outrage over U.S. white supremacy and white nationalism and a concomitant devotion to social and racial justice. His concerns about large-scale immigrant admissions did not stem from the anti-Catholic, antiradical, or ethnic and racial animus that motivated classic restrictionists. Rather, his frustration with robust immigration opportunities was fueled by what he perceived as the ease with which Irish and German newcomers secured work, access to the ballot box, and other membership rights, whereas African Americans received de jure citizenship under the Fourteenth and Fifteenth Amendments and de facto inequality and subjugation. Generations later, we can discern very similar ideas being advanced by African American leaders Bayard Rustin and Barbara Jordan. As chair of the U.S. Commission on Immigration Reform in the 1990s, Jordan advocated reductions in annual admissions because of "the impact of immigration on the most disadvantaged within our already resident society—inner city youth, racial and ethnic minorities, and recent immigrants who have not yet adjusted to life in the U.S." However, she was equally compelling in her defense of noncitizen access to health care, welfare, and other public benefits, arguing that the government should not "lift the safety net out from under individuals who, we hope, will become integral parts of our social community."[22]

Until the 1950s, the country's most prominent labor unions and federations typically aligned with immigration restriction. Their main rationale was that an unfettered supply of immigrant workers undercut the wages, working conditions, and job security of U.S.-born laborers. American Federation of Labor (AFL) president Samuel Gompers observed that "freedom" for workers around the globe required "those devoted to the cause to remain within their own countries and help in national struggles." Immigration restriction supported by *national* labor movements was the only means of protecting domestic workers from "low wages and bad working conditions." In short, the AFL and other labor organizations framed their support for major barriers to new immigration in the social justice terms of guarding the economic well-being of the nation's working-class. By the 1960s, Cesar Chavez provided labor leadership that more closely resembled the convictions of Frederick Douglass. Chavez complained bitterly that undocumented Mexicans were being recruited by agribusinesses to undermine his efforts to organize farm workers, and he urged allies such as Senator Robert Kennedy to strengthen the border, but he also vigorously championed Latinx civil rights.[23]

Rival ideological traditions are a fundamental feature of U.S. immigration politics. Indeed, clashing ideas and beliefs about immigrant admissions and rights have meant that none of the four camps identified has been able to secure significant policy innovation independently. Major legal and policy change is always arduous in an American political system replete with structural veto points, but the deep ideological conflicts over immigration long have made comprehensive reform in this policy realm a reflection of contradictory elements. In the pages that follow, I focus on two periods of policy struggle and reform—the early twentieth century and the 1960s—to illustrate how rival ideological commitments shape and inform U.S. immigration and refugee policy over time.

New Immigration, Rival Camps, and Policy Breakthrough, 1896–1928

In the 1890s, an immigration restriction movement emerged in national politics that boasted grassroots support in every region of the country. Akin to the populist anti-Chinese campaign that swept across the American West two decades earlier, turn of the century nativists railed against new southern and eastern Europeans who they cast as racially inferior and economically threatening. It was a message they honed at public rallies and in newspapers and magazines, one that appealed to conservative nationalists and xenophobes as well as to American Federation of Labor (AFL) leaders and insecure native-born workers.[24] Championing a literacy test and other restrictions designed to bar most southern and eastern European immigrants, Senator Henry Cabot Lodge (R-MA) proclaimed that these measures would protect the nation from economic inferiors who take jobs from U.S. workers. But the economic threat was reinforced by grave demographic perils: "It involves nothing less than the possibility of a great and perilous change in the fabric of our race."[25] Grassroots supporters of Lodge's bill lobbied Congress to enact the literacy test bill, including members of the Immigration Restriction League (IRL), workers from AFL unions, veterans, and farmers.

Of course, a variety of immigration defenders challenged nativist ideas and policy designs. "It is said that the quality of recent immigration is undesirable," outgoing president Grover Cleveland declared. "The time is quite within recent memory when the same thing was said of immigrants who, with their descendants, are now numbered among our best citizens."[26] Ethnic and religious leaders organized huge rallies in cities nationwide in 1898, and Irish, German, Italian, Greek, Jewish, and Catholic speakers highlighted U.S. immigration traditions, ethnic diversity, and the costs of "separating families."[27] Cosmopolitans such as the aging abolitionist William Lloyd Garrison spoke of "rights and justice" for immigrants. Market expansionists depicted robust new immigration as a natural and welcome product of national economic growth. Key business organizations such as the National Association of Manufacturers, steamship companies, and various industrialists joined with ethnic, religious, and social justice groups to form a potent Immigration Protective League. Immigration House members representing urban districts with sizable foreign-born populations pledged to defeat Lodge's bill. With nativists and immigration defenders articulating rival ideas and mobilizing both mass-based support and well-positioned allies in the halls of Congress, major immigration reform produced contentious deadlock and ultimately inaction.[28]

A significant campaign for immigration reform in 1906 followed a similar path, with competing ideas, opposing mobilizations at the grassroots, and polarizing conflict in Washington ending in failure. But immigration restrictionists mounted a renewed push for a literacy test and other hurdles targeting new immigration in the 1910s. Their movement enjoyed support in both elite circles and among mass publics. A federal commission staffed by eugenicists issued findings that fortified nativist claims that southern and eastern European immigration imperiled the nation's future.[29] Commission reports were hailed by restriction-minded social, intellectual, and economic elites who favored new forms of "social control" during the progressive era. They formed an uneasy alliance with labor leaders and craft unions who saw newcomers as threatening to fair wages and working conditions.[30] Another key element of the restrictionist coalition were farm groups and patriotic societies whose members looked at new ethnic enclaves in burgeoning cities with suspicion and dread. As in previous years, business, ethnic, and social justice leaders expressed contrasting ideological convictions and formed a potent lobbying force to defeat literacy test legislation in Congress.[31]

The political fortunes of the immigration restriction movement changed with the onset of World War I. The war itself reduced immigration to the United States from 1.4 million in 1914 to 300,000 in 1916. At a time when national security anxieties were high and calls for unity muzzled many ethnic associations, restrictionist groups, including the AFL, the IRL, patriotic societies, and agrarian associations, stepped up pressure on Congress. A bipartisan coalition of nativist lawmakers in both houses enacted a new law that made admission contingent upon payment of an $8 head tax and passage of a literacy test. Conflict over the measure was broad and very public, and opponents from President Woodrow Wilson to social reformers such as Jane Addams denounced the legislation as inconsistent with U.S. liberal democratic traditions. More privately, when the new requirements slowed the flow of Mexican workers across the nation's southern border, southwestern growers, ranchers, miners, railroad companies, and lawmakers persuaded the Labor Department to waive the literacy test and head taxes for Mexican laborers. In this way, immigration policy innovation publicly met nativist demands while quietly accommodating the labor needs of powerful interests.

When the literacy test failed to limit southern and eastern European immigration, nativists pressed for new reform. During the first Red Scare, immigration restrictionists won passage of an explicitly discriminatory national origins quota system that drastically cut all immigration and reserved most visas for northern and western Europeans. Under the banner of enhancing American unity and security, nativist reformers advanced immigration barriers that reflected a vision of U.S. nationhood rooted in illiberal notions of ethnic, racial, and religious hierarchy. But even as they won stringent limits on new European arrivals, ideological tensions continued to produce legal and policy contradictions. The AFL, the IRL, patriotic societies, and a number of northern lawmakers favored barriers to Latin and South American immigration on protectionist and racial grounds. In contrast, southern and western employers and political representatives supported national origins quotas for overseas immigration but also fiercely advocated for access to cheap Mexican labor.[32] Confronted with stalemate or defeat, the AFL and northern restrictionists agreed behind closed doors to permit Mexican labor migration.[33] The Immigration Act of 1924 ultimately erected formidable barriers to southern and eastern Europeans and reinforced Asian exclusion, but it was decidedly permissive concerning Canadian and Mexican admissions.[34] Anyone with ten years continuous residence in a Western Hemisphere country could enter the United States as a nonquota immigrant.

When the 1924 law neared expiration, the immigration restriction coalition agreed once again to treat Western Hemisphere immigration as an exception to avoid previous conflicts within their ranks. The 1928 law reaffirmed ideological compromise by once again combining sweeping restrictions on European and Asian immigration with few barriers to labor migration from Mexico and other Western Hemisphere countries. In this way, the national origins quota system met both nativist demands and the wishes of potent economic interests. By the early 1940s, southwestern growers and other employers pressed for access to cheap Mexican labor due to war-induced labor shortages. The State Department responded by negotiating a bilateral agreement with Mexico in 1942 that established the Bracero Program, which brought approximately 4.2 million temporary Mexican contract workers to the United States over the next two decades.[35] Ideological tensions over immigration yielded durable policy contradictions.

Conflict, Compromise, and the Immigration and Nationality Act of 1965

For pro-immigration reformers who sought to dismantle racist national origins quotas, the Immigration and Nationality Act (INA) of 1965 was a crucial achievement. President Lyndon Johnson initially hoped to duck immigration reform, but his advisors persuaded him that the quotas were inconsistent with his pledge "to eliminate from this nation every trace of discrimination and oppression that is based upon race or color."[36] Cold War imperatives also influenced this effort because discriminatory immigration quotas "needlessly provide grist for the propaganda mills of Moscow and Peiping."[37] The Johnson administration made immigration reform a top priority after the 1964 election, drawing explicit ties to civil rights. "We have removed all elements of second-class citizenship from our laws by the Civil Rights Act," proclaimed Vice President Hubert Humphrey.

"We must in 1965 remove all elements in our immigration law which suggest that there are second-class people."[38] After legislative wrangling, however, the INA did not end discrimination in U.S. immigration policies any more than the Civil Rights Act made second-class citizenship magically disappear for racial minorities.

During legislative wrangling over the INA, pro-immigration reformers made fateful compromises that satisfied various conservative and reactionary forces in Congress. So it should hardly surprise us that rival and incongruous elements were woven into the INA. In the House, a coalition of restriction-minded southern Democrats and conservative Republicans demanded important concessions for ending the national origins quota system. The "nonquota status" of Mexican immigration, in particular, and Latin American entries, in general, were a prominent concern among restrictionists in both houses of Congress, including nativist southern Democrats in the Senate. With nativists threatening to hold immigration reform hostage in committee, the INA's chief sponsors ultimately relented and agreed to a new ceiling of 120,000 on annual Western Hemisphere immigration.[39]

In addition to new limits targeting Latin American immigration, congressional restrictionists won another major concession: an emphasis on family reunification in the INA. Originally, the Kennedy administration called for immigration reform that increased annual immigration and allocated visas on the basis of special skills or education that benefited national economic interests.[40] Johnson's 1964 State of the Union message reaffirmed the importance of supplanting national origins quotas with skilled immigration: "In establishing preferences, a nation that was built by immigrants of all lands can ask those who now seek admission: 'What can you do for our country?' But we should not be asking: 'In what country were you born?'"[41] Immigrant merit and skills were to replace national origins quotas, but House restrictionists demanded that family reunification become the top priority of a new preference system.[42]

Convinced that family-based immigration was far preferable to discriminatory quotas, the Johnson administration eventually agreed to make skilled immigration secondary to family ties. It was a momentous shift in plans for a new preference system.[43] As David Reimers chronicles, the expectation that family-based preferences would not significantly alter previous immigration patterns was crucial for many lawmakers.[44] Many restrictionists demanded that new legal preference categories emphasize family ties to discourage nonwhite, non-European immigration. As the American Legion reassured its membership, "the great bulk of immigrants henceforth, will not merely hail from the same parent countries as our present citizens, but will be their closer relatives."[45] Few members of Congress anticipated that the new preference system would facilitate an unprecedented surge of Asian and Latin American immigration. The INA defies simple characterization precisely because it is an intricate law with multiple meanings and impacts. It marked a monumental sea change in U.S. immigration policy by ending a draconian national origins quota system explicitly rooted in eugenicist notions of northern and western European superiority. It is equally true, however, that opponents of diverse immigration left their imprints on the INA by winning new limits on Western Hemisphere immigration and by making family ties rather than education and skills the keystone of the legal preference system. The dramatic and unanticipated demographic and societal shifts that these restriction-minded provisions helped spur underscore the INA's transformative, yet variegated, influence on American life.

Conclusion

Despite our current dysfunctions and discontents over deep partisan polarization, American political thought on U.S. immigration defies simple binaries such as restriction versus openness or xenophobia versus xenophilia. Because rival ideological traditions are a fundamental feature of U.S. immigration politics, comprehensive reform proposals regularly have produced conflict and stalemate. Indeed, clashing ideas and beliefs about immigrant admissions and rights have meant that none of the four camps identified has been able to secure significant policy innovation independently. Major legal and policy change is always arduous in an American political system replete with structural veto points, but the deep ideological conflicts over immigration long have made comprehensive reform in this policy realm especially daunting. For generations, campaigns for immigration reform regularly have followed a tortured path of false starts, prolonged negotiation, and frustrating stalemate. In the past, when lightning has struck for enactment of significant policy innovations, passage has hinged upon the formation of "strange bedfellow" alliances that are unstable and that demand difficult compromises addressing rival goals and interests.

As we have seen, this means that even some of the most restrictive immigration laws in American history have included bargains that create openings for international migration and expansive reforms that have featured key restrictions. The National Origins Quota Acts of 1924 and 1928 established a national origins quota system based on ethnic and racial hierarchy. However, in exchange for their pivotal support of these draconian quota restrictions, southern and western lawmakers kept the door open to Western Hemisphere migrants—thereby winning easy access to cheap, tractable Mexican labor for employers in these regions. The INA of 1965 was heralded by immigration champions for dismantling discriminatory quotas and expanding legal admissions, but it was intended to favor European immigrants and also placed new limits on Western Hemisphere migration. It is a pattern that has defined every episode of U.S. immigration reform—from the late nineteenth century to the Immigration Reform and Control Act of 1986 to failed bipartisan efforts of recent decades. Influential works such as Hunt's *Ideology and U.S. Foreign Policy* and Smith's *Civic Ideals* underscore how powerful ideas can shape U.S. law and policy. The rival ideas and epic ideological clashes that immigration fuels in American politics has yielded a durable pattern of incongruous, even contradictory elements being woven into national law and policy over time. The unevenness of U.S. immigration and refugee policy is perhaps a fitting reflection of the unresolved tensions between democratic inclusion or xenophobic exclusion, and between openness and isolation.

Notes

1. See Daniel Tichenor, "Rival Visions of Nationhood: Immigration Policy, Grand Strategy, and Contentious Politics," in *Rethinking Grand Strategy*, ed. Elizabeth Borgwardt, Christopher Nichols, and Andrew Preston (New York: Oxford University Press, 2021).
2. Daniel Tichenor, *Dividing Lines: The Politics of Immigration Control in America* (Princeton, NJ: Princeton University Press, 2002).
3. Daniel Tichenor, "The Demise of Immigration Reform: Policy-Making Barriers Under Unified and Divided Government," in *Congress and Policy Making in the 21st Century*, ed. Jeffrey Jenkins and Eric Pitashnik (New York: Cambridge University Press, 2016), 242–71.
4. Sidney Milkis and Daniel Tichenor, *Rivalry and Reform* (Chicago: University of Chicago Press, 2019), chap. 7.
5. Elisabeth Bumiller, "Bush Would Give Illegal Workers Broad New Rights," *New York Times*, January 7, 2004.

6. To gain a flavor of this variation, see John Higham, *Strangers in the Land* (New Brunswick, NJ: Rutgers University Press, 1955); Cybelle Fox, *Three Worlds of Relief* (Princeton, NJ: Princeton University Press, 2012); Erika Lee, *America for Americans* (New York: Basic Books, 2019).

7. Michael Hunt, *Ideology and U.S. Foreign Policy* (New Haven, CT: Yale University Press, 1987); Rogers Smith, *Civic Ideals* (New Haven, CT: Yale University Press, 1997).

8. Benjamin Franklin, "Observations Concerning the Increase of Mankind," (1751) in *The Papers of Benjamin Franklin*, vol. 4, ed. Leonard Labaree (New Haven, CT: Yale University Press, 1961), 234.

9. "Letters of Agrippa," *Massachusetts Gazette*, December 28, 1787.

10. Josiah Strong, *Our Country* (Cambridge, MA: Harvard University Press, 1963), 42–43.

11. A. Lawrence Lowell as quoted in Morton Kellor, *Regulating a New Society: Public Policy and Social Change in America, 1900–1933* (Cambridge, MA: Harvard University Press, 1990), 230. Anti-Chinese language is quoted in Tichenor, *Dividing Lines*, p.88.

12. Higham, *Strangers in the Land; Lee, America for Americans*.

13. Thomas Paine, *Common Sense and Other Political Writings*, ed. Nelson Adkins (Indianapolis, IN: Bobbs-Merrill, 1953), 21–23.

14. George Washington as quoted in Maldwyn Jones, *American Immigration* (Chicago: University of Chicago Press, 1960), 79.

15. Charles Sumner, "Speech, November 2, 1855," in *The Works of Charles Sumner* (Boston: Lee and Shepard, 1873), 63–74.

16. Hyman Bookbinder as quoted in Tichenor, *Dividing Lines*, 208.

17. Alexander Hamilton, *Papers on Public Credit, Commerce and Finance* (New York: Liberal Arts Press, 1957), 195–97.

18. Andrew Carnegie, *Triumphant Democracy* (New York: Cosimo, 2005), 27.

19. *Congressional Quarterly Report*, March 23, 1996, 798.

20. George W. Bush, "Address to the Nation on Immigration Reform," May 15, 2006.

21. Ilya Somin, "Frederick Douglass on Immigration," *Washington Post*, April 10, 2014.

22. U.S. Commission on Immigration Reform, *Restoring Credibility* (Washington, DC: Government Printing Office, 1994).

23. "Cesar Chavez to Robert Kennedy," August 11, 1968, Robert Kennedy Papers, container 71, John F. Kennedy Presidential Library, Boston, Massachusetts.

24. See the Annual Reports of the Executive Committee of the Immigration Restriction League, 1894–1899, Prescott F. Hall Collection, Houghton Library, Harvard University, Cambridge, Massachusetts.

25. Henry Cabot Lodge, "Speech on Immigration Restriction," *The Congressional Record*, March 16, 1896.

26. Grover Cleveland, "Veto Message," *Immigration: Documents and Case Records*, 199.

27. *New York Times*, March 3, 1898.

28. Higham, *Strangers in the Land*, 105–11.

29. *A Dictionary of Races: Reports of the Immigration Commission*, vol. 5 (New York: Arno Press, 1970); see also Oscar Handlin, *Race and Nationality in American Life* (New York: Little, Brown, 1957), 100–112.

30. "Immigration Referred," *American Federationist*, February 1897, 257; Samuel Gompers, *Seventy Years of Life and Labor* (New York: Dutton, 1937), 156–61.

31. Tichenor, *Dividing Lines*, chap. 5.

32. Mark Reisler, *By the Sweat of Their Brow: Mexican Immigrant Labor in the United States, 1900–1930* (Westport, CT: Praeger, 1976), 40.

33. Reisler, *By the Sweat of Their Brow*, 201.

34. Max Kohler, "Notes," n.d., Max Kohler Papers, box 5, American Jewish Historical Society, Brandeis University, Waltham, Massachusetts.

35. Tichenor, *Dividing Lines*, chap. 6.

36. November 27, 1963, *Public Papers of the Presidents of the United States: Lyndon B. Johnson, 1963–1964*, vol. 1 (Washington, DC: Government Printing Office, 1965).

37. Hart is quoted in Nationalities Services Center, "A New Immigration Proposal," copy in the author's files.

38. Hubert Humphrey as quoted in Tichenor, *Dividing Lines*, 214–15.

39. Michael Feighan, "Highlights of the Immigration Issue," January 18, 1965, copy on file with the author.

40. *Congressional Record*, July 23, 1963, 13132–33.

41. *Congressional Record*, January 8, 1964, 115. See also Abba Schwartz, *The Open Society* (New York: William Morrow, 1968).

42. David Reimers, *Still the Golden Door* (New York: Columbia University Press, 1992), 69–74.

43. *Washington Post*, October 4, 1965.

44. Reimers, *Still the Golden Door*.

45. Deane and David Heller, "Our New Immigration Law," *American Legion Magazine* 80 (February 1966): 8–9.

PART FIVE
Ideologies of Progress

CHAPTER 18

Capital and Immigration in the Era of the Civil War

JAY SEXTON

Thanks to a generation of scholarship, we now know that ideology has mattered a great deal to U.S. encounters with the wider world. Historians have demonstrated that ideology influenced U.S. foreign relations by conditioning how historical actors perceived threat and identified opportunity. Ideology, in this telling, was akin to a lens that tinted what Americans saw when they looked out into the world. To be sure, although elite leaders were key actors in making foreign policy, they were not the only characters who required examination along these lines in foundational works such as Emily Rosenberg's *Spreading the American Dream*, which considered a range of private entrepreneurs as well as public officials, and Michael Hunt's *Ideology and U.S. Foreign Policy*, which explored how cultural production structured the ideological underpinnings of U.S. foreign relations. Works such as those of Rosenberg and Hunt transformed diplomatic history, uncovering the ways in which dynamic and widely shared ideas structured the outward projection of U.S. power.[1]

In this essay, I merge the insights of this line of scholarship with the newer "U.S. and the World" literature on the Civil War era, a period that was conspicuously absent in classic studies of ideology and foreign relations.[2] New studies on the global Civil War era have moved beyond the national frameworks that structured older accounts. This literature has been particularly attuned to cross-border phenomena, such as migration patterns, the development of global capitalism, and networks of transimperial exchange.

Most of all, it has taken as its starting point the simple fact that America's nineteenth-century relations with the wider world were a two-way street: the United States was both an exporter of power (in the forms of territorial annexation, cultural imperialism, and economic expansion) and an importer (a favored destination for migrants, the world's largest market for foreign investment, and an appropriator of foreign reform movements). Nineteenth-century America was in this regard very different from its mid-twentieth-century counterpart, which projected power abroad as never before during a period unusual in U.S. history when its borders were relatively closed to immigrants and its economy exported, rather than sucked in, foreign capital.

There can be no question that the Civil War mattered to the wider world. "At stake," historian Don Doyle recently has written, "were nothing less than the fate of slavery and the survival of the 'last best hope' for the embattled experiment in government by the people. America's Civil War shook the Atlantic world, and its reverberations at home and abroad shaped the world we inhabit today."[3] In this telling, the Union victory empowered the advance of abolitionism and republican self-government outside of the United States. Once the Confederacy had been crushed, the other slaveholding societies in the Western Hemisphere were on borrowed time (slavery ended in Cuba and Brazil in the 1880s).[4] The Union's triumph similarly lent strength to foreign advocates of self-government and political reform. Prominent examples include Mexico, where liberals defeated French-supported monarchists, and Britain, where the franchise was expanded in the Second Reform Act in 1867. "Perhaps it is more than coincidence," the historian James McPherson has argued, "that within five years of that Union victory, the forces of liberalism had expanded the suffrage in Britain and toppled emperors in Mexico and France."[5]

The Civil War's global significance was not limited to how the Union victory promoted abroad the political ideas of liberal republicanism and anti-slavery. Indeed, it is my contention that the least appreciated, but perhaps the most important, global significance of the Civil War is to be found in how it positioned the United States to take advantage of the late-nineteenth-century burst of cross-border exchange that we now call "globalization." The stabilization and reorganization of the nation's political economy made the United States the world's favored destination for migrant labor and capital investment in the half century that followed Appomattox. Post–Civil War America did more than project political ideology and practices abroad; it also sucked up power from abroad like a thirsty sponge.

To understand the ideological dimensions of the global history of the Civil War era requires a multidimensional approach, one that is attuned both to how Americans projected ideas from the inside out, as well as how ideas arrived in the United States from the outside in. Americans articulating political ideas that resonated abroad certainly mattered, but so too did the ideologies of those who chose to migrate to the United States, as well as those foreign financiers who opted to export their capital in its markets. When viewed in this manner, the key ideological texts of the Civil War expand in number. The Gettysburg Address traveled abroad, inspiring liberal nationalists around the globe to heed Lincoln's call to create and defend a "government of the people, by the people, for the people"; but so too did the Homestead Act (1862), which like a magnet drew migrants to the frenetic colonization of the American West. The Emancipation Proclamation advanced the global cause of antislavery, whereas the Public Credit Act (1869) committed the United States to repaying its war debt in specie, thus incentivizing foreign investment from Britain by demonstrating America's adherence to the gold standard, one of the most powerful transimperial ideologies of the nineteenth century.

In this essay, I consider how the varied ideologies of the Civil War period interfaced with one another, as well as how they changed as a result of the geopolitical transformations of this most volatile (and violent) period in U.S. history. Far from there being a single, dominant ideology, multiple ideologies jostled for supremacy in this age of revolutionary change. Antislavery apostles of republican self-government duked it out against southern proslavery ideologues. Advocates of open borders, from within and beyond America's borders, battled against xenophobic opponents of immigration, such as the Know-Nothing Party. Defenders of the gold standard—the ideological heart of nineteenth-century global finance—struggled to maintain dominance against proponents of paper money, who mapped out an ideological case for the new "greenbacks." As you shall see, the ideological conflicts of the Civil War had clear winners, but those on the losing side lived to fight another day.

The United States' conquest and annexation of the northern half of Mexico in 1848 set the stage for the great ideological conflicts of mid-nineteenth-century American politics. The territorial growth of the United States brought with it the poisonous question of the status of slavery in the West. No longer would the U.S. political system be able to contain this morally charged question under the guise of a putatively national ideology of "manifest destiny."

The slavery issue was the most consequential legacy of the war, but it was not the only one, for the geopolitical reconfiguration of the 1840s rapidly transformed the position of the United States in an international economic system that was itself fast changing as a result of British imperial power and the new transimperial technologies of steam and telegraphy. The conquest of northern Mexico and the Oregon settlement primed the pump of the colonization of the North American West, attracting the attention of migrants and capitalists from far beyond the borders of the United States. The discovery of gold in California in late 1848 shifted these processes into hyperdrive: capital began pouring into American markets, not least in the booming sector of railroads, as did migrants and laborers from across both the Atlantic and Pacific.

Push factors from across the Atlantic complemented the newly magnetic draw of the American market. The English banking panic of 1847 and the European revolutions of 1848 shocked financial markets in Europe. With the financial and political infrastructure of the Old World buckling under new strains, the recently depression-plagued and defaulting debtors of the United States, which had been hit particularly hard by the Panic of 1837, began to look like not such a bad option for European capitalists. The result was a sudden infusion of foreign investment in the United States. The yield on U.S. treasury bonds reached a nineteenth-century low in 1851; by 1853 half of the U.S. national debt was held abroad. America's position on transnational money markets, particularly London's Stock Exchange, was enhanced by its enthusiastic embrace of the gold standard, the foundation of Britain's global system of finance. If America's banking system remained chaotic and unintegrated, its commitment to the gold standard during the recent presidency of Andrew Jackson, combined with its increase in specie supplies thanks to the gold rush in California, made the United States an attractive destination for foreign capital. The New York banker August Belmont informed his Rothschild partners in London in 1848 that U.S. securities "now may be considered the safest of any government. . . . I should think that it would be a very desirable thing for yourselves to invest a portion of your fortune in the securities [here]."[6] Belmont reinforced this point by brokering deals in the gold bullion trade between California and London, which his superiors in London ended up selling to the Bank of England to bolster its gold reserves.[7]

The scale of incoming traffic to the United States was even more dramatic with migration flows. The Europe revolutions of 1848—and the accelerating trends of the economic reorganization of central Europe—also pushed migrants, particularly from Germany, to take the plunge of resettling across the Atlantic. But no push factor was greater in this period than was the great humanitarian catastrophe of the mid-Victorian era: the Irish Potato Famine. Deprived of a core source of sustenance, and with the British state failing to provide adequate relief, desperate Irish boarded vessels bound for the other side of the Atlantic. What ensued in the decade of 1845–1854 was the largest immigration wave in U.S. history (as measured by percentage increase in the population that was foreign-born). A remarkable 13 percent of the population of the United States in 1854 had arrived within the preceding decade.[8]

Ideology was not a significant driving force for these transformative geopolitical changes in the mid-nineteenth century. The political architect of U.S. territorial expansion in the 1840s, President James K. Polk, was a hardheaded realist, a pragmatic practitioner of realpolitik as opposed to an ideologue. He appears to have never publicly used the words "manifest destiny" and shied away from framing his statecraft in ideological terms.[9] The surge of foreign investment in the United States during this period was a result of material stimuli and European instability. To be sure, some of the most politically active immigrants of this period were exiled revolutionaries who fled the failed uprisings of 1848. These "48ers" were attracted to America's republican institutions and relative social liberalism. As significant as the 48ers were, however, the majority of those who came to America's shores from the Old World sought the sustenance and stability that was not on offer in the homeland.

If ideology did not cause the era's geopolitical changes, ideological adaptation and conflict was a significant consequence of them. The most obvious example concerned the politics of slavery in the 1850s. Through a complex process of political sorting, the respective sections increasingly, if incompletely, developed distinct ideological lines on the future of slavery in the West. The sudden surge in immigration similarly hardened ideological positions on ethnocultural questions. The influx of predominately Catholic immigrants ignited ethnocultural conflict in the United States, particularly in urban areas of the north, where the densest concentration of recent arrivals were to be found. New wedge issues appeared on the political landscape, including the wait period for naturalization, funding for parochial schools, state deportation of immigrants deemed to be public charges, and public regulation of alcohol.[10] Increased labor competition heightened tensions between immigrants and "native" Americans—it is no coincidence that many of those who most vociferously opposed immigration were those who competed with overseas arrivals on labor markets.

The meteoric ascent of the nativist American Party (or Know-Nothings) prompted advocates of open borders to defend their position. One of the most prominent advocates of immigration was the New York politician William H. Seward, who became a leading proponent of an ideology of open borders and exchange. "I am always for bringing men and States *into* the Union never for taking any *out*," he once declared. Underpinning Seward's position on immigration were political calculations: Seward and his political advisor Thurlow Weed understood that a hardline, anti-immigrant position was untenable in New York, a state with a large and increasing immigrant population. But Seward's embrace of immigration cannot be reduced to politics alone; it was part of a larger vision of national progress that prioritized the material development of the Union. In this telling, the very source of America's power was its ability to attract migrants from around the world who could enhance international commerce and accelerate the nation's development and growth. "The basis of the commerce of the Pacific is the importation of Chinese laborers," Seward declared late in his life, "just as the basis of our European commerce is the importation of Irish or Germans."[11]

The ideological conflicts of the 1850s were not immediately resolved. The alternative possibilities on the future of slavery Lincoln posed in his 1858 "House Divided" speech took four years of warfare to determine:

> Either the *opponents* of slavery, will arrest the further spread of it, and place it where the public mind shall rest in the belief that it is in the course of ultimate extinction; or its *advocates* will push it forward, till it shall become alike lawful in *all* the States, *old* as well as *new*—*North* as well as *South*."

Conflict over immigration temporarily receded due to changing circumstances. Once again, geopolitical shifts conditioned the terrain upon which ideologically charged debates took place. As the Union staggered to the edge of the cliff in the late 1850s, the unprecedented inflow of migrants and capital began to diminish. Ireland began its slow recovery from the famine; those political exiles and economic migrants who desired to leave central Europe had already done so. Then came the Panic of 1857, which greatly diminished the pull northern markets exerted on transatlantic labor and capital.

At this point, the slowdown in incoming traffic of migrants and capital looked like part of the "natural" rhythm of the Victorian cycle of boom and bust, whose vicissitudes often mapped onto political, as well as economic, fluctuations. The story changed with the political earthquakes of 1860–61: the election of Abraham Lincoln, the secession of slaveholding states in the deep South, the bombardment of Ft. Sumter, the secession of several slave-holding states from the upper South, and finally, the beginning of full-on war in America, complete with a naval blockade, a self-imposed Confederate cotton embargo, revenue generating tariffs in the North, and a series of international diplomatic imbroglios that threatened to spread the contagion of crisis across the Atlantic. What *The Economist* called the Panic of 1860 was "in its origin wholly political."[12] The onset of the American Civil War posed the greatest threat to the booming transatlantic economic complex in the century between the end of the Napoleonic wars and the Great War. "I doubt whether we are not as deeply interested in the matter as the parties themselves," remarked Lord Overstone, one of the largest British holders of American securities.[13]

Secession and civil war were the geopolitical earthquakes that halted— indeed, even reversed—the westward transatlantic flows of people and capital that constituted the demographic and economic trend lines of the nineteenth century. Immigration to the United States instantly dried up as would-be migrants thought better of relocating to a war-torn destination that had seen the rapid rise of nativist politicians. The 1860–1862 years "were the lowest in terms of the arrival of European immigrants from 1844 to 1931."[14] Capital not only stopped flowing to the world's greatest debtor nation; it started to flee it. More capital left the American market in this period than entered into it (the only sustained period of time in which this occurred between 1815 and 1914).[15] The gold flight forced the Treasury to suspend specie payments in the first year of the war. The Union's 1862 turn toward paper "greenbacks" not backed by gold was an ominous development in the eyes of European capitalists who held a religious-like faith in the sanctity of the gold standard. The Union's repudiation of the gold standard was widely mocked in Britain. "The Union is flooded with paper money," the *Times* (London) observed with much hyperbole, "it descends like snow in flakes worth half a penny apiece. Cartloads of paper cents issue daily from the Treasury, and are sown broadcast over the Federal states."[16]

At its critical moment of trial, the United States was cut off from its traditional sources of manpower and capital. Necessity, it is said, is the mother of invention. This was certainly the case during America's greatest trial. With the capital markets of the Old World effectively closed, the United States engaged in an unprecedented flurry of innovation in political economy: a national currency was born, taxes were devised, a federation of private banks was created in the National Bank Acts of 1863 and 1864, and, above all, domestic financial markets adapted and grew in order to absorb the flood of war bonds that gushed from the Treasury (some two-thirds of the Union war effort was financed, almost all through domestic sources until the final months of the conflict). It was the Civil War that created modern Wall Street. The exigencies of mobilizing manpower and popular support triggered comparable innovations in central state power and, more so, civil society, which became more nationally integrated and organized as the conflict progressed.

Viewed from the long sweep of nineteenth-century U.S. history, the Civil War years stand out as the moment when the nation not only engaged in a series of integrative changes but also demonstrated the ability to generate its own power. The Union did not require major foreign loans and alliances to emerge victorious. The contrast to earlier periods is worth emphasizing. The Revolution would not have been won without foreign capital and, most of all, the 1778 alliance with France. The Louisiana Purchase would not have been possible without a bridging loan provided by the London Barings. Even the Mexican War was in part financed with foreign capital and won because Comanche power had destabilized Mexican authority, clearing the way for the entry of the United States.

The realization of U.S. power in the 1860s stands apart, of that there can be little question. Yet this generative moment of wartime mobilization and reorganization of political economy did not occur in a vacuum. The power of the Union would not have been what it was without those inflows of the antebellum period. This was particularly the case with the military service of the foreign born. The great 1845–1854 wave of immigration provided the Union with the manpower advantage its armies would require in the war of attrition that was to follow. Fully 25 percent of the Union Army was foreign born, with German and Irish populations being numerically the most significant. Indeed, if one includes soldiers with a foreign-born parent, the figure increases to 43 percent.[17] One can go even further: when African Americans are added to the tally of first and second generation immigrant soldiers, the total is more than half of the mighty Union Army. It is hard to see the Union defeating the Confederacy without the contributions of these "minority" populations, which in fact were a majority of the soldiers who wore blue coats during the Civil War.

The significance of foreign-born military service extended beyond the battlefield. The imperative of raising troops took the wind out of the sails of the Know-Nothing nativism of the 1850s. "Let the nativist bigot think and say what he will," one northern newspaper declared, "the Irish element in America is giving conclusive evidence of devoted attachment to the Union."[18] Union leaders and public officials did more than acknowledge the commitment of immigrant populations; they actively courted them. Recruitment placards were printed in foreign languages; politicians presented the war as part of a transnational struggle for republican government, thereby decoupling the idea of the nation from Anglo-Saxon Protestantism; positions of authority within the Union Army were opened to leaders of immigrant communities—when Lincoln named Alexander Schimmelfennig to a generalship, he did so for reasons of ethnic political outreach, not military leadership.

By the final years of the war, Union leaders did more than just appeal to foreign-born populations at home. They now actively attracted new immigrants. The Union Party platform of 1864 included a pro-immigration plank. On July 4, 1864, Lincoln signed into law an act creating a federal immigrant office in New York that supported business and civil organizations seeking to attract foreign arrivals.[19] The contrast to the Know-Nothing days could not have been starker. As the Civil War placed new strains on the Union, Atlantic migration patterns returned to their customary flow of travel. An estimated 800,000 immigrants arrived in the North during the war, 180,000 of whom joined the Union Army—this was roughly the number of African American troops.

There can be little question that foreign-born military service had an ideological component. The cause of the Union stood as "the last best hope," as Lincoln put it in 1862, for republican self-government in the eyes of many who had fled oppression in the Old World. But the motivations of immigrant populations should not be collapsed into the ideological parameters of native-born American nationalists. Many Irish, for example, interpreted the Union as an extension of Irish nationalism. "It is not only our duty to America but also to Ireland," declared Thomas Francis Meagher to the recruits of the famed Irish Brigade. Indeed, the cause of the Union did not eclipse the interests of ethnic groups during the conflict. Draft riots—most famously that of the Irish in New York in the summer of 1863, but also those staged by Germans in the Midwest—revealed the extent to which immigrant communities acted in their own interests, regardless of the political needs of the Union.

When it came to foreign-born troops in the Union Army, the key ideological text of the Civil War was the 1862 Homestead Act. Immigrants who began the naturalization process were eligible for the 160 acres of land offered by the act. The U.S. foreign service propagated the Homestead Act around the world, drawing in immigrants in the second half of the war. Once again, it was Seward (now secretary of state) who took the lead in promoting immigration, informing his network of consuls and diplomats abroad that the Homestead Act "deserves to be regarded as one of the most important steps ever taken by any government toward a practical recognition of the universal brotherhood of nations."[20] The Homestead Act offered material improvement, but it also encapsulated the ideological pull of the Union. This was the United States that was the land of economic opportunity and social liberalism—the place where the common person had a fighting chance for self-improvement. To their credit, Union leaders understood this, offering material incentives to prospective immigrants. On the last full day of his life, Lincoln informed an Indiana congressman of his desire to encourage immigration "from overcrowded Europe. I intend to point them to the gold and silver that waits for them in the West." Just as his "last speech" signaled a partial embrace of African American political rights, Lincoln's comments here pointed toward a postwar era that would look different from what had preceded it. Nativist bigotry was not dead; but the institutionalized Know-Nothingism of the 1850s had been dismantled.

The story of international finance during the Civil War followed a pattern similar to that of immigration. The capital flight of the 1860–1862 period was followed by a gradual return to the westward flows, which was the trend line of the nineteenth century. European interest in Union war bonds picked up in the final months of the war, with activity focused on the continental money markets of Frankfurt and Amsterdam. By the end of the war, an estimated 10 percent of the Union war debt was held abroad. The uptick in Union bonds in Europe was in part the result of ideological and political considerations. Here was an early rendition of what has come to be known as "ethical investment": it is not a coincidence that foreign investment in the Union increased once the battle lines on slavery had been clarified after 1863. When news of the Emancipation Proclamation reached the Frankfurt *börse*, the U.S. counsel reported a rise in the market "evidently to be ascribed to the energetic anti-slavery proclamation of the President which has been welcomed here with universal approbation."[21] On the flip side, the Confederacy's commitment to slavery made its financial efforts abroad an uphill climb. When the Confederacy finally placed bonds from a modest cotton loan on European markets in 1863, its investors were notoriously secretive of their identities, undermining the political objective of establishing a pro-Confederate lobby of bondholders in Old World capitals.

As with immigration, the political and ideological motives of foreign capitalists merged with hard-headed calculations of material benefit. Investors bought up Union war bonds in the war's final months because there were huge profits to be had: offered at discounts of up to 60 percent, with favorable exchange rates to boot, the Union war bonds that sloshed around Europe's money markets in 1864–65 rank as one of the all-time steals in the modern history of government finance. As European interest in American investments picked up, the United States emerged from the Civil War with a more integrated financial infrastructure, complete with an emerging class of capitalists primed to serve as conduits for foreign investment. The reorganization of the nation's financial system and political economy during the war— the creation of a national currency, the haphazard emergence of a federally regulated banking system, and the influx of Treasury bonds throughout the northern economy—were not intended to attract foreign investment. But these innovations had the effect of short-circuiting the old inefficiencies and logjams of the decentralized financial order of the early republic.

Those "middle men" with knowledge of markets on both sides of the Atlantic were in a particular position to profit from the incoming rush of capital from the Old World as the postwar era loomed. Upstart German American firms, such as J. W. Seligman and Co., funneled capital from Frankfurt and Amsterdam into the U.S. economy. August Belmont, the agent of London Rothschilds in New York, became a major player in the development of Wall Street. The Civil War made J. P. Morgan, who had been an apprentice at a London bank before the conflict but returned to America to make his initial fortune from federal contracts. The subsequent transatlantic growth of the House of Morgan—an old Anglo-American trading firm that evolved into the great power of Wall Street—illustrates how the postwar Union was uniquely positioned to exploit the globalization of finance in the late nineteenth century. What was more was how this new class of financiers attracted foreign capital to the United States through buy-in to the Victorian era's dominant financial ideology: the shrine of the gold standard. Yankee capitalists were the crucial intermediaries not only in selling American projects to foreign financiers but also in pressuring and lobbying their home government to return to the gold standard.

It is now common to argue that the Union victory marked an advance for the ideological causes of abolitionism and republican self-government around the world. This early propagation of American ideas portended the more systematic and widespread exportation of culture and politics in the coming "American century." But this was not the only international legacy of the American Civil War. The settlement of the slavery question and the subsequent political stabilization of the United States in 1865 positioned it to take full advantage of the late-nineteenth-century version of what we now call globalization. In the aftermath of the war, the United States emerged as the most attractive and profitable developing economy in an age in which there were many, not least Canada and Argentina. Post–Civil War America would dominate two of the great international competitions of the ensuing half century: the "scramble for citizens," in which New World nations competed for migrant labor, and what similarly can be called the "scramble for capital," in which developing economies vied to attract foreign investment.[22]

It could have been different. The crisis of the Union, as we have seen, disrupted the economic and demographic flows of the international system in 1860–1862. The capital flight, trade disruption, low immigration, and geopolitical instability of this period offers a glimpse into what the history of North America might have looked like had the conclusion of the Civil War been different. A Confederate victory, or even just an indecisive outcome, might well have produced further conflicts waged for continental supremacy between rival sectional confederacies and their foreign supporters. We will never know what that alternative history might have looked like; the Union victory settled the internal political questions that had plagued the republic since its founding, stabilizing the nation's international position in the process.

The results were immediately apparent when it came to overseas migration to the United States. The decade of the 1860s saw 2.3 million immigrants arrive, most of whom came after the Civil War concluded. The inflows dipped during the economic downturn that followed 1873 but surged once again in the 1880s, during which 5.2 million immigrants arrived. As early as 1870, the percentage of the nation's population that was foreign born surpassed 14 percent. It would remain around this level until 1920, peaking at 14.8 percent in 1890. These immigrants were distinguished from previous arrivals by their ethnic and religious diversity. They came from all corners of Europe, particularly the southern and eastern regions of the continent, as well as from across the Pacific—indeed, the climax of Civil War era pro-immigration sentiment was the 1868 Burlingame Treaty with Qing China that brought in migrant labor to construct the West's burgeoning railroad network. This agreement was championed by William Seward, the great advocate of migration to the United States. The United States more often than not won this era's "scramble for citizens," attracting an estimated 25 percent of international migrants in the long nineteenth century.[23] The Fourteenth Amendment, ratified in 1868, advanced constitutional protections to new arrivals by enshrining the principle of birthright citizenship.

Ideology certainly played a role in the immigration boom after 1865. The draw of the United States in part came from how the war's outcome enhanced its reputation abroad as a liberal and socially open nation. With the stain of slavery and the quasi-aristocratic slave power now removed, the Union reemerged as the world's leading light of political freedom and economic opportunity. In death, Abraham Lincoln became a global celebrity, one who personified the opportunities available to the common man in America. Parents in Britain and Europe named their children "Lincoln"; his speeches, particularly the Gettysburg Address embrace of "government of the people, by the people, for the people," reached into even the most remote corners of the world. At the turn of the century, the Russian author Leo Tolstoy encountered a Circassian tribal chief deep in the Caucasus Mountains who considered Lincoln "the greatest general and greatest ruler of the world . . . a Christ in miniature."[24]

What Lincoln embodied about America was not only the benefits to the common man of its political system of republican self-government but also its material riches and bountiful economic prospects. Lincoln was the archetypal self-made man in economic as well as political terms. Foreign observers found in his ascent from a Kentucky log cabin to the White

House an illustration of the opportunities available for a self-made man in a democratic political system paired with a market-based economy. Here, again, was America as a land of economic opportunity, a place where an immigrant had a fighting chance to move up the social ladder—certainly when compared to their current prospects. More than anything, it was the relative economic prospects on offer that attracted people in the decades after the Civil War. Immigrants also benefited from low fares to the United States and frequent departures of the steamers that serviced American ports. Bolstered by tales of economic opportunity and channeled to New York and San Francisco by the transport networks of a globalizing economy, immigration to the United States became a self-perpetuating phenomenon in the half century that followed the crisis of the Union.

The end of the Civil War had a similar effect on the position of the United States in international capital markets. As we have seen, the credit rating of the Union had begun to improve by the end of the war, but capital markets remained anxious about the United States remaining off the gold standard. Returning to gold required a painful process of retiring paper greenbacks, a deflationary practice of currency contraction that would hit farmers and debtors particularly hard. The Democratic Party was particularly receptive to those opposed to such a deflationary policy that would disproportion-ately advantage Wall Street interests and their foreign allies. The party's 1868 platform embraced an inflationary plan in which it called for the repayment of some old war bonds in depreciated greenbacks. The Pendleton plan, as it was called after its originator, Ohio Democrat George Pendleton, horrified liberal observers and financial interests across the Atlantic. John Stuart Mill, who had stood by the Union in the darkest years of the Civil War, begged Americans to resist the urge to "repudiate" their debt in a letter reproduced in *The Nation* after the 1868 Democratic convention. To Mill, the Pendel-ton plan would "be one of the heaviest blows that could be given to the reputation of popular governments, and to the morality and civilization of the human race."[25]

Ulysses S. Grant and the Republican Party offered a hard-money alter-native in the election of 1868. The party's platform was unequivocal: "the national honor requires the payment of the public indebtedness in the utter-most good faith to all creditors at home and abroad." "It is all that the Bond-holders can expect," August Belmont informed the London Rothschilds.[26] Upon assuming office, Grant did not disappoint. The first action he took was to sign into law the Public Credit Act (1869), which committed the United

States to repaying its war debt in gold. Foreign investment in the United States immediately surged. A congressional report later in 1869 found that nearly half of the U.S. national debt was held abroad, particularly in London. More than a quarter of the nation's net capital growth in the peak year of 1869 came from overseas. The improved credit of the United States kept interest rates on the Civil War debt down and brought specie back into the United States, advancing the Republican Party's agenda of returning to the gold standard (which would not be achieved until 1879). As with migration patterns, capital flows to the United States would ebb and flow in the coming half century. But the macro story was one of unequalled inflows. By the eve of World War I in 1914, foreign investment in the United States totaled $7.1 billion, making America the world's greatest debtor nation.[27] More British capital poured into the United States than into the rest of the British Empire *combined*. Far from a sign of economic dependence, the inflow of foreign capital signaled the unrivaled growth and opportunity of the American market. Foreign capitalists wanted in on the profits.

The postwar boom in immigration and foreign investment, in sum, was lubricated by transimperial ideologies: the opportunity of self-improvement in the America Homestead Act fueled migration; meanwhile, the gold standard America of the Public Credit Act brought in capital from abroad. The ensuing surge in incoming traffic, volatile though it was, became the dominant geopolitical trend of late-nineteenth-century U.S. history.

But every action has an equal and opposite reaction. The quantity, composition, and volatility of the incoming traffic of immigrants and foreign investment thrust those issues to the fore of late-nineteenth-century politics, cultivating counter political movements and ideologies within the United States. Opposition to immigration emerged within labor organizations, who blamed low wages and poor working conditions on new arrivals. Racist xenophobes targeted Chinese immigrants, ensuring that they were denied the right of naturalization. Racialized xenophobia inspired early immigration restrictions, most notoriously the 1882 Chinese Exclusion Act that portended the race-based immigration restriction legislation of the 1920s. The gold standard, as well, attracted more organized and virulent criticism. The nascent coalition behind the Pendleton plan of 1868—farmers, small debtors, and those suspicious of the concentration of wealth and power in Wall Street—formed a number of political organizations, such as the Grangers and the Greenback Party, that advocated for inflationary policies and soft money. Here were the seeds of the political ideology that would find full expression in the form of William Jennings Bryan and the Populists of the 1890s: "We shall answer their demands for a gold standard by saying to them, you shall not press down upon the brow of labor this crown of thorns. You shall not crucify mankind upon a cross of gold."[28]

Conclusion

This foray into the Civil War era yields three general takeaways relevant to this volume's objective of placing ideology at the center of the story of U.S. foreign relations. First, I have argued that ideology must be considered alongside material drivers of change: geopolitics, human mobility, capital flows, and so on. The point is not to prioritize the material over the ideological but rather to emphasize their interdependence. Sometimes ideas determined material outcomes; in other instances, as I have stressed, material developments yielded ideological adaptation. Second, when writing about how ideas conditioned America's engagements with the wider world, historians must take into consideration the ideologies of those outside of the United States. I have argued that the worldviews and ideological perspectives of immigrants and European capitalists had profound implications for America's foreign relations by conditioning patterns of migration and capital flows that were the dominant geopolitical forces of the late nineteenth century. Ideologies, in other words, could be transimperial (such as the gold standard) as well as national.

The third and final takeaway for this volume is that no single ideology structured America's encounter with the wider world. It is perhaps not surprising that an earlier generation of historians—who wrote within the context of a dominate, steroidal nationalism of the Cold War era—emphasized ideological continuity among the makers of American foreign relations. But viewed from the vantage of our current era of political conflict and culture wars, it is perhaps also not surprising that those moments of intense ideological conflict—above all, the Civil War—loom larger in historical consciousness, demanding fresh examination. The Civil War era was a complex and multidimensional battleground of warring ideologies: pro- versus anti-slavery; republicanism versus monarchy; nativism versus open borders; tariffs versus free trade; and greenbacks versus the gold standard. To be sure, the era yielded clear winners: the Union became an antislavery polity committed to settler colonization in North America as well as to tariffs, the gold standard, and relatively open borders to laboring migrants. But if the war's outcome determined what would be the dominant ideologies of the United States in the half century that was to follow, it nonetheless generated counter ideological movements that would continue to structure its politics. Most notable were populist movements that railed against the gold standard and immigration. In sum, the history of ideology and American foreign relations in the era of the Civil War is the story of conflict, not consensus. One suspects that this was not the only period in U.S. history in which this was the case.

Notes

1. Emily S. Rosenberg, *Spreading the American Dream: American Economic and Cultural Expansion, 1890–1945* (New York: Basic Books, 1982); Michael H. Hunt, *Ideology and U.S. Foreign Policy* (New Haven: Yale University Press, 1987).
2. Hunt's examination of the Civil War is only one paragraph long. Hunt, *Ideology and U.S. Foreign Policy*, 36.
3. Don Doyle, *The Cause of All Nations: An International History of the American Civil War* (New York: Basic Books, 2014), 11.
4. Gregory Downs, *The Second American Revolution: The Civil War-Era Struggle over Cuba and the Rebirth of the American Republic* (Chapel Hill: University of North Carolina Press, 2019).
5. James M. McPherson, " 'The Whole Family of Man': Lincoln and the Last Best Hope Abroad," in *The Union, the Confederacy, and the Atlantic Rim*, ed. Robert E. May (Gainesville: University Press of Florida, 2013), 161–62.
6. "Belmont to N.M.R. and Sons, March 20, 1848," T54/275, Rothschild Archive, London.
7. Timothy Alborn, *All That Glittered: Britain's Most Precious Metal from Adam Smith to the Gold Rush* (Oxford: Oxford University Press, 2019).
8. David Potter, *The Impending Crisis, 1848–1861* (New York: Harper and Row, 1976), 241.
9. For this view of Polk, see the classic, Norman Graebner, *Empire on the Pacific: A Study in American Continental Expansion* (New York: Ronald Press, 1955).
10. Tyler Anbinder, *Nativism and Slavery: The Northern Know-Nothings and the Politics of the 1850s* (New York: Oxford University Press, 1992); Hidetaka Hirota, *Expelling the Poor: Atlantic Seaboard States and the Nineteenth-Century Origins of American Immigration Policy* (New York: Oxford University Press, 2017).
11. William H. Seward as quoted in Jay Sexton, "William H. Seward in the World," *Journal of the Civil War Era* 4, no. 3 (September 2014): 418. See also Sebastian

Baird, "The World for Its Mother Country: Responses to Nativism in the Antebellum Period" (master's thesis, University of Oxford, 2013).

12. *Economist*, December 8, 1860, 1357.

13. "Overstone to Norman, January 1861," in *The Correspondence of Lord Overstone*, vol. 2, ed. D. P. O'Brien (Cambridge: Cambridge University Press, 1971), 937–38.

14. Herbert S. Klein, *A Population History of the United States*, 2nd ed. (New York: Cambridge University Press, 2012), 96.

15. Mira Wilkins, *The History of Foreign Investment in the United States to 1914* (Cambridge, MA: Harvard University Press, 1989).

16. The *Times* as quoted in Curtis Wilgus, "Some London *Times* Comments on Secretary Chase's Financial Administration, 1861–1864," *Mississippi Valley Historical Review* 26 (December 1939): 395–98.

17. Doyle, *The Cause of All Nations*, 158–84.

18. Philip S. Paludan, *A People's Contest: The Union and Civil War, 1861–1865* (Lawrence: University Press of Kansas, 1996), 282.

19. Heather Cox Richardson, *"The Greatest Nation of the Earth": Republican Economic Policies During the Civil War* (Cambridge, MA: Harvard University Press, 2009), 165–67.

20. William Seward as quoted in Doyle, *Cause of All Nations*, 177.

21. Jay Sexton, *Debtor Diplomacy: Finance and American Foreign Relations in the Civil War Era, 1837–1873* (Oxford: Oxford University Press, 2005), 125.

22. David Cook-Martín, *The Scramble for Citizens: Dual Nationality and State Competition for Immigrants* (Stanford, CA: Stanford University Press, 2013).

23. Adam McKeown, "Global Migration, 1845–1940," *Journal of World History* 15, no. 2 (June 2004): 156, table 1.

24. Richard Carwardine and Jay Sexton, eds., *The Global Lincoln* (New York: Oxford University Press, 2011), 5–6.

25. John Stuart Mill letter, *The Nation* 7 (October 15, 1868): 308–9.

26. "Belmont to N.M.R. and Sons," May 22, 1868, T57/104, Rothschild Archive, London.

27. Wilkins, *The History of Foreign Investment in the United States to 1914*, 153.

28. William Jennings Bryan, "Cross of Gold" [speech], July 9, 1896, History Matter, accessed December 7, 2021, historymatters.gmu.edu/d/5354/.

CHAPTER 19

The Progressive Origins of Project RAND

DANIEL BESSNER

O n October 1, 1945, four executives from the Douglas Aircraft Company met with Edward Bowles, the highest-ranking civilian scientist in the War Department, and Henry Harley "Hap" Arnold, the Army Air Forces (AAF) commanding general, at Hamilton Field in Novato, California, to discuss creating a national security research program. Although the air forces had spent millions on civilian research during World War II, the service had never furnished much money to scientists in peace. But times were changing. The war, which ended with two atomic bomb explosions, had underlined to Bowles and Arnold that technology was a crucial resource in the AAF's domestic struggle for independence, power, and prestige. To ensure that the air forces had access to the most cutting-edge knowledge, Bowles and Arnold granted Douglas Aircraft $10 million to found a program dedicated to weapons research. No one foresaw that within a decade the project—quickly dubbed Project RAND— would develop into the most influential national security research program in American history.

RAND was the culmination of airmen's decades-long attempt to transform the air forces into a "Progressive" organization defined by the expert and moral use of advanced weaponry.[1] Beginning in the early twentieth century, air officers distinguished themselves from their ground Army counterparts by self-consciously embracing modern techniques and technologies.[2] Airmen's faith in the modern was exemplified in the Progressive theory of airpower that the majority of them endorsed in the interwar years. According to this theory, modern technologies—metal planes, accurate bombsights, powerful engines—enabled the "precision strategic bombing" of an enemy's "vital centers"—the transportation networks, electric grids, materiel-producing industries, and communications centers upon which a country relied to wage war. Destroying an adversary's vital centers, airmen claimed, would end wars rapidly, cheaply, and with as little loss of life as possible. Arnold thus spoke for most of his colleagues when he averred in 1943 that the precision strategic bomber was "the most humane of all weapons."[3]

In addition to its economic and humanitarian benefits, airmen promoted precision strategic bombing because it provided a logical basis for air force independence. If the Progressive theory of airpower was proven correct— that is to say, if precision strategic bombing ended a war absent a ground invasion—it would demonstrate that the AAF had a strategic mission distinct from the traditional Army, to which it remained institutionally subordinate. As Arnold himself once declared, it was "long-range bombardment aviation . . . which, alone, lifts an Air Force from the status of an auxiliary arm to that of an equal" with the Army and Navy.[4]

World War II provided Progressive airpower's advocates with the opportunity to validate their theory. Unfortunately for them, the experience in the European Theater of Operations was disappointing. In war's maelstrom, precision strategic bombing proved impossible, and by 1944 the AAF had switched to area bombing: the indiscriminate bombing of a nation's entire territory. Moreover, the Nazis were defeated only after a costly ground invasion. Nevertheless, the Progressive theory of airpower was saved by the experience in the Pacific Theater of Operations (PTO), where strategic bombing—aided by two atomic weapons—engendered Japan's capitulation. Although bombing ended the war far less cleanly than air officers had predicted, they nonetheless concluded that Japan's surrender validated the thrust, if not the details, of their Progressive theory.[5]

Because Progressive bombing strategy depended on advanced weaponry, airmen, as one analyst put it when describing a later period, "worship[ped] at the altar of technology."[6] Indeed, after World War II Arnold spent his last months as AAF commander institutionalizing his service's research and development (R&D) effort. To do so, he relied on two close associates: Edward Bowles, an MIT professor *cum* War Department official, and Frank Collbohm, a Douglas Aircraft executive. By late 1945, both Bowles and Collbohm had concluded that to remain on the forefront of scientific progress the air forces should fund a civilian group headquartered in industry and dedicated to national security research. This vision excited Arnold, who ordered Bowles and Collbohm to develop the plan for what became Project RAND, which realized airmen's long-held aspiration to make their service into a Progressive institution organized around expertise, innovation, and technology.

The Progressive ideology that shaped Project RAND contained within it a number of assumptions that permeated the military-intellectual complex throughout the Cold War. Perhaps none was more important than the idea that wise policy was a function of bringing the nation's "best" minds together and encouraging them to focus on problems of defense. Put another way, Project RAND, and its manifold offspring, were institutions of the emergent postwar American "meritocracy." To men like Arnold, Bowles, and Collbohm, the future of U.S. national security depended on replacing the old WASP aristocracy with individuals who had proven themselves through academic or administrative achievement. Such a transformation, they assumed, would ensure that the United States overcame all threats as it constructed a just and peaceful world order.

RAND's founders also betrayed a profound scientism. During and after World War II, Arnold, Bowles, and Collbohm affirmed that novel methodologies such as operations research, which applied the scientific method to problems of tactics and strategy, would enable the meritocrats to control—or at least predict and understand—global wars. Although RAND's founders did not naïvely argue that such approaches would eliminate international conflict, they did maintain that the era of scientifically informed war would witness fewer wasteful and destructive struggles than previous epochs. In short, Arnold, Bowles, and Collbohm insisted that science would, in some sense, rationalize war.

To a significant degree, the faith RAND's founders placed in meritocrats and science was a fear-based reaction to the devastation caused during World War II. The advent of highly destructive weaponry, up to and including the atomic bomb, suggested that future wars might eradicate entire populations in the blink of an eye. Arnold, Bowles, and Collbohm managed their technology-induced anxieties by proclaiming their confidence in scientific meritocracy. If the U.S. military could connect itself permanently to the best and the brightest, RAND's founders assumed (or hoped) that the fog of war could be lifted and an atomic World War III could be avoided or, if necessary, won. Project RAND was thus more than a simple collection of experts: it was designed to help guarantee the survival of the United States and the success of the American Century in a newly nuclear world.

Project RAND's story begins with Edward Lindley Bowles (1897–1990). Raised by a country doctor and his wife in Westphalia, Missouri, Bowles was a gifted leader who quickly rose to the top of whatever organization he joined. After serving as a lieutenant in the field artillery during World War I, Bowles matriculated at Washington University in St. Louis, where he received a bachelor of science degree in electrical engineering in 1920.[7] Bowles then moved to the Massachusetts Institute of Technology (MIT) to pursue a master's degree in the same subject. At MIT, he rapidly emerged as a star student, becoming a member of the Institute's faculty before completing his degree in 1921. Soon thereafter he established MIT's undergraduate program in electrical communications, and in 1926 he assumed the directorship of the Institute's Round Hill Research Station, which became a national center for communications research.[8]

Bowles was an ambitious intellectual entrepreneur whose purview extended well beyond MIT. Throughout the interwar era, he consulted for and worked with several of the nation's largest industrial firms, including Atlantic Telephone & Telegraph, Bell Telephone Laboratories, the General Electric Company, International Telephone & Telegraph Company, the Sperry Gyroscope Company, and the Western Electric Company.[9] Bowles's interactions with private corporations convinced him that neither academics nor industrial engineers enjoyed a monopoly of knowledge, and for this reason university–industry collaboration was a crucial means to advance both basic and applied science.

But industry was not the only sector with which Bowles partnered before World War II; the engineer also worked closely with the military. One of Bowles's major concerns at the Round Hill Research Station was to improve aircraft navigation and control.[10] This effort engendered significant interest in the Army Air Corps, which enabled Bowles to meet several rising air officers, including Hap Arnold.[11] This not only helped the engineer learn about the military's concerns but also allowed him to gain a "feeling of the military structure" that he would exploit to great effect during the war.[12] As his relationships with industry and the military suggest, Bowles was an accomplished intellectual entrepreneur. Nevertheless, his success outside the formal structures of MIT prevented him from fully assimilating into the Institute, which would soon create problems for his career.[13]

By the outbreak of World War II in September 1939, Bowles had transformed himself into one of the foremost American experts on electrical communications, which facilitated his entry into government service. In June 1940, Vannevar Bush—the president of the Carnegie Institution for Science and a former MIT professor who had directed Bowles's master's thesis—persuaded President Franklin Delano Roosevelt to create the National Defense Research Committee (NDRC) to organize science for war. Bush, an electrical engineer who kept abreast of developments in electrical communications, believed that radar (an acronym for *radio detection and ranging*) would become a crucial wartime technology if the government properly supported it. As such, he ensured that the NDRC's Section D-1 (Detection), which would unofficially become known as the Microwave Committee (MC), focused on radar research.[14]

Bush admired Bowles and asked his former student to serve as the MC's secretary.[15] Bowles accepted Bush's offer, swiftly learning that his earlier experiences had prepared him well for government service. In particular, because Bowles enjoyed "the confidence of the military, some of [whom were] old hands with whom [he] had worked" for years, his MIT office became "a crossroad between the Microwave Committee and all military agencies."[16] Unfortunately for Bowles, however, his success aroused jealousy in Alfred Loomis, the MC's director, who started to clash with him.

The antagonism between Bowles and Loomis increased until neither could stand to be around the other.[17] Karl T. Compton, MIT's president and the director of the NDRC division responsible for the MC, attempted to attenuate the Bowles-Loomis rivalry by enabling the former to work apart from the latter, to no avail.[18] Tensions came to a head in late 1941 when Bowles dispatched a letter to Compton in which he criticized Loomis and complained that he was doing all of the MC's administrative work.[19] This was the final straw; in early 1942, Compton expelled Bowles from the MC under the pretense that it was too expensive to pay him. Bowles was crushed, concluding that he "was in every sense of the word a ruined individual."[20]

Bowles, it turns out, need not have worried. By the time of his discharge, Secretary of War Henry L. Stimson had developed an interest in radar and hoped to recruit "an expert scientist who is also an expert administrator" to help him understand how best to apply the new technology.[21] Stimson asked his assistant, Harvey Bundy, to identify whom to hire; Bundy hurriedly turned to Bush for recommendations. After briefly considering

Loomis, whom Bundy and Bush rejected because he was Stimson's cousin, they settled on Bowles as the ideal candidate.[22]

On April 1, 1942, only days after Compton dismissed him, Bowles was summoned to Washington, D.C. to interview with Stimson.[23] Bowles was nervous to meet the secretary and upon first arriving in his office was "overawed" by the older man's "Great Spirit."[24] The engineer, however, had little time to wallow in his anxiety because Stimson began to "vigorously cross-examin[e]" him about radar defenses in the Panama Canal Zone.[25] Although he felt like "a country boy" in front of the secretary, Bowles's responses pleased Stimson, who after forty minutes decided that the engineer was "a man of good sense and administrative ability" and asked him to serve as his "expert consultant" for radar.[26] Overwhelmed—Bowles remembered that he "was ready to collapse" by the meeting's end—he nonetheless accepted Stimson's offer, excited finally "to have a job with the great men."[27] Within days, Bowles's office, officially constituted as the Office of the Expert Consultant to the Secretary of War, started operating.[28]

Bowles's office functioned as a classic "adhocracy," "a reactive organization without legal warrant, plan, or explicit governing principles."[29] This improvised style suited the engineer, who since his MIT days had thrived, he admitted, when operating "outside normal institutions and channels."[30] Bowles decided to reproduce within the War Department his interwar experiences at MIT by hiring representatives from academia and industry.[31] Uniting members of these two groups in a single organization, he insisted, was the most effective means to determine how best to utilize radar and other technologies in battle.

Bowles's first task was to analyze how radar could defend against the Nazi U-boats that in early 1942 threatened the Atlantic seaboard.[32] Building off his earlier collaborative experiences at MIT, Bowles urged the creation of a "combat laboratory" that would bring scientists and soldiers together with the AAF to "explore the potentialities of various methods of attacking the German submarine."[33] Hap Arnold, who had long encouraged civil-military collaboration, endorsed Bowles's recommendation and in May established the Sea-Search Attack Development Unit (SADU) at Langley Field, Virginia, to develop the tactics and technologies of anti-submarine warfare.[34] The success of the SADU, as well as the Army Air Antisubmarine Command, which was also created at Bowles's insistence, convinced Stimson that he could trust the engineer; thereafter, the secretary allowed Bowles to expand his purview beyond radar "to examine our

over-all problems and from these to select the ones requiring special attention."[35] Indeed, for much of the war the engineer acted "without reporting
to [Stimson] in detail."[36]

Soon after he began working for Stimson, Bowles learned that just
because a technology existed did not mean it was properly employed at
the front. Moreover, he was concerned that the majority of officers did not
appreciate the potential of new technologies such as radar to revolutionize
tactics and strategy. To rectify these problems, he created what he termed
"Advisory Specialist Groups"—small collections of academic and industrial
experts that were sent abroad and charged with educating officers about
and aiding them in the use of new technologies.[37] Between 1942 and 1945,
Bowles dispatched at least seventeen Advisory Specialist Groups to military
commands all over the world.[38] Never one to shirk his duty, Bowles personally visited, observed, and assisted commands in North Africa, Western
Europe, southern Europe, the Pacific, and India, Burma, and China.[39] By
the war's end, he had established a global network of expertise at the center
of which stood his office.

On their trips abroad, Bowles and his staff developed warm relationships with military personnel that fostered the personal connections that
facilitated academic-industrial-military cooperation during and after World
War II.[40] As Bowles remembered, whenever he was in the field he "was
treated not simply with military courtesy, but as a friend."[41] When Bowles
visited General Douglas MacArthur at his Philippines headquarters, for
instance, the general had Bowles sit next to him at meals, which led to
conversations that compelled the engineer to view MacArthur as "a kindred soul."[42] Such experiences produced, as Bowles aptly put it, "bonds of
understanding" that engendered the affective ties that made the military-
intellectual complex possible.[43]

Bowles's work for Stimson brought him into regular contact with the
military's highest-ranking officers, and he became particularly close with
Hap Arnold, the AAF's commanding general, whom he had known since
his time at the Round Hill Research Station. Bowles and Arnold started
to collaborate intimately in August 1943, when the latter read a report in
which the former lambasted the AAF's communications program.[44] Arnold
concurred with Bowles's criticisms and asked the engineer to "assume overall responsibility for communications in the Army Air Forces."[45] Although
Bowles rejected this offer—it would have required him to stop working for
Stimson—he agreed to act as Arnold's communications consultant.[46]

Bowles's responsibilities quickly grew to encompass other AAF "matters of a technical nature outside the strict field of communications"; in the words of one War Department consultant, he essentially served as the air forces' "Chief Scientist."[47] For his part, Arnold was quite pleased with Bowles's efforts, writing in 1944 that "watching the radio [i.e., radar] experts with careful scrutiny" confirmed to him "the value and importance of these long haired scientists."[48] To Bowles and Arnold, World War II highlighted the significance of scientific-military collaboration to modern warfare, and as the struggle wound down, both began to ask how they could continue such cooperation in peacetime. A Douglas Aircraft Company executive named Frank Collbohm would provide them with a powerful answer.

Franklin Rudolph Collbohm (1907–1990) was the second father of Project RAND. Born to an electrical engineer and a housewife in New York City, Collbohm intended to follow in his father's footsteps when he enrolled in the University of Wisconsin at Madison in 1925.[49] Nevertheless, in college he determined that aeronautical engineering was a more exciting field than electrical engineering and abandoned the latter—and the university entirely—for a career in the aircraft industry.[50] On the advice of a family friend, Collbohm moved to Santa Monica, California, and in 1928 he joined the Douglas Aircraft Company, one of the nation's largest aircraft manufacturers.[51] Collbohm rapidly rose through Douglas Aircraft's ranks and eventually became the "right-hand man" of Donald Douglas, the company's founder and chief executive officer.[52] Collbohm's position had few defined duties, which encouraged him to pursue a diversity of projects: he served as the project engineer for the Douglas Dolphin, a flying boat; established the company's flight-testing department; and personally copiloted the initial flight of the DC-3, the first economically viable American commercial airliner.[53]

Throughout the interwar era the Air Corps regularly contracted with Douglas Aircraft, which allowed Collbohm to meet many air officers, including Arnold.[54] Once the United States entered the war in December 1941, Collbohm became a member of the Office of Scientific Research and Development (OSRD; the NDRC's successor agency) and started to consult for Bowles's office.[55] The executive and the engineer quickly established an effective working relationship based on mutual admiration and respect. Indeed, in 1944 Bowles entrusted Collbohm with one of his office's most important projects: an analysis of extant AAF aircraft capabilities, which eventually came to focus on the Boeing Company's B-29 Super-fortress bomber.

In August 1944, Bowles began to look into forming "a military and civilian group to plan and supervise the execution of a special project for bombing Japan"[56] that would incorporate industrial expertise into strategic planning. To begin this effort, which he dubbed the "Special Bombardment Project," Bowles asked Collbohm and Arthur Raymond—Douglas Aircraft's chief engineer, who was also a consultant for Bowles's office—to undertake a survey of existing aircraft to determine, as Arnold put it, "whether to attack Japan by pilotless aircraft, guided bombs, or B-29's."[57] Collbohm and Raymond were briefed in the AAF's planned operations, were given access to all air forces information, and immediately set to work.[58] At the end of September, they issued a report that concluded that "the B-29 is bound by circumstances to be by far the most important airplane for strategic bomb-ing in the Pacific theater, and a program for exploiting its use to the full should . . . be aggressively carried out" by them. To aid them in this project, they requested that Edward C. Wells, Boeing's chief engineer, be added to their group.[59] Wells was assigned to the project in early October, at which point the three executives turned to analyzing ways to improve the B-29's performance.[60]

Arnold had staked the AAF's future, and his own reputation, on the B-29.[61] By D-Day, it had become apparent that strategic bombing alone had failed to end the war in Europe. The Pacific campaign, which Arnold intended to fight mostly with B-29s, was therefore the last opportunity for the AAF to demonstrate that strategic airpower could force an enemy's capitulation absent a ground invasion. If the AAF accomplished this task, it would prove to outside observers that it deserved independence from the Army. The B-29 was thus the linchpin in the air forces' decades-long struggle to become a coequal military service.

The major problem Collbohm, Raymond, and Wells faced was distance: at the time, all U.S.-controlled air bases were thousands of miles from Japan, which necessitated that the B-29s sent to bomb the island nation carry an enormous amount of fuel. Fuel, however, weighed down the planes and prevented them from holding much ordnance. To reduce the B-29's weight, Collbohm and his colleagues recommended that the AAF remove a signifi-cant amount of equipment from the plane as well as all gun positions save for the tail gun.[62] This "stripped" B-29, the executives contended, would fly faster, higher, and with more bombs—14,000 pounds more—than the standard version of the plane.[63] Bowles endorsed these suggestions, although the air staff proved unwilling to pursue a massive retooling campaign.[64] As such, it was only toward the end of the Pacific war that the AAF employed stripped B-29s in its 315th Bombardment Wing.[65]

Although the Special Bombardment Project did not achieve much in the way of military impact, it was nonetheless important for bringing Collbohm and Bowles together as the war wound down. Indeed, in the winter of 1944–45 Collbohm accompanied Bowles on a trip to the Eastern Hemisphere, in part to examine B-29 operations.[66] The relationship the two formed on this excursion, the trust and conviviality that emerged from spending untold hours together in small planes and at far-flung outposts, provided the personal foundation upon which Project RAND was constructed.[67]

World War II was, famously, the scientist's war. By 1945, a multiplicity of developments—radar, penicillin, napalm, atomic weapons, proximity fuses, etc.—had demonstrated to expert and lay observers alike that scientific research was crucial to the Allies' success. This conviction was driven home in August, when two atomic bombs produced Japanese surrender. To many airmen, Japan's capitulation one week after the annihilation of Hiroshima and Nagasaki proved the substance of Progressive airpower theory correct: strategic bombing ended wars quicker, cheaper, and more efficiently than any other form of warfare. The fact that this victory came at the cost of tens of thousands of innocent lives—that is, it was hardly "precise"—failed to shake airmen's faith in strategic bombing. After all, many concluded, a ground invasion of Japan would have been even more deadly.

At the same time, the awesome power of the atomic bomb engendered widespread fears that, unlike World War II, future wars would be fought and won on very concentrated time scales. In other words, the United States would not again have years to mobilize. In October 1945, for instance, Arnold warned Congress that "the range, speed, and destructive capacity of a powerful [atomic] air force is such that any aggressor by sudden action could disrupt and even obliterate the life of an attacked nation and make it impossible to take effective defense measures."[68] For this reason, Arnold and the majority of his colleagues concluded that the United States must embrace a military posture premised on permanent peacetime mobilization.[69] As Curtis LeMay, the officer in charge of the final bombing campaign against Japan, remembered, the advent of nuclear weapons persuaded airmen that "we had to operate every day as if we were at war, so if the whistle actually blew we would be doing the same things that we were doing yesterday with the same people and the same methods."[70] By the autumn of 1945, manifold military officers had concluded that atomic weapons eradicated the line that traditionally separated war from peace.[71]

Science was considered vital to the effort to guarantee U.S. national security. Even before World War II ended, several government officials affirmed the importance of peacetime scientific mobilization. In November 1944, for example, secretary of war Henry L. Stimson and secretary of the Navy James V. Forrestal together declared that U.S. national security depended on scientists continuing their wartime research during peace.[72] After V-J day, the desire to institutionalize scientists' relationship with the emergent national security state engendered several new organizations, including the Office of Naval Research, the Joint Research and Development Board, the Atomic Energy Commission, and Project RAND.[73]

Bowles was one of the War Department's most vociferous advocates for peacetime scientific mobilization, and in February 1945 he detailed his plan for "establishing an intimate bilateral working relationship" between civilians and the AAF once hostilities ceased.[74] Most important, in this plan he argued that for several reasons the air force itself should not direct peacetime research. First, throughout the war he was disappointed with the service's "lack of self-analysis." Second, he worried that "militarism" could become "a national threat." Finally, he did not believe there was enough talent, money, and organizational fluidity within the AAF to ensure an effective national security research program. As such, Bowles insisted that after the war the aircraft industry should partner with MIT and Harvard to found "an academy to continue a study of air in . . . tactical, strategic, and transport aspects." The work of this academy, he proclaimed, would enable the United States to base its R&D effort "on as rational a foundation as the thinking of our best minds will permit."[75]

Collbohm was likewise anxious about the "exodus of scientists [from government] after the war"—he was certain the geopolitical "situation wasn't going to be all sweetness and light"—and sometime in 1944–45 he concluded that a "mechanism would have to be developed which would make it possible to induce scientists to pursue their careers within a military framework—or at least to continue to devote themselves to problems of national security."[76] Luckily for him, Donald Douglas had expressed personal interest in forming "some kind of a group looking ahead" to the future of air research, and toward the war's end Douglas asked Collbohm to "think about [this group] a little bit."[77] Armed with this vague entreaty, in September 1945 Collbohm—perhaps with Douglas's approval, perhaps without—met with Bowles, who later told Symington:

> Don Douglas had come to a point in life where he wanted, if you will, to leave a noble memorial. [Douglas] had been so impressed with some of these jobs that we had done, in collaboration, that he would like to underwrite the setup and establish a civil corporation to devote itself to military problems, and literally, for the purposes at hand, Air.[78]

Collbohm suggested initiating "a long range broad program on the subject of intercontinental missiles." However, "it was clear," Bowles noted, that Douglas Aircraft "was interested not so much in working on a specific missile as in work of a general research character on the problems looking well out into the future and very much beyond the range of our regular missile projects." Specifically, Collbohm desired "to study the V-2 [*Vergeltungswaffe-2*, a Nazi ballistic missile] techniques . . . so as to examine very broadly their stratospheric transport implications."[79] Bowles was attracted to Douglas's idea of "establishing a basic research organization in air techniques—something that would be of value to the future of air as an instrument of national security"—and was further happy that Collbohm's proposal "fitted in with [his] ideals of the way in which the Military and industry should participate in joint defense planning."[80] In fact, Bowles had discussed setting up an outside group to aid the AAF "many times with General Arnold . . . behind closed doors."[81] Although he had hoped to place his envisioned academy at Harvard and MIT, Bowles chose not to look a gift horse in the mouth and, in Collbohm's words, "paved the way" for this idea with Arnold, considering it "the next logical step" after the Special Bombardment Project.[82]

On September 29, Collbohm and Bowles met with Arnold to officially inform him of their desire to place an air research group at Douglas Aircraft.[83] Of all AAF leaders, Arnold was the most concerned with ensuring the air forces had access to the latest cutting-edge science and technology. As he avowed in a speech given to approximately 250 air officers in January 1945, he was convinced the AAF must organize itself around the "long-haired individuals" "who can think and produce for the air forces the types of aircraft, armament, radar, etc." that won modern wars (and which, everyone listening understood, would ensure air force independence).[84]

He was also interested in avoiding, as Robert Lovett, the assistant secretary of war for air, recalled, the "'Liberty engine' psychology" that had prevailed after World War I, when an oversupply of Liberty engines forced the Air Force "to use these obsolete engines and thereby neglect the continuous development of modern military aircraft."[85] When Arnold learned of Collbohm and Bowles's plan, he endorsed it with enthusiasm, proclaiming "it the most important thing we have to do."[86] Anxious that the postwar fervor for demobilization might lead Congress to deprive him of the funds required to properly support the group, Arnold instructed Collbohm to return immediately to Santa Monica, receive Douglas's approval for the plan, and meet him at Hamilton Field, an air force base north of San Francisco, in two days' time with the "dope" on what Douglas Aircraft needed to guarantee its success.[87]

On October 1, Collbohm, Douglas, Arthur Raymond, and F. W. Conant (Douglas Aircraft's vice president of manufacturing) met with Arnold and Bowles at Hamilton Field to discuss founding "a long-range program . . . directed toward the achievement of an intercontinental guided missile" to be "set up . . . independently of [Douglas Aircraft's] regular engineering activities."[88] Bowles and Collbohm had by this point concluded that their envisioned group would analyze a broad range of issues, but they decided to focus initially on rockets because, as Donald Douglas recalled, Arnold "had the most faith in the coming of missiles" and "had the idea that [AAF] money ought to be spent on missile research."[89] Indeed, Bowles remembered that at the meeting Arnold "emphasized the importance of [creating] an elite program of research going beyond the bounds of conventional delivery [i.e., planes]—that is, a program which would include intercontinental pilotless missiles and related techniques."[90] Bowles and Collbohm were aware of Arnold's concern with rockets and made the canny decision to have this be the focus of their group's first project. But over time, to borrow words Bowles used elsewhere, they wanted their program to move beyond weapons to help the AAF "do its job of strategic thinking" in light of "what science and technology have to offer."[91]

The meeting went smoothly and lasted only an hour and a half.[92] By its conclusion, the participants had determined that the Douglas group would research, design, and eventually develop a rocket prototype. Arnold assigned Bowles the responsibility of ushering the project to fruition and arranged to have $10 million allocated to Douglas Aircraft.[93] The enormous size of the budget, Collbohm remembered, provided the group with "time to prove itself before it ha[d] to go in for" more funds.[94] It also tied the project directly to the AAF.

The Douglas group built on Progressive models of governance in which the state partnered with private experts to solve pressing problems. Yet it also represented a novel form of military-industrial-scientific collaboration. Unlike the NDRC, OSRD, and related efforts championed by Vannevar Bush in 1945–46, the Douglas project depended exclusively on the military for funding and support.[95] Moreover, there was no institution mediating between Douglas Aircraft and the AAF, which guaranteed that the Douglas group would be subject, as Bowles put it elsewhere, to military "direction and discipline."[96] As this suggests, Bowles experienced a change of heart between February, when he expressed concern over the AAF's guiding peacetime scientific research, and October, when he effectively established air force control of the Douglas project. The likely reason for this transformation was that by the latter date Arnold, at Bowles's urging, had entrusted the engineer with institutionalizing the AAF's research effort.[97] In other words, Bowles believed he could trust himself to wisely oversee the Douglas group.

Throughout the autumn of 1945, Bowles worked with AAF generals Carl Spaatz and Ira Eaker to reform the air force structure to support scientific research so the AAF would be able to administer projects such as the inchoate one at Douglas Aircraft.[98] In late November, the three recommended that Arnold create an office dedicated to managing air force R&D. To ensure airmen took this office seriously, Bowles and his colleagues suggested it be placed at the level of deputy chief of staff and directed by Curtis LeMay, who was widely admired for administering the final bombing of Japan.[99] Arnold, who by this point in time "had so much faith in [Bowles] it was dangerous," endorsed these proposals and on December 5 established the Office of the Deputy Chief of Staff for Research and Development (DCS/R&D) with LeMay at its head.[100] This office, Bowles insisted, would "be able to set a pattern in the Air Forces that is truly progressive in the research and development sense."[101]

LeMay's first task was to get the Douglas project, which had become known as "Project X," off the ground.[102] This turned out to be a difficult undertaking. The primary idea behind Project X was that civilians were needed to help shape the AAF's research, development, and procurement efforts. This remit, however, threatened the prerogatives of the Air Technical Service Command (ATSC), which was officially responsible for these activities. Moreover, the ATSC was anxious that the project would connect the air staff's planning division to research and development, further subverting its authority.[103] Indeed, Laurence Craigie, the director of ATSC's Engineering Division, considered Project X a menace that he needed to neutralize. On October 31, he dispatched a letter to Douglas Aircraft inviting the company to "submit a proposal [to ATSC] outlining a one year research program which will result in a practical design" of a family of guided missiles whose characteristics were determined by ATSC.[104] With this request, Craigie affirmed ATSC's authority to tell contractors what, exactly, they should research and develop.[105] Bowles correctly viewed Craigie's gambit as a rejection of "the philosophy of the [Douglas] project" specifically and the "philosophy of . . . progressive research" generally and in the winter of 1945–46 took a firm stand against ATSC.[106]

To settle this dispute, on February 21, 1946, LeMay convened a meeting to which he invited Bowles, Craigie, and Collbohm, among others.[107] At the meeting, Bowles and Collbohm made clear that they wanted Project X to pursue a broad research program that encompassed everything from a "study of available bases, logistics, and tactics" to analyses of the "relative importance of atomic bombs, B-W [biological warfare] and other types of destructive munitions" to "Research and Development of special defensive measures for high velocity missiles, including [a] 'Death Ray.'"[108] As this indicates, between October and February Bowles and Collbohm's plan for the Douglas project had expanded well beyond rockets.[109] Craigie, however, dismissed Bowles and Collbohm's ambitious program and presented a counterproposal that repeated his earlier suggestion that Project X focus on developing guided missiles with ATSC-determined characteristics.[110] This infuriated Bowles, who accused Craigie and ATSC of misunderstanding, or just rejecting, Project X's purpose: to work with, not for, the AAF.[111] Fortunately for the engineer, LeMay concurred with his perspective and informed Craigie in no uncertain terms that the AAF was "not going to tell the contractor what to do, but ask the contractor for advice."[112] With this decision, which Bowles considered "heroic," the stage was set for Project X.[113]

On March 2, 1946, Douglas Aircraft and the AAF signed contract No. W 33–038 ac-14105 (15775), which initiated Project No. MX-791. Unlike traditional air force contracts, which were geared toward the production of specific items, the Douglas project's contract authorized "study and research on the broad subject of intercontinental warfare, other than surface, with the object of recommending to the Army Air Forces preferred techniques and instrumentalities for the purpose."[114] This statement of work, Curtis LeMay remembered, provided the project's analysts with "a real broad spectrum so that they could get into practically anything as long as it pertained to national defense."[115] As Bowles reported to Arnold, "the contract . . . got away entirely from the missile concept."[116] Additionally, the contract made clear that, contrary to initial expectations, the project would concentrate on research, not development.[117] The contract, which covered a period of two years, the maximum allowed by U.S. law, thus established the national security research "academy" that Bowles had first proposed in February 1945.[118]

Project MX-791 was quickly dubbed Project RAND. No one knows for certain from where the designation "RAND" came. The most popular story—and the one promoted by Collbohm and RAND—is that Arthur Raymond developed the name as an acronym for Research ANd Development.[119] (LeMay would joke later that RAND really stood for "research and no development."[120]) Raymond disputed this claim, however, reporting in 1970 that he did suggest the appellation but it was simply "a short name which hopefully wouldn't have other connotations to it." Some people have argued that RAND combined the first and last two letters of Raymond's surname, a charge he vociferously denied.[121] Regardless, after Project RAND became the independent RAND Corporation in 1948 and emerged as the most influential national security think tank of the early Cold War, the name "RAND" would come to symbolize, to critics and supporters alike, the military-intellectual complex of which it formed a central part. With RAND, Bowles and Collbohm established a pattern of military-industrial-scientific collaboration that would define U.S. policy making for the remainder of the American Century.

Notes

1. The idea of the air forces as a "Progressive" organization comes from Mark Clodfelter, *Beneficial Bombing: The Progressive Foundations of American Air Power, 1917–1945* (Lincoln: University of Nebraska Press, 2010). In this chapter, I also rely on Perry M. Smith, *The Air Force Plans for Peace, 1943–1945* (Baltimore, MD: Johns Hopkins University Press, 1970); John F. Shiner, *Foulois and the U.S. Army Air Corps, 1931–1935* (Washington, DC: Office of Air Force History, 1983); Ronald Schaffer, *Wings of Judgment: American Bombing in World War II* (New York: Oxford University Press, 1985); Michael S. Sherry, *The Rise of American Airpower: The Creation of Armageddon* (New Haven, CT: Yale University Press, 1987); Jeffrey S. Underwood, *The Wings of Democracy: The Influence*

of *Air Power on the Roosevelt Administration, 1933–1941* (College Station: Texas A&M University Press, 1991); Geoffrey Perret, *Winged Victory; The Army Air Forces in World War II* (New York: Random House, 1993); Carl H. Builder, *The Icarus Syndrome: The Role of Air Power Theory in the Evolution and Fate of the U.S. Air Force* (New Brunswick, NJ: Transaction, 1994); David E. Johnson, *Fast Tanks and Heavy Bombers: Innovation in the U.S. Army, 1917–1945* (Ithaca, NY: Cornell University Press, 1998); James P. Tate, *The Army and Its Air Corps: Army Policy Toward Aviation, 1919–1941* (Maxwell Air Force Base, AL: Air University Press, 1998); Dik A. Daso, *Hap Arnold and the Evolution of American Airpower* (Washington, DC: Smithsonian Institution Press, 2000); Timothy Moy, *War Machines: Transforming Technologies in the U.S. Military, 1920–1940* (College Station: Texas A&M University Press, 2001); Tami Davis Biddle, *Rhetoric and Reality in Air Warfare: The Evolution of British and American Ideas About Strategic Bombing, 1914–1945* (Princeton, NJ: Princeton University Press, 2002); Yuki Tanaka, introduction to *Bombing Civilians: A Twentieth-Century History*, ed. Yuki Tanaka and Marilyn B. Young (New York: New Press, 2009), 1–7; Ronald Schaffer, "The Bombing Campaigns in World War II: The European Theater," in *Bombing Civilians: A Twentieth-Century History*, ed. Yuki Tanaka and Marilyn B. Young (New York: New Press, 2009), 30–45; Mark Selden, "A Forgotten Holocaust: U.S. Bombing Strategy, the Destruction of Japanese Cities, and the American Way of War from the Pacific War to Iraq," in *Bombing Civilians: A Twentieth-Century History*, ed. Yuki Tanaka and Marilyn B. Young (New York: New Press, 2009), 77–96; Kenneth P. Werrell, *Death from the Heavens: A History of Strategic Bombing* (Annapolis, MD: Naval Institute Press, 2009); Herman S. Wolk, *Cataclysm: General Hap Arnold and the Defeat of Japan* (Denton: University of North Texas Press, 2010); Conrad C. Crane, *American Airpower Strategy in World War II: Bombs, Cities, Civilians, and Oil* (Lawrence: University Press of Kansas, 2016); Melvin G. Deaile, *Always at War: Organizational Culture in Strategic Air Command, 1946–62* (Annapolis, MD: Naval Institute Press, 2018).

2. As Henry Harley Arnold affirmed in a June 1946 speech: "It was through the courage and vision of a body of pioneers interested in the conquest of air that there arose our present military air arm, an arm unhampered by traditions." H. H. Arnold, "The Past Predicts the Future," July 19, 1946, 29–30, folder 5, box 31, Edward Lindley Bowles Papers, Manuscript Division, Library of Congress, Washington, D.C. (hereafter Bowles Papers). On Army officers' technological skepticism and general conservatism, see William Mitchell, *Winged Defense: The Development and Possibilities of Modern Air Power—Economic and Military* (New York: Putman's Sons, 1925), viii–x; H. H. Arnold and Ira C. Eaker, *Army Flyer* (New York: Harper, 1942), 72–73; Johnson, *Fast Tanks and Heavy Bombers*, 57–59, 71, 114–15, 219, 229; Tate, *The Army and Its Air Corps*, 38, 186–88; Moy, *War Machines*, 23.

3. H. H. Arnold to All Air Force Commanders in Combat Zones, "Evaluation of Bombing Methods and Purposes," June 10, 1943, 2, Thirteenth Air Force, box 121, Nathan F. Twining Papers, Manuscript Division, Library of Congress, Washington, D.C.

4. H. H. Arnold to All Air Force Commanders in Combat Zones, "Evaluation of Bombing Methods and Purposes," 1.

5. Curtis E. LeMay, "Remarks By: Maj Gen. Curtis E. LeMay," July 18, 1946, 5, folder IV 3 (B) Gen LeMay's Speeches, box B44, Curtis E. LeMay Papers, Manuscript Division, Library of Congress, Washington, D.C. (hereafter LeMay Papers); Curtis E. LeMay, "Air Power Is Peace Power," August 3, 1946, 2, folder IV 3 (B) Gen LeMay's Speeches, box B44, LeMay Papers; Michael S. Sherry, *Preparing for the Next War: American Plans for Postwar Defense, 1941–45* (New Haven, CT: Yale University Press, 1977), 230–32; Schaffer, *Wings of Judgment*, 174–75; Builder, *The Icarus Syndrome*, 133, 141; Johnson, *Fast Tanks and Heavy Bombers*, 227–28; Biddle, *Rhetoric and Reality in Air Warfare*, 278–80; Tanaka, *Bombing Civilians*, 5; Werrell, *Death from the Heavens*, xiv, 153; Clodfelter, *Beneficial Bombing*, 5, 230–34, 236, 240–42; Crane, *American Airpower Strategy in World War II*, 191; Deaile, *Always at War*, 62, 69–70. Some air officers even presented the atomic attack on Hiroshima as an example of precision strategic bombing. See Lauris Norstad to Carl Spaatz, Telecon MSG NR 9–1, n.d. [August 8, 1945], Personal Collection of Conrad C. Crane, Carlisle, Pennsylvania.

6. Carl H. Builder, *The Masks of War: American Military Styles in Strategy and Analysis* (Baltimore, MD: Johns Hopkins University Press, 1989), 19.

7. Kenneth C. Royall to Secretary, Medal for Merit Board, ~August 15, 1947, folder 5, box 35, 1, Bowles Papers.

8. For Bowles at MIT, see Karl L. Wildes and Nilo A. Lindgren, *A Century of Electrical Engineering and Computer Science at MIT, 1882–1982* (Cambridge, MA: MIT Press, 1985), chap. 6; Alex Soojung-Kim Pang, "Edward Bowles and Radio Engineering at MIT, 1920–1940," *Historical Studies in the Physical and Biological Sciences* 20, no. 2 (1990): 313–37.

9. Henry E. Guerlac, *Radar in World War II: Sections A-C* (New York: American Institute of Physics, 1987), 215–18; Stuart W. Leslie, *The Cold War and American Science: The Military-Industrial-Academic Complex at MIT and Stanford* (New York: Columbia University Press, 1993), 17; Martin J. Collins, *Cold War Laboratory: RAND, the Air Force, and the American State, 1945–1950* (Washington, DC: Smithsonian Institution Press, 2002), 18.

10. Soojung-Kim Pang, "Edward Bowles," 314, 316, 319–23, 330.

11. Edward L. Bowles, "Tape 11-Side B," 1978–1984, 3–4, folder 27, box 84, Bowles Papers; Edward L. Bowles, "My Introduction to Secretary Stimson," December 17, 1982, 1, folder 2, box 37, Bowles Papers; Collins, *Cold War Laboratory*, 18.

12. Bowles, "Tape 11-Side B," 4.

13. For Bowles's reflections on the alienation he experienced at MIT in the inter-war years, see Edward L. Bowles to Karl T. Compton, March 20, 1946, 2–3, folder 6, box 34, Bowles Papers.

14. Irvin Stewart, *Organizing Scientific Research for War: The Administrative History of the Office of Scientific Research and Development* (Boston: Little, Brown, 1948) 12.

15. Bowles, "Tape 11-Side B," 2; Dorothea Wolfgram, "ELB," *Washington University Magazine* (Winter 1980), 36; Roslyn Romanowski, "Transcript of Interview with Edward L. Bowles," March 17, 1982, 10, MIT Museum Archives, Cambridge, Massachusetts.

16. Bowles, "My Introduction to Secretary Stimson," 2; Edward L. Bowles, "Tape 13-Side A," 1978–1984, 10, folder 28, box 84, Bowles Papers.

17. Edward L. Bowles, "Tape 13-Side B," 1978–1984, 1, folder 28, box 84, Bowles Papers.

18. Jennet Conant, *Tuxedo Park: A Wall Street Tycoon and the Secret Palace of Science That Changed the Course of World War II* (New York: Simon & Schuster, 2002), 234.

19. Conant, *Tuxedo Park*, 234–35.

20. Bowles, "My Introduction to Secretary Stimson," 2.

21. Henry L. Stimson, March 30, 1942, 1, vol. 38, March 1, 1942–April 30, 1942, reel 7, Henry L. Stimson Diaries (microfilm), Yale University Library, New Haven, Connecticut (hereafter Stimson Diaries); Robert Buderi, *The Invention That Changed the World: How a Small Group of Radar Pioneers Won the Second World War and Launched a Technological Revolution* (New York: Simon & Schuster, 1996), 144.

22. Buderi, *The Invention That Changed the World*, 144.

23. Henry L. Stimson, April 1, 1942, 1, Stimson Diaries; Bowles, "My Introduction to Secretary Stimson," 2–3. Stimson had learned of Bowles from two sources. The first is Vannevar Bush, Bowles's friend and colleague from MIT, who considered both Loomis and Compton annoyingly arrogant. Recommending Bowles to a high position forced the latter two, who had orchestrated Bowles's dismissal, "to take bitter medicine." The second source is Roger B. Colton, the director of the Signal Corps Laboratories, with whom Bowles was friendly. Bowles learned that when Stimson's office asked the Signal Corps to recommend a person who could help with radar, Colton suggested Bowles. Bowles, "My Introduction to Secretary Stimson," 3–5; Bowles, "Tape 13-Side B," 2.

24. Bowles, "My Introduction to Secretary Stimson," 3.

25. Edward L. Bowles to Frank D. Lewis, September 11, 1942, 1, folder 6, box 29, Bowles Papers.

26. Bowles, "My Introduction to Secretary Stimson," 3; Stimson, April 1, 1942, 1; Bowles to Lewis, September 11, 1942, 1–2.

27. Bowles, "My Introduction to Secretary Stimson," 3–4.

28. At its height, this office employed around eighty consultants. Edward L. Bowles to Henry L. Stimson, July 30, 1946, folder 5, box 31, Bowles Papers.

29. This definition of adhocracy is taken from Gerald Berk, "Building the Problem-Solving State: Bridging Networks and Experiments in the US Advisory Specialist Group in World War II," *Politics & Society* 46, no. 2 (2018): 266.

30. Michael S. Sherry, "Notes on Conversation with Edward L. Bowles," September 3, 1980, 1, Personal Collection of Michael Sherry, Evanston, Illinois.

31. See, e.g., Edward L. Bowles to Henry L. Stimson, "Resume of Consultant Activity," August 23, 1943, 4–6, folder 3, box 30, Bowles Papers.

32. Bowles to Stimson, "Resume of Consultant Activity," 1.

33. Edward L. Bowles to Murray Green, n.d. [1970s–1980s], folder 2, box 37, Bowles Papers.

34. Montgomery C. Meigs, *Slide Rules and Submarines: American Scientists and Subsurface Warfare in World War II* (Washington, DC: National Defense University Press, 1990), 65.

35. Edward L. Bowles to Robert Patterson, May 5, 1947, 1–2, folder 6, box 31, Bowles Papers.

36. Bowles to Stimson, July 30, 1946.

37. Edward L. Bowles to William S. Rumbough, February 6, 1945, 2–3, folder 1, box 31, Bowles Papers. For use of the term "Advisory Specialist Group," see Allen V. Hazeltine to L. J. Henderson, August 26, 1944, folder 7, box 30, Bowles Papers; and Lincoln R. Thiesmeyer and John. E. Burchard, *Combat Scientists (Science in World War II)* (Boston: Little, Brown, 1947), 301. Many of the people who worked for Bowles were also associated with the OSRD and industrial firms. See Edward L. Bowles to Dwight D. Eisenhower, "Military Communications, Related Services, and Organizational Considerations," February 10, 1947, 18, folder 3, box 35, Bowles Papers.

38. Berk, "Building the Problem-Solving State," 286.

39. Edward L. Bowles to Carl Spaatz, November 29, 1943, folder 5, box 32, Bowles Papers; Adjutant General to the Commanding General, Air Transport Command and the Chief of Transportation, Army Service Forces, "Travel Orders," November 10, 1944, 1, folder 4, box 46, Bowles Papers.

40. See, for example, Edward L. Bowles to Ivan Farman, February 14, 1945, folder 1, box 31, Bowles Papers. On Bowles's ability to work well with military officers, see Henry L. Stimson and McGeorge Bundy, *On Active Service in Peace and War* (New York: Harper, 1948), 468.

41. Edward L. Bowles, "Tape 7-Side B," 1978–1984, 3, folder 22, box 84, Bowles Papers.

42. Edward L. Bowles, "Trip Diaries, Pacific Trip," December 27, 1944, 32, folder 3, box 46, Bowles Papers.

43. Edward L. Bowles to William Borden, October 8, 1944, 1, folder 8, box 30, Bowles Papers.

44. For this report, see Edward L. Bowles to H. H. Arnold, "Army Air Forces Communications," June 16, 1943, folder 2, box 30, Bowles Papers.

45. Edward L. Bowles to Henry L. Stimson, August 23, 1943, 1, folder 3, box 32, Bowles Papers.

46. Edward L. Bowles to H. H. Arnold, August 24, 1943, folder 3, box 32, Bowles Papers.

47. Anonymous [Allen V. Hazeltine], "Special Consultant to the Commanding General, AAF, Dr. Edward L. Bowles," n.d. [August 1945], 1, folder 3, box 31, Bowles Papers; "Interview, Arthur Raymond, San Diego, Cal.," August 14, 1970, 6, Henry H. Arnold Collection, no. 168.7330–1607, Murray Green Collection, reel 43826, Air Force Historical Research Agency, Maxwell AFB, Montgomery, Alabama (hereafter AFHRA).

48. H. H. Arnold to Carl Spaatz, September 12, 1944, folder 3, box 33, Bowles Papers.

49. "Franklin R. Collbohm," September 1966, Biographical Materials, box 2, Frank R. Collbohm Papers, RAND Corporation Archives, Santa Monica, California (hereafter Collbohm Papers); Frank Collbohm, "Interview," July 28, 1987, 1–2, RAND History Project Interviews (Acc. 1999–0037), National Air and Space Museum, Smithsonian Institution, Washington, D.C.

50. Collbohm, "Interview," July 28, 1987, 3.

51. "Franklin R. Collbohm," September 1966; Collbohm, "Interview," July 28, 1987, 2–4.

52. "Franklin R. Collbohm Dies, RAND Corporation Founding Leader, Aerospace Pioneer," n.d. [February 1990], 2, Biographical Materials, box 2, Collbohm Papers.

53. Collbohm, "Interview," July 28, 1987, 6, 8–9; Arthur Raymond, compiled by Walter Didur, "Frank and the Pre-RAND Years," in *RAND Alumni Bulletin Supplement* [Special Issue on Frank Collbohm], Spring 1996, 2, Biographical Materials, box 2, Collbohm Papers; Paul A. C. Koistinen, *Planning War, Pursuing Peace: The Political Economy of American Warfare, 1920–1939* (Lawrence: University Press of Kansas, 1998), 186–87.

54. "Interview with Frank Collbohm, Huntington Beach, Calif.," August 17, 1970, 1, Henry H. Arnold Collection, call no. 168.7330–1607, Murray Green Collection, reel 43819, AFHRA; "Statement by Mr. Frank R. Collbohm, Director, The RAND Corporation, on the Origins and History of RAND, with Special Reference to the Roles Played by Mr. H. Rowan Gaither, the Ford Foundation and by Mr. Collbohm," April 12, 1954, 4, History of the RAND Corporation, 1954–1966, box 4, Lawrence J. Henderson Papers, RAND Corporation Archives, Santa Monica, California (hereafter Henderson Papers).

55. "Interview with Frank Collbohm," August 17, 1970, 3–4; Collbohm, "Interview," July 28, 1987, 13; Edward L. Bowles to Frank Collbohm, December 15, 1942, folder 8, box 29, Bowles Papers.

56. Edward L. Bowles to H. H. Arnold, "Special Bombardment Project," August 28, 1944, 1, folder 2, box 33, Bowles Papers.

57. "Interview with Frank Collbohm," August 17, 1970, 3; Collbohm, "Interview," July 28, 1987, 13: Arnold, "The Past Predicts the Future," 8.

58. Arnold, "The Past Predicts the Future," 8–9.

59. Arthur E. Raymond to Edward L. Bowles, "Special Bombardment Project," September 25, 1944, 4, folder 3, box 33, Bowles Papers.

60. Edward L. Bowles to Edward C. Wells, October 4, 1944, folder 4, box 33, Bowles Papers.

61. On Arnold's investment in the B-29, see Thomas M. Coffey, *Hap: The Story of the U.S. Air Force and the Man Who Built It, General Henry H. 'Hap' Arnold* (New York: Viking, 1982), 353–54; Perret, *Winged Victory*, 102–3, 447; Daso, *Hap Arnold and the Evolution of American Airpower*, 195–96; Biddle, *Rhetoric and Reality in Air Warfare*, 266; Wolk, *Cataclysm*, 7–9; Clodfelter, *Beneficial Bombing*, 214; Daniel T. Schwabe, *Burning Japan: Air Force Bombing Strategy Change in the Pacific* (Lincoln, NE: Potomac, 2015), 7.

62. Arthur E. Raymond, concurred by Edward C. Wells and Frank Collbohm, to Edward L. Bowles, "Special Bombardment Project—Interim Report on B-29," October 7, 1944, folder 8, box 30, Bowles Papers. When writing their report, Collbohm, Raymond, and Wells consulted with the mathematician Warren Weaver, who would later prove instrumental in helping set up the RAND Corporation.

63. "Exhibit B" in Raymond, "Special Bombardment Project," 1.

64. Edward L. Bowles to Barney Giles, "B-29 Operations," October 11, 1944, folder 4, box 33, Bowles Papers; Arthur E. Raymond to Frank Collbohm, November 21, 1944, 2, folder 5, box 33, Bowles Papers.

65. Arnold, "The Past Predicts the Future," 9; Bowles to Patterson, May 5, 1947, 2–3; Ralph L. Swann, "A Unit History of the 315th Bomb Wing, 1944–1946," Report No. 86–2460, Air Command and Staff College, Air University, Maxwell Air Force Base, Alabama (March 1986), 27; William Thomas, *Rational Action: The Sciences of Policy in Britain and America, 1940–1960* (Cambridge, MA: MIT Press, 2015), 121.

66. Adjutant General to the Commanding General, Air Transport Command and the Chief of Transportation, Army Service Forces, "Travel Orders," November 10, 1944, folder 4, box 46, Bowles Papers; Raymond to Collbohm, November 21, 1944, 3.

67. For Bowles's take on this trip, see folders 3–4, box 46, Bowles Papers. Collbohm and Bowles had been on friendly terms for years; for instance, on

December 7, 1941—the day the Japanese bombed Pearl Harbor—the two were in California hanging out together on Collbohm's boat. Collbohm, "Interview," July 28, 1987, 12–13.

68. U.S. Congress, Senate, Subcommittee of the Committee on Military Affairs, *Hearings Before a Subcommittee of the Committee on Military Affairs*, 79th Cong., 1st Sess., 1945, 344.

69. See, for example, Edward L. Bowles, "Preliminary Draft," October 12, 1945, 2–4, folder 1, box 43, Bowles Papers.

70. John T. Bohn, "Interview with General Curtis E. LeMay, USAF Retired," March 9, 1971, 29, Oral History Collection, call no. K239.0512–736, reel 30177, AFHRA.

71. This was true of civilians as well. As J. D. Small, who worked for the War Production Board during World War II, wrote to President Harry S Truman in December 1946, the war demonstrated "the necessity for maintaining current, up-to-the-minute, plans for rapid and effective mobilization of our entire national economy should need arise. No matter how remote the prospect of war may be the nation must be continuously prepared for that eventuality." J. D. Small to Harry S Truman, December 5, 1946, 1, Federal Correspondence and Memoranda, 1937, 1946, box 1, David Novick Papers, RAND Corporation Archives, Santa Monica, California.

72. Henry L. Stimson and James V. Forrestal to the President of the National Academy of Sciences, November 9, 1944, folder 5, box 33, Bowles Papers.

73. Sherry, *Preparing for the Next War*, 134–58; Larry Owens, "The Counterproductive Management of Science in the Second World War: Vannevar Bush and the Office of Scientific Research and Development," *Business History Review* 68, no. 4 (Winter 1994): 560; G. Pascal Zachary, *Endless Frontier: Vannevar Bush, Engineer of the American Century* (New York: Free Press, 1997), 322, 329, 336–37; Allan A. Needell, *Science, Cold War and the American State: Lloyd V. Berkner and the Balance of Professional Ideals* (Amsterdam: Harwood Academic, 2000), 103–4; Collins, *Cold War Laboratory*, 8, 45.

74. Edward L. Bowles, "Memorandum for the Files," February 20, 1945, 2, folder 7, box 33, Bowles Papers. Also see Bowles, "Preliminary Draft," 2–4; U.S. Congress, Senate, Subcommittee of the Committee on Military Affairs, *Hearings Before a Subcommittee of the Committee on Military Affairs*, 79th Cong., 1st Sess., 1945, 281–82.

75. Bowles, "Memorandum for the Files," February 20, 1945, 2, 4, 5.

76. Jack Loosbrock, "Interview with Frank Collbohm, RAND Corp, Santa Monica, Calif.," November 4, 1966, n.d. [1], Henry H. Arnold Collection, call no. 168.7330–1607, Murray Green Collection, reel 43814, AFHRA; "Interview with Frank Collbohm," August 17, 1970, 11; "Statement by Mr. Frank R. Collbohm," 2, Henderson Papers.

77. "Interview with Frank Collbohm," August 17, 1970, 11.

78. Edward L. Bowles to Stuart Symington, November 26, 1946, 1, folder 5, box 31, Bowles Papers; "Browles [sic]: RAND," n.d. [early 1970s?], [3, mislabeled as 2], Henry H. Arnold Collection, call no. 168.7330–1607, Murray Green Collection, reel 43814, AFHRA. For a contemporary description that confirms this account, see Edward L. Bowles to H. H. Arnold, September 5, 1946, 1–2, folder 5, box 31, Bowles Papers.

79. Bowles to Symington, November 26, 1946, 1.

80. Bowles to Symington, November 26, 1946, 1; Edward L. Bowles to Bruce L. R. Smith, January 6, 1967, 1, folder 9, box 15, Bowles Papers.

81. Edward L. Bowles, "Tape 17-Side A," 1978–1984, 9–10, folder 32, box 84, Bowles Papers.

82. "Interview with Frank Collbohm," August 17, 1970, 11; Bowles to Arnold, September 5, 1946, 1. Throughout 1946 and 1947, Bowles also dedicated himself to fostering civilian-military collaboration at U.S. research universities. Although this was intellectually connected to Project RAND, it was an independent effort and thus outside the scope of this analysis.

83. "Statement by Mr. Frank R. Collbohm," 4, Henderson Papers. Collbohm also met with, and promoted this idea to, a number of other high-ranking officials, including William R. Purnell, Vannevar Bush, Maxwell Taxlor, Stuart Symington, and Robert Patterson (the latter of whom suggested that Collbohm meet with Leslie Groves, with the idea being that the project would join the Manhattan District, but Groves rejected this plan). See "Statement by Mr. Frank R. Collbohm," 3–4, Henderson Papers; Collbohm, "Interview," July 28, 1987, 16.

84. Tom C. Rives, [Summary of H. H. Arnold Speech Given on January 12, 1945], n.d. [mid-January 1945], 3, folder 6, box 33, Bowles Papers.

85. H. Rowan Gaither, "Summary Notes on Telephone Discussion with Robert Lovett," October 29, 1958, 2, History of RAND Corporation, 1954–1966, box 4, Henderson Papers.

86. Loosbrock, "Interview with Frank Collbohm," n.d.

87. Loosbrock, "Interview with Frank Collbohm," n.d. Also see "Statement by Mr. Frank R. Collbohm," 4, Henderson Papers. For the notes Douglas Aircraft company executives developed for the meeting, see Arthur E. Raymond, "Notes for Conference with Gen'l. H. H. Arnold at Hamilton Field 10-1-45," n.d. [late-September 1945], folder 3, box 34, Bowles Papers.

88. Edward L. Bowles to Robert Patterson, October 4, 1945, 1, folder 3, box 31, Bowles Papers; Bowles to Symington, November 26, 1946, 2.

89. "Reminiscences of Donald Douglas," 1959, 117–18, General Henry H. (Hap) Arnold Oral History Collections, Oral History Archives at Columbia, Rare Book & Manuscript Library, Columbia University, New York; Bowles to Arnold, September 5, 1946, 2; Arnold, "The Past Predicts the Future," 24.

90. Bowles to Symington, November 26, 1946, 1.

91. Edward L. Bowles to [William H.?] Simpson, March 25, 1946, 2, folder 4, box 31, Bowles Papers.

92. Loosbrock, "Interview with Frank Collbohm," n.d.

93. Bowles to Patterson, October 4, 1945, 1–2.

94. "Interview with Frank Collbohm," August 17, 1970, 13.

95. On Vannevar Bush's views on the relationship between civilians, the military, and the government, see Nathan Reingold, "Vannevar Bush's New Deal for Research: Or the Triumph of the Old Order," *Historical Studies in the Physical and Biological Sciences* 17, no. 2 (1987): 299–344; Zachary, *Endless Frontier*, 164–65, 227–28, 263, 328, 335, 355; Needell, *Science, Cold War, and the American State*, 103; Collins, *Cold War Laboratory*, 71–73; Christopher Gainor, *The Bomb and America's Missile Age* (Baltimore, MD: Johns Hopkins University Press, 2018), 73, 76–77, 80.

96. Bowles, "Preliminary Draft," 9. On Project RAND as an institution organized around the interests of the AAF, and to a lesser degree Douglas Aircraft, as opposed to scientists and academics, see Collins, *Cold War Laboratory*, ix, xii, 26–27.

97. Bowles to Patterson, May 5, 1947, 3; Bowles to Patterson, October 4, 1945, 2.

98. Edward L. Bowles to H. H. Arnold, October 24, 1945, 1, folder 3, box 31, Bowles Papers; Edward L. Bowles to H. H. Arnold, November 26, 1945, 1, folder 4, box 31, Bowles Papers; Bowles to Symington, November 26, 1946, 3.

99. Bowles to Arnold, November 26, 1945, 1–2.

100. Michael Sherry, "Notes on Conversation with Edward L. Bowles," September 3, 1980, 3, Personal Collection of Michael Sherry, Evanston, Illinois; A. R. Crawford, Edward L. Bowles, Curtis E. LeMay, and Lauris Norstad, "Memorandum for the Chief of Staff," December 5, 1945, folder 4, box 34, Bowles Papers; Deputy Commander, AAF [Ira C. Eaker] to Deputy Chief of Air Staff for Research and Development [Curtis E. LeMay], "Organization of Office of Deputy Chief of Staff for Research and Development," December 5, 1945, folder 4, box 34, Bowles Papers.

101. Bowles to Arnold, November 26, 1945, 2.

102. "Project 'X,'" December 29, 1945, folder 3, box 34, Bowles Papers. This document is contained in Bowles's papers at the Library of Congress and is situated between an October 31, 1945, letter from Laurence Craigie to Douglas Aircraft and an October 24, 1945, letter from Bowles to Arnold, which suggests that "Project X" was related to what became known as Project RAND. However, one should note that nomenclature was fluid during this moment in U.S. military history, and Project X may or may not have been a common way to reference the Douglas Aircraft project. Also, much of the information in this paragraph comes from Collins, *Cold War Laboratory*, 41–44, 50; David R.

Jardini, *Thinking Through the Cold War: RAND, National Security, and Domestic Policy, 1945–1975* (September 2013), Kindle edition.

103. Bowles to Symington, November 26, 1946, 3.

104. L. C. Craigie to Douglas Aircraft Company, "Proposal for Guided Missile Research Program," October 31, 1945, 2, 1, folder 3, box 34, Bowles Papers.

105. As Bowles later remarked, "there was a dangerous tendency of Wright Field [the ATSC] to want to apply far too much control to the contractee." Edward L. Bowles to Stuart Symington, "Scientific and Technological Resources as Military Assets," October 2, 1946, 3, folder 5, box 31, Bowles Papers.

106. Edward L. Bowles, "Memorandum For: File," March 4, 1946, 1, folder 6, box 34, Bowles Papers; Bowles to Symington, November 26, 1946, 3; Collins, *Cold War Laboratory*, 44–50.

107. Bowles, "Memorandum For: File," 1.

108. "Agenda for Meeting with AAF 2/21/46, Program of Work—1946–1947," n.d. [January-February 1946], 1–2, folder 5, box 34, Bowles Papers. For other ideas concerning RAND's potential early research program, see "Appendix 'A' Outline of Work," in "Research and Development Contract Long Range Air Power," n.d. [winter 1945–46], folder 2, box 35, Bowles Papers.

109. Before the February 21 meeting, it was clear Project X would have a wide purview. For instance, a document likely written by Collbohm in the winter of 1945–46 in anticipation of the project's founding insisted that it should begin its study of "long range air power" "with an analysis of those factors which are primarily of geographic, political, or strategic nature"—such as "the bases available to this country for military installations"—which would enable its members to determine "a logical set of requirements for the [air warfare] system to be designed." "Research and Development Contract Long Range Air Power," n.d. [winter 1945–46], 1–2, folder 2, box 35, Bowles Papers.

110. Bowles, "Memorandum For: File," 1.

111. Bowles, "Memorandum For: File," 1; Bowles to Symington, November 26, 1946, 3.

112. Bowles, "Memorandum For: File," 1.

113. Bowles to Arnold, September 5, 1946, 1. For Collbohm's take on the meeting, see Collbohm, "Interview," July 28, 1987, 18.

114. "Letter Contract No. W-33-038 ac-14105, Douglas Aircraft Company, Inc., Santa Monica, California," March 2, 1946, 1, folder 1946, box 1, Brownlee Haydon Papers, RAND Corporation Archives, Santa Monica, California. Also see "Research and Development Contract Long Range Air Power"; Bowles to Symington, "Scientific and Technological Resources as Military Assets," 3–6; Collins, *Cold War Laboratory*, 40–54.

115. Bohn, "Interview with General Curtis E. LeMay," 6–7.

116. Edward L. Bowles to H. H. Arnold, July 1, 1946, folder 5, box 31, Bowles Papers.

117. Collins, *Cold War Laboratory*, 48–49.

118. Arthur E. Raymond, "For Presentation at First Meeting of RAND Council," December 12, 1946, 1, folder 2, box 44, Bowles Papers.

119. "Interview with Frank Collbohm, Huntington Beach, Calif.," August 17, 1970, 13.

120. Fred Kaplan, *The Wizards of Armageddon* (Stanford, CA: Stanford University Press, 1991), 59.

121. "Interview, Arthur Raymond, San Diego, Cal.," August 14, 1970, 10.

CHAPTER 20

Cold War Liberals, Neoconservatives, and the Rediscovery of Ideology

DANIEL STEINMETZ-JENKINS AND MICHAEL FRANCZAK

T he aim of this volume is to bring clarity to the study of U.S. foreign policy by identifying and understanding its ideological underpinnings. A great irony is that many of the leading mid-twentieth-century Cold War liberal thinkers were fundamentally committed to the idea that, as the left-leaning sociologist Daniel Bell put it, the United States and other rich liberal democracies had reached "the end of ideology." The great post–World War II economic boom in the Western world—in France, *les trentes glorieuses*—proved that class conflict was a problem that could be managed (through economic redistribution) but did not need to be resolved (through revolution). The Soviet economic engine remained impressive, but not enough to excuse the lack of civil and political liberties (to say nothing of the gulags). The end of ideology carried into American foreign policy, as the Kennedy administration's "best and brightest" produced rational plans for an irrational war in Southeast Asia, while promising the emerging "Third World" speedy "modernization" through liberal capitalist development. But it was in the Johnson administration that the end of ideology peaked, as the president simultaneously waged a "War on Poverty" in America and a war on communism in Vietnam and elsewhere.

Our aim in this chapter is to explain the period between Cold War liberalism's ascent in the 1950s and its transformation into a doctrine of neoconservatism by the 1970s. The end of ideology is the key ideology, we argue, for understanding this transformation. First, it explains the political and economic conditions that gave rise to the end of ideology, as the notion appeared in the writings of Daniel Bell, Seymour Martin Lipset, Edward Shils, Raymond Aron, Arthur Schlesinger Jr., and Reinhold Niebuhr. End-of-ideology defenders were divided on its global scope. On one hand were modernization theorists such as Shils and Lipset, who examined the political, economic, and cultural conditions by which the new states could avoid the perils of ideological politics. On the other hand were so-called realist scholars of international relations, most notably Raymond Aron in France and Reinhold Niebuhr in the United States, who believed that the end of ideology was the unique cultural, historical, and political achievement of "Western societies."

We then turn to the domestic and international factors that began in the late 1960s and left Cold War liberalism in a state of crisis and Cold War liberals searching for answers. From roughly 1968 to 1976, the New Left and student protests, détente with the Soviet Union, shame and failure in Vietnam, and a showdown with developing countries over oil prices and a New International Economic Order (NIEO) shattered postwar illusions of never-ending prosperity and national unity.

Some liberal thinkers and political leaders, particularly those involved in the (failed) 1972 campaign of George McGovern and the (successful) 1976 campaign of Jimmy Carter, tried to reinvent liberalism and the Democratic Party through social inclusion and foreign policy restraint. Other Cold War liberals developed a new faith: neoconservatism. In their mind, these liberals were not abandoning the Democratic Party; rather, the party was abandoning them. Figures like Daniel Patrick Moynihan declared themselves "Truman Democrats" to emphasize their fidelity to moderate redistributive liberalism and anticommunism, thereby distinguishing themselves from "radicals" like McGovern. In 1980, most Cold War liberals-cum-neoconservatives did the unthinkable—they voted Republican. Many joined the Reagan administration and played key roles in U.S. foreign policy, particularly regarding human rights and the Soviet Union. Far from its "end" in the 1950s and 1960s, neoconservatives in the 1970s and 1980s rediscovered and repurposed Cold War liberalism for a new project: restoring American power overseas to its 1950s glory days. The price was neoconservatives' commitment to social and economic liberalism at home, which their new coalition partners—Reagan and the New Right—actively sought to dismantle.

Postwar Liberalism Ascendent: Modernization and the End of Ideology

The end-of-ideology debate in the United States was sparked by publication in 1960 of Daniel Bell's *The End of Ideology* and Seymour Martin Lipset's *Political Man* (1960).[1] They argued that the grand ideologies of fascism and Marxism—which they likened to secular religions—were the products of the nineteenth century, a time of deepening misery for the industrial proletariat. However, the social order that emerged after World War II—marked by a prosperous economy, rising standards of living for the middle class, and a growing white-collar sector—had made these counterideologies obsolete. If fascism had been defeated on the battlefield, the aims of socialism could be fulfilled by the postwar economy without any need for confrontational mass politics. The welfare state could deflect revolutionary passions through redistribution; Marxist theories of class struggle would be rendered defunct, or at least confined to university lecture halls.

Before the end-of-ideology debate of the early 1960s, Cold War liberals spent the 1950s developing and defending its assumptions. In the *Irony of American History* (1952), the Protestant theologian Reinhold Niebuhr spoke of the "fluidity of the American class structure" and the decline of "social resentments in the United States." He claimed that power had become "equilibrated" in the United States, as industry and government joined to eliminate extreme "disproportions" and "disbalances" in economic life.[2] In 1957, the historian Arthur Schlesinger Jr., heavily influenced by Niebuhr, proclaimed that "the major problems of economic structure" in the United States "seem to be solved." "Liberalism," Schlesinger observed, "had successfully established its principles"; opposing class forces has been brought into "balance" through the "mixed economy."[3] With the "vital center" firmly in place, the major challenges now confronting liberalism were of a "spiritual" and "cultural" nature. And in 1955, the French liberal Raymond Aron, who was in direct contact with U.S. Cold War liberals through his involvement with the Congress for Cultural Freedom, published his well-known book, *The Opium of the Intellectuals*. Aron declared: "We are becoming ever more aware that the political categories of the last century—Left and Right, liberal and socialist, traditionalist and revolutionary have lost their relevance. They lump together ideas and men whom the course of history has drawn into opposing camps."[4] Aron, too, was convinced that ideological controversies in Western societies were easing to the point of stasis. The welfare state had proven it could reconcile divergent demands and, in turn, deflect revolutionary passions.

Much has been written about the end-of-ideology debate, but less about the divide on its application to the emerging "developing countries."[5] At the very moment Cold War liberals proclaimed that the North Atlantic Community had achieved an end to ideology, the political fate of newly emerging postcolonial states remained undecided—a reality made sober in light of the April 1955 Bandung Conference. For defenders of the end of ideology, the Bandung event inspired a move away from the fight against communism in Western Europe, which had now achieved liberal democratic stability, and toward a fight against global communism. Indeed, Bandung signaled a crucial moment for mid-twentieth-century defenders of the end of ideology. It represented developing countries' emergence as a diplomatic bloc in the Non-Aligned Movement, which occurred prior to formation of the Organization of the Petroleum Exporting Countries (OPEC) in 1960 and the United Nations Conference on Trade and Development in 1964. At this time, "Third World radicalism" had not yet moved away from political self-determination to focus on economic self-determination. In 1955, the type of critique associated with the NIEO of the 1970s was not articulated at Bandung.[6] For most Cold War liberals in the 1950s and early 1960s, it was a given that new states would and should pursue "modernization," or economic growth and development, and that those countries' national governments would necessarily play a major role. The question was chiefly political: who would pay the bill and get the credit, West or East? Faith in a linear model of state-led capitalist development in the developing countries in line with U.S. foreign policy aims was neatly summarized in the title of the Kennedy administration economist Walt Rostow's influential 1960 book, *The States of Economic Growth: A Non-Communist Manifesto*.[7]

No one was more optimistic for modernization's success than Seymour Martin Lipset. In *Political Man*, Lipset unabashedly claimed that "the fundamental political problems of the industrial revolution have been solved" and that the United States represented "the good society itself in operation." For Lipset, the West had entered the end of history: "the very triumph of the democratic social revolution in the West," declared Lipset, "ends domestic politics."[8] Around the time *Political Man* appeared, Lipset published what became one of the most cited social science articles of the century: "Some Social Requisites of Democracy: Economic Development and Political

Legitimacy."[9] The article identifies the structural conditions that are necessary for achieving nonideological democratic governance the world writ over: open class system, high literacy rates, capitalist economy, high participation in voluntary organizations, etc. Like Rostow, Lipset's thesis "sanctioned support for non-democratic developmental regimes in the name of establishing the 'economic preconditions for democracy.'"[10] Although the need for rapid industrialization would make emerging states prone to radical ideologies, Lipset ultimately believed, in the words of Nils Gilman, that "the postideological future of the postcolonial world was already clearly in sight, right here and now in the contemporary United States."[11] An end of ideology for the developing countries presumed, for Lipset, the American model as its telos.

The sociologist Edward Shils was another major end-of-ideology defender who explicitly connected the notion to the development of postcolonial nation-states, especially India.[12] In 1960, the same year that the end-of-ideology debate exploded in the United States, Shils published an article titled "Political Development in the New States," arguing that "modernity entails democracy, and democracy in the new states must above all be equalitarian."[13] The one-to-one connection between modernity and democracy, argued Shils, demanded the dethronement of the rich and traditionally privileged from their positions of long-standing political power. It also required the breaking up of large private estates, progressive income taxation, universal suffrage, and the replacement of monarchies by republics. Shils also made the assumption that modernity entailed disenchantment with religion, which he believed stymied the sense of robust individuality so characteristic of Western societies.[14] In other words, modernization and Westernization were mutually constitutive, and only countries that embraced the former could achieve the latter.

Not all defenders of the end of ideology were interested in exploring its implications for the developing countries; Bell, for instance, stuck to American politics. Other Cold War liberals—particularly "realist" foreign affairs intellectuals—opposed extending the end-of-ideology thesis to developing countries, mainly out of the conviction that those societies were fundamentally incapable of westernization. For Reinhold Niebuhr, power *could* be "equilibrated" in Western liberal democracies precisely because of those characteristics. There could be no liberal equilibrium in the developing countries, however, because most of the thee countries were incapable of liberalism. In *Irony of American History*, Niebuhr characterizes the Middle East as a "decadent Mohammedan feudal order" consisting of "sleepwalking cultures in which the drama of human history is not taken seriously." Niebuhr categorically writes off the entire Asian continent as incapable of Western democracy because the nations that compose it lack the "honesty" necessary for it: "Few of the nonindustrial nations have sufficiently high standards of honesty to make democratic government viable." China, reasoned Niebuhr, embraced Marxism due to its "lack of historical dynamism mak[ing] it an easy prey to communism, particularly among youth."[15]The greater irony, perhaps, is that Niebuhr removes the peoples and societies of developing countries from contemporary history ("sleepwalking") while failing to account for the (very recent) historical factors supporting his own country's fragile equilibrium. Niebuhr cautioned against American liberal crusading abroad—something for which contemporary liberals, most notably Barack Obama, continue to idealize he thought—and his reasoning for this is clear: it would be a lost cause, given the dishonest, decadent, and feudal societies of poorer nations.[16]

But it was the leading architect of the end of ideology in Europe who proved most critical of his American colleagues applying the notion to developing countries. In *Eighteen Lectures on Industrial Society*, Raymond Aron reported that during a trip to India he came away "convince[d] that the major concept of our time is that of industrial society. Europe, as seen from Asia, does not consist of two fundamentally different worlds, the Soviet world, and the Western world. It is one single reality: industrial society."[17] However, for Aron, convergence was primarily limited to the level of industry, not politics. Hence he grew concerned about the political and cultural effects that the demand to industrialize had inflicted on developing countries.[18] "Chinese, Hindus, Moslems," declared Aron, "have been subjugated, humiliated, and exploited by the makers of the machine."[19] In a sharply critical article of U.S. foreign policy that appeared in *Confluence* in 1953, Aron observed that out of a hundred articles appearing in the American press to address Truman's Point Four Plan, "not one can be found which analyses its political conditions."[20] He then rhetorically raised the question whether it is not obvious that the rationalizing of an economy presupposes a certain judicial and political environment. Aron's criticism of the Point Four Plan shares much in common with his critique of Marxism. In fact, Aron specifically described Point Four as the "American ideology":

Does not the error lie in forgetting that freedoms (personal, electoral, etc.), desirable as they may be, do not create the state and cannot flourish in simply any environment. . . . American influence, incapable of supporting the leaders in accord with the true American Ideology is reduced to supporting any available *de facto* potentate.[21]

When Henry Kissinger edited the draft of Aron's article, he found it so critical of the United States that he asked Aron if he could add to it some of Aron's previous material critical of Marxism.[22]

Aron's distancing from his American colleagues enthusiasm over the end of ideology in developing countries is on full display in his response to a paper Edward Shils gave in 1958 at the Congress for Cultural Freedom conference in Rhodes, Greece, titled "Representative Government and Public Liberty in the New States," which was basically a draft version of his 1959 article, "Political Development in the New States." At Rhodes, Aron clearly recognized that Shils's position assumed the imposition of Euro-American values abroad. But what works in the West, stressed Aron, might not necessarily work elsewhere. As he put it, "if democrats are to try to make democracy work elsewhere, especially in Africa and Asia, can we afford to keep our attention focused exclusively on our attractive western features?"[23] Aron went on to suggest that the establishment of parliamentary democracy in the developing states, as things currently stood, was a utopian dream; a pluralistic party system assumed a level of national unity and general agreement that did not exist in the new states. Or "some of the so-called 'new states' have emerged without the minimum of national unity which is necessary for democratic political controversy."[24] The contradiction, as Aron noted, is that liberal values presuppose liberal institutions to maintain them; in developing nations such institutions are typically ineffectual.

Upon hearing Aron's pronouncements at Rhodes, his colleagues wondered if he thought Western-style democracy even possible for the new states. The Swiss journalist Francois Bondy responded that emerging states in Asia and Africa "start at political democracy," which supposedly would lead them down the path to becoming full capitalist economies. "I wonder," Bondy asked, "is the process of starting with the latest model of democracy and then retrieving the early steps of capitalism possible?"[25] Aron's rejoinder to Bondy explicitly illuminates his skepticism regarding Shils's notion of transferring political democracy to the new states:

What I would like to say is that the present experience is without parallel in world history. We take institutions which have grown up slowly
in the West and we transplant them in countries where often neither
the state nor the nation exist and where the tasks to be achieved are
enormous, and were, in fact, never achieved in the West with constitutional procedures and party systems.[26]

Shils was asked for his thoughts concerning Aron's point, which he dodged
by simply mentioning the political conditions of various developing states.[27]
This was eventually followed by Aron's mysterious concluding remarks: "the
most impressive fact, but perhaps depressive too, is that we intellectuals,
coming from all parts of the world, all speak the same language. We use the
same words, the same vocabulary; we work with the same concepts."[28] Aron
thus sought to remind his colleagues of the linguistic particularities of what
they took to be the universal political norm.

Postwar Liberalism in Crisis: Intellectuals Versus the New Left

Even as defenders of the end of ideology were divided over its application
for developing countries throughout the 1950s and early 1960s, they were
generally united in their belief that the United States and Western Europe
had transitioned to a postideological age. Political thinkers and social scientists had found the formula—liberal democracy and regulated, redistributive
capitalism—and the challenge was to refine its functioning. When Daniel
Bell and Irving Kristol launched *The Public Interest* in fall 1965, the idea was
neither to destroy nor protect Cold War liberalism but to refine it. Not yet
the distinctly probusiness neoconservative he would evolve into over the
next decade, Kristol was at the time a self-described "skeptical liberal." Bell,
a fellow "New York intellectual" and City College alum, was then a professor at Columbia University and an avowed "democratic socialist."[29] "The
aim of *The Public Interest* is at once modest and presumptuous," the two
declared in its inaugural issue. "It is to help all of us, when we discuss issues
of public policy, to know a little better what we are talking about—and
preferably in time to make such knowledge effective."[30]

By the end of the decade, liberals' confidence in the end of ideology had
been seriously diminished, both at home and abroad. On March 31, 1968,

President Lyndon Johnson spoke for forty minutes on national television about why America was in Vietnam and the challenges it faced there. At the end of his speech, Johnson dropped a bombshell: "I shall not seek, and I will not accept, the nomination of my party for another term as your president."[31] Galloping inflation and a primary challenge from John F. Kennedy's popular brother, Robert, were other reasons Johnson declined to run again, but the Vietnam War's apparent failure clearly drove Johnson's decision. In fact, RFK's argument against LBJ—that he let the Vietnam War compromise his Great Society—was in fact one Johnson shared about himself, likening the war to a bad mistress taking him away from his real love (ending poverty in America).[32]

Between 1965 and 1968, Kristol, Bell, and other Cold War liberals sharpened their critique of the Great Society in *The Public Interest*'s pages. Reflecting on the publication's early days, Bell summarized their position well: "It's very easy to have ideas. It's harder to translate ideas into programs. It's harder to translate the programs into policy. It's even harder to translate policy into legislation. It's hard to translate legislation into institutions. And it's harder to get the institutions going toward the objectives you had in the first place."[33] However, for end-of-ideology defenders such as Bell, the greatest threat to American liberalism in the late 1960s was not Johnson's overreach through Vietnam or the Great Society but the New Left movement on college campuses.

Bell was no stranger to the New Left; in fact, he was one of their first targets. In 1960, Bell's Columbia University colleague C. Wright Mills wrote a scathing essay in the *New Left Review* titled "Letter to the New Left," in which he derided proponents of the end of ideology as "NATO intellectuals," "smug conservatives," and "tired liberals" who really only cared about stopping socialism. "The-end-of-ideology," he observed, "is based upon a disillusionment with any real commitment to socialism."[34] Like Mills, numerous others on the Left accused Bell and Lipset of promoting technocracy, scientism, and the status quo, and this despite the harsh economic realities of what Michael Harrington had famously described as "The Other America."[35] Indeed, it was the socialist Harrington who was arguably the first to label Bell, Kristol, and others "neoconservatives."[36]

For one week in April 1968, students inspired by New Left thought at Columbia University staged one of the most iconic demonstrations of the decade, occupying administration buildings to protest plans to build a segregated gym in Harlem, as well as the university's contributions to military research during the Vietnam War. Appalled by this revolt against authority, Bell responded by leaving Columbia for Harvard. The student politics of the 1960s brought out Bell's cultural conservatism, which extended far beyond his distaste for rock music or blue jeans. For Bell, the cultural sentiments of the decade represented a radicalization of the individualism and "hedonism" that had characterized aesthetic modernism. Bell believed these sentiments were incompatible with a just economy and a functioning civic life, and he hoped that the restoration of elite rule could rein in their worst excesses. The antiauthoritarian student movements were maddening for Bell because they took as their target the very training grounds for America's elites.

To Bell, the radical movements of the 1960s signified that the elite was under attack and that its legitimacy would have to be restored. As it turned out, Kristol was better suited for this task than Bell, who in 1973 resigned from the magazine the two had founded. Bell had sought to describe analytically what had brought these revolts about, whereas Kristol used his ideas to begin organizing the counter revolt. If, as Bell argued in *The Cultural Contradictions of Capitalism*, shifts in American capitalism had led to the spread of "antibourgeois" cultural trends among the younger generation, Kristol's new project was to bring together right-wing "counterintellectuals" alongside allies in business and government to make the case for capitalism and traditional values. Kristol took Bell's historical interpretation a step further.

As Kristol saw it, well after the campus revolts the New Left radicals continued to spread subversive attitudes, taking advantage of America's changing demographics. For Kristol, the "new class" of white-collar professionals born during the postwar baby boom were particularly susceptible to the radical discontent Bell described, and they were more widely educated than any class in history. Radical intellectuals exploited the impressionability of college-age baby boomers to disseminate an "adversary culture" of hostility toward traditional culture, liberal democracy, and entrepreneurial capitalism.[37] The crisis of the sixties and beyond was in Kristol's eyes nothing less than a cultural coup d'état, in which a small vanguard of radical theorists risked capturing the hearts and minds of the new generation of middle-class and upwardly mobile Americans. For Kristol, the solution to this crisis was a new kind of public thinker, a counterintellectual who could stand up for the majority of Americans that had conservative cultural leanings. Once again, Kristol's neoconservatism involved a variation on the Congress for Cultural Freedom theme of the end of ideology. If the original mission of *The*

Public Interest was to replace ideological passion with scientific knowledge, the mission of neoconservatism as a counterintellectual movement was to contest the radical ideologies for influence over America's middle classes. Kristol intended to defeat the New Left on this territory by mounting a renewed defense of the traditional values he believed Americans still held deep down. "The self-imposed assignment of neoconservatism," as he later put it, was "to explain to the American people why they are right, and to the [left-wing] intellectuals why they are wrong."[38]

Despite these frustrations, in the 1968 elections not even Kristol could imagine voting Republican. Consistent with their Cold War liberalism, he, Bell, and other *Public Interest* regulars (including Lipset) all supported Hubert Humphrey first in the Democratic primaries and then in the general election against Richard Nixon, whom they found offensive in both politics and culture.[39] Even the momentous events of 1968 could not lead these consensus liberals to vote Republican—yet. For it was in the Nixon administration where *The Public Interest* achieved its first great influence, largely through the efforts of a frequent contributor, Daniel Patrick Moynihan.

Born in Tulsa, Oklahoma, in 1927, Moynihan moved to New York City as a child, where he shined shoes before graduating from high school and finding work as a longshoreman. Unlike future friends Kristol, Bell, and Norman Podhoretz (the brash young editor of *Commentary* magazine), the Catholic Moynihan was never a member of the "New York Intellectuals," the fabled group of anti-Stalinist, almost all Jewish, leftist writers and literary critics who debated aesthetics and Trotskyism with equal fervor. After working in New York Democratic Party politics and earning a PhD in international relations, in 1961 Moynihan joined the Kennedy administration—the embodiment of the tough "vital center" liberalism to which he subscribed—as an assistant secretary of labor.

During this time Moynihan gained national attention for a controversial report he authored on Black poverty that made its way to the press. For asserting a causal link between Black family instability and Black poverty, many accused Moynihan of "blaming the victim" (and worse). It did not help that the report became public knowledge in August 1965, the same month as the Watts riots in Los Angeles. Civil rights leader Whitney Young Jr. called Moynihan's thesis a "gross distortion," and the Harvard psychologist William Ryan accused him of harboring a "new ideology" in which Blacks were "savages."[40] "I am now known as a racist across the land," Moynihan despaired to NAACP director Roy Wilkins.[41]

The controversy over the "Moynihan Report" was a turning point in Moynihan's relationship to the Democratic Party. "The reaction of the liberal Left to the issue of the Negro family was decisive," he wrote in a reply to his critics. "They would have none of it. No one was going to talk about their poor people that way." By this time, Moynihan "was a neoconservative in all but name."[42] Like Podhoretz and Nathan Glazer, another close friend and contributor to *The Public Interest* and *Commentary*, Moynihan believed that he had not abandoned liberalism; rather, in its rejection of consensus politics, resistance to internal criticism, and unwillingness to confront its radical elements, liberalism had abandoned him. Following his resignation from the Johnson administration in 1965, the Americans for Democratic Action board member called for a "formal alliance between liberals and conservatives" to combat the "nihilist terrorism" and "erosion of authority" in America's cities and universities. Still preferring the term "liberal dissenter," Moynihan mocked the "mob of college professors, millionaires, flower children, and Radcliffe girls" that he blamed for Johnson's decision not to run for president in 1968.[43]

While Podhoretz declared "full-scale war" on the New Left from the pages of *Commentary*—marking its crowning as the "new conservatives'" principal organ[44]—Moynihan joined the Nixon administration in 1970 as a "special counselor to the president" on race relations and urban affairs. When the press picked up on another memo widely interpreted as urging Nixon to neglect the Black community, for Moynihan, it was history repeating itself as farce. As if he needed another excuse to abandon his sympathies for the American Left, in response to the "benign neglect" memo, Students for a Democratic Society members reportedly threatened to trash his house in Cambridge—the same day that antiwar protesters hung a Viet Cong flag from Peace Corps headquarters in Washington, D.C.[45]

Postwar Liberalism Reinvented: Neoconservatives Versus the Developing Countries

Postwar liberals' feelings of alienation from the Democratic Party and hostility to the New Left animated their politics from 1968 to 1972 more than any other issue. Yet many postwar liberals were about to make an equally significant turn, one that would define them long after the New Left had gone away: support for an interventionist and unilateralist foreign policy, and defense of inequality within an American-led world order. Critically, postwar liberals on the counteroffensive, such as Kristol and Moynihan, drew direct connections between the New Left at home and emboldened developing countries abroad.

Moynihan had perceived the threat as early as 1971 while serving as a UN delegate in the Nixon administration. Observing the passive behavior of State Department representatives toward supposedly anti-Western resolutions of developing countries committees, he told UN ambassador George H. W. Bush that he found "incomprehensible" the idea that the United States was "not willing—or in some perverse way not able—to summon the intellectual competence to defend democracy in a United Nations debate."[46] For the second time in two years, in late 1972 Nixon offered Moynihan the job of UN ambassador. Believing that the "[UN] corpse had already begun to decompose," he turned it down in favor of ambassador to India, Nixon's other offer. His main achievement was the renegotiation of a large food loan India owed to the United States, but his experience abroad left him convinced of a fundamental crisis in U.S.-Third World relations. In letters to Podhoretz and Glazer—now coeditor (with Irving Kristol) of the neoconservative journal *The Public Interest*—he denounced Nixon's and Kissinger's hesitancy to resupply Israel during the 1973 war, the refusal of Europeans to support the United States when it did send arms, and, especially, the anti-Israeli sentiments of the "leftist, 'anti-colonial'" government of Indira Gandhi. "I came here thinking that liberty was losing in the world," Moynihan concluded. "I leave thinking that liberty may well be lost."[47]

On May 1, 1974—International Labor Day—the UN General Assembly adopted the "Group of 77" (G-77) developing countries' resolution calling for "economic decolonization" and a "right to development" through the establishment of a New International Economic Order (NIEO).[48] Acting just months after Arab members of OPEC quadrupled the price of oil, the NIEO's developing countries supporters hoped to negotiate a redistribution of money and power from the Global North—the rich capitalist countries—to the Global South—everyone else but the Communist bloc. Their weapon was control over the price of major commodities, especially oil, that had made possible the United States' and Europe's spectacular prosperity after World War II. "What we aim," explained Venezuela's president and OPEC leader Carlos Andres Perez, "is to take advantage of this opportunity when raw materials, and energy materials primarily, are worth just as much as capital and technology, in order to reach agreements that will ensure fair and lasting balances."[49]

The NIEO captured both the fears and the imaginations of the Washington foreign policy establishment. Anticipating the creation of cartels for other commodities beyond oil, a worsening of transatlantic relations, and turning a global recession into a depression, liberal internationalists went into crisis mode to form a practicable response. The Trilateral Commission (TC), formed in July 1973 with hardly a mention of developing countries in its founding documents or mission statements, in less than a year had shifted its focus to what one report called the "explosion in North-South relations" that "[has] gravely strained the fabric of international economic relations" and "raised the most troubling questions about the world's ability to manage its interdependence through peaceful cooperation."[50] Its main recommendations—more aid for poorer developing countries and more trade and participation in international financial institutions for richer ones—formed the consensus of the 1976 Carter presidential campaign and its chief foreign policy advisor, TC executive director Zbigniew Brzezinski. These recommendations also bore a striking similarity to the strategy adopted by Kissinger (with significant opposition from the U.S. Treasury) in late 1974. In fact, Kissinger was prepared to go even further than the Trilateralists in offering the South concessions, first to prevent it from cutting new deals with oil-desperate Western Europe and second to split what he and West German chancellor Helmut Schmidt termed the "unholy alliance" between OPEC and the developing countries.[51]

For Kristol and Moynihan, the NIEO's call for a world order "based on equity [and] sovereign equality" and designed to "correct inequalities and redress existing injustices" effectively globalized the very issue that had prompted their alienation from the Democratic Party. In a lengthy *Wall Street Journal* piece in May 1975, Kristol condemned the State Department's conciliatory approach as "frightening." Failing to denounce the NIEO's premises was accepting the developing countries' charge that "their poverty is the fault of our capitalism—that they are 'exploited' nations while we are a 'guilty' people." For Kristol, this was the same mistake that liberals in the United States had made in the late 1960s. Far from learning from that "dubious experience with Great Society programs," they were about to repeat it globally:

There is, for instance, a whole flock of "progressive" and socialist economists in American academia . . . trying to launch a [domestic] reform movement through the back door. . . . They feel that if the United States gets itself committed to the propriety and justice of a massive international redistribution of wealth and income, through a "planned world economy," then there is no way it can avoid a commitment to a similar redistributive policy, and a similar commitment to planning, internally. And they are absolutely right.

In other words, U.S. politicians had been endorsing plans to soak the rich at home for years, if not decades, with disastrous results. Pandering to similar demands from the developing countries now—as Kristol accused Kissinger and Brzezinski of doing with the NIEO—would strengthen the forces of illiberalism abroad ("whether communist, socialist, or neo-fascist") and hasten liberalism's decline at home.[52]

Subsequent events reinforced neoconservatives' suspicions. At the World Food Conference in November 1974, the U.S. delegation was faced with sweeping demands for the implementation of the NIEO as a matter of historical justice and human rights, and OPEC leaders refused to discuss oil prices until the United States agreed to comprehensive global negotiations (which it eventually did). One month later, the U.S. delegation found itself outvoted and isolated when the General Assembly (including most of Western Europe) overwhelmingly approved the G-77's Charter of Economic Rights and Duties of States (CERDS), essentially a legal blueprint for the NIEO. In January 1975, Moynihan, at Podhoretz's urging, collected his views on the North-South crisis for a lengthy essay in *Commentary*'s March 1975 issue. (Podhoretz, a gifted publicity hound, called a press conference for the article's release, and days later Moynihan was interviewed on national television.) That same month, U.S. Secretary of State Henry Kissinger invited Moynihan to the White House to talk about his essay, "The U.S. in Opposition," in which he implored U.S. foreign policy leaders to defend the validity of the American-led world order in moral, even Churchillian terms ("Find its equal").[53]

In June 1975, Moynihan joined the Ford administration as ambassador to the UN, where his aggressive posture left the United States isolated from the developing countries and Europe alike, and eventually cost him Kissinger's support. This turned out to be a blessing. "Moynihan has enraged Third World delegates, discomfited his Western European colleagues, and brought cheer to the hearts of Americans," *Time* rhapsodized in a glowing January 1976 profile of "The Fighting Irishman at the UN."[54] The ambassador's attacks on antiliberalism and anti-Americanism at the UN (especially the infamous November 1975 "Zionism as Racism" resolution) brought him wide esteem from other "right-wing liberals" alienated by the Democratic Party's apparent embrace of egalitarianism, multiculturalism, and noninterventionism. As Kissinger had suspected, Moynihan wasted little time in securing political support for a run for office from party power brokers, namely, "liberal Democrats and black leaders so that [he] could address their misgivings about his opinions of socialism and racial issues." In early June 1976, just four months after stepping down, Moynihan declared his candidacy for the Democratic nomination for senator from New York. After narrowly defeating outspoken liberal (and Party favorite) Bella Abzug in the primary, he easily triumphed in the general election over his conservative Republican rival James Buckley—thus making Moynihan "the first neoconservative intellectual to be elected to public office."[55]

The NIEO per se was not a major issue in the 1976 presidential elections, but U.S. policy toward the developing countries certainly was. On the conservative Right, Ronald Reagan blasted incumbent Gerald Ford over his administration's (really, Kissinger's State Department's) efforts to renegotiate the Panama Canal treaties. "We built it, we paid for it, it's ours, and we're going to keep it!" Reagan exclaimed during the Florida Republican primary. In 1975 the neoconservatives were still committed to retaining their influence in the Democratic Party, and once again they rallied around Henry "Scoop" Jackson as their candidate. Coalition for a Democratic Majority (CDM) members Ben Wattenberg and Elliott Abrams ran Jackson's campaign, and the rest of the CDM "did all it could to support him without crossing the legal line of open endorsement." After Jackson's defeat by the little-known Georgia governor Jimmy Carter, the CDM focused their efforts on rewriting the Democratic Party convention platform. "Moynihan, who had just joined the CDM," Vaïsse writes, "worked with Wattenberg . . . to achieve a moderate platform that would not yield on foreign policy issues to pro-Third World leftists. . . . The platform contained no hint of American guilt or apology and no mention of moral equivalence."[56]

Neoconservatives fared worse under Gerald Ford's replacement, Jimmy Carter. Most claimed to have seen Carter as a blank slate in 1976 and were surprised at his foreign policy positions after the nomination. In fact, in the general election Carter endorsed some of their key themes, such as suspicion of detente and support for the human rights of Eastern bloc dissidents. Carter also adopted the neoconservatives' moralistic language, but his usage suggested an interpretation drawn much more from the party's new social egalitarianism and world order liberalism than from the views of the "right-wing Democrats" that had written the convention platform. Like Moynihan before him, Carter attacked the Ford administration's actions during the 1974 World Food Conference. Moynihan had accused the administration of doing too much to placate the developing countries, whereas Carter said it had done too little. Instead of being the "arms merchant of the world," Carter insisted during the televised foreign policy debate with Ford in October, America's "strength derive[s] from doing what's right—caring for the poor, providing food, becoming the breadbasket of the world."[57] For the North-South dialogue, this meant stressing "social and economic" rights as an important part of their human rights program, in the form of new development assistance toward meeting "basic needs."[58] Presented by Carter as a realistic counter to the NIEO, the South nevertheless saw basic needs as a weak consolation prize for global structural reform, and by 1979 North-South dialogue negotiations were again deadlocked.

The Reagan administration offered a new opportunity for U.S. foreign policy neoconservatives—at least those willing to abandon, or set aside, their still liberal views on domestic policy. Moynihan remained a prolabor, New Deal–style Democrat in the U.S. Senate until his death in 2001, but he was an outlier. More common was what Justin Vaïsse calls the "hybrid": people like Norman Podhoretz, Midge Decter, Irving Kristol, and other "first generation" neoconservatives who joined in alliance with Reagan's conservative Republican supporters on issues like the UN, the developing countries, and the Soviet Union. Literally dozens joined the Reagan administration in top national security posts, and neoconservative groups such as the Committee on the Present Danger acted as a crucial pipeline.[59] Some—especially those who had spent time at right-wing think tanks such as the American Enterprise Institute (AEI) and the Heritage Foundation—offered conversion stories about seeing the light of radical market deregulation, but neoconservatives' positive views on food stamps or labor unions had no impact beyond personal conscience. As Seymour Martin Lipset later pointed out: "No neoconservative was assigned [by Reagan] to a post affecting economic or welfare policy."[60]

Remarkably, a *Commentary* essay again facilitated the ascension of another neoconservative Democrat to the top U.S. post at the UN. Jeanne Kirkpatrick's November 1979 article, "Dictatorships and Double Standards"—written shortly after her own stint at AEI, at Kristol's invitation—accused Carter of holding U.S. allies in the developing countries to a higher standard on human rights than its communist enemies and justified support for right-wing, authoritarian developing countries' governments on the basis that they could be "reformed," whereas Marxist or totalitarian ones could not. The self-proclaimed "AFL-CIO Democrat" soon received an enthusiastic phone call from candidate Reagan, who brought her on first as his chief foreign policy advisor and then as U.S. ambassador to the UN (1981–1985).

Conclusion: From the End of Ideology to the End of History

As the communist countries of Eastern Europe collapsed, followed by the Soviet Union itself, the end of ideology experienced a revival. In his influential 1989 essay "The End of History" for the *National Interest*, Stanford political scientist Francis Fukuyama announced with confidence: "What we may be witnessing is not just the end of the Cold War," "but the end of history as such: that is, the end point of mankind's ideological evolution and the universalization of Western liberal democracy as the final form of human government." In making these claims, Fukuyama explicitly sought to distance himself from the end-of-ideology thesis, which he believed entailed a convergence between capitalism and socialism. He instead proclaimed an "unabashed victory of economic and political liberalism."[61] The triumph of the West, he continued, was evident in the exhaustion of alternatives to Western liberalism, the new political landscape in Eastern Europe and China, and the spread of Western consumerism culture all over the world.

Still, Fukuyama's end of history shares significant overlaps with the end-of-ideology thesis. Like defenders of the end of ideology who proclaimed the fluidity of the American class structure in the 1950s, Fukuyama asserted that "the egalitarianism of modern America represents the essential achievement of the classless society envisioned by Marx."[62] Moreover, Fukuyama argued that the global politics of that time indicated to him that all ideological alternatives to liberal democracy were disappearing, and the world was becoming increasingly peaceful. Similarly, Latin America's "lost decade of development" in the 1980s debt crisis demonstrated the bankruptcy of old statist models of economic modernization, whereas East Asia's rapid take-off during the same time proved that free markets and free trade were the only paths to prosperity for rich and poor countries alike. (As Margaret Thatcher insisted again and again:"There is no alternative.") Like Fukuyama, Shils embraced the end of ideology in his own time as a theory of global modernization. Moreover, Fukuyama's insistence that the end of history could not solve the question of human meaning and purpose—"the end of history will be a very sad time"—was little different from Aron's concerns that the nature of modern industrial societies can also too easily spiral into nihilism, cultural decadence, and will to power relativism.[63]

Given their similarities, it comes as little surprise that proponents of the end of history and the end of ideology share similar enemies. In *Identity: The Demand for Dignity and the Politics of Resentment*, Fukuyama argues that liberalism's inherent universalism (i.e., all humans are included in the liberal project) is being undermined by restrictive forms of recognition and resentment based on nation, religion, sect, race, ethnicity, or gender, which has resulted in anti-immigrant populism, the upsurge of politicized Islam, the fractious environment of college campuses, and the turn to white nationalism.[64] This is liberalism's underbelly, Fukuyama argues: illiberal movements seeking recognition and power through liberal means. For Fukuyama, the blame for this tendency falls on the late 1960s and 1970s Western Left, which downplayed or abandoned its working-class economic agenda for one based on culture and identity: "[What] needed to be smashed was not the current political order that exploited the working class but the hegemony of Western culture and values that suppressed minorities at home and developing countries abroad."[65] Unlike the old Marxists, the new cultural Left was more Nietzschean and relativistic, explicit in attacking the Christian and democratic values on which the Western enlightenment had been based. Although Fukuyama says that identity politics have brought welcome reforms, he is up front about the threat it presents to his thesis on the end of history. Most important for our purposes is that early end-of-ideology defenders made the same argument about the rise of the New Left and its impact on the Democratic Party of the 1960s and 1970s. In short, it was the cultural shift of that time that gave rise to today's identity politics; it was also these changes, instigated by the New Left but accepted by middle-class liberals, that discredited the end-of-ideology thesis by the late 1960s.

Notes

1. Daniel Bell, *The End of Ideology: On the Exhaustion of Political Ideas in the Fifties* (Glencoe: Free Press, 1960); Seymour Martin Lipset, *Political Man: The Social Basis of Politics* (Garden City, NY: Anchor, 1960).

2. Reinhold Niebuhr, *The Irony of American History* (Chicago: University of Chicago Press, 1952), 100, 101.

3. Arthur Schlesinger Jr., "Where Does the Liberal Go from Here?," *New York Times Magazine*, August 4, 1957, 36, 38.

4. Raymond Aron, "Nations and Ideology," *Encounter* 16 (January 1955): 24.

5. See H. Brick, "The End of Ideology Thesis," in *The Oxford Handbook of Political Ideologies* ed. M. Freeden, L. T. Sargent, and M. Stears (Oxford: Oxford University Press, 2013), 90–114; Chaim I. Waxman, ed., *The End of Ideology Debate* (New York: Clarion, 1968).

6. Michael Franczak, introduction to *Global Inequality and American Foreign Policy in the 1970s* (Ithaca, NY: Cornell University Press, forthcoming 2022). For this and other misconceptions about Bandung, see Robert Vitalis, "The Midnight Ride of Kwame Nkrumah and Other Fables of Bandung (Ban-doong)," *Humanity: An International Journal of Human Rights, Humanitarianism, and Development* 4 no. 2 (2013): 261–88.

7. Walt W. Rostow, *The Stages of Economic Growth: A Non-Communist Manifesto* (London: Cambridge University Press, 1960).

8. Lipset, *Political Man*, 403, 406.

9. Seymour Martin Lipset, "Some Social Requisites of Democracy: Economic Development and Political Legitimacy," *American Political Science Review* 53, no. 1 (March 1959): 69–105.

10. Nils Gilman, *Mandarins of the Future: Modernization Theory and the Cold War* (Baltimore: Johns Hopkins University Press, 2007), 62.

11. Gilman, *Mandarins of the Future*, 61.

12. For Shils thoughts on the end of ideology, see Edward Shils, "Letter from Milan: The End of Ideology," *Encounter* 20 (November 1955): 52–58. For thinking on India, see Shalini Sharma, "The Chicago School Goes East: Edward Shils and the Dilemma of the Indian Intellectuals, Circa 1956–67," *Modern Asian Studies* 54, no. 6 (November 2020): 2087–2111.

13. Edward Shils, "Political Development in the New States," *Comparative Studies in Society and History* 2, no. 3 (April 1960): 266.

14. Shils, "Political Development in the New States," 286.

15. Niebuhr, *The Irony of American History*, 120, 115, 125.

16. For Niebuhr's influence on Obama, see Jeffrey Stout, "The Ironies of Proximate Justice," in *The Oxford Handbook of Reinhold Niebuhr* ed. Robin Lovin and Joshua Mauldin (Oxford: Oxford University Press, 2021), 603–9.

17. Raymond Aron, *Eighteen Lectures on Industrial Society* (London: Weidenfeld and Nicolson, 1967), 42.

18. Aron's comments on the westernization of Japan are relevant here, see: Raymond Aron, "Mais l'influence occidentale a été, cette fois, incomparablement plus

brutale." "La politique Japonaise simple ou mystérieuse," in *Le Figaro de 1947 à 1977*, November 25, 1953,1111.

19. Raymond Aron, "The Diffusion of Ideologies," in *Political Thought Since World War II* ed. W. J. Stankiewicz (London: Free Press, 1964), 7.

20. Aron, "The Diffusion of Ideologies," 6–7.

21. Aron, "The Diffusion of Ideologies," 8.

22. Henry Kissinger to Raymond Aron: "I am writing to you about your article which has now been translated. I have shown it to a number of possible contributors, all of whom found it extremely challenging. There was only one slight difficulty which I would like to discuss with you. A number of the readers had the impression that you were exclusively concerned with Point Four rather than the general problem of the Diffusion of Ideologies through technical assistance and economic aid. I therefore took the liberty of adding to your article a few pages from your report to the Political Science Association." Kissinger to Aron, *Archives Privées Raymond Aron*, Boîte 152, August 20, 1952.

23. For the Rhodes Conference papers, see Edward Shils, "Intellectuals, Public Opinion and Economic Development," and Raymond Aron, "Political Democracy and Social and Economic Progress," International Association for Cultural Freedom Records, box 408, folder 12, Hanna Holborn Gray Special Collections Research Center, University of Chicago Library, Chicago, Illinois.

24. Raymond Aron, "A Round Table Discussion of the Differences Between East and West," International Association for Cultural Freedom Records, box 409, folder 4 (October 1958, exact date unspecified), 3, Hanna Holborn Gray Special Collections Research Center, University of Chicago Library, Chicago, Illinois.

25. Aron, "A Round Table Discussion of the Differences Between East and West."

26. Aron, "A Round Table Discussion of the Differences Between East and West."

27. Aron, "A Round Table Discussion of the Differences Between East and West," 4.

28. Aron, "A Round Table Discussion of the Differences Between East and West," 6.

29. Irving Kristol, "Forty Good Years," American Enterprise Institute, May 25, 2005, https://www.aei.org/articles/forty-good-years/.

30. Daniel Bell and Irving Kristol, "What Is the Public Interest?" *Public Interest* 1 (Fall 1965):3,(https://www.nationalaffairs.com/storage/app/uploads/public/58e/1a4/9ee/58e1a49eea60e937247032.pdf.

31. Lyndon Johnson, national televised address on March 31, 1968, http://www.lbjlibrary.org/press/rare-video-released-of-president-johnson-rehearsing-historic-march-31-1968.

32. Johnson told the historian Doris Kearns Goodwin this in 1970: "I knew from the start . . . that I was bound to be crucified either way I moved. If I left the woman I really loved—the Great Society—in order to get involved with that bitch of a war on the other side of the world, then I would lose everything

at home. All my programs. All my hopes to feed the hungry and shelter the homeless." Lyndon Johnson as quoted in Doris Goodwin, *Lyndon Johnson and the American Dream* (New York: Harper & Row, 1976), 263. For support, see also Lloyd C. Gardner, *Pay Any Price: Lyndon Johnson and the Wars for Vietnam* (Chicago: Ivan R. Dee, 1995).

33. Daniel Bell as quoted in Joseph Dorman, *Arguing the World: The New York Intellectuals in Their Own Words* (Chicago: University of Chicago Press, 2001), 159.

34. C. Wright Mills, "Letter to the New Left," *New Left Review* 1, no. 5 (September/ October 1960): 19.

35. For a source book of the various participants and themes involved in the end of ideology debate, see Chaim I. Waxman, ed., *The End of Ideology Debate* (New York: Clarion, 1968).

36. Michael Harrington, "The Welfare State and Its Neoconservative Critics," *Dissent Magazine* 20, no. 4 (September 1970): 435.

37. Irving Kristol, "The Adversary Culture of Intellectuals," *Encounter* (October 1979): 27–42.

38. Irving Kristol, *Reflections of a Neoconservative: Looking Back, Looking Ahead* (New York: Basic Books, 1983), xiv–xv.

39. Justin Vaïsse, *Neoconservatism: The Biography of a Movement* (Cambridge, MA: Harvard/Belknap, 2010), 284–85.

40. John Ehrman, *The Rise of Neoconservatism: Intellectuals and Foreign Affairs, 1945–1994* (New Haven, CT: Yale University Press, 1995), 69–70.

41. Gil Troy, *Moynihan's Moment: America's Fight Against Zionism as Racism* (New York: Oxford University Press, 2013), 48.

42. Ehrman, *The Rise of Neoconservatism*, 67.

43. For "formal alliance," see Murray Rothbard, "Confessions of a Right-Wing Liberal," *Ramparts* 6, no. 4 (June 1968), https://mises.org/library/confessions -right-wing-liberal. For "liberal dissenter," see Troy, *Moynihan's Moment*, 49.

44. Justin Vaisse proposes *Commentary*'s 1970 offensive as one of neoconservatism's possible "birth dates." Vaisse, *Neoconservatism*, 70.

45. Troy, *Moynihan's Moment*, 51–52.

46. Troy, *Moynihan's Moment*, 54.

47. Troy, *Moynihan's Moment*, 55–56.

48. UN General Assembly, Resolution 3201, "Declaration on the Establishment of a New International Economic Order," May 1, 1974. For a background of the NIEO's philosophy and terms, see Daniel J. Whelan, "'Under the Aegis of Man': The Right to Development and the Origins of the New International Economic Order," *Humanity: An International Journal of Human Rights, Humanitarianism, and Development* 6, no. 1 (2015): 93–108.

49. "A Letter from the President of Venezuela to the Chairman of the World Food Conference Meeting in Rome," Caracas, November 5, 1974.

50. Richard N. Gardner, Saburo Okita, and B. J. Udink, *A Turning Point in North-South Economic Relations: A Report of the Trilateral Task Force on Relations with Developing Countries to the Executive Commission of the Trilateral Commission*, New York, 1974, 11. In fact, in the TC's first three years, eight out of twelve of its "Trialogue" reports focused on North-South relations.

51. For "unholy alliance," see "Memorandum of Conversation: Energy, Raw Materials, and Development, November 16, 1975" (Rambouillet, France), in *Foreign Relations of the United States, 1969–1976*, Vol. 31. *Foreign Economic Policy, 1973–76*, ed. Kathleen Rasmussen (Washington, DC: U.S. Government Printing Office, 2010), doc. 124.

52. Irving Kristol, "The 'New Cold War,'" *Wall Street Journal*, July 17, 1975, L. William Seidman Files, box 50, Commodities—International, Gerald Ford Presidential Library, University of Michigan, Ann Arbor, Michigan.

53. Daniel Moynihan, "The U.S. in Opposition," *Commentary* 59, no. 3 (February 1975): 31–44. For a detailed account of that article, the Kissinger meeting, and Moynihan's tenure at the UN, see Michael Franczak, "Losing the Battle, Winning the War: Neoconservatives Versus the New International Economic Order, 1974–82," *Diplomatic History* 43, no. 5 (November 2019): 867–89.

54. "A Fighting Irishman," *Time*, January 26, 1976 [clipping], Files of the National Security Advisor, Gerald Ford Presidential Library, University of Michigan, Ann Arbor, Michigan.

55. Ehrman, *The Rise of Neoconservatism*, 91–92.

56. Vaïsse, *Neoconservatism*, 125.

57. "The Second Ford-Carter Presidential Debate, October 6, 1976," Commission on Presidential Debates, https://www.debates.org/voter-education/debate-transcripts/october-6-1976-debate-transcript/.

58. For an overview of this process, see Michael Franczak, "Human Rights and Basic Needs: Jimmy Carter's North-South Dialogue, 1977–1981," *Cold War History* 18, no. 4 (2018): 447–64.

59. Vaïsse, *Neoconservatism*, 187.

60. Seymour Martin Lipset as quoted in Vaïsse, *Neoconservatism*, 207.

61. Francis Fukuyama, "The End of History," *National Interest* 16 (Summer, 1989): 3–4.

62. Fukuyama, "The End of History," 9.

63. Fukuyama, "The End of History," 18; Raymond Aron, *In Defense of Decadent Europe* (South Bend, IN: Regnery, 1977).

64. Francis Fukuyama, *Identity: The Demand for Dignity and the Politics of Resentment* (New York: Farrar, Straus and Giroux, 2018).

65. Fukuyama, *Identity*, 122.

CHAPTER 21

The Galactic Vietnam

Technology, Modernization, and Empire in George Lucas's Star Wars

DANIEL IMMERWAHR

H as any work of popular culture seeped into the U.S. public consciousness like Star Wars has? Rivals are hard to even think of. It's not just the billions in revenues from films, novels, television shows, video games, and merchandising, it's that Star Wars has acquired the sort of cultural heft more common for religious scripture. It passes from parents to children, it's quoted like catechism, and it grows more pervasive with time.

Star Wars intrudes into high politics too. In 1983, Ronald Reagan famously called the Soviet Union an "evil empire."[1] His speechwriter claimed no reference was meant to the "evil galactic empire" described in the first *Star Wars* film's opening crawl, but the resonance was hard to miss—that film had just debuted on cable and *The Return of the Jedi* was about to hit theaters. A month later, Reagan would propose a space-based defense system, which quickly earned the nickname "Star Wars." "The Force is with us," Reagan boasted, quoting the films.[2]

Reagan is not the only major politician to have done so. In 2001, Vice President Dick Cheney told NBC's *Meet the Press* that the government would need to work through "the dark side" to defeat al Qaeda, thereby supplying an oft-quoted metaphor for the Global War on Terrorism's tactics.[3] George W. Bush, Barack Obama, and Hillary Clinton all referenced Star Wars in speeches. Donald Trump ran a special episode of his television show,

The Apprentice, on it, and Joe Biden recruited Star Wars lead actor Mark Hamill to headline a high-profile campaign fund-raiser to defeat Trump.

This doesn't happen with most films. But the Star Wars films were never just films. They were, their creator George Lucas claimed, "a conscious attempt at creating new myths."[4] They've done that well, becoming a shared template for thinking. The Force, the Jedi, the Empire, the Dark Side—these can be mapped onto nearly any set of circumstances.

Yet there's one situation in which Star Wars' references are especially apt. In ways both shallow and deep, the original *Star Wars* trilogy—*A New Hope* (titled *Star Wars* at its 1977 release, then renamed), *The Empire Strikes Back* (1980), and *Return of the Jedi* (1983)—is about U.S. foreign relations. Not only do the films tell of wars, empires, and foreign places but they also address the underlying tenets of U.S. postwar hegemony: that technology is the basis of world power, that traditional societies ought to be modernized, and that the United States is exceptional for being powerful without being imperial. Lucas didn't stumble onto these themes. He started writing the original trilogy during the Vietnam War. That war haunted him, and Star Wars was his response.[5] To the degree that Lucas succeeded in "creating new myths," he did so by rejecting the principles that, in his view, had driven his country to war in Southeast Asia.

Wildly popular cultural artifacts offer windows onto ideologies. The stories that most "make sense" or "feel right" to audiences reflect something important about those audiences' worldviews. In the case of Star Wars, the films show how the Vietnam War was not just a military crisis but an ideological one too. Lucas staged a frontal assault on the midcentury intellectual foundations of U.S. supremacy and, surprisingly, filmgoers loved it. They cheered, too, for what he proposed in its stead: a new basis for U.S. power rooted in a culturally flexible form of anti-imperialism. Lucas proposed heroes whose claims to greatness didn't rest on their modernity, civilizational achievements, or command of advanced technologies but from leading a scrappy rebel alliance against a homogenizing form of hypermodernity. That mythology would endure after the Vietnam War. Writing of far-off times and distant galaxies, Lucas captured his own country in a moment of profound cultural change.

The place to start is with technology. Science fiction, in exploring advanced technologies, often imagines a sunny future.[6] Certainly, that's the sort of science fiction Lucas imbibed as a child. Space adventurers Buck Rogers,

Tommy Tomorrow, and Flash Gordon from the 1930s and 1940s made a deep impression on him with their ray guns and rocket ships. Lucas would begin his first feature film, *THX 1138* (1971), with clips from a Buck Rogers serial, set in the "wonderful world of the future." It was a world, the clips explained, where "a lot of our scientific and mechanical dreams come true."[7]

Lucas didn't need Buck Rogers serials to glimpse that world. He was born in 1944, at the end of a war that had propelled the United States to world leadership and done so by science. World War II ended not as the previous one had, with brutal trench fighting, but with the debut of a spectacular new technology: the atom bomb. The whole war was a scientists' fight, won as much with radar and penicillin as with bullets and artillery shells. Afterward, Dwight Eisenhower boasted of the "world technological leadership" his country had attained—the "unique technological ability to use science" for national defense and for "the improvement of human living."[8]

Men like Eisenhower promised that technology would transform daily life, and it did. Lucas's generation grew up with transistor radios, plastic toys, miracle drugs, dishwashers, and jet planes. As a teenager, Lucas tinkered with cars, souping them up to race. As a filmmaker, he used groundbreaking technologies. Star Wars' special effects dazzled audiences, and Lucas would go on, through his various firms, to oversee many breakthroughs in contemporary filmmaking. Lucas's Industrial Light and Magic handled special effects not only for Star Wars but also for such trailblazing movies as *Terminator 2* and *Jurassic Park*. His firm Pixar led the industry in computer animation. THX, another arm of Lucas's business empire, transformed theater sound. And his prequel Star Wars trilogy (1999–2005) played a large part in converting cinema to digital shooting and projection.

It's easy, given all this, to see Lucas's films and especially Star Wars as "a celebration of American progress and technology," as Peter W. Lee has argued.[9] Yet there was a surprising amount of distance between Lucas's oeuvre and the Buck Rogers serials. Lucas began his first feature film, *THX 1138*, with clips from Buck Rogers set in the "wonderful world of the future," but he quickly cut away to a horrifying dystopia. His high-tech future was one in which workers were kept at their miserable jobs by a combination of sedatives, surveillance, and force—the last administered by robotic police officers with unmoving steel faces.

THX 1138 showed Lucas's wariness of advanced technology. "I'm not a technological guy at all," he confessed.[10] The original Star Wars trilogy features gleaming, futuristic machines, but the state-of-the-art ones belong to the villains. In the first film, the Galactic Empire menaces the rebels with the "technological terror" of the Death Star, a moon-sized battle station that can vaporize planets. As the "ultimate power in the universe," the Death Star has enabled the emperor to dissolve the Senate, abolish the Republic, and rule the galaxy by fear. Alongside it, the Empire deploys a huge starship fleet and an army of storm troopers, who resemble the robot police of *THX 1138*. The villain, Darth Vader, is kept alive by a shiny robotic suit. "He becomes a machine and loses his compassion," Lucas summarized.[11]

The heroes, in contrast, spurn large, capital-intensive technologies. They use spaceships, blasters, and droids but in a markedly different way. Their relationship to technology is artisanal; they're constantly adjusting or fixing their secondhand machines. Lucas shows the act of tinkering over and over, nearly to the point of fetishization. In one of his first scenes, the hero Luke Skywalker repairs droids in his "cluttered and worn" garage (in the screenplay's words).[12] Han Solo and Chewbacca work endlessly on their ship, the *Millennium Falcon* (figure 21.1). Even Princess Leia picks up an arc welder. Lucas took evident pleasure in showing the grease stains—the marks of labor. "George kept emphasizing that he wanted the ships to look like hot rods; they need to look used, greasy, maintained with spare parts, sort of held together with wires and chewing gum," Lucas's art director remembered.[13]

All this flowed from Lucas's teenage years as a hot-rodder, when he "lived, ate, breathed cars," as he recalled.[14] He chronicled those years in his second film, *American Graffiti* (1973). Car culture wasn't about revering powerful technology, though. As the historian Jefferson Cowie has argued, it was a form of protest against automation—"the last place for armchair craftsmen

Figure 21.1 Chewbacca and Han Solo repair the *Millennium Falcon* in *The Empire Strikes Back*.

to use their hands against the swelling tide of the 'degradation of work.'"[15] By the time *Star Wars* premiered, tinkering with and racing modified cars had become a way for blue-collar men to reclaim in their garages a life that, thanks to globalization and auto plant closings, was rapidly slipping away. It's not hard to connect the nostalgic portrayal of gearheads in *American Graffiti* and *Star Wars* to Bruce Springsteen's mournful one in *Born to Run* (1975) and *Darkness on the Edge of Town* (1978).

Lucas dabbled in Springsteen-style pessimism with *THX 1138* but then switched to making upbeat films. Still, Star Wars' bright optimism didn't come from Buck Rogers–style promises of a gee-whiz future. It came from imagining the gearheads winning. The *Millennium Falcon* "may not look like much," but it's the "fastest hunk of junk in the galaxy." "I made a lot of special modifications myself," Han proudly explains while holding a rag. Indeed, the *Millennium Falcon* fires the shot that triggers the second Death Star's explosion in *Return of the Jedi* and helps to destroy the first one in *A New Hope*. Again and again, jury-rigged garage technologies triumph over the spotless, expensive ones preferred by the Empire.

That garage-versus-corporation dynamic resonated with Lucas's own life. From early on, Lucas felt tremendous frustration with the power of Hollywood studios. As Michael Rubin has argued, a main reason Lucas backed digital technology was to wrest the means of production away from the studios.[16] With his own workshop in northern California—the Skywalker Ranch, a super-garage where techies toyed with computers—Lucas could liberate himself from the "sleazy, unscrupulous" executives (as he called them) in southern California.[17]

Lucas took joy in showing the Empire's expensive technologies fail. The first Death Star is a sophisticated planet-killing machine, but it can be destroyed by a single shot to its thermal exhaust port. In the second film, the rebels down a giant imperial walker with tripwire and a harpoon. The trilogy ends with a battle on Endor, when Ewoks capture an imperial base using catapults, slingshots, and bows and arrows. "The whole point was to show how a primitive culture . . . could overcome highly technical people," Lucas remarked. "That was the theme; you have these woodland creatures that are completely nontechnical overcoming the Empire."[18]

The Jedi, too, eschew high technology. They rely instead on the Force, an organic energy field that "binds the galaxy together." When the Jedi fight, explains Luke's mentor Obi-Wan Kenobi, they don't use anything as "clumsy or random as a blaster." They use the lightsaber, "an elegant weapon for a more civilized age," which the Jedi have wielded for "a thousand generations"—each Jedi crafts his or her own. Though Luke flies spaceships, he destroys the first Death Star by turning off his ship's computerized targeting system and using the Force for guidance. "*Star Wars* has more to do with disclaiming science than anything else," Lucas told a reporter the year the film came out. Its heroes have a "totally different way of thinking."[19]

And where did that way of thinking come from? Many sources informed the Force, but there is one Lucas mentioned numerous times: the teachings of Don Juan Matus, a Yaqui shaman from the arid Sonora region of Mexico. Don Juan had been the subject of a series of (possibly fabricated) books by the anthropologist Carlos Castaneda. George Lucas read them all, as did Irwin Kershner, *The Empire Strikes Back*'s director.[20] The books describe how the elderly sorcerer Don Juan trained Castaneda to shut out his rational, scientific mind and gain mystical powers by attuning himself to nature. Lucas told a reporter that the Force was "a Castaneda *Tales of Power* thing" (a reference to Castaneda's fourth volume) and described Obi-Wan as someone who could "do magic, read minds, talk to things like Don Juan."[21] Also like Don Juan, Obi-Wan is "a shabby old desert rat of a man," in the screenplay's words.[22] Luke's training at the hands of Obi-Wan and Yoda (whom Lucas initially conceived as "an old Indian in the desert type") closely resembles Castaneda's own apprenticeship.[23]

Whether by artisanal technologies, Stone Age tools, or gnostic teachings, the heroes best the most advanced military in the galaxy. This is a space fantasy, but it's a far cry from the future of Buck Rogers.

In fact, Star Wars isn't the future at all. One of Lucas's most surprising choices was to introduce every Star Wars film with these words: "A long time ago in a galaxy far, far away." That opening, placing the action in the distant past rather than the far future, offered the films' first hint that they would bear a different relationship to historical time than their progress-oriented science fiction predecessors.

Historical time mattered in Lucas's world because it had served as the backdrop for a great deal of thinking about the United States and its role in the world. So much of U.S. foreign relations since World War II, including the Vietnam War, had been carried out under the banner of modernization—the idea that breaking poor societies free of tradition would make them prosperous and stable. Thus, for modernization theorists, the solution to global instability and poverty was to usher foreign countries through the various historical stages until they became, as W. W. Rostow put it, "high mass-consumption" societies like the United States.[24]

Modernization theory had guided policy making through the Vietnam War, yet it held little sway over Lucas. The heroes of his films aren't progressives seeking to replace a traditional past with a modern future. They're conservatives, aiming to "restore" what was, as *A New Hope*'s opening text explains. At the start of the trilogy, the Jedi are nearly extinct, the "Old Republic" has fallen on "dark times," and an Empire has arisen. The Jedi seek to revive their order, dismantle the Empire, and reestablish the Republic.

The films' preference for old times comes up again and again. The Jedi practice an "ancient religion," their lightsabers are "ancient weapons," and the script describes their base as an "ancient temple."[25] In a galaxy where hyperspace travel is possible, their society is a bizarrely feudal one of knights, lords, and princesses. Lucas based their outfits on traditional Japanese attire. He was particularly influenced by the period films of Akira Kurosawa, set in Japan in the age of the samurai. The Jedi's preference for lightsabers over blasters echoes a Kurosawa trope of samurai nobly sticking with swordfighting, even as their enemies use guns.[26]

Remarkably, the fount of wisdom in this science fiction epic is not a scientist. It's Yoda, a sage who has trained Jedi for eight hundred years. Yoda's teachings stress mastering ancient techniques, not adapting to new technologies. He chides Luke for looking "to the future, to the horizon." In Star Wars, the past, not the future, is the privileged epoch.

It wasn't only in Star Wars that Lucas looked backward. His breakout film, the wildly popular *American Graffiti* (1973), was set in 1962—the last days of sock-hop. The Italian word "graffiti" in Lucas's odd title referred not to spray-painted art (which was only just becoming widespread) but to the etchings that captured daily life in the ancient city of Pompeii before a volcanic eruption buried it.[27] Pompeii was an unexpected reference, yet it underscores just how wrenching and destructive Lucas took the decade after 1962 to be, particularly the Vietnam War. "It was billed as a completely harmless war over *there*; no bomb was ever going to fall on United States soil," he told *Rolling Stone*. "But a huge psychological bomb landed on United States soil, and it changed it forever."[28] *American Graffiti* showed what the country had lost. From the vantage of the early 1970s, the film's producer Gary Kurtz explained, *American Graffiti*'s age of innocence seemed like "ancient times."[29]

If modernizers sought to improve traditional societies, Lucas had a different idea. Immediately after *A New Hope* premiered, he began work with his friend Steven Spielberg on the *Indiana Jones* films, which Lucas conceived and plotted. Harrison Ford starred as Indiana Jones, an archaeologist and expert on lost civilizations. In the films, Jones frequently encounters traditional societies, from bow and arrow wielding Indigenous people in South America to villagers in rural India. Yet Lucas never suggests that Western contact will improve these societies. Jones destroys some ancient sites and restores others, but development—the progressive change that underpinned modernization theory—is entirely off the table.[30]

The same is true of Star Wars. In the third film, *Return of the Jedi*, the heroes travel to the forest moon of Endor and encounter what Lucas called a "really primitive" society.[31] He named that society the Ewoks, after the Miwok people, Indigenous inhabitants of the California area where Skywalker Ranch was situated.[32] The Ewoks act like children and are religious to the point of superstition. But *Return of the Jedi* never proposes developing their traditional society. Rather, the Ewoks prove capable of bringing down the Empire with slingshots.

The film ends with "the little fuzzy wuzzies having a party," as Lucas put it during a story conference.[33] The Ewoks drum and dance, having freed their home from the high-tech Empire. Restoration, not improvement, is the hopeful note on which the original trilogy ends. Lucas would repeat that ending a year later in *Indiana Jones and the Temple of Doom* (1984), with Jones celebrating alongside jubilant Indian villagers whose religious artifacts he has returned.

The Battle of Endor didn't just show a traditional society fighting a high-tech one; it conjured something more specific. "You can look at *Jedi* and see the Vietnam War," noted Lawrence Kasdan, who cowrote the screenplay with Lucas. "You can see the Ewok guerrillas hiding in the jungles, taking on this improper force of mechanized bullies—and winning."[34]

That understanding of the Vietnam War—"mechanized bullies" losing to guerrillas—was common. The United States brought the world's most advanced weaponry to the battlefield: body-heat sensors, laser-guided bombs, planes with wingspans the length of football fields. But nothing worked. "We have the power to destroy most human life on the planet within a matter of minutes," wrote the journalist Ronald Steel, "yet we cannot win a guerrilla war against peasants in black pajamas."[35]

Such thoughts were familiar to George Lucas. As a young man in the San Francisco Bay Area, he lived at the protest movement's epicenter. "We grew up in the '60s protesting the Vietnam War," Lucas remembered.[36] "The draft was hanging over all of us, and we were bearded, freako pre-hippies."[37] Antiwar politics surrounded him. "We all know what a terrible mess we have made of the world," he told *Rolling Stone*. "We all know how wrong we were in Vietnam."[38]

George Lucas's collaborator John Milius remembered that he and Lucas had been "great connoisseurs of the Vietnam War."[39] Indeed, the war cast a shadow over Lucas's early corpus. As Chris Taylor has argued, Lucas in the 1970s had in mind a triptych: three films that would, by examining the past, present, and future, show how much damage the Vietnam War had dealt.[40]

The first was *American Graffiti*, set in the innocent moment just before the 1964 Gulf of Tonkin Resolution led the United States to send combat troops (rather than "advisors") to Vietnam. It's a joyful film, but Lucas throws ice water into the warm nostalgia bath at the end when he reveals the fates of his four teenage male leads. One, Curt Henderson, moves to Canada, choosing exile, presumably to avoid the draft (as Lucas had considered doing himself).[41] Another, Terry Fields, goes "missing in action near An Loc in December 1965."

The second film in Lucas's intended triptych, dealing with the present, was to be *Apocalypse Now*, a documentary-style adaptation of Joseph Conrad's *Heart of Darkness* set in Vietnam. Planning to direct the film, Lucas developed it with John Milius for four years, to the point of drafting a screenplay and scouting locations.[42] It would be, Lucas told interviewers, a "very political film," and he identified his own politics as left-wing.[43] In essence, he explained, it would be more about "man against machine than anything else." It was the story of "technology against humanity."[44]

Lucas never made *Apocalypse Now*. Hollywood backers at first resisted, and by the time funds were found, Lucas had become absorbed in Star Wars. So he passed, leaving his friend Francis Ford Coppola to take over the film. Lucas nevertheless found ways to use his ideas. While working on Star Wars, he plotted and produced *More American Graffiti* (1979), which followed Terry Fields to Vietnam. Although Lucas didn't direct the film, he took over the director's chair for most of the Terry plotline, and he shot it in the grainy documentary style that he'd planned for *Apocalypse Now*.[45] Alongside Terry's dismal plight in Vietnam, the film shows Terry's friends Steve and Laurie back in California turning from PTA parents to police-fighting protestors (figure 21.2). The Bay Area band Country Joe and the Fish appear, singing their antiwar anthem, "I-Feel-Like-I'm-Fixin'-To-Die Rag."

Lucas also found that he could fold his *Apocalypse Now* ideas into *Star Wars*, the final part of his triptych. One reason he felt comfortable handing

Figure 21.2 A police helicopter menaces the protagonists of George Lucas's *More American Graffiti* (1979).

Apocalypse Now over to Coppola is that "a lot of my interest in *Apocalypse Now* was carried over into *Star Wars*," he recalled. "I would essentially deal with some of the same interesting concepts that I was going to use and convert them into space fantasy."[46] Lucas's *Apocalypse Now* would have been "about this totally insane giant technological society that was fighting these poor little people," Lucas said. "They have little sticks and things, and yet they completely cow this technological power, because the technological power didn't believe they were any threat." Lucas adapted this for *Star Wars* by writing the Battle of Endor, which he'd slated originally for the first film. The Viet Cong became Ewoks, "so the main theme of the film was that the Imperial Empire would be overrun by humanity in the form of these cute little teddy bears."[47]

The key is that Lucas saw his own country as the Empire. In his early notes, Lucas described the Empire as "like America ten years from now."[48] Hence Star Wars' place at the triptych's end. *American Graffiti* was the past he yearned for, *Apocalypse Now* was the present he detested, and Star Wars was the future he feared. Lucas made a point of noting how the Emperor Palpatine's throne room was designed to evoke the Oval Office in the White House.[49] He claimed that the corrupt Palpatine was based on Richard Nixon.[50]

Lucas identified the Empire with the United States, and he coded the rebels, particularly the Jedi, as vaguely Asian—Asia having been the setting for the United States' most violent twentieth-century wars. The names Obi-Wan Kenobi and Yoda sounded Japanese, and Lucas took the word Jedi from *jidai-geki*, Japanese period dramas. The name Han, in contrast, seemed Chinese.[51] Lucas considered casting Asian actors to play Luke and Leia and wanted Akira Kurosawa's favorite actor, Toshiro Mifune, for either Obi-Wan or the fallen Jedi Darth Vader.[52] In his 1973 draft of the first film, Lucas described Leia's imperiled home planet as "a small independent country like North Vietnam."[53]

That film premiered right as dissenting Vietnam War movies began to hit screens. Previously, Hollywood's main depiction of the war had been the gung-ho John Wayne production *The Green Berets* (1968). The late 1970s brought a burst of critical films, some set in Southeast Asia, others following disturbed vets back home. These included *Taxi Driver* (1976), *Tracks* (1976), *Heroes* (1977), *Rolling Thunder* (1977), *The Boys in Company C* (1978), *Coming Home* (1978), *Deer Hunter* (1978), *Go Tell the Spartans* (1978), *Who'll Stop the Rain* (1978), *Apocalypse Now* (1979), and Lucas's own *More American Graffiti* (1979). *A New Hope*, released in 1977, set itself apart from the pack with its bright-lines morality and outer space setting. But reviewers could nevertheless decode it. "'Star Wars' is in many respects a film about Vietnam," wrote the *Washington Post*.[54] "The Vietnam parallel is never far," agreed the *London Spectator*.[55]

Technology, modernization, and empire wove together in George Lucas's telling. The United States had grown reliant on large-scale technologies, and rather than progressing with the years, it had declined, becoming an empire. But Star Wars served up hope. The films imagined that small bands of "freedom fighters"—schooled in ancient ways, adopting Asian practices, controlling technology personally, and allying with Indigenous societies—could restore the fallen republic. This vision, though peppy, reflected a profound divergence from the postwar tenets of U.S. foreign relations. It rejected modernization, techno-optimism, and faith that the most powerful country on the planet was also the most virtuous.

To say that Lucas replaced the worldview of his parents' generation with an anti-imperialist vision, however, is not to say that he offered liberation for all. Scholars have been quick to note the racism and sexism that pervade Star Wars. The droids—clumsy figures of fun who address their owners as "master"—draw heavily on old minstrel tropes. Han Solo's loyal Wookiee companion Chewbacca, who participates fully in the action but is sidelined from the honors, is a trusty native. "The Wookiees are more like the Indians, more like noble savages," Lucas told a reporter.[56] The Ewoks offer a cuddlier version of the same stereotype; "I basically cut the Wookiees in half and called them Ewoks," Lucas admitted.[57] And despite her handiness with a blaster, Princess Leia, the sole female lead, appears more as a reward for male heroes than as a hero in her own right.[58]

At the heart of the matter is Lucas's decision to tell the story of U.S. imperialism as a story of white men. Although the Empire's violence is on display as a sign of its moral bankruptcy, the films rarely linger on the victims of that violence. In this, Lucas exhibits a sort of anti-imperialist solipsism. He strenuously opposes empire yet takes little interest in the viewpoint of the colonized who, in the form of the Ewoks, speak only in grunts and gurgles. That is because Lucas's chief objection to the Vietnam War was not what it did to Vietnam. It's what it did to the United States.

A case in point is the fate of Alderaan, Princess Leia's home planet— the planet, under a different name, that Lucas likened in a draft to North Vietnam. In *A New Hope*, the Empire destroys Alderaan with the Death Star to test the weapon's capabilities. This act clearly establishes the Empire's depravity. But what of Alderaan? Leia is initially distraught, yet by her next scene she seems to have forgotten it. As Lucas shows Alderaan only from space, the viewer gets no sense of the lives lived and lost there. An entire planet's obliteration becomes just a backdrop for a moral struggle within the Skywalker family.

Lucas showed a similar lack of interest in imperialism's victims in his one film explicitly about the Vietnam War, *More American Graffiti*. The film is biting in its antiwar politics, especially in its Lucas-directed plotline following Terry Fields to An Loc. Terry undergoes a dramatic shift there. He enlists eager to "kick ass, take names, and eat Cong for breakfast," but, a year later, he concludes that this "isn't my war," fakes his own death, and escapes into the jungle, never to be seen again. It's a Vietnam War story, and it's set in Vietnam, yet Lucas manages to tell it without a single Vietnamese character. The sole glimpse of a Vietnamese person is a photo that Terry's commander proudly displays of a prisoner whom he'd killed. Otherwise, *More American Graffiti* is a Vietnam film immaculately free of Vietnamese people.[59]

There is another, related distinguishing feature of George Lucas's take on Vietnam. After *THX 1138* failed to win audiences, Lucas had a realization. "People don't care how the country's being ruined," he decided. "All that movie did was to make people more pessimistic, more depressive, and less willing to get involved."[60] Lucas continued to believe that "we've got to change the way we live," but he no longer saw frank social criticism as the means to that end. "So then I said, 'Well, maybe I'll take that message and wrap it up in a completely different guise.'" He started making "positive" films. *American Graffiti* and *Star Wars* were set in different universes, but they shared an "effervescent giddiness," Lucas said.[61] And they were massive, industry-changing hits.

The buoyancy in *American Graffiti* comes from its setting in a more innocent time, before the Vietnam War ruined the country. In the original Star Wars trilogy, it comes from the belief that the Old Republic is not irretrievably lost. When a reporter asked Lucas what Star Wars was "ultimately about," Lucas answered with a single word: redemption.[62] The original trilogy starts with "a new hope" in dark times and concludes with what Lucas called the "redemption of a fallen angel," Darth Vader, aka Anakin Skywalker, Luke's father.[63] Although Anakin tries to tempt Luke to the Dark Side, Luke instead turns his father away from it, and Anakin renounces the Dark Side in his final moments. The trilogy ends with Anakin's absolution. After dying, he returns as a smiling apparition, standing benevolently beside the specters of Jedi knights Obi-Wan and Yoda.

From the Skywalkers' perspective, it's a stirring ending, suggesting that innocence can be regained, the nearly extinct Jedi can return, and the son can "redeem his father," as Lucas put it.[64] As a parable for U.S. foreign policy, the tone is similarly hopeful. Republics that have become empires are not doomed, the film insists. The idealistic baby boomers can expiate their parents' sins. The original anti-imperialism of their country can be restored.[65]

Yet, here again, Lucas's solipsism matters. He interprets the theme of empire as an epic moral struggle among would-be imperialists, with everyone else serving as scenery. This allows him to tell Star Wars as a "son saves father" story. But consider the original trilogy's ending from a wider perspective. Anakin has participated actively in the Empire's crimes. He's complicit in mass murder on an inconceivable scale—millions or billions on Alderaan alone, one presumes. His decision to reconcile with Luke and rise up against Emperor Palpatine at the end is surely a step in the right direction. But only by leaving the Empire's victims out can Lucas turn Anakin's story into one of absolution. Seen from Alderaan, Anakin is a galactic *génocidaire*, his last-minute change of heart notwithstanding.

Lucas cares about imperialists' souls, not their deeds. Souls can be saved, hence Lucas's emphasis on hope. This was, after the Vietnam War, a welcome message, as it suggested that the United States might reclaim its ideals, no matter how many lives its wars had needlessly taken. The message fit well with the regenerative rhetoric of the Reagan administration. "It's morning again in America," Reagan's television ads announced. He embraced "the Force," railed against the "evil empire" of the Soviet Union, and backed "freedom fighters" in Afghanistan and Nicaragua, who did indeed resemble the ragtag rebels of Star Wars.[66] Reagan's missile defense program, "Star Wars," would offer, he promised, "a new hope."[67]

Lucas hated this. He unsuccessfully sued over the identification of Reagan's Death Star–like space program with his films. He produced a film, *Latino* (1985), criticizing the Reagan-supported Contras in Nicaragua. But having created a new mythology, Lucas could not control its use. Star Wars galloped on. Under its obliging terms, even the imperialists could imagine themselves as the rebels.

Notes

I thank Michael Falcone, Dexter Fergie, Niko Letsos, Madelyn Lugli, Keith Woodhouse, and the editors for their advice.

1. Remarks at the Annual Convention of the National Association of Evangelicals, March 8, 1983, American Presidency Project, www.presidency.ucsb.edu.
2. Remarks at the National Space Club Luncheon, March 29, 1985, American Presidency Project, www.presidency.ucsb.edu. And see Peter Krämer, "Star Wars," *History Today* 49 (1999): 41–47.
3. Dick Cheney interview on *Meet the Press*, NBC, September 16, 2001.
4. George Lucas interview by David Sheff, 1987, in *George Lucas: Interviews*, ed. Sally Kline (Jackson: University Press of Mississippi, 1999), 153.
5. I've relied especially on three works that place Lucas in the context of the Vietnam War: Chris Taylor, *How Star Wars Conquered the Universe: The Past, Present, and Future of a Multibillion Dollar Franchise* (New York: Basic Books, 2014); Benjamin Hufbauer, "The Politics Behind the Original 'Star Wars,'" *Los Angeles Review of Books* 21, December 2015; and Brian Jay Jones, *George Lucas: A Life* (New York: Little, Brown, 2016).
6. On progress in science fiction, see John Rieder, *Colonialism and the Emergence of Science Fiction* (Middletown, CT: Wesleyan University Press, 2008), chap. 2.

7. This is from the director's version; the theatrical release used a different opener. "*THX 1138*," www.movie-censorship.com/report.php?ID=541751.

8. Statement by the President on Establishing the National Committee for the Development of Scientists and Engineers, April3, 1956, American Presidency Project, www.presidency.ucsb.edu. On U.S. technological leadership, I've learned much from Michael Falcone, "The Rocket's Red Glare: Global Power and the Rise of American State Technology, 1940–1960" (PhD diss., Northwestern University, 2019).

9. Peter W. Lee, "Periodizing a Civil War: Reaffirming an American Empire of Dreams," in *A Galaxy Here and Now: Historical and Cultural Readings of* Star Wars, ed. Peter W. Lee (Jefferson, NC: McFarland, 2016), 168.

10. Michael Rubin, *Droidmaker: George Lucas and the Digital Revolution* (Gainesville, FL: Triad, 2006), 3.

11. Laurent Bouzereau, *Star Wars: The Annotated Screenplays* (New York: Del Rey, 1997), 12.

12. Bouzereau, *Star Wars*, 24.

13. Joe Johnston as quoted in Bouzereau, *Star Wars*, 102.

14. Interview by Kerry O'Quinn, 1981, in *George Lucas: Interviews*, ed. Sally Kline (Jackson: University Press of Mississippi, 1999), 108.

15. Jefferson Cowie, *Stayin' Alive: The 1970s and the Last Days of the Working Class* (New York: New Press, 2010), 341.

16. Rubin, *Droidmaker*.

17. Interview by Jean Vallely, 1980, in *George Lucas: Interviews*, ed. Sally Kline (Jackson: University Press of Mississippi, 1999), 93.

18. George Lucas as quoted in Bouzereau, *Star Wars*, 15.

19. Interview by Stephen Zito, 1977, in *George Lucas: Interviews*, ed. Sally Kline (Jackson: University Press of Mississippi, 1999), 48.

20. Leonard M. Scigaj, "Bettelheim, Castaneda and Zen: The Powers Behind the Force in *Star Wars*," *Extrapolation* 22 (1981): 218.

21. Paul Scanlon, "The Force Behind George Lucas," *Rolling Stone*, August 25, 1977, www.rollingstone.com/movies/movie-news/george-lucas-the-wizard-of -star-wars-2-232011; J. W. Rinzler, *The Making of Star Wars* (New York: Del Rey, 2007), 49.

22. Bouzereau, *Star Wars*, 32.

23. J. W. Rinzler, *The Making of the Empire Strikes Back* (New York: Del Rey, 2010), 22. Connections between the Force training and Castaneda's apprenticeship are documented in Scigaj, "Bettelheim, Castaneda and Zen."

24. W. W. Rostow, *The Stages of Economic Growth: A Non-Communist Manifesto* (New York: Cambridge University Press, 1960), 10. The literature on modernization theory is large; see Daniel Immerwahr, "Modernization and Development in U.S. Foreign Relations," *Passport* (September 2012): 22–25.

25. Bouzereau, *Star Wars*, 88.

26. On Japan and Kurosawa in the films, see Kevin J. Wetmore Jr., *The Empire Triumphant: Race Religion and Rebellion on the Star Wars Films* (Jefferson, NC: McFarland, 2005), chap. 3.

27. Taylor, *How Star Wars Conquered the Universe*, 84.

28. Sheff interview, in *George Lucas: Interviews*, ed. Sally Kline (Jackson: University Press of Mississippi, 1999), 151.

29. Lawrence Meyer and Joel Garreau, "Making Movies with the Same Message as John Wayne and Buddha," *Washington Post*, December 30, 1984.

30. Analyzed in Daniel Immerwahr, "Ten-Cent Ideology: Donald Duck Comic Books and the U.S. Challenge to Modernization," *Modern American History* 3 (2020): 1–26.

31. J. W. Rinzler, *The Making of Return of the Jedi* (New York: Del Rey, 2013), 44.

32. Eric P. Nash, "The Names Came from Earth," *New York Times*, January 26, 1997.

33. Rinzler, *The Making of Return of the Jedi*, 77.

34. Charles Champlin, *George Lucas: The Creative Impulse* (New York: Harry N. Abrams, 1992), 96.

35. Ronald Steel, *Pax Americana*, rev. ed. (New York: Viking Press, 1970), 13. An excellent overview of the Vietnam War's "techno-hubris" is Michael Adas, *Dominance by Design: Technological Imperatives and America's Civilizing Mission* (Cambridge, MA: Harvard University Press, 2006), chap. 6.

36. Peter Biskind, *Easy Riders, Raging Bulls: How the Sex-Drugs-and-Rock 'n' Roll Generation Saved Hollywood* (New York: Simon & Schuster, 1998), 317.

37. Hufbauer, "The Politics Behind the Original 'Star Wars.'"

38. Scanlon, "The Force Behind George Lucas."

39. Margot Norris, "Modernism and Vietnam: Francis Ford Coppola's *Apocalypse Now*," *Modern Fiction Studies* 44 (1998): 732.

40. Taylor, *How Star Wars Conquered the Universe*, 87.

41. Hufbauer, "The Politics Behind the Original 'Star Wars.'"

42. Jones, *George Lucas*, 168–69.

43. Robert Benayoun and Michel Ciment, "Entretien avec George Lucas," *Positif*, September 1977, 60.

44. Scanlon, "The Force Behind George Lucas."

45. Marcus Hearn, *The Cinema of George Lucas* (New York: Harry N. Abrams, 2005), 129.

46. Rinzler, *The Making of Star Wars*, 8.

47. Rinzler, *The Making of Return of the Jedi*, 11.

48. Rinzler, *The Making of Star Wars*, 17.

49. Lindesay Irvine, "In the Shadow of Evil," *Guardian*, November 7, 2005.

50. Biskind, *Easy Riders, Raging Bulls*, 324; Rinzler, *The Making of Empire Strikes Back*, 24.

51. John Baxter, *George Lucas: A Biography* (New York: HarperCollins, 1999), 158. See also Wetmore, *The Empire Triumphant*, chap. 3; and Julien Fielding, "Beyond Judeo-Christianity: *Star Wars* and the Great Eastern Religions," in *Sex, Politics, and Religion in* Star Wars, ed. Douglas Brode and Leah Deyneka (Lanham, MD: Scarecrow, 2012), 25–46.

52. Bouzereau, *Star Wars*, 197; Taylor, *How Star Wars Conquered the Universe*, 146; Rinzler, *The Making of Star Wars*, 69.

53. Rinzler, *The Making of Star Wars*, 16.

54. Jim Hoagland, "The Politics of 'Star Wars,'" *Washington Post*, December 11, 1977.

55. Clancy Sigal, "Anodyne," *London Spectator*, December 24, 1977.

56. Scanlon, "The Force Behind George Lucas."

57. Bouzereau, *Star Wars*, 281.

58. Useful overviews of race/gender include Wetmore, *The Empire Triumphant*; Carl Silvio and Tony M. Vinci, *Culture, Identities and Technology in the* Star Wars *Films: Essays on the Two Trilogies* (Jefferson, NC: McFarland, 2007); Douglas Brode and Leah Deyneka, eds., *Sex, Politics, and Religion* (Lanham, MD: Scarecrow, 2012); and Peter W. Lee, ed., *A Galaxy Here and Now: Historical and Cultural Readings of* Star Wars (Jefferson, NC: McFarland, 2016).

59. The sole Asian character is a photographer with one line of dialogue. However, he speaks fluent English and wears U.S. fatigues—nothing suggests he's Vietnamese.

60. Farber interview, in *George Lucas: Interviews*, ed. Sally Kline (Jackson: University Press of Mississippi, 1999), 42.

61. O'Quinn interview, in *George Lucas: Interviews*, ed. Sally Kline (Jackson: University Press of Mississippi, 1999), 115, 119.

62. Interview by John Seabrook, 1997, in *George Lucas: Interviews*, ed. Sally Kline (Jackson: University Press of Mississippi, 1999), 204.

63. George Lucas as quoted in Bouzereau, *Star Wars*, 271.

64. George Lucas as quoted in Bouzereau, *Star Wars*, 271.

65. This is an interpretation advanced in John Hellmann, *American Myth and the Legacy of Vietnam* (New York: Columbia University Press, 1986), 209–20.

66. Ronald Reagan, Remarks at the National Space Club Luncheon, March 29, 1985; Ronald Reagan, State of the Union Address, February 6, 1985; Ronald Reagan, Remarks at the Annual Convention of the National Association of Evangelicals, March 8, 1983, all from American Presidency Project, www.presidency.ucsb.edu.

67. Ronald Reagan, Address to the Nation on Defense and National Security, March 23, 1983, American Presidency Project, www.presidency.ucsb.edu.

CHAPTER 22

Dual-Use Ideologies

How Science Came to Be Part of the United States' Cold War Arsenal

AUDRA J. WOLFE

T he Cold War wasn't particularly cold, but the term is nevertheless a useful shorthand for a certain kind of thinking that preoccupied national security officials in the United States at the dawn of the Atomic Age.[1] In the late 1940s and early 1950s, U.S. foreign policy strategists used the phrase to invoke a specific kind of conflict, one carried out by "means short of war," by which they meant "war that affects us directly" or, more generously, "nuclear war." Once the Soviet Union revealed that it had acquired an atomic bomb of its own, the global stakes of a "Hot War" between the United States and the Soviet Union seemed too dire to contemplate. "The cold war," NSC 68 warned, "is in fact a real war in which the survival of the free world is at stake."[2]

For U.S. national security officials, Cold War referred to a specific set of political, economic, and psychological techniques, fought both on behalf of and with the ideologies that defined U.S. foreign policy. An ideological war required tools that could promote ideologies. Diplomatic historians have produced compelling accounts of how the United States attempted to appeal to the hearts and minds of global audiences, particularly global elites, using tools as wide-ranging as print propaganda, economics fellowships, and jazz tours.[3] Although campaigns involving science have attracted less attention in the literature, they carried special weight given the unprecedented role of science and technology in the ideologies of freedom and progress that prevailed among U.S. foreign policy elites at the time.[4]

Unlike campaigns involving the arts, literature, or sports, campaigns involving science both conveyed important messages about the nature of freedom *and* opened the door for more concrete expressions of power. Campaigns contrasting the U.S. commitment to scientific internationalism with Soviet scientific nationalism, for example, simultaneously positioned the United States as a beacon for scientific freedom and eased the United States' ability to collect scientific intelligence. This was an ideological choice that produced concrete results for national security.[5]

The same could be said about the very concept of a "cold" war, which combined a dazzling commitment to the language of freedom with a horrifying apparatus for global domination. In this essay, I use the example of science to propose that U.S. ideological campaigns in the Cold War era be considered a form of "dual-use" technology. As usually discussed in the national security community, "dual use" refers to technologies that can be used for either civilian or military purposes. Rockets are dual use because they can be used to launch either weather satellites or nuclear warheads. Global positioning systems are dual use because they enable lost hikers to call for help or drone operators to launch deadly strikes.

Discussions of dual use tend to focus on technologies as *objects*, that is, as stuff.[6] As a historian of science, I embrace a more expansive definition of technology as any tool or process that enables humans to manipulate the world around them. State-supported propaganda easily fits this definition of technology because countries undertake propaganda campaigns specifically to change people's attitudes or behaviors. Propaganda also qualifies as a technology under more conservative definitions of technology as "applied science" because the architects of Cold War era propaganda largely believed themselves to be applying the lessons of communications and social psychology to the real world.[7]

It is by now a cliché to point out that U.S. historians have painted themselves into historiographical corners seeking to either defend or exonerate U.S. actions during the Cold War, and yet this is not a problem that limits itself to U.S. history.[8] Historians of science and technology, perhaps more so than historians in other fields, have long wrestled with the idea that the same kind of knowledge can be beneficial or deadly, depending on who has access to it and why. Particularly when referring to the second half of the twentieth century, the observation that science has many valences—some peaceful, some not—is not particularly novel. A recent work by the historian David Price on anthropology, for example, suggests that the entire discipline of cultural anthropology should be thought of as "dual use" during this time period.[9] What I am suggesting here is that expanding the concept of dual-use technology—an idea at once both quite simple and very powerful—to something as broad as ideology can help historians work through the contradictions and ambivalence that inevitably cloud discussions of U.S. power in the late twentieth century.

When it comes to ideologies of freedom, it's all dual use. There is no way to promote freedom in the name of U.S. hegemony that does not also present the possibility of harm. And nowhere is this more clear than in the case of scientific freedom.

The early Central Intelligence Agency (CIA) understood this. At the time of the CIA's founding, in 1947, the agency's intelligence consumers placed a high priority on scientific and technical intelligence, especially atomic intelligence. They largely credited the Allied victory in World War II to scientific and technical achievements, including radar, the atomic bomb, and the proximity fuse. For this reason, the CIA obtained its first science director, the chemist Wallace Brode, just weeks after opening its doors. But despite an ambitious plan to develop what he referred to as a "Scientific Order of Battle," Brode failed in the position, lasting little more than a year in the job. Beset by interservice rivalries and security roadblocks, Brode could barely staff his office, let alone assess the Soviet threat. In a departure letter to Karl Compton, the chair of the Research and Development Board, Brode warned that neither the CIA nor the various branches of the military trusted scientists who, after all, might have access to useful secrets.[10]

The CIA's problems with science attracted the attention of two major federal reviews of the intelligence establishment. Both the Eberstadt Committee and the Dulles Committee warned policy makers about the high stakes of the lack of concrete information in the field of scientific intelligence. The Eberstadt Committee's report claimed that "failure" in scientific intelligence might "have more immediate and catastrophic consequences than failure in any other field of intelligence." The Dulles Committee took a more practical tack by recommending a more centralized body for gathering and assessing scientific intelligence. These reports, combined with Brode's departure and continuing complaints from Compton, pressured the CIA to organize a new division, the Office of Scientific Intelligence (OSI).

Creation of the OSI on January 1, 1949, gave scientific intelligence a higher priority within the CIA, but otherwise did little to ease the work of Brode's replacement, Willard Machle. Allocated a staff of one hundred,

Machle struggled to recruit scientists willing to work in the relative obscurity and secrecy of an intelligence agency. Like Brode before him, Machle continued to fight turf battles not only with other departmental intelligence units but also with other divisions within the CIA. The Soviet Union's successful detonation of an atomic bomb in August 1949—several years ahead of U.S. predictions—drove home the possibly catastrophic consequences of intelligence failures. Machle resigned in March 1950, having lasted, like Brode, barely fifteen months in the job.

The OSI and its successor, the Directorate of Science and Technology, would eventually become a powerhouse of U.S. intelligence collection and analysis.[11] In the meantime, though, the National Security Council turned to the State Department—not the intelligence agencies—for its urgent needs in scientific intelligence. NSCID 10, issued January 18, 1949, gave the State Department primary responsibility for collecting information on the "basic sciences."[12] State would be responsible for collecting actionable scientific intelligence as well as smoothing channels for international scientific exchanges. State Department officials rightly worried about their ability to carry out this task. They knew they would encounter competition from other agencies, but more to the point, they worried about the difficulty of reconciling intelligence with diplomacy, and they also worried, out loud, about the challenges of isolating "outstanding scientists" from what they described as the "taint" of intelligence collection. And there was a practical obstacle as well: foreign contacts would presumably not cooperate with scientists suspected of being intelligence operatives.

State turned to Lloyd Berkner, a radio engineer known for his administrative acumen, for possible solutions. Berkner had deep ties to defense policy and the government's intelligence needs; among other things, he had served on the postwar committee that coordinated the Army's and Navy's requests for intelligence.[13] Berkner's landmark report, "Science and Foreign Relations," released in April 1950, established an ambitious agenda for the role of science in the State Department that put emerging ideas about scientific freedom to use. The main body of the report recommended more opportunities for international exchange, fewer restrictions on exchange of technical information, and increased U.S. participation in international conferences. The so-called Berkner Report forthrightly acknowledged that "certain benefits which are essential to the security and welfare of the United States, stem from international cooperation and exchange with respect to scientific matters." A classified appendix made explicit that the point of all of this was to gather scientific intelligence. The idea was that private citizens, acting in their roles as private scientists freely mingling on the international stage, would offer the most reliable source of scientific intelligence. Scientists should be encouraged to go about their routine business, and the U.S. government should encourage or even create opportunities for scientists to have "free and open discussions" with their international colleagues.[14]

For most of the 1950s, the National Academy of Sciences took on the role of administrative helpmeet for this project of scientific intelligence via scientific internationalism, providing the State Department and the CIA with everything from weekly lists of U.S. scientists traveling abroad to personnel recommendations for international conferences. By 1954, the National Academy's Office of International Relations derived its primary support from a contract with the State Department in exchange for "various" kinds of assistance. With the National Academy's help, American science became much more international in the 1950s. But it's worth remembering that this was never scientific internationalism for the sake of scientific internationalism. It was scientific internationalism for the sake of anticommunism. Scientific internationalism, like scientific freedom, is dual use.

The story that I have told thus far arguably does not fit under the headline of "ideological Cold War" at all, given that it involves a quest for actionable scientific intelligence. Notice, however, how the plans depended on certain assumptions about how science should operate in the world. The Berkner Report, a document designed to facilitate the expansion of U.S. state power, took the trouble to explain that the State Department's activities should not interfere with scientists' "natural" inclination to cross borders. "The Department," the report explained, "should not interpose itself between the scientist and the achievement of his objective of free flow of information." Rather, the free flow of information had been blocked by "certain situations in the modern world," an oblique reference to the various styles of authoritarian government that proliferated in the mid-twentieth century.[15] Seeking to understand why the United States, and only the United States, had developed an atomic weapon during World War II, leading scientific administrators like Berkner and his comrade-in-arms, Vannevar Bush, developed a folk philosophy of science that contrasted what they regarded as the wholesome practice of science in the United States with its corrupt counterparts in Nazi Germany and the Soviet Union. Successful science policy, they argued, depended on scientists' "freedom of inquiry," "freedom from government control," and "freedom from dogma."[16]

These messages about the nature of scientific freedom in the West, and the perils of science under communism and fascism, should rightly be considered an ideology of science. As such, this language soon found its way into U.S. propaganda, particularly propaganda carried out by scientists. In the fall of 1950, for example, the Genetics Society of America held a four-day "Golden Jubilee of Genetics" to celebrate the fiftieth anniversary of the "rediscovery" of Gregor Mendel's so-called laws of inheritance. This was the text. The subtext of the event, which was recorded for international broadcast by Voice of America, was to contrast the achievements of Western genetics with the sorry state of genetics in the Soviet Union. Ever since August 1948, when Communist Party favorite Trofim Lysenko announced that Stalin himself had endorsed his (fabricated) theories of inheritance, genetics in the Soviet Union had been subject to a party line. Institutions shut their doors, scientists lost their jobs, and research programs went underground. Given the timing, it was easy—too easy—for American ideologues to paint of all Soviet science with the brush of Lysenkoism, and American science as its opposite.[17]

This contrast between authoritarian science in the Soviet Union and scientific freedom in the United States become a central touchstone of U.S. ideological campaigns in the 1950s. The very first session of the CIA-backed Congress for Cultural Freedom's marquee meeting in Berlin, for instance, was titled "Science and Totalitarianism" and featured a rousing condemnation of Lysenkoism delivered by the American geneticist (and former communist) H. J. Muller. Muller, a world-renowned *Drosophila* researcher who had the bad timing to be in Berlin in 1933 and in Moscow in the late 1930s, rarely bothered to distinguish between the evils of fascism and communism; the title of his presentation was typical of a certain style of Cold War jeremiad.[18] As Muller told the crowd, "this right to think differently, to question, and to *express* our disagreements is the primary moral basis for the development of science and, indeed, all that is valuable in the intellectual life of man." Later, Muller would travel to India and Japan on the Congress for Cultural Freedom's behalf, recruiting sympathetic scientists to the cultural front. In 1953, the congress held a successful convocation on "Science and Freedom" in Hamburg, Germany, bringing together 110 scientists from nineteen countries to debate the appropriate balance between pure and applied research, academic freedom in an age of state-supported science, and scientists' moral responsibility. The event was, by all accounts, a tremendous success.[19]

In a contemporary climate in which scientists around the world find their fact-based work challenged by conspiracy theorists, industry hacks, and venal politicians, it feels uncomfortable, even dangerous, to point out that there's something troubling about the notion of "Science and Freedom" as fashioned by U.S. propagandists. For the record, then: Scientific research should not be subject to party lines. Science functions better under conditions of democracy than under authoritarianism. To say that notions of scientific freedom had to be constructed and maintained is not to say that they are not desirable. At the same time, the U.S. government was not supporting these sorts of messages about the nature of science to enact a normative vision of the philosophy of science. The Congress for Cultural Freedom's programs in science, like their programs in other areas of intellectual life, were meant to convince intellectuals around the world that liberal democracy as practiced in the West—that is, capitalism—offered better opportunities to build moral and satisfying creative careers than either socialism or communism.[20] If we take the phrase "hearts and minds" literally, this was both an emotional appeal to the people U.S. national security experts assumed would be making decisions abroad (the "hearts" part) and a calculated effort to divert technical expertise from socialist and communist governments (the "minds" part). Like so many other aspects of the ideological war, U.S. promotion of scientific freedom was simultaneously utopian and deeply cynical. It was dual use.

How difficult it is, even now, to acknowledge that ideologies of academic and scientific freedom were themselves part of U.S. propaganda. I say "part of," not "creations of"; of course, scientists and intellectuals trumpeted their independence from government control well before the Cold War. Nevertheless, for the first two decades of the Cold War, it is fair to say that the values of elite scientists and U.S. propagandists overlapped. Scientists who fit certain institutionally approved categories—white, male, straight, able-bodied, politically nonconfrontational—could receive nearly unlimited funds to investigate whatever they wanted, with relatively little government interference, as long as they limited their critiques of the government to safe terrain. In return, these same elite scientists tacitly agreed to contribute to the national interest, even if that national interest took the form of promoting scientific freedom.

It took some time for the rest of the government to catch up to the intelligence community's vision of scientific freedom as a tool for global domination. In 1955, for example, the U.S. Atomic Energy Commission attempted to prevent Muller from delivering a paper on the genetic dangers of fallout at the Geneva Conference on Peaceful Uses of Atomic Energy. (Aside from his side-hustle as a first-rate propagandist, Muller had been awarded a Nobel Prize in 1946 for his work demonstrating that radiation could cause genetic mutations.) Administrators feared that Muller's comments could be used in campaigns on behalf of a nuclear test ban, but they underestimated the dangers of muzzling a well-known champion of scientific freedom on the international stage. Muller, ever the savvy ideologue, worked out a perfect solution: He delivered his comments from the floor, thereby demonstrating that scientists in the United States had the right to criticize their own government. Did bucking the will of the Atomic Energy Commission take courage? Certainly. Did his actions also reinforce the message that he had been delivering via the CIA's and the Voice of America's platforms for years? Absolutely.[21]

At least until the late 1950s, the U.S. commitment to a scientific front in the ideological Cold War was halting, underfunded, and largely driven by the interests of the scientists (like Muller) who led the campaigns.[22] The CIA's relatively small-scale cultural operations bypassed congressional budget scrutiny. Two exceptions, the International Geophysical Year and Atoms for Peace, proved the rule: Congress, the military, and the foreign policy establishment could only be persuaded to back ideological campaigns involving science if they had a strong national security component. Atoms for Peace— a program that the historian Kenneth Osgood has described as "quite possibly the largest single propaganda campaign ever conducted by the American government"—did triple duty as an ideological campaign, a nonproliferation program, and an intelligence channel.[23] U.S. involvement in the International Geophysical Year—orchestrated by none other than Lloyd Berkner—was designed to do something similar in the realm of space. The successful U.S. launch of an artificial satellite would simultaneously promote international scientific cooperation, collect militarily useful scientific data, and establish the freedom of the skies (a necessary step toward ensuring the legality of the military's planned reconnaissance satellites). But even with their obvious psychological overtones, both of these programs directly contributed to U.S. defense priorities. They promoted security first, ideology second.

The global response to the Soviet *Sputnik* forced the United States to rethink its priorities when it came to science. Eisenhower and his advisors fully expected the Soviets to beat the United States into space; what they hadn't anticipated was the impact that launch would have on the reputation of the United States. In a detailed survey of world opinion conducted just weeks after the launch, the U.S. Information Agency (USIA) reported that Soviet claims of scientific and technical superiority, and Soviet propaganda in general, had gained credibility. U.S. allies openly speculated whether the balance of scientific achievement and military might had shifted to the Soviet Union. "American prestige is viewed as having sustained a severe blow," USIA reported.[24]

The situation forced U.S. authorities to take prestige seriously, with lasting consequences for both domestic and international science policy. On the domestic front, government agencies across the board added science advisors. Congress ramped up funding for high school science education, graduate fellowships, and basic research. The most dramatic shifts, however, came in ideological campaigns. President Eisenhower ended his 1958 State of the Union address with a rousing call for a U.S.-led but international "Science for Peace" program. The USIA hired a science advisor and declared 1958 a "Year of Science." A host of government agencies from the Atomic Energy Commission to the National Science Foundation brainstormed ways to signal the U.S. commitment to global peace through scientific programming, and nongovernmental groups such as the National Academy of Sciences and the Rockefeller Foundation asked how they could help. Behind closed doors, the psychological warfare strategists at the Operations Coordinating Board discussed the best ways to coordinate these overt programs with the CIA's ongoing covert work on behalf of science.

A remarkable number of ambitious programs involving science and scientists, many of which had no discernable relationship to defense needs, emerged from these discussions. One of the most telling involves the efforts of the Asia Foundation to translate and adapt U.S. biology textbooks for high school classrooms across noncommunist Asia. Nominally a development-focused nonprofit incorporated in California, the Asia Foundation was in reality one of the CIA's largest proprietary organizations from its founding in 1954 until its cover was blown in 1967. Operating under the codename DTPILLAR, the foundation spent approximately $8 million a year backing the work of Asian-led organizations and their American partners in countries located on the perimeter of the People's Republic of China. From the mid-1950s through the late 1960s, the Asia Foundation partnered with almost any voluntary organization headed by Asians that might plausibly support the development of civil society, from 4-H clubs to seed exchanges.[25]

Educational reform programs meshed particularly well with the Asia Foundation's mandate to cultivate democratic institutions, foster economic growth, and strengthen relationships between Asian and American elites. The program's officers were keen to fund translations and adaptations of a series of post-*Sputnik* high school science textbooks that had originally been developed for American teenagers. No matter the specific subject, these textbooks stressed what educators referred to as the "nature of inquiry" over rote memorization. Even before the textbooks found their way into American classrooms, the USIA and USAID were distributing drafts to libraries and educators throughout the world. The Asia Foundation invested heavily in the biology textbooks, funding some combination of teacher training programs and/or textbook adaptation in Afghanistan, Ceylon, Hong Kong, India, Japan, South Korea, the Philippines, and Taiwan.

The ready availability of these modern, accessible, locally specific textbooks changed the way high school biology was taught around the globe, replacing rote memorization with inquiry-based learning. Popular with local technocrats, these textbooks subtly conveyed American scientific values, contrasting empiricism with authoritarianism and basic research with applied research. Programs such as these operated at multiple levels. The elaborate adaptation process strengthened ties between foreign technocrats and U.S. educators, extending U.S. hegemony. In Washington, the technocrats and modernization theorists running organizations such as USAID posited that this textbook approach to scientific rationality would prepare a new generation of Asian students and teachers for an economic takeoff that would usher in U.S.-style capitalism. And last but hardly least, by offering material support for overseas educators' desire for professional respect and national autonomy, the textbook programs concretely demonstrated American goodwill. Somewhat remarkably, the Asia Foundation's partnerships with Asian educators continued even after the Asia Foundation's ties to the CIA were reported in 1967.[26] Not even the taint of a CIA connection could dampen international technocrats' willingness to pursue development through science-based education.

Programs like these defy easy historical analysis. This was by intent. During this time period, officials at the USIA actively theorized the multivalent nature of diplomacy involving science. A 1958 memo describing the potential for the textbook programs, for example, describes the program as a "method of using science and technology in support of general Agency and country objectives in the Far East." Although scientists, science teachers, and government officials were the primary target audience for this "method," the USIA hoped that educational programs would also influence the general public at large, "which needs to be reminded of the preeminence of non-Communist nations in science and technology, and to have explained the differences between a technological society oriented to the needs and desires of the people, and one oriented solely toward the objectives of the state." On the next page, the author of the report notes that "there is every indication that [American] scientists will be delighted to cooperate."[27]

In the context of this document, the United States is supposed to be the "technological society oriented to the needs and desires of the people," and the Soviet Union the one "oriented solely toward the objectives of the state." Yet, at least in this in-house document, the USIA theorized that positioning science as a tool to serve the people could, in fact, further state objectives. In a "Basic Guidance Paper" on science and technology issued around the same time, the USIA advised all foreign posts that programming on science should emphasize how science and technology could "improve the general welfare, not only in the United States, but the world over." The paper distinguished between science, which constituted research undertaken for its own sake, and technology, which is "only the means to an end." "Science," the guidance paper advised, "is neither for nor against, moral nor immoral. Science is apolitical."[28]

These were remarkable statements to be issued in the name of a government propaganda agency. At the height of the ideological Cold War, science and politics had become so closely intertwined that government officials announced the impossibility of them having anything to do with one another. It is ludicrous, yet somehow powerful; repulsive, yet enticing. This careful distinction between science and technology allowed the United States to open up its policies involving scientific cooperation and scientific exchange: If science is for knowledge, and technology for power, then *technology*, rather than *science*, is the thing whose dissemination should be controlled. The concept of dual-use technologies owes its existence to the idea that technology, but not science, can be weaponized—and yet this idea was itself intended as an ideological weapon.

There are, of course, many ways to talk about ideas that contradict themselves. The concept of "apolitical science" might, for instance, be considered a Butlerian binary in which the distinction between the two (science and politics) is primarily enacted through performative scripts.[29] In this essay, however, I have suggested that we might more profitably consider this problem through the familiar national security idiom of dual use. It's not so much that "science for freedom" and "science in the interests of U.S. power" are opposites but that they are exactly one and the same. The language of dual use implies that the problem is not with the underlying thing (whether an object or an ideology) but with who is using the thing, and for what purpose.

I suggest this language not to privilege national security thinking but because the simplicity of the concept allows us to give name to a phenomenon that we witness running throughout the history of U.S. foreign policy but find difficult to discuss. Although some ideologies (for instance, white supremacy) have no possible redeeming purpose, many of the ideologies that the United States advanced over the course of its history, especially during the Cold War, contained at least the possibility of liberation if only they could be combined with notions of collective justice. An absolutist perspective that either embraces or rejects particular ideologies *because they were promoted by the United States* distorts the historical narrative and does little to further the cause of justice, in the United States or elsewhere. As with a 3-D printer that can be used to manufacture either medical supplies or assault rifles, the rhetoric of scientific freedom can be used both to protect marginalized scientists from powerful bureaucrats and to defend elite researchers' turf.

Science is not inherently oppressive, nor is it inherently liberatory. This is a rather different thing than saying, as the USIA did in 1958, that science is apolitical. Rather, it is the most political thing imaginable to say that there is a future in which science *can* be liberatory if and only if it is based on the consent of those subject to its powers.

Even as we rightly question the label of Cold War and interrogate the notion of freedom, we would do well to continue to grapple with what the concept meant to Cold War era thinkers whose ideological positions, particularly about the nature of scientific freedom, continue to resonate in the present moment. Scientific insights arguably drove the technological threats that frightened U.S. policy makers into supporting a Cold War; today, those same insights have left us with a terrible environmental legacy and an increased nuclear threat. But we desperately need science's empirical, fact-based approach to solving real-world problems, including the existential threats of climate change and global pandemics. Rejecting Cold War binaries of science as the opposite of technology, of science as the opposite of politics, can help us envision a new future that binds the fate of scientists to those of all people. Science isn't either/or; science is both/and. The ideology of science and ideologies of freedom, more generally, are and always have been dual use.

Notes

1. Paul Thomas Chamberlin, *The Cold War's Killing Fields: Rethinking the Long Peace* (New York: Harper, 2018).
2. Neil H. Peterson et al., eds., "Document 85: Note by the Executive Secretary to the National Security Council on United States Objectives and Programs for National Security (NSC 68) [TOP SECRET]," in *FRUS 1950*, vol. 1 (Washington, DC: Government Printing Office, 1998), https://history.state .gov/historicaldocuments/frus1950v01/d85.
3. Highlights from this rich literature include Walter L. Hixson, *Parting the Curtain: Propaganda, Culture, and the Cold War, 1945–1961* (New York: St. Martin's, 1997); Scott Lucas, *Freedom's War: The American Crusade Against the Soviet Union* (New York: New York University, 1999); Penny M. Von Eschen, *Satchmo Blows Up the World: Jazz Ambassadors Play the Cold War* (Cambridge, MA: Harvard University Press, 2004); Kenneth Osgood, *Total Cold War: Eisenhower's Secret Propaganda Battle at Home and Abroad* (Lawrence: University Press of Kansas, 2006); Laura A. Belmonte, *Selling the American Way: U.S. Propaganda and the Cold War* (Philadelphia: University of Pennsylvania Press, 2008); Nicholas J. Cull, *The Cold War and the United States Information Agency: American Propaganda and Public Diplomacy, 1945–1989* (New York: Cambridge University Press, 2008); David Ekbladh, *The Great American Mission: Modernization and the Construction of an American World Order* (Princeton, NJ: Princeton University Press, 2010); Michael E. Latham, *The Right Kind of Revolution: Modernization, Development, and U.S. Foreign Policy from the Cold War to the Present* (Ithaca, NY: Cornell University Press, 2011); Jason Parker, *Hearts, Minds, Voices: US Cold War Public Diplomacy and the Formation of the Third World* (New York: Oxford University Press, 2016).
4. The literature on science and the Cold War is vast. For entry points, see Audra J. Wolfe, *Competing with the Soviets: Science, Technology, and the State in Cold War America* (Baltimore, MD: Johns Hopkins University Press, 2013); Naomi Oreskes, introduction to *Science and Technology in the Global Cold War*, ed. Naomi Oreskes and John Krige (Cambridge, MA: MIT Press, 2014), 1–9.
5. I explore this topic at length in Audra J. Wolfe, *Freedom's Laboratory: The Cold War Struggle for the Soul of Science* (Baltimore, MD: Johns Hopkins University Press, 2018). For other perspectives, see Joseph Manzione, "'Amusing and

Amazing and Practical and Military': The Legacy of Scientific Internationalism in American Foreign Policy, 1945–1963," *Diplomatic History* 24, no. 1 (2000): 21–55, https://doi.org/10.1111/1467-7709.00197; John Krige, "Atoms for Peace, Scientific Internationalism, and Scientific Intelligence," *Osiris* 21, no. 1 (2006): 161–81, https://doi.org/10.1086/507140; John Krige, *American Hegemony and the Postwar Reconstruction of Science in Europe* (Cambridge, MA: MIT Press, 2006); Ronald E. Doel and Allan Needell, "Science, Scientists, and the CIA: Balancing International Ideals, National Needs, and Professional Opportunities," in *Eternal Vigilance? 50 Years of the CIA*, ed. Rhodri Jeffrey-Jones and Christopher Andrew (Portland, OR: Frank Cass, 1997).

6. See, for instance, the essays in Jonathan B. Tucker, ed., *Innovation, Dual Use, and Security: Managing the Risks of Emerging Biological and Chemical Technologies* (Cambridge, MA: MIT Press, 2012).

7. In Project Troy, for example, the State Department assembled a crack team of physical and social scientists to develop strategies for psychological warfare. Their report addressed both technical issues, such as how to circumvent Soviet jamming of Voice of America broadcasts, as well as content, such as how the United States might use Stalin's death to its advantage. See Allan Needell, "'Truth Is Our Weapon': Project Troy, Political Warfare, and Government-Academic Relations in the National Security State," *Diplomatic History* 17 (1993): 399–420, https://doi.org/10.1111/j.1467-7709.1993.tb00588.x.

8. Diplomatic historians have been urging each other to move past this framing for almost as long as the framing has existed. See, for instance, Odd Arne Westad, "Exploring the Histories of the Cold War: A Pluralist Approach," in *Uncertain Empire: American History and the Idea of the Cold War*, ed. Joel Isaac and Duncan Bell (New York: Oxford University Press, 2012), 51–59.

9. David H. Price, *Cold War Anthropology: The CIA, the Pentagon, and the Growth of Dual Use Anthropology* (Durham, NC: Duke University Press, 2016).

10. The material in this and the next six paragraphs is adapted from Wolfe, *Freedom's Laboratory*, 38–55.

11. Jeffrey T. Richelson, *The Wizards of Langley: Inside the CIA's Directorate of Science and Technology* (Boulder, CO: Westview Press, 2002).

12. C. Thomas Thorne Jr. and David S. Patterson, eds., "Document 429: National Security Council Intelligence Directive No. 10 (January 18, 1949)," in *FRUS, 1945–1950, Emergency of the Intelligence Establishment* (Washington, DC: Government Printing Office, 1996), https://history.state.gov/historicaldocuments/frus1945-50Intel/d429.

13. For a biography of Berkner, see Allen A. Needell, *Science, Cold War, and the American State: Lloyd V. Berkner and the Balance of Professional Ideals* (Amsterdam: Harwood Academic, 2000).

14. The complete (open) portion of the Berkner Report was published as Lloyd V. Berkner, Douglas Merritt Whitaker, and National Research Council (U.S.), *Science and Foreign Relations: International Flow of Scientific and Technological Information*, General Foreign Policy Series 30 (Washington, DC: U.S. Department of State, 1950). For a more concise (and accessible) version, see Lloyd Berkner, "Science and Foreign Relations: Berkner Report to the U.S. Department of State," *Bulletin of the Atomic Scientists*, October 1950, 293–98. For the classified appendix, see Lloyd Berkner, "Appendix: Scientific Intelligence [SECRET]," April 18, 1950, RG 59 (U.S. Department of State) A1 3008A, General Records Relating to Atomic Energy Matters, box 64, folder "Science and Foreign Relations," NARA II, College Park, Maryland.

15. Berkner, "Science and Foreign Relations."

16. Wolfe, *Freedom's Laboratory*, 30–33.

17. Wolfe, *Freedom's Laboratory*, 69–72.

18. For biographical background on Muller, see Elof Axel Carlson, *Genes, Radiation, and Society: The Life and Work of H. J. Muller* (Ithaca, NY: Cornell University Press, 1981); for the rhetorical punch of "totalitarianism" in this context, see L. K. Adler and T. G. Paterson, "Red Fascism: The Merger of Nazi Germany and Soviet Russia in the American Image of Totalitarianism, 1930s–1950s," *American Historical Review* (1970): 1046–64.

19. Wolfe, *Freedom's Laboratory*, 78–81.

20. Essential histories of the Congress for Cultural Freedom include Peter Coleman, *The Liberal Conspiracy: The Congress for Cultural Freedom and the Struggle for the Mind of Postwar Europe* (New York: Free Press, 1989); Frances Stonor Saunders, *The Cultural Cold War: The CIA and the World of Arts and Letters* (New York: New Press, 1999); Giles Scott-Smith, *The Politics of Apolitical Culture: The Congress for Cultural Freedom, the CIA, and Post-War American Hegemony* (New York: Routledge, 2002); Hugh Wilford, *The Mighty Wurlitzer: How the CIA Played America* (Cambridge, MA: Harvard University Press, 2008); Sarah Miller Harris, *The CIA and the Congress for Cultural Freedom in the Early Cold War: The Limits of Making Common Cause* (New York: Routledge, 2016); Giles Scott-Smith and Charlotte Lerg, eds., *Campaigning Culture and the Global Cold War: The Journals of the Congress for Cultural Freedom* (New York: Palgrave Macmillan, 2017).

21. Wolfe, *Freedom's Laboratory*, 96–97.

22. The material in this and the next six paragraphs is developed from Wolfe, *Freedom's Laboratory*, 96–102; 135–56.

23. Osgood, *Total Cold War*, 156; Krige, "Atoms for Peace."

24. USIA Office of Research and Intelligence, "World Opinion and the Soviet Satellite: A Preliminary Evaluation," October 17, 1957, RG 306 (USIA), P 243, Office of Policy and Plans: Program Coordination Staff, Office of the Advisor

for Science, Space, and the Environment, box 9, folder "Satellites: Sputnik," NARA II, College Park, Maryland.

25. "FOIA Doc_0001088621," February 6, 1990, 0001088621, http://www.foia.cia.gov/sites/default/files/document_conversions/89801/DOC_0001088621.pdf.

26. Wallace Turner, "Asia Foundation Got CIA Funds," *New York Times*, March 22, 1967.

27. "Science and Technology in Support of Country and Agency Objectives in the Far East," November 1958, RG 306 (USIA), P 243, Office of Policy and Plans: Program Coordination Staff, Office of the Advisor for Science, Space, and the Environment, box 3, folder "IOP/A Basic Paper 1958," NARA II, College Park, Maryland.

28. George V. Allen to All USIS Posts, "Science and Technology: A Basic Guidance Paper," November 18, 1958, RG 306 (USIA), P 243, Office of Policy and Plans: Program Coordination Staff, Office of the Advisor for Science, Space, and the Environment, box 3, folder "IOP/A Basic Paper 1958," NARA II, College Park, Maryland.

29. Judith Butler, *Gender Trouble: Feminism and the Subversion of Identity* (New York: Routledge, 1990).

Conclusion

"Empires need ideologies," Benjamin Coates writes, "and the American empire is no exception." This volume explores how ideologies sustained, cloaked, and undermined the U.S. empire, and so much else of the nation's relations with the world. Contributors identified and unpacked many of the ideologies that the United States contained, inspired, and provoked. They demonstrated the variety and complexity of this process and its consequences for the U.S. and the world.

Eclecticism is a virtue in a book examining a category as capacious as ideology in America's foreign relations. Whereas Michael Hunt's foundational scholarship on ideology and U.S. foreign policy aimed to demonstrate the influence of ideology on elite policy makers, this book's approach to ideological transmission and reception looks further and wider, focusing on a tighter sets of connections by examining the integral role of ideas and the place of ideology in U.S. foreign policy.

In addition to foreign policy elites, such as politicians, think tankers, and diplomats, the voices we have encountered in this collection include activists, organizers, home economists, nineteenth-century children, blue-collar workers, housewives, and infantry soldiers. Our intention has been to broaden our field of analysis so that it captures the vibrant and heterogeneous field that is the "United States in the World" today.

One of the great virtues of a wide-ranging collection is how common themes emerge across ostensibly dissimilar topics, eras, and approaches.

A key example is "civilization," the central focus of the chapters by Benjamin Coates and Nicholas Guyatt and touched upon by Emily Conroy-Krutz and Daniel Immerwahr. In 1993, the political scientist Samuel Huntington wrote a controversial and influential article in *Foreign Affairs* (later published as a book) about a coming civilizational crisis that he called the "Clash of Civilizations." Huntington considered how civilizational discourse has informed U.S. foreign policy, but his approach, although it caused a major stir in policy and political science circles, has not attracted much attention from historians.[1] This book, in contrast, demonstrates that notions of "civilization as ideology" have had a profound impact on the United States' relations with the world. As Coates observes, invocations of civilization can be traced "from a messianic optimism inscribed in a variety of nineteenth-century civilizing missions to an anxious defensiveness in the face of successive twentieth-century existential threats." Historically, civilization has often been little more than a thinly veiled rationale for oppression.

The impossibility of disentangling economics (a hard causal factor) from ideology (which is supposedly softer) is another common theme across the book. In *American Foreign Policy and Its Thinkers*, Perry Anderson faulted the current generation of diplomatic historians for neglecting the Wisconsin School—the body of work that privileges economic causation and was ushered in by the publication of William Appleman Williams's *The Tragedy of American Diplomacy*—and focusing too much on ideology as a driver of U.S. foreign policy.[2] His principal target, oddly, was Odd Arne Westad, who is attentive to economics *and* ideology (as a former Michael Hunt student, how could he not be?). But our collection suggests that economics versus ideology is a false binary.

There is a compelling argument to be made, we believe, that many of the foreign policy disputes—over free trade through the nineteenth and twentieth centuries, as Marc-William Palen shows in chapter 5, the pull of the U.S. economy and its post–Civil War political model, as Jay Sexton demonstrates in chapter 18, and the power exerted by neoliberalism and neoconservatism in the post–Cold War period, as Penny Von Eschen (chapter 15) and Daniel Steinmetz-Jenkins and Michael Franczak (chapter 20) make clear—are immensely important *and* ideological to their very core. Ideologies related to the material drivers of economics, we find, have tended to align with ideological competition over who and what "counts" as American. As Daniel Tichenor shows in chapter 17 on "contentious designs," ideologies around immigration reveal fresh insights about the "intermestic," the terrain that blends the domestic with the international and reminds us of the crucial importance of domestic politics for foreign policy, which often has been commingled with disputes about economic policies and interests.

Race and racism have been pivotal to the ideological forces sweeping through the foreign policy history covered in this book. Even before the founding of the United States, as Matthew Kreur makes clear in chapter 1, racial hierarchies and power were closely intertwined, often in unpredictable ways. Race, ethnicity, and racism were integral animating ideas at the intersection of domestic and international—they helped to shape contact between peoples and served to propel the colonizing of North America. Such colonization was cast in civilizational terms, superior (Anglo-Saxon) peoples claiming these spaces and resources alongside a role in "tutoring" lesser peoples. As these notions developed, the U.S. population changed and grew rapidly, as did race-based chattel slavery, such that racism and prejudice against nonwhite peoples became instantiated in law, politics, and society in entrenched structures.

Eventually, ideas about who and what counts as "American" slotted into notions of freedom and national security and created vectors for advancing land claims, "strenuous" imperial foreign policies, furthering slavery, and thus amplifying often radically unequal wealth accumulation. Racism and racial hierarchical thinking were not monolithic; they generated multivalent ideological forces as well, notably abolitionism and the civil rights movement. So we see in this historical record a push and pull that did not amount to narrow opposition or dualism. Brandy Wells's examination of Flemmie B. Kittrell's internationalism is a case in point (chapter 12). It reveals how some Black American diplomats aimed to develop policies and promote ideas about egalitarianism that rejected simplistic racist assumptions and helped to fulfill America's foundational principles of the inalienable rights of all.

Another ideological propensity that appears and reappears throughout the volume is unilateralism, which here we can understand as proceeding without care for or genuine interest in the views of others. Christopher Nichols demonstrates how unilateralism courses through the history of U.S. foreign policy like few other ideational forces (chapter 9). Penny Von Eschen hones in on a particular moment at the end of the Cold War, when the hardwired unilateral instincts of the Reagan and Bush administrations precluded the making of a genuinely different new world order (chapter 15). The epitome of that moment might be the concept of a New World Order (NWO) promulgated by George H. W. Bush during the Gulf War as part of the first large scale post–Cold War multilateral military operation, including both U.S. and Russian forces. Imaobong Umoren (chapter 11) explores how the leader of a small island state in the Caribbean actively encouraged America's unilateralist predilections to command its attention and support. Although Jeremi Suri's emphasis is on "freedom" not "unilateralism" (chapter 14), there is little doubt that the era of "freedom over" was driven by U.S. unilateralism, even when alliance systems were involved.

Suri's focus on freedom is nevertheless vital to a volume on ideology and U.S. foreign policy. As far as presidential rhetoric is concerned, freedom is America's comfort blanket. But it is more than that—it is a word that can be seen as a sort of fishing bob when closely analyzed in historical context. It reveals movement under the surface—interpretations of American mission, democracy, racial hierarchy, capitalism, empire, and much more. It has served to inspire some of the best and the worst actions in U.S. foreign relations history, from democracy promotion and humanitarian relief to intervention and occupation. This brings us to an observation by Raymond Haberski Jr. (chapter 13) that ideology is "the moment when you speak a language and do not know you're doing it." This can be seen in invocations of freedom and civilization, which serve as signifiers of robust, complicated ideological commitments. But it can also be explored in terms of the themes of fear and insecurity, which are vividly presented by Andrew Preston (chapter 8) and Michaela Hoenicke-Moore (chapter 3). This, in turn, illuminates an essential finding in this book: to secure a more complete view of the historical development and impact of ideologies, we must move beyond elites and examine everyone—from everyday citizens and GIs to low level bureaucrats and even filmmakers.

Offering up a neat didactic conclusion would be a problematic way to end a book such as this. Each of the authors understands ideology differently, and this has spurred several paths of inquiry, featuring varied protagonists and themes, some of which overlap and some of which do not. Historical subfields, like all subfields, have an inbuilt tendency to regard their methods and purpose as particularly important and cutting-edge. No such one-upmanship is evident here. The contributors to this volume can be situated in many different fields: cultural, intellectual, social, diplomatic, domestic, and with specific reference to gender, race, and religion. Each demonstrates in different ways, through various methods, the vital importance of ideology in the history of U.S. foreign relations more broadly. This is perhaps the only single note on which it is possible to end.

Notes

1. Samuel Huntington, "The Clash of Civilizations?," *Foreign Affairs* 72, no. 3 (Summer 1993): 22–49.
2. Perry Anderson, *American Foreign Policy and Its Thinkers* (London: Verso, 2015).

Acknowledgments

For their support of this project and the international conference at Oregon State University in 2019 that brought the thinkers and ideas together to develop this book, we thank the OSU College of Liberal Arts and Dean Larry Rodgers, the OSU School of History, Philosophy, and Religion and Director Nicole von Germeten, and the OSU Center for the Humanities. We also thank the University of East Anglia's School of History for facilitating David Milne's research on this project. We also want to acknowledge and thank C-SPAN for their coverage of the conference.

We are grateful for the support of sponsors and friends, such as Patrick and Vicki Stone, and a range of institutions, notably the Andrew Carnegie Corporation. We owe special thanks to the Richard Lounsbery Foundation, which helped to underwrite our conference and to provide the time and space for the editors to conceive, write, and revise the book, as well as to collaborate on public writing and engagement efforts regarding the role of ideas in U.S. foreign policy and in discussing ideas about science and their place in U.S. foreign relations.

We want to thank and recognize our brilliant designer Dougal Henken for his efforts on the designs that helped to make this venture stand out. We extend special thanks to Natalia Bueno, Suzanne Giftai, and Joy Jensen for support related to the conference and in the writing of this book. Miriam Lipton was a great help as we completed the final version of the book.

We also thank and want to recognize Danielle Holtz. During her time as a postdoctoral fellow at the OSU Center for the Humanities, she contributed significantly to our thinking about this subject, to draft chapters, and to the conference that helped to give rise to this book.

At Columbia University Press we'd like to thank Stephen Wesley for his faith in this project and for his editorial vision. We also thank Leslie Kriesel, Ben Kolstad, and the excellent team that has shepherded this book to completion.

The contributors to this volume have been exceptional and are owed tremendous thanks, not just for their astute insights but also for their collaborations in conversation with each other and with us to make the volume more cohesive and compelling. Personally, this volume emerged from the two editors' conversations during conferences over many years; it has been a special thrill to finally bring these ideas together in collaboration, and we very much hope readers enjoy and learn from it, as we have. We had to sacrifice quite a bit at times to make this happen, so our families are owed appreciation, and we thank Lily Sheehan, Emma Griffin, and Anna and Benedict Milne.

Contributors

Christopher McKnight Nichols is Professor of History and Wayne Woodrow Hayes Chair in National Security Studies, Mershon Center for International Security Studies, at The Ohio State University. Nichols previously was a professor at Oregon State University, where he directed the Center for the Humanities. Nichols is an Andrew Carnegie Fellow and an Organization of American Historians Distinguished Lecturer. Nichols is a frequent commentator on the historical dimensions of contemporary politics and foreign policy. Nichols is author or editor of six books. He recently published *Rethinking American Grand Strategy* (2021), and his best known book is *Promise and Peril: America at the Dawn of a Global Age* (2011, 2015). Nichols is currently working on a book on early Cold War domestic and foreign policy and a sweeping history of global anti-imperialism.

David Milne is professor of modern history at the University of East Anglia. He is the author of *America's Rasputin: Walt Rostow and the Vietnam War* (2008) and *Worldmaking: The Art and Science of American Diplomacy* (2015). He is currently writing a biography of the *Chicago Tribune* journalist, Sigrid Schultz, for Oxford University Press.

Daniel Bessner is the Joff Hanauer Honors Associate Professor in Western Civilization in the Henry M. Jackson School of International Studies at the University of Washington. He is the author of *Democracy in Exile: Hans Speier and the Rise of the Defense Intellectual* (2018).

Benjamin Coates is associate professor at Wake Forest University, where he teaches courses on legal history and the history of the United States and the world. He is the author of *Legalist Empire: International Law and American Foreign Relations in the Early Twentieth Century* (2016) and is currently working on a history of economic sanctions.

Emily Conroy-Krutz is an associate professor of history at Michigan State University. She is the author of *Christian Imperialism: Converting the World in the Early American Republic* (2015).

Penny Von Eschen is William R. Kennan Jr. Professor of American Studies and professor of history at the University of Virginia. Her books include the forthcoming *Paradoxes of Nostalgia, Cold War Triumphalism and Global Disorder Since 1989* (Spring 2022); *Satchmo Blows Up the World: Jazz Ambassadors Play the Cold War* (2004), and *Race Against Empire: Black Americans and Anticolonialism, 1937–1957* (1997).

Michael Franczak is a postdoctoral fellow in global order at the University of Pennsylvania's Perry World House. His first book, *North-South: Global Inequality and American Foreign Policy in the 1970s* is forthcoming in early 2022. His current project asks how China and climate change shaped U.S. grand strategy in the 1990s and beyond.

Nicholas Guyatt is professor of North American history at the University of Cambridge. His books include *Bind Us Apart: How Enlightened Americans Invented Racial Segregation* and *The Hated Cage: An American Ordeal in Britain's Most Terrifying Prison*. He is also the editor of the forthcoming *Oxford Illustrated History of the United States*.

Raymond Haberski Jr. is professor of history and director of American Studies and director of the Institute of American Thought at IUPUI. He is the author or editor of seven books and a founding member of the Society for U.S. Intellectual History. A former Fulbright Distinguished Chair in American Studies at Copenhagen Business School, he is at work on a coauthored book tentatively titled "Philanthropy and the Public Good."

Michaela Hoenicke-Moore is associate professor of history at the University of Iowa where she teaches U.S. foreign policy and the histories of Europe and the United States in the twentieth century. She is the author of *Know Your Enemy: The American Debate on Nazism, 1933–45* (2009), which won the 2010 SHAFR Myrna Bernath Book Award. Her current book project, *The Varieties of Patriotism: Americans Debate Their Country's*

Role in the World from the "Good War" to Vietnam, is a study of foreign policy views at the grassroots level.

Daniel Immerwahr is professor of history at Northwestern University. He is the author of *Thinking Small: The United States and the Lure of Community Development* (2015) and *How to Hide an Empire: A History of the Greater United States* (2019).

Matthew Karp is associate professor of history at Princeton University and the author of *This Vast Southern Empire: Slaveholders at the Helm of American Foreign Policy* (2016). Currently, he is at work on a book about the birth of the Republican Party in the 1850s.

Matthew Kruer is assistant professor of early North American history at the University of Chicago. He is the author of *Time of Anarchy: Indigenous Power and the Crisis of Colonialism in Early America* (2021).

Melani McAlister is professor of American studies and international affairs at George Washington University. She is author or editor of four books, including *The Kingdom of God Has No Borders: A Global History of American Evangelicals* (2018) and volume 4 of the forthcoming *Cambridge History of America and the* World (coedited with David Engerman and Max Friedman). She currently serves on the board of directors of the American Council of Learned Societies, and on the editorial boards of *Modern American History, Diplomatic History*, and *American Quarterly*.

Marc-William Palen is a historian at the University of Exeter. He is editor of the Imperial & Global Forum and codirector of History & Policy's Global Economics and History Forum. His works include *The "Conspiracy" of Free Trade: The Anglo-American Struggle over Empire and Economic Globalisation, 1846–1896* (2016). His current book project, under contract with Princeton University Press, explores the global intersections of capitalism, anti-imperialism, and peace activism since the mid-nineteenth century.

Andrew Preston is professor of American history at Cambridge University, where he is a Fellow of Clare College, and 2020–21 president of SHAFR. He is the author or editor of nine books, including *Sword of the Spirit, Shield of Faith: Religion in American War and Diplomacy* (2012).

Katharina Rietzler teaches at the University of Sussex, England, and is coeditor of the essay collection *Women's International Thought: A New History* (2021) and the anthology *Women's International Thought: Toward A New Canon* (forthcoming).

Daniel Steinmetz-Jenkins is an assistant professor in the College of Social Studies at Wesleyan University. His current book is titled *Impossible Peace, Improbable War: Raymond Aron and World Order* (forthcoming).

Jay Sexton is the Kinder Institute Chair in Constitutional Democracy at the University of Missouri and emeritus fellow at Corpus Christi College, Oxford University. The author of *A Nation Forged by Crisis*, *The Monroe Doctrine* and *Debtor Diplomacy*, Sexton lives in Columbia, Missouri.

Jeremi Suri holds the Mack Brown Distinguished Chair for Leadership in Global Affairs at the University of Texas at Austin, and is based in the university's Department of History and the LBJ School of Public Affairs. Suri is the author and editor of ten books on politics and foreign policy, including *The Impossible Presidency: The Rise and Fall of America's Highest Office*, which was widely reviewed across the United States. His writings appear in the *New York Times, Washington Post, Atlantic, Wired, Foreign Policy*, and other media, and he hosts a weekly podcast, "This Is Democracy" (http://jeremisuri.net).

Daniel Tichenor is the Philip H. Knight Chair of Social Science and program director of the Wayne Morse Center of Law and Politics at the University of Oregon. His most recent books are *Rivalry and Reform: Presidents, Social Movements, and the Transformation of American Politics* (2019) with Sidney Milkis, and *Democracy's Child: The Control, Iconography, and Agency of Young People in U.S. Politics* (forthcoming) with Alison Gash.

Imaobong Umoren is associate professor of international history at the London School of Economics and Political Science. Her research interests focus on politics, race, and gender in the modern Caribbean and Black internationalism. Umoren's first book, *Race Women Internationalists: Activist-Intellectuals and Global Freedom Struggles* (2018), was awarded the Women's History Network (UK) book prize for the best first book on women's/gender history in 2019. She is currently working on a political biography of Eugenia Charles.

Brandy Thomas Wells is assistant professor of history at Oklahoma State University. She specializes in the histories of the twentieth century United States, African American, African diaspora, and gender and sexuality. She is currently writing a book tentatively titled "The World Is Going to Hear from Us: Black Women and the International Pursuit of Freedom and Equality."

Audra J. Wolfe is the author of *Freedom's Laboratory: The Cold War Struggle for the Soul of Science* (2018) and *Competing with the Soviets: Science, Technology, and the State in Cold War America* (2013). A Philadelphia-based writer, editor, and historian of science, her work has appeared in the *Washington Post*, *Atlantic*, *Slate*, popular podcasts, and other popular and scholarly venues. She is a frequent commentator on issues related to U.S. science policy.

Index

Air Technical Service Command
(ATSC), 398–99

AJC. *See* American Jewish Committee

Alaska, 289

Almond, Gabriel, 3

Althusser, Louis, on ideology, 5–6

Amartefio, Evelyn, 254

American Association of University
Women (AAUW), 98–99

American Board of Commissioners for
Foreign Missions (ABCFM), 212,
216, 219, 229n8

American Colonization Society, 138

American Committee to Keep Biafra
Alive, 326

American Enterprise Institute (AEI), 428

American Federation of Labor (AFL),
354, 355, 357

American Free Trade League (AFTL), 123

American Graffiti (film), 438–39, 441, 443

American Initiatives Project, 269

American Jewish Committee (AJC),
322; on Israel, 328, 330; on Nigeria-
Biafra war, 338–39; on Palestine, 330

American Jewish Emergency Effort for
Biafran Relief, 329

American Negro Leadership Council
on Africa (ANLCA), 336

American Proposition, 269–70, 274

American Reporter, 252

America's Town Meeting of the Air,
92–93

AME-Zion, 336

Amistad, 136

Amoco, 316

ANC. *See* African National Congress

Anderson, Carol, 248

Anderson, Perry, 470

Andrews, Fannie Fern, 101

Anekwe, Simon, 334–35, 337

Anglo-Indian wars, 36

ANLCA. *See* American Negro
Leadership Council on Africa

anticolonialism, 17–18

anticommunism, 82–83, 104, 233,
293, 304; of E. Charles, 240–42;
neoliberalism and, 241; Red Scare, 357

Anti-Corn Law League (ACLL), 118,
119–20

Anti-Defamation League, 328–29

anti-imperialism, 80–81, 85, 116–18,
122–23, 136; of J. Q. Adams, 137–38;
of Lucas, 445–48

Anti-Imperialist League (AIL), 123

antislavery movement, 369; ideology
of, 152–54; Lincoln and, 161; mass
partisan politics and, 153

Anyanwu, Donatus U., 335

apartheid, South African, 300, 313

Apocalypse Now (film), 443–44

Appomattox, 368

Arab-Israeli war of 1967, 17, 323,
330–36, 339; Tanenbaum on, 331–33

Arafat, Yassir, 311

aristocracy, 119

Armey, Dick, 353

Army Air Antisubmarine Command,
390–91

Army Air Forces (AAF), 385, 386, 388;
Arnold on, 393; Bowles on, 396–98

Arnold, Henry Harley, 385–86, 387,
401n2; on AAF, 393; Bowles and,
391–92; on missiles, 397–98

Aron, Raymond, 20, 413; Kissinger and,
432n22; on Point Four Program,
417; Shils and, 418–19

Ashley, James, 161

Asia Foundation, 460; CIA ties of, 461

Asian immigrants, 360

al-Assad, Bashar, 3

Atkinson, Edward, 119, 121

Atlantic Charter, 292

Atomic Energy Commission, 395,
458–59, 460
Atoms for Peace, 459
ATSC. *See* Air Technical Service
Command
autonomism, 197
Awolowo, Obafemi, 325
Azikiwe, Nnamdi, 336

B-29, 393–94
Bacevich, Andrew, 76, 85
Bacon, Nathaniel, 36
Bahamas, 233–34
Balch, Emily Greene, 96
Balkan Ghosts (Kaplan, R.), 315
Bandung conference, 338, 345n58, 415
baptism, *221*, 223
Barbados, 231
Barbour, James, 147
Baroda University, 251–53
Barre, Siad, 315
Bayou of Pigs, 232, 236
Beard, Charles, 115–16; on
unilateralism, 191
Beecher, Henry Ward, 121
Bell, Daniel, 20, 413, 414, 416–17; on
end-of-ideology, 419–20; New Left
and, 420–21
Bell, Duncan, 146
Belmont, August, 370, 377
Belt and Road initiative, 135–36
Bennett, John, 332
Berkner, Lloyd, 45, 455
Berkner Report, 455–56
Berlin, Isaiah, 281, 295; on freedom,
283–84
Berlin Wall, 307
Bernardin, Joseph Cardinal, 265
Biafra, 322; activism supporting,
325–26; African American support
for, 336–37; aid to, 329–30; Israel

as similar to, 324. *See also* Nigeria-
Biafra war
Biden, Joe, 25n4, 128, 129, 436;
unilateralism and multilateralism
under, 186–87
Biden Doctrine, 204n11
Biopatong Massacre, 313
Bish, Milan, 236
Bishop, Maurice, 231, 235
Black Boys, 42–43
Black-Jewish Alliance, 336–39
Black nationalism, 79, 83, 336
Black Women's Oral History
Interviews Project, 256
Blaine, James G., 121
Blinken, Anthony, 186
Bolshevik Revolution, 97
Bolton, John, 170, 185
Bonaparte, Napoleon, 193
Bondy, Francois, 418
Bookbinder, Hyman, 352
Borah, William, 197
Born to Run, 439
Bosnia, 315
Bourdieu, Pierre, 327
Bourne, Randolph, 196
Bowles, Edward, 385–87, 406n67; on
AAF, 396–98; Arnold and, 391–92;
at MC, 389–90; at MIT, 388–89; at
War Department, 390–92, 395
Boxer Uprising, 227
Bracero Program, 358
Brandt, Joseph, 43
Brauer, Kinley, 152
Bremmer, Ian, 187
Bretton Woods system, 4
Brewer, Susan, 77
Brickner, Balfour, 332
Bright, John, 118, 125
Brode, Wallace, 454–55
Browning, Edmond, 274

Brunauer, Esther Caukin, 99

Bryan, William Jennings, 382

Bryant, William Cullen, 119

Brzezinski, Zbigniew, 425, 426

Buchanan, Patrick, 351

Buck, Peal S., 101

Buckley, James, 427

Bunche, Ralph, 252

Bundy, Harvey, 389–90

Burlingame Treaty, 379

Burnham, Forbes, 238

Burroughs, Nannie Helen, 97

Bush, George H. W., 186, 304, 472; on ANC, 313; on environmentalism, 306–7; on exceptionalism, 311–12; on immigration, 353; interventionism under, 315–16; on Iraq, 304; just war theory used by, 274; Mandela and, 309–14; Soviet Union and, 309

Bush, George W., 1, 64, 76, 77, 179, 186, 196, 198, 435; on freedom, 294–95; on immigration, 348; on terrorism, 294

Bush, Prescott, 311

Bush, Vannevar, 389, 398, 456

Bush Doctrine, 198

Butler, Judith, 302–3

Butler, Pierce, 350

Calhoun, John C., 119

California Anti-Chinese Convention, 351

California gold rush, 370

Canton, 136–37, 140, 141, 145

capital, free labor and, 154–58

capitalism, 74–75, 293; democracy linked to, under neoliberalism, 317

car culture, 438–39

Carey, Henry, 120

Caribbean, 231–32; Reagan on, 233–34

Caribbean Basin Initiative (CBI), 233; neoliberalism and, 235

Caribbean Community (CARICOM), 234–36

Carnegie, Andrew, 353

Carnegie Council, 268

Carnegie Endowment for International Peace, 123

Carter, Jimmy, 62, 307

Cartwright, Marguerite, 254

Castaneda, Carlos, 440

Castro, Fidel, 311

Catholic Caritas International, 326

Catholic Church, 15, 267–68; Catholic immigrants, 371–72; Jewish people and, 328; on just war theory, 264; pacifism in, 264–65; on Vietnam War, 265; Weigel on, 269

Catholic Relief Services, 329

Catt, Carrie Chapman, 125

Caute, David, 173

CBC. See Congressional Black Caucus

CBI. See Caribbean Basin Initiative

CDM. See Coalition for a Democratic Majority

Central America, 240

Central Intelligence Agency (CIA), 239, 293, 457; Asia Foundation ties to, 461; founding of, 454; science and, 454–55, 459–60

CERDS. See Charter of Economic Rights and Duties of States

"Challenge of Peace, The," 264–65

Charles, Eugenia, 14, 231, 235–36; anticommunism of, 240–42; Reagan and, 239–40

Charles I (King), 35

Charles II (King), 35, 37–38

Charter of Economic Rights and Duties of States (CERDS), 426

Chavez, Cesar, 355

Cheney, Dick, 435

Cherokee, 45, 56

democracy: capitalism linked to, under neoliberalism, 317; Douglass on, 160–61; emancipation as democratic revolution, 158–63; hegemony and, 293–94; ideology and, 16–18; interventions in name of, 304; participatory, 1; Seward on, 159; Shils on, 416; slavery and, 158–59; weakening of, 316

Democratic Party, 380, 427, 430

Denny, George V., 92, 104

Detroit, 310

Detzer, Dorothy, 92

developing countries, 61; end-of-ideology and, 415–19; neoconservatism and, 423–29

Dewey, John, 104

DFP. *See* Dominica Freedom Party

DLP. *See* Dominica Labour Party

Doctrine of Discovery, 31

Dominica, 231–32; U.S. relations with, 241

Dominica Freedom Party (DFP), 233

Dominica Labour Party (DLP), 233, 240–41

Dominican Defense Force, 236

Dongan, Thomas, 40

Dorsey, Susan Miller, 102

Douglas, Donald, 392, 395–96, 397

Douglas, Michael, 241

Douglas, Stephen, 157

Douglas Aircraft, 385, 396–97, 409n102

Douglas Dolphin, 392

Douglass, Frederick, 12, 153, 159; on Chinese American rights, 354; on democracy, 160–61; on immigration, 353–54

Doyle, Don, 368

Dreads, 236

DTPILLAR, 460

dual-use technology, 453, 462; science as, 463–64

DuBois, Rachel, 102

Du Bois, W. E. B., 58–59, 162

Dugan, Robert, 266–67

Dulles Committee, 454

Eaker, Ira, 398

Earth Day, 307

Eastern Europe, revolutions in, 300–301

Eastman, Crystal, 124–25

Eberstadt Committee, 454

Eckes, Alfred, 126

Eddy, Mary Baker, 100

education: intercultural, 101; of women, 98–99, 101; women's international citizenship and, 103–4

Egypt, 331

Eighteen Lectures on Industrial Society (Aron), 417

Eisenhower, Dwight, 62, 253, 437, 459–60

emancipation, as democratic revolution, 158–63

Emancipation Proclamation, 121, 369

Emergency Quota Act of 1921, 201

Emerson, Ralph Waldo, 119, 121, 352

emotions, 172–73, 182n25

Empire Strikes Back, The (film), 436, 440

end of history, 294, 429–30

"End of History, The" (Fukuyama), 429

end-of-ideology, 412–13; Daniel Bell on, 419–20; debates on, 414–15; developing countries and, 415–19; Lipset on, 415–16

End of Ideology, The (Bell, D.), 414

Engel, Jeffrey A., 311–12

Engels, Friedrich, 124

English banking panic of 1847, 370

environmental damage, from Cold War, 306–8

Great Society, 420, 425, 432n32

Great War, 373

Greece, 293

Greeley, Horace, 121

Greenback Party, 381–82

greenbacks, 369, 373

Green Berets, The, 445

Grenada, 231; Great Britain on, 238–39;
U.S. invasion of, 236–38

Grossman, Lawrence, 328, 331

Grotius, Hugo, 45

Grow, Galusha, 158

Guinea, 253

Gulf War, 311–12, 472

Gutierrez, Luis, 352

Habib, Adam, 313

Hague Peace Conference, 58

Haley, Nikki, 170

Hamill, Mark, 436

Hamilton, Alexander, 187, 193,
352–53

Hamilton, Anne Burrows, 103

Hamiltonianism, 193–94

Hammer, Ellen, 100

Hani, Chris, 313

Harding, Warren, 60, 200

Harrington, Michael, 420

Harris, William, 36

Harvard/Radcliffe Bureau for
International Research, 99

Haudenosaunee, 40

Hauerwas, Stanley, 273; Neuhaus and,
274–75

Havana, 312

Havel, Vaclav, 17, 315; on nationalism,
316; on NATO, 308–9; on U.S., 299,
305–6, 308–9

Hawaii, 211

heathenism, 214, 215, 225

Heerten, Lasse, 326

hegemonic freedom, 291–94

hegemony: defining, 304; democracy
and, 293–94; ideology and, 302;
U.S., 300

Hehir, J. Bryan, 265, 270

Herberg, Will, 329

Heritage Foundation, 428

Herring, George, 200, 207n38; on
unilateralism, 191

Heschel, Abraham Joshua, 328

Hickenlooper, Bourke, 82

higher education, of women,
98–99, 101

Hill, Christopher, 170

Hinduism, 216

Hiroshima, 394

history, end of, 429–30

Hixson, Walter, 76

Hobbes, Thomas, 172

Hoffman, Phillip, 335

Holborn, Louise, 99

Hollinger, David, 86

Holocaust, 327, 334

Homestead Act, 288, 376, 381

Hoover, Herbert, 60–61, 199, 200

Horizons Unlimited Tour, 255–56

Horrocks, Allison Beth, 247

House, Edward, 59

House Divided speech, Lincoln, 372

Howard University, 249, 252,
255, 258

Hoyter, John, 38

Hull, Cordell, 12, 117, 125–26

humanitarianism, 323, 327

Humphrey, Hubert, 358–59, 422

Hunt, Michael, 21, 81, 115–16, 152,
349–50, 361, 367; on culture,
173; on foreign policy, 76–77; on
ideology, 2–3, 74–75, 175, 215, 469;
on nationalism, 78–79

Huntington, Samuel, 64, 304, 351

National Bank Acts, 374
National Committee on the Cause and Cure of War, 99
National Conference of Christians and Jews, 328–29
National Council of Churches, 274, 332
National Council of Negro Women (NCNW), 246, 253–55
National Council of Women, 97
National Interest, 429
nationalism, 85; African Americans and, 79, 83, 336; contestation of foreign policy and, 78–79; ethnonationalism, 351; Havel on, 316; Hunt on, 78–79; ideology of, 74, 78–79; religion and, 79–80
National Origins Quota Acts, 361
National Press Club, 177
National Science Foundation, 460
national security, 385–86
National Security Act of 1947, 16, 293
National Security Council, 455
Native Americans. *See* Indigenous peoples
NATO. *See* North Atlantic Treaty Organization
Nazi Germany, 61, 323, 390
NCNW. *See* National Council of Negro Women
Nearing, Scott, 124
Necotowance, 34
negative freedom, 283
neo-Cobdenism, neoliberalism compared with, 127–28
neoconservatism, 20, 273, 294–95; developing countries and, 423–29; under Ford, 427–28; on just war theory, 263; liberalism and, 412–13; neoliberalism and, 316; under Reagan, 428–29; rise of, 412–13
neoliberalism, 17, 299; anticommunism and, 241; capitalism and democracy

under, 317; CBI and, 235; false consciousness in, 303; freedom and, 314–15; history of, 303–4; ideology of, 300, 303; individual in, 303; naturalization of, 300; neo-Cobdenism compared with, 127–28; neoconservatism and, 316; origin of, 127; Reagan and, 303–4
Neuhaus, Richard John, 266–68, 270, 273; Hauerwas and, 274–75; on PFSS, 271; on religion, 268
neutrality, 81, 285; unilateral, 194
Neutrality Act (1794), 193
New Deal, 61, 81–82, 175
Newell, Harriet, 220
New Hope, A (film), 436, 441–42
New International Economic Order (NIEO), 413, 415, 425, 427
New Jewel Movement (NJM), 234
New Left, 2–3, 413, 430; Daniel Bell and, 420–21; Kristol on, 421
New Left Review, 420
New Nationalism, 289
New Right, 413
New World Order (NWO), 472
Nicaragua, 448
Nicholas (Tsar), 156
Nichols, Christopher McKnight, 123
Niebuhr, Reinhold, 20, 75, 82, 85, 332, 413; on class conflict, 414; on Middle East, 417; on power, 416–17
NIEO. *See* New International Economic Order
Nigeria: African Americans support for, 336; decolonization of, 325
Nigeria-Biafra war, 17, 323; AJC on, 338–39; end of, 326; Jewish people on, 327, 329–30, 334; scholarship on, 326–27; start of, 325; Tanenbaum on, 329–30
Nightline, 311

Rorty, Richard, 80
Roseau Pond Case-Hatton Garden Project, 240
Rosenberg, Emily, 367
Rossinow, Doug, 343n29
Rostow, Walt, 415, 441
Rothberg, Michael, 327
Round Hill Research Station, 388, 391
Rousseau, Jean-Jacques, 16
Rubin, Michael, 439
Russian Revolution, 290–91
Rustin, Bayard, 354
Rutherford, Mildred Lewis, 103
Ryan, William, 422

SACP. *See* South African Communist Party
SADU. *See* Sea-Search Attack Development Unit
Sampson, Edith Spurlock, 254
Savage, Gus, 237
Savarin, Charles, 235
Savord, Ruth, 100
Schäfer, Axel, 267
Schlafly, Phyllis, 104, 105
Schlesinger, Arthur, Jr., 20, 413; on class conflict, 414
Schloepflin, Rennie, 229n8
Schmidt, Helmut, 425
Schultz, Sigrid, 100–101
Schurz, Carl, 12, 155
Schwartz, Abba, 352
science: as apolitical, 462–63; CIA and, 454–55, 459–60; defining, 453–54; as dual-use technology, 463–64; freedom and, 454, 456–57; as propaganda, 458; in Soviet Union, 456–57
science fiction, 436–37
scientism, 18, 19, 387, 420
Scoon, Paul, 237
Scowcroft, Brent, 311

Scudder, J., 215, 225; on India, 216–17
SDI. *See* Strategic Defense Initiative
Seaga, Edward, 14, 232, 234–35, 241
Seal of the Dominion of New England, *37*
Sea-Search Attack Development Unit (SADU), 390–91
Second Reform Act, 368
self-determination, 162
self-interest, power and, 199–202
self-sufficiency, 199
Seminole Indians, 146–47
Sequoyah, 45
Seward, William, 12, 153, 156–57, 289, 376, 379; on democracy, 159; on immigration, 372
Sexton, Jay, 138
Shane, Scott, 262
Shanghai, 224
Sherry, Michael, 263
Shils, Edward, 20, 413, 429–30; Aron and, 418–19; on democracy and modernity, 416
Shklar, Judith, 172
shock therapy, 314
Shultz, George, 239
Singh, Nikhil Pal, 75
Sixty Minutes, 239
slavery, 119–20, 152, 288; J. Q. Adams on, 138–39; Civil War and end of, 368, 370; democracy and, 158–59; emancipation as democratic revolution, 158–63. *See also* abolitionism
Small, J. D., 407n71
Smith, Adam, 12
Smith, Emily, 224
Smith, Rogers, 350, 361
Smoot-Hawley Tariff, 125, 200
socialism, 305; free trade, 122–26
socialist internationalism, 124

Tate, Merze, 99, 101, 252; Kittrell and, 256–57
Taylor, Chris, 443
TC. *See* Trilateral Commission
Tea Party, 75–76, 348
technology: defining, 453–54; dual-use, 453, 462–64; Lucas on, 436–38; propaganda as, 452–53; in Star Wars, 436–40, 445
Tecumseh, 146–47
Tel Aviv, 330–31
terrorism, 309; G. W. Bush on, 294
Texas, 139–40, 148
Thatcher, Margaret, 239, 303, 429
Thomas, Norman, 125
Thompson, Dorothy, 95, 100–101
Thompson, E. P., 5
Thompson, John A., 175
THX 1138 (film), 437–38, 446
Tolstoy, Leo, 379
totalitarianism, 316
Toynbee, Arnold, 55, 64
trade liberalization, U.S., 126. *See also* free trade
Tragedy of American Diplomacy, The (Williams, W. A.), 115–16, 470
Tranquillitas Ordinis (Weigel), 270, 271
transnationalism, 196
Trans Pacific Partnership, 200
Treason Act, 240
Treaty of Middle Plantation of 1677, 36, 38, 39
Treaty of Nanjin of 1842, 137
Treaty of Wanghia, 1844, 146
les trentes glorieuses, 412
Trilateral Commission (TC), 425
Trinidad and Tobago, 238
Truman, Harry, 81–82, 129, 176, 306, 317, 407n71
Truman Doctrine, 293

Trump, Donald, 64–65, 128; on freedom, 282; immigration under, 348; on North Korea, 170; unilateralism of, 185–86
tuberculosis, 250
Turkey, 293, 315
Turner, Henry, 59
Twain, Mark, 58–59, 124
Tyler, John, 57
Tyrrell, Ian, 138

U-boats, 390–91
UDC. *See* United Daughters of the Confederacy
Uganda, 220
Ugarte, Manuel, 195
UMT. *See* universal military training
Underwood-Simmons Tariff, 125–26
unilateralism, 13, 17, 471–72; Beard on, 191; of Biden, 186–87; under B. Clinton, 203n5; defining, 188–89; executive power and, 196; Herring on, 191; history of, 187–88, 191–96; as ideology, 201–2; isolationism and, 197–99, 207n38; McDougall on, 191; multilateralism and, 196; under Obama, 203n5; origins of, 191–96; power and, 193; reciprocal actions, 198–99; of Trump, 185–86
unilateral neutrality, 194
Union, 368; foreign-born troops in army of, 376; immigration in, 372–73; paper money in, 373–74; victory of, 378. *See also* Civil War
unipolarity, U.S., 299, 304; after Cold War, 300; exceptionalism and, 304
United Daughters of the Confederacy (UDC), 103
United Nations, 128, 255, 316